Praise for this Book

"This book will save parents and teachers many hours of aimless searching, and provide the peace of mind that they are providing their kids with the highest quality of what's available on the Internet."

Susan Calcari
Internet Scout, InterNIC Net Scout Services

"Jean Armour Polly has done a big part of what every parent wishes he or she had time to do—explored and assessed many sites for their suitability for K-8 use. While nothing is guaranteed, this is a great help in 'pre-surfing' a large number of sites, helping you find the gold in the ocean of Internet information."

Vint Cerf,
Senior vice-president, MCI Data Architecture; Internet Society Trustee and Internet pioneer

"Jean Armour Polly is one of the few people writing about the Internet who really knows what she's talking about! She was there from the start—and has probably logged more time surfing the Net than anyone I know. For kids, parents, and teachers, this book is just what the librarian ordered. I know it will be a big help to us at AskERIC."

Mike Eisenberg, Ph.D.
Professor, School of Information Studies, Syracuse University; Director, ERIC Clearinghouse on Information & Technology and the AskERIC Internet Education Information Service

"Finally, a cyber-map for kids even their parents will enjoy! Jean Armour Polly makes the Internet a lot more 'kid friendly.'"

Ira Flatow
Host of public radio's "Science Friday"

"If anybody in the world is qualified to teach us about kid-friendly resources on the Internet, it's Jean Armour Polly. A librarian, a mother, a Net enthusiast for many years, she's been grappling with issues of usefulness, age-appropriateness, educational value, usability, for years. A great resource for teachers and parents of children with hungry minds."

Howard Rheingold, author of best-sellers Virtual Reality *and* The Virtual Community, *founding Executive Editor of* HotWired

"An indispensable and reassuring guide for parents who want to turn their kids loose on the Internet."

Guy Kawasaki
Apple Fellow

"Amongst a flood of Internet books, Polly's stands out as instrumental and of true value."

Brendan Kehoe
author of Zen and the Art of the Internet

"This is a wonderful guide that opens a storehouse of knowledge—about almost every conceivable subject. Even better, it is a virtual encyclopedia that kids AND adults will benefit from using. I love it!"

Charles R. McClure
Distinguished Professor, School of Information Studies, Syracuse University

"All I can say is NEAT. Your book is both timely and right on target in meeting a serious need. In the future, I'll plan on carrying it with me when I go 'on the road' as the K-12 'card catalog' for the Internet."

Don Mitchell
frequent speaker on the use of the Internet in K-12 education

True Tales of Internet Adventures
Starring Librarians, Teachers, Parents, and Kids Who Use This Book

We thought you might like looking over my shoulder at some of the great responses we've had from the first edition. Most of the following came from School Library Media Specialists who are also KidsConnect volunteers. KidsConnect is a technology initiative from AASL (American Association of School Librarians) in cooperation with the ERIC Clearinghouse on Information and Technology at Syracuse University. Blythe Bennett, the Coordinator of the KidsConnect project, sent out a "call for true adventures using the book" and this is some of what we got back in e-mail. They are reprinted here with permission of their authors. If you have a true tale of your own, please write to me (**mom@netmom.com**).

Book Takes a Shine to Pigs!

The book has been invaluable to me both as a K-12 school librarian in a very rural school and a KidsConnect volunteer. One specific example was a question I had about the raising and care of show pigs. I floundered around for a while trying to find the answer, when the whole time it was there in the book! I was able to answer the question and am happy to report that the pigs are all doing well, growing fast and eating a lot! Thanks for your dedication to the task.

Carole L. Ashbridge
Library media specialist; KidsConnect volunteer, Sackets Harbor, New York

Librarian in Texas Helps Kids in Hong Kong

I would like to thank you for making this book available to KidsConnect volunteers. It is fantastic! I am forwarding one of my recent questions from a 3rd grade teacher at a school in Hong Kong who was looking for some sites about China.

Hi,
We're a Grade Three class in Hong Kong trying to look for sites about China that aren't all "news" that adults like to read. We want to find Web sites that will give information, pictures and things to do about The Silk Road, The Great Wall, different areas of China and other stuff. Can you help us?

I used some sites I found in your book, and added a few more sites of my own. The teacher was very grateful for the assistance from KidsConnect, and it must be gratifying to you as it is to me that we are helping kids learn all over the world! The students at my elementary school have enjoyed browsing through your book, also. For some of our recent school projects, I have helped teachers find information on butterflies and whales using your fascinating book. We are all amazed at the wealth of information we are able to tap into for our curriculum using the Internet, and your book is a very helpful guide. Thanks for making all of these great sites available to us!

Marcia Garman Zorn
Librarian, Shady Oaks Elementary School, Hurst, Texas

Book Helps Child Whisper to Horses

I am a librarian with KidsConnect and experienced a very touching situation with a young girl who had a sick horse. She wrote to KidsConnect seeking advice on how to care for her sick foal (bottle feeding) and how to understand the whole situation. Yes, it brought tears to my eyes! I used your book for kids and investigated all your suggestions related to horse care. NetVet was recommended again and again so I was happy to tell the child about that resource.

Carol Simmons
KidsConnect Librarian, Rush, New York

Sydney, Australia 2000 Olympics: Net-mom is Rested and Ready!

A student came in to me to find the Sydney 2000 Olympic symbol. We used a search engine to try and find this, with no luck. I then took out your book and looked up "Olympics" and there was the Sydney 2000 Olympics Official Home page, and right at the top was the Olympic symbol. Success! So, both the student and I were very impressed. I think your book is a wonderful idea, it's very clearly set out.

Dale Hauser
Teacher Librarian, Concordia College, Toowoomba, Queensland, Australia

Connecticut Kids Join Net Groups to Save Environment

This book has given me an opportunity to demonstrate another example of resources available in our Media Center. Specifically, we have found sources rich in content and exciting in appearance for the Environmental Unit. Students were excited about the potential of joining programs to promote environmental awareness, something they never would have known anything about had they not had your book. We salute you for your time and your efforts!

Carol Weinshel
Media Specialist, Helen Keller Middle School, Easton, Connecticut

THE INTERNET KIDS & FAMILY YELLOW PAGES

SECOND EDITION

ABOUT THE AUTHOR

Jean Armour Polly is an internationally recognized expert on the Internet from a user's point of view. She wrote the original "Surfing the Internet" back in 1992 and is documented as the holder of the first published use of the phrase. Jean was one of the first two women elected to the Internet Society Board of Trustees.

As Net-mom, she is a private consultant, researcher, and speaker. Recent clients have included The Bertelsmann Foundation, America Online, and Disney Online. She is also a senior advisor to the Morino Institute. Jean recently served as cochair of the Children's category of the international Global Information Infrastructure Awards competition.

Jean cohosts a weekly call-in radio show called "The On-Ramp" with John Levine, author of *Internet for Dummies*. If you are outside the listening area of the station (Syracuse, New York), you can listen to it over the Internet by following the easy instructions on the show's home page at *<http://iecc.com/radio>*.

Formerly the Director of Public Services and Internet Ambassador at NYSERNet, Inc., Jean was coprincipal investigator on the landmark study, "Project GAIN: Connecting Rural Public Libraries to the Internet" (1994) and producer of the accompanying video.

Prior to that, Jean was a public librarian for 16 years. She is cofounder emerita of PUBLIB, the oldest and largest Internet discussion list for public librarians.

During Jean's watch, the Liverpool (New York) Public Library began many innovative programs, including an electronic BBS (1983–85), a public computer lab (1981–present), and a circulating software collection (1984–present), which was later named in her honor.

Jean received her B.A. in medieval studies at Syracuse University in 1974 and her master's degree in library science from the same university in 1975.

She is a member of the American Library Association and is a former director of the Library and Information Technology Association's board.

A popular and entertaining regular on the demo and speaking circuit, Jean has jacked into the Net in places as diverse as Alaska, the Czech Republic, Italy, Hawaii, and historic booth number one at Rogers Frontier Bar in Old Colorado City, Colorado.

She lives on a hill in central New York, above a woods full of raccoons, fox, and deer. Mom to an 11-year-old son, Stephen, Jean also enjoys her cats, ducks, and a garden pond full of goldfish and lilies. Her husband, Larry, leads a microcomputer repair and support group at a local university and is system administrator of the netmom.com and pollywood.com server network at home. More about Jean is available at her home page: *<http://www.netmom.com/>*.

Communications about this book should go to **mom@netmom.com**.

THE INTERNET KIDS & FAMILY YELLOW PAGES

SECOND EDITION

Jean Armour Polly

Osborne/McGraw-Hill

Berkeley New York St. Louis San Francisco Auckland Bogotá Hamburg London
Madrid Mexico City Milan Montreal New Delhi Panama City Paris São Paulo
Singapore Sydney Tokyo Toronto

THE INTERNET KIDS & FAMILY YELLOW PAGES

SECOND EDITION

OSBORNE/MCGRAW-HILL
2600 TENTH STREET
BERKELEY, CALIFORNIA 94710
U.S.A.

For information on translations or book distributors outside the U.S.A., or to arrange bulk purchase discounts for sales promotions, premiums, or fund-raisers, please contact Osborne/**McGraw-Hill** at the above address.

Publisher
Brandon A. Nordin

Editor-in-Chief
Scott Rogers

Project Editor
Janet Walden

Editorial Assistant
Ann Sellers

Copy Editor
Kathryn Hashimoto

Proofreader
Pat Mannion

Indexer
David Heiret

Computer Designers
Roberta Steele, Sylvia Brown

Illustrators
Leslee Bassin, Roberta Steele

Series Design
Peter F. Hančík

4567890 QPD QPD 998

ISBN 0-07-882340-4

Check with Us

Computer files (making up the pages you see on the World Wide Web) are stored in directories on remote servers all over the world. Sometimes people move these files to different places, so you need to find where they have been moved.

We regularly check every site in this book, to see if it is still there. If it isn't, we try to locate where it has moved. If it's gone, I find something else and replace it. Net-mom will never leave you adrift on the Net!

I let you know about these changes at my Web site: <http://www.netmom.com/>. If you can't get to my home page at www.netmom.com, try its mirror site at <http://www.well.com/user/polly/>.

For my son Stephen

and my mother,

who both have a lot to teach about love

and respect for children.

Put it before them briefly so they will read it, clearly so they will appreciate it, picturesquely so they will remember it, and, above all, accurately so they will be guided by its light.

Joseph Pulitzer

Table of Contents

Acknowledgments

There are a number of people I want to thank, and this is the page where I get to do that.

You wouldn't be holding this book in your hands if it weren't for my husband, Larry Polly. He pulled the ethernet around the house, made sure the servers were running, developed the database for the project, and ran the entire production side of the book manuscript. It was a mammoth task, and he never lost his sense of perspective and humor.

And to my almost 11-year-old son, Stephen, a big hug and thanks for giving Dad and me the time to do something for kids all over the world.

I would be remiss if I did not thank my friend Steve Cisler at Apple Computer, Inc., for continually pushing my thought and action toward finding my own Right Path.

Mario Morino, chairperson of the Morino Institute, believed in this project from the start. I'd like to thank the Morino Institute for financial and moral support. Lots of people say they are behind children's issues, but Mario rolls up his sleeves and gets busy. Watch the man closely, he's a visionary.

From Osborne/McGraw-Hill, I would like to thank Scott Rogers, editor-in-chief, for continued support, even though he hasn't managed to send me on a book signing tour of South Pacific Island bookstores—yet. Also bugging him to do that is Anne Ellingsen, who does all the public relations for the book. If you've read a review, heard me on the radio, or seen me on TV, Anne was probably responsible. So, she will have to come along on the signing trip, too! Senior project editor Janet Walden, copy editor Kathryn Hashimoto, proofreader Pat Mannion, and indexer David Heiret should be praised for the time they took with the book and the care and commitment they displayed towards making it right for families.

Thanks go to my friend Harley Hahn, author of about a zillion computer and Internet books. Harley was a ready source of counsel and encouragement. And he has his own sportswear line.

Now that I think of it, so does John Levine, author of *Internet for Dummies* and many other computer books. Maybe it's a trend. John's deep understanding of the computer book publishing industry, and how to work with it anyway, was a great source of comfort.

To Pat McManus, a tip of the wizard's hat and a big thank you from Net-mom.

To Vicki, Diane, Peg, Melinda, and all the girlfriends, thanks for the support.

To Dewayne, thanks for coaching me on How to be an Entrepreneur 101.

Thanks also to DHL, the courier company used by Osborne/McGraw-Hill. Specifically, Betsy Kosecki, Paul Auber, Claretha Cargo, and Bob Humeniuk. They really helped in shipping out edited material, review copies, and so much more.

I also want to thank Mom for providing support services, including cooking a few dinners and washing the dishes.

I want to acknowledge the work of members of the original research team, whose work also appears in this book: Brian M. Harris, Gayle Keresey, Vicki Kwasniewski, Bernie Sloan, and Mark A. Spadafore.

Thanks to Blythe Bennett of KidsConnect and the KidsConnect librarians: Barb Benkert, Carole L. Ashbridge, Marcia Garman Zorn, Barbara Troisi, Carol Simmons, Carol S. Surges, Dale Hauser, Carol Weinshel, Carolyn Haney, Janice Etscovitz, Jo Ann Wahrman, Kathy Tobiason, Kay Salling, Marlene Lazzara, Mary Deault, Mary Ann Albertine, Michelle Kowalsky, Nelda Brangwin, Sally Ray, Jane Henderson, Rosemary Schmiedeler. Also Jane Taylor (and her mom, Martha Taylor) and teacher Jan Bittner.

To the kids at my son's school: see, some moms *do* write books!

Additional young advisors include Maureen, Colin, and Dylan; Brian; Maureen, Christian, and Justin; Jill and Todd; Chris and Sara; T.J.; David; Ruth; Jacob; Trevor; Jeremy; Matt; Kyle, Nikki, and Noah; and Tyler.

Finally, thank you to the parents, families, teachers, and librarians who bought the first book and made it a best-seller. Kids do belong on the Net.

Respectfully,

Jean Armour Polly
Jamesville, New York
April 1997

About the Research Team

Kitty Bennett is a news researcher and intranet server administrator at the *St. Petersburg Times* in Florida. She first journeyed into the Internet about six years ago, and she now spends many hours a week there doing her work and having fun. Last year, she spent a week in Vladivostok, Russia, teaching Russian journalists how to use the Net to do news research for the Art Pattison Foundation–sponsored conference, "New Media for a New World." A proponent of free community computer networks, she was part of the group that helped to establish a Free-net in the Tampa Bay area. Kitty also worked on the first edition of this book.

Peg Elliott has a master's degree in library science from Syracuse University and currently divides her work time between the Liverpool Public Library, where one of her responsibilities is designing their Web page, and the Dewitt Community Library, where she is a substitute reference librarian. She also conducts an information research service out of her home. Peg is committed to promoting the enhanced use of Internet resources for information and educational purposes and seeks opportunities for the positive use of the Internet as an information tool. In her spare time, Peg is an active volunteer on PTA/PTO committees in each of her three children's schools. Peg is originally from California, and although she has lived in upstate New York for more than 25 years, she dreams of the time when she and her husband will retire their snow shovels and move to a warm and sunny climate. Peg also worked on the first edition of this book.

Ron Evry is a writer whose work appears regularly in *COMBO MAGAZINE* (where he writes about comics and the Internet), *The Comics Journal,* and *Hogan's Alley Magazine.* He is often seen doing special reports on the nationally syndicated *Flights of Fantasy* TV show. He is also the Web page editor for the National Cartoonists Society and the creator of a shareware comic book font called Witzworx, which can be downloaded at *<http://www.clark.net/pub/revry/witzworx.html>.* Ron is vice president of Washington Apple Pi and learned how to create his first Web page using an Apple IIgs and writing HTML code using AppleWriter. He runs the computer lab at Antietam Elementary School in Woodbridge, Virginia, and you can drop in on the school's home page at *<http://www.pen.k12.va.us/~revry/antietam.html>.* Ron also worked on the first edition of this book.

Jan K. France is a volleyball nut and ski bum wannabe, although in real life she's a Mac computer programmer in Colorado. She and her husband, Ray, an information systems manager, have two teenagers who usually couldn't care less about computers. But the kids do love to surf the Net! Jan owns a software company specializing in educational products for children, parents, teachers, and home schoolers. Read the product descriptions and download demos at her home page: *<http://www.dimensional.com/~janf/>.* Jan also worked on the first edition of this book.

Charles and **Frankie Grace** have been surfing the Net for many years now and have reviewed Web sites for an online service. They share a love of theater, music, and the outdoors. In fact, they've camped from Tennessee to Alaska twice and plan to do it again. They have a daughter, Heather, in Alaska (now you know the reason for the mega camping trips) and a son, Philip, in Mississippi. They share their home with two dogs, one cat, and a beta (2.2). Charles has been teaching fifth grade for 22 years with the Shelby County schools. That's where he met Frankie, a professional musician and former teaching assistant. They moonlight as theater technicians and online/data researchers.

John Iliff is system administrator and head of reference at Pinellas Park Public Library *<http://snoopy.tblc.lib.fl.us/pppl/pppl.html>* in Florida. He is cofounder emeritus of PUBLIB, the oldest and largest listserv for public librarians around the world. A former chimney sweep, auto worker, and social worker, he became a librarian after obtaining a master's degree at the University of South Florida. He now lives in a beach shack on Coquina Key, where he picks oranges off his tree almost every day of the year. His wife, Karen (a nurse), and his son, Michael, try to beat him to the modem every night. John also worked on the first edition of this book.

Steve Marks is a former high school teacher and coach who has worked for the State University of New York in television and media production. He has combined these experiences by delving into the world of teleconferencing and distance learning. His wife, Susan, and their four boys, Michael, Andrew, Stephen, and Matthew, enjoy music, sports, and, of course, working with the computer and surfing the World Wide Web! Steve also worked on the first edition of this book.

Neal Meier, a sophomore at Weld Central Junior/Senior High School in Keenesburg, Colorado, keeps busy with any and every extracurricular activity possible. These activities include being sophomore class president and participating in the science fair, Future Business Leaders of America, band, speech, and the Knowledge Bowl. He maintains a 4.0 average and "a somewhat decent social life." Neal is always looking toward the future and what it holds for him.

Keith Parish is a Christian husband, father, writer, musician, and "soldier" in a FORTUNE 500 company, living in Memphis, Tennessee, and loving God, his wife, Sarah Ellen, and their three children, Sarah Emily, Hannah, and Isaac. In 1983, when he first saw the words he'd just typed glowing back in phosphor green on a personal computer screen, a rush of adrenaline surged through his system that he hasn't forgotten since. And now, the jolt of what the Internet has done to personal computing is enough to get him excited all over again.

Larry M. Polly manages the campus microcomputer support group at the State University of New York Health Science Center, at Syracuse, New York. He created and manages the original campus gopher and is webmaster of the www.netmom.com and www.pollywood.com Web sites. A self-taught Unix programmer, he also manages a variety of other servers at the university. When he is not dodging Jean's cats, he enjoys soldering old electronic parts together with his son, Stephen, age 11. He also enjoys traveling to exotic locales.

Stephen Jade Polly, age 11, served as the Kid Advisor and arbiter of humor in this book. He likes to use the Net to learn about science, and his favorite season is Hawaii. His cat, Pooshka, is incredibly large.

Laurel Sharp is a children's and reference librarian who loves to play and hear all kinds of music. She lives with her husband, three sons, and Apples the dog in central New York. Laurel also worked on the first edition of this book.

Diane Towlson is a graphic artist, with a bachelor of fine arts degree from the Rochester Institute of Technology. She is a staff artist and computer wrangler at Onondaga County Parks, where her very cool boss, Jon, helps her and her coworkers create "Special Places for Year-Round Adventure" in the central New York area. When Diane is not online or hawking her fabric masks at art shows, she can be found vacationing in the land of sun, salsa, and Lime 'n' Chili taco chips (which for some reason are not sold east of the Mississippi). Diane also worked on the first edition of this book.

Introduction

What's different about the second edition of this book?

It's bigger! This book has almost 3,400 resources, making it almost twice the size of the first edition. We revisited every site in the first edition and made sure it still qualifies for inclusion under our selection policy. And we've added lots of new entries in almost every category.

There are also more than 230 Net Files—fun trivia questions whose answers can be found all over the Net. (Don't worry, the answers are printed upside down!)

It's up to date! We regularly check every site in this book, to see if it is still there. If it isn't, we try to locate where it has moved. If it's gone, I find something else and replace it. Net-mom will never leave you adrift on the Net!

I let you know about these changes at my Web site: <http://www.netmom.com/>. If you find something that doesn't seem to be working, try the tips later on in the "Troubleshooting" section. If they don't help, check my Web site. Chances are, if there is a consistent problem with a site, we've noticed it and found the solution.

It has more cool stuff! You say you don't have time to read the whole book? I've added my Special Don't-Miss Hotlists for all your favorite topics. We've pulled out the ten best Web resources for:

- Homework help
- Kids who love art and music
- Kids who love comics, cartoons, and animation
- Kids who love games, toys, and interactive stuff
- Kids who love reading, writing, or writing to pen pals
- Kids who love science
- Kids who love sports
- Parents
- Preschoolers
- Teachers

If you look at the hotlists, you can be sure you're hitting the highlights of the Web for that topic.

You'll also find 16 features called "Postcards from the Net." These are behind-the-scenes looks at some of your favorite sites and the folks responsible for them. Net resources like those of the National Zoo or the Exploratorium science museum don't just happen. People build them, dream about them, improve them, and really care about the kids who use them. We've tracked down the webmasters, gotten their pictures, and asked them all kinds of questions about their sites. These unique postcards are scattered throughout the book.

At the back of the book, you'll see two special sections: "Countries of the World" and "Parenting and Families."

Spend some time in our completely new "Countries of the World" section. We've explored thousands of Web sites from governments, embassies, travel agencies, and individuals, looking for the best resources on each country. We've found some fascinating information, including Armenian wedding customs, the national dog of South Korea, and how Canadian kids near the Arctic Circle get to sleep when the sun stays above the horizon all night.

Following the "Countries of the World" section is a special section that contains all the parenting and family life resources, so they will be easier to find. This part of the book has sites on everything from adoption to home schooling, from health to practical parenting. It also has an introductory section called "The Secret Garden: What Parents Ask Me About Kids and the Internet," which includes a collection of questions parents have asked me about the Internet and my answer to each one. I will tell you about parental filtering software, unwanted e-mail and how to stop it, magic cookies, and much more. Check it out.

WHAT'S DIFFERENT ABOUT THIS BOOK?

Other books are collections. This book features *selections*. You're holding the first and only book of Internet resources for kids and families selected by a librarian. You'll find a thoughtful and intuitive organization of Internet knowledge here, driven by the questions I used to answer at the public library reference desk.

I selected these sites with care, respect, and yes, love. I was thinking hard about kids and parents worldwide. I was thinking about inclusion, and tolerance, and disturbing events on the news. I believe that the Net can help humans learn to get along and that there is hope for a better world ahead.

WELCOME KIDS!

It's great to meet you. I can't wait to show you some of my favorite places on the Net!

First, though, you need to know that the Net changes all the time. Some places I thought were cool when I wrote this book might not be the same by the time you follow in my footsteps. So if, on the Net, you find yourself someplace that just doesn't "feel right" to you, or you are "talking" to someone and start to feel uncomfortable with what is going on, go get a parent, teacher, or caregiver. If no one is around, just turn off the computer.

The good news is, while you're reading this, I'm still finding outstanding new places for the next edition of this book. Please think of me as your friend—come on, let's explore!

WELCOME PARENTS, TEACHERS, AND CAREGIVERS!

Because of my unique background as a public librarian, Internet pioneer, and mom, I wrote this book because I believe kids belong on the Net. There has been some movement to ban kids from the Net entirely, and I believe that is entirely wrong. Still, I know that there are places on the Net that I would not want my son to go to without me. There are places in the city where I live that I wouldn't let him go to alone, either.

So, I set out to find places on the Net that were built expressly for children or where people of any age could find value. You're holding in your hands thousands of such locations. Almost all of them are Web sites; the handful remaining are gopher, ftp, or other archives. They are located all over the world, from Washington, D.C. to Moscow. You'll visit servers on tiny Pacific islands, one inside the Vatican, and an Internet video camera aimed at a research station on Antarctica. You'll visit the Library of Congress, NASA, the British Museum, and even some school and family home pages.

SELECTION POLICY: WHAT YOU WILL FIND IN THIS BOOK

Every good library needs a selection policy, so naturally, we have one. Here it is.

This book selects resources for its collection that, in general, meet the following standards:

■ They include compelling, engaging material for children from preschool through eighth grade, or approximately

ages 3 to 14. (Also included are many sites for general audiences of all ages as well as sites for adults in the "Parenting and Families" section.)

■ They display outstanding organization and navigation/search capabilities.

■ They use a judicious mix of graphics and text, so that they will be useful to a user with text-only Web access. Many times these resources will offer a text-only option.

■ They are authoritative and list their sources.

■ They are timely and have a date on them.

■ They exist on a stable Internet site with good connectivity.

SELECTION POLICY: WHAT YOU WON'T FIND IN THIS BOOK

I have explored all these sites myself, in great detail. This book does not knowingly include resources that contain violent, racist, sexist, erotic, or other adult content.

Additionally, I have not included resources involving sexuality and gender issues. In the "Parenting and Families" section, you will find health information, such as a text-based discussion on puberty. My research informs me that most parents want to decide how, and when, to introduce their children to these topics, so I have respected that. If you feel otherwise, please see the "Internet: Search Engines and Directories" section of the book for guidance on finding things on the Net.

You'll see that I have marked some entries with a note called "A caution to parents." Some sites contained too many links for me to follow to their ends. Please be sure to preview these sites yourself.

However, the Internet is always in motion, and resources may change. Something I found appropriate for inclusion in the book today may be inappropriate tomorrow. So, I cannot guarantee that your Internet experience, based on my recommendations, will always meet your needs.

I strongly recommend that parents, caregivers, and teachers always use the Internet alongside their children and preview sites if at all possible.

Still, let me say that when in doubt, I left the site out. I was guided by the following, which I found on a server in Honolulu.

You cannot make people see stuffs they no can see. So, jus worry about yourself...no make hassles, treat everyone like how you like be treated, and everything should be okay dokey.

—Bu La'ia

Some outstanding material for kids is on the Net, and much of it is in this book. The Net is BIG, though, so if you don't find your favorite subject, or your favorite site, it's possible I haven't discovered it yet. You can e-mail me and tell me why it's your favorite, and maybe it will get into the next edition.

So, go have fun with the kids—I hope you like the book. Please write and let me know: **mom@netmom.com**

WHAT YOU NEED TO KNOW TO USE THIS BOOK

This book won't teach you how to use your Net browser; there are too many of them. I use Netscape, but you may use Internet Explorer, America Online, Lynx, or some other application. If you just know how to use your browser, you can find out how to use the Internet. Go to the "Internet— Beginner's Guides" section of this book and start learning.

You need to know what a "smiley" is. Here's one coming at you :-) Now, put your left ear on your left shoulder and look at those characters again. See the little smiley face? This is a "winkie" ;-) and it means we're joking about something. We use these throughout the book. You can read more about smileys in the "Internet—Netiquette, Folklore, and Customs" section of this book.

TROUBLESHOOTING

At the beginning of the "Parenting and Families" section is a special feature called "The Secret Garden: What Parents Ask Me About Kids and the Internet." In it, and among other things, I explain how Web pages get from host computers to your desktop and what can go wrong in between.

Unfortunately, I can't help you with connectivity problems. Contact your Internet service provider and ask them to help you with setting up your browser or configuring other Internet software applications. They may also be able to help you with modem settings or other hardware-related concerns.

However, I can help you with the following problem:

I typed in the address, but it doesn't work. I got "404 Not Found," "Not found on this server," "No DNS entry exists for this server," or some other cranky-sounding message. What should I do?

If you come across this problem, just follow these steps:

1. Try it again. The Internet isn't perfect. Along the way, from where the information lives to your computer, something may have blinked.

2. Check your spelling. Many of these addresses are long and complex, so it's easy to make a mistake. You might try having another person read you the address while you type it.

3. Make sure you are careful to use capital letters or lowercase when they are printed in this book. They are not interchangeable, and the computer won't recognize a file called "foo.html" if you have typed "FOO.HTML."

4. Check to see if perhaps I have found where the page has gone. The updates to this book are all at <http://www.netmom.com/>

5. The location or file name may have changed since I visited the page. That means its address will be different. Computer files (making up the pages you see on the World Wide Web) are stored in directories on remote servers all over the world. Sometimes people move these files to different places, so you need to find where they have been moved.

And if you're pretty smart (and you are, because you've got this book), you'll know four tricks to help you find pages that have moved.

Trick #1: Solve File Name Change Problems

The first trick is to shorten the address and look there. Say that you've been looking for Dorothy and Toto's home page. It used to be at:

http://land.of.oz.gov/munchkinland/mainstreet/dorothy.html

Perhaps Dorothy has changed the name of her home page, so you want to go "back" a level and look around. Try this:

http://land.of.oz.gov/munchkinland/mainstreet/

That takes you "higher" in the directory path, and you may be able to find where Dorothy has moved from there. On the "mainstreet" Web page, you might see several new choices:

/the.scarecrow.html
/the.tin.man.html
/the.cowardly.lion.html
/dorothy.and.toto.html

Great! Dorothy's just changed the name of her home page to include her little dog, too. Choose that one, and make a note of it for future visits. Write the changes directly into this book; I won't mind. Another mystery solved!

If you still can't find what you're looking for, try going back another level. You may have to try several levels back until you locate what you want.

Trick #2: Solve Server Name Change Problems

It's also possible that the Wizard of Oz has ordered that the new name of the World Wide Web server containing everyone's home page will now be called "www.land.of.oz.gov," instead of "land.of.oz.gov." That creates a problem for people looking for home pages under the *old* server name, which isn't there anymore. How are you supposed to find it?

Fortunately, the crafty old Wizard chose a common name change. If a computer server's name is going to be changed, it's often given a prefix to reflect the type of service it runs. Common prefix names are gopher (for those operating Gopher servers), or ftp (for those offering File Transfer Protocol), or www (for sites running Web servers.)

If you don't know what the new server name might be, try *guessing*, using one of these prefixes. For a Web server, try putting "www." in front of whatever name it originally had (unless it already had that prefix). For example, here's the old name:

http://land.of.oz.gov

Here's your guess at the new name:

http://www.land.of.oz.gov

Bingo—that was it! Be sure to make a note of the change in this book, so you won't have that problem again.

Trick #3: Use Search Engines

If none of the above works, it's possible that Dorothy has taken her home page someplace else. In that case, the previous two tricks won't work, since you will no longer find an entry for her anywhere in the Land of Oz domain.

Your next trick involves trying one of the Net search or Net directory indexes, such as Infoseek, Yahoo, and AltaVista. Many of them are listed under those Net buttons on Netscape's browser. If you are using another browser, it probably has similar choices to help you search the entire World Wide Web. Look in the section of this book called "Internet—Search Engines and Directories" for more information on searching techniques.

Choose one of the search engines, and search on the word "dorothy." Chances are, she's put her home page on a computer server in her new domain. Wow, the search returns hundreds of pages containing the word "dorothy." How do you know which one you want, without having to look through all of them?

You would look at the original entry for Dorothy's home page in this book. We have been very careful to print

whatever Dorothy used as her home page title. It is very possible that she is still using that home page title, even though it is located on a different computer server. We don't really have a home page for Dorothy in this book, but to continue the example, let's say this is the original entry's home page title:

Dorothy and Toto's Wicked Good Adventure

Go to one of the search indexes again. Instead of just searching on "dorothy," try the page's title as it is printed in this book. You want to make the search engine look for the entire phrase "Dorothy and Toto's Wicked Good Adventure." You don't want to search on "Dorothy," "Toto's," "Wicked," "Good," and "Adventure" separately. If you did that, you would get hundreds of items again; we are trying to narrow it down, and searching on the entire phrase will help do that. Check the directions for the particular index you are using (typically, a Help button will take you there); many of them allow you to keep the entire phrase together by putting it between quotation marks. So, for example, you would try this:

Search on: "Dorothy and Toto's Wicked Good Adventure"

Or: "Dorothy and Toto"

Or: "Wicked Good Adventure"

If that doesn't work, you can try to guess what Dorothy might have said in the *content* of her home page. She probably talks about Toto, the Scarecrow, the Tin Man, and the Lion in there somewhere. Therefore, these words will be indexed, and you should be able to use that knowledge when you search using one of the indexes.

Go back to your search engine (we like Infoseek or the advanced mode of the AltaVista search engine for this). Try the following (be sure to check the Help files to learn the correct way to phrase your search):

Search on: Dorothy AND Toto AND Scarecrow

Or: Dorothy AND Lion

Or: Dorothy AND Scarecrow AND Lion

Trick #4: Check with Us

When all else fails, don't forget to look on my home page at <http://www.netmom.com/>. While you were trying all these tricks, we may have already found where the page has been moved. If you can't get to my home page at www.netmom.com, try its mirror site at <http://www.well.com/user/polly/>.

These are just some tips to help you find where Dorothy's gone. I know they will help!

For Homework Help

Here's emergency info for kids who need quick facts for homework assignments. Check it out!

Biography.com
http://www.biography.com/
Got a name? Get the facts! Here's a searchable online database from A&E TV and the *Cambridge Biographical Encyclopedia.*

CNN Interactive
http://www.cnn.com/
There's no better place than this to get the latest current events and news information. Read about the top news stories by category, get news summaries in the daily news almanac, or search to get a list of recent news articles by keyword. The video vault has some really cool stuff, too.

HomeWorkHelper! Welcome!
http://www.homeworkhelper.com/
Here you can submit your question, select any or all of the six source types, and GO. For older students, there is also a link to the Electric Library and Researchpaper.com, the Internet's largest collection of topics, ideas, and assistance for school-related research projects.

Internet Public Library Reference Center
http://ipl.sils.umich.edu/ref/
This site links to sites all over the Net, so be prepared to take some time to check all the different sources at the Internet Public Library.

IPL Citing Electronic Resources
http://www.ipl.org/classroom/userdocs/internet/citing.html
Using the Net to find information for research projects is great, but how do you cite all those electronic resources? This useful list from the Internet Public Library will show you the way.

Kids Web - A World Wide Web Digital Library for Schoolkids
http://www.npac.syr.edu/textbook/kidsweb/
What's your assignment? Here you'll find a short list of links arranged by subject category: arts, sciences, social studies, reference, sports, and some fun and games, too.

Knowledge Adventure Encyclopedia
http://www.adventure.com/library/encyclopedia/
It's 8 P.M. and the local library is closed. You left your textbook in school and your family doesn't own a set of encyclopedias. Don't panic! Try this online encyclopedia—you can search by keyword or phrase.

Library of Congress World Wide Web (LCWeb) Home Page
http://lcweb.loc.gov/
This is the ultimate library and your link to just about everything! You can search the American Memory historical collection for help with your history homework, but there are also international exhibitions, government resources, links to all the state libraries, online reading rooms on lots of topics, and LC Marvel's gopher-based, subject access to Internet sites.

Research-It! - Your one-stop reference desk
http://www.itools.com/research-it/
This site's cool! Spell a word, conjugate a verb, find a quote, or locate facts about a famous person. More than 15 quick reference tools are all rolled into one easy-to-use site.

StudyWEB
http://www.the-acr.com/studyweb/studyweb.htm
This site is sure to have something you can use, with more than 10,000 research-quality links listed by subject category. The Reference Shelf is a good place to start, but the brief reviews of each site will also help you select just the right place to look.

For Kids Who Love Art and Music

A huge creative community is out there on the Net! Be part of the arts, crafts, and music scene in cyberspace.

Aunt Annie's Crafts Page
http://www.auntannie.com/
She won't pinch your cheeks and talk about how much you've grown! Aunt Annie *will* give you ideas, patterns, and great directions for making interesting crafts. She has a new project for you each week, and it's not the usual "handprint in the plaster" craft. Many are paper crafts, like table decorations, paper hats, or toys. Who could ask for a cooler aunt?

Carlos' Coloring Book Home
http://www.ravenna.com/coloring/
Did you ever use a computer and the Internet to color? At this site, you can color a birthday cake, a snowman, and other fun pictures on the World Wide Web with your computer! The best thing about this coloring book is that you can color over and over, and the pages don't fall out!

The Crayola Art Education Page
http://www.crayola.com/art_education/
Inspirations! When you look at this site, you'll be amazed at all the ways you can use crayons, markers, watercolors, and other art products. There are examples of other kids' drawings, too.

Eyeneer Music Archives
http://www.eyeneer.com/
Here are links to world music, contemporary classical, new jazz, and American music. Each link will keep you busy exploring for a good while. In the International Music Archive, photos, sound samples, and descriptions of instruments abound. You can see and hear a Chinese qin or a Japanese shakuhachi. Elsewhere, look for biographical information, photos, QuickTime video, interviews, and information on new recordings.

Joseph Wu's Origami Page
http://www.datt.co.jp/Origami/
Where else could you find a picture of an origami Swiss Army knife, or paper dragons, wizards, and sea anemones? Admire these figures as sculpture, or try and make your own. You'll find origami diagrams, photographs, and places to buy a great variety of paper and books here.

Mark Kistler's Imagination Station
http://www.draw3d.com/
The real world is in three dimensions: objects have width, length, and depth. In a drawing, you have only two dimensions to work with: length and width. You have to use special techniques to simulate the third dimension of depth. No problem—Mark's here to give you 3-D drawing lessons. You say you can't even draw a straight line? Mark claims it doesn't matter. Soon you'll be talking about the 12 Renaissance secrets of 3-D drawing right along with him!

RCA: Idiot's Guide to Classical Music
http://www.rcavictor.com/rca/hits/idiots/cover.html
Did you know that when you listen to the Elmer Fudd theme song ("Kill da wabbit! Kill da wabbit!") you're really tapping your foot to "Ride of the Valkyries" by Wagner? You probably recognize more classical music than you'd think! Listen to some of the sound bites at this site, and see which ones you know from TV commercials, shows, and movies. You'll also find a Beginner's Guide to Classical Music at this site.

Songs for Scouts
http://www.macscouter.com/Songs/index.html
Gather 'round the campfire and share some singing. Here are silly songs, lots of gross songs, and songs that are just plain fun. If you want the definitive version of "Greasy Grimy Gopher Guts," look no further.

WebMuseum: Bienvenue! (Welcome from the curator)
http://sunsite.unc.edu/wm/
Browse through an incredible collection of famous paintings and other artwork. See the *Mona Lisa*, the most recognized piece of art in the world, or listen to classical music in the auditorium. You can even take a mini-tour of Paris! The opening page of the WebMuseum includes a list of its mirror sites. Choose one close to you to provide a faster connection.

Welcome to Piano on the Net '97
http://www.artdsm.com/music.html
Would you like to learn how to play the piano or how to read music? You can! The first few lessons don't even require a piano, but for later lessons you will want a piano. Even a small portable keyboard will do. This easy, reassuring series of modules includes QuickTime movies, audio files, even online metronomes to keep you on time with the music.

For Kids Who Love Comics, Cartoons, and Animation

Cartoon Corner
http://www.cartooncorner.com/
Step-by-step cartoon character drawing lessons and sections on what cartoonists do make this a terrific site for budding cartoonists of all ages!

The Comic Strip
http://www.unitedmedia.com/comics/
Every week they make families around the world laugh. They have names like Snoopy, Dilbert, and Marmaduke. Who are these wacky characters? They are the drawings that make up the comic strips in your newspaper. Catch up on your favorite comic strip characters, and see what they are doing on the Internet. Find out about the artists and how they thought up the characters, and play games based on the comic strip. Then take a detour from the main page to the National Cartoonists Society, where the *real* cartoonists behind the strips hang out!

Draw and Color with Uncle Fred
http://www.unclefred.com/
"Uncle Fred" Lasswell has been drawing the "Barney Google and Snuffy Smith" comic strip since 1934, and it still stays on the cutting edge of today's technology. His Web page includes numerous fun cartoon drawing lessons and features from his videodisk of the same name. Even the youngest of Web surfers will have no trouble drawing these characters.

DC Comics
http://www.dccomics.com/
DC Comics is the home of such superhero greats as Superman and Batman, along with many others. We wonder if they ever go out for lunch together. If you want to know what's new at their comic book company, stop in here. You will find some of those trendy new cyber trading cards, as well as sound clips and more!

Garfield Online
http://www.garfield.com/
This purr-fect home page is hosted by a big fat hairy deal: Garfield! Check out the recipes for Garfield's favorite food (lasagne) and read some great jokes. Still can't get enough of this cantankerous kitty? Grab a Garfield screen saver for your computer!

Marvel Universe Online
http://www.marvelcomics.com/marvel.html
Do X-Men have anything to do with X-Files? We don't think so, but then we haven't read everything at this site! Silver Surfer, Ghost Rider, and Spider-Man are all part of the Marvel Comics universe. This new site promises games in the near future, maybe by the time you read this. Right now you can find cyber trading cards and info on the characters. Web-sling your way to this site as soon as you can!

The Non-Stick MGM Cartoons Site
http://www.nonstick.com/mgm/
Here is everything you always wanted to know about Tom and Jerry, Droopy, and all the other classic MGM cartoons and how they were made. The site features downloadable sounds and graphics and includes links to other terrific animation pages as well.

RON KURER'S TOON TRACKER HOME PAGE
http://ftp.wi.net/~rkurer/index.html
With so many long-forgotten animated cartoons of the past showing up on cable TV these days, this site is a gold mine of information on many of them. Find pages devoted to Mighty Mouse, Beany and Cecil, Clyde Crashcup, Clutch Cargo, Bullwinkle, Woody Woodpecker, and dozens more!

The Simpsons
http://www.foxnetwork.com/simpsons/simpson2.htm
Bart is just a good kid with a "few bad ideas...that are still being reviewed by the Springfield district attorney." Better get over to the official Fox Network Simpsons Web page before you have a cow! You'll find some fun Simpson games, news about the show, and contests here in virtual Springfield.

Warner Bros. Kids
http://www.kids.warnerbros.com/
Anyone with the slightest interest in animated cartoons needs to drop in here. The step-by-step tour of how a cartoon gets made is the World Wide Web at its best! The site also includes Looney Tunes Online Karaoke and Looney Tunes Web Postcards!

For Kids Who Love Games, Toys, and Interactive Stuff

???? Welcome to the Adventure ????
http://www.post-mystery.com/about.html
Ready to go on a mission to save an endangered animal? All right! Trouble is, you don't know what kind of animal you're trying to save! If you follow the clues and answer a few simple questions, you might be able to save the Mystery Critter before the poachers snag it!

The Amazing Fish-Cam!
http://www1.netscape.com/fishcam/fishcam.html
Yes, from wherever you are on the Web, you can watch fish swim around a tank in someone's office. These fish can be viewed by two different cameras (you get to pick), or you can choose the Continuously Refreshing Fish-Cam if you have Netscape 1.1. Ah, a nice, salty glass of refreshing fish-cam—there's nothing quite like it!

Platypus Children's Garden
http://www.peak.org/~platypus/in.html
Do you like puzzles? Here you'll find mazes, word search puzzles, jigsaws, and more. Many of them were designed for kids, by kids! You'll also find family activities, music, pages that *talk* and *sing* (if you have the right plug-ins and hardware), and much more. We particularly enjoyed the "Shareware Carol." This site is available in English and Spanish, and some songs are in Japanese.

Cyber Jacques' Cyber Seas Treasure Hunt
http://www.cyberjacques.com/
Avast ye, me hearties, from whatever else you're doing, and come try the games at Cyber Jacques' seagoing arcade. They all require Shockwave, so you'd best have a current version or you'll be walking the plank real soon! What's here? In Fish, you throw pies at a bear but avoid the flying fish jumping up between the two of you. In What's Inside, you take apart a pirate to see what's underneath (a hamster running around an exercise wheel is one thing we found) and retrieve letters to a word puzzle. Figure out the secret word, and you've won! You'll find several more equally wacky games here.

Discovery Online, Keiko — Keiko Cam
http://www.discovery.com/area/keiko/whale1.4.html
Did you ever see the *Free Willy* movies about the whale that was rescued from a small dispay aquarium? Did you know that "Willy" is really named Keiko, and he now lives in a two-million-gallon aquarium in Oregon? You can look at him every day. The text explains why Keiko, a boy, has a name that is usually a girl's name. You're right—it was a mistake!

Happy Puppy's Front Porch
http://happypuppy.com/
Happy Puppy brings you a list of computer gaming software and home pages of many of the video and computer game software companies on the Net. You'll find lists for Mac and PC games and info on new versions of your favorite games as they are announced. Other software archives listed here have cheat codes, shareware, demos, and upgrades available for those in need of too much fun!

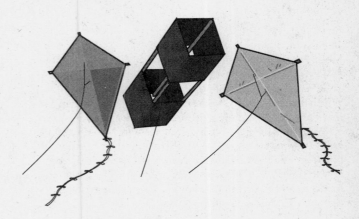

Interactive Model Railroad - MAIN
http://rr-vs.informatik.uni-ulm.de/rr/
This one is pretty cool. You get to give commands to an actual model train at the University of Ulm in Germany! You pick the train you want to control, tell it which station to go to, and if you're quick (and lucky) enough, you're in charge. A box on the page gives the domain name of whoever happens to be controlling the train at the time.

Minifig Generator
http://www.legopolis.com/minifig/
This neat interactive site uses Lego body parts and JavaScript so you can have fun picking heads, torsos, and legs to create your own mini figure. How about a pirate's head on a doctor's lab coat, with skeleton legs? You can make your own choices or let the computer randomly pick its own. You can then name your creation and build it so that you can print out a copy. Cool, huh?

Virtual Mr. Spud Head
http://www.westnet.com/~crywalt/pothead/pothead.html
Similar to Mr. Potato Head, this site lets you choose other vegetables. Try a mustache on an artichoke or maybe some spectacles on a pumpkin. Not a veggie fan? You could try a famous politician, too!

Virtual Pet Home Page
http://www.virtualpet.com/vp/
If you can't have a real pet, maybe you can own a virtual pet! The Tamagocchi "Lovable Egg" has become a real craze in Japan, and all signs point to overwhelming popularity when the little pastel-colored eggs are introduced to the U.S. this summer (as Tamagotchi). What are they? Check this site for pictures of them, plus information on all known types of virtual pets. You can download free demos of some of them.

For Kids Who Love Reading, Writing, or Writing to Pen Pals

OK, so reading, writing, and pen pal exchanges have been around forever, right? Yes, but with the Net, they've never been easier or more fun. If you love the written word and the thrill of correspondence sent and received, don't miss these sites. Warning: No flabby brains allowed!

Children's Bestsellers
http://www.bookwire.com/pw/bsl/childrens/
current.childrens.html

What are kids reading today? Now *Publishers Weekly* puts its Children's Bestsellers List on the Net. For picture book, fiction, paperback series, and nonfiction, you'll get the week's top ten sellers, with title, author, publisher, price, and ISBN number. There's also the all-time children's best-sellers in paperback and hard cover (*The Pokey Little Puppy*, 14 million copies—wow!).

Children's Literature Web Guide
http://www.ucalgary.ca/~dkbrown/

This comprehensive, highly acclaimed site will help you find what seems to be anything and everything about children's literature. It is simple, fast, well organized, and aided by a good search engine. If you're into reading, there's no place like this Net home.

The Electric Postcard
http://postcards.www.media.mit.edu/postcards/

Stop by this postcard rack, select a topic, browse the pictures, address it to an e-mail buddy, write a message, and with a mouse click, it's there. You can even put in Web links and pictures of your own if you're "HTML-savvy."

For Young Writers
http://www.inkspot.com/~ohi/inkspot/young.html

If you dream about writing, or if you write and you want your writing to be better or published or just appreciated by others, it's all here! Get advice from professional writers and editors. Participate in chat sessions and discussions with other young writers. Find links to other useful writing sites. Submit your work to the Young Writer's Collection for Web publication. You may even get your first, paying writing gig by visiting the Paying Markets page. Capital!

How A Book Is Made
http://www.harpercollins.com/kids/book.htm

Have you ever wondered how an idea for a book makes it from the author's mind to print and, finally, the hands of an eager reader? Author and illustrator Aliki and her book-loving cats take you through all the steps. This colorful and informative part of the site is great fun. But don't miss the powerful thoughts from author Patricia MacLachlan on what it is to be a writer and how life feeds the creative process.

IPL Youth Division
http://www.ipl.org/youth/

IPL stands for Internet Public Library. Like a great library, this "cybrary" has cool exhibits (like how a car is built), book talk (book reviews "by kids, for kids"), Story Hour (where you can read and hear online stories), and plenty of ways, old and new, to explore the world.

KidPub WWW Publishing
http://www.kidpub.org/kidpub/

The title of this site says it all. If you want to read lots (10,000 submissions in the archive at last count) of writing published by kids from all over, stop in and enjoy these original works. Maybe you want to see your own name and work in print, er, pixels. This is the place to submit it. Or maybe you'd like the fun of contributing a paragraph to an unfolding, collaborative story.

Maddy Mayhem's PenPal List!
http://nebula.on.ca/madbo/penpal.htm

A part of the safe and fun Maddy Mayhem's Kids' Stuff site, the PenPal List is a good place to go to learn about others and the world around you as you exercise the art of writing. If you're age 17 or under, fill out a form with information about yourself and your interests, click a button, and zap—you've just joined the group. Scan the list of correspondents or use your browser's find feature to look for that certain pen pal who shares your interests. But remember, read Maddy's reminders about how to be safe meeting people on the Net. Reach out and write someone!

NGS - WORLD Magazine
http://www.nationalgeographic.com/ngs/mags/
world/world1.html

This is definitely not your parents' *National Geographic*. This is your *National Geographic*. Learn far-out facts like how a doctor in Texas is developing a way to "grow" vaccines into fruits (better than a sharp stick in the arm). This site keeps you coming back with jokes, riddles, pictures, and interesting stories and facts. Grab it!

Stone Soup, the magazine of writing and art by young people
http://www.stonesoup.com/

"The beautiful magazine by young writers and artists!" This is how this site's authors describe *Stone Soup*. We couldn't agree more. *Stone Soup* is a magazine/e-zine made up of poems, stories, and book reviews by writers up to age 13. Its form and content are exceptional. Might your work qualify? Submission policy and prices paid are described.

For Kids Who Love Science

DAN'S WILD WILD WEATHER PAGE
http://www.whnt19.com/kidwx/
Want to know how clouds are formed or what to do if you are caught in a lightning storm? Just see Dan! He has info on almost any weather occurrence. From hurricanes to air pressure, Dan has it covered with colorful diagrams and graphics. Teachers and parents might just learn a thing or two, as well.

Exploratorium: ExploraNet
http://www.exploratorium.edu/
Do you know what makes a fruit fly grow legs out of its head? How would you like to take a light walk and exploring the world of shadows? The Exploratorium, in San Francisco, is a huge hands-on science laboratory for kids of all ages. Discover the many interesting wonders that they have ported to the Web!

Home Page of VolcanoWorld
http://volcano.und.nodak.edu/vw.html
How do you become a volcanologist? Just ask Mr. Spock for lessons, of course! Well, not quite. Look at this site to find out what becoming a volcanologist is all about and what courses you'll need to take. Also you'll learn about computers (hey, you're halfway there, since you wouldn't be reading this if you didn't know about computers already). Oh yeah, there's also the BEST information here about volcanoes, including lessons and activities for teachers and students.

The MAD Scientist Network
http://medinfo.wustl.edu/~ysp/MSN/
Do you have a question about science that is stumping everyone you ask? Or maybe you have a really simple question you're too embarrassed to bring up in class. Look no further. You have just stumbled onto the solution. This site is a collaboration of scientists around the world gathered to answer your questions. You can search the archives and see if your question, or one like it, has already been answered.

Missouri Botanical Garden Learning Network
http://www.mobot.org/MBGnet/index2.htm
A *biome* is the collection of creatures and plants living in a particular region. Explore six different biomes here: grassland, rain forest, taiga, deciduous forest, desert, and tundra. You'll learn about the features of each area and its plants and animals. You don't have a clue what living in the taiga is like? Ask a kid at a school in Finland or Russia—links to schools in each biome area are included here!

Neuroscience Resources for Kids
http://weber.u.washington.edu/~chudler/introb.html
When you bite into a chocolate bar, how do you know it's delicious? How do you know to say "Ouch!" when you get stung by a mosquito? Little sensors, called *neurons,* are all over your body, and they carry messages to your brain through a system of nerves. Your brain then sorts everything out. This resource is crammed with great info about brains, your senses, spinal cords, and careers in neuroscience. Be aware, though, that many of these folks go to school for 20 *years* before they become neuroscientists!

Science Friday Kids Connection
http://www.npr.org/programs/sfkids
Every Friday, science guru Ira Flatow hosts a radio show on National Public Radio, called (what else?) "Science Friday." The companion Web site for kids is a real treasure for all listeners! Interested in the show topic? Find study questions, links, and resources to find out more about it. Recent topics have included comets, identifying smashed bugs on your car windshield, and HAL, the robot from the movie *2001: A Space Odyssey.*

StarChild: A learning center for young astronomers
http://heasarc.gsfc.nasa.gov/docs/StarChild/StarChild.html
This is a wonderful beginner's guide to astronomy. It's written for smaller children and presents itself in an easy-to-read text. This site includes sections on general astronomy, Earth, planets, stars, galaxies, the Sun, and more. Use these pages to introduce a child (or brother or sister) to the wonders of space. You may even learn some new stuff yourself.

Welcome to Cockroach World
http://www.nj.com/yucky/roaches/
"Ewww, gross!" Wait just one minute. Maybe they aren't so disgusting. They're even a little cool. Facts, multimedia presentations, quizzes, and more await you at the place that's proud to call itself the Yuckiest Site on the Internet.

Zia Kid's Experiments Page
http://www.zia.com/tech/exp/default.htm
If you're looking for a way to dazzle the rest of the class with your science fair know-how, get your safety goggles on and take a look here! You'll learn how to make raisins dance, grow crystal cubes and needles, and examine the attraction of magnetic breakfast cereal. Most of these kitchen chemistry experiments are based on a series from the American Chemical Society, so you know it's not just science, it's GOOD science!

For Kids Who Love Sports

Play 'em. Watch 'em. Talk about 'em. Listen to 'em. Sports are the best. The Web has your sport, whether it's hot air ballooning, juggling, or one of the more popular team sports. We made the call: these sites are the winners!

The AudioNet Sports Guide
http://www.audionet.com/sports/
You missed the big game? Check here to see if an audio broadcast is available. Some are live; others are here whenever you tune in. You'll also catch online shows with coaches and players, as well as special reports.

CNN - Sports
http://www.cnn.com/SPORTS/index.html
Get the top stories in the world of sports from CNN. From auto racing to rugby to yachting—even the more unusual sports get attention here.

ESPNET SportsZone
http://espnet.sportszone.com/
This looks like a newspaper, with cover stories and more inside. ESPNET covers all the major sports and many of the minor ones. Live audio feeds, chats with sports figures, and replay movies make it an entertaining way to get your sports. Bet your newspaper doesn't do that!

GORP - Great Outdoor Recreation Pages
http://www.gorp.com/
Do you love adventure *and* sports? Then turn to the great outdoors for the excitement you seek. How about high-country skiing? Or kayaking down a white-water river? Is hang gliding your dream? Is rock climbing your quest? Give an extreme sport a try here at GORP.

INTERNATIONAL SOCCER NET
http://207.67.226.117/soccernet/
Stay fit with stretching and conditioning tips. Read interviews with soccer greats. Get news about the World Cup. Link to college, pro, and international teams. What a kick!

Major League Baseball MLB@BAT
http://www.majorleaguebaseball.com/
If you're into card collecting, baseball video games, improving your game, fantasy baseball, or just hanging out with the stars—it's all here. Just put your mitts on the mouse!

NFL.COM: Front Page
http://www.nfl.com/
Get to your favorite NFL teams fast at this official site. When we popped in to the Denver Broncos' page, for instance, it had lots to offer. Audio clips from the players, stats, schedules, results, and special stories are updated often. Here comes Elway. Go for the TD!

OLYMPICS Home Page
http://www.olympic.nbc.com/
The Olympics roll around every few years, so there's always something to look forward to or highlights from the past to look back on. NBC's official site has special moments, results, athlete profiles, and fun facts.

Sports Illustrated for Kids
http://pathfinder.com/SIFK/
This magazine goes far beyond its print edition. They've got the cover stories, sure. But they've also got sports games that you can play online, as well as puzzles, movies, and sound clips. (Singing football players? Spare us!)

The Unofficial Michael Jordan Picture Gallery
http://rossby.metr.uoknor.edu/~jbasara/mike/jordan.html
Normally we wouldn't concentrate on just one sports figure. But for Michael Jordan...well, we just had to make an exception. See Michael dunking the ball. See Michael shooting a free throw. See Michael soaring through the air. See Michael driving around an opponent. See Michael smiling. You've got to love this guy!

For Parents

If you just want the skinny, the bottom line, and the cut-to-the-chase best sites on the Net for parenting, keep reading.

Canadian Parents Online
http://www.canadianparents.com/
Here is a good place for parents to help each other in a comfortable, community atmosphere in which to connect and communicate about diverse issues, such as stepparenting, foster parenting, or handling special needs children. Be sure to check out the Library for monthly feature articles or ask one of the resident experts questions about nutrition, family finances, or child rearing.

Educational Resources For Parents
http://www.execpc.com/~dboals/parents.html
Wow, talk about one-stop shopping! There are more than 160 links to sites of interest to parents, grandparents, and other caregivers. Articles range all the way from preparing yourself for parenthood to preparing your child for college, and every possible stage in between. There are links to organizations, such as the National PTA and scouting, online magazines, and book reviews.

Family Planet
http://family.starwave.com/
This daily online family and parenting magazine has it all: feature articles on both the fun and the serious sides of parenting in the twenty-first century. If you've been bitten by the travel bug, enjoy the local events calendars, children's museums, and festivals listings for many major U.S. and international cities.

Family.com
http://family.com/
Is the way to your child's heart through his or her stomach? Even if it's not, you'll enjoy the recipes and nutrition information here, along with the special feature articles on computing, education, and general family issues. "Get the Local Angle" by linking to more than 100 regional parenting publications.

Fathers' Resource Center: Home Page
http://www.visi.com/~frc/
Whether you are a new dad, a single dad, or a seasoned dad, this site has something for you. The quarterly online newsletter, Father Times, offers insightful articles and advice designed to "support, educate, and advocate" fathers. The list of links to other father-focused resources, personal stories, and online magazines is great.

The National Parenting Center
http://www.tnpc.com/
If you are like most parents, you have doubts and concerns about medical, educational, and behavioral issues involving your child. Here you can read the daily *ParentTalk Newsletter* for comprehensive and responsible guidance from nine of the world's most renowned child-rearing authorities. You can also participate in one of the Parenting dialog rooms.

ParenthoodWeb — The WWW Community for Parents and Families
http://www.parenthoodweb.com/
Here new parents and parents of young children can "Ask the Pros," browse the Library for child care and parenting articles, find out about children's product recalls, and participate in the open discussion board. Don't miss the links to software and movie reviews.

The Parenting Community: PARENTS PLACE.COM
http://www.parentsplace.com/
So, you've survived parenting your terrible two-year-old, but how do you cope with the terrifying teen years? Parents, this is definitely one to bookmark! As your kids get older, you won't outgrow this site, which offers information beyond early childhood issues and includes those issues of most concern to parents of teens. There are chat rooms, reading rooms, health and education news, family activities, and even recipes.

Parents Page
http://www.currents.net/community/family/parent.html
Do you need to know how to get a family Internet account? Are you looking for educational software reviews? This computer-oriented parenting site offers links to Internet filtering sites and software, *Computer Currents* articles for parents, and a hodgepodge of other interesting links.

Positive Parenting (On-Line)
http://www.positiveparenting.com/
All of us who are parents know that dealing with kids can be a real battle of the wills. This site provides support and advice on how to handle the most difficult situations with your kids and includes a great set of parenting links.

For Preschoolers

Preschoolers are gourmets when it comes to computers. They want something more than what they can already do on paper. We looked for totally engaging, thinking activities when selecting these sites.

Billy Bear Storybooks - Free Fun & Games Page
http://www.worldvillage.com/kidz/bilybear/wgames.htm
The graphics here are superb! Kids can play games online or offline on paper. "Make Your Own Cartoon Bear" and the "Mix & Match Em Up" games are sure to be winners.

CTW The Official Home of Sesame Street
http://www.ctw.org/
Home to the *Sesame Street* Web site, there is also a link to CTW's new preschool series, *Big Bag*. Numerous activities are here: an interactive storybook, online games, and coloring pages. The topics button leads to a list of advice and tips from experts. This site has laughs for parents, too!

Hop Pop Town
http://www.kids-space.org/HPT/
Precious musical games let preschoolers record a song or experiment with notes and instruments. A writing activity makes a cute, illustrated story. It's easy to use with a little adult and kid help: the kids learn about music and the mouse; the adults learn how to think more creatively!

I Spy
http://www.lexmark.com/data/spy/spy.html
Pictures on this site contain lots of objects and make for a fun game. To play, just say "I spy..." and mention an item. Parents can make it easy or gradually more difficult as their child gains the skill of visual discernment. A list of items to be found is included for each picture.

LITTLE EXPLORERS by Enchanted Learning Software
http://www.EnchantedLearning.com/Dictionary.html
The younger set can click on any letter in the alphabet and link to *oodles* of activities. This is an interactive picture dictionary with hours of fun just waiting behind the letters.

Mr. Edible Starchy Tuber Head Home Page
http://winnie.acsu.buffalo.edu/potatoe/
or Java version at
http://westnet.com/~crywalt/SpudHead/SpudHead.html
To play, just click on the desired nose, eyes, or ears. Clicking on the potato head makes the part appear. Kids know the drill!

Mister Rogers' Neighborhood
http://www.pbs.org/rogers/
Parents, print out the coloring pages and art projects for the preschoolers in *your* neighborhood. Then get great ideas from the "Plan and Play Activities." They present ways to explore a theme like "Mad Feelings" or "Everybody's Special."

Nikolai's Web Site - Home Page!
http://www.nikolai.com/nnn.htm
The kids will find lots of creative stuff to do here! Make finger puppets, print out and build a town or a circus, cook easy recipes, dress paper dolls, read stories. Watch out for pirates!

Preschool Pages - At Home Moms
http://www.intex.net/~dlester/pam/preschool/
  preschoolpage.html
Crafts for little hands, finger plays, recipes, games, and online stories are just a few of the ideas we found here. Parents will love these on a rainy day!

Theodore Tugboat
http://www.cochran.com/TT.html
Little ones can make choices in the online stories about this tugboat. Do they want to visit a barge or a big ship? Do they want to make friends or look for a job? Also included is Berit's Best Sites for Children, a collection of more than 500 links.

For Teachers

You don't even have time for lunch, so how are you supposed to digest all this Internet stuff? Start with these teacher-oriented sites as your staples. Bon appetit!

Access Excellence
http://www.gene.com/ae/
Focusing on the biological sciences, the activities collection is truly excellent. Online "seminars" put you in touch with scientists and other teachers. Offerings include "Local Habitats," "Science of Amber," and "Emerging Diseases." Collaborative classroom projects like "Fossils Across America" help in sharing resources.

Cisco Educational Archive and Resources Catalog
http://sunsite.unc.edu/cisco/edu-arch.html
OK, you've got this great new computer sitting in front of you, with a super-fast modem. Now, how do you actually use it for your day-to-day teaching? Are you looking for information about the dilophosaurus? Or perhaps you want to find out more about civil rights? Don't waste any time—go right to the door of the Virtual Schoolhouse! Investigate your questions here and "CEARCH" using a very fast search engine. Cisco's done an excellent job of collecting great resources for kids, teachers, and parents. You'll also find a list of online schools and links to their home pages. You may never have heard of Cisco, but your Internet service provider has, and chances are good that much of your Internet traffic travels through Cisco equipment. Cisco often announces special grants and other opportunities for schools here, so check often.

Internet Resources for Special Educators
http://www.interactive.net/~wader/sped.htm
OK, in your classroom you've got two gifted students, five with ADD, one with cerebral palsy, four learning-disabled kids, and three with behavior disorders. How do you mainstream them all? This collection will point you to the support you need.

Kathy Schrock's Guide for Educators - Home Page
http://www.capecod.net/schrockguide/
The links in this guide are organized according to subject area. If you teach World History, for instance, you'll get a breakdown of Web pages, from the "Ancient World Web" to "World War II: The World Remembers." A list of new pages each month will point you to the latest and greatest.

PBS Teacher Connex
http://www.pbs.org/tconnex/
There are so many TV programs! How do you select the best ones for your classroom? Here are descriptions of the shows on public television, grouped by month or subject area. Teacher guides, info on taping rights, and links to related sites—they're all here in one place.

Quest: NASA K-12 Internet Initiative
http://quest.arc.nasa.gov/
NASA presents you with ways to use the Internet in your classroom. Ongoing projects to connect K–12 classrooms are all built around the space theme. Offerings include Web chats, teaching tips, curriculum materials, and a pipeline to NASA experts.

TEACHERS HELPING TEACHERS
http://www.pacificnet.net/~mandel/
Don't you just hate to read "advice" from someone who has never set foot in the classroom? Instead, here are your peers, who know *exactly* what you're going through and how to help. It's very practical!

Urban Education Web
http://eric-web.tc.columbia.edu/
UEweb is connected with the ERIC (Educational Resources Information Center) clearinghouses. They offer vast numbers of articles, manuals, and other publications about urban education. Just one example is their "Strong Families, Strong Schools" handbook. One of UEweb's best features is its searchable ERIC databases. These hold lesson plans, publications, and educational research. Of course, if you'd rather gopher right to the ERIC files, you can also go to: gopher://ericir.syr.edu/

Web Sites And Resources For Teachers
http://www.csun.edu/~vceed009/
All subject areas are covered here, but let's take math as an example. You get not only lesson plans but also online math applications, like a calorie calculator and even a magic square checker. Online board games such as Mancala (the great strategy game that teaches critical thinking) and dozens of puzzles will challenge your students to go beyond worksheet math.

Web66 Home Page
http://web66.coled.umn.edu/
Are you new to the Information Superhighway? Wondering how to integrate it into your classroom? Web66 will help you get connected with other K–12 classrooms. Route your course instead of wandering all over the Web!

AFRICAN AMERICANS

The Universal Black Pages

This site collects African American spoken word, music, art, entertainment, and historical resources. You'll also find lots about the Diaspora, which refers to the spread of Africans around the world by slavery and other means. Now their descendants find themselves separated by geography but joined by cultural and historical roots. Prepare for a rich experience here!

http://www.gatech.edu/bgsa/blackpages.html

CULTURE
Africa Online: Kids Only

At this site, you can find a key pal at a school in Africa! Did you know that over 1,000 different languages are spoken in Africa? For some quick lessons in Kiswahili, some fun word search and other games, and biographies of Nelson Mandela and other famous Africans, check this site.

http://www.africaonline.com/AfricaOnline/kidsonly.html

African Wedding Guide

Some couples are choosing to add touches of African culture to their wedding ceremonies. If someone in your family is getting married soon, make sure he or she sees this site. You'll find information on choosing African fabrics, using symbols, and incorporating African traditions into today's weddings.

http://www.melanet.com/melanet/wedding/

Black English

Black English, or Ebonics, has gotten a lot of attention lately, since the Oakland school board created a policy about it. Is it slang? Is it just poor English? Is it a language of its own? This page of lecture notes argues that it is a unique language with complex grammar rules and vocabulary. What do you think? There is also a link to the Oakland school board policy here.

http://www.west.net/~joyland/BlkEng.html

The Encyclopedia of African Music

Spanning musical styles from the entire Black diasphora, you'll hear everything from the Kenyan national anthem to Jamaican reggae and Brasilian samba at this most comprehensive site! But wait, there's more: lots of country-specific information, including languages, history, and geography. There are way too many links here for Net-mom to check them all, so explore with caution and with a parent.

http://matisse.net/~jplanet/afmx/ahome.htm

HISTORICAL FIGURES
African American Historical Figures

Learn about 12 famous African American men and women from the nineteenth century at this site.

http://www.webcom.com/~bright/source/blackfac.html

African American
Historical Figures

Did you know that Mary Church Terrell was the first president of the National Association of Colored Women or that Mary Ann Shadd was the first Black woman editor of a North American newspaper? Read about other African American pioneers at AFRICAN AMERICAN HISTORICAL FIGURES!

African American inventors, inventions, and patent dates

This is a list of some African American inventors and their patented inventions. These inventions include a pencil sharpener, refrigeration equipment, elevator machinery, and railroad telegraphy discoveries.

http://www.ai.mit.edu/~isbell/HFh/black/
events_and_people/009.aa_inventions

A
B
C
D
E
F
G
H
I
J
K
L
M
N
O
P
Q
R
S
T
U
V
W
X
Y
Z

A
B
C
D
E
F
G
H
I
J
K
L
M
N
O
P
Q
R
S
T
U
V
W
X
Y
Z

African American Online Exhibit Homepage

Profiles of Significant African Americans in Science, Medicine, and Technology were developed by students at the University of California at Irvine. This site also has a great timeline of events, inventions, and people, and you'll find educational opportunities and organizations in support of African Americans pursuing a career in the sciences.

http://sun3.lib.uci.edu/~afrexh/AAhomepage.html

Burlington City, New Jersey - History

Read about Cyrus Bustill and Oliver Cromwell of Burlington, New Jersey. Bustill, a baker, supplied American troops with baked goods during the Revolutionary War; his great-great-grandson was Paul Robeson. Cromwell served in the Revolutionary War, and George Washington personally signed his discharge papers. Washington also designed the medal that was awarded to Cromwell. Read about the Oliver Cromwell Black History Society, which operates today.

http://bc.emanon.net/cgi-bin/burl/_history

Events and People in Black History

What happened this week in Black history? You can also search on a name, and if you're lucky, there will be a short biography!

http://www.ai.mit.edu/~isbell/HFh/black/bhist.html

The Faces of Science: African Americans in the Sciences

This site gives you biographical information for about 100 African Americans who have made important contributions to science. The articles are well-documented, and their sources are cited. You can also see a selection of patents issued to some of these scientists.

http://www.lib.lsu.edu/lib/chem/display/faces.html

Ronald E. McNair

Dr. McNair was mission specialist aboard the 1984 flight of the space shuttle Challenger. Read about his life at this site.

http://www.aad.berkeley.edu/uga/osl/mcnair/
   Ronald_E._McNair.html

HISTORY
The African-American Mosaic

The Library of Congress is in Washington, D.C., and it has a huge collection of materials, some of which cover about 500 years of African history in the Western Hemisphere. The materials include books, periodicals, prints, photographs, music, film, and recorded sound. This exhibit samples these materials in four areas: Colonization, Abolition, Migrations, and the Work Projects Administration period. You'll be able to look at pages from original materials, such as an abolitionist children's book. Sometimes it's useful to look at these original materials, also called "primary sources," for yourself, rather than use books other people have written about these same sources—this way, you're closer to what really happened. This site has lots to use for school reports!

http://lcweb.loc.gov/exhibits/african/intro.html

AFROAM-L Griot Online [Afrinet]

In Africa, a *griot* is a highly respected person who has memorized the history, culture, songs, lineages, and other details about a village or a people. In the same oral tradition, this site collects maps, text, pictures, and a timeline. Millions of Black people throughout the Caribbean, South America, and North America share a common history, which this site tries to retell in words and pictures.

http://www.afrinet.net/~griot/

Anacostia Museum HomePage

Did you know that February is Black History Month? This site will give you many examples of the contributions of African Americans to U.S. history and culture. You will discover online exhibits of inventions, art, music, and more. The museum is located in Washington, D.C. Hint: Click on the Exhibitions and Programs menu choice and not the navigation bar at the bottom.

http://www.si.edu/anacostia/anachome.htm

> **Computers are dumb, people are smart.**

CNN Million Man March - Oct. 16, 1995

On October 16, 1995, Nation of Islam leader Louis Farrakhan called thousands of African American men to go to Washington, D.C. to make their voices heard. This historic event is chronicled here. CNN's site includes pointers to the "official" MMM site but adds audio and video to the print record. Read many related stories, quotes, and support material, such as biographies of some of the main participants.

http://www3.cnn.com/US/9510/megamarch/march.html

Education First: Black History Activities

This comprehensive and thoughtful collection of links in support of Black History Month will take you all over the Web on a Treasure Hunt to find the answers to some very big questions. You'll also find information on many prominent Africans and people of African descent, from Bob Marley to Nelson Mandela. This site has study questions and activities for classes as well.

http://www.kn.pacbell.com/wired/BHM/AfroAm.html

National Civil Rights Museum

Take the Virtual Tour to discover what it was like when African Americans had to sit at the back of the bus and avoid "Whites Only" restaurants, swimming pools, and drinking fountains. As bizarre as this seems to us now, before the Civil Rights Movement of the 1960s, this was standard, everyday life in many places in the U.S. The Freedom Summer of 1964 included student sit-ins, boycotts, and marches. This museum in Memphis, Tennessee, re-creates some of the sights, sounds, and scenes of that era. Remember, the struggle for civil rights continues around the world today, and it involves people of many races.

http://www.mecca.org/~crights/ncrm.html

AMPHIBIANS

See also PETS AND PET CARE

Frogs and Other Amphibians

Ahh—the sweet singing of frogs in the springtime…but did you know that frogs are disappearing all over the world? This phenomenon has been linked to depletion of the ozone layer in the atmosphere, which lets too much ultraviolet light through, which harms the frogs. Recently, scientists have also discovered a connection between the health of frogs and a buildup of ozone in the lower atmosphere due to pollution. Watch your frogs carefully, everybody— they are important! Did you know that Australian tree frogs give off a chemical that helps heal sores when it's put on a person's skin? Doctors expect to find lots of other ways the chemical can be used. You'll find additional links that lead to information about rain forest amphibians and Australian frogs. You can even make your way to the Interactive Frog Dissection Kit, where you can test your knowledge of frog anatomy by playing the Virtual Frog Builder Game.

http://fovea.retina.net/~gecko/herps/frogs/

NET FILES

What words with no vowels are acceptable in the game of Scrabble?

HMMM-HMMM

Answer: Here are a few: "brr," used to indicate coldness; "shh," used to urge silence; "tsk," a scolding exclamation; "psst," used to attract someone's attention; and "crwth," an ancient stringed musical instrument. Check http://www.yak.net/kablooey/ scrabble.no.vowels.txt for more from the San Jose Scrabble Club!

A
B
C
D
E
F
G
H
I
J
K
L
M
N
O
P
Q
R
S
T
U
V
W
X
Y
Z

A
B
C
D
E
F
G
H
I
J
K
L
M
N
O
P
Q
R
S
T
U
V
W
X
Y
Z

Herp Link- Care Sheets and FAQ's

What's the best way to care for that nifty newt you have just bought? This site tells you all about how to care for various kinds of frogs, salamanders, and other amphibians. Further down in the list you'll find reptile care sheets—even how to take care of your very own alligator, if you have one (but we don't recommend it!). This site has numerous unchecked links.

http://home.ptd.net/~herplink/care.html

FROGS AND TOADS

Froggy Page

Do you love frogs? Do you jump at playing a game of leapfrog? Would you leap at a chance to learn how to make an origami jumping frog? Want to meet some famous frogs and read froggy tales? This is the ultimate frog lover's site. Check out the frog jokes or visit the Cyberpond, home of Sue the Tadpole. Ribbit! Croak! Jugarum! Go to the Froggy Page and hear all kinds of frogs singing.

http://www.cs.yale.edu/HTML/YALE/CS/HyPlans/
loosemore-sandra/froggy.html

Froggy Page

Frogs in the news! Why are frogs slowing down the plans for the Olympics in Sydney, Australia? Why do residents of a town in Connecticut want to build a six-foot tall statue of a frog? What's the deal with the Toad Plague in Russia? Be informed; get slimed! Check out the Froggy Page.

The Interactive Frog Dissection

Did you ever wonder what's inside a frog? Now you can look for yourself. There's a special way to take animals apart to learn about them, and it's called dissection. Learn to identify the locations of a frog's major organs. Click on one button and watch movies of dissections. Click on another button and practice what you've learned. Only one frog had to lose its life for this Web page, and many dissections can be performed over and over, by kids all over the world.

http://curry.edschool.Virginia.EDU/go/frog/

SALAMANDERS AND NEWTS

Autodax: Salamander Feeding

Visit a scientific research lab, where the spotlight is on salamanders and how they feed. High-speed movies of various types of salamanders feasting on termites, waxworms, and crickets make for an interesting if not appetizing educational experience!

http://violet.berkeley.edu/~deban/salfeed.html

Salamander Care in Captivity

There are over 100 kinds of salamanders commonly found in the U.S. In general, they like cool, damp areas, and they come out mostly at night or after a rain. This page describes how you can keep these shy amphibians in captivity, though Net-mom suggests you keep them only for a day or so and then let them go.

http://www.users.interport.net/~spiff/caretxt/
salcare.html

Salamanders and Newts

Salamanders may live in the water, but eventually they turn into land dwellers. Newts are generally aquatic. Don't confuse them with lizards! Lizards have scaly skin and claws, while these fragile animals have smooth skin and delicate feet. Did you know some newts have lived for over 50 years in captivity? This page gives hints on the care and feeding of these interesting creatures, which many people keep as pets.

http://www.poly.edu/~duane/zoo/amphibians/
sal_newt.html

AMUSEMENT PARKS

See also DISNEY

Institute of Future Technology

If you've never had an opportunity to visit Universal Studio's world-famous theme park and production studio, here's your chance! An interactive tour of Back to the Future: The Ride, Doc Brown's wild trip through time, will take you down into live volcanoes and bring you way too close to long-extinct dinosaurs. Hint: Don't eat lunch before looking at this site!

http://www.univstudios.com/btf/

National Amusement Park Historical Association

Here's a group dedicated to saving old amusement parks, on the theory that a once-amusing ride can never, ever cease to be amusing. Read about the history of amusement parks and some of your favorite rides.

http://www.sgi.net/napha/

Paramount's Great America - Santa Clara, California

This park in Northern California has a lot going for it. It has the largest IMAX theater in the world, the largest and most expensive carousel in the world, and the only stand-up coaster west of the Mississippi. It also has award-winning roller coasters, such as the Top Gun—an inverted looping coaster—and our personal favorite, the Green Slime Mine Car Coaster!

http://shipofools.lit.cwru.edu/woc/pga/index.html

Santa Cruz Beach Boardwalk

The Santa Cruz Beach Boardwalk in Santa Cruz, California, lets you take a walk into America's past. Check the live videocam to see what the weather's like in Santa Cruz today. Maybe you'll see the classic 1911 Looff Carousel or the 1924 Giant Dipper roller coaster. If you are interested in going to Santa Cruz, you can plan your whole vacation (including hotel information) right from this page!

http://www.beachboardwalk.com/

Six Flags Theme Parks

They say that 85 percent of Americans live within a day's drive of a Six Flags theme park; there are now eight of them, all over the United States. They are part of the Time-Warner family, so you'll see Batman, Superman, and all your favorite Looney Tunes characters when you visit. From this jumping-off point, you can take a virtual vacation at all of the parks and explore the similarities and differences of each. You'll find a park calendar, a list of the latest and greatest rides, a suggested "perfect day" itinerary, directions to each park, and job opportunities!

http://www.sixflags.com/

Welcome to Huis ten Bosch

This is the largest theme park in Japan. For some reason, it's based on the theme of Holland, with its canals and historic buildings. Wander around and click on things—you may end up at a ride, a restaurant, or a palace!

http://www.bekkoame.or.jp/~suga/htbe1.html

NET FILES

It's stored in Washington, D.C., inside a heavy-gauge stainless-steel container, which is pumped full of argon gas instead of plain air. The container is kept in a carefully controlled environment at 49.5 degrees Fahrenheit and 49 percent relative humidity. Special quarter-inch Plexiglas sheets filter out ultraviolet light.

What on earth is inside?

Answer: Actually, two items are inside, both of them drafts of Lincoln's Gettysburg Address, in the Library of Congress collection. You can see the storage containers and read about the rare documents inside them at
http://www.loc.gov/exhibits/G.Address/gapres.html

A
B
C
D
E
F
G
H
I
J
K
L
M
N
O
P
Q
R
S
T
U
V
W
X
Y
Z

Welcome to Universal City Hollywood

Did you ever want to explore a real movie studio's backlot? You'd find old props and scenery, closets full of costumes, and maybe some new things they are working on, like—DINOSAURS! Visit the virtual Jurassic Park ride from here, as well as the world-famous Universal Studios tram ride. It will take you into the fist of King Kong, through the gaping maw of Jaws, and spit you out just in time to escape an earthquake and a very believable flood! It's all in fun, but if you prefer a tamer type of entertainment, you can download some interactive games here and stay at home.

http://www.mca.com/unicity/

In medieval times, knights wore suits of armor as protection in battle. Since all knights looked alike with their armor on, they needed some way to tell each other apart at a distance. A coat of arms was originally a silk T-shirt worn over the armor. This garment had a picture of items important to the knight's family, arranged in specific ways and in various colors, which also had meaning. Everyone in the same family wore the same coat of arms. In the Bible, Adam was the first man and Eve was the first woman. Did either have a coat of arms?

Answer: Heralds in medieval times thought every important person should have a coat of arms. So, although it was thousands of years later, they decided to assign arms to Adam and Eve. Adam's shield is plain red and Eve's is plain silver. See the shields at http://www.fred.net/jefalvey/jeffhera.html

CAROUSELS
1911 Looff Carousel Page

Along the Boardwalk in Santa Cruz, California, is a National Historic Landmark. It's a hand-carved carousel, and you can read about its history here. See a few close-ups of some of the horses, and download a QuickTime movie of the carousel in action.

http://www.beachboardwalk.com/looff.html

Carousel!

Everyone has seen carousel horses, but did you know that some carousels have frogs, roosters, and fantastic creatures like sea monsters on them? Find out about the history of carousels, see some detailed wooden horses, and listen to carousel music—guaranteed to make you smile! This site tells you where antique carousels can still be found and ridden. They are something of a rare species, since many old carousels have been taken apart and the horses and other figures have been sold. Maybe you can help save an old carousel in your town.

http://www.carousel.org/

ROLLER COASTERS
Coasters.Net

It all starts innocently enough. You get into a little car, you slowly click-clatter click-clatter up the track to the top of a huge and dangerous mountain, when all of a sudden, you're at the top and the whole world is below you. It might be nice to enjoy the view, but with a rush of wind, you're catapulted over the hill, screaming out your last breath, speeding towards uncertain doom at the bottom. You twist, you turn, you wish you had not eaten lunch. At last, the car slows and it's all over. You hear yourself yell, "AGAIN!" Roller coaster fans will love this page, complete with reviews of coasters all over the world. You'll also find frequently asked questions, photos, statistics, and an overview of roller coaster history right here. This is a "no hands" Web site, and remember, in cyberspace, no one can hear you scream!

http://www.coasters.net/

ANCIENT CIVILIZATIONS AND ARCHAEOLOGY

See also HISTORY—ANCIENT HISTORY

ABZU

ABZU is a "guide to resources for the study of the Ancient Near East available on the Internet." This guide is based at the Oriental Institute in Chicago. Resources are indexed by author, directory, region, and subject. The resources also include online journals, online library catalogs, and museum collections online. Check out the 3-D models of the pyramids and the animated fly-throughs of the sites at <*http://www-oi.uchicago.edu/OI/DEPT/RA/ABZU/ ABZU_REGINDX_EGYPT_IMG.HTML*>.

http://www-oi.uchicago.edu/OI/DEPT/RA/ABZU/ ABZU.HTML

The Ancient World Web: Main Index

This site is chock-full of links to information about the ancient world. Topics include ancient documents, architecture, and cooking. In addition, links are provided to information about geography, history, the history of science, military, money, sciences, theater, towns, and cities. What a great surfing stop for students of ancient history!

http://atlantic.evsc.virginia.edu/julia/ AncientWorld.html

NET FILES

In a recipe, what does the symbol XXX mean?

Answer: No, it's not when you throw in a mystery ingredient of your choice! It's the symbol for light, fluffy confectioners' sugar. Check http://foodstuff.com/pearl/glos-x.html for a great food glossary.

Archaeology

How do archaeologists take a few items from a pile of rubble and re-create an entire picture of how people lived long ago? This explanation from the TV show *Newton's Apple* includes many resource ideas as well as a glossary. There are also some hands-on activities to help you learn how historic sites are surveyed and, sometimes, excavated.

http://ericir.syr.edu/Projects/Newton/11/archeogy.html

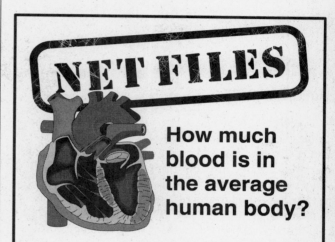

NET FILES

How much blood is in the average human body?

Answer: The average human has about five liters of blood. About 55 percent of your blood is plasma. Check out the inside story on blood at http://sln.fi.edu/biosci/blood/blood.html

ArchNet: WWW Virtual Library - Archaeology

ArchNet, housed at the University of Connecticut, is a virtual library for all things archaeological. Look up resources by geographic region or by subject. This is a don't-miss site for budding archaeologists. Indiana Jones probably stops here all the time!

http://spirit.lib.uconn.edu/ArchNet/ArchNet.html

Go climb a rock in OUTDOOR RECREATION.

A B C D E F G H I J K L M N O P Q R S T U V W X Y Z

Exploring Ancient World Cultures

Move the mouse, punch the buttons, and be prepared to enter a different world. Eight cultures from the past can help you to understand the cultural diversity of today. Go on a journey through time to visit the following ancient cultures: the Near East, India, Egypt, China, Greece, the Roman Empire, the Islamic World, and Medieval Europe. Although the text is very dense, you'll get a lot of information from the photos and thoughtful links to other places on the Net.

http://eawc.evansville.edu/index.htm

ANCIENT AMERICA

MayaQuest

Who were the Mayans, and what happened to their civilization? This site tells you all about the history and cultures of this lost nation. The ancient Maya had an apparently healthy culture from around A.D. 250. They were masters of mathematics, building huge pyramids in the jungles of what is now Mexico and Central America. They had complex astronomical calendars and engineering for improving agriculture. During the ninth century, their civilization collapsed. No one knows exactly where they went or what happened to them. From this site, you can follow an expedition team called MayaQuest, searching the jungle for archaeological answers in 1995, 1996, and 1997.

http://www.mecc.com/mayaquest.html

Shawnee Minisink Site

How did people live 10,000 years ago? What did they eat? What were their houses like? This Web page features an archaeological dig in the Delaware Water Gap area near what is now the border of Pennsylvania and New Jersey. The dig, conducted by the American University Department of Anthropology, reveals the history of the region, exactly what was dug up, and how the artifacts were pieced together to show a picture of that time period's culture.

http://www.american.edu/academic.depts/cas/anthro/
sms/sms.html

ANCIENT EUROPE

Flints and Stones

Do you have the "right stuff" to survive in Stone Age times? Meet the shaman, who will show you what life is like in his village of Ice Age hunters and gatherers. You'll also meet the archaeologist, who will show you how he interprets the lives of the village folk from the objects, art, and other signs they have left behind. Everyone thinks cavemen were big, hairy guys who carried clubs and dragged women around by the hair. This site explodes that myth and others. You'll also be able to take a Stone Age food quiz—hmmm, should you eat that mushroom or not?

http://www.ncl.ac.uk/~nantiq/menu.html

ANCIENT GREECE

Ancient City of Athens

This colorful site presents a photographic archive of the archaeological and architectural remains of ancient Athens, Greece. The owner of the Web page, Kevin Glowacki, is also one of the photographers. He gives rights to students to use these images, as long as the source is cited. The photographs are all GIF images and illustrate the topography and monuments of ancient Athens. Further details are given. This is a landmark site for any student studying ancient Greece. However, there are a lot of color illustrations, so be patient waiting for the page to load. It's well worth the wait!

http://www.indiana.edu/~kglowack/Athens/Athens.html

Perseus Project Home Page

The Perseus Project is "an evolving digital library on Ancient Greece" that is headquartered at the Department of Classics at Tufts University. Information is offered about art and archaeology as well as primary texts and Greek dictionaries. Included are pictures and descriptions of 523 coins, 1,420 vases, 179 sites, and 381 buildings. This is a don't-miss site for anyone studying ancient Greece!

http://medusa.perseus.tufts.edu/

A
B
C
D
E
F
G
H
I
J
K
L
M
N
O
P
Q
R
S
T
U
V
W
X
Y
Z

ANCIENT ROME
ROMARCH List Home Page

Romarch, housed at the University of Michigan, is the home to Web resources about Roman art and archaeology from 1000 B.C. to A.D. 700. General-interest resources include central sources of information and images, museums, society, as well as culture, religion, law, and war. Resources that are especially good for students are marked. A geographic approach to the sources is available, but beware: You may accidentally stumble into a site in another language!

http://www-personal.umich.edu/~pfoss/ROMARCH.html

VIKINGS
The Viking Network Web

Experience the Viking way of life: raiding, trading, and exploration. This site is aimed at kids and teachers all over the world who are interested in Viking heritage and culture. You'll find some e-mail discussions to meet other kids interested in Vikings, too. Did they wear horns on their helmets, or not? Find out here!

http://odin.nls.no/viking/vnethome.htm

NET FILES

If you were to go fishing for a glacier, what kind of bait would you use?

Answer: Ice worms, of course! These little critters are the only animals that live inside glacial ice. You can read a bit more about them (alas, there's no picture of one) at http://www.whistler.net/glacier/worms.html

ANTHROPOLOGY

People and Environmental Change on the Northern Great Plains

Anthropologists study people, their cultures, and the setting in which they live. A community, whether a small band of hunters or a large sprawl of city dwellers, always affects the land. This gem of a site explores the Great Plains area of the U.S. and traces the hand of man upon it. You'll learn about these vast grasslands and the human habitation of them. Beginning with the first peoples thousands of years ago, through the Dust Bowl of the 1930s, to today—see what you can predict for the future based on what has happened in the past.

http://www.usd.edu/anth/epa/index.html

Relationship Terms

When describing a culture, you might begin by studying the basic social unit: the family. You're pretty clear on your parents, your brother and sister, and maybe even your aunts and uncles. But where do your first cousins come in—and what's this "once removed" stuff? If you've gotten a little fuzzy on relationships and the terms that describe them in our Western culture, check here. Can you really be your own grandpa?

http://www.nacs.net/~stbrown/relation.htm

UCSB Anthropology Cool Web Sites Feature

The study of families, cultures, and communities is called cultural anthropology. There's also physical anthropology and archaeology. This colorful, well-designed page has unearthed many of the most interesting and important anthropological sites, annotating and organizing them for easy accessibility. Here you'll find links described and cataloged in alphabetical order, by topical and geographical focus, and by departmental and museum sites. The museum sites are especially worth visiting.

http://www.sscf.ucsb.edu/anth/netinfo.html

A
B
C
D
E
F
G
H
I
J
K
L
M
N
O
P
Q
R
S
T
U
V
W
X
Y
Z

AQUARIUMS

See also FISH

Fish Information Service (FINS) Index

That little goldfish you bought has outgrown its bowl, so you're going to get it a new tank. Visit this archive of information about aquariums! It covers both freshwater and marine, tropical and temperate fish tank culture. You'll find beginning to advanced information, especially on marine and reef tanks. Click on a picture to identify a fish and get more information, or use the glossary full of aquarium terms. Be sure to see the live video from a camera overlooking a garden pond, and check out the live Fish Cam activity at a saltwater tank in someone's office.

http://www.actwin.com/fish/

The Florida Aquarium

Watch out! Whew, didn't you see that stingray? You almost stepped on it! Because stingrays live in shallow offshore water, beachgoers often step on them by accident and get stung. Stingrays will lie partly buried in the sand, with only their eyes, spiracle, and tail exposed. Stingray stings are easy to avoid, though— just shuffle your feet as you wade. Learn more about stingrays and other creatures that inhabit Florida's waterways. Ask the Aquarium experts a question or check out one of many experiments and games available for kids of all ages.

http://www.sptimes.com/aquarium/

The Monterey Bay Aquarium Home Page

Did you ever wonder what it would be like to swim with fish—even sharks? Would you dare feed them? Watch your hand, that shark looks hungry! Look at the sea otter pup—isn't it cute? Visit the Monterey Bay Aquarium Home Page and get a diver's-eye view of hand-feeding the fish in the Kelp Forest Tank. Watch the QuickTime movies as divers hand-feed various sharks, rockfish, and eels that inhabit the underwater seaweed forests.

http://www.mbayaq.org/

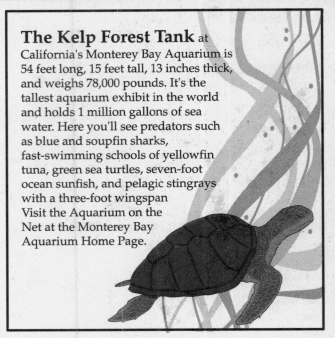

The Kelp Forest Tank at California's Monterey Bay Aquarium is 54 feet long, 15 feet tall, 13 inches thick, and weighs 78,000 pounds. It's the tallest aquarium exhibit in the world and holds 1 million gallons of sea water. Here you'll see predators such as blue and soupfin sharks, fast-swimming schools of yellowfin tuna, green sea turtles, seven-foot ocean sunfish, and pelagic stingrays with a three-foot wingspan Visit the Aquarium on the Net at the Monterey Bay Aquarium Home Page.

The New England Aquarium Home Page

Perched on the wharf in Boston Harbor is the New England Aquarium. You can join Stefan on a virtual whale watch—maybe you'll see some humpbacks on your day trip out on the water. When you come back, you can see the Giant Ocean Tank inside. It's over four stories high and contains more than 200,000 gallons of water! The 45-year-old sea turtle, Myrtle, can usually be found snoozing on the bottom, so be sure to look for her.

http://www.neaq.org/

**Looking for the
State Bird
or the State Motto?
It's in the UNITED STATES
section.**

Sea World/Busch Gardens Animal Information Database

Do you ever wish you could visit Sea World in either Florida, Ohio, Texas, or California? You can find out about all kinds of fish here and also learn about parrots, polar bears, gorillas, lions, and more. Interested in setting up a tropical saltwater aquarium? This page tells you how to keep an aquarium as a hobby. Write, e-mail, or phone Shamu the Killer Whale to ask questions about the ocean and marine animals. Try your hand at the animal information quiz and receive a free animal information booklet. Check out the wide variety of educational programs and curriculum materials on endangered rain forests, ecosystems, and habitat. Surprise your grandmother with her very own pet coral reef—find out how to grow one at this site!

http://www.seaworld.org

ARCHITECTURE

World-Wide Web Virtual Library: Architecture

The resources here will guide you from the covered bridges of New Hampshire to the architecture of Islam. You'll find yourself looking at churches in Australia, contemporary buildings in Hong Kong, and Soleri's desert Arcosanti experiments. What a great way to experience many different architectural building styles all at once!

http://www.clr.toronto.edu:1080/VIRTUALLIB/ARCH/ proj.html

BRIDGES

The Building of the San Francisco Bay Bridge

The San Francisco–Oakland Bay Bridge opened to traffic in November 1936. It was called "the greatest bridge in the world for the versatility of its engineering." This bridge is one of seven toll bridges in the Bay Area that connect the city to its surrounding suburbs and are key to making San Francisco the city it is today. You'll see photos here of the building of this historic bridge.

http://www.wco.com/~jray/baybridg/baystart.htm

Where on earth can you climb *inside* a huge elephant and live to tell your friends about it?

Answer: Lucy is a famous elephant-shaped building in Margate City, New Jersey. She dates back to 1888, built by a realtor to advertise his business development plans! It took one million pieces of lumber for the structure and 12,000 feet of tin for the elephant's skin. You can climb up spiral staircases inside the legs to get to the rooms inside. Get a picture of Lucy to color at http://www.historychannel.com/kids/landmarks/lucy.html

Confederation Bridge- The Northumberland Strait Bridge

Eight miles long, it's the longest continuous multispan marine bridge in the world. It links the Canadian mainland of New Brunswick Province to Prince Edward Island. Ferries have been the only other way to get vehicles to and from the island. This site will tell you all about the construction of the bridge, which opens in June 1997. There is even a lottery to be one of the first to cross it!

http://www.peinet.pe.ca/SCI/bridge.html

May the forces be with you in PHYSICS.

A
B
C
D
E
F
G
H
I
J
K
L
M
N
O
P
Q
R
S
T
U
V
W
X
Y
Z

A
B
C
D
E
F
G
H
I
J
K
L
M
N
O
P
Q
R
S
T
U
V
W
X
Y
Z

Covered Bridges

Why are some bridges covered? To avoid rot, according to Dr. McCain, who also says that the structures were once called "kissing bridges." Take the Northeastern Chester County Driving Tour and read about the renovation of Bartram's Bridge. Stop by the Covered Bridges page today and enjoy your virtual tour of the bridges of various counties in Pennsylvania, Oregon, and New Hampshire.

http://william-king.www.drexel.edu/top/bridge/cb1.html

Newton's Apple- Bridges

How do bridges stay up? London Bridge didn't. It was always falling down, falling down. What are the different kinds of bridge designs, anyway, and why would you pick one over another? If you're ready to build your very own bridge, better stop here first. Create a blueprint and model of your bridge before you begin construction. This *Newton's Apple* TV show will help!

http://ericir.syr.edu/Projects/Newton/12/Lessons/
  bridges.html

NET FILES

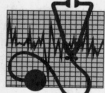

How many times will your heart pump in your lifetime?

Answer: According to the Franklin Institute's *The Heart: An Online Exploration*, it will beat two and a half billion times. That's a lot of ba-bump, ba-bump. If you want to learn just about everything there is to know about the heart, take a look at http://sln.fi.edu/biosci/heart.html

CASTLES AND PALACES
Castles on the Web

King Arthur, eat your heart out! If you want to know anything (and we mean *anything*) about castles, this is the page for you. You'll find Castle Tours, Castle of the Week, Castle Questions and Answers, Castle Image Archive, and Castles for Sale. Maybe you can look up your family's ancestral castle. There's also a Glossary of Castle Terms so that even the novice castle lover can feel at home. Hey! Watch out for the (splash) moat.

http://fox.nstn.ca/~tmonk/castle/castle.html

CHURCHES, MOSQUES, AND SYNAGOGUES
Cittá del Vaticano

Take a virtual tour of St. Peter's Basilica in Rome, Italy, designed by Michelangelo. See photos of the domes and vaults, piazzas, and gardens at this multilingual site.

http://www.christusrex.org/www1/citta/0-Citta.html

Dome of the Rock

Built in A.D. 692, the Dome of the Rock is one of the great Muslim monuments. The building looks like an enameled, multicolored jewel, capped by a shining golden dome. The Dome protects and houses the Sacred Rock of Jerusalem sandstone at the summit of Mount Moriah. Muslims believe that the prophet Muhammad, guided by the archangel Gabriel, traveled to Jerusalem and rose to the presence of God from this Rock. The site is also sacred to other faiths, as it was formerly the location of the Temple of Solomon. This site also details costumes, foods, and other important sites in early Muslim history.

http://jeru.huji.ac.il/ee21.htm

Be an angel and check what we've found in RELIGION.

Washington National Cathedral

On the highest point in Washington, D.C., is a beautiful interfaith cathedral. It is decorated with 107 carved stone gargoyles and untold numbers of grotesques. A grotesque is like a gargoyle, except it has no pipe inside, and the water runs over the outside of the carving. The cathedral also has wonderful stained glass windows inside. The western rose window contains over 10,500 pieces of glass! Along the inside aisle is another window commemorating the flight of *Apollo 11*. It holds a real piece of moon rock! In addition to many U.S. presidents, Dr. Martin Luther King, Jr. and Indira Gandhi have spoken from the pulpit. Helen Keller is among the famous Americans buried beneath the cathedral.

http://www.cathedral.org/cathedral/

Westminster Abbey - Place of Worship, and House of Kings

This London landmark has been the site of every British coronation since 1066. Many kings and queens are entombed at the Abbey, notably Elizabeth I. You'll also find Chaucer's grave in the Poets' Corner, along with those of other famous English authors, including Lewis Carroll. The Abbey has been the scene of numerous royal ceremonies, including royal weddings and other occasions. Admire the inspiring Gothic architecture as you wander around with the other tourists at this site.

http://www.westminster-abbey.org/

GARGOYLES

Gargoyle Home Page

Have you ever seen a gargoyle? Gargoyles have been added into the roof lines of large buildings since the eleventh century. Originally, they were placed for functional purposes—they helped drain water off the roof. They also had symbolic religious significance. Today, gargoyles are still used as decorations on buildings. Tour the Gargoyle Home Page and find out more about the history and design of these little monsters. Be sure to keep an eye up as you walk along the street—you never know what may be looking back down at you!

http://ils.unc.edu/garg/garghp4.html

GOVERNMENT AND PUBLIC BUILDINGS

Moscow

The Kremlin is an architectural marvel located in Moscow, Russia. Its walled city is the site of Red Square, cathedrals, and many government buildings. Take a virtual tour and learn some fascinating facts about this complex. Don't miss the world's largest bell!

http://www.geom.umn.edu/~ipavlovs/Russia/Moscow/moscow.html

Tower of London Virtual Tour

The Traitor's Gate. The Bloody Tower. The Ceremony of the Keys. The Crown Jewels. What an incredible history this building has. The Tower of London has been a treasury, a prison, and a government building for a thousand years. It is said that if the ravens that inhabit the Tower green ever leave, the Commonwealth of Great Britain will fall. You can take a tour of the Tower and its grounds right here. But don't scare the ravens!

http://www.voicenet.com/~dravyk/toltour/

NET FILES

Everyone knows the Liberty Bell is cracked.

How did that happen?

Answer: It cracked the first time it was test rung, while still at the English foundry where it was cast in 1752. It was given to a Philadelphia foundry to be recast in 1753. It was then hung in the tower of Philadelphia's Independence Hall. The most important time it rang was on July 8, 1776, when it called people to hear the first public reading of the Declaration of Independence. Over the years, the crack in the bell became worse and worse, until by 1846 it was too damaged to be rung. There are several known recordings of the bell. Its sound was broadcast to all parts of the country on June 6, 1944, when Allied forces landed in France. Every year, it is symbolically "tapped" on the Fourth of July. Read more at http://libertynet.org/iha/_bell.html

Virtual Tour of the US Capitol

This page lets you tour the U.S. Capitol in Washington, D.C. You can take a Guided Tour or explore using a Tour Map, which allows you to have control over what you visit. You'll learn the history of the building, too. On September 18, 1793, George Washington laid the first cornerstone for the Capitol. The dome is made of cast iron and was erected during the Civil War. The pictures of the construction of the building are fascinating.

http://www.senate.gov/capitol/virtour.html

LIGHTHOUSES

Bill's Lighthouse Getaway

It's a foggy night, a ship is lost amid the black waves, with shoals and rocks somewhere out ahead. Suddenly, the darkness is pierced by a friendly light in the distance. It's the lighthouse! Checking the navigational map, the ship's captain notes the location of the lighthouse on shore and is able to steer clear of danger. Part of American lore and legend, lighthouses all over America (and now, Ireland) can be visited via this home page. You'll find pictures and descriptions of lights from New England, through the Great Lakes, around the South Atlantic, and to the West Coast. There are also links to Lighthouse Societies and something about the history of the Fresnel lens, which produces the powerful light needed.

http://zuma.lib.utk.edu/lights/

The WWW Virtual Library: The World's Lighthouses, Lightships & Lifesaving Stations

Are lighthouses all over the world? You bet—and this site will let you visit a lot of them. Learn all about the history of lighthouses and lightships from a real lighthouse keeper! Lightships are just that: very well-lighted ships stationed at sea, guarding shoals and other navigational hazards.

http://www.maine.com/lights/www_vl.htm

TUNNELS

Journey Through the Channel Tunnel

This is a tourist's-eye view of a trip through the tunnel under the English Channel. On December 20, 1994, the author traveled from London-Waterloo to Paris-Gare du Nord by Eurostar train, returning the same day. This site has lots of pictures of the journey as well.

http://www.elec.rdg.ac.uk/~stssjs/ctr.html

ART

The Art of Motion Control

Imagine having a robot that does your chores for you. How about a robot that cuts sheet metal or uses an airbrush? Artist Bruce Shapiro has designed a series of robotic tools that allow him to create artwork. He has built an egg engraver, a plasma torch, and even an automated etch-a-sketch. With these tools, he makes metal sculpture, engravings, and more. See pictures of the tools and the artwork they've made. You can send Bruce e-mail—maybe he can build a robot that does your homework for you!

http://home.iaxs.net/bshapiro/

Draw a Trochoid

Do you love to draw patterns? A mechanical toy that traces the path of one circle as it moves around another circle will draw complicated patterns for you. When your parents were kids, they had to draw these using clumsy toys that were actually geared tools. Their pens and gears were always slipping, and it took forever to draw the final image. Now you can do it by typing in numbers and hitting the Generate Image button. Isn't technology wonderful?

http://www.vanderbilt.edu/VUCC/Misc/Art1/trochoid.html

A B C D E F G H I J K L M N O P Q R S T U V W X Y Z

A B C D E F G H I J K L M N O P Q R S T U V W X Y Z

Fresco Workshop

Do you know what a fresco is? It isn't a can of diet soda or a city in California. It's a form of artwork, and—get this—it's painted right on the walls. Traditionally, plaster is poured in layers and is tinted as it dries. The end result is a lasting piece of art. The world's earliest known frescoes are the cave paintings of Lasceaux, France. They were made some 30,000 years ago—that's old! Historically, the technique was developed in ancient Greece, and it was incorporated into Minoan and Roman artwork. This series of pages takes you through the process step by step, as a group of people create a fresco of a playground scene.

http://www.artswire.org/Community/afmadams/afm/
fresco.html

NET FILES

*Every year
The Worshipful Companies
of the Vintners and Dyers
participate in an unusual and
ancient ritual on the
River Thames in London.*
What is it?

Answer: *This group is charged with the royal duty of rounding up and taking a census of all the swans! For many centuries, mute swans in Britain were raised for food, like other poultry. Individual swans were marked by nicks on their webbed feet or beak, which indicated ownership. Somewhat like cattle brands in the American West, these markings were registered with the Crown. Any unmarked birds become Crown property. The swans are rounded up at a "swan-upping," and although they are no longer used for food, the Royal Swanherd continues the tradition to this day. Check* http://www.airtime.co.uk/users/cygnus/muteswan.htm *for more information.*

CAVE ART
Discovery of a Palaeolithic painted cave at Vallon -Pont-d'Arc (Ardèche)

Admit it, you would love to draw all over the walls in your home. The only problem is that you would get in trouble. A long time ago, kids your age didn't have crayons or finger paint. In fact, ancient civilizations apparently encouraged drawing on the walls. At least 17,000 years ago, cave people drew all over this cave, and their artwork can still be seen today. These paintings were discovered by archeologists in the Ardèche gorges of southern France. The photographs are gorgeous, too.

http://www.culture.fr/culture/gvpda-en.htm

CERAMICS
KUTANI

Kutani is a very attractive form of Japanese pottery. The enameled vases look like jewels when they emerge from the kiln. The KUTANI pages show the elaborate process that leads to a finished piece of ceramic art. You can view a map of Japan showing Terai-Machi (the cradle of Kutani) and see a picture of the tools used in Kutaniware. Explore the history of the process and see examples of this beautiful art form.

http://www.njk.co.jp/kutani/

Virtual Ceramics Exhibit

What's the last thing you built with clay? What turns a piece of clay into art? The Virtual Ceramics Exhibit is an online art show for works in clay. Click on the pictures and read why the artists made the pieces. Warning: This site is very graphics-intensive, and the pictures take a long time to load.

http://www.uky.edu/Artsource/vce/VCEhome.html

**Lose yourself in a Museum.
SCIENCE has them all.**

A
B
C
D
E
F
G
H
I
J
K
L
M
N
O
P
Q
R
S
T
U
V
W
X
Y
Z

DRAWING AND PAINTING

See also COLOR AND COLORING BOOKS

Extended Tour

Have you ever been caught drawing on the wall? Can you imagine someone being paid to paint pictures on one? The ceiling of the Sistine Chapel in Rome, Italy, is considered to be one of the most incredible works of art in human history. It was painted by Michelangelo in the 1500s. It took him many years to paint it. Take the tour, download the images, but please don't draw on the wall.

http://www.christusrex.org/www1/sistine/0-Tour.html

Kali

Math is fun! Kali is a geometry program written at the Geometry Center. It makes cool symmetrical patterns (suitable for framing or just coloring) based on your instructions, which are easily entered by clicking on pictures and buttons.

http://www.geom.umn.edu/apps/kali/about.html

Mark Kistler's Imagination Station

The real world is in three dimensions: objects have width, length, and depth. In a drawing, you have only two dimensions to work with: length and width. You have to use special techniques to simulate the third dimension of depth. No problem—Mark's here to give you 3-D drawing lessons. You say you can't even draw a straight line? Mark claims it doesn't matter. Soon you'll be talking about the 12 Renaissance secrets of 3-D drawing right along with him!

http://www.draw3d.com/index.html

METAL AND JEWELRY CRAFT

Artist-Blacksmith's of North America

This is the home page of the Artist-Blacksmiths' Association of North America. Besides making common items, such as nails and hooks, blacksmiths of long ago made ornate latches, gates, hinges, frames, handles, knobs, and more. Look at "blacksmithing lessons" in the Education section to see some of the tools and how they are used today.

http://wuarchive.wustl.edu/edu/arts/blacksmithing/
    ABANA/

MUSEUMS

Asian Arts

See the rich art of many cultures in this electronic journal devoted to Asian arts. You'll be linked to online museum exhibits, articles about new discoveries, and many graphics of traditional Asian art. Explore the different media that the artists used. Weavings, sculpture, metal engravings, masks, paintings, clay tablets, carvings, and more await you.

http://www.webart.com/asianart/

Ghost of the de Young

If you think visiting an art museum sounds more boring than, say, sorting out the letters in your bowl of alphabet soup, then you should read this online comic book. Seems Irene and Farley are trying to take Irene's daughter, Olive, to the De Young art museum in San Francisco's Golden Gate Park. Olive wants to go to Disneyland instead! Mom and Farley leave Olive on a lobby bench (with a guard nearby) while they visit a special exhibit. Suddenly, the ghost of Mr. De Young himself appears to take Olive on a very special tour of some of the museum's masterpieces! Follow along on this humorous 72-page story. Hint: Load all the pictures first, then read them with the family.

http://www.thinker.org/fam/education/publications/
    ghost/index.html

Leonardo da Vinci Museum

You may know him as the inspiration for one of the Teenage Mutant Ninja Turtles. But the real Leonardo da Vinci didn't even have a shell. Although famous for painting the *Mona Lisa,* he also designed a helicopter, a hang glider, a parachute, and several other contraptions that didn't actually get built until hundreds of years later.

http://www.leonardo.net/museum/

POLLUTION stinks.

The Metropolitan Museum of Art

Let's read the tour brochure: "The Metropolitan Museum of Art's collections include nearly three million works of art spanning 5,000 years of world culture, from prehistory to the present." Hmmm, maybe we should think about spending the whole day exploring this one site! This world-class art museum is located in New York City. If you visit the virtual version, you'll see suits of armor, Egyptian antiquities, Asian art, twentieth century art, sculpture, and lots of famous art masterpieces. Want a closer look? Check the education section at <*http://www.metmuseum.org/htmlfile/education/edu.html*> for a family tour to some very interesting Winslow Homer paintings, and learn lots more about the kids pictured in them and the times when they lived! This site is also available in Japanese.

http://www.metmuseum.org/

Museums Index at World Wide Arts Resources

From this jumping-off point, you can explore over 950 museums all over the world! You'll find art museums galore, but you'll also experience science, folk, maritime, and other specialized exhibits if you explore the lists. Many countries from Africa to Asia are represented.

http://wwar.com/museums.html

National Museum of American Art

Look at all those paintings of yours that Mom has hung proudly on the refrigerator! One day you may become a famous American artist. Then your work would become part of a tradition of American art, and it might find a home in this museum. The museum boasts a grand collection of the best artwork produced by American artists. Which page will your artwork be on? Maybe the White House Collection of American Crafts, or part of the permanent collection? Browse these pages, and take a walk through history.

http://www.nmaa.si.edu/

Get on board, little children, in RAILROADS AND TRAINS.

There are over 37,500 works of art in the collection of the National Museum of American Art!

You can view over 500 artworks at their home page.

The Robert C. Williams American Museum of Papermaking

Young Roman students did their homework on wax tablets. Thanks to innovative thinking in China over 1,700 years ago, today you turn your homework in on paper. By the time you are out of school, students will probably hand in their assignments on computer disks. The American Museum of Papermaking highlights the development of papermaking. From clay tablets to the modern paper mill, follow the winding history of paper. After all, without paper how would you make paper airplanes?

http://www.ipst.edu/amp/

The comic strip "Peanuts" was first printed on October 2, 1950. In what year did Snoopy the beagle first appear standing on two legs instead of four?

You'll find more Snoopy facts at
http://www.unitedmedia.com/comics/peanuts/timeline/

Answer: Snoopy first stood on two legs in 1958.

A
B
C
D
E
F
G
H
I
J
K
L
M
N
O
P
Q
R
S
T
U
V
W
X
Y
Z

Splendors of Christiandom

The Vatican, an independent city-state, is located in Rome, Italy. It has its own postage and souvenir coinage, but it is best known as being the worldwide center of Roman Catholicism. The Head of the Catholic Church, the Pope, lives here. The world-famous Vatican Museums are here; the Popes have been collecting art since 1503, so there is a lot to see! If you go to the Vatican, you'll have to wait in line to get in, but here in the virtual museum, you can walk right in. View over 500 images of paintings, tapestries, and sculptures. The Sistine Chapel paintings are at *<http://www.christusrex.org/www1/sistine/0-Tour.html>*.

http://www.christusrex.org/www1/splendors/splendors.html

NET FILES

You're making a new recipe for dinner, but the cookbook has some words you've never heard of. What, for example, is a roux?

Answer: According to *Webster's Dictionary*, it's a "cooked mixture of flour and fat," and it's pronounced "roo." Get out the butter and learn more new words at http://gs213.sp.cs.cmu.edu/prog/webster?roux

WebMuseum: Bienvenue! (Welcome from the curator)

Browse through an incredible collection of famous paintings and other artwork. See the *Mona Lisa*, the most recognized piece of art in the world, or listen to some classical music in the auditorium. You can even take a mini-tour of Paris! The opening page of the WebMuseum includes a list of its mirror sites. Choose one close to you to provide a faster connection.

http://sunsite.unc.edu/wm/

SCULPTURE
Ball Run Sculptures

If we said, "Kinetic sculpture," you might say, "Huh?" How about marble runs—do you know what they are? No? OK, then how about those cool machines you see in museums, airports, and malls with the balls that travel around mazes of tracks, doing strange things like ringing bells, inflating balloons, traveling in elevators, only to get to the bottom and travel up to the beginning again? *Now* you know what we mean! This no-frills page is a collection of what kinetic art resources reside on the Web. You can also use it to plan your vacations around visiting these fun sculptures, since it includes a checklist by city and state. Don't miss the audio-kinetic Tower of Bauble at the Vancouver Science World at *<http://www2.portal.ca/~raymondk/Spider/QuickTime2/scienceWorld.html>* and be sure to listen for the gongs, xylophones, and cymbals. If you can wait long enough, you can see a QuickTime VR movie of the area, but, alas, not the sculpture in action!

http://www.msen.com/~lemur/ball-runs.html

Walter S. Arnold / Sculptor—Virtual Sculpture Gallery

Have you ever tried to hold as still as a statue? Statues are a form of art called sculpture. A sculpture starts as a block (usually wood or stone) and ends up as a piece of art. Walter S. Arnold is a sculptor who makes all sorts of art. He sculpts a lot of really neat things, such as gargoyles and park fountains. Learn about the tools sculptors use under the Resources link at "carving tools." Stop by the Virtual Sculpture Gallery and treat yourself to a very creative collection of art and ideas.

http://www.mcs.net/~sculptor/home.html

STAINED GLASS
The Chagall Windows

The Synagogue of the Hadassah-Hebrew University Medical Center, in Jerusalem, is lit by sunlight streaming through the world-famous Chagall Windows. Marc Chagall, the artist, worked on the project for two years. The Bible provided his main inspiration. The Chagall Windows represent the 12 sons of the patriarch Jacob, from whom came the Twelve Tribes of Israel. Chagall's brilliantly colored windows also have floating figures of symbolic animals, fish, and flowers. See this beautiful example of stained glass art without having to wait for a sunny day!

http://www6.huji.ac.il/md/chagall/chagall.html

TEXTILE ARTS
Textiles Through Time

What if we didn't have any malls? Where would people go to buy their clothes? Throughout most of history, people have had to make their own clothes, fabric, and fibers. This site links museum textile collections around the world. See handmade fabrics, including clothing, quilts, ceremonial artifacts, and a whole lot more. You'll also find links to the Bayeux Tapestry, Hmong needlework, and exquisite Japanese kimonos.

http://www.interlog.com/~gwhite/ttt/tttintro.html

Welcome to the World Wide Quilting Page

Of course you know what a quilt is, but do you know what goes into making one? Did you know that quilts can be computer designed, watercolor painted, or tie-dyed, and they can even have pictures transferred onto them? The page has a detailed how-to section with every step of the process, from basic quilt design to advanced stitch technique. Peek in and see the shameful losing quilt in the Worst Quilt In The World Contest!

http://ttsw.com/MainQuiltingPage.html

ASIAN AMERICANS

See also HOLIDAYS—ASIAN HOLIDAYS

CERN/ANU - Asian Studies WWW Virtual Library

Interested in the Pacific island of Tonga, or maybe the country of Malaysia, or perhaps Japan? Check this site for resources for school reports.

http://coombs.anu.edu.au/WWWVL-AsianStudies.html

Kid's Window

This little window on things Japanese will bring a smile to your face. Learn several origami folded figures, select items from a Japanese restaurant menu, and hear some Japanese letters and words.

http://jw.nttam.com/KIDS/kids_home.html

CULTURE
Asian Astrology

Find out about Chinese, Vietnamese, and Tibetan calendar and astrological systems here. You'll also find calendar conversion utilities and information on Asian divination. The site also has an informative FAQ on Feng Shui, the art of locating buildings according to the most favorable geographic influences. Recently, this practice has migrated to interior decoration. To find out whether you should relocate your bed or not, check here.

http://users.deltanet.com/~wcassidy/astro/astroindex.html

Body Language and Gestures in Asia and the Pacific

How well can you speak "body language"? If your mom were to cross her arms, frown, and start tapping her foot, you'd be able to read her body language well enough to tell she was mad! In other cultures, various body motions or gestures may mean something completely different than they do to you. This site focuses on proper body languages of the Asia-Pacific region. Find out how to cross your legs in Singapore, how to accept a gift in Korea, and when to applaud in China.

http://www.worldculture.com/gesturea.htm

A
B
C
D
E
F
G
H
I
J
K
L
M
N
O
P
Q
R
S
T
U
V
W
X
Y
Z

Chinese Historical and Cultural Project, San Jose, CA, US

The Golden Dragon is reawakening! Discover how this 200-foot long, historic creature appeared at Chinese festivals around the turn of the century. And now it's coming back! Have a look at the colorful modern photos as well as the historic photos and get a glimpse into Chinese history and culture. Teachers note: There are also complete lesson plans and materials for use in the award-winning Golden Legacy program.

http://www.dnai.com/~rutledge/CHCP_home.html

Hmong Textiles

The Hmong people of Vietnam and Laos have a language, but it is a spoken language, not a written one. So, their culture passes down its stories by telling them orally, or by telling them in cloths. Here are some cloths made by Hmong Americans and native Hmong. What stories might they be telling?

http://www.lib.uci.edu/sea/hmong.html

Living in Tokyo is....

This excellent winner from last year's Cyberfair was created by over 40 kids from a school in Japan. They will tell you from experience that living in Tokyo is fun, delicious, interesting, challenging, and inspiring! You'll discover the fascinating material they present on Japanese customs, theater and music, sumo wrestling, foods, and more.

http://cyberfair.gsn.org/smis/contents.html

Teaching (and Learning) About Japan

Festival puppets, flower arranging, the tea ceremony: these are all traditional parts of Japanese culture. But what do you know about popular things kids in Japan like to do? This site gives an overview of the traditional and the popular! A caution to parents: Characters in Japanese children's stories (anime, Manga) often die and do not live happily ever after. Also, not every link has been reviewed from this site.

http://www.csuohio.edu/history/japan.html

WWW Hmong Homepage

The Hmong come from China, Thailand, and Laos. This is a collection of resources relating to the history, culture, and language of the Hmong people, many of whom have emigrated to the U.S. Check the photographic archives and the news links to read current information about the Hmong.

http://www.stolaf.edu/people/cdr/hmong/

ASTRONOMY, SPACE, AND SPACE EXPLORATION

The Astronomical Society of the Pacific

So, you think you might be interested in astronomy? Well, things are looking up! The Astronomical Society of the Pacific is here to help. This organization has been serving astronomers for over 106 years. They publish *The Mercury*, a monthly magazine, and *The Universe in the Classroom*, a free quarterly newsletter for teachers. Of course, there's also loads of information for astronomers here on their Web site.

http://www.aspsky.org/

The Astronomy Cafe

Do you have what it takes to be an astronomer? Do you have the same interests and curiosities that astronomers have? Ask the Astronomer, and you might just find the answers right here. Dr. Sten Odenwald starts by telling you about his childhood and how a TV show sparked his own interest in astronomy. He tells you how his knowledge of mathematics and astronomy developed through college and then describes his career as a research scientist and astronomer. You can also read about the experiences of other astronomers and how they became interested in astronomy. Lots of links, articles, and other astronomy resources for you here!

http://www2.ari.net/home/odenwald/cafe.html

NET FILES

Who or what is Al Dente?

Answer: Al dente means "to the tooth" in Italian. It is a phrase that describes perfectly cooked pasta, which should be slightly chewy. Find out more at http://www.eat.com/cooking-glossary/al-dente.html

Naked Eye Astronomy

If you're serious about learning about astronomy, you should read this introductory essay. It will give you older kids a good perspective on what astronomy is all about. It starts with the concept of time and distance, which is important if you want to learn the whys and hows of astronomy. If there's something you don't understand, try reading it with your parents and then explain it to them. We're sure they will appreciate it. ;-)

http://lsnt7.lightspeed.net/~astronomy/naked-eye/naked-eye.html

SKY Online - Sky Publishing Corporation

If you really want to know what's up in the sky this week, today, NOW!, then you've got to visit this site. This is the publisher of *Sky & Telescope* magazine and other magazines, books, star atlases, and much more. Included are check tips for backyard astronomers, including how to find and see the Russian space station *Mir* as it orbits overhead. You can also track the latest comet sightings, meteor forecasts, and eclipse data. There is a fabulous collection of links, too. If it's happening in space or astronomy this week, you'll find something about it here.

http://www.skypub.com/

SKYWATCHER'S DIARY

Are you interested in astronomy but don't know where to look? Would you like to know what interesting events are happening in the night sky? Check out this site for a day-by-day list of what to look for and where to look for it. The list is updated each month and includes an archive of past diaries. Check out the archive near the end of the month to take a peek at next month's diary.

http://www.pa.msu.edu/abrams/diary.html

Space Calendar (JPL)

Keep this calendar on hand if you like to keep up with what's happening in space. If you check out September 16, 1997, for example, you'll find that the closest full moon for 1997 will be that night. The calendar also lists anniversaries of past space events, along with upcoming earthly meetings and conventions of space-related activities.

http://NewProducts.jpl.nasa.gov/calendar/

Space Environment Center Home

Check out today's space weather! Here's a partial listing for October 31, 1995: "The geomagnetic field should remain disturbed for the next three days. Generally active to minor storm conditions are forecast. Periods of major storming are expected for high latitudes. Energetic electron fluxes at geosynchronous orbit should increase to high levels late on 31 Oct." Not exactly what you might hear on TV, but it's how the weather in space is described by the scientists who study it. You'll also find images of the Sun and charts showing how strong X rays from space are today. Don't forget to wear your shades!

http://www.sel.bldrdoc.gov/

Beanie Babies rule in TOYS.

A B C D E F G H I J K L M N O P Q R S T U V W X Y Z

A B C D E F G H I J K L M N O P Q R S T U V W X Y Z

StarChild: A learning center for young astronomers

This is a wonderful beginner's guide to astronomy. It's written for smaller children and presents itself in an easy-to-read text. This site includes sections on general astronomy, Earth, planets, stars, galaxies, the Sun, and more. Use these pages to introduce a child (or brother or sister) to the wonders of space. You may even learn some new stuff yourself.

http://heasarc.gsfc.nasa.gov/docs/StarChild/
StarChild.html

Your brother always stands too close to the dart board when he plays. What's the rule about how far back you're supposed to stand?

Answer: According to the Darts Basics area of the CyberDarts page, "The official throwing distance, for most countries, is 2.37 meters, as measured along the floor, from the face of the dartboard. In feet, this is 7 feet, 9-1/4 inches. The height of the board, to the center of the bull, is 173 centimeters, or 5 feet, 8 inches." You can read more of the rules at http://www.cyberdarts.com/basics/dartsbasics.html

AURORA BOREALIS
The Aurora Page

Shimmering curtains of light in the night sky—it's the Aurora Borealis! Find out about Aurora Borealis sightings and forecasts. Various Aurora maps and images are here, including images taken from the space shuttle. Ever heard the northern lights? They also make sounds! Learn all about the theories on why this happens. There's even a survey for those lucky people who have "heard" one.

http://www.geo.mtu.edu/weather/aurora/

COMETS AND METEORS
Build Your Own Comet

If your parents won't let you stay up late to look for comets and meteors on a school night, maybe you can get your teacher to help you make one during the day, in class! This "comet recipe" includes dry ice and ammonia, so you'll need some help working with these materials, which need careful handling. You'll also find tips for introducing this activity to the classroom and comets facts and other links to educational resources.

http://www.noao.edu/education/igcomet/igcomet.html

Comet Introduction

Comets! They're made up of rock particles and frozen gases—it's cold out there in space! They orbit around the Sun, but instead of traveling in a circle, like planets, their orbit takes them very close to the Sun, then very, very far away. The show starts when they get close enough to the Sun for their frozen gases to start to "boil" away. These boiling gases are part of what forms the bright tail that blazes across the sky. Find out more about comets, and look at pictures of some of our recent visitors, including Comet West, Comet Shoemaker-Levy 9, Halley's Comet, and others.

http://bang.lanl.gov/solarsys/comet.htm

What is the sound of one router flapping?

Comet Hale-Bopp is coming!

Zinging its way through the sky at two million miles per hour is Comet Hale-Bopp, and lots of kids saw it in spring, 1997. If you weren't one of them, it's not too late! You can see a GIF of it here, and read lots of information on this spectacular visitor to our solar system.

http://www.skypub.com/comets/hb01.html

Comet Shoemaker-Levy Home Page (JPL)

For centuries, comets have been well known by the astronomers that scan the night skies, searching for its mysteries. Gene and Carolyn Shoemaker and David Levy spotted something on March 24, 1993 that was to become a major event. The comet they identified was found to have an orbit around Jupiter. Only this time, it was on a collision course! The fragmented comet, P/Shoemaker-Levy 9, after intense observation and study, collided with Jupiter between July 16 and July 24, 1994. It took over a week for all the fragments to reach the planet, but it provided a light show for anyone with a strong enough telescope pointed in the right direction. See the results here.

http://www.jpl.nasa.gov/sl9/

Comets.Asteroids.and.Meteoroids

Do you want just an overview of facts about comets and meteors? Check here for basic coverage, including such information as how many meteors fall to Earth each day (tons!), how many meteors you can expect to see an hour during the Perseid shower every August (68 at maximum), and what the heck a tektite is (a glassy rock that may be the remains of a meteor or a comet fragment—scientists are still arguing about it).

http://spacelink.msfc.nasa.gov/Instructional.Materials/
    Curriculum.Materials/Sciences/Astronomy/
    Our.Solar.System/Small.Bodies/
    Comets.Asteroids.and.Meteoroids

The truth is out there in UFOS AND EXTRATERRESTRIALS. Maybe.

The Cosmic Football

Scientists often explore the ice of Antarctica for micrometeorites. These tiny space travelers are so small, you need a microscope to see them! They have to be collected and studied under very special conditions so that they are not contaminated. This is the story of one very unusual micrometeorite and the British scientist who unraveled its mystery. See if you can follow the clues and make the correct hypothesis about how it got its distinctive shape.

http://www.nhm.ac.uk/sc/cf/cf1.html

Small Bodies

Did you ever make a wish on a "falling star"? It isn't a star, of course, but a meteor—a bit of rock captured by Earth's gravity, burning as it enters our atmosphere. Sometimes these space rocks don't burn completely, and they can reach Earth. When this happens, they are known as meteorites. You can get a close-up look at some well-traveled rocks at this site, which also features fascinating Hubble Space Telegraph photos of Comet Shoemaker-Levy 9 fragments hitting Jupiter in 1994. Compare various portraits of Comet Halley, the world's most famous comet, which swings by Earth about every 75 or 76 years. The spectacular 1910 appearance over Flagstaff, Arizona makes the more recent 1986 visitation look like a fizzled firecracker!

http://pds.jpl.nasa.gov/planets/welcome/smb.htm

ECLIPSES
Educator's Guide to Eclipses

Have you ever seen an eclipse? It's certainly an eerie event. It takes the Moon, the Sun, and Earth to make an eclipse. A solar eclipse happens when the Moon gets between Earth and the Sun and casts a shadow on Earth. A lunar eclipse happens when Earth gets between the Moon and the Sun and casts a shadow on the Moon. All three objects have to be lined up just right in the sky for this to happen. Read about eclipses and discover the special words astronomers use to describe the event.

http://bang.lanl.gov/solarsys/edu/eclipses.htm

A B C D E F G H I J K L M N O P Q R S T U V W X Y Z

May 10th, 1994 Eclipse

It was a dark day in New Mexico on May 10, 1994. No, the weather wasn't bad—it was a total solar eclipse! Scientists and astronomers traveled there from all over the world just to get a good look. To see the rare event that caused all this excitement, check out this site.

http://www.ngdc.noaa.gov/stp/ECLIPSE/eclipse.html

PLANETARIUMS

Adler Planetarium & Astronomy Museum Web Site

The Adler Planetarium opened in 1930 in Chicago and was the first planetarium to open to the public in the Western Hemisphere. This well-done page tells you about the available shows and what's on exhibit. Read about upcoming events and programs. If you're ever in the area, be sure to pay a visit.

http://astro.uchicago.edu/adler/

NET FILES

What special bean was once used as money, and where?

Answer: Cacao beans, from which chocolate is made. Cacao trees are believed to have originated in South America, and they were so valuable that the Aztecs used them as money. According to the Seeds of Change site at http://horizon.nmsu.edu/garden/history/cacao.html "They also roasted and ground the cacao bean and added vanilla pods, water, pepper, and other spices to make a drink, but it wasn't until 1492 that sugar was added...to make it sweet, and it wasn't until more than 150 years later that the English people began making the drink with milk instead of water!"

Loch Ness Productions: Planetarium Web Sites

Have you ever been to a planetarium show? You sink back in your seat, then the lights go down and the stars come out across the domed ceiling of the planetarium. It's a special treat each and every time you go. Here is a list of planetariums around the world, sorted by location. Find the planetarium closest to you to see what shows are available. If you're going on a trip, check out the schedule of a planetarium near your destination. Enjoy the show.

http://www.lochness.com//pltweb.html

SOLAR SYSTEM AND PLANETS

How Big is the Solar System?

Let's say you had a bowling ball to represent the Sun and a peppercorn to represent Earth, and you chose other objects to stand in for the other planets. Do you think you could make a scale model of the solar system that would fit on a tabletop? No. Well then, would it fit in your classroom? Still no. OK, how about your school playground? Truth is, you would need 1,000 yards (or slightly less than a kilometer in the metric version) to perform this fascinating and unforgettable "planet walk." This is a great activity for a family picnic, too, since it's fun for both children and adults. Complete instructions are provided here!

http://www.noao.edu/education/peppercorn/ pcmain.html

Mars Atlas home page

Fasten your seat belts. The Mars shuttle will be leaving just as soon as you get the courage to start clicking! You'll soon be served with a map of Mars that you can click to zoom in on. Then move around by selecting directional arrows. Stay as long as you like on Mars. You can either pack a lunch or just go to the fridge if you get hungry. Hint: The actual map link is further down the page, in the To Get Started section.

http://ic-www.arc.nasa.gov/ic/projects/bayes-group/ Atlas/Mars/

A B C D E F G H I J K L M N O P Q R S T U V W X Y Z

The Nine Planets

Here's a site with pictures of all the planets and their moons and much, much more. How did they get their names? Find out what planets are made of and which are most dense, brightest in the sky, and so on. Many of the words are linked to a glossary; just click on a highlighted word for an explanation. Also find out which planets have the best prospects for supporting life. Earth is listed first!

http://seds.lpl.arizona.edu/nineplanets/nineplanets/nineplanets.html

Primer on the Solar Space Environment

How well do you know our nearest star? Have you ever wondered how long the Sun will last before it burns out? How big are sunspots? Are they bigger than your school? Visit this site for a comprehensive description of the Sun as an energy source and its effects on life on Earth. Did you know that geomagnetic storms on the Sun can alter current flow in pipelines and really confuse homing pigeons?

http://www.sec.noaa.gov/primer/primer.html

Solar System Live

This is Solar System Live, and they mean it! You can tell the computer to draw a picture of the solar system almost any way you'd like it. You can even see what it looked like in the past or what it will look like sometime in the future, by giving it that date. If you're adventurous, you can even get a stereo view, but you'll need to train yourself how to look at the twin pictures—this may take a bit of practice or help from someone older, but it's worth it. You can even include a comet in the drawing to discover how it travels through the solar system on its long journey.

http://www.fourmilab.ch/solar/solar.html

Sun

It's big, it's hot, and it's the brightest thing around. No, we're not talking about glow-in-the-dark slime. We're talking about our very own star: the Sun. The Sun makes plants grow and keeps us warm. It's over 4.6 billion years old and is big enough to hold 1.3 million Earths. Read all about what it's made of and how it works.

http://bang.lanl.gov/solarsys/sun.htm

The Sun

It's pretty hot stuff! With a temperature of 15 million degrees Kelvin at its center, the Sun is the source of energy for all life on Earth. Each second, the Sun burns enough fuel to produce 386 billion-billion megawatts of energy (that's a lot of light bulbs!). But don't worry, it has enough fuel to burn another five billion years. There are many more interesting facts here to discover about the Sun.

http://seds.lpl.arizona.edu/nineplanets/nineplanets/sol.html

Views Of the Solar System

What do you think of when you hear the word "Mars?" Mars, ahh yes, one of my favorite candy bars. How about "Pluto?" Hey, that's Mickey's pet dog! "Saturn?" My dad's got one of those in the garage. OK, now what do they all have in common? They're all planets, of course! Did you know that Mars has volcanoes and that the biggest one is 15 miles high (the biggest one on Earth is only six miles high)? Did you know that (at least until 1999) Pluto is closer to the Sun than Neptune? Scientists also think that Pluto's atmosphere freezes and falls to the ground when it gets further away from the Sun—imagine shoveling clouds off your front walk! Did you know that you can drive a Saturn, but you can't make it sink? At least not the planet—it floats. There's lots more here, including many images and animations of planets, comets, and asteroids.

http://bang.lanl.gov/solarsys/

Welcome to the Planets

This collection centers on images taken from NASA's planetary exploration program. There are different annotated views of each planet, including close-ups. You'll also find pictures and facts about the spacecraft NASA used to take these photos, including Mariner, Viking, Voyager, Magellan, Galileo, and the Hubble Space Telescope.

http://pds.jpl.nasa.gov/planets/

Wolves are a howl in MAMMALS.

A
B
C
D
E
F
G
H
I
J
K
L
M
N
O
P
Q
R
S
T
U
V
W
X
Y
Z

A
B
C
D
E
F
G
H
I
J
K
L
M
N
O
P
Q
R
S
T
U
V
W
X
Y
Z

Woman in the Moon

You may have heard of the Man in the Moon, but have you ever seen the Woman in the Moon? Some people think she's actually easier to see! She looks a little like Wilma Flintstone to us, but study the pictures here and see what you think.

http://www.tufts.edu/as/wright_center/
  georgepage.html

SPACE EXPLORATION AND ASTRONAUTS

History of Space Exploration

Humans have been observing the stars for hundreds of years. It wasn't until 1959, with *Luna 1*, that we were able to actually break away from the gravity of Earth to visit another heavenly body—the Moon. In 1968, *Apollo 8* made the first manned space flight around the Moon. Read about all the other spacecraft that we have launched in our quest for knowledge about our universe.

http://bang.lanl.gov/solarsys/history.htm

NET FILES

What are zoonoses?

Answer: No, they're not elephant trunks, alligator snouts, or even parrot beaks. Zoonoses are viruses, infections, or diseases that can be passed from an animal to a human. For example, there are lots of things you can get from your cat! The good news is that zoonoses are very hard to "catch." Read more about it at http://www.clock.org/~ambar/off/zoonoses.html

Jim Lovell and the Flight of Apollo 13

This is a brief biography of astronaut Jim Lovell, from his childhood to his retirement. Read about how his interest in rocketry developed into a love for flying and space travel. Jim's most famous mission was the ill-fated *Apollo 13* flight to the Moon. This disastrous flight ended with the crew "escaping" back to Earth by way of the lunar module that was supposed to land on the Moon. Various links are included that explain more about some of the terms used in the story.

http://www.mcn.org/Apollo13/Home.html

Space FAQ 12/13 - How to Become an Astronaut

Being an astronaut must be a cool job. But how do you get to be one? Getting a Ph.D. and being a flight pilot are two very important qualifications for becoming an astronaut. Good eyesight and excellent physical condition are also a must. Also, don't be shy—astronauts need to be able to speak to the public. This page tells you all about how to impress NASA to get a job as an astronaut.

http://www.cis.ohio-state.edu/hypertext/faq/usenet/
  space/astronaut/faq.html

Space Shuttle Clickable Map

Isn't it amazing how much stuff we recycle these days, when we used to throw it away? NASA is doing the same thing with the space shuttle. NASA recycles the booster rockets after they fall into the ocean and fly the main cabin and cargo bay back to use again and again. This page has a clickable picture of a space shuttle, which will take you on a descriptive tour of its different parts. Explore the shuttle and find out what makes it click, er, tick.

http://seds.lpl.arizona.edu/ssa/space.shuttle/docs/

If you forgot the words to "gopher guts" try lyrics in MUSIC AND MUSICIANS.

Space Shuttle Launches

Here's the official schedule for all upcoming space shuttle launches. This site also describes each of all the past flights. Find out about the crew and cargo for each of the missions. You'll also see descriptions of the scientific experiments the astronauts performed while in space. Some of these experiments include studying the growth of crystals in microgravity and the effects of gravity on the growth of newt eggs (flight STS-65).

http://www.ksc.nasa.gov/shuttle/missions/
    missions.html

The Ultimate Field Trip - Section 1

Here's a field trip that you're unlikely to forget. Astronaut Kathy Sullivan is your host and guide on this incredible journey. She tells you about her decision to switch careers from marine biologist to astronaut. As she talks about her experiences as mission specialist aboard the space shuttle, she guides you on a tour of Earth photos taken from the shuttle. Kathy describes each photo in her own personal way, which gives you a special insight to her own experience.

http://ersaf.jsc.nasa.gov/uft/uft1.html

SPACE PHOTOS AND IMAGES

ASP List of NGG Images

The Astronomical Society of the Pacific (ASP) offers a list of space images, many of them with descriptions and sky locations. This collection includes images from the Hubble Space Telescope and observatories around the world. Browse and discover the wonders that exist out in the universe!

http://www.aspsky.org/html/resources/ngc.html

Astronomy Picture of the Day

Today we see an image of NGC 4261, a Hubble Space Telescope photo of a neighboring galaxy that has a giant black hole at its center. Tomorrow will be a picture called "24 hours from Jupiter." Guess we'll have to return tomorrow to see that one. The descriptive captions are peppered with links to other materials.

http://antwrp.gsfc.nasa.gov/apod/astropix.html

Chesley Bonestell Gallery

Do you ever watch old Hollywood movies about outer space? You know, the ones where the rockets look like firecrackers. Since people hadn't even started to explore space yet, moviemakers had to rely on imagination when they wanted to show the surface of an alien planet. Most of those outer space scenes were filmed against painted backdrops. To film Martians in their natural habitat, for example, movie directors dressed actors in silly costumes and plopped them in front of the paintings of Chesley Bonestell. His work isn't just a great backdrop for 1930s movies—it helped shape the way scientists design space suits and rocket ships.

http://www.secapl.com/bonestell/Top.html

JSC Digital Image Collection

So many pictures, too little time! This is the Johnson Space Center's collection of space images taken from various space missions. Over 10,000 press release images and 300,000 Earth observation images are available. You'll see pictures here from the first Mercury flight to the latest space shuttle mission. If you know your latitude and longitude, you might be able to find a space photo of where you live. (You can get your latitude and longitude for most places in the U.S. at the How Far Is It? page at <http://www.indo.com/distance/> if you want to check.) You can also try the Search option and click on a map to find photos of that area.

http://images.jsc.nasa.gov/

SEDS Messier Database

This would definitely make E.T. feel homesick: 110 images of the brightest and most beautiful objects in the night skies. This is the Messier catalog of star clusters, galaxies, and nebulae. Charles Messier started this catalog in the eighteenth century as a collection of objects that were most often mistaken for comets. It serves as an excellent reference list for both beginner and seasoned astronomers. You'll also find the celestial position for each object, which will help you locate it in the sky.

http://seds.lpl.arizona.edu/messier/Messier.html

A
B
C
D
E
F
G
H
I
J
K
L
M
N
O
P
Q
R
S
T
U
V
W
X
Y
Z

A
B
C
D
E
F
G
H
I
J
K
L
M
N
O
P
Q
R
S
T
U
V
W
X
Y
Z

STARS AND CONSTELLATIONS

Milky Way Galaxy

Did you know that they named our galaxy after a candy bar—or was it the other way around? Anyway, our Earth is part of the solar system that centers on the Sun, our closest star. Our Sun is only one of a few hundred billion stars that make up the Milky Way galaxy. If you think that's big, the Milky Way (the galaxy, not the candy bar) is only one of millions of galaxies in the universe.

http://lsnt7.lightspeed.net/~astronomy/
   milkyway.description/milkyway.description.html

Out of This World Exhibition

You may have heard the names of some of the star constellations: the Big Dipper, Taurus the Bull, and Aquarius, to name a few. You may have even seen their figures drawn along with the stars that form them. Probably not like the figures you'll find here. These pages are filled with etchings and drawings of star charts and maps from hundreds of years ago. They show the constellations drawn with detailed figures and objects. Early astronomers might not have had the fancy instruments we have now, but they sure had imagination!

http://www.lhl.lib.mo.us/pubserv/hos/stars/
   welcome.htm

The Universe in the Classroom, Spring 1986

Can you imagine weighing 10,000 tons? That's how much you would weigh if you were able to stand on one of our neighboring stars, Sirius B. Although this star is only about the size of our Earth, it weighs almost as much as our own Sun. That tremendous weight is what gives it such strong gravity. Our Sun is over 300 times brighter than Sirius B. However, Sirius A, its twin, is twice as big as our Sun. Sirius A would look over 20 times brighter if it were in the same spot as our Sun. If these facts sound interesting, there's lots more here about these and other stars that share our corner of the universe.

http://www.aspsky.org/html/tnl/05/05.html

TELESCOPES AND OBSERVATORIES

HST Greatest Hits 1990-1995 Gallery

They say on a clear day, you can see forever. However, astronomers would rather do without the air, no matter how clear. Light waves get distorted as they travel through the air, and it's hard to get a good picture when you're trying to see very far away. That's the idea behind the Hubble Space Telescope (HST). With a powerful telescope in orbit above the atmosphere, scientists can get a much better picture of our universe. The images are sent back to Earth electronically. This way, they are not affected by the atmosphere. Be sure to check out the telescope's greatest hits!

http://www.stsci.edu/pubinfo/BestOfHST95.html

Mount Wilson Observatory

Located above Los Angeles, California, this observatory has been at the forefront of astronomy for many years. The lights in nearby L.A. are about as bright as a full moon, so observations are limited to bright objects such as nebulae or star clusters. Still, scientific competition to use the telescopes at this facility is fierce! On the virtual tour, you'll visit all the 'scopes on the mountain. Plus, you'll get a tour of the Monastery, which is the building where scientists sleep when not performing their duties. The building is divided into two parts: the "day" side (for scientists who sleep at night and work during the day) and the "night" side (for scientists who sleep during the day and use the telescopes at night).

http://www.mtwilson.edu/index.html

Telescopes

Read all about reflection, refraction, parabolic mirrors, and spherical aberration. These are some of the definitions used to describe telescope features and how they are made. Telescopes need to magnify light from weak, distant sources and make the images visible to the observer. There's a lot more available on astronomy if you click on "Return to lecture notes homepage" at the bottom of the page.

http://lsnt7.lightspeed.net/~astronomy/telescopes/
   telescopes.html

UNIVERSE
Black Holes

You can check in, but you can't check out! As far back as 1793, astronomer Rev. John Mitchell reasoned that if something were big enough, its gravity would be so strong that even light could not escape. Since then, Einstein's Theory of Relativity has helped explain how this is possible. These objects are now called black holes. Some scientists think that black holes are formed from stars that collapse into themselves when they burn out. That's hard to imagine, but we're finding out more and more about black holes all the time. Maybe you'll be the one who makes a big discovery someday about the mystery of black holes.

http://www.aspsky.org/html/tnl/24/24.html

Everyone knows diamonds are made out of carbon, right? And so is graphite, the "lead" in your pencil. How can one be so hard and the other so soft, if they are both made out of the same thing?

Answer: It all depends on the chemical structure of the carbon. Scientists are experimenting with a new carbon structure, called buckminsterfullerene (or fullerene for short, also known as "buckyballs"). This structure looks something like a geodesic dome, which was invented by Buckminster Fuller. One cool thing you can do with buckyballs is put other atoms inside the buckyball "cage." This can create all sorts of new materials, with interesting properties! Read more about buckyballs and other structures at http://www.lbl.gov/MicroWorlds/MaterialWorld/MatWorld.html in the Material World section.

AVIATION AND AIRPLANES

Airlines of the WEB -- Marc-David's Chunk of the Web

Every airline with a Web page is collected here! Cruise links to all the big airlines (Delta, United, TWA, British Airways), and check out the little ones. You'll find Tigerfly, the U.K.-based "world's smallest airline." You'll learn lots of airline statistics here too, like how much airlines spend on food per passenger and current monthly statistics about which airlines generally take off and land on time.

http://w2.itn.net/airlines/

AirNav: Airport Information

Type in the three-letter airport code for the airport you want, and you'll get detailed information back. If you don't know the code, you can just type in the name of the nearest city. You can try to look for nearby balloonports, gliderports, heliports, seaplane bases—pretty much everything but a starship dock! You'll get back a map of the airport, its radio frequencies, runway descriptions, yearly traffic statistics, and more, including a list of obstructions in the general area, such as tall radio towers or buildings. You'll also find out if migratory birds or animals are sometimes on the runways.

http://www.airnav.com/airports/

Aviation Enthusiast Corner

Whoa—did you see that precision flying team, the U.S. Air Force Thunderbirds? Those F-16 Fighting Falcons sure do put on a great air show! If you want to learn more about this drill team in the skies and see when they will be coming to your area, then check this Web site. You'll also find the schedules of lots of other air show performers, plus specifications on different types of aircraft. There are also links to aircraft manufacturers, aviation museums, and lots more. Warning: This site is graphics-intensive and takes a long time to load.

http://aeroweb.brooklyn.cuny.edu/air.html

A
B
C
D
E
F
G
H
I
J
K
L
M
N
O
P
Q
R
S
T
U
V
W
X
Y
Z

The Blimp

Have you ever noticed that large sporting events tend to attract blimps, like flies around a picnic? The blimp carries a joystick-controlled camera, which gets a live overhead shot of the playing field. You may have seen the MetLife Blimp—it has everyone's favorite beagle, Snoopy, on it. But is it Snoopy One or Snoopy Two? There are two MetLife blimps, one based on each coast. While they normally are tasked to help televise sporting events, the Western Snoopy recently helped track some whales as part of an environmental research project. This site will tell you all about the blimp's construction, its history, and how the heck they park it!

http://www.metlife.com/Blimp/blimp-toc.html

Flight Training Information

Wow—you're taking a flight lesson! The weather is nice, but the winds are from 15 to 20 mph, which means plenty of practice with crosswinds. Yikes, too crooked—better go around and try it again. What does it take to be a pilot, anyway? Read the diary of a student pilot and find out. A very informative graphic describes all those confusing-looking gauges in the cockpit.

http://www.wolfenet.com/~tegwilym/FlyLesson.html

LANDINGS

What in the world is a flight plan? Well, a flight plan helps you prepare for the best route of flight before taking off, just as you would map out your summer vacation road trip. A flight plan will include items such as departure and destination airports, navigation aids, fuel consumption rates, and wind information. This will aid in a safer flight for all. You can download software to assist with flight planning, or you can stay on the ground and use the flight simulator games available here. Make your reservations now; this is a feature-rich site!

http://www.landings.com/aviation.html

NATIONAL AIR & SPACE MUSEUM HOMEPAGE

See pictures and learn about milestones in aviation. For example, Charles Lindbergh was one of the most famous pilots in history. In his plane, *Spirit of St. Louis*, he was the first to cross the Atlantic alone. He took off from Roosevelt Field, in New York State, early on the morning of May 20, 1927. After 33½ hours, Lindbergh landed at Le Bourget Field, near Paris, welcomed by a cheering crowd. This was the first solo crossing of a major ocean by air, and it was a very big deal at the time. Come in for a landing at this online museum, where you'll also see famous spacecraft and even a real moon rock! The National Air and Space Museum is part of the Smithsonian Institution, and it is located in Washington, D.C.

http://www.nasm.edu/

Time Line

Look, it's a bird! No, it's a plane! In fact, it's a whole bunch of things that fly. From the Montgolfier brothers' hot-air balloon (built in 1783) to the world's largest passenger airplane, the Boeing 747, you'll discover it all here. You'll learn the history of flight and the people and technology behind it. Warning: This page is graphics-intensive, and it comes all the way from the Science Museum of London.

http://www.nmsi.ac.uk/on-line/flight/flight/history.htm

BALLOONING
Morris's Ballooning Info Page

Up, up, and away! Look at all the beautiful balloons. This is the place to discover the wonderful world of ballooning. You'll learn about the Kodak Albuquerque International Balloon Fiesta, the largest ballooning event in the world. You'll meet the pilots and crew of Serenity, a balloon based in Fort Collins, Colorado. Want to buy a secondhand, used balloon? A resource is here for that, too.

http://www.unm.edu/~mbas/BALLOON.HTML

Have an order of pi in MATH AND ARITHMETIC.

The StarChild team of Laura A. Whitlock, Joyce W. Dejoie, Jesse S. Allen, and Elizabeth (Libby) Truelove. This was the first time that they were ever all in one place at the same time!

"The very first draft of these pages was created as a demonstration model, but it was not selected for funding. In truth, we then forgot that these pages were still around until (to our surprise!) we were informed that they were being heavily used!"

ASTRONOMY, SPACE, AND SPACE EXPLORATION

StarChild: A Learning Center for Young Astronomers

Webmasters: Jesse S. Allen, Joyce W. Dejoie, Elizabeth (Libby) Truelove, and Laura A. Whitlock

http://heasarc.gsfc.nasa.gov/docs/StarChild/StarChild.html

How many people work on your pages?

Four of us work on the pages. Libby Truelove and Joyce Dejoie create all the text. Laura Whitlock and Jesse Allen maintain the site and add new images and animations. We get about 1,000 hits every day but we have had days with as many as three or four times that number.

If this isn't your main job, what do you do?

Jesse Allen works on the education sites our group (the High Energy Astrophysics Science Archive Research Center at NASA's Goddard Space Flight Center) produces. His undergraduate training is in astronomy and his master's degree is in education.

Joyce Dejoie's main job is teaching 6th grade math and science at Lakeside Middle School in Evans, Georgia. Her undergraduate training was in psychology, and she also has a specialist in education.

Libby Truelove has two jobs: teaching 8th grade math and science at Lakeside Middle School in Evans, Georgia and being a veterinarian! She has a doctorate in veterinary medicine, and has been taking education courses.

Laura Whitlock works on restoring data from old X-ray and gamma-ray astronomy satellites so that it can be used by scientists all over the world. She created and leads the development of the High-Energy Astrophysics Learning Center education web site. She oversees the development of StarChild. She also mentors a local high school student in a research project in X-ray astronomy. Plus, she's a working astronomer! She enjoys analyzing data which come from neutron stars and black holes. She has a bachelor's and doctorate in physics.

Do you have a family?

Allen: Married, keeps thirty-gallon fish tanks which house his Japanese Koi: Lord Admiral Nelson, amongst others.

Dejoie: Married, two sons (Michael and Tony).

Truelove: Married, one daughter (Randi), and a furry brown dog named Annie.

Whitlock: Mom to the world's best Dalmatian, Oppenheimer. You can see him pop up in the web site from time to time!

If you could invite three people throughout history to your house for dinner, who would they be?

Allen: Michael Faraday (chemist and experimental physicist), Herbert Hoover (31st President of the U.S.), and Benjamin Banneker (inventor, mathematician, compiler of almanacs, astronomer).

Dejoie: Barbara Jordan (Congresswoman, educator, constitutionalist), Confucius (Chinese philosopher), Flip Wilson (comedian).

Truelove: "Pistol Pete" Maravich (one of the fifty greatest basketball players of all time), Maya Angelou (poet, writer, activist), and John F. Kennedy (35th President of the U.S.).

Whitlock: Leonardo da Vinci (artist and inventor), St. Joan of Arc (French patriot and martyr), and Helen Keller (writer and educator who overcame blindness and deafness).

A
B
C
D
E
F
G
H
I
J
K
L
M
N
O
P
Q
R
S
T
U
V
W
X
Y
Z

BIOLOGY

Cell Basics

Cells are the basic building blocks of life. You need a microscope to see most cells and the tiny structures inside them, which are called *organelles*. This page, part of a biology hypertextbook for the Massachusetts Institute of Technology, gives you an overview of cell biology. See the differences between plant and animal cells, and if you're really into it, go back to the home page for this resource and learn about photosynthesis, genetics, and more! Want to see more pictures and text about cells? Try *<http://lenti.med.umn.edu/~mwd/cell.html>* for another online Cell Tutorial.

http://esg-www.mit.edu:8001/bio/cb/cellbasics.html

The Heart: An Online Exploration

The heart is more than just a symbol for Valentine's Day. It's the pump that keeps your life's blood flowing throughout your body. Your blood distributes food to your cells and carries away the waste. Since it can't move on its own, it would be quite useless without the heart to keep it moving! Visit this page to read about the heart and all its functions.

http://sln.fi.edu/biosci/heart.html

Introduction to Virtual FlyLab

Have you heard someone say, "he has his father's eyes" or "his mother's smile"? That's because the child is made from genetic instructions contributed by each parent. They combine in different ways, so you'll see people in the same family look similar to each other, but not exactly the same—unless they are twins. Confused yet? This whole science is called genetics, and scientists learned a lot about its rules by studying fruit flies and their offspring (that's their kids). We know it sounds weird. You can try it yourself here. What happens when you mate a purple-eyed fruit fly to one with fluffy wings?

http://vflylab.calstatela.edu/edesktop/VirtApps/
VflyLab/IntroVflyLab.html

Neuroscience Resources for Kids

When you bite into a chocolate bar, how do you know it's delicious? How do you know to say, "Ouch!" when you get stung by a mosquito? Little sensors, called *neurons*, are all over your body, and they carry messages to your brain through a system of nerves. Your brain then sorts everything out. This resource is crammed with great info about brains, your senses, spinal cords, and careers in neuroscience. Be aware, though, that many of these folks go to school for 20 *years* before they become neuroscientists!

http://weber.u.washington.edu/~chudler/introb.html

How many senses do you have? Perhaps you hear, see, smell, touch, and taste? Maybe you have a "sixth" sense (or maybe that's *nonsense*). Anyway, we "sense" that soon you'll be traveling to the Neuroscience Resources for Kids Page to find out more!

MICROSCOPES
Early History of the Lens

Sure, we could tell you all about the person who first thought of using a lens to magnify things, or when eyeglasses came into vogue (earlier than you might think!). Or we could tell you about the dude who later invented the microscope. But wouldn't you rather check it out yourself? Lots of pictures and fascinating facts about early optics and scientists are here for you to explore.

http://www.duke.edu/~tj/hist/c1.html

Molecular Expressions: Images From the Microscope

Yoo-hoo! I'm right down here, right under your nose. No, silly, not on the floor—under the microscope. Take a look at me and a bunch of other images on the Molecular Expressions page. How about a close-up of that microprocessor chip inside your computer? It's here! So is a microscopic tour of beers of the world, as they appear under polarized light. There's more, including how to set up a microscope of your own.

http://micro.magnet.fsu.edu/

If you want to visit another world without leaving home, check out Molecular Expressions: Images from the Microscope.

SCIMEDIA: Light Microscopy

You'll find a great little diagram here with all the parts of a microscope. This site also has links to info on lenses, electron microscopy, and more.

http://www.scimedia.com/chem-ed/imaging/lmicrosc.htm

BIRDS

See also FARMING AND AGRICULTURE—POULTRY; PETS AND PET CARE

The Aviary

Join the flock here for a large variety of information about birds. Whether you own a companion bird or enjoy watching wild birds, this home page is a gathering place and resource center for all bird lovers. You'll find information about bird illness and on how to keep your bird safe, as well as food and nutrition tips. You'll discover the importance of toys for your pet bird and learn about wild bird rescue. Fly on over and ask an avian vet a question about your pet bird today.

http://theaviary.com/

How fast does a glacier move?

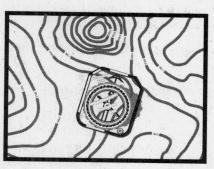

Answer: The fastest moving glacier, the Quarayaq in Greenland, moves about 2.7 to 3.3 feet per hour. Most glaciers move much slower than that. Surprisingly, scientists didn't know glaciers moved at all until 1827. A Swiss scientist built a small hut on a glacier. When he came back three years later, the hut had moved more than 100 yards downhill! Read more fun glacier facts at http://www.whistler.net/glacier/coolfact.html

Common Birds of the Australian National Botanic Gardens

It's such a nice day for a walk in the garden. What beautiful birds! And listen—their songs are so pretty. The Australian National Botanic Gardens are so peaceful, it almost feels as if you are actually there. Watch out, though. During the spring breeding season, male magpies protect their territory by "swooping" intruders: a painful experience for those unlucky enough to be hit. Did you know that the tongue of the New Holland honeyeater has a "brush" at the end, which helps it gather the sweet nectar in flowers? Visit the gardens and learn about the other fascinating birds in the sanctuary.

http://osprey.anbg.gov.au/anbg/birds.html

Strike up the band in MUSIC AND MUSICIANS.

A B C D E F G H I J K L M N O P Q R S T U V W X Y Z

The National Audubon Society Sanctuary Department

Did you know that the greatest threat to wild birds is the loss of habitat? Imagine walking along and seeing a close-up of a wood stork in a cypress tree or a sandhill crane family taking a walk along the river sandbar. Visit this home page and learn about sanctuaries across the United States that protect these wild birds and other wildlife. Take time out to enjoy the scenery and wildlife in these refuges.

http://www.igc.apc.org/audubon/xsanc.html

The North American Breeding Bird Survey-95.1

This survey says nearly 63 percent of wetland bird species are increasing in numbers! This site offers a large-scale survey and source of information about population changes of North American birds. It is also a tool for learning about birds, with pictures of common birds of North America. The coolest part, though, is the more than 50 audio files of common birdsongs and birdcalls.

http://www.im.nbs.gov/bbs/bbs.html

__H__ave you ever heard a birdsong and wondered who wrote the music? You might find its composer at The North American Breeding Bird Survey-95.1, where they have over fifty of the latest bird tunes on file for your listening pleasure.

"Use the source, Luke!" and look it up in REFERENCE WORKS.

The Pet Bird Page (Parrots)

Thinking about buying a bird for a pet? If so, this is the place to stop before making your purchase. They'll help you choose the bird that's best for you. You'll find important information on what to feed your bird and on how to train it as well as guidelines to finding a good vet. You'll have an opportunity to talk to professionals and experienced breeders in the chat room, and you'll learn about the daily and periodic care required for your feathered friend.

http://hookomo.aloha.net/~granty/

Everybody loves budgies, those colorful little birds also known as parakeets. Budgie is short for budgerigar, which is from an Aboriginal word which translates as "good eating." If you'd rather admire and not eat your budgies, try perching on The Pet Bird Page (Parrots).

Satellite Tracking of Threatened Species

"Graak, #12345, last seen March 15, 1995 at 19:48:22." This is a sample of monitoring a migratory, threatened species. The bird's activity, latitude, and longitude can be measured via satellite data transmissions. Discover why and how these birds are being tracked by visiting this interesting site!

http://sdcd.gsfc.nasa.gov/ISTO/satellite_tracking/

Programs, reviews, theme songs, and more in TELEVISION.

BIRD WATCHING
Backyard Bird Feeding

The bird food store has so many choices: black oil sunflower, safflower seed, niger seed, or maybe peanut hearts. How do you sort it all out? The good news is that you don't have to sort the various seeds—the birds do that for you! You'll find a handy guide to what species of birds like which foods plus some tips about feeders and placing them in the right spots to attract the most birds.

http://www.fws.gov/~r9mbmo/pamphlet/feed.html#0

Bird Song Mnemonics

When you go on a bird watching hike, odds are that you'll hear a lot more birds than you'll see. Wouldn't it be cool to be able to identify a bird by the sounds it makes? For example, you're out for a walk in the woods and you hear a bird that seems to be singing, "Sweet Canada, Canada, Canada"—instantly, you know that's a white-throated sparrow. Or maybe you're walking in the meadow and hear a high-pitched "chortle-deeeeee," drawn out on that last syllable. You know at once that's a red-winged blackbird. How did you get so smart? You've memorized a list of birds and little hints to help you remember what their songs sound like. One's available on this home page! The fancy word for memory-joggers like these is *mnemonics*.

http://www.1000plus.com/BirdSong/birdsong.htm

GeoGraphical Birding Guide

Shhh!—be very quiet—we don't want to disturb the golden eagle nest or the babies in it. Look, four baby eaglets! Watch out, here comes their mom to feed them! The GeoGraphical Birding Guide has information about the distribution and population changes of birds all over the world. It also has tools for learning about birds, with pictures and quizzes on bird identification. Use the clickable map to find out about birding hot spots and information in your state.

http://www-astronomy.mps.ohio-state.edu/~ignaz/
    birds/ABA/ABA.html

NET FILES

On the Internet, nobody knows you're a frog. Craving some "Bee Grubs in Coconut Cream"? Where on Earth can a frog find a cookbook?

Answer: At the Froggy Page, of course! "Marinate bee grubs, sliced onions, and citrus leaves in coconut cream containing some pepper. Wrap in pieces of linen and steam. Serve as a topping for rice." It doesn't suggest where a frog might get some linen, though.
http://www.cs.yale.edu/HTML/YALE/CS/HyPlans/loosemore-sandra/froggy/recipes.html

Virtual Birding in Tokyo

Wouldn't it be fun to see what kinds of birds are in other kids' backyards—say, in Tokyo, Japan? This site lets you compare your local birds to their counterparts on the other side of the world! Does the puddle duck mallard you have strutting around your park pond look the same as the ones in Japan? Find out here at this beautiful site.

http://ux01.so-net.or.jp/~koike/

BIRDHOUSES
HOMES FOR BIRDS

Home, home on a metal pole? Sure, if you're talking about a birdhouse! Did you know that more than two dozen North American birds will nest in birdhouses? Stop by this Web site, and you will discover very complete advice about how to design a birdhouse to attract different types of birds to your neighborhood.

http://www.bcpl.lib.md.us/~tross/by/house.html

A
B
C
D
E
F
G
H
I
J
K
L
M
N
O
P
Q
R
S
T
U
V
W
X
Y
Z

HotSpot for Birds - Bird Houses, Feeders, and Birds and Supplies

Everyone needs a home, even our fine feathered friends, the birds. You'll find that different types of birds require different types and placements of their homes. A birdhouse is appreciated by its tenants, and boys and girls, young and old, can also enjoy the presence of a birdhouse—and no batteries are required!

http://www.lainet.com/hotspot/bhcare.htm

NC State University - NCCES - Working With Wildlife - Building Songbird Boxes

Did you know that you can build houses for specific kinds of birds? Just by varying the diameter of the entrance hole, you can make a house for bluebirds, flycatchers, or flickers. You also have to make the hole a certain distance above the floor of the birdhouse. There are other building considerations to keep in mind for various species. Check this site for plans and specifications for birdhouses and predator guards for them. Then place your new homes in the trees and fields in March or April, while the birds are still home-hunting! For larger birds, such as woodpeckers and owls, see the instructions for Woodland Wildlife Nest Boxes at <http://www.ces.ncsu.edu/nreos/forest/steward/www17.html>.

http://www.ces.ncsu.edu/nreos/forest/steward/
   www16.html

DUCKS, GEESE, AND SWANS
Carter's Rare Birds

Duck, duck, goose! You probably know Daffy Duck, Donald Duck, and even Mother Goose, but let's look at some of the less-famous ducks and geese, such as cackling Canada geese, cinnamon teal, American widgeons, and wood ducks. Stop by this site and meet some of these birds and hear what they sound like. You'll learn about their nests and eggs and also about their status in both the wild and in captivity.

http://www.rarebird.com/carter/

North West Swan Study

Do you know what a cob is, besides something corn grows on? What's a pen, besides something you write with? A *cob* is an adult male swan, and a *pen* is an adult female swan. The three to seven eggs the pen lays is called a *clutch,* and young swans are called *cygnets.* To learn more about swans, visit this page, and listen to the warning call swans give humans who get too close to their nests.

http://www.airtime.co.uk/users/cygnus/swanstud.htm

In Greece, do people celebrate Christmas by decorating a tree?

Answer: Christmas trees are seldom seen in Greece. More common is a wooden bowl containing a cross wrapped in a sprig of basil (an aromatic herb). The bowl has some water in it to keep the plant fresh. According to the Christmas Around The World home page, "Once a day, a family member, usually the mother, dips the cross and basil into some holy water and uses it to sprinkle water in each room of the house." This ritual is done to keep pesky spirits, called Killantzaroi, away from the house. They do things like put out hearth fires, make milk sour, and generally cause trouble. Luckily, they only come out for the 12 days of Christmas, and since they come down the chimney, keeping the fire burning the entire time is also a good deterrent. Read more at http://www.christmas.com/greece.html about Christmas traditions.

EAGLES, FALCONS, AND HAWKS
Old Abe the War Eagle

During the Civil War, many military units adopted an animal mascot. Usually it was a dog or a goat, but the Eighth Wisconsin Infantry Regiment had something really unique: a bald eagle, which they named "Old Abe," after President Abraham Lincoln. You can read about Old Abe's war stories and see pictures. Old Abe's legacy lives on in the logos of Wisconsin companies, in replicas at the Wisconsin State Assembly and elsewhere, and in the names of school sports teams. Additionally, the insignia patch of the U.S. Army's 101st Airborne Division, originally formed in Wisconsin during World War I, carries a graphic of Old Abe. According to this page, the "Screaming Eagles" saw extensive action in World War II and the Vietnam and Persian Gulf Wars.

http://badger.state.wi.us/agencies/dva/museum/cybergal/oa-main.html

The RAPTOR CENTER at University of Minnesota

You find a hawk with an injured wing. What do you do? You need to call a special kind of animal doctor, called a *wildlife rehabilitator*, who helps the bird get better so it can be released to the wild again. This site tells you what to do in an emergency, but the most important rule is that the less contact you have with the bird, the better its chances of survival will be. You can also call the Raptor Center 24 hours a day to get advice. They treat many sick or injured birds of prey, also known as *raptors*. For example, a bald eagle was found with a severe bacterial infection. The Raptor Center cured it and released it the next month. Years later, the same lucky bird was found caught in a steel-jawed trap, and it had another visit to the Raptor Center. The injury was successfully treated, and the eagle was once again released in February 1995. Visit this Web site to find more materials about the Raptor Center and the birds they treat, including information about endangered/threatened birds and the environmental issues that affect them.

http://www.raptor.cvm.umn.edu/

Computers are dumb, people are smart.

SERRC'S Home Page

Did you ever wonder how injured wild birds are rehabilitated? What if they don't fully recover? Visit the Southeastern Raptor Rehabilitation Center (SERRC) and discover what it takes to rehabilitate injured birds before they can be released to the wild. Meet the special permanent residents that will never be released due to the severity of their injuries. Learn the importance of raptors and how you can help ensure that these birds get the finest care available. Maybe your class could participate in the Adopt-A-Raptor program!

http://www.vetmed.auburn.edu/raptor/

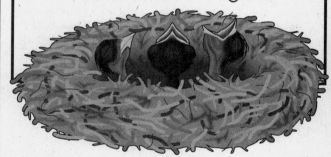

Adopt a raptor today! Find out more about how these birds of prey need your help and what you can do for them at SERRC's Home Page.

OTHER BIRDS
Hummingbirds!

Did you know that in the spring male hummingbirds start heading north as early as three weeks ahead of the females and immature birds? This is so the male can scout ahead for food for the females and young during migration. For more information on attracting hummingbirds to your yard, hummingbird feeders, the natural history of hummingbirds, and more, visit this outstanding hobbyist's page.

http://www.derived.com/~lanny/hummers/

A B C D E F G H I J K L M N O P Q R S T U V W X Y Z

NET FILES

How tall is the Oscar award, and how much does it weigh?

Answer: The Academy Awards statuette known as "Oscar," is 13 1/2 inches tall and weighs 8 1/2 pounds. It was born at a Hollywood banquet on May 11, 1927, one week after the Academy of Motion Picture Arts and Sciences was organized. At that meeting, Louis B. Mayer, president of Metro-Goldwyn-Mayer (MGM) Studios, urged that the Academy create a special film award. Cedric Gibbons, an art director for MGM, quickly sketched a figure of a knight holding a crusader's sword standing atop a reel of film, whose five spokes signified the five original branches of the Academy (Actors, Directors, Producers, Technicians, and Writers). Learn more about the award winners at http://www.ampas.org/ampas/awards/history.html

The Penguin Page

We all know what macaroni and cheese is, but have your ever heard of macaroni penguins? They live in the Antarctic and nearby islands, and they eat crustaceans, fish, and squid. Visit the Aggressive Behavior section and discover the difference between the "sideways stare" and the "alternate stare" given by penguins to other penguins and other animals. You'll also learn about various penguin species and their predators.

http://www.vni.net/~kwelch/penguins/

It never rains on the PARADES in cyberspace.

OWLS

Jamie Stewart's Screech Owl Page

What a wonderful collection of photos, taken of a family of screech owls nesting near Jamie Stewart's house! Be sure to fill out the guest book, and tell Jamie you saw his page referred to in this book. When you do this, you get to see another cute owl picture!

http://www.voicenet.com/~jstewart/scrchowl/
scrchowl.html

NC State University - NCCES - Working With Wildlife - Owls

Do you know a barn owl from a screech owl? You will if you visit this site! A barn owl has a heart-shaped face and can be between 15 to 20 inches tall. A screechie, on the other hand, has tufted ears and is much smaller—only about 10 inches long. You can learn to build owl houses here and help increase the owl population where you live. Let's owl build some bird houses soon!

http://www.ces.ncsu.edu/nreos/forest/steward/
www22.html

Purdue On-Line Writing Lab Web Server Owl Info Page

Whoo, whoo is the largest of them all? With a wingspan of six feet, six inches, the eagle owls are the largest of the owl family. Stop by this site for an introduction to owls, and check out the wonderful gallery of owl pictures. Did you know that an owl's eyes are almost immovable and that some owls can turn their head completely upside down? Whoo, whoo knew?

http://owl.trc.purdue.edu/Images/Picture-Gallery.html

What is the sound of one router flapping?

BOATING AND SAILING

See also SPORTS—CANOEING AND KAYAKING;
SPORTS—ROWING AND SCULLING;
SPORTS—WIND SURFING

Age of Sail Page

Your *Treasure Island* book report is finished, and it would be great to put a graphic on that title page. Or maybe you've written your very own pirate story! If your report or story is on sailing, boating, tall ships, pirates, or adventure on the high seas, then here's your source for great clip art. There is also an unchecked list of links to related boat pages. "Aaaay, me bucko! Have at it!"

http://www.cs.yale.edu/homes/sjl/sail.html

Interactive Marine Observations

This site falls into the category of the truly amazing. A network of sea buoys and CMAN (Coastal Marine Automated Network) stations is maintained by the National Data Buoy Center (NBDC), a division of NOAA (National Oceanic and Atmospheric Administration). The observations are updated continuously, and an eight-hour history is usually available for each station. They report temperature, dew point, wind (sustained and gust) direction and speed, surface pressure, wave heights, and the period between waves. How are the waves off Maui, Hawai'i? What's the temperature off Anchorage, Alaska? Or you can check even closer to home, if you're going boating in the coastal waters of the U.S. or maritime Canada.

http://www.nws.fsu.edu/buoy

VIDEO AND SPY CAMS let you look in on interesting parts of the world.

Navigation Information Connection (NIC)

The U.S. Army Corps of Engineers sponsors this informative site, which offers maps of navigable rivers in the U.S. as well as daily reports on the status of navigation locks along those rivers. Never seen a lock in operation before? They allow boats to go around waterfalls or rapids by providing a water "elevator" for the boat to climb or descend the river. There are diagrams and pictures of locks here; the shortcut is <*http://www.ncr.usace.army.mil/ navdata/locpic.htm*> if you wish to bypass the other interesting resources.

http://www.ncr.usace.army.mil/nic.htm

Ocean Challenge/Class Afloat

If your teacher told your class to go get your coats because you're going on a field trip, you'd probably be pretty excited, right? What if he or she led you right onto the deck of a tall ship and said to get comfortable because you are all going on a round-the-world cruise? Still interested? You're then told that your class is going to be the crew and that you'll be gone for months! That's exactly what's happening to 33 high school kids, their teachers, and only eight actual, old salt crew members. You can follow the progress of their journey on the Net and even ask them questions. Meet the kids, read their ship diaries, and enjoy this classroom afloat.

http://www.oceanchallenge.com/ca9697/classafl.htm

Sailing Online Services

Where's the *bow*? What if your *scupper* is plugged? How do you know when to *luff*? If you're going to be talking to boaters or sailors (or if you're going to be one), then you'll have to check out this site. And you thought you were a sailor because you knew your *port* (left) from your *starboard* (right)! Sail on over and find the definition of any sailing word.

http://www.ov-m.com/sos/dictionary.html

The Web in Pig Latin? Make it so in LANGUAGES AND ALPHABETS.

A B C D E F G H I J K L M N O P Q R S T U V W X Y Z

A
B
C
D
E
F
G
H
I
J
K
L
M
N
O
P
Q
R
S
T
U
V
W
X
Y
Z

The Semaphore Flag Signaling System

You want to say "Hi" to your buddy in a boat across the bay, but it's too far to yell. You could use the semaphore alphabet and two flags to send messages. How? Boaters spell words by holding a flag in each hand and moving them into different positions. An *H* is made by holding the right-hand flag out straight and the left-hand flag down and across the body. You can learn the whole semaphore alphabet from the pictures and descriptions you'll find at this page. Get your flags and practice!

http://osprey.anbg.gov.au/flags/semaphore.html

United States Power Squadrons®

Can you pass the online navigation quiz offered by the Power Squadron? Try it. You'll be asked which color running light is on the port side and similar questions. You can compare your scores with others and, no, you don't have to sign your name! If your score could use some improvement, check for a local Power Squadron group near you. They offer free classes in boating and sailing safety and navigation. You can preview what will be taught in the classes here.

http://www.usps.org/

How many mosquitoes can one little brown bat catch in one hour?

Answer: It can catch 600 mosquitoes! Read more fascinating bat trivia at http://www.batcon.org/trivia.html

Young Sailor

Ah, the slap of the waves against your boat, the wind in your face, the cry of the gulls overhead as the sun shines on and on. Sailing—there's nothing like it! This site provides online chapters from the book by the same name. You'll learn how to choose a boat, how to be fluent with nautical terms, the inside story on ropes and knots, and, oh yes, basic sailing.

http://www.yachtnet.com/journal/youngsailor/
youngstoc.html

BOOKS AND LITERATURE

Children's Bestsellers

What are kids reading today? Now *Publishers Weekly* puts its Children's Bestsellers List on the Net. For Picture Book, Fiction, Paperback Series, and Nonfiction, you'll get the week's top ten sellers, including the title, author, publisher, price, and ISBN. There's also the All-Time Bestselling Children's List for paperback and hardcover books. (*The Pokey Little Puppy* is at number one with 14,000,000 copies. Wow!)

http://www.bookwire.com/pw/bsl/childrens/
current.childrens.html

Children's Book Awards

Every year, thousands of books are written for kids. Most of the books are good, but trying to decide which books to borrow from the library can be difficult. Fortunately, there are several organizations that pick the finest books for children each year. These books are judged best by a variety of criteria, including which are best for young children, elementary-school-aged kids, etc. Some of the awards for the best children's books are listed on the Internet, and you can find convenient links to many of those lists here. Besides the Caldecott and the Newbery Awards, you'll find the Coretta Scott King Award, and the Laura Ingalls Wilder Medal winners. This year there are also many international awards, plus awards given to books selected by kids. If you're looking for a good book to read, take a glance here!

http://www.ucalgary.ca/~dkbrown/awards.html

Children's Literature Selections Page

This page features first chapters of some of the books selected as Newbery Award and Honor Books Winners by the American Library Association's Association for Library Service to Children. It doesn't include all winners, just those available from Dial-A-Book. Links include background on the Newbery Awards, the terms and criteria used to select winners, and information about the committee that selects the books. There is an option to order some of the books online, but check your local library first!

http://www1.psi.net/ChapterOne/children/

Children's Literature Web Guide

This is the FIRST place to look for Internet resources related to books for children and young adults! Here you will find online children's stories, information about authors and illustrators, children's book awards, and lots of lists. Also available at this site are lists of book discussion groups, sources for book reviews, online resources, publishers, booksellers, and children's literature associations. David K. Brown updates this site frequently and provides a convenient What's New section.

http://www.ucalgary.ca/~dkbrown/

How a Book is Made

These pages give you an inside look at how a book is published. Illustrations from Aliki's book, *How a Book Is Made*, help to tell the story. Cats pose variously as a book's illustrator, author, and editor, as well as workers in production, advertising, and sales. They show the steps involved in the writing and publishing of a book! You can also see how a pop-up book is made in the Noodles section of this page.

http://www.harpercollins.com/kids/book.htm

Author, author, lend me your words. If you like writing, and want to find out what it's all about, check out How a Book Is Made.

IPL Youth Division

Welcome to the Internet Public Library, or IPL! Join the Story Hour and read from a selection of five stories, including "Do Spiders Live on the World Wide Web?," *The Tortoise and the Hare*, and "Molly Whuppie." Got a book report coming up soon? Completed FAQs for Avi, Matt Christopher, Robert Cormier, Lois Lowry, Phyllis Reynolds Naylor, Daniel Pinkwater, and Jane Yolen are available. Biographical information for David Lee Drotar, Timothy Gaffney, Katherine Paterson, Gary Paulsen, and Seymour Simon is also found here.

http://www.ipl.org/youth

NET FILES

Why has **Darth Vader** been spotted hanging around the Washington National Cathedral?

Answer: Don't worry, everyone knows he's there. Get out your binoculars. That's him high up on the Northwest Tower: he's a grotesque, which is similar to a gargoyle. The design was one of four winning suggestions by kids. Find out about the others at http://www.cathedral.org/cathedral/kids/gargoyles.shtml

A
B
C
D
E
F
G
H
I
J
K
L
M
N
O
P
Q
R
S
T
U
V
W
X
Y
Z

A
B
C
D
E
F
G
H
I
J
K
L
M
N
O
P
Q
R
S
T
U
V
W
X
Y
Z

Stone Soup, the magazine of writing and art by young people

Stone Soup is a well-known magazine of stories, poems, and artwork by kids, for kids. Here at their home page you can peek at a sample issue, plus read some online stories and poems. Maybe you'll be able to send them some of your own work! There is nothing like seeing your name in print next to something you wrote, whether it's printed in a magazine, a book, or on the Net!

http://www.stonesoup.com

ADVENTURE STORIES

Choose Your Own Adventure

Sixth graders wrote this interactive adventure. Cruise along with Buzz Rod in his candy apple red Dodge Viper. He's pretty upset after a fight with his parents. He sees a bright flash of light—look out! To find out what happens after Buzz loses control of his car, surf on over to Hillside Elementary School. Every time you click on the Random SpaceTime Warp button, you will find a different ending to Buzz's story. You find out what happens to Buzz, and you can also read about the author of each ending and hear sound effects recorded by the authors.

http://hillside.coled.umn.edu/class1/Buzz/Story.html

Theodore's Tugboat stories

Theodore Tugboat is the star of a Canadian television series. In this set of links, Theodore and part of the story appear on each page. At the end of each page, you get to choose which of two things Theodore will do next! This choice is offered on almost every page, so you'll be actively involved in the story and its ending.

http://www.cochran.com/theosite/IStory.html

Never give your name or address to a stranger.

CLASSICS

Kindred Spirits: The LM Montgomery Home Page

The Kindred Spirits WWW site is dedicated to the works and life of Lucy Maud Montgomery (or LMM, for short), the Canadian author of the *Anne of Green Gables* series. Here you will find information about Cavendish, which is the model for Avonlea. A comprehensive FAQ contains a list of all of Montgomery's works, books about her, and other materials based upon her characters and her works. Other links take you to The Road to Avonlea Home Page, a LMM Art Gallery, as well as information about Ontario, where LMM lived as an adult, and PEI (Prince Edward Island), where she grew up.

http://www.upei.ca/~lmmi/cover.html

NET FILES

What is the function of the "hat" in the card game called Hungarian Tarokk?

ANSWER: Only on the Net would you learn this one! Tarokk is played with a deck of 42 cards. "An important part of the apparatus of this game is the hat, which should look as silly as possible. The traditional version is a sort of Austrian hunting hat with too many large feathers stuck into it at odd angles, but anything ridiculous-looking will do. Any player who has the XXI of trumps captured by an opponent's Skíz must wear the hat until someone else suffers the same misfortune." For a description of the deck and the rules, go to http://www.netlink.co.uk/users/pagat/tarot/paskiev.html off the Card Games home page.

My Little House on the Prairie Home Page of Laura Ingalls Wilder

Whether you're a fan of the book or the television series, you need to visit this little house on the cyberprairie to find out everything about Laura Ingalls Wilder and her life. You'll be able to track her travels from the big woods to the prairie, chronicled in her book series about Ma, Pa, Mary, and, of course, herself. You can visit the Heritage Sites, which are now located in the places Wilder describes in her novels.

http://www.vvv.com/~jenslegg/index.htm

Ozcot Home Page

L. Frank Baum, the author of the Oz books, called his California home Ozcot. This home page contains a list of Oz books by the author. The major feature of this site is a set of text-only HTML files to *The Wonderful Wizard of Oz* and *The Marvelous Land of Oz*.

http://www.best.com/~tiktok/

NET FILES

How do blind people know if they have a $1 or a $10 bill?

Answer: According to the National Federation of the Blind, many blind people fold the bills in a special way. They ask the bank or store clerk to indicate to them which bills are fives, which are tens, and so on. Then, they don't fold a $1 bill at all and they fold a $5 bill the long way, a $10 bill the short way, and a $20 bill both ways. With this system, they can tell what's in their wallets. For more interesting information about how kids cope with blindness, check out ftp://nfb.org/ftp/nfb/futref/pastfr/95spiss.txt

The Page at Pooh Corner

Somewhere in the Internet's Hundred-Acre Wood is The Page at Pooh Corner. It's the home of information about A. A. Milne's Winnie-the-Pooh books. Find general information about Pooh and facts about author Milne and the illustrator, E. H. Shepard. Learn about the area in England where the Pooh stories are based and the real Christopher Robin. Sing along with your favorite Disney Pooh songs or download pictures of Pooh and his companions. This page also gives you links to more sites that feature Pooh, that "tubby little cubby all stuffed with fluff."

http://www.public.iastate.edu/~jmilne/pooh.html

Piglet Press Audio Books

Jump on this page and prepare to be swept away by a Kansas twister and totally immersed in Oziana. Piglet Press has gone way beyond the call of duty in promoting their small collection of Oz audio tapes by putting together a most thorough collection of pictures, descriptions, and notes to L. Frank Baum's beloved series of books. There are pages devoted to each and every Baum book as well as material on those done by Ruth Plumly Thompson and other successors. Look up specific characters, places, and things from the first 14 books via the 878-page Encyclopedia Oziana, reference the movies (several have been made), get details about Baum himself, and find out about two different international Oz Clubs. There are also sample sound files from the Piglet tapes, sections on Baum's songs and short stories, and a bibliography. To exit from the page, just click your heels together and say, "There's no place like home..."

http://www.halcyon.com/piglet/

Treasure Island

It's a tale of adventure, pirates, tropical islands, and murder! "If this don't fetch the kids, why, they have gone rotten since my day," said Robert Louis Stevenson, when he wrote this book in 1881. The book is available online at this site. Besides a biography of the author, you'll find links to sites about pirates, islands, and buried treasure! This finely designed site also has some rainy-day suggestions for things to do—besides reading, of course.

http://www.ukoln.ac.uk/treasure/

A B C D E F G H I J K L M N O P Q R S T U V W X Y Z

A
B
C
D
E
F
G
H
I
J
K
L
M
N
O
P
Q
R
S
T
U
V
W
X
Y
Z

Winnie the Pooh - An Expotition

Explore this interactive map of the "100 Aker Wood" and try to find and visit all 20 wonderful places. Check out the Bee Tree, Rabbit's house, and the ever-popular Heffalump Trap! You'll find interactive games and more at each site.

http://worldaccess.com/pooh/welcome.html

Winnie the Pooh- An Expotition

They all went off to discover the Pole, Owl and Piglet and Rabbit and All; It's a thing you Discover, as I've been tole By Owl and Piglet and Rabbit and all. Want to go along? March right over to Winnie the Pooh- An Expotition and join up!

The Wizard of Oz-- Carminati Elementary School

Visit this site for the fabulous illustrations by the kindergarten and first-grade kids at Carminati Elementary School in Tempe, Arizona. They retell *The Wizard of Oz* in a way that will delight you. Notice that Dorothy sometimes has ruby slippers (as in the movie) and other times has silver slippers (as in the original book)!

http://seamonkey.ed.asu.edu/oz/wizard1.html

May the forces be with you in PHYSICS.

CONTEMPORARY FAVORITES
Goosebumps on the Web!

Are you a fan of R. L. Stine? His *Goosebumps* series is the subject of this home page. Follow creepy links that lead you to Stine's biography, his photo, and the transcript of an online Halloween chat with Stine. Also read a ghoulish chapter from recent books in his series. Did you know you can get *Goosebumps* from TV? A link includes synopses of the TV episodes, identifying the book featured. Did you hear a noise? We're sure we heard something...

http://place.scholastic.com/goosebumps/index.htm

Go to Goosebumps on the Web! for a thrilling look at R.L. Stine's *Goosebumps* book and TV series.

HarperCollins Children's Books: The Big Busy House

The Big Busy House Web site gives you the latest news from this publisher of children's books. Read sample chapters from their *X-Files* series or from other new titles. Or read information about how classics like *If You Give a Mouse a Cookie* were developed. Check out the author interviews and add that info to your next book report. There's a lot at this site—you might even enter and win one of the contests!

http://www.harpercollins.com/kids/

The Roald Dahl Index

Did you enjoy any of the following movies: *James and the Giant Peach, Charlie and the Chocolate Factory,* and *Matilda*? Did you know that they were all written by the same author: Roald Dahl? Learn about his life, read reviews of the books and movies, and find out how to make "Stinkbug Eggs" for your next party!

http://www.tridel.com.ph/user/bula/rdahl.htm

MYSTERIES

Booklover's Den: The Booklover's Virtual Reading Room

Links from the Booklover's Den give a mystery fan information about a ton of series books and other mysteries. Series featured include Nancy Drew, Trixie Belden, Judy Bolton, and the Dana Girls, as well as the Hardy Boys, Encyclopedia Brown, and The Three Investigators. The author of these Web pages, Biblioholics, is also starting a free online newsletter about children's series.

http://members.aol.com/biblioholc/Den.html

ONLINE BOOKS

Many full-text, public domain books appear on the Internet. Some are collected as part of Project Gutenberg <http://www.promo.net/pg/>, while others are in the Online Book Initiative <gopher://ftp.std.com/11/obi/book>. Another large collection is at Carnegie Mellon <http://www.cs.cmu.edu/books.html>.

Most of the books you will find are retrieved as flat text files. If you prefer reading them as HTML hypertext, try the archives at <http://www.cs.cmu.edu/People/rgs/rgs-home.html> or <http://www.cs.cmu.edu/books.html>. These resources tell you whether the files are text or HTML.

We have selected some classic children's books from these huge collections: look for your favorites!

Barrie, J.M.

Peter Pan
gopher://wiretap.spies.com/00/Library/Classic/peter.txt

Burnett, Frances Hodgson

Sarah Crewe
gopher://wiretap.spies.com/00/Library/Classic/crewe.txt

The Secret Garden
gopher://wiretap.spies.com/00/Library/Classic/garden.txt

Burroughs, Edgar Rice

Tarzan of the Apes
http://www.cs.cmu.edu/People/rgs/tarz-table.html

Irving, Washington

The Legend of Sleepy Hollow
gopher://wiretap.spies.com/00/Library/Classic/sleepy.txt

Kipling, Rudyard

The Jungle Book
gopher://wiretap.spies.com/00/Library/Classic/jungle.rk

London, Jack

The Call of the Wild
gopher://gopher.vt.edu:10010/02/117/6

Porter, Gene Stratton

A Girl of the Limberlost
gopher://wiretap.spies.com/00/Library/Classic/limber.gsp

The BookWire Electronic Children's Books Index

Many online children's books are collected here, including Mark Twain stories and Hans Christian Andersen fairy tales.

http://www.bookwire.com/links/readingroom/echildbooks.html

Time magazine's annual "Man of the Year" has also been a woman and even an idea from time to time. Guess who the first woman was. (Hint: A king loved her so much that he gave up his throne to marry her.)

Answer: Wallis Warfield Simpson was Time's first "Woman of the Year," for the year 1936. Find out more at http://pathfinder.com/time/special/moy/1939.html

A
B
C
D
E
F
G
H
I
J
K
L
M
N
O
P
Q
R
S
T
U
V
W
X
Y
Z

A B C D E F G H I J K L M N O P Q R S T U V W X Y Z

Classics for Young People

Many books your parents read as kids are collected here; some of the ones they may remember include the *Wizard of Oz* books, *The Wind in the Willows*, and *Treasure Island*. You'll also find the *Anne of Green Gables* stories, and *Alice in Wonderland*. Maybe you can read these books to your parents just before you tuck them in for their naps!

http://www.ucalgary.ca/~dkbrown/storclas.html

FAIRROSA'S CYBER LIBRARY

You'll find lots of links to online kids' books, such as *A Little Princess*, *Peter Pan*, and *A Journey to the Center of the Earth*. One of the coolest things, though, is the selection of links to authors' home pages. Need some biographical author info to complete your book report? Try here!

http://www.users.interport.net/~fairrosa/

Incomplete Online Works of Edgar Allan Poe

This home page collects many of Poe's works, including his poetry and short stories. Some of the works are available in HTML; all are available in ASCII. Access to Poe's writings is alphabetical, so you can quickly find what you're looking for. Surf on over to read "The Raven" or another one of Poe's 122 poems and stories!

http://www.comnet.ca/~forrest/works.html

PICTURE BOOKS

Alex's Scribbles - Koala Trouble

Alexander Balson wanted to write some stories about Max, a koala bear who's always getting into trouble. Alex is only five years old, so he got some help from his parents. Together they have created a fine Web page for your enjoyment. Alex's illustrations really make the interactive story come alive!

http://www.peg.apc.org/~balson/story/#adv

Candlelight Stories

Storybooks right on the Web! The illustrations are beautifully done by the author of this site. It's amazing how kids can learn to use the mouse when they are reading these stories. Try "Sally Saves Christmas" for a look at what happens when a little girl travels on a moonbeam. As you look at each page, try asking your little brother or sister what will happen next—will Sally decide to follow the Moon Queen? You can also get your own stories published on this site!

http://www.CandlelightStories.com/

Children's Stories

Lucy Van Hook is a really cranky pirate. She wants to steal the King's cookies. Where can they be hidden so her evil plan will fail? Kids of all ages will enjoy the tales here. When you finish the story, you can enjoy making the cookies—the recipe is included!

http://www.itsnet.com/~outward/childstory.html

Concertina - Books on the Internet

Concertina is a Canadian children's publisher. Current titles featured include *Waking in Jerusalem*, *I Live on a Raft*, *My Blue Suitcase*, and *The Song of Moses*. Additional links tell the reader about the authors and illustrators as well as the design techniques used to create the online versions of the book. Each book includes the illustrations and all of the pages. *Waking in Jerusalem* is enhanced by the addition of sound clips for each page.

http://www.iatech.com/books/

Cyber-Seuss Page

Welcome to the world of "the great glorious and gandorious...Dr. Seuss!" You remember him as the author of *The Cat in the Hat*, *The Grinch Who Stole Christmas*, *Green Eggs and Ham*, *Fox in Sox*, and *Yertle the Turtle*. See a photo of the author, read quotes from him, and visit Dartmouth, where Theodor Seuss Geisel (Dr. Seuss) went to college. Check out the scavenger hunt and other contests. Admire the collection of Seuss images, and if you still want to read more, peruse the list of Dr. Seuss books in print!

http://www.afn.org/~afn15301/drseuss.html

Green Eggs and Ham has been a favorite breakfast of ours since as far back as we can remember. Rumor has it that's a long time, so you know this is a tried-and-true feast. Read all about this and more recipes for treats you can enjoy at any meal at the Cyber-Seuss Page.

Disney's Serialized Storybooks

Quick, name some of your favorite movies. Chances are that some of the ones you mention are available as online books! New online storybooks from Disney are placed here every month. Currently, you can read *Aladdin, Toy Story, Oliver & Company, The Lion King, 101 Dalmatians, The Hunchback of Notre Dame, Pocahontas,* and *The Rescuers Down Under.*

http://www.disney.com/DisneyBooks/new/StoryBook/
    StoryBook.html

The Fairy Tales of Ika Bremer

"Stop, Don't Read This Page." Who could resist a story that begins like that? It's scary but not too scary. Here you'll find off-the-edge tales about wacky planets, a princess with no hair, and some really baaaad riddles! This site is in English, German, and Spanish.

http://www.ika.com/stories/

Be an angel and check what we've found in RELIGION.

Grandad's Animal Book Contents

Grandad, Thomas Wright, lives on the Hawaiian island of Maui. He's written an interactive animal English alphabet book, in which a picture of an animal is shown with each letter of the alphabet. You know the drill: Z is for Zebra. But you'll also find a vocabulary list, notes on classifying animals, and facts about various classes of animals. You can also choose a letter of the alphabet and then identify which animal begins with that letter of the alphabet. There is also a version of this page in Spanish.

http://www.maui.com/~twright/animals/htmgran.html

IPL Story Hour

Bored? Parents not telling you any good stories anymore? Just want to read something new? Point your browser towards the IPL (Internet Public Library) Story Hour. Many traditional stories are available, as well as newer ones. Some are illustrated by kids, too!

http://ipl.sils.umich.edu/youth/StoryHour/

NET FILES

What is the official dance of the State of South Carolina?

(Hint: It's not the Macarena!)

Answer: *It's square dancing! Square dancing is a traditional form of family entertainment and fun in South Carolina. Its many variations include squares, rounds, clogging, contra, line, and other historical or "heritage" dances. Check http://www.lpitr.state.sc.us/square.htm for more of the state's symbols.*

Theodore Tugboat

Here's a tugboat with a smile and appealing eyes, straight from the Canadian TV series. Toddlers will love the interactive story, in which they get to choose what happens next. Downloadable coloring book pages sail via the Net to your printer or graphics program. Little ones can even get their own postcard in the mail from Theodore Tugboat himself! Warning: If you have a slower connection, be sure to set your browser not to autoload images.

http://www.cochran.com/TT.html

PLAYS AND DRAMA

Reader's Theater

Looking for a play you can perform with the rest of your class? This site has nine complete plays for grades two through eight. A wide range of subjects is covered, from folktales to science fiction. Most are adapted from short stories by Aaron Shepard.

http://www.ucalgary.ca/~dkbrown/readers.html

Shakespeare

Ah, the Bard himself comes to the Net! Visit this site for the complete works of Shakespeare. You can search the texts, find lists of his plays (chronologically and alphabetically), read Bartlett's familiar Shakespearean quotations, as well as find a picture of William himself. The list of Shakespeare's works is divided into comedy, history, tragedy, and poetry. After you choose a play, you will move to a Web page where you can read one scene per page. The text includes hyperlinks to the glossary, making it easy to understand what Shakespeare was writing. This is a don't-miss destination for all drama students.

http://the-tech.mit.edu/Shakespeare/

When the play's the thing,
the Shakespeare page
is the server to visit.

Theatre Central

All the world's a stage at this site, which contains links to theatre-related pages from all over the world. This site is dedicated to all kinds of theatre, from professional companies to scholastic groups to online magazines. It's updated weekly by its owner, Andrew Kraft. You can find schedules of theatre companies and information about associations, people involved in theatre, educational resources, stagecraft, publications, and film resources. This is a great site if you're interested in drama!

http://www.theatre-central.com/

POETRY

Grin's Message

Grin the dolphin will rhyme his way into any preschooler's heart. He conveys messages about ecology and kindness via several aquatic animals. The poem is accompanied by lovely drawings. Put this site in your bookmarks, because once you introduce children to it, they'll want to access it again and again!

http://www2.opennet.com/schoolhouse/grin/
   Welcome.html

Online Songs and Poetry for Children

There was an Old Man with a beard,
Who said, 'It is just as I feared!
Two Owls and a Hen, four Larks and a Wren,
Have all built their nests in my beard!'

You'll find Edward Lear's limericks and poems here, plus many other collections from poets such as Robert Louis Stevenson, Lewis Carroll, and Walter de la Mare.

http://www.ucalgary.ca/~dkbrown/storsong.html

Poetry Gallery

Are you a poet? Do you want to publish your poetry so the world can read it? Then this is the place for you! Read poems written by other kids. Send in your masterpiece, and soon you can read your own poem on this page.

http://mgfx.com/kidlit/kids/artlit/poetry/index.htm

POETRY—HAIKU

Haiku Homepage

Haiku is a form of poetry that began in Japan but is popular all over the world. How poets can evoke so many thoughts in only 17 syllables amazes us. Tips for aspiring haiku writers are given here. One of the links leads to The Haiku Attic, where you can post poems to share with others.

http://www.dmu.ac.uk/~pka/haiku.html

The Shiki Internet Haiku Salon

Shiki Masaoka, a haiku poet, was born in Japan in 1867 and helped popularize the arts as well as haiku, Japan's short poem form. Haiku consists of three lines of five, seven, and five syllables each, and it usually includes a special word to evoke the season. Here is a haiku we made up about the Internet:

The Net's a garden.
See, my modem light is on,
Netscape slowly blooms.

Now you try it!

http://mikan.cc.matsuyama-u.ac.jp/~shiki/

POETRY—JUMP ROPE RHYMES

JUMPROPE Hypertext archives

Cinderella, dressed in green,
Went upstairs to eat ice cream.
How many spoonfuls did she eat?
One, two, three...

Do you jump rope? You may want to look at this collection of old and new rhymes kids use to keep rhythm while they jump rope. They have been contributed from all over the world, and you can add ones you know. Some are very old, and some aren't considered "politically correct" anymore, but all are interesting. Peek into the past of Splits and Red Hot Peppers, in the days before Double Dutch. For information on jump rope associations and competitions today, see U.S.A. Jump Rope Home Page at *<http://www.ortech-engr.com/USAJRF/>*. Do not miss the action photos, especially the Subway trick, which seems to defy gravity!

http://www.uwf.edu/~stankuli/jrope/jumprope.htm

POETRY—ONLINE

Here are some excerpts from some famous poems. Visit the associated site to read the complete work.

Angelou, Maya
"Inauguration Poem," January 20, 1993

Here on the pulse of this new day
You may have the grace to look up and out
And into your sister's eyes, into
Your brother's face, your country
And say simply
Very simply
With hope
Good morning.

gopher://english.hss.cmu.edu/00ftp%3AEnglish.Server% 3APoetry%3AAngelou-Inauguration%20Poem

NET FILES

What's a *potpourri?*

Answer: Pronounced "po-poo-ri," potpourris and sachets are little bundles of dried herbs, flowers, and spices. They scent rooms and closets, make terrific gifts, and are easy to put together. All you need is a jar or a handkerchief, some herbs and spices, and the directions, located at http://www.azstarnet.com/dillards/momday/heart.htm For more recipes, try http://www.geocities.com/SoHo/1721/potpourri.html and http://www.bigtop.com/kids/recipes1.html

A
B
C
D
E
F
G
H
I
J
K
L
M
N
O
P
Q
R
S
T
U
V
W
X
Y
Z

Carroll, Lewis (Charles Lutwidge Dodgson)
"Jabberwocky"

*'Twas brillig, and the slithy toves
    did gyre and gimble in the wabe.
All mimsy were the borogoves,
    And the mome raths outgrabe.
"Beware the Jabberwock, my son!
    The jaws that bite, the claws that catch!
Beware the Jubjub bird, and shun
    the frumious Bandersnatch..."*

gopher://english.hss.cmu.edu/00ftp%3AEnglish.Server%
    3APoetry%3ACarroll-Jabberwocky

Frost, Robert
"Stopping By Woods on a Snowy Evening"

*Whose woods these are I think I know.
His house is in the village, though;
He will not see me stopping here
To watch his woods fill up with snow...*

gopher://wiretap.spies.com:70/00/Library/Classic/
    Poetry/woods.p

Kilmer, Joyce
"Trees"

*I think that I shall never see
A poem lovely as a tree...*

gopher://wiretap.spies.com:70/00/Library/Classic/
    Poetry/trees.p

Kipling, Rudyard
"If"

*If you can keep your head when all about you
    Are losing theirs and blaming it on you;
If you can trust yourself when all men doubt you,
    But make allowance for their doubting too...*

gopher://wiretap.spies.com:70/00/Library/Classic/
    Poetry/if.p

Lear, Edward
"The Jumblies"

*They went to sea in a Sieve, they did,
    In a Sieve they went to sea:
In spite of all their friends could say,
On a winter's morn, on a stormy day,
    In a Sieve they went to sea...*

gopher://english.hss.cmu.edu/00ftp%3AEnglish.Server%
    3APoetry%3AEdward%20Lear-The%20Jumblies

Longfellow, Henry Wadsworth
"Paul Revere's Ride"

*Listen my children and you shall hear
Of the midnight ride of Paul Revere,
On the eighteenth of April, in Seventy-five;
Hardly a man is now alive
Who remembers that famous day and year...*

gopher://english.hss.cmu.edu/00ftp%3AEnglish.Server%
    3APoetry%3ALongfellow-Paul%20Revere

NET FILES

What do ice, a thick layer of honey, petroleum jelly, and a thick paste made of water and baking soda all have in common?

Answer: They are all suggested as first aid for minor burns at First Aid Online. The best advice for you comes from your family doctor, but this site may also interest you: http://www.prairienet.org/~autumn/firstaid/

"The Song of Hiawatha"

Should you ask me,
whence these stories?
Whence these legends and traditions,
With the odors of the forest
With the dew and damp of meadows,
With the curling smoke of wigwams,
With the rushing of great rivers,
With their frequent repetitions,
And their wild reverberations
As of thunder in the mountains?
    I should answer, I should tell you...

gopher://wiretap.spies.com:70/00/Library/Classic/
    hiawatha.txt

"The Village Blacksmith"

Under a spreading chestnut-tree
    The village smithy stands;
The smith, a mighty man is he,
    With large and sinewy hands;
And the muscles of his brawny arms
    Are strong as iron bands...

gopher://wiretap.spies.com:70/00/Library/Classic/
    Poetry/village.p

Moore, Clement
"The Night Before Christmas"

Is there anyone who doesn't know this beloved classic, which begins:

'Twas the night before Christmas,
when all through the house
Not a creature was stirring, not even a mouse...

gopher://gopher.vt.edu:10010/02/125/1

Stevenson, Robert Louis
A Child's Garden of Verses

Many of these poems you can read to your little brothers and sisters. The first one starts:

In winter I get up at night
And dress by yellow candle-light.
In summer quite the other way,
I have to go to bed by day...

gopher://wiretap.spies.com:70/00/Library/Classic/
    child.rls

Wordsworth, William
"The Daffodils"

I wandered lonely as a cloud
    That floats on high o'er vales and hills,
When all at once I saw a crowd,
    A host, of golden daffodils...

gopher://wiretap.spies.com:70/00/Library/Classic/
    Poetry/daffo.p

"Lines Written in Early Spring"

I heard a thousand blended notes,
While in a grove I sate reclined...

gopher://ftp.std.com:70/00/obi/book/
    William.Wordsworth/lines.in.spring

NET FILES

Who is Blossom Galbiso?

(Hint: You have her to thank for one of your favorite games!)

Answer: She's the Hawaiian teacher who popularized POGs, or milkcaps, in 1991. You can see a photo of Blossom and read her own essay about the birth of POGS at http://www.ukulele.com/blossom.html

Get on board, little children, in RAILROADS AND TRAINS.

NET FILES

What insect is being used to help design fighter jets?

Answer: Dragonflies are able to change direction very quickly in flight. Engineers at the University of Tennessee are trying to find out how to make jets do the same by studying dragonfly wings. They "fly" large models of these insects in wind tunnels to study how their wing shape keeps them up. Read about the project at http://loki.ur.utk.edu/ut2kids/dragonfly/dragonfly.html

POETRY—NURSERY RHYMES

Dreamhouse: Nursery: Books: Rhymes

Everyone loves these gentle rhymes of childhood. The rhymes are subdivided by subject, including animals, bedtime, folks and things they do, food, places to go, and weather and things around us. An alphabetical listing is available as well as a list of recommended books. The rhymes chosen are favorites of the collector and her children. This is a useful site for finding those elusive words you can't quite remember from a long-forgotten nursery rhyme!

http://pubweb.acns.nwu.edu/~pfa/dreamhouse/
nursery/rhymes.html

Beanie Babies rule in TOYS.

Nursery Rhymes for Our Times

According to Douglas Crockford, most nursery rhymes are archaic because of their language. He says the rhymes fail to teach kids about the one thing they need in order to live full productive lives: technology. Crockford rewrites 11 nursery rhymes to make them relevant for modern children. A sample rhyme from his page rewrites Old King Cole:

Mister Cole has remote control
And remote control has he
He gets CNN
He gets HBO
And he gets his MTV.

http://www.communities.com/paper/nursery.html

Are you beeping?
Are you beeping?
Brother Jack?
Brother Jack?
Get your pocket pager.
Get your pocket pager.
Call them back.
Call them back.

Poetry always reflects its cultural context, and this is one you can find at Nursery Rhymes for Our Times.

SCIENCE FICTION

The Good Reading Guide - Index

This is a comprehensive index to works by science fiction authors arranged by author. It includes standard authors as well as many children's authors, including Lloyd Alexander, John Christopher, Madeline L'Engle, C. S. Lewis, and Ursula K. LeGuin. While not all of the lists are complete, this is an excellent site for finding other titles by your favorite science fiction authors. You can also read comments other people have about the authors and their works.

http://julmara.ce.chalmers.se/SF_archive/SFguide/

Tigger (Grace Sylvan) produces the Children's Software & More pages; look for her cartoon-style graphics online.

"I've found the Web very exciting—all those people sharing information from all over the world—and any individual can really make an impact."

COMPUTERS—SOFTWARE ARCHIVES

Children's Software & More!

Webmaster: Grace Sylvan

http://www.gamesdomain.com/tigger/ sw-kids.html

Who came up with the idea for your page or project?

When I first got on the Web, I was very excited by what I saw. I went looking for sites about children's programs, and everything I found at the time was very limited. I'd already been posting a list of the programs I'd found fun for my kids to the misc.kids.computer newsgroup, so I decided to publish them on the Web. I was impressed with the organization of utexas mac archive, and began a similar site specializing in children's programs.

How many people work on your pages? Does it take a lot of time? How many hits do you get a day?

I work on my pages. My daughter sometimes helps by making seasonal pictures and/or editing clip art (she's only seven, and she loves to do artwork, on the computer and off). It is a full-time job. As of December, 1996, I'm getting about 4,500 visitors to my front page every day.

If this isn't your main job, what do you do, what is your training?

I'm a Mom, that's my main job. In what seems like another lifetime, I held a variety of jobs, including systems management, user training, technical writing, and user interface design.

Do you have a family? A dog? A lizard?

I live with my husband and two children in San Jose, CA. My daughter has a pet guinea pig, and we also have a fish tank with tropical fish.

What are your hopes and fears for the future of the Internet?

I've found the Web very exciting—all those people sharing information from all over the world—and any individual can really make an impact. A problem is organizing it all—there are now hundreds of excellent pages on most topics—but then again, it's like books at the library—I don't need to read all the excellent books on a topic to use the resource well.

When you're not using the Net, what do you like to do?

Spend time with my family—reading to my children, learning things with them, doing art projects with them. I also sew most of my own clothing and clothing for my family.

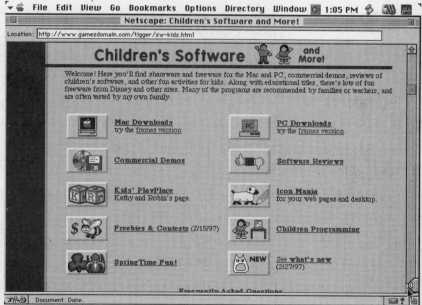

A
B
C
D
E
F
G
H
I
J
K
L
M
N
O
P
Q
R
S
T
U
V
W
X
Y
Z

CARS

Automotive Makes and Models

The Yahoo directory of car manufacturers lists familiar names, such as General Motors, Toyota, and Volkswagen. You'll also find the Kia, the DeLorean, and the Lada—they are all here. Hey, there are even some links on Hummers! Naturally, this vast array of links has not been checked for family-friendliness, so your mileage may vary.

http://www.yahoo.com/Recreation/Automotive/
    Makes_and_Models/

AUTOZonLINE Classic Car Museum

There are cars, and then there are *classic* cars. This site has pictures of the coolest classic cars ever. There's even a 1926 Nash and a 1926 Chrysler (yes, they had cars in 1926). And they look just like the Viper…not! Try their sister site for information and links to other great car sites around the Net at *<http://www.theautoguide.com/>*.

http://www.azl.com/autozonline/carbarn.html

Car and Driver

Cars are fun to look at and interesting to talk about; *Car and Driver* magazine writes about them every month. Driving is fun too, unless you get stuck in traffic. You may not be a driver yet, but you know you will be. You need a place to find out what's happening in the world of cars this year, this month, today! This site has great resource information on every kind of car you can think of, and it also has "Daily Auto Insider" with today's news on cars. Shockwave games, links, car shows—it's all here. Drive on in, there's a parking space!

http://www.caranddriver.com/hfm/

Car Culture

This is an educational site that's fascinating and fun. "Crossing Six Continents with Tacoma Jim & Jo" takes us along on a drive around the world—next stop, Mongolia! Oh, this site is sponsored by Toyota, and you can learn a lot about them, too.

http://www.toyota.com/carculture/

NET FILES

Every August, kids from all over the world can't wait to get to Akron, Ohio, and go as fast as they can down a 954-foot hill.

Why?

http://pages.prodigy.com/VJND22A/htmsoap4.htm

Answer: They're in the World Championships of the All-American Soap Box Derby! You won't find any motorized vehicles here—these are gravity-powered! Three division winners get to wear the traditional gold championship jackets at the end of Derby Day. Read more about it at

Cartalk.com

Would you let Click and Clack, the Tappet brothers, work on your family car? They have a very funny radio show, newspaper column, and Web site all about car maintenance and repair. And oh, yes, they used to run a garage in Cambridge, Massachusetts; now, only one brother works there (the other one got tired of breathing exhaust fumes). The Web site has clips from the radio show, advice columns, and other useful stuff, like car reviews, a directory of truly great mechanics, and—what's this?—a guide to raising kids. Maybe they should stick to cars!

http://www.cartalk.com/

Looking for the State Bird or the State Motto? It's in the UNITED STATES section.

Engine Catalog Page

"Start your engines. Are you ready to go? Start your engines. Are you ready to go? Press on the pedal and the fuel will flow. Down goes the piston, in comes the gas. The mixture is compression and you'll go really fast!" That's part of "The Engine Song." You can hear it at this site while you watch animations of fuel injectors, pistons, crankshafts, and other parts of the internal combustion engine. A lesson plan is available for teachers and parents.

http://www.ca.sandia.gov/carnival/html/
eng-catpg.html

Ford Worldwide Connection: Historical Library

The history of the world-famous Ford Motor Company would be a great topic for your history, technology, or science report, or…wait a minute—you don't need a report due to go to this site! It's got awesome information, pictures, and stories about cars from 1903 right up to today. For the real sports car fan, the "Jaguar Historical Library" is here, too.

http://www.ford.com/archive/intro.html

Introduction to Alternative Fuel Vehicles

What if your family didn't have to drive to the gas station anymore? What if you had an electric car and could just plug it in? Electric cars exist right now! There are lots of other alternative fuels, too, such as ethanol, methanol, propane, natural gas, and of course solar power. No dilithium crystals yet, but somebody somewhere is probably working on it, and when there is news about it, that news will be here! The California Energy Commission has an excellent series of pages on energy, but the connection is typically very busy and slow. Try it when it's nighttime in California.

http://www.energy.ca.gov/energy/afvs/vehicles.html

What is the sound of one router flapping?

License Plates of the World

Sure, you may be familiar with Maine's red lobster, or Georgia's peach, or maybe even Hawaii's rainbow—but what does an Argentine license plate look like, or a Mongolian one, or…well, you get the picture. You *will* get the picture if you visit this Web site! You will also like The License Plate Collector's Home Page at <*http://users.aol.com/EdE/plates.htm*> where you can find out how to get inexpensive sample plates from state motor vehicle departments. Unfortunately, the addresses are not here, but look in this book under the "United States" heading for the official page of the state you're interested in—the address is probably listed there.

http://danshiki.oit.gatech.edu/~iadt3mk/index.html

THE PM ZONE HOMEPAGE

You can see next year's models *now* and classic cars too? This must be the PM Zone's Automotive section, where you can get the latest on all the cars out there from *Popular Mechanics* magazine. *Popular Mechanics* surveys users and reports on cars, which means that you get the real story on how the cars perform from the people who drive them and not just from the manufacturer. They report on every kind of car—from Ferrari Spiders to Dodge Caravans—and they spy on the new models, so you can be the first to see them. Put the key in, start 'er up, and head into the PM Zone.

http://popularmechanics.com/

Everyone is talking about the new car being unveiled next fall, but nobody has seen it. Is it just a revamp of this year's model, or is it really as hot as they claim? You might just get that sneak preview at The PM ZONE HOMEPAGE.

Investigate the "Spy Reports" in the Automotive section for the latest information.

A
B
C
D
E
F
G
H
I
J
K
L
M
N
O
P
Q
R
S
T
U
V
W
X
Y
Z

CATS

See also MAMMALS—CAT FAMILY; PETS AND
PET CARE

Cat Fanciers Web Site

Crazy about cats? This is the place for you! It will give
answers to questions you didn't even know you had.
It contains information about cat breeds, colors, cat
shows, the welfare of animals, and lots of other
cat-related subjects. Are you concerned about the
feline leukemia virus? It is considered to be the most
common cause of serious illness and death in
domestic cats, but don't worry, you can't catch it—the
virus is specific to cats only. You'll find lots of links to
everywhere, including cat health information at
veterinary schools around the world.

http://www.fanciers.com/

Cats! From Wild to Mild

The Natural History Museum of Los Angeles County
has a new exhibit in 1997, and it is all about cats.
Encyclopedia-type entries for 19 feline species from
around the world are represented here, including
jaguars, lions, tigers, leopards, bobcats, and wildcats,
as well as house pets. You can see wonderful color
pictures of the cats, plus range distribution maps for
each. Many of them are endangered species; for
example, only 50 Florida panthers are estimated to be
left in the wild. Some still exist on the Web, though, as
you'll find a collection of links for each species. Do
you have a cat? Chances are that you do or that you
know someone who does. About 65.8 million cats live
in the United States, which beats the 54.9 million
dogs. Garfield would be so pleased!

http://www.lam.mus.ca.us/cats/

rec.pets.cats FAQ Homepage

This is the FAQ from the Usenet cats newsgroup,
arranged in HTML so it's easy to read. Find out all
about cat breeds, colors, health, training, and more!

http://www.zmall.com/pet_talk/cat-faqs/

CAT SHOWS
/OFF: Online Feline Fanciers

Your cat is so beautiful! Do you want to enter your
pet in a cat show? Be sure to stop by this site first and
find out how to get started showing your cat under
Cat Fanciers' Association (CFA) rules. Read up on
breeder information and learn about CFA scoring and
how titles are earned. If you think you are ready to
enter the realm of cat shows, check out CFA's show
schedule, and good luck!

http://www.clock.org/~ambar/off/

CHEMISTRY

General Chemistry

Do you love chemistry? Does the idea of equilibrium,
states of matter, or quantum mechanics give you
goose bumps? If that's the case, then this page is for
you! Here you'll find a multimedia course on
chemistry that should satisfy even the most intense
chemistry nut.

http://www-wilson.ucsd.edu/education/
    gchem/gchem.html

MathMol

Everything around you is made of chemicals—from
your computer to your favorite book to you! Scientists
are learning more and more about how chemicals
work by understanding the math of molecules. You
may wonder why learning math, algebra, or geometry
makes any sense, but they are the keys to
understanding much of chemistry. The resources here
let you visualize and manipulate important
molecules. You'll never look at your math book the
same way again!

http://www.nyu.edu/pages/mathmol/

Sheffield ChemDex

This site is a huge collection of links, news, and resources on chemistry. You'll also find pages on the history of chemistry, software to help you learn about chemistry, and more. We want to point out the WebElements 2.0 Periodic Table. It is notable because of the graphics and other visualization information for each element. In the Other Periodic Tables links, you will find sources for software that will help you learn the names and properties of the elements discovered so far! There is also a song that helps you to do this; find it here. Not all links have been checked.

http://www.shef.ac.uk/~chem/chemdex/index.html

NET FILES

Your grandpa has sent your dad a ticket for a lottery drawing out of state. How can you find out if your family has won?

Answer: Check http://www.usatoday.com/ leadpage/lottery/lotto.htm for lottery winners in over 30 states. Good luck!

Understanding Our Planet Through Chemistry

How do scientists know the age of Earth or when a meteor struck our planet? How can scientists predict and understand volcanoes—when no one can look closely at an eruption and survive? The answers to these and many other questions about our planet can be found in the study of chemistry. To learn more, take a peek at this site.

http://helios.cr.usgs.gov/gips/aii-home.htm

EXPERIMENTS
Bread Chemistry

Everyone likes bread: it's great as toast, makes for good sandwiches, and sometimes is excellent for missiles in a food fight. Bread, though, is a good lesson in chemistry. Every time bread is made, all kinds of interesting chemical reactions result. Don't loaf around! Check out this episode from the award-winning *Newton's Apple* TV program for a lesson in bread as science.

http://ericir.syr.edu/Projects/Newton/12/Lessons/
   bread.html

Physical Science and Chemistry Lesson Plans

You have to do a science fair demonstration, and you think a chemistry experiment is the way to go. Problem is, what experiment should you do? Wouldn't it be great if you could get hold of a teacher's lesson plans for chemistry experiments? Well...you can! You'll find a whole slew of great experiments at this gopher page. Be careful, though, and always check with an adult before doing these experiments. You can never be safe enough when it comes to mixing chemicals.

gopher://ec.sdcs.k12.ca.us:70/11/lessons/
   UCSD_InternNet_Lessons/
   Physical_Science_and_Chemistry

Solving Dissolving Activity - Science Museum of Minnesota

How can rainwater make an acid and dissolve rock? Actually, that's how many caves are formed. Here is an experiment to try at home that will explain how, complete with pictures and instructions. Be sure to ask for help from a parent or teacher.

http://www.sci.mus.mn.us/sln/ma/sdact.html

The truth is out there in UFOS AND EXTRATERRESTRIALS. Maybe.

A B C D E F G H I J K L M N O P Q R S T U V W X Y Z

A
B
C
D
E
F
G
H
I
J
K
L
M
N
O
P
Q
R
S
T
U
V
W
X
Y
Z

The World of Chemistry

The Chemical Institute of Canada and the Halifax West High School have teamed up to present 15 different experiments you can try at home or in school. For example, how do chemists test substances to find out what they are made of? Try the Unknown Powder experiment—you'll need an adult to help you set it up, so you don't already know which powder is which! Hint: The secrets behind all the experiments are in the Teacher's Notes sections, which are in the Investigation areas. This site is available in English and French.

http://www.schoolnet.ca/math_sci/chem/worldofchem/

Zia Kid's Experiments Page

If you're looking for a way to dazzle the rest of the class with your science fair know-how, put your safety goggles on and take a look here! You'll learn how to make raisins dance, grow crystal cubes and needles, and examine the attraction of magnetic breakfast cereal. Most of these kitchen chemistry experiments are based on a series from the American Chemical Society, so you know it's not just science, it's GOOD science!

http://www.zia.com/tech/exp/default.htm

PERIODIC TABLE OF THE ELEMENTS

The Periodic Table of the Elements on the Internet

Chemistry is easy to understand—it's "elementary." Actually, chemistry *is* all about elements, the primary parts of all chemicals. For years, scientists have learned what the elements of chemistry are, and they've grouped the elements in a chart called the periodic table. To see all of the elements and their properties, take a look at this page, written by a ninth-grader! It's easy to use, and you'll learn much. For another version, including the top five requested elements, visit *<http://the-tech.mit.edu/Chemicool/>*.

http://users.boone.net/yinon/default.html

PLASTICS AND POLYMERS
Slime Time

Polymers are chemicals that we use all the time. Plastic is a polymer, nylon is a polymer, the keyboard of your computer is probably largely made of polymers. The greatest polymer of all, though, is SLIME! No kidding. You can read all about slime, and polymers, on this page, produced by Mr. Lemberg's first period chemistry class in Washington State's Battle Ground Public School.

http://www.bgsd.wednet.edu/WWWSchools/phs/doc/
    chem/doc/slime.html

SOLIDS, LIQUIDS, AND GASES
Microworlds- Exploring the Structure of Materials

Scientists are learning more and more about the world by studying its tiniest parts. By looking at atoms and molecules, scientists find out why some objects are hard, some are brittle, and some are strong. You can view this miniature world here. You'll see a new machine that is helping to explore inner space, and you can also view discoveries about materials you use every day.

http://www.lbl.gov/MicroWorlds/

CIRCUSES AND CLOWNS

See also JUGGLING

CIRCUSTUFF Juggling and Circus On-Line

Interested in circus tricks? Start your clowning around here. At this site, you can download digital animations of juggling tricks. You can slow the animation down and even freeze the frames to be sure you "catch" every move. You'll also find juggling props to keep you busy for a long time!

http://www.demon.co.uk/circustuff/

A B C D E F G H I J K L M N O P Q R S T U V W X Y Z

NET FILES

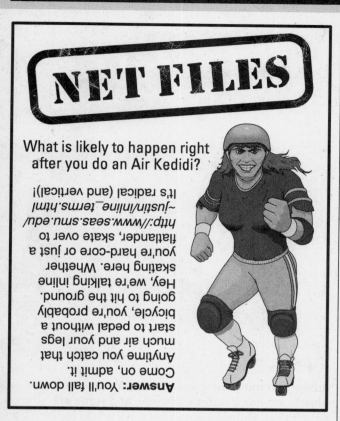

What is likely to happen right after you do an Air Kedidi?

Answer: You'll fall down. Come on, admit it. Anytime you catch that much air and your legs start to pedal without a bicycle, you're probably going to hit the ground. Hey, we're talking inline skating here. Whether you're hard-core or just a flatlander, skate over to http://www.seas.smu.edu/~justin/inline_terms.html It's radical (and vertical)!

Cirque du Soleil

Since its beginning in 1984, over ten million people have seen a Cirque du Soleil show. They have performed all over the world, and often several of their circus companies are touring at any one time. What makes Cirque du Soleil so different? For one thing, there are no animal acts. For another, this is a reinvented circus, one that is part theatre, part magic, part imagination, and mostly just plain fun! To see the impossible become reality, visit this site and find out when they are coming to a town near you.

http://www.cirquedusoleil.com/

If you forgot the words to "gopher guts" try lyrics in MUSIC AND MUSICIANS.

Clowns of America International Home Page

Send in the clowns. What, you forgot to order the clowns? Help, we need emergency clowns! No time to waste—just log on to this site and check the clown directories for a clown near you. If you need to replace your supply of clown noses, oversized elf shoes, or lapel flowers that shoot water, look no further than the Clown Mall. Don't miss the fascinating history of clowns, where you'll learn the origin of the phrase "jump on the bandwagon."

http://www.clown.org/

The FSU Flying High Circus Home Page

Did you know you can go to college *and* be in a circus at the same time? At Florida State University, you can! Learn about lots of circus tricks performed by students. Some stunts—such as triple somersaults on the flying trapeze and seven-man pyramids—are so hard that lots of professional circus performers won't even try them. What's really surprising is that most of the students haven't had any circus training before joining the Flying High Circus. Don't miss the "cloudswings," especially the kind done without a net. Other circus schools around the world are also listed, as well as links to related sites, like unicycle and juggling home pages.

http://mailer.fsu.edu/~mpeters/fsucircus.html

The Great Circus Parade - Wisconsin's National Treasure

Hey, look at this poster. It reads: "Come to the Great Circus Parade! A two-hour processional over a three-mile route, authentically re-creating turn-of-the-century circus street parades. Features 60 historic wagons, 700 horses, cavorting clowns, wild animals in cage wagons, and the fabulous 40-Horse Hitch." Sounds like FUN! Look over there—isn't that Buffalo Bill Cody in that beaded buckskin jacket? You can learn something about circus history, including circus trains, at this colorful, animated site. If you have Java, you'll also hear vintage calliope music!

http://circus.compuware.com/

A
B
C
D
E
F
G
H
I
J
K
L
M
N
O
P
Q
R
S
T
U
V
W
X
Y
Z

Juggling Information Service

The three ingredients of becoming a juggler are: practice, practice, and this Web site. Here you'll find the home pages of fellow jugglers, a collection of juggling pictures in the gallery, juggling videos in the movie theater, and much more. Ask for juggling help, and you'll get helpful suggestions from other jugglers. Have fun, and don't forget to check out "The Instant Jugglers' Manual"—warming up, four balls, five balls, you're on the way to being a juggler!

http://www.juggling.org/

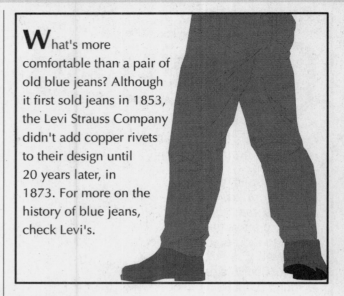

What's more comfortable than a pair of old blue jeans? Although it first sold jeans in 1853, the Levi Strauss Company didn't add copper rivets to their design until 20 years later, in 1873. For more on the history of blue jeans, check Levi's.

CLOTHING

The History of Costume by Braun & Scheider

Your school is having an Ancient Rome day and you don't know how to tie your toga? No problem, just drop in here, where there are 500 costumes pictured, from ancient times through the 19th Century. The original German text was written in the Victorian period. This page concentrates on the pictures, which are detailed. Whether you intend to dress as a 14th Century German Knight, or a late 19th Century Swiss Heidi, you'll find a model here! Hint: choose the TEXT version, which loads faster, then focus on the time period you need to explore.

http://www.siue.edu/COSTUMES/history.html

Levi's

Although Levi's jeans have been around for over a hundred years, they just got this Web site up and running, and it is packed full of fun stuff. Explore the "jean-eology" historic timeline offered through the "faded" link in History. Take the "Inner-seam" tour to see how the company comes up with their television commercials. Check out what's happening in the world of fashion through the "street" link.

http://www.levi.com/menu

COSTUME
Art Deco-Erté

When you think of a special event costume, you probably think of Halloween. In Hollywood, movie stars put on costumes for special events, such as parties or awards ceremonies. The costumes they wear today are usually just tuxedos and gowns. Long ago, famous people used to incorporate a lot more imagination into their costumes! Designers such as Romain de Tirtoff, better known as Erté, went to great efforts to create one-of-a-kind costumes. Erté was an Art Deco fashion creator, and this site is full of great costume ideas.

http://www.webcom.com/ajarts/welcome.html

Textiles Through Time

What if we didn't have any malls? Where would people go to buy their clothes? Throughout most of history, people have had to make their own clothes, fabric, and fibers. This site links museum textile collections around the world. See handmade fabrics, including clothing, quilts, ceremonial artifacts, and a whole lot more. You'll find links to the Bayeux Tapestry, Hmong needlework, and exquisite Japanese kimonos.

http://www.interlog.com/~gwhite/ttt/tttintro.html

CODES AND CIPHERS

See also WORDS

Morse Code and the Phonetic Alphabets

Morse code was invented by Samuel Finley Breese Morse as a way to send messages over telegraph lines. Morse is known as the inventor of the "electromagnetic recording telegraph," although he had help from others. The first message transmitted over a telegraph line was in 1844. "What hath God wrought" went 36 miles, from Washington, D.C. to Baltimore, Maryland, in code sent by Morse himself. What happens if you make a mistake in sending code? You can't erase or backspace, so to indicate that a mistake has been made and tell the receiver to delete the last word, send .... (eight dots).

http://www.soton.ac.uk/~scp93ch/refer/alphabet.html

There's lots of stuff below the street: wires, pipes, and tunnels. Access to them is through an opening in the street called a **manhole**. Why is a manhole round? Why isn't it square?

Answer: *According to Dr. Math, it's so the manhole cover won't fall through the hole and hit something underneath! A circle is the only shape that won't fall through its own hole. If it were a square, for example, you could drop it through diagonally, because the diagonal diameter of a square is longer than the diameter straight across. Other polygons will have diameters of different lengths, allowing you to turn the cover so that the shortest diameter of the cover lines up with the longest diameter of the hole, allowing it to fall through. Read more from Dr. Math at* http://forum.swarthmore.edu/dr.math/problems/mosh26.html

Morse Code Translator

Type in your name and get it translated into Morse code. Or, if you're a real code wizard, type in the dots and dashes and have it translated back into readable text. .-- --- .-- is "wow" in Morse code! There is also a very informative link to phonetic alphabets, which police and military units use in telecommunications.

http://www.soton.ac.uk/~scp93ch/refer/ morseform.html

National Cryptological Museum

Years ago, the road signs pointing to the CIA (the spy guys—the Central Intelligence Agency) building in Virginia said, "Bureau of Public Roads." Everybody knew what is was, but nobody was willing to admit it publicly. A lot of this has changed. The National Security Agency, a similar government agency that does all kinds of James Bond-type things, opened in 1993 this public museum devoted to secret codes and code breaking. This page has a nice sampling of museum exhibits, complete with photographs. You'll see once-secret cryptology devices, such as the Cipher Wheel, the Black Chamber, and Enigma. Museum hours and instructions on how to get to the place (including a map) are available here as well. Thank goodness they didn't put the directions in code!

http://www.nsa.gov:8080/museum/

What is the Black Chamber?

Despite its ominous-sounding name, it was a highly secret MI-8 code-breaking project during the 1920s. Herbert O. Yardley worked for the Army and the State Department and broke the diplomatic codes of several different nations, including Japan. Before the meetings of the Washington Naval Conference of 1921–22, the U.S. State Department broke the codes detailing the Japanese bargaining position. Everyone was dumbfounded, because the Americans seemed to be reading the minds of the Japanese. They were, of course. The Japanese quickly figured this out and changed their codes. Find out more at the National Cryptological Museum home page.

A
B
C
D
E
F
G
H
I
J
K
L
M
N
O
P
Q
R
S
T
U
V
W
X
Y
Z

A
B
C
D
E
F
G
H
I
J
K
L
M
N
O
P
Q
R
S
T
U
V
W
X
Y
Z

Some Classic Ciphers and Their Weaknesses

Using a secret code can add intrigue and excitement to the rather ordinary activity of sending a note or letter to a friend (especially via e-mail). While personal computers have made it possible for anybody to have access to encryption programs, sometimes it's just more fun to use a code that you can scribble on a piece of paper. Some of these ciphers go back to the time of Julius Caesar, and a good handful of them can be found on this page. Each code is simply explained, and each is taken apart—deciphered—as well. Even more fun than writing in code is breaking someone else's. Here, you can learn how to use the Caesar, Vigenère, Augustus, and Playfair ciphers, among others, and you'll also find out what it takes to rip them up. Then for people who really want to keep a secret, there is a link to modern encryption systems for e-mail, such as PGP (Pretty Good Privacy).

http://rschp2.anu.edu.au:8080/cipher.html

The Story of the Beale Ciphers

The Beale ciphers hold the key to one of the greatest unsolved puzzles of all time. The story goes that around 1820, a fellow named Beale hid two wagon-loads of silver, gold, and jewels someplace near Roanoke, Virginia. He left three coded letters, supposedly detailing the location of the treasure, with a trusted friend. Then he left for the West and was never seen again. One of the letters, describing the treasure, has been deciphered. It is in a code based on the Declaration of Independence. It is believed the other letters are similarly coded to the same document or other public documents. You can read about the status of the Beale ciphers, and you might want to try solving them yourself (if you find this treasure, please let us know!). More stories of the searchers are at the main level of this page, at <http://www.rev.net/~brent/index.htm>.

http://www.rev.net/~brent/story.htm

Well-informed lizards, snakes, and other herps read the REPTILES resources.

NET FILES

In 1991, what was the fastest steel roller coaster in the world?

Answer: *The Steel Phantom at Kennywood in West Mifflin, Pennsylvania, gets top honors at 80 mph. This coaster also ties with the Desperado at Buffalo Bill's in Jean, Nevada, for having the longest drop at that time: 225 feet. For more stomach-lurching statistics on the roller coasters at Kennywood, see* http://www.kennywood.com/coasters.html

Collectors Universe

This site claims to be "the largest collectible oriented site on the Internet." Whether this assertion is true or not, if you collect coins, stamps, comics, or trading cards, this page is not to be missed. Using professional-quality, vividly colored graphics, each separate "universe" link includes lists of dealers, shows, classified ads, news, and chat sections and clubs. They also have promised to be on the cutting edge with innovations that will "change collectibles on the Internet forever." This may be worth checking out every once in a while just to see what they mean!

http://www.collectors.com/

The Land of the Lunchboxes

Long before we had lunch boxes made of plastic, as we do today, we had lunch boxes that were made out of metal. They had cool things on them, too, such as the stars of TV westerns, comedies, and cartoons. You may have some of these lurking about in cabinets and basements, and you should definitely dig them out. Not only are they interesting and colorful, but they are very collectible, and some are worth lots of money! This page shows you the history of metal lunch boxes, which carried many a peanut butter and jelly sandwich to school, five miles through the deep snowdrifts, when Dad was young. A caution to parents: There is a mild language glitch on this page when the author gets a little emotional about the death of metal lunch boxes back in 1985.

http://www2.ari.net/home/kholcomb/lunch.html

Learn About Antiques and Collectibles

Have you ever been to a flea market? They don't sell fleas there, just lots of old things people have in their basements, garages, and attics. At these types of sales, you can find everything from old clothing to jewelry to toys to fishing gear. Sometimes you will be able to find a treasure inside a pile of junk! How do you know what to look for? You could take along an expert, or you could study this Web page before you go. It will give you the basics on how to talk to antique dealers, plus what to look for in collecting various items, including dolls, marbles, tools, and more.

http://willow.internet-connections.net/web/antiques/

Nerd World : COLLECTIBLES

The nerds at Nerd World have done it again! They have put together the most incredible set of links dealing with a cornucopia of collectibles. If you're looking for Web sites about ship models, real or model railroads, gold coins, old magazine art, carousel horses, radio-controlled vehicles, paper ephemera, cards, card games, signs, comics, phone cards, PEZ dispensers, historic newspapers and books, dolls, stamps, clocks, and much, much more, then be sure to drop in here. Parental advisory: This is a large site with many links, and they have not all been checked.

http://www.nerdworld.com/nw768.html

NET FILES

ACROSS the water, you see a distant fellow boater holding a yellow and red flag in each hand, out straight from his sides. Is he trying to tell you something?

ANSWER: He might be. If he is signaling you using the semaphore flag system, he is sending the code for the letter "R." Want to know what the rest of his message is? Better check http://155.187.10.12/flags/semaphore.html to find out!

Welcome to the Scout Patch Auction

Last time you were rummaging in Grandma's attic, you found a lot of old Boy Scout stuff. There were a lot of old merit badges, pins, and even some old manuals. "That's a lot of junk," said Grandma. "Just throw it out." But you want to check the Net first. Hey, this merit badge is worth over $3,000! You may have a real treasure chest there and not even know it. The Scout Patch Auction tracks sales of Boy Scout and Girl Scout memorabilia, so start here.

http://www.tspa.com/

A B C D E F G H I J K L M N O P Q R S T U V W X Y Z

A
B
C
D
E
F
G
H
I
J
K
L
M
N
O
P
Q
R
S
T
U
V
W
X
Y
Z

COIN COLLECTING

Coin Collecting FAQ Part 1

Have you already put together a nice collection of coins, or did you just stumble onto a few old ones in your change? Not really sure what to do with them? Roll on over to this page and get some of the more basic coin collecting questions answered. "How can I determine what a coin is really worth?" and "How can I sell my coins?" are two of the questions that are answered here, clearly and with logic and detail.

http://www.telesphere.com/ts/coins/faq.html

You've got a good start on a coin collection, but some of them are pretty dirty. Should you clean your coins? Probably not. Collectors today value the originality of a coin, and any attempt to clean a coin may alter this originality and lower its value. Read more about this controversy and many other questions about numismatics at the **Coin Collecting FAQ Part 1** page.

Numismatics Home Page

Coin collecting is an international activity, and this is a good place to look for information and links to numismatic hobbyists around the globe. Here you'll find links to discussion lists, news, pictures of coins, and a special link to an international Web-based currency converter!

http://www.cs.vu.nl/~fjjunge/numis.html

OPTICAL ILLUSIONS: now you see them, now you don't!

One-Minute Coin Expert

Scott Travers has excerpted one entire chapter from his popular book, *One Minute Coin Expert*, on this site. He answers many frequently asked questions from both beginner and experienced coin collectors. Most of these questions are based on ones he has often been asked on radio and television programs. The information posted here is solid and useful, and of course it is designed to entice you to buy the book and get the rest of what you need to become a "one-minute coin expert" yourself. One of the tips he recommends for kids is that they join the Young Numismatist coin collecting club (it's free). Send a postcard with your name, address, age, and telephone number to: Lawrence J. Gentile, Sr., 542 Webster Avenue, New Rochelle, NY 10805. His program for kids includes "free seminars, free coins, free books, and a wealth of information that youngsters find helpful."

http://www.inch.com/~travers/1min.htm

U.S. CoinNection Home Page

Whether you're a beginner or a pro at collecting coins, this page will have something of interest. There is a history of U.S. coins from colonial times to the present day, as well as articles such as "How are U.S. coins graded?" Every month, a specific coin series is highlighted, such as Liberty-head nickels. A glossary explains coin terms, and an FAQ answers questions about how to get started in this popular hobby!

http://ppp.jax-inter.net/coin/

SHELL COLLECTING

Sea Shells

Tony Printezis has graciously put together this page of detailed photographs of his shell collection. The unique thing about his collection is that it doesn't exist! Printezis has devised a computer program from scratch that creates delicate, multicolored images of seashells, which look like they came off a magical beach. Click on the thumbnails and see full-screen pictures of these shells.

http://www.dcs.gla.ac.uk/~tony/ss/

Shelling on Sanibel-Captiva Islands

Florida's Sanibel Island lacks offshore reefs and a perpendicular heading, compared to its neighbor islands, which makes it a natural interceptor of shells from the South Seas. People come from all over the world to comb Sanibel's beaches for washed-up natural treasures. Find out about the Bailey-Matthews Shell Museum and other information for the traveler, and learn how to do the Sanibel Stoop!

http://www.usa-chamber.com/sanibel-captiva/
shelling.html

Can you do the Sanibel Stoop?
Stand on the shore, bend over, and scoop up
a handful of rare and beautiful sea shells found
on Florida's Sanibel Island.
Kick off your flip-flops and head over to
Shelling on Sanibel-Captiva Islands
to find out more.

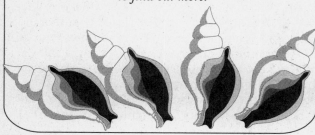

SPORTS AND OTHER TRADING CARDS

Sports Collectibles by Nerd World Media

Links to dozens of sports collectible sites can be found here, many of them specializing in sports cards. The intriguing thing is that some of these pages on the Nerd World list are professional commercial sites while others are strictly amateur, done for the love of the hobby. They're all great. This is the place to start looking for sports card information, whether you want to buy, sell, get questions answered, or just chat with other collectors. Not all links were checked.

http://www.tiac.net/users/dstein/nw430.html

Welcome to Beckett Online

For over a decade, Dr. James Beckett and his organization have tracked and published the prices of baseball, football, basketball, hockey, and many other sports trading cards. BeckWorld offers a free membership that allows visitors to drop in and dig up information on selected popular cards. A paid subscription plan is also available for unlimited online searches in their extensive guides.

http://www.beckett.com/

STAMP COLLECTING

Stamps and Postal History Page

Bob Swanson has a collection of stamps, cancellations, first-day covers, and postcards that would make any collector drool, and he has put lots of the best images right here. He has a monthly "Mystery Cover" and links to the American Philatelic Society, the Military Postal Society, and plenty of other fascinating stamp-oriented sites. If you want to try scanning in your own stamps, you'll find advice on that, too.

http://www.cris.com/~Swanson/posthist.html

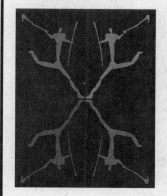

Some early scientists thought they grew from seeds dropped by stars. Others were sure these objects were carved from stone by ancient, forgotten artists. What are they?

Answer: *Fossils. You can even make your own fossils using the handy recipe at this site. First you take a dead insect, follow the simple instructions, and wait about 400 million years. Check* http://rs6000.bvis.uic.edu/museum/exhibits/ttt/T T T 1b.html *for an explanation.*

A
B
C
D
E
F
G
H
I
J
K
L
M
N
O
P
Q
R
S
T
U
V
W
X
Y
Z

A
B
C
D
E
F
G
H
I
J
K
L
M
N
O
P
Q
R
S
T
U
V
W
X
Y
Z

Welcome to the National Postal Museum

Clicking on the crumpled envelope on this site's welcome page will bring you into one of the Smithsonian Institution's newest museums! It's organized into five major galleries that tell the story of postal history, and it includes a great collection of rare and wonderful stamp images. In many ways, the study of U.S. postage stamps is the study of American history and tradition. Whether you collect stamps or just use them to mail letters, you'll find a visit to this site well worth the time.

http://www.si.edu/postal/

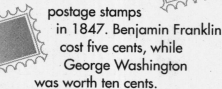

The Penny Black and the [Two] Penny Blue were the world's first adhesive postage stamps, issued in Great Britain in 1840. They featured a portrait of a very young Queen Victoria. The U.S. issued its first postage stamps in 1847. Benjamin Franklin cost five cents, while George Washington was worth ten cents. The Smithsonian Institution's National Postal Museum offers a glimpse into the intriguing—and sometimes sticky—world of stamps and stamp collecting at Welcome to the National Postal Museum.

Real surfers get their feet wet in OUTDOOR RECREATION.

COLOR AND COLORING BOOKS

See also ART—DRAWING AND PAINTING

Carlos' Coloring Book Home

Did you ever use a computer and the Internet to color? At this site, you can color a birthday cake, a snowman, and other fun pictures on the World Wide Web with your computer. The best thing about this coloring book is that you can color over and over, and the pages don't fall out!

http://www.ravenna.com/coloring/

Color Communication

Red means "stop" and green means "go"—everyone knows that without giving it much thought. But did you know that color can affect the way you feel? It can make you feel relaxed or jumpy. It can make you feel interested or bored, even make you feel warmer or colder! And color sometimes means different things in different countries: for example, black is the color of grief and mourning in the U.S., while in some Asian countries the appropriate color is white. Find out more about the fascinating world of color here. Hint: Click on "Color Matters" to get into the main part of the tutorial.

http://www.lava.net/colorcom/color.html

Color Theory

When you mix paints, you already know that if you mix red and blue you get purple, and if you mix blue and yellow you get green, right? That works with paint, but it doesn't work when you mix different colors of light. Light is a different story: for example, red and green light make yellow. How can that be? It's all explained in words and pictures here. This is important stuff to know if you want to print pretty color pictures in magazines, calendars, and even on the cover of this book!

http://www.pubserv.washington.edu/Color.Theory/Color.Theory.html

Color Theory

This page gives an excellent introduction to the color wheel: the three primary colors (red, blue, and yellow), the three secondary colors (purple, green, and orange), and the six tertiary colors (red-violet, red-orange, yellow-orange, yellow-green, blue-green, and blue-violet). You'll learn about complementary and contrasting colors, warm and cool color schemes, and shades and tints. What color is your favorite?

http://web1.andrew.cmu.edu/user/dw4e/color/color.html

NET FILES

Mastodon, mammoth, bison, and musk ox traveled one way, passing the camels, horses, and cheetahs going in the other direction. What were they doing?

http://tyrrell.magtech.ab.ca/tour/iceages.html

Answer: They were migrating across the land bridge that connected Asia and North America during the ice age, when massive ice packs covered more of the earth's surface than they do today. Falling sea levels exposed enough land to make the connection possible. The first group of animals came to North America from Asia, while the second group originated in North America. Behind both groups were humans, chasing their respective food sources! The chilling truth is out there at http://tyrrell.magtech.ab.ca/tour/iceages.html

Explore underwater archaeology in SHIPS AND SHIPWRECKS.

NET FILES

What's the world's record for the number of balls a juggler's been able to keep in the air at one time?

http://www.juggling.org/records/records.html

Answer: The record is 12 balls, 12 catches! Bruce Sarafian, in 1996, authenticated this to the Juggling Information Service with a personal video. Read about more records for juggling clubs and rings at http://www.juggling.org/records/records.html

Crayola * Crayola * Crayola * Crayola

What's your favorite Crayola color? How do they make crayons anyway? In 1903, the Binney & Smith company manufactured the first box of Crayolas. Explore the history of Crayolas, read the latest "Colorful News," and learn about Crayola trivia. Uh-oh! You've left a bunch of crayons on the back seat of your family car, and now they've melted! On the Crayola page, you can find out how to remove the stains. Make fun stuff from ideas right out of *Crayola Magazine*. You don't even have to color between the lines! Check the new Heroes contest, where you can name a new color after a person you admire.

http://www.crayola.com/crayola/

Kendra's Coloring Book

Coloring used to be so hard. There's that "stay within the lines" thing. Plus, it can be tough to find the right color crayon or marker. When you do find it, it's always broken or out of ink. If you make a mistake, you might as well start over. Your worries are over at this site. All you have to do is pick a picture, select a color, and click where you want the color to go. No more worrying where you left the "peach."

http://www.gcg.com/misc/colorbook/

A B C D E F G H I J K L M N O P Q R S T U V W X Y Z

A
B
C
D
E
F
G
H
I
J
K
L
M
N
O
P
Q
R
S
T
U
V
W
X
Y
Z

Pocahontas coloring book main page

Would you like to make your own Pocahontas coloring book? Disney has created black-and-white pictures of Pocahontas, John Smith, Meeko, and Flit from the movie *Pocahontas*. You can copy them to your computer and color them in a paint program, or you can print them out and color them on paper.

http://www2.disney.com/DisneyPictures/Pocahontas/
   coloring_book/coloring.html

COMICS AND CARTOONS

Cartoon Corner

How do people get jobs as cartoonists? Seems like a terrific job, using crayons and markers all day and thinking up funny things. This site will tell you the secrets of cartooning, but you have to promise *not* to tell anyone else! Learn some drawing tips, and try to guess some tricky riddles here.

http://www.cartooncorner.com/

CBS Kidzone

What cartoons are on CBS? *Timon & Pumbaa* (from *The Lion King*), *The Mask*, and those all-time great crime fighters—*Teenage Mutant Ninja Turtles*! There are some fun games involving these characters, plus downloadable graphics, too.

http://www.cbs.com/cbskidzone

The Comic Strip

Every week they make families around the world laugh. They have names like Snoopy, Dilbert, and Marmaduke. Who are these wacky characters? They are the drawings that make up the comic strips in your newspaper. Catch up on your favorite comic strip characters, and see what they are doing on the Internet. Find out about the artists and how they thought up the characters, and play games based on the comic strip. Then take a detour from the main page to the National Cartoonists Society, where the *real* cartoonists behind the strips hang out!

http://www.unitedmedia.com/comics/

DC Comics

DC Comics is the home of such superhero greats as Superman and Batman, along with many others. We wonder if they ever go out for lunch together. If you want to know what's new at their comic book company, stop in here. You will find some of those trendy new cyber trading cards, as well as sound clips and more

http://www.dccomics.com

Why is the Library of Congress' Legislative Information on the Internet named "Thomas"?

Answer: "Thomas" is named in honor of Thomas Jefferson. He was the third President of the United States and drafted the Declaration of Independence. The inscription "In the spirit of Thomas Jefferson, a service of the U.S. Congress through its Library" can be found at the THOMAS home page at http://thomas.loc.gov/

Felix the Cat Home Page

Long before Garfield ever tasted his first bite of lasagne, Felix the Cat was a favorite. He appeared in newspapers as early as 1923! In fact, according to this page, Felix was used as the first test image on early TV experiments in the RCA laboratories. Now he's back on TV, and Felix is one popular cat. Read about him and his magic bag here.

http://www.felixthecat.com/

Become one with the Net.

Fox Kids Cyberstation

The Fox Network has some great taste in 'toons, since they broadcast Net-mom's favorite: *The Tick*! But you may also like *Carmen Sandiego*, *The X-Men*, *Taz-Mania*, *Batman and Robin*, and *Casper*, among others. You can find some fun sound files and get news on the shows here.

http://www.foxkids.com/home.htm

Garfield Online

This purr-fect home page is hosted by a big fat hairy deal: Garfield! Check out the recipes for Garfield's favorite food (lasagne) and read some great jokes. Still can't get enough of this cantankerous kitty? Grab a Garfield screen saver for your computer!

http://www.garfield.com/

Hergé

Let's go on an adventure! Tintin is a bold, youthful character who finds himself constantly in the middle of excitement. He travels around the world with his pet dog Snowy, solving baffling mysteries. Tintin was created in 1929 by Belgian artist Hergé. Originally, it was a newspaper comic strip, but it has recently become an animated series. Read about the development of Tintin, and see some of the wonderful drawings.

http://www.netpoint.be/abc/herge/

Looney Tunes Karaoke

Your favorite Looney Tunes characters from Warner Brothers probably include Bugs Bunny, Tweety Bird, and Daffy Duck. Everyone always forgets that after Looney comes TUNES—and now you can sing right along with those characters, karaoke-style! This hilarious site is sure to make you smile.

http://www.kids.warnerbros.com/karaoke

The Marvel Universe Online

Do X-Men have anything to do with X-Files? We don't think so, but then we haven't read everything at this site! Silver Surfer, Ghost Rider, and Spider-Man are all part of the Marvel Comics universe. This new site promises games in the near future, maybe by the time you read this. Right now you can find cyber trading cards and info on the characters. Web-sling your way to this site as soon as you can!

http://www.marvelcomics.com/marvel.html

Mother Goose & Grimm

Does your dog eat out of the garbage can? If so, then your dog has something in common with Grimm! Mother Goose and Grimm are the lovable duo that appear in newspapers around the world as well as on Saturday morning cartoons. At this site, you can read biographical information about Mother Goose, Grimm, Atilla, and Mike Peters (the guy who draws these zany characters).

http://www.grimmy.com/

The Simpsons

Bart is just a good kid with a "few bad ideas...that are still being reviewed by the Springfield district attorney." Better get over to the official Fox Network Simpsons Web page before you have a cow! You'll find some fun Simpsons games, news about the show, and contests here in virtual Springfield.

http://www.foxnetwork.com/simpsons/simpson2.htm

TBS Kids' Disaster Area

The TBS (Turner Broadcasting System) Web site is a real Disaster Area—at least, that is what they call their kids' site on the Web! You're probably a fan of a lot of TBS cartoons, including *The Jetsons*, *Scooby Doo*, or *Captain Planet*, so you'll love this site. If you have never heard of any of these, check out the games and contests anyway for some guaranteed fun.

http://www.turner.com/tbs/disaster/

A B C D E F G H I J K L M N O P Q R S T U V W X Y Z

A
B
C
D
E
F
G
H
I
J
K
L
M
N
O
P
Q
R
S
T
U
V
W
X
Y
Z

This week's Zany Zoo

If animals could talk, what would they say?
The Zany Zoo is a weekly cartoon, featuring a cast of
zoo animals and the strange things they do. See the
animals' perspectives on such things as kangaroo
hiccups and punk penguins. Join zookeeper John
Johnson, his assistant Mike, and veterinarian Maria as
they interact with this wonderful group of characters.
Check the archive for additional funnies!

http://www.psnw.com/~jmz5/zz/

Warner Bros. Animation 101

Do you love to watch cartoons? Do you ever wonder
how cartoons are made? Go on a tour and watch the
whole process. See how the pictures go from pencil
sketches to handpainted art. Follow along as voices,
sound effects, and music are added. Just watch out for
falling anvils!

http://www.wbanimation.com/cmp/ani_04if.htm

Cartoons sure have a lot of sound effects!
Did you know that the ones they use over and
over are stored on computers? Then, whenever
they are needed in a cartoon, they are "played"
with a special computer-connected piano
keyboard. Other sound effects are created on
the spot. Draw on Warner Bros. Animation 101
for more information.

Welcome to the XPage

X-Men? Look no further. All you could possibly want
to know about "X-Men" comics (and other comics,
too) is here. Somewhere. At least we think so,
although we have not checked all the links.

http://www.mallorn.com/~m-blase/xpage/

You Can With Beakman and Jax

Put on your thinking cap and log on to this site.
This newspaper feature has become so popular,
there is now a *Beakman's World* TV series! Check out
important historical facts in the You Can Calendar.
Discover the answers to important questions, like
"What are fingernails made of?" Help Beakman and
Jax with their research project. See pictures from the
Hubble Space Telescope, and read about what the
pictures show and what they mean.

http://www.nbn.com/youcan/

COMPUTERS

alt.folklore.computers FAQ

The word "folklore" generally conjures up images of
Davy Crockett or Paul Bunyan. While not as rustic,
the world of computers is just as rich in legends and
lore. This Usenet newsgroup has amassed a barrage of
legends, and this site puts the most popular of them
into easy-to-follow HTML format. Learn the truth
about the NASA probe that rumors say was destroyed
because of a computer typo. Who really wrote
MS-DOS? Find out about the origins of Usenet and
Unix, various computer firsts, and where in the world
Jolt's high-caffeine cola is illegal.

http://www.best.com/~wilson/faq/

**I wonder what the
QUEENS, KINGS, ROYALTY
are doing tonight?**

Did you hear about the guy who missed the chance to sell his operating system to IBM (which instead used Bill Gates's MS-DOS), because he was flying around in his airplane at the time?

What is the longest discussion thread *ever* in a newsgroup?

Where can you buy slide rules these days? Find out the fascinating answers to these and other questions at alt.folklore.computers FAQ.

Computer Anatomy 101

From the people who brought you The Interactive Frog Dissection page, we now present computer anatomy for beginners! In this brief tutorial, you'll see under the cover of a typical computer and learn what the inside of a hard disk looks like, among other things. At the end you can take a quiz and test your new skills.

http://curry.edschool.virginia.edu/~phr7x/
Computer101/home.html

The Computer Museum

In an old building on Museum Wharf in Boston sits a walk-through computer. The trackball is as big as your sofa. The keyboard is as big as your school bus. And you ought to see the size of that motherboard. Welcome to the Computer Museum! You can visit its Web page and get a taste of the exhibits there. Here's a twist: When you enter this site, you can put in a name (any name will do) and you can put in the name of your country or your ZIP code if you are in the U.S. This Web page keeps track of all connected users, and when you select "Who's Out There?" you will get a world map with all current users—if you have a Java-enabled browser. You can click on Paolo from Brazil or Geoff from Australia or Sarah from the U.K. and send a message. Then you can explore the galleries together! For a timeline of computer history, don't miss <*http://www.tcm.org/history/timeline/index.html*>.

http://www.tcm.org/

Dave's Guide to Buying a Home Computer

How do you figure out which computer is the right one for you? What size and speed of microprocessor do you need? You don't want to waste your allowance money on a computer that is more than you need, but you do want a system that will be usable for a number of years. Read this guide for tips and suggestions on purchasing and installing a PC. Find out what to ask the store salesperson and what to look for in features. The opinions expressed are just that—opinions—but you'll find some valuable information here.

http://www.css.msu.edu/pc-guide.html

NET FILES

What does "All That" mean in street-speak?

Answer: It means "the top banana, the coolest person in the world." For example: "Ever since she started playing in that band, she thinks she's all that." Find out more current slang and submit new words you and your friends use at http://www.jayi.com/jayi/Fishnet/StreetSpeak/SSdata.html

You can always count on the info in MATH AND ARITHMETIC.

A B C D E F G H I J K L M N O P Q R S T U V W X Y Z

A
B
C
D
E
F
G
H
I
J
K
L
M
N
O
P
Q
R
S
T
U
V
W
X
Y
Z

Introduction to PC Hardware

Are today's computers a *RISC*? How much *cache* do you need to buy a computer? *IDE*'d like a bigger hard drive, but what kind? Is our spelling that bad, or are we trying to make a point? Well, it so happens that those "misspelled" words are computer terms that you can read about on this Web page. You'll learn all about the various types of memory and how they are used in a computer system. Read about what's inside a microprocessor chip and about the different kinds of hard drives. By the time you're through, you'll be able to impress the salespeople in your local computer store—and maybe get a good deal to *boot*.

http://pclt.cis.yale.edu/pclt/pchw/platypus.htm

IPL Youth Division: Do Spiders Live on the World Wide Web?

Take your baby sister to story time at the University of Michigan's Internet Public Library! This picture book dictionary will help her learn the difference between the mouse on your desk and the mouse in your barn. In case you were wondering, the one in the barn eats up all the corn, while the one on your desk eats up all your time.

http://ipl.sils.umich.edu/youth/StoryHour/spiders/
  mousepg.html

THE JARGON FILE

In the beginning, computers were understood by only a small group of insiders. These insiders developed their own language and made up their own words, all of which served to further isolate them from the rest of the world, which was, after all, a distraction from computers and programming. ;-) For years, hacker lore and legend has been collected into this file. It's even been published in book form, as *The Hacker Dictionary*, which you can find at *<http://www.ccil.org/jargon/>*. Now it has made it to the Web, and you will laugh at the funny computing terms and lingo heard daily in machine rooms all over the Net. Some have even made it into popular conversation! You can search the file for specific terms or just browse for fun. Parental advisory: some of these terms have mildly racy origins.

http://www.fwi.uva.nl/~mes/jargon/

Ever attended a disk drive race?

In the olden days of computing, disk drives were about the size of washing machines. Bored programmers wrote routines to command the drive heads to seek back and forth on the disks, which built up a momentum that often allowed the drives to totter across the floor. Walking drive races are a legendary part of computing history, and you can read more at THE JARGON FILE.

RING!OnLine| Computer Advisor

Here's some advice on how to buy a computer. This two-part column will help you if you're looking for your first computer or looking to upgrade that old "slowpoke." How much RAM do you need, how big a hard drive should you get, and what is a cache, anyway? Check this site to find out.

http://www.ring.com/vts/advisor/main.htm

Mr. Spock agrees it is highly logical to want to know all about STAR TREK, STAR WARS, AND SPACE EPICS.

The Virtual Museum of Computing

The world's largest museum devoted to computers is appropriately located in Downtown Hyperspace. Don't worry about putting coins in the parking meter. Just stroll around and check out the ever-growing collection. You'll find galleries featuring local virtual exhibits, corporate histories, and entire wings with histories of computing organizations and societies, plus general computer history. Special exit doors here will take you to a couple of dozen other online computing museums. While there is no virtual snack bar here yet, you can drop in on an assortment of selected computer-oriented newsgroups to chat about what you've seen. You'll even find a gallery of mousepads old and new! Parental advisory: This is a large site with many links, and they have not all been checked.

http://www.comlab.ox.ac.uk/archive/other/museums/
computing.html

NET FILES

How **BIG** is the audio-animatronic stegosaurus on the Jurassic Park ride at the Universal Studios theme park?

learn if it's a carnivore or a vegetarian.
http://www.mca.com/unicity/attractions/jp/ and
over to the Jurassic Park ride facts site at
stories tall, and, gee, it's coming your way! Run
Its pal, the incredible Ultrasaurus, is over five
Answer: It's 18 feet tall and over 40 feet long.

AMIGA
Amiga Report Magazine

The Amiga may be the phoenix of computers, rising out of the ashes to new heights. It never achieved the measure of popularity in the U.S. that it did in Europe. But the purchase of the rights to the once-discontinued system by the Amiga Technologies group has created the possibility of new developments. Whether you already own an Amiga and are looking for sources of support and new software (there are Web browsers for Amiga users!) or you are just interested in keeping track of what's happening, drop in on this site regularly.

http://www.omnipresence.com/Amiga/News/AR/

Aminet at ftp.wustl.edu

"Aminet is the Internet's largest collection of Amiga software." Check out the recent uploads list to keep up to date with your favorite shareware. Visit the "Tree of Aminet directories" for a list of their archives sorted by category. A search tool and help files are also available for those Amigaphiles in need of Amiga files.

http://ftp.wustl.edu/~aminet/

APPLE II
Apple II Resources

While Apple Computer may have discontinued the Apple II line a few years ago, millions of these workhorse machines are still in use in homes and schools everywhere. Plenty of new Apple II hardware and software is still being developed. Nathan Mates has collected as many Apple II links as he could find, including newsgroups, FTP sites chock-full of programs and information, lists of BBSs, and companies producing Apple II products. The FAQ here is a labor of love. Once the corporate slogan for Apple Computer, "Apple II Forever!" seems to be a fact of life for the dedicated bunch of folks you'll find here.

http://www.visi.com/~nathan/a2/

A
B
C
D
E
F
G
H
I
J
K
L
M
N
O
P
Q
R
S
T
U
V
W
X
Y
Z

A B C D E F G H I J K L M N O P Q R S T U V W X Y Z

ARTIFICIAL INTELLIGENCE

Cog, the Robot

Back in 1921, playwright Karel Čapek coined the word "robot," and since then, books, movies, and television programs have all speculated about the form these mechanical creatures will take. Now a group of researchers at the Massachusetts Institute of Technology's Artificial Intelligence Lab are actually attempting this feat. *Artificial intelligence* is the process in which a computer takes in information and uses it to create new knowledge—a simulation of human thinking. Cog the Robot is a collection of sensors and motors that attempt to duplicate the sensory and manipulative functions of the human body. Coupled with artificial intelligence programming, Cog may eventually succeed in bringing science fiction's fantasies to reality. Move over Data, here comes Cog!

http://www.ai.mit.edu/projects/cog/Text/
cog-robot.html

The Riddle of the Sphinx was this:

"What goes on four feet, on two feet, and three, But the more feet it goes on, the weaker it be?"

What is the answer?

Answer: The riddle's answer is MAN! He crawls (four feet) as a baby, walks (two feet) as an adult, and uses a cane (three feet) when he is old. You can read more about the riddling Greek Sphinx (but not this answer, which we found in the current paper edition of the Brewer Dictionary of Phrase and Fable) at http://www.bibliomania.com/Reference/PhraseAndFable/data/1167.html#sphinx
(This Greek Sphinx was a sea monster, while the more familiar Egyptian Sphinx was half human, half lion.)

Everyone's heard of the 4-H Club. What are the four H's?

Answer: In 1911, they stood for "Head, Heart, Hands, and Hustle . . . head trained to think, plan and reason; heart trained to be true, kind and sympathetic; hands trained to be useful, helpful and skillful; and the hustle to render ready service, to develop health and vitality." Now, however, they signify Head, Heart, Hands, and Health. The 4-H four-leaf clover emblem was patented in 1924. Read more about the program at http://www.fourhcouncil.edu/nhistory.htm

ATARI

What's an Atari 8-bit?

The Atari 8-bit computer was a natural outgrowth of the company's phenomenally popular game cartridge machine. In fact, all of these machines, whether the 400, 800, or any of the XL or XE series, had a port or two for popping in game or program cartridges. Plenty of folks are still getting lots of mileage out of them, and this site is a great starting point if you're wondering what you can do with the one Dad just bought at a garage sale. It includes plenty of links to active Atari 8-bit home pages as well as the important "Atari 8-bit Omnibus."

http://zippy.sonoma.edu/~kendrick/nbs/whatisatari/

Don't be irrational, check on the numbers in MATH AND ARITHMETIC.

HARDWARE AND SOFTWARE COMPANIES

Apple Computer

This is the computer "for the rest of us" that launched the mouse, the graphical user interface, and the networked laser printer into the consumer mainstream. Apple's home page has product information to help you choose a system and a technical support area to help answer questions. You'll also find downloadable upgrades to Apple software and information on the "cool Apple technologies" that Apple is working on to improve their products for the future. Apple has been an advocate of the education market ever since 1977, with the introduction of the Apple II. Since then, they have continued to embrace education with their product lines, including the Macintosh and Power Macintosh. A 1993 "Technology in Public Schools" report showed that "93 percent of public school students attended institutions that use Apple computers." Additionally, the Apple Classrooms of Tomorrow (ACOT) research program is a collaboration among public schools, universities, research agencies, and Apple Computer, Inc. itself. For the past ten years, ACOT has studied technology's impact on education. A compilation of the lessons learned is available for a few dollars. It's called "Changing the Conversation about Teaching, Learning & Technology: A Report on 10 Years of ACOT Research." The ordering information is at *<http://www.research.apple.com/research/proj/acot/>*. Other research studies are also available. Find out more about Apple's educational programs at Apple's Education K12 page in the Solutions area at *<http://ed.info.apple.com/education/>*.

http://www.apple.com/

Guide to Computer Vendors

Want to write to the programmers of your favorite game, to suggest some new features? Here they are: over a thousand computer hardware and software vendors with Web pages ready to be accessed with a click. It's all filed with an easy-to-use alphabetical index, and as a bonus, a telephone directory lists several thousand computer companies. Want more? Link to the computer magazine list maintained on this page, and drop in on your favorite periodical's Web site! Not all links have been viewed.

http://guide.sbanetweb.com/

Microsoft in Education

In February 1975, Bill Gates and Paul Allen completed the first computer language program written for a personal computer: a BASIC interpreter for the Altair. In 1981, Microsoft shipped MS-DOS 1.0 for IBM's new personal computer. In the years to come, MS-DOS became the standard operating system bundled with the millions of PCs shipped to businesses and individuals. In 1985, Windows was introduced to the public. Since then, Microsoft has shipped millions of copies of Windows. Needless to say, Microsoft is the largest software company in the world! Check out these K–12 pages and see what Microsoft is doing in the way of sponsoring programs to promote education, computers, and networking.

http://www.microsoft.com/education/

Software Publishers

About 500 North American software companies are listed in this index. The companies are listed alphabetically, and each listing contains general company information plus a list of their software products, along with descriptions and pricing. A link to the company's home page is also included, if one is available. ElJen Publishing, Inc., the publisher, also offers a Windows CD version of this directory, which includes more in-depth descriptions for each product.

http://www.softwarecenter.com/library/companies.htm

MACINTOSH

Cult of Macintosh*

An unofficial evangelistic effort promoting the Macintosh is actively attempting to place page mirrors on every continent. Frequently updated, it has become a friendly all-around resource for Mac users, with hundreds of links to just about anything a Mac user could desire. Try one of these mirrors if you have trouble connecting:

<http://www.gulf.net/~stone/mac/>
<http://ucsu.Colorado.EDU/~jungd/cult/>
<http://www.dakota.net/~schnaidt/cult/>

http://cult-of-mac.utu.fi/

A
B
C
D
E
F
G
H
I
J
K
L
M
N
O
P
Q
R
S
T
U
V
W
X
Y
Z

MacFixIt (Home Page)

Eventually, every computer owner will run across a problem and will need some kind of support. We like the info at this site, which is constantly being kept up to date.

http://www.macfixit.com/

Macintosh Educator's Site

Billed as an "educators" page, anyone with a Mac (and even those without one) will have a blast visiting here. Short descriptions are provided for each of the links, which include all the major Macintosh archives, magazine pages, and help sites, as well as Science, General Education, and Fun pages.

http://www.hampton-dumont.k12.ia.us/web/mac/

The ULTIMATE Macintosh

Hundreds of Macintosh-related links are piled on this one page, making it possible to conduct a search using your browser's Find command (on Lynx, use the / command). The best thing about this page is the What's HOT! section, which provides up-to-the-minute news and links to the latest information (including promotions from Apple and major vendors) and software updates. Not all links have been viewed.

http://www.velodrome.com/umac.html

MAGAZINES

Yahoo—Business and Economy:Products and Services:Magazines:Computers

Sorry for the long URL, but here's the direct link to Yahoo's online list of computer-related magazines on the Net. (Be sure to save the bookmark for this so you don't have to retype it.) Check out your favorite, or find some new interesting magazines to browse through. Of course, a search function can help you find a word or topic of interest. Be sure to select the "Search only in Personal Computers" button, unless you want to search all of Yahoo.

http://www.yahoo.com/Business_and_Economy/
   Products_and_Services/Magazines/Computers/
   Personal_Computers/

NET FILES

What do you get when you don't iron your moose?

Answer: A Bullwinkle! Find more jokes like this at http://starcreations.com/stardreams/kidzweb/kw-03.htm

PC COMPATIBLES, MICROSOFT WINDOWS

IBM Corporation

Here's where the personal computer (PC) all started. IBM introduced the PC in 1983. Today, computers based on the same design account for about 85 percent of the microcomputer market. Talk about popular! Before the PC, and even now, IBM's stronghold has been with big-business computers that run governments, corporations, banks, and other institutions. Explore this Web site to see what this computer giant is up to these days.

http://www.ibm.com/

What TIME is it, anyway?

Welcome to Gateway 2000 USA

Did you know Gateway computers are shipped in boxes that look like they are part dairy cow? What's with those cows, anyway? Ted Waitt's family had been in the cattle business for many generations. When he created a new computer company, Gateway 2000, he brought some of his heritage with him. Apparently, he also brought some luck with him, because his company is now the largest seller of computers through direct marketing.

http://www.gw2k.com/

The Windows 95 QAID

"How much RAM is required to run Windows 95?" "I lost multiboot option, how do I get it back?" These are two of the many questions that are answered on this Question-Answer Information Database (QAID). The questions are listed by category, such as CD-ROM, booting, printers, and sound. You'll also find news, tips and tricks, and other Windows 95-related areas to browse through. Some of the dialog can get quite technical, but then, computers can get that way sometimes. The QAID is also available for download, allowing you to search for answers while offline.

http://www.kingsoft.com/qaid/win40001.htm

NET FILES

What is an **afuche** *drum?*
What does it look like?

Answer: It's a small, squat cylinder with a handle and a corrugated metal surface. A long string of beads wound loosely around it makes a scrabbly, swishy note when you shake it. There's a great picture at http://www.cse.ogi.edu/Drum/encyclopedia/a.html You can also find out what a *shekere* is, among other things.

Windows95.com

Despite the name, this page is not owned or operated by Microsoft. Using the familiar Windows interface, visitors can click and get help on a variety of topics regarding Windows 95, including the straight lowdown on what kinds of computers should, and should not, use it. There are discussion forums and live chat areas, links to 32-bit shareware, a glossary, and lots of information for beginners. You can download *Win95 Magazine* or a Windows 95 demo for Windows 3.1 users, and new users can purchase Quick Tutors 95, an interactive online help program.

http://www.windows95.com

SOFTWARE ARCHIVES
Children's Software and More!

Families who drop in on this site will find it a severe test of the storage capacity of their hard drives. :-) A wealth of kids' software is available on the Internet, and this is the place to look. This extensive, fully annotated collection gives each program its own page, including age recommendations, program sizes, and shareware fees, if any. The page is divided between Mac and PC archives, and a third section is devoted to downloadable commercial demo programs. This last section includes links to many pages of kids' software review sites.

http://www.gamesdomain.com/tigger/sw-kids.html

CNET resources—software central

This is an intro page to the shareware.com software archives. We've pointed to this page because of its three sections at the bottom of the page, called "virus check?," "survival kits," and "beginner's guides." Each section has a Mac- and PC-specific selection that contains valuable information on downloading software, especially for first-time users. For those "experts" out there, the direct link to the archive is *<http://www.shareware.com/>*. Enjoy!

http://www.cnet.com/Resources/Software/

A B C D E F G H I J K L M N O P Q R S T U V W X Y Z

A
B
C
D
E
F
G
H
I
J
K
L
M
N
O
P
Q
R
S
T
U
V
W
X
Y
Z

Galt Shareware Zone

If you're looking for reviews on shareware software for Windows 3.x or Windows 95, you might try this extensive collection. You can look for the hottest game downloads and the hottest recommended downloads, and you can wander through over 500 screen savers. You can also get a free newsletter that highlights each month's new additions to the archive. Parents, check it out: some of these games are of the Mortal Kombat variety.

http://www.galttech.com/

Happy Puppy's Front Porch

Happy Puppy brings you a list of software and home pages of many of the game software companies on the Net. You'll find lists for Mac and PC games and info on new versions of your favorite games as they are announced. Other software archives listed here have shareware, demos, and upgrades available for those in need of too much fun!

http://happypuppy.com/

INFO-MAC Hyperarchive ROOT

Over the years, info-mac has become the master list for Macintosh software archives, with mirror sites around the world. Now you can use your Web client to search or browse this mirror collection at MIT. This is a great way to find shareware, demos, clip art, help, and information about Macintosh. If you own a Mac, this will become one of your favorite links.

http://hyperarchive.lcs.mit.edu/HyperArchive.html

Oak Software Repository

Check out this archive site for access to just about all the DOS and Windows software available. Besides listing many of the other software archives, you can browse the legendary SimTel archives here with your Web browser. The SimTel collection goes back to the early DOS years, and it is one of the largest collections of PC programs and information in the world. Of course, a search function is available to help you find the "needle in the haystack" you might be looking for.

http://www.acs.oakland.edu/oak.html

SHAREWARE! GAMES! FREEWARE! - JUMBO!

Shareware? What's that? You can try out shareware software before you buy it. Sometimes the shareware version will do everything that the full version will do. Jumbo also has lots of free programs for most computers and operating systems. It's easy to find what you want, since everything is classified by subject. The short descriptions will help you find that arcade game, er, math tutorial you want!

http://www.jumbo.com/

TUCOWS

Tucows says it is the world's most popular collection of Internet software for Windows 95, Windows 3.1, and Macintosh software—and we believe it! This collection is mirrored at over 150 sites around the globe, so pick a site close to you. (Another suggestion is to pick a server located somewhere where the local time is in the middle of the night—that server will probably not be overloaded.) This is your source for plug-ins, helper applications, and games.

http://www.tucows.com

TIMEX SINCLAIR
ZX81 Home Page

At first glance, the ZX81, more commonly known in the U.S. as the Timex Sinclair computer, appears to be a sleek and snappy palmtop. Actually, this tiny, membrane-keyed device is a desktop computer, and at one time it sold like hotcakes. As the first computer in history to break the $100 price barrier, over a million were purchased. They came with a "whopping" one kilobyte of RAM and used cassette tapes to store data—no floppies or hard drives. Writing programs for the machine was an exercise in precision coding. If you've found a ZX81 in the attic or at a garage sale, this is the page to turn to for lots of fascinating information about it and where to go for help in using it. We had two of them. Net-mom's Dad often enjoyed showing us cool programs he wrote for it, while we were still figuring out the manual for our Apple IIe. Loading from cassette tape was quite a trick, though. This was back in the olden days, when we had to trudge through the snow to buy RAM....

http://www.gre.ac.uk/~bm10/zx81.html

UNIX

UNIX 101: UNIX by Example

Unix is a very popular operating system, found in many variations for many types of computers. Unix commands are different than the ones you may be used to, but you may need to know a little tourist Unix as you travel around the Net. You can learn just enough Unix here.

http://he1.uns.tju.edu:80/unix101/

UNIXhelp for users

Excuse me, but you "grepped" my file while I was "rm"ing it! Unix geeks like to talk like that a lot. But, we admit, Unix is cool. Because of its power, Unix is the operating system that is used by engineers and networking professionals most often. Unix systems don't have to "add" TCP/IP to "plug" into the Internet—it's their native networking language. Now try to guess what operating system was used to expand the Internet into what it is today. You're right, it's Unix. Unix was even used to run Jurassic Park in the movie. At this site you can learn basic Unix commands and be able to translate what the Unix wizards are saying.

http://www.geek-girl.com/Unixhelp/

VIRTUAL REALITY

Hot Virtual Reality Sites

Watch out! A giant batwinged bird is about to swoop down and talk to you. Does that sound impossible? It's not impossible when you are wearing specially designed helmets and data gloves that allow you to view virtual worlds. This page is dedicated to virtual reality news, movies, books, arcade games, hardware, and software. Be careful, those spotted pigs look like they want to play. This list of links is extensive and has not been checked.

http://www.nist.gov/itl/div878/ovrt/hotvr.html

NET FILES

You've always wondered if your brother is an alien from outer space. Now you get your photos back and sure enough, he's got glowing red eyes! What should you do?

Answer: Don't call NASA yet. According to Kodak, this effect sometimes occurs when you use a flash. It's actually the reflection of light from the flash off of the blood vessels inside the subject's eyes. To reduce "red-eye," you need to reduce the size of your subject's pupils so there won't be so much reflective surface available. Increase the light level in the room by turning on all of the lights, or have your subject look at a bright light just before you take the flash picture. Also, some cameras have a red eye reduction feature. To eliminate red eye from pictures you have already taken, you need to manipulate the image electronically. If you have the equipment available to you, you can do it yourself, or you can take the prints to a Kodak digital enhancement station at a retail store. Call Kodak for locations, and visit http://www.kodak.com:80/catHome/faqs/faq.shtml for answers to more frequently asked questions about film and photography!

What is VRML?

It's virtual reality (VR) on the World Wide Web, and stands for Virtual Reality Modeling Language. You can experience the look and feel of VR at the Hot Virtual Reality Sites page.

"Use the source, Luke!"
and look it up in
REFERENCE WORKS.

A
B
C
D
E
F
G
H
I
J
K
L
M
N
O
P
Q
R
S
T
U
V
W
X
Y
Z

A
B
C
D
E
F
G
H
I
J
K
L
M
N
O
P
Q
R
S
T
U
V
W
X
Y
Z

CONSUMER INFORMATION

See also MONEY

Consumer World

OK, you've bought that skateboard you've been wanting. Now it won't even roll! Hustle over to this site to find out what you can do about it. It doesn't matter that you're a kid. You have consumer power, and manufacturers listen to consumers, regardless of their age. While you're there, you can also find out how to avoid online scams, determine if the skateboard has been recalled, and link to the Better Business Bureau. You'll also find out how to contact many companies and other sources of consumer information. Be sure to show this site to your parents—they will love it.

http://www.consumerworld.org/

COOKING, FOOD, AND DRINK

See also COLLECTORS AND COLLECTING

The Dinner Co-op Home Page: for cooks and food-lovers

What's Dad making for dinner? The next time he has no idea, help him try the links on this page. For one thing, there are recipes—LOTS of recipes! We haven't checked all the links, but this site certainly has some interesting stuff. For example, can the color of food suppress your appetite? Have you ever noticed that besides blueberries, no blue food exists in nature? Our brains are just not keyed into seeing a blue thing as a food source. If you want to eat less, put a blue light in your dining room or eat from a blue plate. This page suggests you put a little food-grade food coloring into the water the next time you cook some spaghetti, and try it out on yourself! Don't forget the blue M&M "meatballs"! Find it at <http://www.lava.net:80/~colorcom/appmatters.html>.

http://dinnercoop.cs.cmu.edu/dinnercoop/
   home-page.html

Food Lover's Glossary

Have you ever read a recipe in a cookbook and come across an ingredient that's unfamiliar? This site is a collection of terms to make reading recipes easier. From "abalone" to "Zuppa Inglese," the glossary provides mouth-watering definitions. The terms cover all types of food from all walks of life. There are recipes for every meal of the day and every course of the meal, plus some delightful extras. Check your knowledge against the glossary, but be warned: Don't do it on an empty stomach.

http://foodstuff.com/pearl/gloss.html

HomeArts: Eats

Who doesn't like food? When you think about food, do you think about what is on the plate or how it got there? This site puts together information about food, collected from *Redbook, Good Housekeeping, Country Living*, and other great sources of food news. There are tons of hints on cooking and food preparation for you to explore.

http://homearts.com/depts/food/00dpfdc1.htm

Quasi Comprehensive Candy Bar Wrapper Image Archive

Here's a guy who is easily amused. He collects candy bar wrappers, scans them, and puts them on the Web. Apparently, he's not the only one: he has links to people who do the same thing for gum wrappers, European candy, and Mentos! If you can get past the M&M's, Skittles, Snickers, and Kit-Kats, you may need the Pepto-Bismol pink background.

http://www.math.okstate.edu/~kbradle/snacks/

WELCOME TO Epicurious

You still can't find that extra-special recipe for your doll's dinner party? The publishers of *Bon Appetit* and *Gourmet* magazines give you recipes and a restaurant forum, and they share tips on how to make being in the kitchen a rewarding experience. Check the recipe file and search the forum to locate those hard-to-find holiday cookies. Get basic cookery tips from the original *Fannie Farmer* cookbook!

http://www.epicurious.com/

NET FILES

Do Fish Sleep?

Answer: According to the Florida Aquarium, "Fishes don't sleep like we do, but reef fishes have active and inactive times. Some prefer days; others are active at night. The reef is like a motel with day guests who leave at dusk when night guests arrive." For more answers about fish and ocean life, check http://www.sptimes.com/Aquarium/FA.3.1.html

COOKING FOR BEGINNERS

Big Top's Fun Recipes

If you're having a party or other special occasion, why not take a chance and try some Keroppi Frozen Treats or some Hello Kitty Chocolate Truffle Hearts? The Big Top Frozen Krazy Punch sounds delicious, and the Wacky Popcorn would be a great snack for watching TV.

http://www.bigtop.com/kids/recipes1.html

Blondee Cooks with Kids

Check Blondee's easy pizza recipes, porcupine salad, and butter graham crackers. These nutritious snacks and finger foods are fun to make and delicious, too. You can also send in your own recipe, and Blondee may choose it for her online cookbook!

http://www.familyinternet.com/recipie/bkids.htm

Cooking With Kids - Recipe Links

Visit this site to find over 20 Web sites with easy recipes for kids and interested adults or anyone who is just learning to cook! You'll find recipes for holidays and regular days, breakfasts, lunches, and dinners.

http://www.intex.net/~dlester/pam/recipe/
recipeskids.html

KidsHealth Kid's Recipes

KidsHealth is one of the best family sites on the Net, and their recipes page doesn't disappoint. Whether you're looking for a breakfast treat (pancakes, oatmeal) or a dinner delight (chili, macaroni and cheese), you'll find some great ideas here. Don't miss the snacks either, especially Ants on a Log and Train and Trail Mix.

http://kidshealth.org/kid/games/recipe/index.html

FOODS AND DRINKS

Ben & Jerry's Ice Cream, Frozen Yogurt and Sorbet HomePage

Admit it. How many times have you run to the grocery store because you needed a Ben & Jerry ice cream cone? Now you can get it here without leaving your seat. If you love their ice cream, you will love their site. It's chock-full of the philosophy and wit that makes them so popular. Find out who these guys are, and play with their fun stuff. If you still grieve over the discontinuation of your favorite flavor, make sure to visit the flavor graveyard and find peace of mind knowing that at least they have gone to the great Web page on the Net. If you get a craving for the real thing, don't even try to lick the screen—just go to the store like everyone else. Funny thing, though. They make over 50 products, but only 34 of them are available in supermarkets. For the rest, you have to go to one of their Scoop Shops. Their hottest ice cream flavor is Chocolate Chip Cookie Dough!

http://www.benjerry.com/

A
B
C
D
E
F
G
H
I
J
K
L
M
N
O
P
Q
R
S
T
U
V
W
X
Y
Z

A
B
C
D
E
F
G
H
I
J
K
L
M
N
O
P
Q
R
S
T
U
V
W
X
Y
Z

Butterball

Which do you prefer: light or dark meat? ("Hey!" says the turkey, "It's all the same meat to me!") Turkey is not only a very popular food during the holiday season, it's also a great meal any time of the year. ("Yeah, well so is vegetarian pizza!") Turkey is great, because after the first meal, the leftovers are good for a zillion sandwiches and a delicious soup. ("Ever heard of falafel, pita, and hummus?") At this page, you will find great stuffing recipes, gravy recipes, carving tips, and creative garnishing ideas. ("I'm outta here!")

http://www.butterball.com/

Did you know that the first meal on the Moon was turkey? Astronauts Neil Armstrong and Buzz Aldrin feasted on roast turkey from foil packets. They apparently didn't have any cranberry sauce, though. Stuff yourself with more facts at the Butterball page.

Candy USA

If you eat all that good, healthy food Mom gives you, maybe she'll let you have a treat for dessert. Until then, visit this site, where you'll learn a lot about candy and chocolate. There are candy statistics, nutritional info, candy in the news, and even candy contests! According to this site, "The best-selling kids' candy these days is anything an adult wouldn't normally choose to eat: super sour suckers, candies that color the mouth, anything blue raspberry-flavored, and anything with 'gross out' appeal." Is that true for you and your friends?

http://www.candyusa.org/

CheeseNet

You can slice it, grate it, melt it, and of course you can eat it. What's your favorite way to eat cheese? How is cheese made? Read about the cheese making process, or tour the cheese picture gallery. Read about the differences among cheeses around the world. If you have questions, you can send them to "cheeseologist Dr. Emory K. Cheese" in the Ask Dr. Cheese section. You might be amused by the cheese poetry, then again, maybe not.

http://www.wgx.com/cheesenet/

Dole's 5 a Day

Do you mind your peas and carrots? Learn the nutritional values of the fruits and vegetables that you eat every day. Then fun stuff awaits when you meet Adam Apple, Bobby Banana, and their friends. Try the 5 A Day Game along with them, as they point out how important they are to your well-being. Try some of the delicious recipes provided, and you'll want to bring these friends to your dinner table every day! There's also a virtual tour to the Dole Salad factory—oops, watch out for that radicchio—at <http://www.dole5aday.com/about/factory/factory.html>.

http://www.dole5aday.com/

It was a breakthrough back in 1913. Henry Ginaca, engineer and inventor, unveiled his masterpiece: a machine that could peel, core, and pack 35 pineapples per minute. Wow, the people at the Dole factory were ecstatic! The Ginaca Machine is still used in pineapple canneries today. Dole is more than pineapples, though: check out the Dole's 5 a Day home page.

Food and Cooking Menu

Everything you ever wanted to know about pork, but were afraid to ask Mom, is here. Get some free recipes sent to you by mail (go to "You're Invited" to get these freebies). While you're at this site, look around at all the recipes and pictures. Yum!

http://www.nppc.org/foodandcooking.html

What are the most endangered species in the world (not counting your little brother)?

Frito-Lay

Frito-Lay is more than just corn chips. Their site offers fun, interactive advertising games. You can create your own "dream date" ("Is your dream date punk or preppie?"). Use corn chips to spice up your recipes, and create Chili Pie or a Fiesta Burger. Ever wonder who invented the pretzel? It was invented by a monk in A.D. 610. In other news, Frito-Lay goes through seven and a half *million* pounds of potatoes every day to make potato chips. That's a lot of Ruffles!

http://www.fritolay.com/

Godiva Chocolatier

See how sweet life can be. Godiva Chocolate welcomes you to their playground for chocolate lovers. They tempt your palate with chocolate recipes, trivia, and an online catalog for instant gratification. If only the Web would implement those aroma attribute protocols! You will never forget another anniversary or birthday if you register with their free gift reminder service. If that still isn't enough, they have plenty of links to other chocolate sites to help satisfy your cravings.

http://www.godiva.com/

Hershey Foods Corporation

Crunchy, creamy, drippy like hot fudge or steaming like cocoa—what could be more delicious than chocolate? Where do they make chocolate? Lots of places, but one of them is in Hershey, Pennsylvania, at Hershey's Chocolate Town, U.S.A. This site has fun facts about chocolate at <http://www.hersheys.com/~hershey/hcna/facts/> and a tour of the largest chocolate factory in the world at <http://www.hersheys.com/~hershey/tour/plant.index.html>. This site offers a text-only option for those with slower connections.

http://www.hersheys.com/~hershey/

It never rains on the PARADES in cyberspace.

A
B
C
D
E
F
G
H
I
J
K
L
M
N
O
P
Q
R
S
T
U
V
W
X
Y
Z

M&M's® Factory

When you eat M&M's, which colors do you eat first? Which colors do you avoid? Take a tour of the M&M factory, and play some funny Shockwave games like "Melt the Candy Bar." If you don't have Shockwave, just download the games (Windows or Mac) for use later. Remember, virtual M&M's don't melt in your hand *or* your mouth, but you'll be hungry for some serious chocolate after you visit this site! You can also get screen savers and wallpaper to make sure there is always chocolate in the house when you want some.

http://www.m-ms.com/factory/

The M&M/Mars Factory tour is delicious! Over 2.6 million M&M candies go to the printing machine per hour to receive their "m." Check out the Bakery recipe of the month at M&M's® Factory and peruse the baking hints for techniques on making impeccable cookies. Sign up for a free recipe book, and take a tour of the manufacturing plant to find out just how those little "m's" get on there.

Nabisco: America's Favorite Food Company!

Are you a twister or a dunker? Any way you eat Oreos, they are America's favorite sandwich cookie treat! Discover the stories behind how your favorite snacks came to be—like Fig Newtons, Barnum's Animal Crackers, and Chips Ahoy cookies. Nabisco also offers a section for healthy living, cooking tips, and recipes, and they challenge you to lots of fun games, including finding the Nabisco antenna-thing in *Where's Waldo?*-type crowd pictures.

http://www.nabisco.com/

Oscar Mayer CyberCinema

If you wish you were an Oscar-Mayer wiener, you'll want to spend a lot of time at this site. There are the usual recipes, contests, and company jabbering, but what caught our eye was the interactive History of the Wienermobile. With or without Real Audio, it's hot! The first hot dog on wheels toured the streets of Chicago in 1936. It was only 13 feet long. By the 1950s, the Wienermobile had grown to 22 feet. It had a sound system and a sunroof. By 1958, though, it finally got what it had been lacking all these years. No, it wasn't mustard—it was a bun! Six "Wienebagos" were touring the world by 1988, with the comforts of onboard microwave ovens and other conveniences. In 1995, the latest model was 27 feet long and 10 feet high. We cannot do any better than to quote from the home page: "The model underwent tests in the wind tunnel at the California Institute of Technology in Pasadena and could really, theoretically speaking, haul buns as it reached speeds in excess of 90 miles per hour." Hot dog!

http://www.oscar-mayer.com/

The Pie Page

When is the best time for pie? If you answered, "Anytime!" you are definitely going to enjoy this site, which has recipes for all of your favorite dessert pies and even one for venison pie...mmmm. Seriously, you'll find tips for better pie making here. There's also a step-by-step tutorial on how to make a perfect pie crust.

http://www.teleport.com/~psyched/pie/pie.html

Yum, everyone likes pie! Did you know that a glass pie plate is the best kind to use when you're baking one? Find out more at The Pie Page.

NET FILES

What are stovebolts and why would you find them in the ocean?

Answer: They are the knobby tubercles on the upper jaw of a humpback whale. They appear in distinctive patterns and are used to distinguish whales from each other. No one knows their exact function, but they are thought to be touch-sensitive hair follicles. You can see a picture at http://www.neaq.org/KIDS/vt.ww.stove.html

The Story of Milk

Cows make milk to feed their baby calves. But after the baby is eating other food, the cow continues to make up to eight gallons of milk a day! Cows are milked in a special room called a *milking parlor*, and their milk is pumped to stainless steel holding tanks and immediately chilled to 38 degrees. It waits until the milk tanker truck comes to pick it up. This happens twice a day. When it gets to the milk processing facility, the milk goes through two other steps, homogenization and pasteurization, but you'll have to read about those at this Web site. The main level has cow-related Shockwave games and other fun.

http://www.moomilk.com/tours/tour1-0.htm

> ## Ask not what the Net can do for you, ask what you can do for the Net.

This Page Stinks!

You know that smell from a mile away—it's garlic! Garlic has a wonderful flavor. It makes spaghetti and pizza taste great. It's also good for chasing away garden pests, and it may even be helpful in avoiding cancer. Garlic is also legendary for repelling vampires. Find out more about this fascinating food. The Garlic Page has recipes, health facts, growing tips, and, of course, garlic news. Don't, please don't choose the link from this page labeled "Surprise." We warned you. Although perhaps there might be one of you out there interested in the effects of garlic on medicinal leeches.

http://garcia.broadcast.com/garlic/

Welcome to the Burlingame Museum of Pez Memorabilia

Have you ever had PEZ? They are a fruit flavored candy and are best known for their famous collectible dispensers. The first PEZ dispensers didn't have any heads at all, and now there are over 250 different models. The PEZ Exhibit has detailed pictures of all of the dispensers, with the date of manufacture for each one. You can see which dispensers were made when your parents, and maybe even your grandparents, were born!

http://www.spectrumnet.com/pez/

INTERNATIONAL
EXPO Restaurant Le Cordon Bleu

Are you hankering for some French cooking? Do you want to try some recipes for true gourmet chefs? These recipes are for expert cooks, so don't ask your parents to help you whip up some *Feuilletés de Saumon aux Asperges* after they've just come home from a hard day at the office. These recipes are for special days when everyone is ready for a treat. The site includes recipes for seven special days of cooking. Imagine, a whole week of French food. *Bon appétit!*

http://sunsite.unc.edu/expo/restaurant/restaurant.html

A B C D E F G H I J K L M N O P Q R S T U V W X Y Z

A
B
C
D
E
F
G
H
I
J
K
L
M
N
O
P
Q
R
S
T
U
V
W
X
Y
Z

GUS Gourmet Cookbook

Is your mouth watering for some Chinese food? Here's something even better than takeout! Each week, this site presents one new Chinese recipe that you can make at home. It even shows you how it will look. Get out your chopsticks for a great time!

http://www.gus.net/cook/cook.html

Hawaii's Favorite Recipes

Come tune into Aunty Leilani's Cooking Show and find recipes for tasty Hawaiian dishes. Check out the Internet Island Fruit Salad or the Pineapple Cream Cheese Pie. Although it is more fun to cook these recipes while wearing a traditional Hawaiian print shirt, a lei, sandals, and a straw hat, the results are just as good if you don't. Be sure to drop in and get your name in Hawaiian here, too!

http://www.hisurf.com/Recipes.html

Mama's Cookbook

Do you want to be a great cook? Mama's Italian cookbook is a great place to start! It has recipes for all your favorite Italian meals, plus cooking and pasta glossaries for beginners. If you're not sure which one you want, you can let Mama pick "one of her favorites." There is also a searchable database of recipes if you know what you want and don't want to hunt through the list to find it.

http://www.eat.com/cookbook/

Recipes for Traditional Food in Slovenia

Can you point to Slovenia on the world map? Can you name any Slovenian foods? Get with the program! Check out the recipes for traditional food in Slovenia. There are pictures of the foods and downloadable sound files of the names for many of the dishes. You'll find recipes for all kinds of foods, including a wonderful spring soup and a delicious fish stew.

http://www.ijs.si/slo/country/food/recipes/

Rolling Your Own Sushi

Do you know how to eat with chopsticks? If not, don't worry—sushi is a wonderful finger food. Sushi is a Japanese delicacy that is fun and relatively easy to make. A common misunderstanding about sushi is that it is raw seafood. There is a form of sushi called *sashimi*, which does have raw seafood, but this is different than sushi. Sushi is delicious and (don't tell your parents) it's good for you. Warning: Making sushi involves the use of a sharp knife; be sure to let your parents help you prepare your sushi.

http://www.rain.org/~hutch/sushi.html

What are the ingredients for a California Roll?

If you said imitation crab, avocado, cucumber, rice, and nori (toasted seaweed sheets), you'd be a winner! Find out all about Rolling Your Own Sushi.

VIDEO AND SPY CAMS let you look in on interesting parts of the world.

A
B
C
D
E
F
G
H
I
J
K
L
M
N
O
P
Q
R
S
T
U
V
W
X
Y
Z

SPECIAL DIETS

Asian Kashrus Recipes

Cooking Kosher is a very precise and delicate operation. Finding recipes can be a tedious task. With this collection of Asian Kosher recipes, the job is made easy. There are dozens of recipes for cooking food in a variety of cuisine. Thai, Chinese, and Vietnamese are just a few of the delicious styles listed.

http://www.kashrus.org/recipes/recipes.html

Low-Fat Lifestyle Forum Home Page

Do you hate to eat food that is classified as good for you? The truth of the matter is that "good for you" isn't all liver and spinach. There are a lot of arguments about what "healthy eating" means, but most agree that a low-fat lifestyle is best. This site has cooking and eating tips, as well as recommended cookbooks and loads of easy recipes.

http://www.wctravel.com/lowfat/

The Vegetarian Society UK

Ewwww! Do you dread being told to eat your veggies? Do Brussels sprouts make you hide in the closet? Vegetarian cooking doesn't have to mean tons of icky green food. The Vegetarian Society of the United Kingdom has assembled a list of tasty recipes for every meal, from breakfast to dessert. These pages are also loaded with important facts about nutrition. You'll find some animal rights information here too.

http://www.veg.org/veg/Orgs/VegSocUK/info.html

How many onions should you put in an asparagus and peanut strudel?

One (yum!). Find out about this and other delicious vegetarian recipes at The Vegetarian Society UK.

NET FILES

You'd like to do a neat trick, but you need a piece of equipment with a spoke, a honda, and a loop to do it.

What in the world are those?

Answer: They are the parts to a rope lasso! Check out
http://www.juggling.org/books/lasso/HTML/chap1.html#SECTION0051000000000000000000
for more on this cowboy skill.

CRAFTS AND HOBBIES

See also PEACE

Aunt Annie's Craft Page (tm)

She won't pinch your cheeks and talk about how much you've grown! Aunt Annie *will* give you ideas, patterns, and great directions for doing interesting crafts. She has a new project for you each week, and it's not the usual "handprint-in-the-plaster" craft. Many are paper crafts, like table decorations, paper hats, or toys. Who could ask for a cooler aunt?

http://www.auntannie.com/

The Web in Pig Latin? Make it so in LANGUAGES AND ALPHABETS.

A B **C** D E F G H I J K L M N O P Q R S T U V W X Y Z

Kid Crafts

It may not look like much, but this is it! Recipes for imitation Play-Dough, fake GAK, finger paint, slime, pretend silly putty, and cinnamon ornament dough—it's all here! There is also a recipe for something you can eat, called "Singing Cake." We haven't tried it, but it "sounds" like fun! Sure, you'll find tons of craft ideas here, too. Another version, with even more recipes for fun, is Arts and Crafts Recipes at *<http://www.intex.net/~dlester/pam/preschool/ preschoolideas2.html>*.

http://ucunix.san.uc.edu/~edavis/kids-list/crafts.html

Slime Time!

If you can't wait to be slimed, ooze over to the Kid Crafts home page and prepare some of the slime recipes. You'll learn something about the behavior of polymers in the process.

POLLUTION stinks.

Where did the word "geyser" originate?

Answer: The Geysir, which means "gusher," is a geyser located in Haukadalur, Iceland. All other geysers in the world were named after it. It erupts only rarely these days, but when it does, the water and steam may reach 200 feet in the air! Go to *http://www.wku.edu/www/ geoweb/geyser/location.html* and read all about geysers around the world. There's also a colorful map of worldwide geyser locations.

Kid's Craft Links - At Home Moms Page

There is a wealth of craft ideas here for kids of all ages. They have everything from holiday crafts to bean bags to finger puppets to...well, you get the idea we like this site! One of our favorites is the Michaels Kids Club link at *<http://www.michaels.com/kids/ kid-main.html>*. Michaels is a huge craft store, and they are always dreaming up new ways for you to use their materials. At their Web site, though, you are just using recycled electrons, and there is never a mess to clean up. Don't miss the make-and-decorate-it-yourself gingerbread architecture game—we played with it for a long time, but then we got hungry and had to stop.

http://www.intex.net/~dlester/pam/craft/ craftlinkskids.html

You Can Make Paper

Have you ever seen homemade paper? The rough, uneven edge (called a *deckle*) gives it that homemade look. You can recycle old newspaper or other printed materials into paper pulp. You can even throw in a bit of yucca, lawn grass, flowers, or other plants. Then make your own homemade, natural paper. Try it here!

http://www.nbn.com/youcan/paper/paper.html

NEEDLECRAFT AND SEWING

Welcome to the World Wide Quilting Page

Who would be crazy enough to take something whole, cut it up into a lot of little pieces, and then sew it all back together again? Quilters! What they end up with usually looks pretty spectacular—unless you are the person who created the winning quilt in the Worst Quilt in the World Contest (see it here!). This site provides you with all the information and resources needed to keep you from winning next year's contest.

http://quilt.com/MainQuiltingPage.html

Wonderful Stitches WWW

Are you hooked on cross-stitch or needlepoint? If the answer is yes, then this site is guaranteed to keep you in stitches. Check out what other stitchery enthusiasts have been creating with their busy fingers, then try out some of the decorative stitches featured in the monthly sampler. If you are in need of supplies or want to join a needlework group, put down your needle and look here!

http://www.needlework.com/

ORIGAMI

Arts & Crafts Class

Origami is the Japanese art of paper folding. The word literally means "to fold" (*oru*) "paper" (*kami*). Find a few sheets of square paper, and you can get started with some easy paper-folding projects. Here's an origami crane and a *yakko* (yes, a *yakko* and that's not someone who talks too much!). This site provides graphics and helpful instructions to show you how to fold them.

http://jw.stanford.edu/KIDS/SCHOOL/ART/
kids_arts.html

Joseph Wu's Origami Page

You don't care if you ever see another folded paper crane in your life! OK, relax, you don't have to fold any more cranes. Now you're ready for some intermediate and advanced origami projects. From this page you can download incredible diagrams and instructions for a windmill, butterfly, or basket, among other things!

http://www.datt.co.jp/Origami/

PAPER AIRPLANES

DSW Games

"Next time someone tells you to go fly a kite, you can fly a paper airplane instead!" This graphically amusing site gives you two airplane templates to print out and fold, "guaranteed to make you the Red Baron of the office!" You may need a paper clip and some tape to help trim your flyer, too.

http://www.dsw.com/airplane.htm

Paper Airplane Hangar Page

This site is the ultimate site for learning about, building, and—best of all—flying paper airplanes. You'll find step-by-step instructions, safety tips, and of course, LINKS!

http://www.cs.man.ac.uk/~yeomansb/planes/

CREATION STUDIES

Creation Science

How did life on Earth begin? Some scientists believe life evolved over millions of years. Others believe there are some real problems with the theory of evolution. For instance, how did life originate from dead chemicals? How could man have come from the apes? To see the arguments against the theory of evolution, go to this site.

http://emporium.turnpike.net/C/cs/

EVOLUTION VS. CREATION SCIENCE

Have you ever thought about how Earth began? Or how all the plants and animals came to be? Creation scientists are those who believe that it all came about as described in the Bible. To help form your own theories, investigate this site.

http://web.canlink.com/ocrt/evolutio.htm

A
B
C
D
E
F
G
H
I
J
K
L
M
N
O
P
Q
R
S
T
U
V
W
X
Y
Z

CULTURAL DIVERSITY

Guide to Museums and Cultural Resources on the Web

The Natural History Museum of Los Angeles County invites you to take a virtual tour of all the continents (including Antarctica) and explore museums in each. You may peek inside the Wool Museum in Australia, check out the Information Highway exhibit in Canada, or visit an art museum in Singapore. This will give you a good idea of how many different cultures are in the world and an understanding of what each has to teach.

http://www.lam.mus.ca.us/webmuseums/

NET FILES

"Don't linger too long at the pewter wash basin at the station. Don't grease your hair before starting or dust will stick there in sufficient quantities to make a respectable 'tater' patch. Tie a silk handkerchief around your neck to keep out dust and prevent sunburns. Don't imagine for a moment you are going on a pic-nic; expect annoyance, discomfort and some hardships. If you are disappointed, thank heaven."

http://wellsfargo.com/fr/frsty/ch1/

Answer: These are some of the hints given to passengers traveling by stagecoach from St. Louis, Missouri, to San Francisco, California, in 1877. The trip generally took about 24 days! Read more about it at

---

Get on board, little children, in RAILROADS AND TRAINS.

CURIOSITIES AND WONDERS

Birthstones

Did you know that if you were born in April, your lucky birthstone is the diamond? To find out more about various gemstones and their properties, check this site.

http://mineral.galleries.com/birthsto.htm

The Jackalope Page

Have you ever seen something that looks like a rabbit with antlers? Chances are good that you've never seen such a beast. Do they really exist? Some kids in Wyoming have put together some information on jackalopes, so check it out and see what you think! (Here's a hint, though: You can only hunt jackalopes on June 31.)

http://monhome.sw2.k12.wy.us/projects/jackalope.html

The Notorious Spam Cam

Spam is a registered trademark of a fine product manufactured by the Hormel company. Every month or so, some people with too much time on their hands take out some Spam and put it on a plate with other food items. Then they leave this plate out to decompose. Every afternoon they take another picture of the plate and put it up on the Web. By the 25th day or so things look pretty gruesome. Molds of all colors, fungus, even some things science has not identified yet—this is what you're likely to see as the days lurch on. Don't let your baby sister watch. Please.

http://www.fright.com/cgi-bin/spamcam

Seven Ancient Wonders of the World

Everyone's heard about them, but who can name them? Well, there are the Pyramids, of course, and uh…hmmm. Luckily, there is a list of all of them here, along with pictures and links. Since there are not many of the ancient wonders of the world around anymore, you'll also find a list of the Modern Wonders of the World, as well as the Natural Wonders of the World. There are also pictures and links for wonders such as these: the Great Wall of China, Victoria Falls, and the Eiffel Tower.

http://pharos.bu.edu/Egypt/Wonders/

If you could invite three people throughout history to your house for dinner, who would they be?

"The Three Stooges, just for the pie fights at the end of the meal!"

PARENTING AND FAMILIES—FAMILY FUN

GusTown

Webmasters: Jeff Malkin, Lisa Hoffman, Pat Lewis, R.G. Kelley, Anthony Tarantino, Emme Levine, and Tom Pollock.

http://www.gustown.com

Who came up with the idea for your page or project? Was it you? How did the idea originate?

Gus and the CyberBuds had their first adventure in CyberTown. Since then they have been to Cyberopolis, the Kooky Carnival, CyberStone Park, and the Megarific Museum. The crew at Modern Media Ventures has always been busy working on the Learning Adventure Series, but when the Web started to take off, Gus and the Buds wanted to start a new adventure on the Net. So, GusTown was born.

How many people work on your pages? Does it take a lot of time? How many hits do you get a day?

We have a team of about seven people who work on GusTown. The site is updated once a quarter, and this takes about two weeks to do from brainstorming for ideas to programming the pages. We have been getting hundreds of visitors per day.

You must hear from people all over the world! Can you think of an unusual request, question, or comment someone has sent to you?

We are very happy to say that people from all over the world have been joining the CyberBud Club. We have new members from Australia, Canada, Chile, England, Hong Kong, India, Indonesia, Iran, Israel, Korea, Kuwait, Malaysia, New Zealand, Philippines, Scotland, Singapore, Sweden, Switzerland, Venezuela, and all over the United States.

If this isn't your main job, what do you do, what is your training?

We come from a variety of backgrounds including teaching, filmmaking, art, and music.

What's the one thing you'd really like to do on your page but have not yet implemented?

Gus and the CyberBuds have a large collection of their own original music. The crew at Modern Media Ventures is currently looking into using real-time audio to transmit some of these original songs. When it's done, Gus will be your DJ and you will choose the line-up of tunes.

What are your hopes and fears for the future of the Internet?

We hope that the Net will continue to become available to more and more people and that small companies and individuals with their own small Web pages will always find a home on the Net. We are also concerned about lack of privacy and children's safety on-line.

When you're not using the Net, what do you like to do?

When we are not on the Net we like to play pool, go bike riding, cook, play music, and hang out with our pets.

If you could invite three people throughout history to your house for dinner, who would they be?

The Three Stooges, just for the pie fights at the end of the meal.

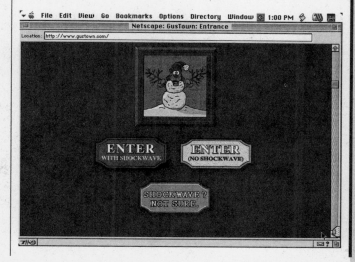

DANCE

Dance Clipart - Introduction

What fun! If you are writing a newsletter or an article for your school paper, or if you want to try making your own stationery at home, here are over 130 dance-related images you can download. You'll even find dance cartoons, symbols, and organization logos with dancers to choose from. So clip away!

http://www.cs.unc.edu/~leech/dance/clipart/

You're at a picnic, and boy is it hot! You want a can of soda, so you go to the ice chest to get one. All the ice has melted, and the cans are in cold water. You notice all the diet soda is floating, while the stuff with real sugar in it has sunk to the bottom.

Why is that?

http://www.zia.com/tech/exp/c0692.html

experiments at

certain volume. You can learn more and try some cool chocolate milk. Density is the amount of mass in a milkshake with ice cream is denser than a glass of substances. You know that a glass of chocolate called density, and chemists use it to identify various weigh more, so it sinks to the bottom. This property is same. The extra sugar in the regular soda makes it hold the same amount of soda, they don't weigh the **Answer:** Although both cans are the same size and

Wet or dry, give AMPHIBIANS a try!

Dancing for Busy People

You may have heard of square dancing, but how good is your round dance? When someone yells, "Hey, how about a Sicilian circle!" do you jump on the dance floor, ready to go? Whether your mescolanza needs a makeover or your line dance needs to be straightened, visit this site to get an encyclopedia of popular community dances, instructions, and links to other featured Web sites!

http://www.henge.com/~calvin/

The European Dance Server

Try to keep your feet still while you explore this page—we dare you! You'll find links to ballroom dancing, square dancing, round dancing, and contra dancing. Try a Highland fling or maybe a samba. Dance your way through cyberspace, and start here.

http://www.dance.co.uk/

The Performer's Edge Magazine

Are you interested in dancing competitively but don't know how to get started? Are you already performing but still get nervous during auditions? You might also be wondering about foot and ankle problems in dance, or how to sew those beautiful costumes you want to wear. This site may answer your dance questions. *Performer's Edge* started in 1991 as a regional publication. Now it's internationally circulated as an invaluable how-to resource guide for students and teachers of dance. The online site includes excerpts of the news briefs and articles from the most recent bimonthly issue, and it lists the table of contents from all prior issues. Each issue contains information about dance performance and auditions, professional career possibilities, costuming, dance medicine, and more. If you are a serious dancer, you won't want to miss this one.

http://arts-online.com/edge.html

The Web in Pig Latin? Make it so in LANGUAGES AND ALPHABETS.

A B C D E F G H I J K L M N O P Q R S T U V W X Y Z

STOMP - SEE WHAT ALL THE NOISE IS ABOUT

Oh, man! Your parents are dragging you to see some stage show at the theater, and you think you'll be bored. All of a sudden, some guys come out on stage banging on trash cans and pipes, dancing a rhythm with push brooms, and in general making so much noise that no one hears you when you yell, "Hey! Who *are* these guys?" You've just been introduced to STOMP, the hot new dance show from the British Isles. This Web page lets you hear some fantastic beats created with everyday materials, and if you go to the study area of this site you'll find some sound and noise experiments that you can try at home.

http://www.usinteractive.com/stomp/home.html

AFRICAN DANCE

C. K. Ladzekpo - African Music and Dance

"The Africans Are Coming, The Africans Are Coming" is the largest seasonal, professional African cultural arts extravaganza in the U.S. Directed by C. K. Ladzekpo, the African Dance Ensemble has been performing since 1973 and continues to stand for tradition and creativity. Dance, especially ethnic dance, is characterized by music, costume, and tradition, and you'll find all of that here! Lots of video (and audio) clips feature the colorful and vibrant dance and percussion ensemble music of West Africa.

http://cnmat.cnmat.berkeley.EDU/~ladzekpo/

BALLET

Body and Grace

Here you can learn about the history of the American Ballet Theatre (ABT) through photographer Nancy Ellison's electronic exhibition, "Body and Grace." This is a wonderful collection of photos, which starts with the ABT's beginning in 1940 and includes such historical greats as Agnes de Mille, as well as portraits of the current ABT hierarchy: principals, soloists, and corps de ballet.

http://www.i3tele.com/photo_perspectives_museum/
    faces/bodyandgrace/html/abt.html

CyberDance — Ballet On The Net

If ballet is your life, you may want to take a break from your barre exercises long enough to check out this wonderful collection of U.S. and Canadian classical and modern ballet resources. Included is a complete list of professional, regional, and school-affiliated ballet companies. You'll find their addresses and phone numbers, ticketing information, and their touring schedules. The link to the Boston Ballet, among others, even includes a spotlight on their solo and principal dancers. Find out what motivates 20-year-old Pollyana Ribeiro to keep trying new things. It doesn't stop there: you'll find articles, reviews, FAQs, e-zines, and lots of great links, including one to the New York Public Library, which boasts the best dance collection in the world!

http://www.thepoint.net/~raw/dance.htm

ARTHUR Mitchell

made history as the first African American male to become a permanent member of a major ballet company when he joined the New York City Ballet in 1955. His talents helped him rise quickly to the position of principal dancer. When Dr. Martin Luther King, Jr. was killed in 1968, Mitchell decided to do something to provide children in Harlem (in New York City) with the kinds of opportunities he had been given. That same summer, he began giving dance classes in a remodeled garage. The next year, he founded the Dance Theatre of Harlem. Now, this world-renowned organization has grown into a multi-cultural facility, serving students and dancers from the United States as well as from around the world. Learn more about this dance company, and others, at Cyber-Dance—Ballet on the Net.

A
B
C
D
E
F
G
H
I
J
K
L
M
N
O
P
Q
R
S
T
U
V
W
X
Y
Z

A
B
C
D
E
F
G
H
I
J
K
L
M
N
O
P
Q
R
S
T
U
V
W
X
Y
Z

NET FILES

Who invented the first pretzel?

Answer: Legend has it that a sixth-century Italian monk used to give out these doughy treats to children who were good during Mass. The pretzel shape is supposed to represent arms crossed in prayer, and the three holes represent the Father, Son, and Holy Spirit. It may be the world's oldest snack food! Read more about the pretzel and its fascinating history at http://libertynet.org/iha/_pretzel.html

WebMuseum: Degas, Edgar

Edgar Degas was a French Impressionist painter in the late 1800s, and he's acknowledged as a master of drawing the human figure in motion. What better subject for his paintings than the ballet dancer? This special Degas exhibit includes works from the Fogg Museum in Cambridge, Massachusetts, the Metropolitan Museum of Art in New York, the National Gallery in Washington, D.C., and the Musée d'Orsay in Paris. Come browse and enjoy these wonderful pastel drawings and oil paintings portraying the grace and form of ballet dancers on stage and off. While you're in the WebMuseum, be sure to check out the works by other famous painters as well.

http://watt.emf.net/wm//paint/auth/degas/

POLUTION STINKS

FOLK DANCING

The Bassett Street Hounds Morris Dancers

As early as the 1500s, groups of dancers in the Cotswold region of western England were donning their bells and colorful ribbons and welcoming the spring season with a ritual folk dance. Morris dancing on the Net now boasts a worldwide representation from well over 100 teams. Read more about the history of Morris dancing and its various styles (Cotswold, Border, Longsword, and Northwest), all of which are part of the Hounds' repertoire. From this site, you can connect to a searchable archive of the Morris Dance Discussion List and "all known" other Morris-related Web pages.

http://web.syr.edu/~htkeays/morris/hounds/index.html

NET FILES

Each box of Barnum's Animal Crackers contains 22 cookies, with an assortment of 17 animals. How many animals can you guess?

Answer: According to the Nabisco page of Animal Cracker History at http://www.nabisco.com/museum/barnums.html you may find any of the following animals in your box: tiger, cougar, camel, rhinoceros, kangaroo, hippopotamus, bison, lion, hyena, zebra, elephant, sheep, bear, gorilla, monkey, seal, and giraffe. But it wasn't always like that. Learn how the animal lineup has changed since the cookies were first made in 1902.

California Heritage Dancers

Most "folks" in the United States don't know much about their own folk dance heritage. Dances done by the earliest settlers are all but forgotten, and the California Heritage Dancers aim to change all that. Their repertoire includes dances from the earliest Colonial times to the modern day. You'll see costumes and hear tunes from the Appalachians in the early 1800s. You'll hear some foot-stompin' calls from frontier Western dances, and you'll be amazed at some of the gowns, petticoats, and other clothing women used to wear to dress up! Did you know that automaker Henry Ford was a great square dancer?

http://www.heritagedance.com/index.html

NET FILES

Twin sisters of identical height walk into the same room. All of a sudden, one of them looks tiny, while one is a giant! Their parents are upset, but they calm down when one of the twins points out that it's only an Ames Room.

What's that?

Answer: It's a specially constructed room that creates an optical illusion. It's named for American psychologist Adelbert Ames, Jr., who was the first to build one, back in 1946. If you look into the room through a carefully placed peephole, the person standing in the left corner always appears small, while the person in the opposite corner looks much bigger. The room looks like it's a normal rectangle—but the floor, windows, ceiling, and doors are all trapezoids! Read more about this tricky room and how you can build one at http://www.illusionworks.com/amesrm.htm

Take a ride on a Carousel in AMUSEMENT PARKS.

I F D O Home Page

Folk dancing is both fun to watch and fun to do. The International Folk Dancers of Ottawa bring together the traditional social dances and authentic music of many countries and cultures. Here you can find schedules and other information about folk dancing in Ottawa and then link to lots of other folk dance resources on the WWW. Check out Chang's Folk Dancers HomePage and step-hop-step to the "Salty Dog Rag" at <http://www.fmdata.com/bbrux/changs/>. Song Chang was born in Sweden and began his International Dance Group in the basement of his San Francisco home in 1938. Then, go halfway around the world (without even leaving your chair) to try some Scottish country dances at a server in Germany at <http://www.tm.informatik.uni-frankfurt.de/strathspey/what-is-scd.html>!

http://lucas.dfl.doc.ca/ifdo.html

Web Cloggers

OK, now you shuffle, step, step...then shuffle, step, shuffle, step...right foot then left. Traditionally associated with the Southern Appalachian Mountains, clogging (or clog dancing) is becoming more popular with young and old all around the world. This site is a great place for cloggers to find out what's happenin'. You'll find lists (and links) to upcoming events and clogging-related merchandise, books and videos, plus there's lots of space for clogging instructors and dance groups to post their own information. So come on, let's dance! If you're still unclear on clogging, check <http://members.aol.com/mdevin/clogtext.html> "What is Clogging?" for an explanation of what cloggers look like, what they wear, and what's on their feet!

http://www.clogging.com/

Lost your marbles? Find them in GAMES AND FUN.

A
B
C
D
E
F
G
H
I
J
K
L
M
N
O
P
Q
R
S
T
U
V
W
X
Y
Z

HULA AND POLYNESIAN DANCING

Hawai'i's H4 - Hula Section

Aloha from Hawaii! The *hula* (Hawaiian for "dance") expresses the culture of the islands in a unique combination of colorful costumes and rhythmic hip and arm movements. This "photo album" contains screen shots from the TV coverage of the Twentieth Annual Queen Liliuokalani Keiki Hula Festival and Competition. You don't have to cross the *moana* (ocean), *kai* (sea), or *mauna* (mountain) to enjoy the spirit of the hula—just grab your *lei* (wreath of flowers worn around the neck) and point your browser toward this colorful site!

http://www.hotspots.hawaii.com/hula.html

NATIVE AMERICAN DANCE

Pow Wow Dancing

The powwow drum brings the heartbeat of the Earth Mother to the gathering of Native American tribes. You can see many traditional dances at these spiritual festivals, from the colorful and exciting Fancy Dress dance to the sacred Kiowan Gourd Dance. This site explains some of the dances and the traditions surrounding the costumes. You'll also learn proper etiquette regarding the drum and the head singer. Check the schedule to see if a powwow is planned near your home!

http://www.scsn.net/users/pgowder/dancing.htm

TAP DANCE

E-TAP! PRODUCTIONS' TAP DANCE PAGE

This site not only tells you about tap dance, it also lets you *hear* the various steps and variations. Remember: step right, shuffle, step left—and don't wear sneakers to tap class!

http://www.imperium.net/~papadali/

The wonderful world of worms may be admired in the section called INVERTEBRATES.

Tap Dance Homepage

Did you know that May 25 is National Tap Dance Day, signed into law by President Bush in 1989? Don't wait until then to find all the neat information about tap dancing at this site. If you're getting your shim sham confused with your paddle and roll, then refer to the Tap Steps glossary (and instructions) to set you straight. The Sites and Sounds of Tap section includes video clips and recordings. There's an events calendar, book list, tap trivia, and lots more. The Who's Who section lists tap companies and has bios of some of tap's greatest from today and yesterday, such as Gregory Hines, Hank Smith, Fred Astaire, and Bill "Bojangles" Robinson, whose birthday was—you guessed it—May 25, 1878!

http://www.allegheny.edu/~corrp/tap/

"My toes are the sticks, and the floor is the drum," says Ira Bernstein, dancer. Not just any *dance*, though. Ira does tap dancing, Appalachian clogging, English clogging, French-Canadian step dancing, Cape Breton step dancing, Jitterbug swing dancing, and Cajun and Zydeco dancing. Because the sound of each dance is just as important as the look of it, he wears a variety of footwear when he performs: tap shoes, wooden clogs, fiberglass-tipped shoes, and rubber boots. These produce different tones, volumes, and dynamics of sound necessary for the different dances. You can hear a brief audio clip of Ira clog dancing in the Sounds of Tap area on the Tap Dance Homepage.

Salute the nations of cyberspace in FLAGS.

DINOSAURS AND PREHISTORIC TIMES

Dinosaur Art and Modeling

Now here's something different! If you really love dinosaurs, you won't want to miss these exhibits. Here are the works of the world's most well-known dinosaur artists and model makers, including animatronic model makers, known for creating the moving dinosaurs in movies. Lifelike paintings, action sculptures, and life-size models created for museums are all included here.

http://www.indyrad.iupui.edu/dinoart.html

The Dinosaur Society

Usually, people join wildlife societies to help save endangered species; this organization helps save animals *already* extinct. Read all about Sue the dinosaur: seems she died about 65 million years ago, and her fossilized remains were discovered in 1980, near Faith, South Dakota. There was a dispute about who really owned the skeleton, the FBI seized her, and she's being held, pending an auction! You can read all about it here. You can also visit a dig and join the Society online.

http://www.dinosociety.org/

The Dinosauria

Can we start making new live dinosaurs from DNA, as in the movie *Jurassic Park*? No way! There's a lot of good scientific reasons why cloning dinosaurs would be impossible. Visit "Dinosaurs—Movies vs. Reality" at <http://www.ucmp.berkeley.edu/diapsids/popular.html> to find out why. Packed with scientific information about dinos and prehistoric times, some of the exhibits here are narrated by scientists.

http://www.ucmp.berkeley.edu/diapsids/dinosaur.html

Visit historic sites via the Net in HISTORY.

The Field Museum of Natural History

Virtually visit the "Life Over Time" exhibit at the Field Museum of Natural History! Watch movies of the albertosaurus, the moropus, the triceratops, the camel, and the sabertooth cat. Test your knowledge of the prehistoric age. Enter the sweepstakes to start a new species, and listen to mammoth bone music. A teachers' guide to the exhibits provides a bibliography, so you can read more about the dinosaurs and other prehistoric animals.

http://www.bvis.uic.edu/museum/

The Field Museum of Natural History Exhibits

Where can you see pictures of dinosaurs, hear their names pronounced, and then watch them run? You can do all of this and more by visiting the exhibit pages at the world-famous Field Museum of Natural History. Here you can see birds dodge Jurassic dinosaurs and listen to the Triassic forecast (1-900-CLIMATE) on the dinosaur weather report. Tours include the following: "Life Before Dinosaurs"; "Dinosaurs!"; "Teeth, Tusks, and Tarpits: Life After Dinosaurs." Make tracks to go see it!

http://rs6000.bvis.uic.edu/museum/exhibits/Exhibits.html

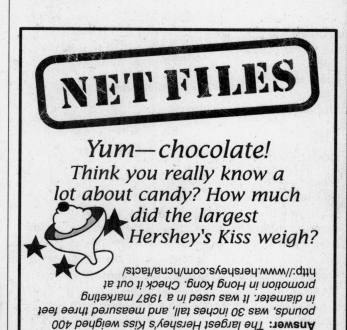

A
B
C
D
E
F
G
H
I
J
K
L
M
N
O
P
Q
R
S
T
U
V
W
X
Y
Z

NET FILES

What is the largest soap bubble ever made?

SOAP

Answer: David Stein holds the official Guinness record for the longest bubble: 50 feet by 2 feet in diameter. He used his own patented invention, The Bubble Thing. See some pictures at http://bubbles.org/fpbhpd.htm

Funky Dinosaur Land

You want the best links, articles, reference material, and pictures of dinos on the Net? It's here, it's *all* here, in one fantastic dino delight! It will take a while to download the page of art, because it displays thumbnails of all of the dino pictures. You won't find a photograph of a real, live dinosaur, though. Do you know why?

http://www.comet.net/dinosaur/

Hadrosaurus

Where in the world was the first, nearly complete skeleton of a dinosaur found? It was found in Haddonfield, New Jersey. In the summer of 1858, vacationing fossil hobbyist William Parker Foulke led a crew of workmen digging "shin deep in gray slime." Eventually he found the bones of an animal, larger than an elephant, that once swam and played about the coastline of what is now Pennsylvania. Read about the discovery that started our fascination with dinosaurs!

http://www.levins.com/dinosaur.html

Honolulu Community College Dinosaur Exhibit

Sometimes it's great to read all about dinosaurs. And sometimes it's more fun to look at pictures. Hey, how about looking at all kinds of fossils and sculptures while someone reads to you? Here you can see the dinosaur bones and sculptures while listening to one of the exhibit's founders talk about them! These fossils are replicas of the originals at the American Museum of Natural History in New York City.

http://www.hcc.hawaii.edu/dinos/dinos.1.html

Introduction - The Mammoth Saga

This virtual exhibition of mammoths, other animals, and plants of the ice ages is based on an exhibition held at the Swedish Museum of Natural History in Stockholm, Sweden. In it, you'll explore the U.S. Midwest of 16,000 years ago and take a look at a woolly rhinoceros, a sabertooth cat, and ancient reindeer. Siberian nomads lived in huts made of mammoth bones, and you can see a re-creation of one here! There are also nice links to other places on the Web that will help you learn more.

http://www.nrm.se/virtexhi/mammsaga/
    welcome.html.en

The Official Royal Tyrrell Museum Web Site

Take a virtual tour of this famous museum in Alberta, Canada. You can stay on the guided tour, or you can use the virtual maps to go from exhibit to exhibit in any order you want! There are fantastic dinosaur exhibits with lots of pictures, and you'll find information on the second floor in Dinosaur Hall. In addition to all of the dinosaurs, you can visit a *paleoconservatory*, which is a greenhouse full of primitive plants. Try the link to Dinosaur Provincial Park, where most of the museum's exhibits have been excavated.

http://tyrrell.magtech.ab.ca/

Do you know the way to San Jose? If not, check a map in GEOGRAPHY.

DISNEY

See also AMUSEMENT PARKS; MOVIES

Disney - Disney.com Home Page

Oh yes, the magical world of Disney! The Walt Disney Company produces movies, television shows, and music, and they are nearly all fun. If you want to keep up on the latest from the folks at Disney, take a look at their official home page. You'll find clips from recent Disney movies, which you can play on your computer. You can listen to recordings from the Disney Channel. You can also get all kinds of great graphic images of your favorite Disney characters. There is much, much more. If you like Disney, this is a must-see.

http://www2.disney.com/

Hidden Mickeys of Disney

Look at a picture of Mickey Mouse: notice that his head is made of three circles—a big one for the head and two smaller ones for his ears. Did you know that the people who designed the Disney theme parks have hidden Mickey Mouse all over the place? It's true. At the Magic Kingdom, Epcot Center, Disney–MGM Studios, and even in the Disney hotels, Mickey Mouse's image is hidden in all kinds of unusual places. At Disney World, these three circles are concealed everywhere, from lakes to ceiling fans. Check this site to find out where Mickey is hiding, plus loads of other Disney secrets!

http://www.oitc.com/Disney/

John's Mostly Mermaid Page

John has collected just about everything on Disney films such as *The Lion King, Sleeping Beauty, Aladdin,* and *Beauty and the Beast.* He has complete scripts for many of these movies, so you can print them out and follow along with the movie when Ariel (*The Little Mermaid*) says, "Walking around on those...what do you call them...feet?" The main focus here is on Ariel, but he does try to give other movies equal time. Lots of graphics are here for you to download, plus links to other Disney sites around the Net.

http://http.tamu.edu:8000/~jvs6403/

The Ultimate Disney Link Page

Disney is all over the Internet. This site is a good place to begin exploring Disney Internet sites. Here you'll find links to Disney theme parks, a hodgepodge of Disney fan pages, and connections to just about anything else that's Disney. Created by Disney World cast member Ed Sterrett, this truly is the ultimate Disney site!

http://www.magicnet.net/~tudlp/

A Visit to Yesterland

Disneyland hasn't always been as it is now. New attractions have been added and old ones have been replaced. Some of those old attractions were really good, and it's too bad they are gone. With the magic of the Internet, though, you can visit many of those attractions here. You can wander into Adventure Through Inner Space, take a ride on the Flying Saucers, or mosey down the People Mover. You'll learn when these and other rides started and ended, and you'll get a good idea of what Disneyland was like for your parents or maybe your older brothers and sisters.

http://www.mcs.net/~werner/yester.html

NET FILES

What's the longest-lived mammal on Earth? What's the second longest-lived mammal?

Answer: Man has the longest life of all mammals, but the spiny anteater comes in second with a life expectancy of 50 years. Read more about this unusual egg-laying mammal at http://edx1.educ.monash.edu.au/~juanda/vcm/gary.htm

NET FILES

Which would you rather be in the middle of: "Mills Mess" or "Burke's Barrage"?

Answer: Actually, if you aren't a juggler (and a good one at that), you'd better not get in the middle of either one! These are two difficult juggling tricks. Hey, don't even worry if you're just starting out, you'll find juggling help and information at http://www.juggling.org/

Walt Disney Pictures

The folks who brought you *Pocahontas*, *The Lion King*, *A Goofy Movie*, and *Toy Story* have their home page here. There's a bunch of video, sound, and color images of movies that have been released and also of movies currently in production. If you're hopelessly "techno-clueless" and can't get your audio or movie files to play, Disney's help files can really help (click on the HELP button). Find out how to see the video and hear the movie themes by linking to whatever software you need.

http://www.disney.com/DisneyPictures/

Curl up with a good Internet site.

Welcome to Walt Disney Records

"Be Our Guest" at this treasure chest of sounds from Disney movies. Whether you're in the mood for just "The Bare Necessities" (*The Jungle Book*) or something a little more exotic like "Hakuna Matata" (*The Lion King: Rhythm of the Pride Lands*), you'll find it here. Samples of all the latest music are available, but don't forget about the music from oldies such as *Fantasia* and *Mary Poppins*. Also, you'll find some information about each movie and how it was made.

http://www.disney.com/DisneyRecords/

THEME PARKS

Disneyland Paris

Disneyland Paris gives folks in Europe a more convenient opportunity to visit a Disney park. A picture tour of Disneyland Paris and information about the park are available here. Until the official Web page comes online at *<http://www.disney.fr/dlp/>* if you'd like to visit Disneyland Paris, this is the Web page for you!

http://www.informatik.tu-muenchen.de/
~schaffnr/etc/disney/

Disneyland Park - Anaheim, California

Disneyland is the first of all the Disney parks, and some claim it has a special charm no other can match. At this Web site, dedicated Disneyland fan Doug Krause has pulled together a slew of information and pictures for anyone interested in visiting Disneyland in California. You'll find the usual park info here, plus some really unusual stuff. For example, there's a list of the memorabilia inside the Disneyland Fortieth Anniversary time capsule, which won't be opened until 2035. There's also Walt Disney's own chili recipe, so get in here and chow down!

http://www2.best.com/~dijon/disney/parks/disneyland/

SLIME is a polymer, as anyone who's read CHEMISTRY knows!

Tokyo Disneyland Official Home Page

Disneyland's Japanese version is called Tokyo Disneyland. With all the appeal of other Disney parks, you can see the sights of Disneyland—the Far East version. It's fun to see what's familiar and what's different at this park. There are also some interactive games you can play. This site is available in English as well as Japanese and Chinese.

http://www.tokyodisneyland.co.jp/

Walt Disney World Home Page

Going to Disney World? At this site, you'll find out everything you need to know about The Magic Kingdom, Epcot, Disney–MGM Studios, plus other attractions in the Orlando, Florida, area.

http://www.travelweb.com/thisco/wdw/wdwhome/wdw.html

DOGS AND DOG SPORTS

See also MAMMALS—WOLVES AND DOG FAMILY; PETS AND PET CARE

2000 DOG NAMES: Naming Your Puppy

Dad says you can keep that puppy who followed you home; now all you need is a name. Let's see, how about Sammy? That's the most popular dog name in North America, according to this Web site. Of course, if you want a really unusual name, you could pick one of the thousands of names here, like Angstrom or maybe Tsunami. This site also ranks dog breeds by their intelligence. The Border collie is listed first—after *your* dog, of course!

http://vanbc.wimsey.com/~emandel/dognames/

Belgian Games

Stupid dog tricks—sure, this site has some really silly tricks, but you'll find some useful ones here, too. How about teaching your dog to start pawing you when your alarm clock goes off? You could teach your dog to collect your toys and put them away for you or to look for your mom's lost car keys. Or you could teach your dog to nod on command; then, when you ask your furry friend to respond to a question like "Aren't I the best, smartest, and most good-looking owner you could ever have?" the dog will always nod an enthusiastic "Yes!" The directions for how to teach these tricks are at *<http://www.hut.fi/~mtt/training.html>*.

http://www.hut.fi/~mtt/belg_tricks.html

Canine Companions National WebSite

Have you ever seen a blind person and guide dog team? Did you ever wonder how dogs for the blind are trained? How about a hearing or signal dog, who teams up with deaf people? These animals go to their owners to signal when a noise is heard. They will signal on ringing door bells and phones, smoke alarms, crying babies, and much more. There are also therapy dogs and special canine companions who know how to help disabled people. Find out about this very interesting class of working dogs here!

http://www.caninecompanions.org/

PetChannel: Dogs

Does your dog love to watch the Pet Channel on TV? Then your dog will really wag his or her tail at this Web version! If you're looking for a canine companion, you can look through pages on over 200 breeds. There are also links to dog names, health care, dog food companies, and much more. You can also submit your own dog poetry, stories, and tributes to your pet. If you want to make your own home page to honor your dog, you can build one here.

http://www.petchannel.com/dogs/index.htm

Take a closer look through the microscope in BIOLOGY.

AMPHIBIANS! Visit the Froggy Page before you croak.

A
B
C
D
E
F
G
H
I
J
K
L
M
N
O
P
Q
R
S
T
U
V
W
X
Y
Z

A
B
C
D
E
F
G
H
I
J
K
L
M
N
O
P
Q
R
S
T
U
V
W
X
Y
Z

Professional Dog Networks

Gee, those puppies in the pet store look awfully cute! But wait—before you buy a registered dog, you should know a lot more, and you may not find the answers in the pet store. Some breeds have medical problems that are genetically passed on to the pups. How do you know you won't be getting a puppy with these health problems—many of which can be expensive to treat, if not life-threatening to your best pal? The best way to avoid these problems is to buy from a trustworthy dog breeder. These folks will often let you meet your pup's mom and dad, as well as show you their medical test results and health records. A good breeder will know about and discuss any genetic problems with the breed you're investigating. Maybe you're looking for a quiet dog or an energetic dog. Breeders often "temperament test" their puppies, and they can help match you with a dog that fits your personality.

This site lists breeders for various recognized dog breeds, but you could also find a list in an established dog magazine at the bookstore or public library. You should know that there are "good" pet stores as well as "bad" dog breeders. But the important thing is that you need to know a lot about where the dog's been and his parents' health background. At this page, you'll also find information about the many "breed rescue clubs" around the world. These are people who love, for example, golden retrievers. They "rescue" these dogs from animal shelters and try to place them in adoptive homes. You'll also learn about groups that try to find homes for retired racing greyhounds.

http://www.prodogs.com/index.htm

Pug Park

The admission booth to this amusement park says "Pugs: FREE! Humans FREE when accompanied by a Pug!" Pick up your map to Pug Park and learn all about these little dogs and their big fans. Although focused on pugs, the general information about dog care provided in this site applies to every breed. Don't miss the pug bumper cars or the recipes for pug cakes and cookies.

http://alohi.ucdavis.edu/~len/pugpark/pugpark.html

Online LIBRARIES rock!

rec.pets.dogs FAQ Homepage

This comprehensive site will give you information on everything, from picking the best breed for you to showing your dog in obedience trials to health care. The Working Dogs area will tell you about sled dogs, search and rescue dogs, and even narcotics-sniffing dogs. Don't bark up the wrong tree—curl up with your puppy and this Web site!

http://www.zmall.com/pet_talk/dog-faqs/

Don't try to get your sled dogs running by yelling "MUSH!"

The word the dogs are expecting is "HIKE!" Now you're moving! Mushers know that to turn teams right, they yell "Gee," and for a left turn, "Haw!" You'll have to check the Working Dogs area of the **rec.pets.dogs FAQ Homepage** to find out how to get them to slow down!

Welcome to the AKC

The AKC is the largest registry of purebred dogs in the United States. Here you'll find a list of the breeds they recognize, a roster of recent obedience and show winners, and information on the AKC's many educational activities. You'll also find a list of breed clubs and contacts, as well as a breeder's directory.

http://www.akc.org/

EARTH SCIENCE

GLOBE Home Page

GLOBE stands for Global Learning and Observations to Benefit the Environment. It's an environmental education and science partnership of students, teachers, and scientists initiated to increase environmental awareness throughout the world and to contribute to a better understanding of Earth. Students take measurements and make observations of the weather at their schools and share their data via the Internet with other students and scientists around the world. All the details are patched together to make a view of the world as it's seen through the student findings at 3,000 schools in over 40 countries.

http://www.globe.gov/

NET FILES

What did Nero, emperor of ancient Rome, use to improve his viewing of the gladiators?

Answer: *The emperor was known to use a large emerald to give him a better view of the "the games." Concave gemstones were discovered to be useful as magnifying lenses in ancient times. Beam over to* http://www.duke.edu/~tj/hist/hist_mic.html *to read more about the history of lenses and optics.*

GSC Atlantic's Earth Science Site of the Week

This is a growing one-stop earth science shop, where you'll find links to everything from atmospheric studies to volcanology. Check out the current site of the week or visit the past site archive. There's an easy-to-use subject index as well as chronological listings. You can nominate your favorite earth science site for inclusion, too!

http://agcwww.bio.ns.ca/misc/geores/sotw/sotw.html

CLIMATE—ACID RAIN
You Can & Acid Rain

How can rain be an acid? It starts out as regular rain, but then it falls through air pollution. It becomes a weak acid that can dissolve marble, kill trees, and ruin a lake's entire ecosystem. You can help. Here's how to make an acid finder and how to test rainwater. Let Beakman and Jax explain this phenomenon, first identified in England in 1872. Smoke from burning coal was the cause then, as it remains now.

http://pomo.nbn.com/youcan/acid/acid.html

CLIMATE—GREENHOUSE EFFECT
Air

Someone in a colder climate might think the greenhouse effect is a good thing, especially for those who don't like the cold. However, there are consequences connected with having more planetwide heat than usual, and this doesn't just mean less snow to play in. Find out all about the greenhouse effect at the Australian Environmental Resources Information Network.

http://kaos.erin.gov.au/air/air.html

DAY AND NIGHT
Earth and Moon Viewer

When it's 10 A.M. and bright and sunny in Florida, what's it like in Japan? Stop by this site and ask their server, which will show where it's light and dark any place in the world. You can choose the satellite location to view from, or you can tell it to look at Earth from the Sun's or Moon's perspective. You can even create a custom request and specify the desired longitude and latitude you want to see; the computer then picks the best viewpoint.

http://www.fourmilab.ch/earthview/vplanet.html

ECOLOGY AND ENVIRONMENT

The Green Page

Developed by high school students, this is an annotated guide to many of the best environmental science Web pages and projects out there. They don't hold back on their opinions of the ones they don't like, either!

http://www.vcomm.net/enviro/greenpg.html

Harlem Environmental Access Project Home Page

Did you know that a family of four throws away 80 to 150 pounds of garbage a week? If we recycle rather than buy new items, we can generate less garbage. This home page and its parent page, The Environmental Defense Fund, at <http://www.edf.org> has Fast Facts on recycling and many other resources on environmental issues, such as rain forests and renewable energy. Don't miss the instructions for starting a composting program in your school!

http://www.edf.org/heap/

NET FILES

What are turkey wings, lion's paws, buttercups, and pear whelks?

Answer: They are a few of the more than 160 varieties of shells you might find along the beaches of Florida's Sanibel-Captiva Islands. You can see pictures and learn more at http://www.usa-chamber.com/sanibel-captiva/shelling.html

Missouri Botanical Garden Learning Network

A *biome* is the collection of creatures and plants living in a particular region. Explore six different biomes here: grassland, rain forest, taiga, deciduous forest, desert, and tundra. You'll learn about the features of each area and its plants and animals. You don't have a clue what living in the taiga is like? Ask a kid at a school in Finland or Russia—links to schools in each biome area are included here!

http://www.mobot.org/MBGnet/index2.htm

National Wildlife Federation: Education, Teacher Resource

Looking for projects and information on a variety of environmental subjects? Check these out: air, habitat, people and the environment, wildlife and endangered species, and water. Sound good? Each topic includes general background information, class activities, fun facts, and a glossary of terms. How about a random riddle from Ranger Rick? There are also suggestions of things you can do to help!

http://www.igc.apc.org/nwf/ed/

Teacher and Student Home Page

Earthwatch takes ordinary people on extraordinary research expeditions. Of course, you pay for the privilege of counting katydids or helping to save a coral reef. But when you get back, you'll have a great story to tell about how you spent your summer vacation! This page archives some of the field notes and lesson plans developed from past trips, and it's interesting to see which ecological "hot spots" they will attend to next.

http://www.earthwatch.org/ed/

GEOLOGY

US Geological Survey: Ask a Geologist

Have you ever wondered why earthquakes happen in some places but not in others? Why does Hawaii have volcanoes but Florida doesn't? Just ask a geologist. This page tells how to e-mail your questions to a United States Geological Survey scientist for an answer. Before you send your mail, be sure to read about what kinds of questions to ask and how to ask them.

http://walrus.wr.usgs.gov/docs/ask-a-ge.html

GEOLOGY—EARTHQUAKES

Record of the Day

Where in the world was the biggest earthquake today? The answer is just a click away. This site will show you the most recent large earthquake recorded by the Cal Tech Seismological Laboratory in California. You can look at the actual graph that was recorded by their seismograph. Hmm, where *are* the Ryukyu Islands? Maps show you where the earthquake's epicenter was. Be sure to check often. Earthquakes are happening around the world all the time.

http://www.gps.caltech.edu/~polet/recofd.html

Seismic Event Bulletins

How many earthquakes do you think occur in the world every day? Probably a lot more than you realize. Seismic activity is monitored day and night, and any recorded activity is posted to this site within 48 hours of each event. Check here and you'll be surprised to find there's a whole lot of shakin' goin' on.

http://www.cdidc.org:65120/web-bin/recentevents

Seismo-Cam

Want to know what's shaking in L.A.—literally? Live shots of a seismograph as it's tracking activity in the Los Angeles, California, area can be monitored here. If nothing's happening while you're watching, you can look at some archived shots from past events, including some BIG temblors. There are also lots of great links to sites with info on earthquakes, including one at the University of Nevada that explains how the seismographs work, at <http://www.seismo.unr.edu/Webcam/explanation.html>.

http://www.knbc4la.com/seismo/

VirtualEarthquake

How do scientists figure out where the starting point, or *epicenter*, of an earthquake was? In this cool simulation, you pick the general region for your test earthquake (California, Japan, Mexico). Use the easy-to-follow instructions to examine seismograms and pinpoint the epicenter as well as the relative strength of your quake.

http://vflylab.calstatela.edu/edesktop/VirtApps/
    VirtualEarthQuake/VQuakeIntro.html

GEOLOGY—FOSSILS

Charlotte, The Vermont Whale: Directory of Exhibits

Just how did a whale get in Vermont, which has no seacoast? Find how the bones of this 12-foot beluga whale ended up buried in Charlotte, Vermont, about 10,000 years ago. Very nice descriptions with drawings show how the whale probably died and was eventually preserved and fossilized in the sediment.

http://mole.uvm.edu/whale/TableOfContents.html

Teeth, Tusks, and Tarpits

Early scientists thought fossils were carved by ancient artists or were seeds dropped from stars. Chicago's famous Field Museum of Natural History explains fossils and gives a recipe for making your own. Of course, you'll need a dead animal or plant and a million years or so to wait, but go ahead, try it at home!

http://rs6000.bvis.uic.edu:80/museum/
    exhibits/ttt/TTT1b.html

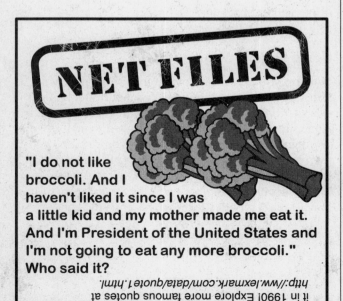

NET FILES

"I do not like broccoli. And I haven't liked it since I was a little kid and my mother made me eat it. And I'm President of the United States and I'm not going to eat any more broccoli." Who said it?

http://www.lexmark.com/data/quote1.html.

Answer: George Bush, the 41st U.S. president, said it in 1990! Explore more famous quotes at

GEOLOGY—GEMS AND MINERALS

Rock 'U'

Rocks are our friends, says this tutorial on various types of minerals. This site explores diamonds, oxides, and silicates, though not in great detail. Still, you'll find interesting stuff, like how to turn amethyst into citrine and how quartz was used to detect submarines during World War I.

http://ahs1.lft.k12.la.us/science/rocku/rocku.html

Do you know the difference between a rock and a mineral?

A mineral is always the same, the world over. A rock, on the other hand, may be made up of a few or many minerals. You can pick up similar rocks right next to each other, and they may be made of different minerals. Mine Rock 'U' for more gems of knowledge!

Smithsonian Gem & Mineral Collection

Gems and jewels: before they become treasures, they look like, well, rocks. You might be able to spot a diamond in the rough if you study this site. You'll see a collection of pictures and descriptions of rocks and minerals from the Smithsonian Institution's National Museum of Natural History in Washington, D.C. This is a long Web page with lots of small pictures, but it's worth the wait. You can also click on each small picture to get a larger picture of that mineral. Hint: If you have a slow connection, turn images off before you open the page, then click on the name of the mineral to see the picture.

http://galaxy.einet.net/images/gems/gems-icons.html

GEOLOGY—GEYSERS

Geysers

A *geyser* is simply a hot spring that erupts, shooting water into the air. There are only about 700 geysers left in the world! Four hundred of them are located in Yellowstone National Park, but they can also be found in such faraway places as Siberia and Chile. Find out how a geyser builds up steam, and discover why geothermal energy production has destroyed many of the geyser fields and threatens some of the few remaining ones. See what happens when they leave the water running? ;-)

http://www.wku.edu/www/geoweb/geyser.html

GEOLOGY—VOLCANOES

Geology—Volcanoes

From here, it's safe to explore several different volcano labs, including Cascades Volcano Observatory, Alaska Volcano Observatory, and Hawaii Volcano Observatory. You might feel some heat, but that's probably just your computer monitor! In Alaska, things were hot during the 1995-1996 winter: they were monitoring several active volcanoes on both sides of the North Pacific, including Pavlof and 40 others! You'll see satellite maps of activities and plume trails almost as they occur at this amazing site.

http://geology.usgs.gov/

Home Page of VolcanoWorld

How do you become a volcanologist? Just ask Mr. Spock for lessons, of course! Well, not quite. Look at this site to find out what becoming a volcanologist is all about and what courses you'll need to take. Also, you'll learn about computers (hey, you're halfway there, since you wouldn't be reading this if you didn't know about computers already). Oh yeah, there's also the BEST information here about volcanoes, including lessons and activities for teachers and students.

http://volcano.und.nodak.edu/vw.html

Wet or dry, give AMPHIBIANS a try!

Mount St. Helens

Imagine that you're living near Mount St. Helens, a sleeping volcano, and suddenly it blows up! There's dust and debris everywhere, mud slides, and boulders shooting into the air. Read exciting stories from people who were there. Sponsored by Educational Service District 112 in Vancouver, Washington, this graphics-intensive site provides maps, photos, and classroom projects to help bring this devastating eruption to life. The site is also supported by NASA, the National Forest Service, and Volcano World.

http://volcano.und.nodak.edu/vwdocs/msh/msh.html

NET FILES

Who is credited with inventing the concept of computer programming?

Answer: Ada Byron Lovelace (1815-1851) is credited with the invention of programming, for her work with Charles Babbage's "analytical engine." A military programming language, Ada, is named in honor of her. Read more about this mathematician at http://www.scottlan.edu/lriddle/women/love.htm

DINOSAURS are prehistoric, but they are under "D."

LAND FEATURES—CAVES AND CAVING

Ape Cave

Ape Cave is a special geologic formation called a lava tube. Formed when Mount St. Helens (Amboy, Washington) erupted 1,900 years ago, it is 12,810 feet long—that's almost two and a half miles! It is the longest intact lava tube in the United States and the second longest in the world. You can read all about its amazing features, such as sand castles, "lava-sicles," and lava balls. Don't miss the creatures of Ape Cave, which include cockroaches, millipedes, and cave slime. There have never been any apes in Ape Cave, however. The name came from a local youth group that explored Mount St. Helens, climbing all over it like monkeys!

http://volcano.und.nodak.edu/vwdocs/msh/
    ov/ovb/ovbac.html

Mammoth Cave National Park Home Page

"Captain, Spock here. According to the informative sign, I am exploring the longest recorded cave system in the world. There seem to be more than 336 miles mapped, but sensors indicate much more to this labyrinth. I chart my location as Kentucky. My Star Fleet tricorder reads ambient temperature at 53 degrees Fahrenheit. Here is a sign; I will read it aloud: 'Violet City Lantern Tour, 3 hours, 3 miles (strenuous). A nostalgic tour into a section of the cave that is not electrically lit. The tour features saltpeter mining, prehistoric exploration, historic tuberculosis hospital huts, and some of the largest rooms and passage ways in the cave. The first half-mile follows the Historic Tour route. Do not bring flashlights. Restrooms not available.' No rest rooms? Illogical. Beam me up. No, wait—it says that other tours are available; some are handicapped-accessible and some are short, fun walks for kids, too. And they have rest rooms!"

http://www.nps.gov/maca/macahome.htm

Never give your name or address to a stranger.

A
B
C
D
E
F
G
H
I
J
K
L
M
N
O
P
Q
R
S
T
U
V
W
X
Y
Z

Virtual Cave

Now you can explore the mineral wonders of the perfect cave without leaving your house or school! This site has pictures of many geologic features besides stalactites and stalagmites. For example, you'll see popcorn, bathtubs, and cave pearls. For a bat-free cave experience, try spelunking here. There's also a handy list of public "show caves" arranged by state so that you can find a real cave to visit.

http://www.goodearth.com/virtcave.html

STALACTITES are the ones that hang "tite" from a cave's ceiling. For another way to remember which ones grow up and which hang down, explore the Virtual Cave!

LAND FEATURES—DESERTS
Desert Biome

What is a desert like? It's a land of temperature extremes, usually very rocky and dry. How do deserts form? What kind of plants and animals live there? Because it's so hot during the day, many desert animals live underground most of the time, and others are active only during the cool night. These are the types of questions answered at this page, prepared by the Missouri Botanical Garden. Visit other deserts the easy way—in the links section!

http://www.mobot.org/MBGnet/vb/desert/index.htm

An Inside look at the Arizona-Sonora Desert Museum

When you hear the word "desert," does it conjure up visions of sand dunes? Even Africa's Namib, perhaps the sandiest desert in the world, is only about 30 percent dunes! In Arizona's Sonora Desert, sand covers only 1 or 2 percent of the area. It doesn't mean there are no plants, either. Sloping and flat desert lands host so many plants, you can't walk without bumping into bushes! Also, flowers bloom most of the year. Learn more about the interrelationships of the plants, animals, and geology of this arid environment, as presented by the Arizona–Sonora Desert Museum.

http://Ag.Arizona.EDU/ASDM/inside.html

LAND FEATURES—GLACIERS
Blackcomb Glaciers - Main

Did you know that 75 percent of the fresh water in the world is trapped in glaciers? Glaciers are not just found near the polar caps. They also exist along the equator, although only at the high altitudes. Find out how a glacier forms and what happens when glacier meets volcano. You'll find lots of "cool" glacier facts here! The Blackcomb Glacier is in British Columbia, Canada.

http://www.whistler.net/glacier/

Did you know that 75 percent of the world's fresh water is locked up in glaciers? That's equivalent to 60 years of nonstop rain all over the world! Dig into the **Blackcomb Glaciers–Main page**, and watch out for the ice worms.

LAND FEATURES—MOUNTAINS

Shangri La Home Page

Welcome to a real-life Shangri-La! Around long before people created boundaries, the Himalayas are not just rock and snow but a breathtaking range of mountains teeming with life. The exclusive home of the spiny babbler bird, they also lay claim to some impressive records, including the highest mountain and the deepest canyon. Learn more about the geography and inhabitants of this beautiful region and discover how humankind has left a mark on these majestic peaks.

http://aleph0.clarku.edu/rajs/Shangri_La.html

LAND FEATURES—POLAR REGIONS

Australian Antarctic Division

Discover why these Australian scientists put on their parkas and went way down under to set up shop in Antarctica. Their research includes issues of global change, management of the marine ecosystem, and protection of the Antarctic environment. It's tough to go to the Pole for a research season, and you can read all about life there to see if it's for you at *<http://www.antdiv.gov.au/aad/exop/sfo/separation/separation.html>*. Learn more about their expeditions, and find out why they are so interested in what those penguins just had for lunch.

http://www.antdiv.gov.au/

International Arctic Project

On March 7, 1995, Will Steger and his team began a trek across the top of the world on an expedition to the North Pole. The goal was to raise awareness of the global importance of the Arctic. Huskies and dog sleds hauled their gear over 2,000 miles of frozen tundra, and their mission took four months. Their journey is chronicled in this informative site. You'll see maps of the trip and read entries from the diaries, and you'll never think about the North Pole the same way again! Although you should start at the Web site, the journals and other text materials are at the attached gopher: *<gopher://gopher.igc.apc.org:70/11/environment/misc/iap>*.

http://www2.scbe.edu.on.ca/arctic.html

Live From Antarctica2

This site lets you take a virtual visit to the South Pole as well as several scientific outposts in Antarctica. This collection of links is outstanding. You'll learn about penguins, plankton, and polar ice, and you can also learn about how you'd prepare to go to the Pole: what you'd need to pack and how you'd go about getting there. For example, at *<http://quest.arc.nasa.gov/antarctica/team/april/>* join April Lloyd, a third-grade teacher from Charlottesville, Virginia, on the adventure of a lifetime. April describes her journey to New Zealand and then to McMurdo Station in Antarctica. Her journey takes her all the way to the South Pole, where she takes part in the first ever, live television broadcast from that site.

http://quest.arc.nasa.gov/antarctica2/main/related/index.html

Did you know that the Antarctica contains 90 percent of Earth's ice and has regions drier than the Gobi Desert?

Find out more about the way cool world of Antarctica at Live From Antarctica2!

The Polar Regions

Dress up warm to visit this site, which covers the Arctic and the Antarctic regions. You'll find everything from Santa Claus (who lives at the North Pole) to information on dog mushing. Follow various polar expeditions, and explore scientific research stations and projects involving schoolchildren all over the world. You'll find lots about wildlife and polar land forms here. Truly a labor of love, this site welcomes you to learn more about all things arctic.

http://www.stud.unit.no/~sveinw/arctic/

A
B
C
D
E
F
G
H
I
J
K
L
M
N
O
P
Q
R
S
T
U
V
W
X
Y
Z

A B C D E F G H I J K L M N O P Q R S T U V W X Y Z

Virtual Antarctica

This is a slick resource, with audio and cool Web graphics sure to grab your attention. This site documents an expedition to Antarctica as seen though the eyes, cameras, diaries, and e-mail of the participants. You'll find lots here on geology, weather, and wildlife, as well as history. Hint: The shortcut index is at
<http://www.terraquest.com/va/guidebook/site.html>. This is a don't-miss site!

http://www.terraquest.com/antarctica/

LAND FEATURES—RAIN FORESTS

MBGnet's Rainforest Biome

When you think about a rain forest, you probably think about a tropical jungle, right? Sure, this site will tell you all about those kinds of rain forests. But did you know that a temperate kind of rain forest exists in cooler parts of the world? These types are located along sea coastlines. In the U.S., you'll find one that stretches for 1,200 miles between Alaska and Oregon. In this type of forest, you will find redwoods, the world's tallest trees! Explore the features and creatures of all kinds of rain forests at this page, prepared by the Missouri Botanical Garden. Don't miss the extensive list of links to info on rain forests both tropical and temperate.

http://www.mobot.org/MBGnet/vb/rforest/index.htm

Welcome to the Rainforest Action Network Home Page

You may have already heard that there are more kinds of plants and animals in tropical rain forests than anywhere else on Earth. And you probably already know that about half of all the world's species live in rain forests. But did you also know that in the rain forest you can find an antelope that's as small as a rabbit, a snake that can fly, and a spider that eats birds? The Kids' Corner is packed with just this kind of wild information about the rain forest, and it has lots of pictures of the creatures and native people living there. We all have a big problem, though: rain forests might be gone by the time you grow up. They're already disappearing at the rate of 150 acres per minute! Find out what you can do to help.

http://www.ran.org/ran/

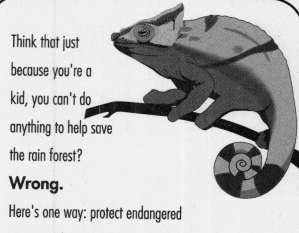

Think that just because you're a kid, you can't do anything to help save the rain forest?

Wrong.

Here's one way: protect endangered species in the rain forest by asking your family not to buy anything made of ivory, coral, reptile skins, tortoise shells, or cat pelts. Go to Welcome to the Rainforest Action Network Home Page to find out more ways.

LAND FEATURES—SWAMPS AND BOGS

Okefenokee Joe's Natural Education Center

Between northern Florida and southern Georgia lie the 700 acres of the Okefenokee Swamp, home to critters as diverse as coral snakes, alligators, and—yes, TOURISTS! You'll be amazed at the dark, mirrorlike water of the swamp, with its overhanging trees draped in swaying strands of Spanish moss. Explore old Seminole canoe routes and learn about the fragile ecology of this very special area. Don't miss hearing the swampwise music of "Okefenokee Joe" while here, but don't turn your back on that gator!

http://www.gravity783.com/joe1.html

Computers are dumb, people are smart.

WATER

Wise Use of Water - Brochures

The world is three-quarters water, isn't it? That means there is plenty to go around, right? Well, if you're talking about water that's healthy for us to drink, it's really in short supply. Consider the millions of people in the world, all of them thirsty. Now think of all the animals and birds in the world, all of them thirsty. Hmmm—better use that water wisely. Here's a list of tips and ideas to help you conserve this natural resource for future dried-out kids on hot, summer days. This site is also available in French.

http://www.cciw.ca/glimr/metadata/
    water-wise-pamphlets/intro.html

WATER FEATURES—OCEANS AND TIDES

Education Center Activities: Let's Make Waves

Water doesn't make its own waves; wind stirs up those waves and swells! If you have ever sailed, you know that the windier the day, the more waves there are. Through some simple experiments designed with kids in mind, you can use a fan and marbles to create waves and model the movement of energy through water. These activities should help you sailors remember that the wind in your sail also causes the waves beneath your boat!

http://www.hmco.com/school/rdg/gen_act/ocean/
    wave.html

Ocean Planet Homepage

How many forests grow in the deep sea? Plenty—they're forests made of kelp and other seaweed. These kelp forests are home to many sea creatures, just like the trees on land that shelter and provide homes for many birds and animals. Kelp forests also need good-quality water to survive; pollution and overharvesting are a threat to them. Visit the Smithsonian Institution's National Museum of Natural History in Washington, D.C. This is their Ocean Planet exhibit, where you can read about the kelp forest and much more.

http://seawifs.gsfc.nasa.gov/ocean_planet.html

NET FILES

How many pounds of steel are used to make a midsize car body?

Answer: The midsize Toyota Camry has 550 pounds of steel in its body (in 970 different parts). Drive on over to http://www.toyota.com/carculture/ built.html and learn all about automaking and a lot more!

Tomorrow's Forecast

What's controlling tomorrow's weather? Winds? Air pressure? Nope. The answer is the oceans, which cover two-thirds of our planet. They affect our weather more than anything else on Earth. Their existence is what makes life itself possible. This site has a number of lesson plans for teachers (or enthusiastic students). The lesson plans include projects and experiments centered around how the ocean affects our lives and our planet.

http://educate.si.edu/art-to-zoo/oceans/cover.html

Find historic documents and spell-check them for fun in HISTORY.

A B C D E F G H I J K L M N O P Q R S T U V W X Y Z

A
B
C
D
E
F
G
H
I
J
K
L
M
N
O
P
Q
R
S
T
U
V
W
X
Y
Z

Why is the Ocean Salty

You could describe seawater as being a very diluted soup of pretty much everything on Earth: minerals, organic matter, even synthetic chemicals. Here's the strange thing: the ocean has the same degree of saltiness everywhere. There isn't one place that is saltier than another. Where did the salt come from? If freshwater rivers and streams keep flowing into the sea, why doesn't the sea become less salty? Find out here!

http://www.ci.pacifica.ca.us/NATURAL/SALTY/
salty.html

ENDANGERED AND EXTINCT SPECIES

Endangered Species

In the United States, 613 plants and 433 species of animals are on the threatened and endangered lists (as of December 1996). *Extinct* means they are gone from planet Earth forever. *Endangered* species are animals and plants that are in danger of becoming extinct. *Threatened* species are animals and plants that are likely to become endangered in the future. Learn which species are listed as threatened and endangered where you live, in the United States, and internationally. Find out how each animal or plant became endangered and what you can do to help prevent their extinction.

http://www.nceet.snre.umich.edu/EndSpp/
Endangered.html

Endangered Species Home Page

Why is it so important to protect the various species of fish, wildlife, or plants facing extinction? They have educational, historical, recreational, and scientific value to all of us, that's why! Stop and learn about the different recovery plans and activities for species on their way back from the brink of extinction. You can also check the current status of endangered and threatened plants and animals here.

http://www.fws.gov/~r9endspp/endspp.html

It's not all bad news at the National Wildlife Service's **Endangered Species Home Page.** California condors are coming back! In 1987, only 27 of these huge birds were left in the whole world. By 1996, the number had increased to 121, and a successful captive breeding program continues to offer encouragement that the species will survive.

???? Welcome to the Adventure ????

Ready to go on a mission to save an endangered animal? All right! Trouble is, you don't know what kind of animal you're trying to save! If you follow the clues and answer a few simple questions, you might be able to save the Mystery Critter before the poachers snag it. You'll need some help from the World Wildlife Fund of Canada, and you'll need some luck and the right equipment to succeed at this fun adventure. Be warned that this game takes quite a while to play. The good news is that you can bookmark the place where you get tired and come back later to play the game from that point.

http://www.post-mystery.com/about.html

Whooooooo will you find in BIRDS?

World Wildlife Fund

Want to hear a black rhino sneeze? Want to see what's on and off the endangered species list worldwide? Get in here and see what this organization does to help animals and environments all over the globe. Destruction of tropical forests means the winter habitat of your favorite spring songbirds is at risk. What will happen to the summer tanager and the northern warbler if their winter home disappears completely? Find out how you can help.

http://www.wwf.org/

ENERGY

ENERGY QUEST—Energy Education from the California Energy Commission

What was Ben Franklin's energy-saving invention? Join Ben in a word game to find out the answer. He also has other games, crafts, and even a Declaration of (Energy) Independence. This site has activities and games about different kinds of energy, from wind to solar and nuclear to hydroelectric! This site is a must for the energy-efficient, but it loads very slowly.

http://www.energy.ca.gov/energy/education/eduhome.html

FUSION ENERGY

Did you know that the Sun is a fusion power plant? Solar energy is produced by a reactor in the Sun's core with a temperature of 15 million degrees Celsius. It would be great to be able to produce energy this way on Earth. Scientists are working on it, but they have a long way to go. They have already achieved the necessary temperatures—as high as 510 million degrees, more than 20 times the temperature at the center of the Sun. Now, the problem is keeping the deuterium-tritium fuel magnetically suspended inside the reactor. Say that ten times! Who knows, maybe you'll be the one to solve this problem. Will fusion power plants be the energy source of the future?

http://www.pppl.gov/oview/pages/fusion_energy.html

"Every time you look up at the sky, every one of those points of light is a reminder that fusion power is extractable from hydrogen and other light elements, and it is an everyday reality throughout the Milky Way Galaxy." Carl Sagan, *the famous astronomer, said that. How are we doing on producing fusion power here on Earth? Get an update at the FUSION ENERGY site!*

Maine Solar House

This is Bill Lord's solar house. He built this house in southern Maine, on a property specially chosen for the project. Everything was planned with the goal of constructing a house that would make the most out of solar energy. Descriptions and diagrams show how he uses heat from the sun to warm the house and produce his own electricity. He even sells electricity to the power company when he has a surplus!

http://solstice.crest.org/renewables/wlord/

Watch the building of a solar house on the Maine Solar House page. You will see it take shape, from the dream and planning stages to the building of the house to actually living in the home. The owners of this solar house in Maine actually **make** money from the power company!

A
B
C
D
E
F
G
H
I
J
K
L
M
N
O
P
Q
R
S
T
U
V
W
X
Y
Z

A B C D E F G H I J K L M N O P Q R S T U V W X Y Z

Renewable Energy Education Module

For sale to a good home: five types of renewable energy. Choose yours today, before the world runs out of energy! You have a choice of solar, wind, hydroelectric, geothermal, or biomass energy. Shots and history are included, suitable for a beginner.

http://solstice.crest.org/renewables/re-kiosk/
index.shtml

NET FILES

What are the major food groups?
(Isn't one of them chocolate?)

ANSWER:
The Food Pyramid lists six food groups:
- Bread, cereal, grains, pasta
- Fruit
- Vegetables
- Meat, poultry, fish, dry beans
- Milk, cheese, yogurt
- Oils, fats, sweets (yes, that's chocolate, but eat only a little!)
Find out more at http://lfcinfo.health.org/brochure/pyramid.htm

Rocky Run Energy Projects

There are all kinds of things kids can do for energy. Drink more soda? No—that's not the kind of energy we have in mind! These students from Virginia have an energy-efficient house online as part of a village that they're designing. You can click on a room in the house and get energy-saving tips. Virginia has three different kinds of power plants. How many do you have where you live?

http://k12.cnidr.org/gsh/schools/va/rrms/energy.html

ETIQUETTE AND CUSTOMS

Home and Family: Parenting - Table Manners Through the Ages

When your mom tells you to stop playing with your food, that's about good table manners. In the 1700s, a Colonial mom would have said: "Grease not thy fingers or napkin more than necessity requires..." "Smell not thy meat nor put it to thy nose..." "Spit not in the room but in the corner," and, well, you get the idea. Compare table manners from the eighteenth century and 25 years ago with current standards here!

http://homeandfamily.com/features/parent/
tablemanners.html

Japanese Customs - Table Manners

If you are invited to a traditional Japanese dinner, you'll want to know how to behave so that you won't offend your hosts. This page will tell you what the hot towel is for, how to use chopsticks, and why you don't want to put soy sauce on your rice. Compare this with the table manners you use in your home.

http://www.shinnova.com/part/99-japa/abj21-e.htm

Learn2 Set a Table

Which side does the fork go on? Does the knife edge go towards the plate or away from it? You'll find the answers to these and other mysteries of life as you learn to set a table. This is not just a casual breakfast table, mind you, but a full-fledged formal dinner table with lots of silver and glassware! Practice the napkin-folding tricks and really show off a terrific table.

http://learn2.com/06/0608/0608.html

Learn2 Use Chopsticks

We used to feel ridiculous using chopsticks, but not anymore! While we once had to spear our shrimp tempura, now we deftly handle even the smallest morsels of sticky rice. And it's all because of the terrific techniques taught at this page!

http://learn2.com/06/0607/0607.html

Moon Travel Handbooks: Trans-Cultural Study Guide

It's all too easy to assume that people in other countries have the same customs as you do. But once you've found yourself saying or doing something that seems innocent at home but provokes anger somewhere else, you may wish you'd studied a bit more before traveling. This guide was put together by a group called Volunteers in Asia, but it works well for just about anywhere. This is a list of hundreds of questions you could ask in order to systematically study another culture.

http://www.moon.com/trans_cultural/

EVOLUTION

Evolution Entrance

The University of California at Berkeley has set up a separate "exhibition area" for the subject of evolution in its online Museum of Paleontology. Here you are greeted by Charles Darwin speaking of the course of evolution being much like a "great tree of Life." From there, you can link to sections on Dinosaur Discoveries and Systematics (the classification system used in charting the families of species) and find out about the most important scientists to develop this field.

http://www.ucmp.berkeley.edu/history/evolution.html

Mutant Fruit Flies

Great, now it's teenage mutant ninja fruit flies! The basis for evolution is the ability of some individuals to adapt and change, which may result in a genetic mutation of the species. To demonstrate the varieties of genetic mutation, San Francisco's Exploratorium has transferred this amazing exhibit to their Web site. Detailed color illustrations of naturally mutated fruit flies graphically demonstrate better than pages of text how this phenomenon works. Just when you thought it was safe to go near the fruit bowl... If you want to try it yourself, visit the Virtual Fly Lab at <http://vflylab.calstatela.edu/edesktop/VirtApps/VflyLab/IntroVflyLab.html>.

http://www.exploratorium.edu/exhibits/mutant_flies/mutant_flies.html

The Sci.Bio.Evolution Home Page

Two Usenet newsgroups have rousing discussions of evolution: this one and talk.origins (see following entry). You'll find links to the archives of each group here, ready to download. Check the link to Niel's Geologic Timelines at <http://hea-www.harvard.edu/QEDT/niel/scales/geohist1.ascii> if you're always confused about whether the Paleozoic came before the Cenozoic. There are also links to two of Darwin's most important texts, *Voyage of the Beagle* and *The Origin of Species*. But you may like the formatting better at <http://www.literature.org/Works/Charles-Darwin/origin/>.

http://weber.u.washington.edu/~jahayes/evolution/index.html

NET FILES

What **lighthouse** is also one of the **Seven Wonders** of the ancient world?

Answer: The Lighthouse of Alexandria, on the island of Pharos, off Egypt, is one of the Seven Wonders of the ancient world. Built around 300 to 220 B.C., it was as tall as a modern-day 40-story building, making it the tallest structure in the world at that time. It had a miraculous mirror lit by the sun during the day and by fires at night. The light could be seen 35 miles away. By the mid-1400s it was in ruins, and for a long time its exact location was not known. In September 1995, French divers announced they had found large pieces of granite underwater, believed to be pieces of the ancient lighthouse. Find out more at http://pharos.bu.edu/Egypt/Wonders/pharos.html

A
B
C
D
E
F
G
H
I
J
K
L
M
N
O
P
Q
R
S
T
U
V
W
X
Y
Z

A
B
C
D
E
F
G
H
I
J
K
L
M
N
O
P
Q
R
S
T
U
V
W
X
Y
Z

The Talk.Origins Archive

People love to argue about whether the theory of evolution is "true" or not. This newsgroup is one of the places where this discussion goes on. (Check the entries for "Creation Studies" in this book for more information.) Though you probably won't want to enter into this newsgroup's conversation, the FAQ section is interesting, and you can check out a nice collection of fossil images and other related links. An interactive browser and a keyword file searcher are included here to make things easy.

http://earth.ics.uci.edu:8080/origins/faqs.html

EXPLORERS AND EXPLORING

1492 Exhibit

This Library of Congress display examines Columbus, the man and the myth. Why do we talk about the "discovery" of America when people were living there all along? What was life like in the America that Columbus encountered? What changes, immediate and long term, befell both the Europeans and the people of the Americas?

http://sunsite.unc.edu/expo/1492.exhibit/Intro.html

Exploration of the Americas Title Page

This shows that kids can create a Web site where no other exists! A fifth-grade class in New York has created an encyclopedia of exploration that has no rivals on the Net. It's divided into sections: northeastern North America, southeastern North America, Mexico and western North America, and South America. Some of the explorers you'll read about include Cabot, Hudson, La Salle, Ponce de León, and Cortéz.

http://pen1.pen.k12.va.us/Anthology/Div/Albemarle/
Schools/MurrayElem/ClassPages/Prudhomme/
Explorers/exploretitle.html

Explorers

There's not a lot of content here, but you'll find info on Cook, Columbus, Magellan, and a few others, as well as maps and politically correct commentary. You'll have to type in the name of the explorer you need. For more on Magellan, try <http://www.nortel.com/entprods/magellan/ferdinand/MagellanBio.html>.

http://www.adventure.com/library/encyclopedia/

The Heroic Age: A Look at the Race to the South Pole

Soon after the North Pole was reached by Robert E. Peary in 1909, the race was on to see who could get to the South Pole first. This page looks at three explorers: Ernest Shackleton, Robert Scott, and Roald Amundsen. All three attempted to reach the South Pole in the early 1900s, but only Amundsen and Scott made it. Investigate their strategies and what went wrong, or right, in each case. There is still more detail at <http://magic.geol.ucsb.edu/~geo10/Students/race.html>.

http://magic.geol.ucsb.edu/~geo10/Students/
heroic.html

The La Salle Shipwreck Project

The Texas Historical Commission has quite a find on their hands! They are excavating a shipwreck believed to be that of the *Belle*, one of the ships brought by the French explorer René Robert Cavelier, sieur de La Salle. La Salle was the explorer who claimed the Mississippi and all its tributaries for France. His ship was lost in 1686. It lies in about 12 feet of water in a bay about halfway between Galveston and Corpus Christi. Archaeologists built a special double-walled coffer dam around the wreck, then pumped out the water in the middle of this "doughnut." They were then free to explore and carefully record their findings. You can read about La Salle and the recovery of his ship and its artifacts at this very special site!

http://www.thc.state.tx.us/belle/index.htm

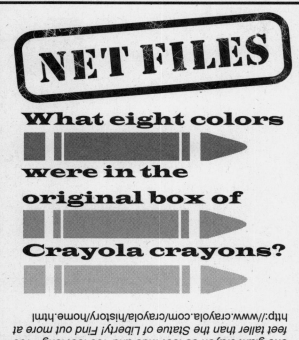

NET FILES

What eight colors were in the original box of Crayola crayons?

http://www.crayola.com/crayola/history/home.html
feet taller than the Statue of Liberty! Find out more at
one giant crayon 35 feet wide and 400 feet long—100
encircle the globe four and a half times, or to make
an average of five million daily. That's enough to
produces more than two billion crayons each year—
Binney & Smith, maker of Crayola products,
yellow, and green.
Answer: *Black, brown, blue, red, purple, orange,*

Lewis & Clark Trail

This is an ambitious project from Washington State, which began in October 1995. It has begun to collect information about the lives and times of Meriwether Lewis and William Clark. During the years 1804–1806, Lewis and Clark led the first transcontinental expedition to the Pacific coast. In commemoration of the 190th anniversary of the explorations, the journey is being re-created online. Their most fascinating travel journals are here, as well as some suggested classroom projects. What was life like on the trail before hiking boots and lightweight backpacks existed?

http://134.121.112.29/wahistcult/trail.html

Salute the nations of cyberspace in FLAGS.

New South Polar Times

This site offers a dramatic account of man's touch on the Antarctic Continent, from the earliest dog sled explorers to modern scientists in airplanes. Fascinating stuff, the story is better than Saturday superhero cartoons, and it's all true! Be sure to read astronomer Chris Bero's hilarious FAQ on life in Antarctica at *<http://205.174.118.254/nspt/question/chrisfaq.htm>*. Here's a sample: "How much are you paid for going to the South Pole?" "Not enough! Trust me kids, get it in writing before you start working at the pole. Also, don't make the same mistake I made. There is no such thing as Antarctic dollars!"

http://205.174.118.254/nspt/home.htm

Rune Stone

Columbus was a latecomer to the Americas; the Vikings had been here long before. Want proof? Look at the Heavener Rune Stone, in a state park near Heavener, Oklahoma. A Viking land claim was apparently made there about A.D. 750. It is believed that these Norse explorers crossed the Atlantic, sailed around Florida into the Gulf of Mexico, and entered the Mississippi River. From there, they explored its tributaries, the Arkansas and Poteau Rivers, leaving five or so rune stones along the way. At least, that's the theory. See what you think!

http://admin.hps.osrhe.edu/hps/htmls/runtest.htm

Terraquest

Tired of reading about all those musty old explorers from long ago? This site allows you to go along on some fantastic present-day journeys. You'll find pictures, virtual reality panoramas, audio, and text that documents real expeditions with real people just like you! Try virtual Antarctica and discover the wonders of the South Pole. Or perhaps you'd like a sea voyage to the virtual Galápagos Islands—learn about how this remote island's unique animals helped Charles Darwin formulate his theories of evolution. If that's not enough, tag along with blind mountaineer Erik Weihenmayer as he scales the 3,000-foot sheer wall of El Capitán in Yosemite National Park.

http://www.terraquest.com/

A B C D E F G H I J K L M N O P Q R S T U V W X Y Z

A
B
C
D
E
F
G
H
I
J
K
L
M
N
O
P
Q
R
S
T
U
V
W
X
Y
Z

Colleen Dick, webmaster
of the bilingual Platypus
Children's Playground

"I think people can make an effort to seek out and patronize the business of small excellent pages. It is a great grassroots medium, and it can stay that way, but not if people only visit the big sites that pop up in the ads and first on all the search pages."

GAMES AND FUN
Platypus Children's Playground
Webmaster: Colleen Dick
http://www.peak.org/~playtypus/in.html

Who came up with the idea for your page or project?

I came up with the idea for a family page to attract visitors to my shareware site. I confess to being a gadget junkie—when any new plug-in comes along I just have to try it! I have also started putting Spanish translations on my pages for my many friends in Mexico.

How many people work on your pages? Does it take a lot of time? How many hits do you get a day?

I do most of the work on my pages. My four children (ages 4-13) help by coming up with graphics, doing limited editing, and designing puzzles and mazes. They also test the pages, just as they always did with my shareware. My 11-year-old son has started playing with JavaScript—I hope he makes something robust and good enough to post before too long.

You must hear from people all over the world! Can you think of an unusual request, question, or comment someone has sent to you?

Someone once complained because I had moved a graphic and he had a link to it which no longer worked, so he said I was responsible for messing up his Web site! But seriously, I get a kick out of getting e-mail from Canada, England, Chile, Spain, Mexico, Japan, Norway, France, and South Africa, just to name a few.

If this isn't your main job, what do you do, what is your training?

This page isn't really my job, because I don't get paid anything for it. Most importantly I am a mother to four kids. My official training is in speech science and linguistics with a minor in music. I do have a graduate degree in software engineering and have worked in computer speech synthesis among other things in the past, but what I really wish I could do was make a living singing classical music. Right now I do Web sites for other companies and sometimes give workshops on Web multimedia.

Do you have a family? A dog? A lizard?

I have a husband, Tom, daughter Jean (13), son Connor (11), son Eamon (8), and daughter Eleanor (4). We have a cat named Squeaker. There are also a number of invertebrates on our property, but we really aren't on a first-name basis with them.

What are your hopes and fears for the future of the Internet?

I'm just afraid that as the Net shifts into commercial gear, the big powerful companies will find ways to force small companies off, or render them otherwise ineffective. I think people can make an effort to seek out and patronize the business of small excellent pages. It is a great grassroots medium, and it can stay that way, but not if people only visit the big sites that pop up in the ads and that are first on all the search pages.

If you could invite three people throughout history to your house for dinner, who would they be?

I would love to invite Jesus Christ, Mahatma Gandhi, and Mother Teresa.

FAMILY HOME PAGES

Children's Stories, Poems, Pictures and Sounds

This is a great place to start your Internet searching. From their home in England, the Bowens have included links to a variety of resources. You'll find resources from writing children's books to chocolate, from teddy bears to the Smithsonian Institution. And the list goes on! Both daughters (Emma, age eight, and Alice, age ten) have individual home pages that include their own stories and artwork and other things. There are even more links to other family home pages.

http://www.comlab.ox.ac.uk/oucl/users/
   jonathan.bowen/children/

CyberKids Home

"Monster in the Park," "Mixed-Up Zoo," "Beyond the Barrier of Time," "Scary Stories That Make Your Mom Faint"—these are only some of the great stories written by kids that your family can read together in this online magazine. Like any magazine, there are writing and art contests, software and product reviews written by kids for kids, and cookie recipes, too. In addition to the fictional stories, the feature articles have crossword or word search puzzles along with them, to make learning about something new even more fun. The CyberKids Launchpad will link you to lots of other neat sites listed by subject area. If you have thoughts or ideas you want to share with other readers, be sure to send them in.

http://www.cyberkids/.com

Elizabeth's Snow White Page

Elizabeth says, "Surfing the Internet lets me be free and go anywhere I want! Without my wheelchair or walker." Eleven-year-old Elizabeth has Down syndrome and cerebral palsy, but from her wheelchair, she travels all over the world. With the help of her two big brothers, Chris and Ryan, she has developed her own home page. Elizabeth helps prove how computers can help challenged kids really express themselves and become more independent.

http://www.ECNet.Net/users/gjmuzzo/lizzie1.htm

Heather's Happy Holidaze Page!! For Kids Only!!

Heather is not yet seven years old, and she came up with the concept and design of this neat home page all by herself! With a little help from her dad and mom, it's been up and running since September 1995. Pictures go with each of her favorite holidays, so children of all ages can enjoy this site. You'll find scary Halloween links and a search for Tom Turkey for Thanksgiving. For some little-known tree facts, traditions, and folklore, be sure to try her links for Christmas. Heather's 14-year-old brother has his own Web page, too. Jason's is on snakes and reptiles, which is full of everything you'd ever want to know about these cold-blooded creatures. Both Heather and Jason are already saving for college by getting corporate sponsors for their pages!

http://www.shadeslanding.com/hms/

Jackson's Page For Five Year Olds

Jackson has pictures with each of his links to help preschoolers "read" his page—which includes things most kids will be interested in (like Legos, Hot Wheels, and Power Rangers). But don't stop there. Be sure to look at the Signal Flag and Semaphore game. Then keep digging until you get to the Ports and Harbor Pilots Home Page. Buried in the "other interesting maritime sites" is a fun link to the Pirate Page with information on real pirates and their ships.

http://www.islandnet.com/~bedford/jackson.html

Kids' Space

What fun—this is everybody's home page! Here you and your family (or teacher) can submit music or drawings and hear and see what other children around the world have done, too. The Story Book is where you can write your own stories, using the pictures and themes provided each month. There is even a beanstalk that keeps growing each month in the Craft Room. You can pick an artwork and create a story for it, or you can pick a story already written and draw a picture for it. All commands at this site include pictures with them, so even the youngest child who may be still developing reading skills can enjoy this interactive learning experience.

http://www.kids-space.org/

A B C D E F G H I J K L M N O P Q R S T U V W X Y Z

A
B
C
D
E
F
G
H
I
J
K
L
M
N
O
P
Q
R
S
T
U
V
W
X
Y
Z

The Martin Family Home Page

Visit the multicultural Martins in Canberra, Australia! "Like many other families, we are a blended unit— David brought Bruce with him when he married Julie, and now there is Rex as well. In other ways though, we may not be so typical. Bruce's Mum is an Aboriginal lady from Aurukun in far northern Australia, and the continuing personal connections not only of Bruce himself but of all of us are very important aspects of all our lives." The family seems to be equally at home in the city or "the Bush," and you can see pictures of their life in both worlds. You'll find lots of links here about Australian and Aboriginal resources.

http://ourworld.compuserve.com/homepages/
David_Martin/homepage.htm

The Petry Family Home Page

The Petry family is from Kentucky. You can listen to Megan, age 11, playing her violin! You can read about Japanese culture and customs, as younger brother Douglas has a pen pal from Japan. The many links to other family pages from around the world are great. Don't forget to check out the parent/teacher resources listed here, too.

http://www.iglou.com/petryfam/

Rachel's Page

Rachel lives in Chicago, Illinois, and she is a typical 12 year old. She is in her school chorus and she loves cats. She has a "cool site for the time being," which doesn't change daily but changes only when she finds another cool site. Kids' WB cartoon site was her cool site for two months until she discovered BHI TEENS 90210, a site that offers free personal Web pages to kids under 18 and will include things such as a monthly newsletter and music page. Along with links to other fun places for kids, Rachel includes a long list of links to other kids' pages, especially for those 10 to 14 years old with similar interests.

http://www.mcs.net/~kathyw/rachel.html

The Teel Family WWW Site

The Teel family is obviously proud of their home state of Alaska! They have included information about the animals that live there, a list of books with Alaskan themes for preschoolers and older kids, and many links to other Alaskan sites. The kids are home schooled, so their home page has useful curriculum links, art and crafts projects, and lots more. This is one of the BEST family home pages on the Net.

http://www.teelfamily.com/

TnT-Tristan and Tiffany's Daily Cool Stuff For Kids

This brother and sister team live in British Columbia, Canada. They have taken turns picking children's Web sites and then rating them so many "poodles" out of five. A site rated five poodles is really great! Tristan is ten years old and Tiffany is seven. Some of their previous TnT selections include Miss Piggy's Home Page, Sports Illustrated For Kids, and The Gargoyles Home Page.

http://www.polar7.com/tnt/

FARMING AND AGRICULTURE

See also GARDENS AND GARDENING; HORSES AND EQUESTRIAN SPORTS

Farm Fun Page

At Davis' Farmland in Massachusetts, you can discover what's old in farming: rare and endangered farm animal breeds. At the level we've chosen, you can click on a variety of common farm animals and hear the sounds they make; click on "more animal sounds" to hear elephants, lions, and other nonbarnyard creatures! You can also download coloring pages of farm life and activities, plus play a farm crossword puzzle.

http://www.ziplink.net/~farmland/farmfun.htm

OSU's Breeds of Livestock

Oklahoma State University's breed archive is extensive. You'll find pictures and info on breeds of the following animals: horses, cattle, swine, sheep, goats, and poultry. Oh, yes, did we mention the "other" category? There you'll find llamas, donkeys, and—buffalo! But let's talk cattle. Everyone's heard of the Jersey cow: "With an average weight of 900 pounds, the Jersey produces more pounds of milk per pound of body weight than any other breed." They have a nice photo here, too. But have you ever heard of the Australian Friesian Sahiwal? It's a breed being developed in Australia for use in tropical areas. How about the Florida Cracker/Pineywoods, the Florida equivalent of the Texas longhorn? Visit this site for a virtual barnyard of breeds.

http://www.ansi.okstate.edu/breeds/

WWW Library - Livestock Section (Youth)

Are you interested in 4-H or maybe even a career in animal science? This is the place for you! You can learn about sheep and wool, check out the National Dairy Database, or get information on your favorite breed of livestock. Maybe you'd like to attend the Judging Camp this summer for hands-on experience. Not sure about the livestock-judging thing? Kids gain a lot from competing on a livestock evaluation team. It builds character, and it may even give you confidence if you are shy or tone you down a bit if you are a little less reserved. Don't forget the genetics simulation called Cowgame. You can download a DOS program that lets you pick the bulls and cows you want to breed and then shows you the calf results.

http://www.ansi.okstate.edu/library/youth.html

BEEKEEPING
Billy Bee Honey Products Limited - Canada's #1 Honey

To *bee* or not to *bee*...but the question is, what do you know about bees? Worker honeybees have many jobs in taking care of their hives. They do the feeding, cleaning, guarding, the long-distance and short-distance flying; they carry pollen, produce honey, and build the honeycomb. To learn more about beekeeping, visit this site, and *bee* careful!

http://www.billybee.com/

A
B
C
D
E
F
G
H
I
J
K
L
M
N
O
P
Q
R
S
T
U
V
W
X
Y
Z

CATTLE

Big Dave's Cow Page

Cow lovers alert! People's fascination with cows tends to *mooo*ve in the direction of humor, using pictures, sounds, poetry, and songs. This site contains all of that and more, including information for that *udder*ly serious scholar in search of bovine research.

http://www.gl.umbc.edu/~dschmi1/links/cow.html

The Story of Milk

Cows make milk to feed their baby calves, but even after the baby is eating other food, the cow continues to make up to eight gallons of milk a day! Cows are milked in a special room called a *milking parlor*, and their milk is pumped to stainless steel holding tanks and immediately chilled to 38 degrees Fahrenheit. Then the milk tanker truck comes to pick it up. This happens twice a day. When it gets to the milk processing facility, the milk goes through two other steps, homogenization and pasteurization, but you'll have to read about those at this Web site. You'll find cow-related Shockwave games and other fun at the main level.

http://www.moomilk.com/tours/tour1-0.htm

CROPS, PRODUCE, AND ORCHARDS

The Corn Growers Guidebook (Purdue University)

The corniest people in the United States bring you everything you need to know about the top crop: corn. Maybe you want to raise corn, or you need a corn recipe or a corn song. Perhaps you want to find out what products have corn in them or what ancient civilizations used corn. Well, you've *corn* to the right place. When you have had your fill of corn, you can link to the maize page and read about—more corn.

http://www.agry.purdue.edu/agronomy/ext/corn/cornguid.htm

Don't Panic Eat Organic

Farmer, don't harm your environment. Nature's pesticides include ladybugs, which eat aphids, and owls, which catch rodents. Did you know that barn owls are called "flying cats"? You can also use "companion" plants, which help to repel bugs from each other! By understanding and using the natural biological systems on a farm, you can leave the sprays and chemicals on the store shelf and let nature do most of the work. Let these certified organic farmers show you how to cultivate in harmony with your surroundings.

http://www.rain.org/~sals/my.html

Jim's Farming Page

If you don't live close to a farm, you probably have no idea what a "harrower" is or how corn and beans are grown and harvested. Farmer Jim takes you on a tour of his fields through the growing season. See the big equipment Jim uses. If you explore this resource a little further, you can "Ask a Farmer" a question and see some neat agricultural links.

http://toybox.asap.net/farmsite/field.html

NET FILES

In the Tournament of Roses Parade in Pasadena, California, each float must be completely covered with flowers or other organic material. What's the average number of flowers on each float?

Answer: An average float requires up to 100,000 blossoms. More than one-half million roses are used in each parade, according to the home page at http://www.mech.nwu.edu/fac/sirota/rose/roseinfo.html

GOATS
Goats

It has some quirky habits, smells a little, and has been hanging around you all day. Do you call the police? No, all the poor goat wants is a good scratch between the shoulders! The Irvine Masa Charros 4-H Club raises dairy and pygmy goats and knows what a rewarding experience raising goats can be. With the dedication and knowledge demonstrated at this site, how can anyone not approve of these kids raising *kids*?

http://www.ics.uci.edu/~pazzani/4H/Goats.html

LLAMAS
LlamaWeb, Llamas on the Internet!

Llamas make wonderful pets. They are used as pack animals, golfing caddies, and watch or guard animals. Their coat fiber is used to produce rugs, ropes, and sweaters and other clothing. All camelids (the camel family of mammals) have a bad reputation for spitting. Usually they spit at other llamas, though, and not at people in particular. Be careful not to get in the middle of a spitting contest between two camelids! Stop by to learn all about raising these interesting animals, and vote for the cutest baby llama.

http://www.webcom.com/~degraham/

POULTRY
Poultry Page

If you are more interested in what breed of chicken crossed the road rather than why it crossed the road, then strut on over to the Featherside Farm and inspect their collection of colorful chick pics and descriptions. If you say there is more to poultry than fowl chickens, you're right! They've also included ducks, geese, turkeys, and peafowl guaranteed to smooth your feathers. Hint: Take the link back to the home page to view a dancing chicken.

http://www.cyborganic.com/People/feathersite/
Poultry/BRKPoultryPage.html

Watch your step in DANCE.

SHEEP
Sheep

If you are looking for a farm animal to raise, take a good look at the multipurpose sheep. Stay warm with wool sweaters made from their fleece. Feast on cheese produced from their milk. Stop mowing the lawn; instead, let sheep keep your grass closely clipped. Get your daily exercise by walking a mile a day with your lamb. Make a profit when you take them to the market. "BAAAAAA!" OK, the sheep request that you skip that last one. Here is where 4-Hers show you how fun and rewarding sheep raising can be.

http://www.ics.uci.edu/~pazzani/4H/Sheep.html

SWINE
Bacon Links, Life & Potbellied Pig FAQ and Resource Page

Does the thought of swine make you swoon? Does having a pig as a pet make your day? Then a pot-bellied pig is the way to go. Read about where the pot-bellied pig came from, see other people's pigs, and join the Pot-Bellied Pig List, where you can talk to others who think hogs are heaven.

http://www.voicenet.com/~johnpac/bacon.html

NET FILES

What national park has more geysers than any other place on Earth?

Answer: Don't get steamed up, but Yellowstone in Wyoming/Montana/Idaho has over 400 geysers. Yellowstone was the first national park in the world, established in 1872! Read all about this famous and amazing place at http://www2.wku.edu/www/geoweb/geyser/about2.html

A
B
C
D
E
F
G
H
I
J
K
L
M
N
O
P
Q
R
S
T
U
V
W
X
Y
Z

Did you know...

President Harry Truman once said, "No man should be allowed to be President who does not understand hogs." Even if you don't have political aspirations, you can learn a lot about pigs here. Peruse pig trivia, discover porcine pithy sayings, and meditate on the history of pork. Hogwash? Not here.

http://www.nppc.org/hog-trivia.html

The city of Cincinnati, Ohio, was so strongly associated with pork production that it was nicknamed Porkopolis. Read more intriguing pig facts at the Did you know...page.

Pigs

Are you interested in raising pigs for fun and/or profit? The 4-Hers in this site learn integrity, good sporting, and communication through raising hogs. Investigate the steps required to start your own pig raising venture, what breeds are available, and how to care for these large but gentle swine. And don't forget the added bonus (forget the health spa): unlimited free mud baths!

http://www.ics.uci.edu/~pazzani/4H/Pigs.html

Do you know the way to San Jose? If not, check a map in GEOGRAPHY.

FESTIVALS AND FAIRS

The Gathering of the Clans

Scroll down to the Highland Games part of this page. 'Tis a stirring sight, indeed: the gathering of the clans, marching behind the drums and blaring bagpipes. You can sample Scots recipes, admire clan tartans, listen to folktales, and watch a dancer step nimbly over crossed swords. Try the caber toss if you're very strong, throw the stone, or pitch the sheaf in these traditional games of Scotland. Learn about them, as well as Gaelic culture in general, at this site.

http://www.tartans.com/culture.html

Internet 1996 World Exposition

You may have learned all about the various world's fairs and expositions of the last century. The idea was to show people what new inventions—like railroads, telephones, lights, and cars—could do for them. Well, if you've been wondering what this new invention called the Internet can do for you, then welcome to this site. It's a world's fair for the Information Age. One of the most important parts of this expo is the Global Schoolhouse Pavilion, which links schools around the world, showcases young artists, and features activities to help kids learn (and like) the Internet.

http://park.org/

KTCA Productions: PowWow

Please rise, as the flags and eagle staffs enter the arena for the powwow. It's OK, everyone is welcome at Native American powwows. Learn about the dance, regalia, drum, and song of powwows. If you're thinking about attending a powwow, this page will teach you its customs. Learn more by reading the entries in the "Native Americans and Indigenous Peoples" and the "Dance" sections in this book.

http://www.ktca.org/powwow/

Shrewsbury Renaissance Faire

Art thou off to the faire? Don't forget your Renaissance-era costume and your muffin hat (you can learn to make one here). Yum, those gingerbread cookies look good! Care for some fried dragon scales? What is your U.S. currency worth in Elizabethan English pounds? See what goes into a reenactment of a sixteenth-century Welsh village—this one is located near Corvallis, Oregon. Remember to learn history by playing *faire*, anon!

http://www.peak.org/shrewsbury/

NET FILES

In modern times, which famous people have been born on December 25?

Answer:

❂ Rod Serling, creator of *The Twilight Zone*
❂ Conrad Hilton, founder of the Hilton hotel chain
❂ Louis Chevrolet, auto racer and designer, whose name is on General Motors cars
❂ Clara Barton, founder of the American Red Cross

And many others. Find out who shares your birthday at http://www.eb.com/bio.html

---

SLIME is a polymer, as anyone who's read CHEMISTRY knows!

World's Columbian Exposition:

Back in 1893, a wonderful fair took place in Chicago, Illinois, and it was called the Columbian Exposition. It introduced the American public to the wonders of the day: electric lights, the cotton gin, typewriters, and all manner of nineteenth-century technology. It was also the first appearance of food products we know so well today: carbonated soda, hamburgers, Juicy Fruit gum, Cracker Jacks, and Aunt Jemima syrup, among many others. There were strange displays, too, such as a map of the United States "made entirely of pickles" and "not one, but two Liberty Bell models—one in wheat, oats, and rye, and one entirely in oranges." Take a virtual visit to the past here! You'll find a thoughtful essay and more pictures at World's Columbian Exposition: Idea, Experience, Aftermath, *<http://xroads.virginia.edu/~MA96/WCE/title.html>*

http://users.vnet.net/schulman/Columbian/
   columbian.html

FISH

See also AQUARIUMS; OUTDOOR RECREATION—FISHING; SHARKS

The Amazing Fish-Cam!

Something fishy is happening on the Net right now! See a live picture of a saltwater fish tank in Lou's office. Who is Lou? No one knows, but his fish tank is famous. Can you spot a moray eel or maybe a "humuhumunukunukuapua'a" (humu-humu-nuku-nuku-apu-a'-a), which is the state fish of Hawaii?

http://www1.netscape.com/fishcam/

Fish FAQ

Did you know that salmon generally lay from 2,500 to 7,000 eggs, depending on the species and its size, or that some lobsters hardly move more than one mile? What is the most common fish in the sea? Why do scientists classify fish? How long do fish live? How is the age of a fish determined? Visit the profusely illustrated home page, where you'll find the answers to all these questions and more. You'll discover how porcupine fish inflate themselves, too!

http://www.wh.whoi.edu/homepage/faq.html

A B C D E F G H I J K L M N O P Q R S T U V W X Y Z

A
B
C
D
E
F
G
H
I
J
K
L
M
N
O
P
Q
R
S
T
U
V
W
X
Y
Z

Foam Bath Fish Time

Kevin Savetz plays with bathtub foam fish toys. You will too, at this site, which will tell you the time in several time zones—using FISH. Just get in here and see one of Net-mom's all-time favorite Internet toys!

http://www.northcoast.com/savetz/fish/fishtime.cgi

marine-biology Fishes

What's the *porpoise* of this site? Well, if you can't tell a yellowfin tuna from a cookie-cutter shark or a ratfish from a queenfish, then your troubles are over! This Cal Poly marine biology site has descriptions and photos of many common Pacific fish.

http://www.calpoly.edu:8010/cgi-bin/db/db/
marine-biology/Fishes:/templates/index

The Salmon Page

The Riverdale Elementary School in Oregon loves salmon: catching it, cooking it, and saving it and its environment. They have also illustrated the page with colorful fishy paintings. For a collection of unchecked links about this king of fishes, cast your line here!

http://www.riverdale.k12.or.us/salmon.htm

Underwater World Home Page

Want to go on an underwater diving adventure in the Galápagos Islands? Go to this site, and don't forget your fins! You'll escape the deadly chomp of the scariest sharks in the sea. You can help some freaky fishes finish their family album by matching names with pictures, then add your name to the freaky fishes' friends hall of fame. Did you know that fish have no eyelids? They can't blink, wink, or close their eyes to sleep. Learn what a lobster eats, how a clam shell grows, how oysters make pearls, and answers to other fishy questions.

http://pathfinder.com/pathfinder/kidstuff/underwater/

FITNESS AND EXERCISE

Fitness Fundamentals

The President of the United States wants you to be physically fit! The President's Council on Physical Fitness and Sports is an organization whose single goal is to help Americans become fit—to aid citizens in learning how to be physically healthy. One of the many resources the Council provides is the booklet at this site. It provides all the basics in starting an exercise and fitness program for people of all ages, including figuring out what your target heart rate during exercise should be.

http://www.hoptechno.com/book11.htm

Reebok Guide to Fitness

Good ol' walking—putting one foot in front of the other—is a great way to stay fit. Extensive walking for exercise, though, requires preparation, including stretching exercises and goal setting. It's all illustrated for you here. Check out this site to get some ideas on how to plan to walk your way to fitness. And take your dog out with you—dogs like fresh air, too!

http://www.reebok.com/spfit/walkfit/
walkreebok1.html

STRETCHING AND FLEXIBILITY

When you exercise—whether you're going for a run or a short jog or you're dancing up a storm—stretching your muscles before you begin is important. At this page on the World Wide Web, you'll learn everything there is to know about stretching and how muscles contract. You'll also learn about fast and slow fibers, connective tissue, and cooperating muscle groups. As a matter of fact, if you read all this, you'll be a foremost expert on this subject!

http://www.ntf.CA:8082/papers/rma/
stretching_toc.html

Take a closer look through the microscope in BIOLOGY.

Welcome to turnstep.com!

One, two, three—kick!! Aerobic exercises get your heart beating and your lungs heaving, and they make your muscles strong. Many aerobic exercises are fun when done to music as dance steps that tone your body. You can learn some new aerobic steps and a ton about aerobics by checking out this Web page.

http://www.turnstep.com/

FLAGS

Ausflag - For Further Information

Vexillology is the study of flags, and many people find it a topic of deep consequence. This site gives some general flag terms, plus worthwhile links to flag resources all over the Net. You can also see the winners in an unofficial contest to design a new flag for Australia. Also try the Heraldry and Vexillology Page at <*http://www.du.edu/~tomills/flags.html*>. There, you'll find out why flags are flown at half-mast, which flags get to fly higher than others, and more.

http://www.ausflag.com.au/info/info.html

Betsy Ross Home Page

Betsy Ross is credited with having sewn the very first U.S. flag in 1776. But did she? You can learn about the questions surrounding this cherished American figure, as well as take a virtual tour to her house in Philadelphia. Apparently George Washington wanted six-pointed stars on the flag, as they appear on his original pencil sketch. Betsy recommended five-pointed stars instead. Everyone scoffed, saying that the stars were too hard to draw, let alone cut. Then the committee with Washington stood amazed as Ross folded a piece of paper, made one snip with scissors, and unfolded a perfect five-pointed star! You can learn the secret of this trick at <*http://www.libertynet.org/iha/betsy/flagstar.html*>.

http://www.libertynet.org/iha/betsy/

The Flag of the United States of America

For a country that is barely over two hundred years old, the United States has a vast and rich accumulation of lore and tradition regarding its flag. Old Glory gets its due from this page in red, white, and blue embellishment. Images of every single official and unofficial U.S. flag are stored here, as well as a variety of documents, songs, poems, speeches, and letters. Red Skelton's famous version of the Pledge of Allegiance can be found here, as well as the information you'll need if you'd like to acquire a flag that has flown over the Capitol. A series of intriguing questions and answers are posted here, along with the (complete!) words to the National Anthem. The site also carries "opposing views" about flags, national symbols, and patriotism.

http://www.icss.com/usflag/

Did you know that you can buy a flag that has flown over the U.S. Capitol?
It doesn't stay up there very long, just a minute or so, but think of the tradition and history and, heck, the fun of having a flag like that! You can even request a flag that has flown over the Capitol on your birthday or other special occasion.
The flags cost between $7.50 and $18.75 plus shipping, and the ordering information can be found at The Flag of the United States of America Page.

Flags

This site features just about every flag from every nation in the world, each as a separate downloadable, full-color, inline GIF image. Other information for each nation from the *World Factbook* can be found here as well.

http://www.adfa.oz.au/CS/other/flg/

A B C D E F G H I J K L M N O P Q R S T U V W X Y Z

A
B
C
D
E
F
G
H
I
J
K
L
M
N
O
P
Q
R
S
T
U
V
W
X
Y
Z

Flags

Dyed-in-the-wool flag fans will find some delightful goodies on this Australian page. Besides a fine selection of international flag images, you'll find sections featuring motor racing flags, international maritime signal flags ("I am discharging explosives!"), and the complete semaphore flag code—all graphically displayed.

http://osprey.anbg.gov.au/flags/flags.html

Microscopic Flag Icons for the KIDLINK WWW

Here you will find more than 75 tiny flag icons representing countries participating in the KIDCAFE and KIDLINK discussion list projects. This page loads rapidly, since the GIFs are so small. You can use these to dress up your school reports or home pages!

http://www.kidlink.org/WWW/miniflags.html

NAVA Presents - The Flags of the Native American Peoples of the United States

Over 500 Indian nations are recognized by the U.S. government, and some of them have their own flags, which are shown and described here. The Nez Perce have a salmon and a deer on their flag, as well as an eagle, which is sacred to their nation. There is also a drawing of Chief Joseph, one of the greatest Indian leaders. The Iroquois flag has linked squares, symbolizing the nations of the Iroquois confederacy, designed to look like linked wampum shell beads. There are many more flags to admire at this unique site!

http://www.nava.org

Quinn Flags and Banners

Chances are good that your local mall doesn't have a flag store. This site is where you will probably want to go when the occasion calls for purchasing a flag, whether it's the Stars and Stripes, a state flag, the Jolly Roger, sports flags, or flags from many nations. You can even get the flag for Vatican City here! Flag poles, mounting brackets, and indoor display equipment are all available here as well. There are also some guidelines on flag etiquette.

http://www.qflags.com/

USPS and other Nautical Flags

Have you ever seen a tall ship "dressed"? That means it has all its colorful flags and pennants flying for a special occasion. Those flags also represent a common maritime language. Some flags stand for letters, numbers, or words. Some combinations of flags have special meanings, too. Check this site to see messages like "I am on fire!" or "I need a tow." You'll also learn a lot about nautical flag etiquette, as well as international and U.S. flag customs in general. This excellent site is prepared by the U.S. Power Squadron.

http://www.usps.org/f_stuff/flag.html

Welcome to FOTW (Flags of the World)

If you were going to design a flag for cyberspace, what would it look like? Fans of this site have chosen one—see what you think. We also liked one of the losers (the one with the two crossed computer mice), but there is no accounting for taste. You'll also find pages and pages of flags of the world here, too. An extra bonus: you'll see national symbols, anthems, and other patriotic links for many countries!

http://flags.cesi.it/flags/

FOLKLORE AND MYTHOLOGY

BREWER: Dictionary of Phrase and Fable

Are you forever forgetting the Riddle of the Sphinx? Want to know who Apollo was? Can't wait to find out what the seven wonders of the ancient and medieval worlds were? The current edition of this classic book is one of Net-mom's favorites. The 1894 edition is online and searchable!

http://www.bibliomania.com/Reference/PhraseAndFable/

AMPHIBIANS! Visit the Froggy Page before you croak.

The Encyclopedia Mythica

This encyclopedia on mythology, folklore, and magic contains well over 1,800 definitions of gods and goddesses, supernatural beings, and legendary creatures and monsters from cultures and beliefs all over the world. You'll find Chinese, Etruscan, Greek, Haitian, Japanese, Latvian, Mayan, Native American, Norse, Persian, Roman, Welsh, and other mythologies here. Check up on gnomes, unicorns, fairies, and other legendary beings in this award-winning reference source!

http://www.pantheon.org/mythica/

Gryphons, Griffins, Griffons!

This page is dedicated to *gryphons*, mythological beasts with the head, forelegs, and wings of an eagle and the hindquarters, tail, and ears of a lion. They are symbols of strength and vigilance in mythology. Sections of this home page include gryphons in literature, art, and architecture and other gryphon sightings on the Internet. Fly over to this site to check out these wondrous beasts!

http://sashimi.wwa.com/~tirya/gryphon.html

Myths and Legends

This impressive set of links contains pointers to resources from Australian Aboriginal myths to modern science fiction and fantasy. It is the single, best source for a comprehensive listing of world mythological resources. You'll find Celtic, Slavic, Greek, Roman, Norse, and many other kinds of stories here. A caution to parents: This site had too many links for us to explore individually.

http://pubpages.unh.edu/~cbsiren/myth.html

Reed Interactive's Online Projects

On this page, you'll find creation stories and traditional wisdom as told by school children from around the world. Included are animal legends, creation stories, tales about the environment, and other stories. Stories have been submitted by children from Australia, Iceland, Canada, Alaska, and Israel.

http://www.ozemail.com.au/~reed/global/
mythstor.html

FAIRY TALES

Cinderella Project: Home Page

You may have seen Disney's animated story of Cinderella, but do you know that there are lots of other pictures and stories about her? Here is a collection of 12 different versions of the story, some with illustrations. She's really an old lady: the earliest version here is dated 1729!

http://www-dept.usm.edu/~engdept/cinderella/
cinderella.html

Cinderella fans should drive their carriages immediately over to the Cinderella Project: Home Page! This site is a text and image archive containing a dozen English versions of the Cinderella tale. The texts may be read horizontally (one version at a time) or vertically (one episode at a time) for comparisons among the versions. You can also choose to look at only the images. This is a good site to visit if you'd like to read variations on a common fairy tale.

Dinos rule in DINOSAURS AND PREHISTORIC TIMES.

A
B
C
D
E
F
G
H
I
J
K
L
M
N
O
P
Q
R
S
T
U
V
W
X
Y
Z

A
B
C
D
E
F
G
H
I
J
K
L
M
N
O
P
Q
R
S
T
U
V
W
X
Y
Z

Faerie Lore and Literature

Move over, Tinkerbell, this is the fairyland of legend and literature! Check the archive of fairy drawings, Irish and other fairy tales, and the fairy dictionary. You'll also find the texts of Andrew Lang's *Red Fairy Book* and *Yellow Fairy Book.* Read about some funny fairies and some that aren't so nice. Don't believe in fairies anymore? Some of us do, and you can even see a photo of one at a Texas Renaissance Fair here (well, sort of). A caution to parents: There are also some links to Wiccan fairy stories included in this very complete collection of stories, poems, and lore.

http://faeryland.etsu.edu/~earendil/faerie/

Tales of Wonder

This site features folk and fairy tales from around the world. Geographic areas represented include Russia, Siberia, central Asia, China, Japan, and the Middle East. Tales from Scandinavia, Scotland, England, Africa, India, and Native American nations are also included. The source used for the stories is listed. This is an excellent site for exploring the world of folk and fairy tales.

http://www.ece.ucdavis.edu/~darsie/tales.html

Every time you baby-sit your little brother, he wants a story, and you've told him all the stories you know! Get some new ones at Tales of Wonder, which contains folk and fairy tales from around the world. You'll find stories from China, Scotland, Japan, and the Middle East, as well as many stories told by Native Americans.

KING ARTHUR

Avalon: Arthurian Heaven

Avalon is the mystical isle where King Arthur was taken after he was mortally wounded in battle. According to legend, Arthur is still sleeping in Avalon until a modern-day hero can awaken him. This home page offers lots of information for Camelot fans, including FAQ, a list of Arthurian names, the ten rules of chivalry, and some Arthurian shields. Other types of references you can find here are books, articles, and other media, including *First Knight.* Don't forget to read the link to information about copyright of this home page if you're going to use this information in a school report!

http://reality.sgi.com/employees/chris_manchester/arthur.html

*Interested in the Knights of the Round Table and their quest for the Holy Grail? Avalon is where the once and future King Arthur sleeps until awakened by a future hero, to ride across the moors of Britain once again. Could that hero be you? **Avalon: Arthurian Heaven** gives beginners a firm footing in Arthurian legend via book lists, multimedia, and links to other sites exploring the mystery and legend behind the Celtic hero. Remember the tenth Rule of Chivalry, which is: **Thou shalt be everywhere and always the champion of the Right and Good and the foe of Injustice and Evil!***

The Teel Family of Alaska, webmasters of the ever-enjoyable Snow Page and more.

"Someone wanted to know what language we speak in Alaska, if we have seen any polar bears, and if the northern lights dance when you clap!"

FAMILY HOME PAGES

The Teel Family WWW Site

Webmasters: Susan, Matthew, Sarah, Caleb, and Ricky Teel

http://www.teelfamily.com/

Who came up with the idea for your page or project?

My husband Matthew came up with the original idea, and I found that we all loved working on the Web site.

How many people work on your pages? Does it take a lot of time? How many hits do you get a day?

I do the largest amount of work, but Matthew does the guest book and his pages. Sarah and Caleb each do all the work on their pages, and Ricky has a little help from Mom! Our site receives an average of over 400 unique visitors per day reading an average of 44.84 documents each, or 19,327 documents per day. A large percentage are from outside the United States.

You must hear from people all over the world! Can you think of an unusual request, question, or comment someone has sent to you?

Someone wanted to know what language we speak in Alaska, if we have seen any polar bears, and if the northern lights dance when you clap!

What is your favorite resource on the Net?

Aunt Annie's Craft Page <http://www.auntannie.com/>.

If this isn't your main job, what do you do, what is your training?

Life ;-)

What's the one thing you'd really like to do on your page but have not yet implemented?

An interactive goal chart that homeschoolers could use to set and print their goals for the day.

Do you have a family? A dog? A lizard?

We have a dog, two cats, a gerbil, a lizard, and fish.

What are your hopes and fears for the future of the Internet?

I hope that it remains a place where the average person can still have a voice. My fear is that the monolithic commercial sites will overpower the individual sites.

When you're not using the Net, what do you like to do?

Crafts, teach, read, garden, go on outings with the kids.

If you could invite three people throughout history to your house for dinner, who would they be?

Abe Lincoln (16th President of the United States), Moses (Old Testament religious leader), Ben Franklin (scientist and statesman).

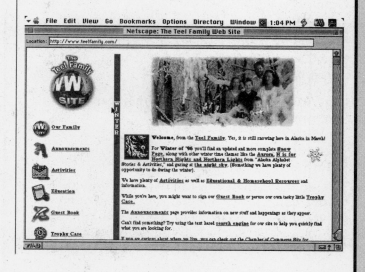

A
B
C
D
E
F
G
H
I
J
K
L
M
N
O
P
Q
R
S
T
U
V
W
X
Y
Z

GAMES AND FUN

@ Thunderbeam Kids' Software: Your quest for the perfect kids' software ends here!

These games, rated by kids, require Java-enabled browsers. If your computer is Java-enabled, take your pick, from classic skill games to arcade games to games that challenge your math and verbal abilities! If you don't like getting eaten by snakes, forget Planet Sisyphus. We did like Thimblerig, where a die is under one of the Pepsi cups, which seem to be square dancing in front of you. Which cup? You'll go nuts, but it's fun!

http://www.thunderbeam.com/web/k/javacorral/
    index.html

ACEKids_Java_Games

Is your browser Java-enabled? If you're not sure, this page explains how you can tell. Make sure you don't enable Java without asking your parents first, since there are lots of reasons they may have chosen to disable it. But if you've got it, you can play Master Mind, Connect Four, Stars, and Hit Me!

http://www.acekids.com/javagame.html

Billy Bear Storybooks - Free Fun & Games Page

The graphics here are superb! You can play these games online or offline on paper. The "Make Your Own Cartoon Bear" and the "Mix & Match Em Up" games are sure to be winners.

http://www.worldvillage.com/kidz/bilybear/
    wgames.htm

Build-a-Monster

This is a sweet little game to amuse the little kids in your family. Pick a head for your monster—how about that frog? OK, now pick a body—do you like that chicken? Now, which feet should you pick? Yikes, that makes a very strange-looking monster, but it won't scare anyone!

http://www.rahul.net/renoir/monster/monster.html

Children's Playground

Do you like puzzles? Here you'll find mazes, word search puzzles, jigsaws, and more. Many of them were designed for kids, by kids! You'll also find family activities, music, pages that *talk* and *sing* (if you have the right plug-ins and hardware), and much more. We particularly enjoy the "Shareware Carol." This site is available in English and Spanish, and some songs are in Japanese.

http://www.peak.org/~platypus/in.html

Cyber Jacques' Cyber Seas Treasure Hunt

Avast ye, me hearties, from whatever else you're doing, and come try the games at Cyber Jacques' seagoing arcade. They all require Shockwave, so you'd best have a current version or you'll be walking the plank real soon! What's here? In Fish, you throw pies at a bear but avoid the flying fish jumping up between the two of you. In What's Inside, you take apart a pirate to see what's underneath (a hamster running around an exercise wheel is one thing we found) and retrieve letters to a word puzzle. Figure out the secret word, and you've won! You'll find several more equally wacky games here.

http://www.cyberjacques.com/index.html

NET FILES

What can you get from one bushel of corn?

Answer: A backache, if you try to lift it by yourself! A bushel of corn weighs about 56 pounds and contains approximately 72,800 kernels. Most of the weight is the starch, oil, protein, and fiber, along with some natural moisture. From that one bushel you could make: 32 pounds of cornstarch or 33 pounds of corn sweetener or 2.5 gallons of fuel ethanol, plus 11.4 pounds of 20 percent gluten feed, 3 pounds of 60 percent gluten meal, and 1.6 pounds of corn oil! You'll find this answer at http://www.ohiocorn.org/usage/bushel.htm

The Electric Origami Shop

Actually, this site is not about origami at all, but the stuff here will bend your mind. Check the Fridge Gallery, where you can display your art in cyberspace. None of those tacky magnets are needed—just a bit of cyberglue and your imagination. Or take the temperature of the mood of the Internet today—is it blissfully unaware, grumpy, or happy? Add your mood. Be sure to seed some alien snow, and watch it grow into drifts before your eyes!

http://www.ibm.com/Stretch/EOS/

Games Kids Play

Remember that game you played at camp last summer? It was called Steal the Bacon, wasn't it? Or was it Red Light/Green Light? Maybe you're mixing it up with What Time Is It, Mr. Wolf? If you're a little hazy on the rules of those terrific games you had fun playing once—and then forgot—visit this site. You'll find an archive of the best kids' games EVER!

http://www.corpcomm.net/~gnieboer/gamehome.htm

Happy Fun Physics Ball

Here's another strange Java game. Click on the Happy Fun Ball and drag your mouse over to the nearest wall of the game square. Now release the button. Happy Fun Ball bounces off the wall. Not impressed yet? OK, now click on Happy Fun Ball and drag it as fast as you can around and around the screen. Now let it go. Keep doing it. Happy Fun Ball has some random tricks that you'll see, sooner or later.

http://links.math.rpi.edu/java/students/sander/
    Friction/

I Spy

Before we all wondered where Waldo was, we loved a game called I Spy. Now that game's come to the Web, and it's perfect entertainment for young children. Choose a picture, say, a screen full of colorful postage stamps. The first player looks at the picture and says, "I spy a rocket!" Player two points to the stamp with the rocket on it, if he or she can find it. Then it's player two's turn: "I spy a stamp with a dog!" And so on. See if you can find the stamp with Mt. Rushmore!

http://www.lexmark.com/data/spy/spy.html

Kid's Corner * Oasis Telecommunications, Inc.

Here is one wing. Where is the other one? Hmm, the body goes here, and oops, leave room for the antennae to go here! Can you guess what kind of puzzle we're doing and what picture we will have when we are done? Check it out, and while you're here, try a hangman game and a very nice collection of links.

http://kids.ot.com/

Mr. Edible Starchy Tuber Head Home Page

If you are a big fan of Mr. Potato Head, this is the next best thing. Select online options for eyes, ears, hair, and so on to determine what your Mr. ESTH looks like. The author of the page has also created stories about Mr. ESTH, as well as places he's been spotted in the movies and on TV! Now it comes with a link to a cheap imitation: Mr. Edible Fibrous Stalk Head, at <http://smurfland.cit.buffalo.edu/hot-bin/cel>.

http://winnie.acsu.buffalo.edu/potatoe/

NET FILES

What's the world's longest insect?

check http://info.ex.ac.uk/~gjlramel/six.html over a foot long! To find out more incredible facts, (*Pharnacia serritypes*), the female of which can be the longest insect in the world is the Stick insect **Answer:** According to The Insect Home Page,

A B C D E F G H I J K L M N O P Q R S T U V W X Y Z

A B C D E F G H I J K L M N O P Q R S T U V W X Y Z

PonyShow's Kids - Paradox's Puzzles

Paradox has created some really charming puzzles here. If you like to look for hidden animals and objects in drawings, try Pop's Pizza Puzzle or the Secret of the Spiral Notebook. Other puzzles attempt to teach math concepts such as tangents or repeating images, but they are not interactive. For more fun, go back out to the main page at <http://www.ponyshow.com/kidsnet/websitea.htm> and read stories, write to pen pals, or try more links!

http://www.ponyshow.com/kidsnet/puzzle/puzzle.htm

Professor Bubbles' Official Bubble Homepage

You don't need a lot of skills to learn to blow soap bubbles, right? So what is with this guy who calls himself "Professor"? Turns out he really is an expert. At his home page, he reveals the ultimate soap solution for making the most colorful, sturdy bubbles. He explains how to make your own bubble-blowing tools from soup cans and coat hangers (ask your parents for help). You don't even need anything special—he teaches you how to blow bubbles using only your HANDS! But wait, there's more. Check the bubble FAQ, bubble games, and the other wonders of the Bubblesphere.

http://bubbles.org/

Virtual Mr. Spud Head

Similar to Mr. Edible Starchy Tuber Head, this site lets you choose other vegetables. Try a moustache on an artichoke, or maybe some spectacles on a pumpkin. Not a veggie fan? You could try a famous politician, too!

http://www.westnet.com/~crywalt/pothead/pothead.html

Where's Waldo?

That Waldo—he's lost again! Can you find him at the circus? He's hidden in the crowd somewhere. Maybe if you click on some of these objects, they will make noises—try it! After you find Waldo at the circus, try the geography game. There are downloadable demos for both Mac and Windows platforms, or you can play the games online.

http://www.warneractive.com/index.html

BOARD GAMES
The Gateway to Othello

This Swedish site lets you play Othello, or Reversi, against the computer. You can also read about rules, strategy, and tournaments and view a list of the world's best (human) players at some of the linked sites.

http://www.pt.hk-r.se/~roos/othello1/

Marcel's WebMind

This is a Web version of the popular Master Mind game. You can play this game right over the Internet! The objective is to break the "code" by finding the right combination of colors. The computer will show a black peg, which means that you have the right color in the right position, or a white peg, which means that you have the right color in the wrong position. You can play at several different skill levels, too, and this version gives you hints.

http://einstein.et.tudelft.nl/~mvdlaan/WebMind/WM_intro.html

Play Chess against tkChess

If you know your rooks from your pawns, you'll definitely want to make your move here. There are two versions: one is Java-enabled, so you can drag your pieces around; the other should work fine on both text and graphical browsers, but be sure to read the FAQ to find out how to use the algebraic notation system, which is easier than it sounds. You'll also find links to other Net chess pages, including one that will let you challenge another online player so you can play in real time.

http://pine.cs.yale.edu:4201/cgi-bin/chessplayer/

San Jose Scrabble® Club No. 21

Did you know that "a'a" is an acceptable Scrabble word? It's a type of rough, cinderlike lava. If you're a fan of the game, this page will go a long way to settle arguments and food fights over which word is legal or not. This page provides links to other Scrabble pages on the Web and even has information on the world championships! The Scrabble FAQ at <http://www.teleport.com/~stevena/scrabble/faq.html> links you to other clubs around the world as well as to more and more Scrabble and crossword puzzle links.

http://www.yak.net/kablooey/scrabble.html

Welcome to Connect Four

Tired of the same old tic-tac-toe? Then maybe you'd like to try Connect Four. Play against the computer and see if you can outsmart it—we couldn't! The best thing about playing over the Net is that you never lose the game pieces.

http://csugrad.cs.vt.edu/htbin/Connect4.perl

CARD GAMES
Card Games

This page is an excellent place to get the rules of many different types of card games from all over the world. If you have a question about who goes first in Go Fish, then this is the page for you! A caution to parents: Not all of the world's card games have family-friendly names.

http://www.netlink.co.uk/users/pagat/

The House of Cards

Do you ever just sit alone on a rainy day and realize that there is nothing else to do but play Solitaire? If you only knew *how* to play Solitaire! Think of this site as the place you can go to learn the rules of card games new, old, and never before heard of.

http://www.sky.net/~rrasa/hoc.html

Did you know

that jokers were added to American card decks in the 1870s? You can learn about different types of decks and try out lots of fun card games at The House of Cards!

DARTS
CyberDarts

Do you see bull's-eyes when you surf the Net? Maybe you'd better turn off the computer and take a walk outside, in actual reality! If you're *looking* for bull's-eyes, though, you've come to the right place. This is the page for those who are obsessed with the game of darts. This page includes press releases from the American Dart Association, a listing of international dart groups (you can find one near you), and wild and crazy dart stories. It's a must for dart enthusiasts. Links are too numerous, and we could not check them all.

http://www.cyberdarts.com/

FRISBEE
Freestyle Frisbee

Ever notice how Frisbees never come with directions? How do you learn those cool tricks? Now you can visit this Web site and learn from the experts. Put a spin on it, and don't forget the silicon spray!

http://www.frisbee.com/

The History of the Disc

Ever wondered who invented the toy Frisbee? It began life as either a pie plate or a cookie tin lid from the Frisbie Pie Company in New Haven, Connecticut, long ago in the early 1870s. You can read the incredible history of this toy here and even see the original patent. Never heard of a "patent"? This page explains it all!

http://www.upa.org/~upa/upa/frisbee-hist.html

An Introduction to the Sport of Ultimate

"When a ball dreams, it dreams it's a Frisbee!" And you thought it was just a simple game. This stuff is serious fun. Ultimate had a modest beginning back in 1968 in New Jersey at Columbia High School. By 1972, the game had escalated to an intercollegiate sport, and today it's played in over 30 countries around the world. As with any sport, there are rules, but the list is short and the play is simple. Check it out!

http://radon.gas.uug.arizona.edu/~hko/upa/intro.html

A B C D E F G H I J K L M N O P Q R S T U V W X Y Z

A B C D E F G H I J K L M N O P Q R S T U V W X Y Z

National Capital Air Canines

Don't leave your dog home when you want to play—take your pet along! This page features world-class disc dogs in action photos. Bone up on how to train your dog to catch and fetch a flying disc!

http://www.vais.net/~krobair/ncac.htm

GRAFFITI
Graffiti Walls

Let's be honest. Graffiti is ugly: it makes buildings and signs look hideous. On the other hand, it is kind of fun to be able to leave a mark somewhere. The problem is that graffiti makes whatever is marked look ugly. Now, through the wonder of the Internet, you can leave your mark and never worry about defacing property. It's at this site, and there is one for kids aged 11 and younger and one for kids aged 12 and up. Spray paint, scratch, do what you like. It's designed for fun with no unsightly mess to clean up! The walls are closely monitored for appropriate content to keep the site enjoyable for all.

http://www.kidscom.com/newkc/wall.html

NET FILES

What color is a giraffe's tongue?

Answer: *It's black, and it's over 20 inches long! Read up on giraffes at* http://www.wolfe.net/~ohwell/giraffe.html

HORSESHOE PITCHING
Horseshoe Pitching Information Site

You can't just borrow shoes from the pony in the paddock; you've got to use regulation horseshoes if you want to play with folks from the National Horseshoe Pitchers Association (NHPA). According to this home page, the horseshoes used by the NHPA are very different from shoes actually used on horses— they are much bigger. Any shoe used in a tournament must not exceed 7 1/4 inches in width and 7 5/8 inches in length. The opening of the horseshoe can't be wider than 3 1/2 inches from just inside both points of the shoe. Most of them weigh about 2.5 pounds. For more of the fine points of horseshoe pitching, trot on over here!

http://user.holli.com/~tsearsxx/
    Horseshoe-Pitching.html

Rules of Horseshoes

Here are the court dimensions, rules, and scoring for the game of horseshoes. It's everything you'll need to set up the game. Add two steel stakes, a set of horseshoes, some sand for the pits, and a yard. A partner is also a must. No room for a horseshoe pit where you live? Try the smaller-size variant: washers! The link to that page is at <http://www.bro.net./washers/>.

http://www.ece.neu.edu/personal/stricker/
    horseshoes/horseshoe_rules.html

MAZES
Glenn Teitelbaum's Maze

Hang a left—no, a right! Now you're lost (you can always use that BACK key on your browser). Have fun exploring these interactive mazes, but watch out for The Minotaur. Every now and again The Wumpus will turn up and show where you are on the map. Unfortunately, the Wumpus will run away again—with the map!

http://www.pb.net/usrwww/w_tglenn/maze.htm

Visit the CHEMISTRY section periodically.

PeterCat's Maze of Treasures

Gosh, which way should you go? You have a choice of three directions: should you try the Twisting Little Maze of Passages, the Maze of Little Twisting Passages, or the Twisty Maze of Little Passages? Sometimes when you choose a direction, a "treasure" Web site is selected, and you can choose to go "off-maze" to check it out. Choose the right directions, and angels and leprechauns will escort you to the exit! A caution to parents: Not all the "treasure" sites have been checked; kids should use this site with their parents.

http://www.servtech.com/public/petercat/maze/

POGS AND MILKCAPS

Milkcaps, the Hawaiian Phenomenon

Has the game of milkcaps, or POGS, hit your school yet? Don't worry, it will; or maybe this fad has come and gone where you are. This very easy game has kids everywhere clamoring for POGS, POGS, and more POGS! But did you know that the game may have started 600 years ago in Japan? Find out about the mother of POGs, Blossom Galbiso, who reinvented the game for schoolchildren.

http://www.ukulele.com/milkcaps.html

STONE SKIPPING

North American Stone Skipping Association

"If you can throw a stone at the water and make it touch down and lift off, just once, you have skipped a stone and thereby join one of the most ancient recreational activities of humankind," says Jerdone. He's the current Guinness world record holder for stone skipping! In 1994, he made a small piece of flat black slate jump 38 skips, on the Blanco River in Texas. This site tells you all about the history of stone skipping, also known as "Ducks and Drakes" in England, "ricochet" in France, and "stone skiffing" in Ireland. It even tells you how to challenge the world record holder and asks you to send in your favorite stone skipping locations so they can be mapped worldwide. The huge links list off this page has not been checked.

http://www.ccsi.com/yeeha/nassa/a1.html

Sitting on a beach, you idly pick up a small flat stone and shoot it across the surface of the water. Wow! It sure skipped a lot of times! Could be a world record! Check the North American Stone Skipping Association's home page and read lots of interesting things about skipping stones.

STRING FIGURES
World-Wide Webs

Everybody's taken a loop of string and played Cat's Cradle with a friend. Here's a collection of string figures from around the world to keep you busy all afternoon! Try The Banana Tree or Four Boys Walking in a Row, both from Pacific islands.

http://www.ece.ucdavis.edu/~darsie/string.html

GARDENS AND GARDENING

See also FARMING AND AGRICULTURE

The Butterfly Guide

You love butterflies, especially when they visit your yard. You wish they'd stay around longer, though. This site tells you what kinds of plants you need in your garden to attract caterpillars and butterflies, especially the really pretty and unusual ones. For example, if you want the beautiful, light blue spring azure butterfly to hang around, you need to plant aster, butterfly weed, and dogwood trees.

http://www.butterflies.com/guide.html

A
B
C
D
E
F
G
H
I
J
K
L
M
N
O
P
Q
R
S
T
U
V
W
X
Y
Z

Canoe Plants / Introduction and Contents

When early Polynesian explorers set out for Hawaii, a journey of thousands of miles, they traveled in wooden canoes. They took with them, among other things, 24 species of plants thought to be essential to life. These "canoe plants" of ancient Hawaii included *awapuhi kuahiwi* (shampoo ginger), *ko* (sugar cane), and *niu* (coconut). They were all the new settlers needed for their food, rope, medicine, containers, and fabrics. Here's a guide to these life-sustaining plants. There are also fascinating links to early Polynesian wayfinding over these vast ocean reaches.

http://www.hawaii-nation.org/canoe/canoe.html

Carnivorous Plant Database

Imagine this if you can: a little fly takes a break from buzzing around by coming to rest on the leaf of a beautiful pink plant. What the fly doesn't know is that the leaf is very sticky. Slowly, the leaf edges curl up around the fly. Gulp. It's been eaten—by a plant! Trapping insects for food is what "carnivorous" plants do. They live in poor soil, so they have to get their nutrition from somewhere (or something). Here, you can see what they look like. A fun thing to do at this site is to click on "Database Entry Formats" to find the right abbreviation for where you live. Then enter the abbreviation into the search box to see if carnivorous plants are anywhere near you. If so, keep your pet flies tied up inside! There are also links to other sites on the Net with even more information and pictures of carnivorous plants.

http://www.hpl.hp.com/bot/cp_home/

**Looking for
the State Bird
or the State Motto?
It's in the
UNITED STATES section**

Hydroponics! Hydroponics! Hydroponics! IUWF On-Line!

OK, you've got no dirt, no sunshine, and no space. No way can you start a garden, right? Wrong. Hydroponics to the rescue. Hydro-what? "Hydro," as in water, and "ponics," as in the Greek word *ponos*, which means labor. But you don't have to work very hard to grow plants hydroponically, which just means growing them in water mixed with fertilizer—no dirt is required. Plants use a lot of energy tunneling their roots into the dirt to get food. With the hydroponic method, vegetables, fruits, flowers, and herbs get big and fat by lying back and letting their roots hang down in some very nutritious water. Imagine making strawberry shortcake in the middle of January, with organic strawberries grown from your own "water farm" in your bedroom closet! Take a look at this site to find out how.

http://www.viasub.net/IUWF/index.html

HYPERGARDEN

So what if you've got a black thumb—you can always go hang out in the Hypergarden, created by the students at the Electronic Imaging Lab of Metropolitan Community College in Omaha, Nebraska. Here you'll find a weird but beautiful bunch of images using parts of actual gardens—like trellises—and fractal forms. Huh? What's that? A *fractal* is a geometric shape—like certain kinds of triangles, snowflakes, trees, clouds, and mountains—that can be divided into parts that each look like the shape you started with. If the spooky Addams Family has a garden, this is what it looks like.

http://www.unomaha.edu/~gday/hypergarden.html

KinderGARDEN

This is a treasure trove of gardening links and projects just for kids and families, brought to you by Texas A & M. Whether growing a salad on your windowsill or sprouts in an eggshell, you'll find easy-to-understand projects here. There's even more: games, puzzles, and advice on the best gardening books for kids.

http://aggie-horticulture.tamu.edu/kinder/index.html

A
B
C
D
E
F
G
H
I
J
K
L
M
N
O
P
Q
R
S
T
U
V
W
X
Y
Z

Search the WebGarden Factsheet Database

Yikes! Your carrots have weevils all over them, and the bottoms of your tomatoes are covered with black spots. Who ya gonna call? Ohio State University's WebGarden Factsheet Database, that's who. It's a mega-collection of over 5,000 links to gardening fact sheets from the United States, Canada, and all over, complete with a handy little search form. In the case of your weird tomatoes, for example, all you have to do is type "tomatoes" and "black spot" into the title part of the form and choose "vegetables" as the category for expert advice and instant relief (bet you're watering too much or too little). Try the WebGarden main pages for a gardening dictionary and more on watching your garden grow.

http://hortwww-2.ag.ohio-state.edu/hvp/Webgarden/
   FactsheetFind.html

Seeds of Change Garden

What's a Seeds of Change garden? It's a combination of green thumb and cultural exchange. Before Columbus arrived in the New World in 1492, there were "Old World" plants native to Europe and "New World" plants native to the Americas. People's food choices were limited to what grew nearby; if oranges didn't grow in their village, for example, they would never get to taste one. Exploration and trade with other nations changed all that. Read about how schools are growing Old World and New World gardens and a third garden based on seeds from traditional fruits and vegetables saved from their home kitchens. This terrific site will tell you all about the history of food crop plants and how you can create your own Seeds of Change garden! You'll find recipes here, too.

http://horizon.nmsu.edu/garden/welcome.html

**Did the groundhog
see his shadow?
Find out if it will be an
early spring in HOLIDAYS.**

The Telegarden

Now here's a garden for the '90s, where Web cruisers gather to plant seeds and water plants by the remote control of an industrial robotic arm. This started as a real garden at the University of Southern California, although for 1997 it has moved to a server in Austria. The idea is to bring together a community of people to help tend a "shared garden." Click on "Guest Entrance" at the bottom of the page. You can explore the garden by clicking on a drawing of the robotic arm. This moves the arm—and a camera—to give you an up-to-the-minute picture of what's going on.

http://www.usc.edu/dept/garden/

See a live image of the Telegarden, an interactive garden that began life at the University of Southern California.

It's in Austria this year, but you can visit it over the Web.

It's tended by a robot controlled by World Wide Web users!

**Get to know some famous
AFRICAN AMERICANS.**

A B C D E F G H I J K L M N O P Q R S T U V W X Y Z

A B C D E F G H I J K L M N O P Q R S T U V W X Y Z

NET FILES

Where are the oldest bells in North America?

Answer: According to the Change Ringing Information page, "The oldest bells in North America are at The Old North Church, in Boston. They were hung in 1745. In the ringing room today hangs a copy of a 1750 charter in which the guild of ringers agreed upon a democratic organization of the tower. Paul Revere's is the second signature on that contract. Perhaps his association with ringing is the reason he had a key to the tower [to give to his friend] that fateful night …." This refers to the "one if by land, two if by sea" lanterns hung in the tower of the Old North Church, which signaled Revere, on the opposite shore, to warn the colonists that the British were coming! Read more about it at http://web.mit.edu/bellringers/www/html/change_instruction.html

The Time Life Gardening Library

OK, you live in Colorado and have a shady front yard. You really like red flowers, but your soil is very poor. Is there anything you can plant? Search the Electronic Encyclopedia's database of thousands of plants to find out which ones will work, what they look like, and how to take care of them. Maybe you already know the name of the plant you want to grow and are just looking for some watering or pruning tips. Everything you need to know is here! When nothing can grow outside, search for a house plant in the House Plant Pavilion. If your parents find out about this site, watch out: you may get to do some weeding. But remember, a weed is just a plant for which a use has not yet been discovered.

http://pathfinder.com/vg/TimeLife/

BOTANIC GARDENS

Boyce Thompson Southwestern Arboretum

If you're one of those people who think a cactus is just a prickly, ugly weed and the desert is a dry wasteland of sand, may we suggest taking a cyberwalk through Arizona's Boyce Thompson Southwestern Arboretum? There's not very much water to go around in the desert, but most deserts are not deserted! Many scientists think that the variety of life in the desert is second only to that found in the tropics. You won't want to miss the cactus garden, with its 800 different cacti, including tall saguaros, ground-covering prickly pears, and squat, spiky hedgehogs. So that the cactus can conserve what little water it has, some of its flowers last only one day—and that day happens to be captured here in lots of beautiful pictures.

http://ag.arizona.edu/BTA/btsa.html

The Butchart Gardens

A garden in an old rock quarry? Come to Vancouver Island, off the west coast of Canada, and see for yourself. Over a million bedding plants are used each year to ensure continuous bloom. And they plant 100,000 bulbs every fall to make a spectacular springtime display!

http://vvv.com/butchart/

NET FILES

How do two traditional Maoris greet each other?

Answer: They don't shake hands or wave; they rub noses. Check out proper gestures and other cultural behavior at http://www.worldculture.com/gesasia.htm so you'll look and feel right at home when you visit another country!

Introduction to the Australian National Botanic Gardens

Ever hear a kookaburra laugh? The call of this bird is one of the most famous sounds of the Australian bush. You can listen to the calls of the kookaburra, the currawong, the peewee, and a bunch of other very strange birds at the Australian National Botanic Gardens. Birds love the gardens because it's a safe place, filled with lots of native plants and habitats that give them food and shelter. You can also find out how Aborigines—who have lived in Australia for at least 40,000 years—gathered everything they needed to live a healthy life from the land. At least half of what they ate came from plants, and one of the ways they encouraged new plants to grow was to burn all the old plants to the ground! And speaking of plants, don't miss the kangaroo paws and the wattles, just two of the many different kinds of plants grown halfway around the world.

http://osprey.erin.gov.au/anbg/anbg-introduction.html

NET FILES

DID you know that sunspots rotate around the Sun? How long does a sunspot take to go completely around and get back to where it was?

ANSWER:
A sunspot takes 27 days to rotate around the Sun's surface. Read all about sunspots at http://www.sel.bldrdoc.gov/primer/primer.html

The New York Botanical Garden

Back before there was a New York City, a forest covered the whole island of Manhattan. Of course, there isn't much of a forest left these days, but 40 acres of the natural, uncut, 200-year-old forest has been saved at the New York Botanical Garden just as it was. The garden, one of the oldest and biggest in the world, also has 27 specialty gardens featuring everything from rocks to roses, all of which you can visit online. Make sure you read all about the garden's scientists, who travel the world looking for medicinal plants that may help to fight cancer and other diseases.

http://pathfinder.com/vg/Gardens/NYBG/

Welcome to the Missouri Botanical Garden's Learning Network!

This site is awesome. For example, explore the virtual biomes. A *biome* is a collection of plants and animals that live together in a specific region. Visit the desert, the tundra, the temperate forest, the grasslands, the rain forest, and the taiga. What's the taiga? It's the largest biome of all, stretching across parts of Canada, Europe, Russia, and Asia. The summers are warm and the winters are cold (with an average temperature of below zero six months of the year!). It doesn't have as many different kinds of animals and plants as the other biomes; still, you can learn all about moose, red fox, and other species that do thrive in this land. Wouldn't it be great to talk to some kids who lived in the taiga biome? You can! There are partner schools for each biome, so check them out.

http://www.mobot.org/MBGnet/

HOUSE PLANTS
Time Life's House Plant Pavilion

Some scientists think we humans have a natural urge to make our houses like the surroundings of our earliest ancestors: lots of clean, warm, humid air and a green landscape. This site is a good place to get started if you want to turn your house into a jungle. Newbies will learn how to grow everything from *acalypha* (otherwise known as a copperleaf) to *zantedeschia* (that's a golden calla lily). You'll also learn a lot about the history of houseplants, which goes back a long, long way.

http://pathfinder.com/vg/TimeLife/Houseplants/

A B C D E F G H I J K L M N O P Q R S T U V W X Y Z

A
B
C
D
E
F
G
H
I
J
K
L
M
N
O
P
Q
R
S
T
U
V
W
X
Y
Z

GENEALOGY AND FAMILY HISTORY

EVERTON'S GENEALOGICAL HELPER: online edition

Here's the online version of the world's largest genealogical magazine, *Everton's Genealogical Helper*. Sure, it's not the print version, which usually runs around 300 pages, but some great features and lots of help for beginning genealogists are available—for free! Recent issues explained how to find your Scandinavian ancestors and talked about Jewish resources on the Internet.

http://www.everton.com/ghonline.html

NET FILES

Where was cheese first made?

Answer: It was probably first made in the Middle East. Cheese was known to the ancient Sumerians in 4000 B.C. The ancient Greeks credited Aristaeus, a son of Apollo and Cyrene, with its discovery; it is also mentioned in the Old Testament of the Bible (don't eat cheese *that old*, though). You can read all about the aromatic world of cheese at CheeseNet

http://www.wgx.com/cheesenet/info/

If you feel funny, think what we went through when we wrote the JOKES AND RIDDLES section!

FHC Listing

Where's the biggest collection of genealogical material in the world? The Family History Library in Salt Lake City, Utah, is the biggest one of its kind. The library is part of the Church of Jesus Christ of Latter-Day Saints. The Church thinks it's very important to find out about family history, so they send researchers around the world to copy public records. You can see these records in person by going to a Family History Center—a branch of the Family History Library—near you. There's at least one in every U.S. state, and there are others in the British Isles, New Zealand, Australia, Canada, and other countries. They're free and open to the public. Take a look at this list to find one close to you.

http://www.genhomepage.com/FHC/fhc.html

The Genealogy Home Page

Ever thought about drawing your family tree? No, not the one in your front yard! We're talking about your relatives. Picture a tree with you at the bottom. On the first two branches are your parents. On the next highest branches are their parents, who are your grandparents. Farther up the tree are their parents, or your great-grandparents. Guess, what—that tree reaches up higher than you can see! Get started here with help from experienced family researchers, called *genealogists*. Computers and the Internet are two of the most important tools being used today by genealogists. You can get your own free family tree tracking software here and learn how to be part of a project to share family histories over the Net. The project already includes millions of names! Wouldn't it be amazing if someone's already working on your family history? Find out here.

http://www.genhomepage.com/full.html

Guide for Interviewing Family Members

"Who was your best friend?" That's just one of the questions you need to include on a family history questionnaire. What are the other 118? Check this site, print out the questions, then go visit your grandma and grandpa for some amazing stories. Don't forget to bring your tape recorder or your videocamera!

gopher://ftp.cac.psu.edu/00/genealogy/roots-l/
   genealog/genealog.intrview

Helm's Genealogy Toolbox - Introduction

Sure, your dog has a pedigree, but do you? Search for your family name and history here. You may find out your friends should be calling you Duke, Prince, or Princess! Would you like to see what your grandparents' (or maybe even great-grandparents') birth or death certificates looked like? Find out how to send away for your own copies. And if your family has its own coat of arms, the section on heraldry will explain what all those colors and symbols mean.

http://genealogy.tbox.com/genealogy.html

NET FILES

Little Bo Peep has lost her sheep and doesn't know where to find them! They probably went to the country that has the most sheep in the world. Where is that, anyway?

Answer: Australia has the most sheep: over 138 million! Don't let anyone pull the wool over your eyes—go to "About Wool" off http://www.ansi.okstate.edu/library/youth.html to find out about sheep breeds and wool production.

IMC's Family Associations & Publications

Ever wonder what it would be like to go to a huge family reunion and meet relatives from all over the country? Maybe there's one being planned right now for your family name. To find out, just go to this site and click on the first letter of your last name. If there is an association for your family, the name and address for the person in charge will be listed.

http://www.memphismemphis.com/genealogy/family/main.htm

GEOGRAPHY

MAPS
THE MAP CASE

This is a project presented by the Bodleian Library Map Room in Great Britain. The Bodleian Library is one of the oldest libraries in the world, and it contains the seventh largest collection of maps. This is a perfect site if you have a report on British history, and they have some unusual maps from the New World, too. For example, there's Boston, Old Montréal, and "Part of Virginia Discovered ... by John Smith 1612" (maybe Pocahontas helped him draw it!).

http://www.rsl.ox.ac.uk/nnj/mapcase.htm

Mapmaker, Mapmaker, Make Me a Map

If you wanted to get to your friend's house but didn't know the way, how would you get there? One way would be to have your friend write the directions on a sheet of paper. That might work if your friend only lived a few blocks away, but it could get very complicated and wordy if he or she lived farther away. The answer: draw a map! This page tells you how maps are made and explains some of the terms used in mapmaking. You'll also find out about the different kinds of maps and how they are used.

http://loki.ur.utk.edu/ut2kids/maps/map.html

MapQuest

Get customized maps for places all over the world using the interactive atlas. You can get street-level information covering 78 countries and 300 international travel destinations. It's outstanding, it's fun, and it's free! There's also a TripQuest driving planner. How long have you been begging Mom and Dad to drive you to Disneyland? Maybe they say, "Oh, it's so far, and we'd get lost on the way." No problem. Just go to this site, type in the name of your town, and type in the nearest city to Disneyland (Anaheim, California, is close enough). Magically, you'll get back not only a map but also detailed driving directions, complete with the mileage of each segment! It works for U.S. and Canada only (driving to Disneyland from Halifax, Nova Scotia is 3,574.6 miles). Unfortunately, you can't drive from Hawaii, but you get the idea.

http://www.mapquest.com/

A
B
C
D
E
F
G
H
I
J
K
L
M
N
O
P
Q
R
S
T
U
V
W
X
Y
Z

A
B
C
D
E
F
G
H
I
J
K
L
M
N
O
P
Q
R
S
T
U
V
W
X
Y
Z

NAISMap Home Page

If you ever wanted to make a detailed map of a country, this is the perfect place for you. You'll use your forms-capable browser to instruct a Graphical Information System (GIS) what you want it to do. Here you can build many different maps of Canada and learn tons about geography in the process. Want to know the Canadian range of the grizzly bear or the location of wetlands? Try this site!

http://ellesmere.ccm.emr.ca/naismap/naismap.html

National Geographic Society Map Machine

Everyone knows how wonderful the National Geographic Society's maps are. Now many of them are online. Need a quick map, facts about a country, state, or province, and a picture of its flag? You'll find it right here at the Map Machine Atlas. Try View From Above (then click on the spinning globe) for colorful maps of the world pieced together from satellite images, digitally enhanced to make it a global cloudless day! You can also get political and physical maps, as well as view some maps of yesteryear in the Flashback area off the main table of contents.

http://www.nationalgeographic.com/ngs/maps/
cartographic.html

The Perry-Castañeda Library Map Collection

Available from the University of Texas Library, this collection includes maps from around the world and links to some of the best map collections on the Internet. Check out the historical maps and the current events maps of Bosnia and Iraq. If you need a map, start here!

http://www.lib.utexas.edu/Libs/PCL/Map_collection/
Map_collection.html

Rare Map Collection

Of course, maps have been around for a long time. You can view one of the finest collections of historic maps on the Internet at this University of Georgia Web site. Included are some great maps of U.S. Civil War battlefields, as well as material on Colonial and Revolutionary America.

http://www.libs.uga.edu/darchive/hargrett/maps/
maps.html

TIGER Map Server Browser

This site will give you color maps with cities, highways, lakes, and other features clearly marked, based on 1992 data. Try searching by ZIP code, latitude-longitude, as well as city name. You can mark your maps with a variety of symbols. It's also linked to the Census Bureau's *U.S. Gazetteer*, with information on population. You can save your map as a GIF image (select that button, then click on the map itself) and print it. Enclose it with your next letter to Santa or your relatives or anyone else who needs directions to your house!

http://tiger.census.gov/cgi-bin/mapbrowse-tbl

USGS: What Do Maps Show

This site has comprehensive lesson plans and hands-on student activity sheets for students—all related to understanding maps. You can also download student map packets, which you can print out for use with the lessons. This is a great geography teaching and learning tool.

http://info.er.usgs.gov/education/teacher/
what-do-maps-show/WDMSTGuide.html

Xerox PARC Map Viewer

Quick—you need an emergency map of Idaho to complete your homework! Relax, this site gives you public domain, copyright-free maps on demand, for the United States and world regions, using several different projections. The maps show only coastlines, rivers, and borders; they don't have marked cities or roads. For those using a text-only browser, the following hint is suggested by Xerox's Palo Alto Research Center: Select the Map Viewer's "Hide Map Image" option and then the "Retrieve Map Image Only" option. Some browsers will then allow you to save the image to a file on your computer.

http://mapweb.parc.xerox.com/map/

DISNEY: a man, a plan, a land!

Heather Shade, a first grader with one of the most popular kids' sites on the Internet, Heather's Happy Holidaze.

If you could invite three people throughout history to your house for dinner, who would they be? "The real Barbie, the elves from Santa's workshop, and Sleeping Beauty."

FAMILY HOME PAGES

Heather's Happy Holidaze Page - For Kids Only!!

Webmaster: Heather Shade

http://www.shadeslanding.com/hms/

Who came up with the idea for your page or project?

Me! I got the idea because my brother had a Web site and I wanted one too! I wanted mine to be about holidays because I like them so much.

How many people work on your pages? Does it take a lot of time? How many hits do you get a day?

I come up with ideas for each holiday, design the games, and pick out the pictures and sounds for them. My mom and dad make the Web pages and I have to like them before we put them on the Internet.

My site gets about 6,000 hits a day but was as high as 40,000 per week in October and November.

You must hear from people all over the world! Can you think of an unusual request, question, or comment someone has sent to you?

One man who writes children's books wrote me and asked if I knew the words to the song "The worms crawl in.. the worms crawl out..." I did, of course!

What is your favorite resource on the Net?

I like many different things. I sometimes do my school work by using the Internet and for games. I now like the Microsoft Web site but we have most of their games.

If this isn't your main job, what do you do, what is your training?

I'm in first grade. I go to school.

What's the one thing you'd really like to do on your page but have not yet implemented?

Put music on every page or on every holiday!

Do you have a family? A dog? A lizard?

I have a mom and a dad and my brother is Jason. We have two cats, seven turtles, and my brother has three snakes! See

his Web site at <http://www.shadeslanding.com/jas/>. It's called Jason's Snakes and Reptiles.

What are your hopes and fears for the future of the Internet?

I hope I can win a lot of Internet awards. My fear is that the government will make it cost too much for people.

When you're not using the Net, what do you like to do?

I like to play games, watch TV, collect Barbies, draw, and read.

If you could invite three people throughout history to your house for dinner, who would they be?

The real Barbie, the elves from Santa's workshop, and Sleeping Beauty.

HEALTH AND SAFETY

Kidshealth Kids Section

This is the best kids' health resource out on the Net. Now, you might be thinking, "Diseases, ick! Why would I want to visit a Web page about health?" Well, haven't you always wanted to know what causes hiccups? The answer's here! And what if we said the Shockwave games here are awesome? Play Plak Attack: shoot toothpaste or crack your floss whip to fight back at the plaque monsters and keep your teeth healthy. Or try the animations about how your body works. Hit the kitchen for some healthy recipes (try Ants on a Log or Pretzels), or read some reviews of hot toys and see how they rate on the Fun-o-meter. There is a LOT more here; we recommend the whole site for learning about nutrition, feelings, and lots of ways to stay healthy.

http://kidshealth.org/kid/

NET FILES

How many meteors fall to Earth each day?

Answer: According to Dr. Harry B. Herzer III, of the NASA Aerospace Education Services Project, the number is probably more than you think.

It's estimated that 1,000 to more than 10,000 tons of meteoritic material falls to Earth every day! Luckily, most of this material is very tiny, like particles of dust. They are so small, their fall is slowed by air resistance, so they don't burn as they descend. They settle gently to the ground, and you may be walking on them without ever knowing it.

http://spacelink.msfc.nasa.gov/Instructional.Materials/
Curriculum.Materials/Sciences/Astronomy/Our.Solar.System/
Small.Bodies/Comets.Asteroids.and.Meteoroids

Welcome to Health Issues

What happens when students in Ms. Seno's sixth-grade class at Madison (Wisconsin) Middle School write about health issues? You get some really great articles about all kinds of important ways to stay healthy. Find out about: acupuncture (an ancient Chinese medical art); hydrocephalus (a disease of fluid buildup in the skull); prostate cancer (cancer in the prostate gland in men); basketball injuries (ever heard of jumper's knee?); steroids (drugs that are killing and hurting athletes); tennis elbow (it's a lot more painful than you think); hunting dangers and safety (animals are not the only ones unsafe in the woods during hunting season). Check out these health topics written by other kids!

http://198.150.8.9/healthissues.html

ACUPUNCTURE

Acupuncture

Nobody likes seeing needles at the doctor's office—it usually means getting a shot or vaccination. The Chinese, though, have been using needles to *ease* pain and cure diseases in an ancient medical art called *acupuncture*. Learn the story behind this 5,000-year-old medical practice in a report by sixth grader Paul Braun. Who knows, maybe you'll want to get poked by needles in a doctor's office after you read this!

http://198.150.8.9/acupuncture.html

BEDWETTING

Bedwetting

Bedwetting is embarrassing! Did you know that 15 percent of all kids older than three years old wet the bed? It's true, and there are reasons for this. To learn more about bedwetting, check out the page produced by the American Academy of Child and Adolescent Psychiatry. This page is available in English, French, and Spanish.

http://www.psych.med.umich.edu/web/aacap/
factsFam/bedwet.htm

A B C D E F G H I J K L M N O P Q R S T U V W X Y Z

DENTAL CARE

Ask the Dentist Home Page

There is nothing better than a beautiful set of choppers. After all, how can you eat corn on the cob or bite into a big, juicy apple if your teeth aren't in tip-top shape? You can look over other questions to the dentist or ask your own. What's toothpaste made of? Should you pull out your loose tooth? What's the deal with that fluoride goop they put on your teeth? The answers are here!

http://www.parentsplace.com/readroom/dentist/
index.html

The Tooth Fairy

Some children believe that when they lose a tooth, it should be left under their pillows for the Tooth Fairy. She takes the tooth and may leave behind some coins. There is a lot about that gentle story at this Web site. You will also find quick tips on how to keep your teeth healthy and cavity-free. How often should you brush your teeth, and what's that gunky stuff called plaque? Learn how to floss, and remember: the only teeth you have to floss are the ones you want to keep!

http://www.toothfairy.org/

DISABILITIES

Cerebral Palsy Tutorial

Cerebral palsy, also known as CP, is a medical condition causing uncontrolled muscle movements. It's not a disease, and you can't "catch" it from someone who has it. People with CP have it all of their lives. Many times kids who have CP use wheelchairs around school, and sometimes they can't speak clearly. To learn more about CP, take a look at this site.

http://galen.med.virginia.edu/~smb4v/tutorials/
cp/cp.htm

DEAFKIDS

Most people don't understand what it's like to be deaf. Join other kids at this site who know exactly what it is like to be deaf. Spend a little time on these lists for some written conversation!

List Address: deafkids@sjuvm.stjohns.edu
Subscription Address: listserv@sjuvm.stjohns.edu

The Disability Connection

Now we're talking MICE! Mice of different sizes and speeds, remote-controlled mice, and head-controlled mice. But don't look here for information about cute, little, furry rodents, or toys, or the latest on hypnosis—this site is for you and your family if you're looking for adaptive technology solutions for your computer. The Mac Access Passport is a comprehensive database of access products. You'll find expanded keyboards and other neat gadgets for the physically challenged, innovative software for the visually impaired, and lots of special education software. There is a list with links to popular shareware for you to download and a list of organizations that provide other adaptive technology resources. You may also want to check out the new Convomania site, a digital campfire for kids with disabilities who think "being sick sucks!" It's at <http://www2.apple.com/disability/convomania.html>.

http://www2.apple.com/disability/welcome.html

NET FILES

How many gallons of salt water are in the aquarium at Epcot's DiveQuest?

Answer: Six million gallons. That's enough to fill Spaceship Earth (the giant geodesic golf ball) with room to spare. Find more wet facts at http://www.scubadiving.com/destinations/usaorlando.html

A
B
C
D
E
F
G
H
I
J
K
L
M
N
O
P
Q
R
S
T
U
V
W
X
Y
Z

A
B
C
D
E
F
G
H
I
J
K
L
M
N
O
P
Q
R
S
T
U
V
W
X
Y
Z

Future Reflections

The biggest hassle with being blind is not the lack of eyesight; it's the lack of understanding by other people. For anyone interested in what's happening with blind kids, *Future Reflections* is *the* magazine for blind children and their parents. It is available on the Internet, sponsored by the National Federation of the Blind. What color is the sun? How do you do arithmetic in Braille? Know what blind kids know!

http://nfb.org/reflects.htm

National Sports Center for the Disabled

If you love outdoor recreation, adventure, and freedom, then read about all of the fun programs sponsored by the National Sports Center for the Disabled. The NSCD, a nonprofit organization located in Winter Park, Colorado, celebrated its 25th year of "enabling the spirit through sports" in 1995. If you're a winter sports fan, you can join their Ski Pals Program, where disabled and able-bodied kids of ages eight to fourteen hit the slopes. If skiing, snowboarding, or snowshoeing aren't for you, then how about the Family Camp in June? You and your family can enjoy white-water rafting or hiking on nature trails designed to accommodate any special needs. There's even a rock climbing course for the blind and visually impaired.

http://www.nscd.org/nscd/

FIRST AID

First Aid Online

Ouch! Insect bites, scrapes, cuts, sprained ankles, nose bleeds, and other injuries are never fun. When these bumps and bruises happen, always go to a trusted adult. Then, take a look at this site. You'll learn how to bandage a cut, how to help your baby sister if she puts an eraser in her ear, or how to take the sting out of a sunburn. Remember that no online service is a substitute for your doctor, but for minor injuries, this is a good place to remember.

http://www.prairienet.org/~autumn/firstaid/

HUMAN BODY

anatomy

What's your body's biggest organ (and we don't mean pipe organ)? It's your skin! You probably don't think too often about your skin, but it's there holding your body like a great big wrapper. To see your skin from the vantage point of an electron microscope, take a look at the "ultrastructure of skin" from this page at the Mie University (Japan) School of Medicine. Get a close-up look at the various skin layers and see what happens if they get infected.

http://www.medic.mie-u.ac.jp/derma/anatomy.html

Anatomy

Your body is so amazing. It's a combination of muscles, bones, arteries, and various organs, including your great brain. To get an inside peek at some parts of your incredible body, take a look at this page from Levit Radiologic-Pathologic Institute. Your body looks a whole lot different from the inside! Hint: The term "inferior brain" just means it is looked at from below; "superior brain" means the view is from above.

http://rpisun1.mda.uth.tmc.edu/se/anatomy/

NET FILES

Who invented the first solar energy collector?

Answer: *The Swiss scientist Horace de Saussure invented the first solar collector, or "hot box," in 1767. Read more about solar and other types of energy at* http://www.crest.org/renewables/re-kiosk/solar/solar-thermal/history/index.shtml

The Heart: An Online Exploration

Probably the only time you think about your heart is when you run fast and you feel it beating in your chest. Or maybe you think about your heart when you put your hand over it and you feel it go thump, thump. Even if you don't think much about your heart, everybody knows the heart is important. After all, without hearts, what shape would valentines be? To learn all kinds of cool things about the heart, check out the Franklin Institute's info. You'll never take your heart for granted again!

http://sln.fi.edu/biosci/heart.html

Puberty in Boys

It happens to every boy. All of a sudden, his voice starts croaking, his Adam's apple starts growing, and peach fuzz turns into whiskers. These changes are due to puberty. To learn more about puberty in boys, read the text-only information provided by Planned Parenthood of Ontario. You may want to talk this over with someone you trust, like a parent, teacher, or pastor.

http://www.ncf.carleton.ca/freenet/rootdir/menus/
social.services/ppo/info/sex/s103.txt

Puberty in Girls

As a girl grows into a woman, her body changes in many ways. This change is puberty, and sometimes it can be scary and confusing. To learn about puberty, read the text-only information here, provided by Planned Parenthood of Ontario. You may want to talk this over with someone you trust, like a parent, teacher, or pastor.

http://www.ncf.carleton.ca/freenet/rootdir/menus/
social.services/ppo/info/sex/s101.txt

VA Image Browser

Did you ever wonder what your body would look like with transparent skin? Did you ever wonder what your heart looks like while it's beating inside your chest? You don't have to wonder any longer! At this site, you can see images (including moving pictures) of these and many other parts of the human body.

http://www.vis.colostate.edu/cgi-bin/gva/gvaview/

ILLNESS AND DISEASE

Asthma in Children

Asthma is no fun: wheezing, coughing, struggling to breathe; anyone with asthma knows what problems this illness causes. To learn about asthma, take a look at this site, provided by the Children's Medical Center of the University of Virginia. You'll see cool graphics and hear some great audio files, including what the doctor hears when listening through the stethoscope.

http://galen.med.virginia.edu/~smb4v/tutorials/
asthma/asthma1.html

NET FILES

The mail must go through!

These days, letters traveling around the U.S. go by airplane, but it wasn't always like that. When did airmail service start in the U.S., and which cities had it first?

Answer: In 1918, you could have a letter sent via airmail to these cities: New York, Washington, D.C., and Philadelphia. Commercial passenger air service developed as a spin-off from airmail postal service. Find out more at
http://www.si.edu/postal/collect/movemail.htm

Want a snack? Learn to make one in COOKING, FOOD, AND DRINK.

A B C D E F G H I J K L M N O P Q R S T U V W X Y Z

A
B
C
D
E
F
G
H
I
J
K
L
M
N
O
P
Q
R
S
T
U
V
W
X
Y
Z

Bugs in the News!

What is microbiology? It's the study of really, really little "critters" that can only be seen under a microscope. This includes stuff like bacteria and viruses. Ick, you say? You might be surprised to know that bacteria are our friends. In fact, bacteria are absolutely necessary for all life on this planet—but not too many of them, and not the "wrong" kinds in the "wrong" places. You'll learn what an antibiotic does and what to expect from viruses such as the flu. You'll read the very latest on breaking "bug" news stories, such as that live bacteria they found in an insect trapped in amber for millions of years. Just like *Jurassic Park!* (Look in the General Interest..... area.)

http://falcon.cc.ukans.edu/~jbrown/bugs.html

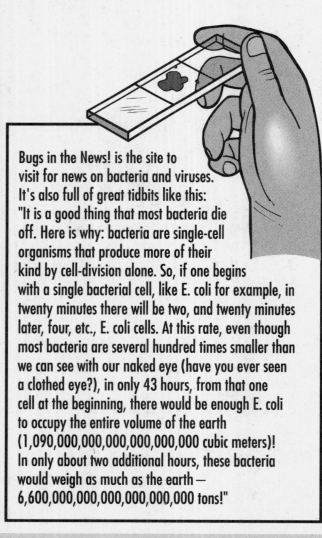

Bugs in the News! is the site to visit for news on bacteria and viruses. It's also full of great tidbits like this: "It is a good thing that most bacteria die off. Here is why: bacteria are single-cell organisms that produce more of their kind by cell-division alone. So, if one begins with a single bacterial cell, like E. coli for example, in twenty minutes there will be two, and twenty minutes later, four, etc., E. coli cells. At this rate, even though most bacteria are several hundred times smaller than we can see with our naked eye (have you ever seen a clothed eye?), in only 43 hours, from that one cell at the beginning, there would be enough E. coli to occupy the entire volume of the earth (1,090,000,000,000,000,000,000 cubic meters)! In only about two additional hours, these bacteria would weigh as much as the earth — 6,600,000,000,000,000,000,000 tons!"

CELLS Alive!

You get a bad case of the sniffles, and your doctor gives you a shot of penicillin. Ouch! That hurt, but in a few days you feel better. What happened? To see how penicillin works and to learn plenty of information about cells, take a look at this site. If you're really sharp, you'll also find the "anatomy of a splinter" section!

http://www.comet.chv.va.us/quill/

Communicable Disease Fact Sheets

Ahh chooo! Nobody likes getting sick. Chicken pox, mumps, influenza (that's the long way to say the flu) are among the many illnesses you can catch. Sicknesses you catch are called *communicable diseases*, and you can learn about lots of these from this info provided by the New York State Department of Health. So, remember to always cover your face when you sneeze, wash your hands before you eat, and be health-smart!

http://www.health.state.ny.us/nysdoh/consumer/
    commun.htm

KidsHome

This part of the Internet is just for kids who have cancer, HIV, and other serious illnesses. Meet other kids who hate taking their medicine. Share some stories and poems: welcome to KidsHome.

http://wwwicic.nci.nih.gov/occdocs/KidsHome.html

Welcome to the On-line Allergy Center

Itchy skin, red eyes, runny nose, and headache are all symptoms of allergies. You may wonder why Mother Nature would ever let people suffer with allergies, but according to Dr. Russell Roby, allergies happen because your body is working extra hard to keep you healthy! Get the facts about allergies, so the next time you sneeze after the lawn is mowed you can understand why.

http://www.sig.net/~allergy/welcome.html

NUTRITION
10 Tips to Healthy Eating and Physical Activity

Is a big, gooey, pepperoni pizza part of a healthy diet? For pizza lovers, thank goodness, it is! According to the International Food Information Council Foundation, pizza can be used with other foods to keep you healthy. And the ten tips are only the beginning. You'll also learn how to evaluate food advertising, so you won't be fooled into eating the prize and playing with the cereal.

http://ificinfo.health.org/brochure/10TIPKID.HTM

SAFETY
Jeff Sam's Child Safety & Parenting Page

Here's everything from rollerblade safety to how to treat a sunburn, plus tips on how to keep your baby brother amused in the store while your dad shops for groceries. You'll find tons of stuff at this site!

http://www.enforcers.com/childsafety/

KIDestrians™

Did you know you have kid brakes? They keep you from stepping off the curb before looking both ways. How do you learn to use them? Learn how to be safe on the streets, when crossing railroad tracks, and in many other traffic safety situations by practicing these activities with your parents.

http://tdg.res.uoguelph.ca/g-police/kid_intr.html

The Missing Kids Database

Some families are looking for their missing children. Check their photos. Have you seen any of these kids? Maybe you can help! This site lets you search by state, physical description, and other characteristics. If you have a Web page of your own, check the How You Can Help area. It will tell you how to put a link at your page that will show photos of recently missing kids to your Web site visitors, like the pictures on milk cartons.

http://www.missingkids.org/

My 8 Rules for Safety

What are "Checking first," "Using the buddy system," and "Trusting your feelings"? These are three of the eight rules for safety developed by the National Center for Missing and Exploited Children. To stay safe, it's important to stay with friends when you are outside, to always tell your parents or caregiver where you are going, and to trust your feelings if you think something is wrong. This site is presented by Child Find Canada. You'll also find rules for older kids and how to keep safe on the Net.

http://www.discribe.ca/childfind/educate/8tips.hte

NET FILES

What plants attract butterflies?

Answer: *Many flowering plants attract butterflies, and others help feed their caterpillars. Some of these are milkweed, lantana, lilac, cosmos, goldenrod, and zinnia. You can find out more at* http://www.butterflies.com/guide.html *if you flutter by!*

Operation Lifesaver

Trains are fascinating, but dangerous. Did you know that a big 150-car freight train traveling at 50 mph can take up to 1.5 miles to come to a complete stop? In the U.S. there are about 6,000 deaths and injuries per year involving trains and cars or pedestrians walking on the tracks. Most train accidents occur when the train is traveling 30 mph or slower. Even at 30 mph, the approximate stopping distance is 3,500 feet or two-thirds of a mile! Operation Lifesaver educates adults and kids on trains and train safety. Make tracks to visit here soon.

http://www.oli.org/oli/

A
B
C
D
E
F
G
H
I
J
K
L
M
N
O
P
Q
R
S
T
U
V
W
X
Y
Z

A
B
C
D
E
F
G
H
I
J
K
L
M
N
O
P
Q
R
S
T
U
V
W
X
Y
Z

OUDPS Kid Safety Topics Menu

Sometimes it's hard to stay safe and play safe. What do you do if a bully starts picking on you? What do you do if you are in an accident? What do you do if a stranger contacts you on the Internet? Find the answer to these and many other safety questions on this site, provided by the University of Oklahoma Department of Public Safety. If you read all the information here, you'll be a safety expert!

http://www.uoknor.edu/oupd/kidsafe/kidmenu.htm

Smokey Says

Who can prevent forest fires? Only you, of course! You need to know how to safely handle matches and fire, and Smokey the Bear and his friends can help you learn how. Try the Shockwave games, and you won't get burned, even though this site is *hot*!

http://www.smokeybear.com/

Before 1889, Italian pizzas were topped with olive oil, cheese, and basil. Who came up with the idea of putting tomato sauce on pizza, and why?

Answer: *According to Seeds of Change at* http://horizon.nmsu.edu/garden/recipes/pizza.html *"Tomato made its debut as a pizza topping in 1889 when Raffaele Esposito, a famous baker, made a special pizza topped with tomato, mozzarella cheese, and basil for Queen Margherita (the pizza still retains her name today). Incidentally, the color of the toppings corresponds to the colors of the Italian flag—tomato red, white cheese, and green basil!"*

SLEEP DIFFICULTIES
Children's Sleep Problems

Sleep is a good time for dreams, when your body rests for a new day of fun. Sometimes, though, sleep is interrupted by nightmares, sleepwalking, or even really bad dreams called sleep terrors. If you would like to learn more about sleep problems that kids have, take a look here. This page is available in English and French.

http://www.psych.med.umich.edu/web/aacap/factsFam/sleep.htm

HISTORY

See also ANCIENT CIVILIZATIONS AND ARCHAEOLOGY

1492 Exhibit

"1492: An Ongoing Voyage" is an exhibit at the Library of Congress. Explore the New World before the Europeans got there, what happened when they arrived, and how both the Old and New Worlds were forever transformed by their contact. This is a hypertext exhibit that includes both text and GIF images. It's a good resource for information about Columbus and the early history of America. Read more in the "Explorers and Exploring" section of this book.

http://sunsite.unc.edu/expo/1492.exhibit/Intro.html

> "We're flooding people with information. We need to feed it through a processor. A human must turn information into intelligence or knowledge. We've tended to forget that no computer will ever ask a new question."
> —Admiral Grace Hopper

Any-Day-in-History Page of Scope Systems

Want to know who shares your birthday or what famous events throughout history happened the day you were born? Just visit this site and type in the month and year you want. For example, famous people born on February 8 include author Jules Verne, actor James Dean, and actress Audrey Meadows, who played Alice in *The Honeymooners*. Find out when and where these folks were born, too; Meadows, for example, was born in China. You can also find out who died on this day (Mary, Queen of Scots) and find out what important historical events took place. On February 8, the Boy Scouts organization was incorporated (1910), radio first came to the White House (1922), and Walt Disney Studios was formed (1926). Know anyone with a brand-new baby? Give the proud parents a printout of their baby's birth date!

http://www.scopesys.com/anyday/

The History Channel®

Who says history's boring? If you get this cable channel, you know the truth is out there! Even if you don't have cable, you can visit this Web site. There are activities for kids (including contests) and classrooms. Plus, explore listings to places where you can see historic events and time periods re-created and background info on many of the History Channel's special programs. Check the coloring book with pictures of historic sites. Try This Day in History (little menu bar box at the bottom of the page—type the date you want), and get historical facts, plus the top ten in music for past years. Even if you think you have no interest in history, stop in—we think you'll be pleasantly surprised.

http://www.historychannel.com/

Sharpen your digital crayons for COLOR AND COLORING BOOKS!

History/Social Studies Web Site for K-12 Teachers

Wow! Finally, an easy way to learn and teach social studies. Subjects available in the menu include archaeology, diversity sources, electronic texts, genealogy, geography, government, and kids and students. Also included are general history, non-Western history, European history, American history, and news and current events. Announcements and relevant TV specials are also listed. Impress your social studies teacher by introducing him or her to this excellent site!

http://www.execpc.com/~dboals/boals.html

ANCIENT HISTORY

Exploring Ancient World Cultures

This site is an excellent introduction to ancient cultures in cyberspace. Eight cultures are represented: the Near East, India, Egypt, China, Greece, the Roman Empire, the Islamic World, and Medieval Europe. Anthony Beavers, an assistant professor at the University of Evansville (Indiana), has tried to provide a variety of resources with balance among the cultures. Some of the Internet sites included in this home page are materials for the study of women in the ancient world, world art treasures, a collection of world scripture, and The International Museum of the Horse. This home page is rich in information for the student of ancient history. Think you're pretty good? Take one of the ten-question online quizzes on Genesis, Greek mythology, or another subject!

http://eawc.evansville.edu/

NET FILES

"If you would not be forgotten as soon as you are dead and rotten, either write things worth reading or do things worth the writing."
Who said it?

American at http://sln.fi.edu/franklin/rotten.html
own advice! Learn more about this famous
scientist, and statesman, certainly followed his
Answer: Benjamin Franklin, who, as an inventor,

A
B
C
D
E
F
G
H
I
J
K
L
M
N
O
P
Q
R
S
T
U
V
W
X
Y
Z

HISTORIC DOCUMENTS

Declaring Independence: Drafting the Documents

You know the Declaration of Independence, written on July 4, 1776. It begins: "When in the course of human Events, it becomes necessary for one People to dissolve the Political Bands which have connected them with another...." The colonists didn't one day just wake up and decide to send this letter to King George III of England. This Library of Congress exhibit presents a chronology of events. You'll find fascinating information about how the documents were drafted, plus photos of important objects. Some of these include fragments of the earliest known draft, the original draft, and various prints relevant to the exhibit, as well as correspondence from Thomas Jefferson. Did you know he was the one who wrote the original? For the actual text, see the National Archives at <http://www.nara.gov/exhall/exhibits.html> or <http://www.law.emory.edu/FEDERAL/independ/declar.html> if you want a transcription with the original "Dunlap Broadside" capitalizations preserved.

http://lcweb.loc.gov/exhibits/declara/declara1.html

EuroDocs: Western European Primary Historical Documents

Venetian sailing directions from 1499? A medieval illuminated manuscript? If you're looking for something newer, how about a World War I archive, or D-Day documents from World War II? The links at this Brigham Young University (Utah) Library home page connect to Western European historical documents that are transcribed, scanned in, or translated. The documents are in the public domain. This home page is an excellent starting place for students who are researching Western European history and want to use primary source material.

http://library.byu.edu/~rdh/eurodocs/homepage.html

Ask not what the Net can do for you, ask what you can do for the Net.

The Gettysburg Address

The Library of Congress has devoted this page to President Abraham Lincoln's Gettysburg Address. Lincoln was invited to dedicate the Union cemetery only three weeks before the ceremony, so he did not have much time to write the speech. View the working drafts of the eloquent speech Lincoln eventually delivered. You'll also see the only known photo of Lincoln taken at Gettysburg, Pennsylvania. These precious original documents have been preserved for future generations; find out how! The text of the Gettysburg Address is at <http://www.msstate.edu/Archives/History/USA/19th_C./gettysburg-address>.

http://lcweb.loc.gov/exhibits/G.Address/ga.html

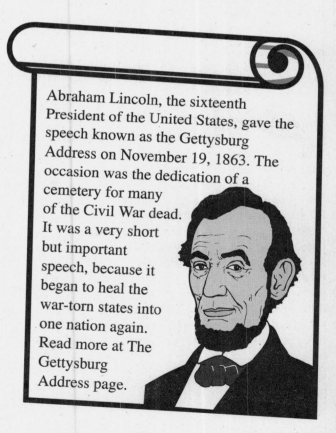

Abraham Lincoln, the sixteenth President of the United States, gave the speech known as the Gettysburg Address on November 19, 1863. The occasion was the dedication of a cemetery for many of the Civil War dead. It was a very short but important speech, because it began to heal the war-torn states into one nation again. Read more at The Gettysburg Address page.

Crack open CODES AND CIPHERS.

THE HISTORICAL TEXT ARCHIVE

Choose the area of the world you're interested in—click—wow, here is an archive of that country's, or region's, important documents and resources. Try this for elusive information you haven't found anywhere else. The Women's Studies links contain several Godey's Lady's Books from the 1850s. Parents: not all links have been checked.

http://www.msstate.edu/Archives/History/

What were women reading in the 1850s? Many of them loved to look through the Godey's Lady's Books, and now several are online. Here's part of an etiquette column, regarding proper behavior in the theater:

"We may as well mention here, for the sake of the other sex, that loud thumping with canes and umbrellas, in demonstration of applause, is voted decidedly rude. Clapping the hands is quite as efficient, and neither raises a dust to soil the dresses of the ladies, not a hubbub enough to deafen them." You can find more at *http://www.history.rochester.edu/godeys/*, which is a link off **THE HISTORICAL TEXT ARCHIVE** page.

What is the sound of one router flapping?

Inaugural Addresses of the Presidents of the United States

George Washington's second-term inaugural speech remains the shortest on record, requiring only 135 words. William Henry Harrison delivered one of the longest, speaking for an hour and 45 minutes in a blinding snowstorm. He then stood in the cold and greeted well-wishers all day; he died a month later, of pneumonia. Read the speech here, but make sure you keep your hat on! Project Bartleby, at Columbia University in New York, houses a home page containing the inaugural addresses of the presidents. Also included is an article about presidents sworn in but not inaugurated and the Oath of Office itself. This is a good site for finding inaugural factoids, such as the revelation that Geronimo, the great Apache, attended the inauguration of Teddy Roosevelt and that attendees at Grover Cleveland's second inaugural ball were all agog at the new invention: electric lights!

http://www.columbia.edu/acis/bartleby/inaugural/

Magna Carta

In 1215, the English barons were fed up. They thought that their king had gone too far, on more than one occasion. They wanted a line drawn that would explain the difference between a king and a tyrant. They defined laws and customs that the King himself had to respect when dealing with free subjects. That charter is called the Magna Carta. It's made it all the way from 1215 to the Net, as part of the Treasures Digitisation Project at the British Library. You can view the whole manuscript and read a translation of it. A brief history and further reading are included.

http://portico.bl.uk/access/treasures/magna-carta.html

From another galaxy? Learn about Earth in the ASTRONOMY— SOLAR SYSTEM AND PLANETS area!

A B C D E F G H I J K L M N O P Q R S T U V W X Y Z

A
B
C
D
E
F
G
H
I
J
K
L
M
N
O
P
Q
R
S
T
U
V
W
X
Y
Z

National Archives Online Exhibit Hall

The National Archives and Records Administration (NARA) is a nationwide system that preserves United States government records of permanent value. The online exhibits help to bring some of the rich and varied holdings of the National Archives to the public. In the Exhibit Hall, you will find some cool special exhibits: for example, "The Charters of Freedom" features the Declaration of Independence, the Constitution of the United States, and the Bill of Rights. You'll also find a special exhibit on the Emancipation Proclamation, issued by President Abraham Lincoln, which ended slavery. Other featured documents include the 19th Amendment and Japanese surrender documents. Visit this site for firsthand looks at the historic documents of the United States, several of them written in longhand!

http://clio.nara.gov/exhall/exhibits.html

What languages are spoken in Vatican City?

Answer: The main languages are Italian and Latin. And don't forget Monastic Sign Language, which is used by those in religious orders who have taken a vow of silence. You can learn a lot about languages and where they are spoken at http://www.sil.org/ ethnologue/

U.S. Founding Documents

We like this archive of U.S. documents, particularly for its searchable version of the Constitution of the United States. Do you know where your 19th Amendment is? You'll also find the Federalist Papers and the Declaration of Independence.

http://www.law.emory.edu/FEDERAL/

US Historical Documents

The University of Oklahoma Law Center hosts "A Chronology of United States Historical Documents." The chronology begins in the pre-Colonial era, with the Magna Carta and the Iroquois Constitution, and concludes with the State of the Union Address given by President Bill Clinton in 1997. Along the way, you'll find The Mayflower Compact, the famous "Give Me Liberty or Give Me Death" speech by Patrick Henry, The Monroe Doctrine, The Emancipation Proclamation, and Martin Luther King's "I Have a Dream" speech. Take a peek at the "other" verses of the National Anthem, too:

Oh! thus be it ever, when freemen shall stand
Between their loved homes and the war's desolation!
Blest with victory and peace, may the heaven-rescued land
Praise the Power that hath made and preserved us a nation.
Then conquer we must, for our cause it is just,
And this be our motto: "In God is our trust."
And the star-spangled banner forever shall wave
O'er the land of the free and the home of the brave!

http://www.law.uoknor.edu/ushist.html

Various Historical Documents

Jon Shemitz, who also runs a Home Schooling Web site at <http://www.midnightbeach.com/hs/>, has put the U.S. Declaration of Independence, the Constitution of the United States, and the United Nations Convention on the Rights of the Child, into HTML (HyperText Markup Language) so that the documents can be read more easily with a Web browser. This presentation also makes the documents easy to search!

http://www.midnightbeach.com/jon/histdocs.htm

You know something the Net doesn't. Make your own home page!

HISTORIC SITES

Alexander Palace Time Machine

Once, a second-grade boy visited the library and found a book about the great tsars of Russia. He became fascinated with their stories and their palace lifestyle. As time went on, he read everything he could about the great palace, hoping someday to visit Russia to see it for himself. Incredibly, this boy grew up to do that very thing, and now he's written a comprehensive Web page all about it. This outstanding multimedia tour will give you a look into the past as you explore the life and times of Tsar Nicholas II and his family and friends.

http://www.travelogix.com/emp/batchison/
BobHome.html

NET FILES

"Uncle Sam" is a drawing of a man wearing a flag suit, and in cartoons he is often used to represent the United States, if the U.S. were a person. Early drawings were based on a real person, who happened to be a clown. Who was he, and what famous phrase is also associated with him?

Answer: According to the Clowns of America International, "Dan Rice (1823–1901) was a clown of the Civil War era. Rice had a goatee and wore a patriotic costume he referred to as his flag suit. Political cartoonist Ogden Nash based his drawings of Uncle Sam on Rice and his costume. [Rice] campaigned for Zachary Taylor for President. One of the things he would do was invite Taylor to ride on the circus bandwagon in the circus parades. Local politicians would clamor to ride as well, hoping his popularity would benefit them. People would comment, 'Look who's on Taylor's bandwagon,' inspiring the phrase 'Jump on the bandwagon.'" Find out more at http://www.clown.org/history.html

America's Homepage!! Plymouth, Mass

Take a virtual tour of "Plimoth Plantation." In this living history museum, all the employees dress and act as they would in 1627! Visit the re-created village and farm site, then tour other Plymouth and Pilgrim historical resources. Some of the best biographical and other information is in the Historical Reference area. The only thing missing from this page is a good clear picture of Plymouth Rock, but we have pointed out this oversight to the webmaster, so maybe by the time you read this you can gaze on a photo of a gray rock with 1620 carved in it.

http://media3.com/plymouth/

Colonial Williamsburg Home Page

What would it be like to be suddenly transported back in time to the 1700s? For fun, you would play cards and board games, or you'd work puzzles; outside, you would roll hoops, walk on stilts, and play a rousing game of ninepins bowling. What kinds of foods would you eat? How would people behave—are manners the same now as they were back then? What kind of job would you have? Experience the eighteenth century by visiting this site! Colonial Williamsburg is a living history museum in Virginia, where the people dress and act as if they were living in Colonial times. They have to know a lot about history to do that, and some kids work at the museum, playing the roles of kids back in the 1700s. This is a great site to learn how people lived in early American times.

http://www.history.org/

Ford's Theater NHS Home Page

The theater where President Lincoln was shot is now a National Historic site. If you scroll down to the bottom of the page, you will learn some fascinating facts about the assassination. Why was there no guard—or was there? Where is the chair Lincoln was sitting in? And where is the bullet that killed him? The surprising answers are all here. This site offers information in 11 languages besides English.

http://www.nps.gov/foth/

A B C D E F G H I J K L M N O P Q R S T U V W X Y Z

A
B
C
D
E
F
G
H
I
J
K
L
M
N
O
P
Q
R
S
T
U
V
W
X
Y
Z

GORP - National Historic Trails

Ever wondered if you could find any of the old pioneer routes, like the Oregon Trail? You can! To this day, some of the old wagon ruts are still visible, and you can walk in the footsteps of early settlers during the westward expansion of the United States. You'll find maps and detailed descriptions of the Oregon Trail, plus the following: Santa Fe Trail; Trail of Tears; Iditarod National Historic Trail; Juan Bautista de Anza National Historic Trail; Lewis and Clark National Historic Trail; Mormon Pioneer National Historic Trail; Nez Perce National Historic Trail; and the Overmountain Victory National Historic Trail.

http://www.gorp.com/gorp/resource/us_trail/
  historic.htm

Great American Landmarks Adventure

At this page you can download pages of historic landmarks to color. But it's not the usual type of famous landmark. Here you'll find some really weird stuff, such as a huge elephant-shaped building (Margate City, New Jersey) and Independence Rock (Casper, Wyoming), where folks traveling along the Oregon Trail got out of their covered wagons long enough to scratch their names. You'll find the U.S. Capitol here, but you can also choose to color Taos pueblos. If you send in your drawing, they may put it on the Web. Check it out!

http://www.historychannel.com/kids/landmark.html

Historic Mile

Take a tour of over 50 famous landmarks in Philadelphia, Pennsylvania! You'll visit Independence Hall, where the Declaration of Independence was signed, and see Betsy Ross' House, where some say she sewed the very first American flag. Along the way, stop in at the Pretzel Museum for a quick snack.

http://libertynet.org/iha/virtual.html

> ## Attention everyone. The Internet is closing. Please go play outside.

Historic Mount Vernon—The Home of Our First President, George Washington

Seeing where our first president lived makes him more real to us. Walking up his front steps, lounging on his lawn—these things connect us to a real person instead of an historical figure. Maybe you can't visit Mount Vernon, Virginia, in person, but you can stop in via the Net. At Mount Vernon, you can take a tour, read some astounding facts, and even work out a Washington word search puzzle. You can also learn about archaeology at Mount Vernon and explore related links. The Mount Vernon virtual tour includes the East Front, the large dining room, study, master bedroom, gardens, the Washingtons' tomb, and a slave memorial. Washington was the only one of the Founding Fathers to free his slaves.

http://www.mountvernon.org/

Did Washington really chop down a cherry tree?

How about that "throwing the silver dollar across the Potomac River" story—is that bogus?

True or false—he had wooden teeth?

All of these are false. One thing is true, though: many people wanted to crown Washington as King; he declined, accepting the presidency instead. Read more facts you never knew at the pages of Historic Mount Vernon—The Home of Our First President, George Washington.

I-CHANNEL—ELLIS ISLAND

Between 1892 and 1954, Ellis Island was the gateway to America for over 12 million immigrants. Before they could set foot in America, they had to be "processed" on this island in the New York harbor. This meant a three- to five-hour wait, medical and legal questions, and inspections. Some were eventually turned away. Learn about the journey, the processing center, and life in the new land at this excellent example of multimedia education. You will hear audio recollections of some of the immigrants themselves. There is also an "immigrants' cookbook" with recipes such as cabbage rolls and gingersnaps.

http://www.i-channel.com/ellis/

NET FILES

St. Edward's Crown is the coronation crown of England, first used in 1661. It was used when Queen Elizabeth II was crowned in 1953. How much does the crown weigh? (Hint: It is made from solid gold.)

Answer: The crown weighs 2.2 kilograms (nearly five pounds) and is set with 444 semiprecious stones. You can read more about the British Crown Jewels at http://www.royal.gov.uk/faq/faq2.htm and see a picture at http://www.royal.gov.uk/faq/index.htm#JEWELS.

Moscow

Tour the Moscow Kremlin Exhibition! Inside, you'll find wonderful pictures and stories. Some of the sites you will see and read about are the Cathedral of Annunciation, Red Square, the Residence of the President, the Senate Building, and the Tsar-Cannon.

http://www.geom.umn.edu/~ipavlovs/Russia/
  Moscow/moscow.html

National Civil Rights Museum

The National Civil Rights Museum is located at the Lorraine Motel (Memphis, Tennessee), where Dr. Martin Luther King, Jr., was assassinated on April 4, 1968. Here you will find continuing exhibits, events, and links of interest. The virtual tour is arranged in chronological order. You'll learn about the Montgomery bus boycott, the freedom rides, Dr. Martin Luther King, Jr., the student sit-ins, the march on Washington, and the Chicago freedom movement. You can take a chronological tour or choose the exhibit you want to see. Each exhibit has a short paragraph about the subject and why it is important in civil rights history.

http://www.mecca.org/~crights/ncrm.html

National Trust for Historic Preservation

Many historic sites are old—so how come they look so nice? Because people like you care enough to save them from deterioration. This is called *historic preservation*. This resource will help you find out how to save historic sites in your area. For international sites, a more direct source is the International Council on Monuments and Sites at <http://www.icomos.org/>.

http://www.nthp.org/

Old Sturbridge Village

Do you think it would be fun to live in the past? Why not visit the nineteenth century and see how you like it? You can experience the sights and sounds of this re-created New England village by taking a virtual visit. Let's visit the blacksmith shop—can you hear the clang of the hammer on the anvil? Listen for the team of horses pulling a sleigh. Why not stroll over to the confectionery shop for some horehound drops or rock candy? Got a question? Ask in the Kids Club, where you'll also find puzzles and a mystery sound contest! If you visit the real Sturbridge Village in Massachusetts, you'll find a fascinating living history museum, where all the kids and other villagers dress, talk, and act like they are living in 1830.

http://www.osv.org

A B C D E F G H I J K L M N O P Q R S T U V W X Y Z

A
B
C
D
E
F
G
H
I
J
K
L
M
N
O
P
Q
R
S
T
U
V
W
X
Y
Z

The Statue of Liberty

Give me your tired, your poor,
Your huddled masses yearning to breathe free,
The wretched refuse of your teeming shore.
Send these, the homeless, tempest-tost to me,
I lift my lamp beside the golden door!

This is part of the poem inscribed on the Statue of Liberty. It was written by Emma Lazarus, and you can find the complete verse at this site. The Internet needs a good resource on the Statue of Liberty! There are a few factoids at this site, written by kids, at *<http://www.kusd.edu/s_projects/statue_liberty/statue_liberty.html>*. Don't forget to check out magician David Copperfield's amazing "vanishing" of the statue at *<http://www.digiweb.com/~dannyb/illusions/liberty.html>*.

http://www.brigadoon.com/~sjparish/library/
   polish1.htm

Temple of Liberty: Building the Capitol for a New Nation

Visit the Capitol, courtesy of the Library of Congress. The United States Capitol was envisioned as a "Temple of Liberty" by George Washington and Thomas Jefferson. Read the various proposals for how this most important of all U.S. public buildings should look. Then study the approved plans and visit the porticoes and the wings of our Capitol as it was built. The original building took 34 years, six architects, and six presidents to build. When you're finished touring this historic site, you'll be an expert, and your feet won't be tired!

http://lcweb.loc.gov/exhibits/us.capitol/s0.html

Tower of London Virtual Tour

The Traitor's Gate. The Bloody Tower. The Ceremony of the Keys. The Crown Jewels. What an incredible history this building has. The Tower of London has been a treasury, a prison, and a government building for a thousand years. It is said that if the ravens that inhabit the Tower green ever leave, the Commonwealth of Great Britain will fall. You can take a tour of the Tower and its grounds right here. But don't scare the ravens!

http://www.voicenet.com/~dravyk/toltour/

United States Holocaust Memorial Museum

The United States Holocaust Memorial Museum in Washington, D.C., offers general information on this painful chapter of world history. The education page offers a guide to teaching about the Holocaust, a brief history, FAQ, a heartbreaking article about children in the Holocaust, and a videography. An online reservation form for groups is available. Parents: Descriptions may be too graphic for youngsters.

http://www.ushmm.org/

Vatican Exhibit Rome Reborn

Rome is one of the most glorious cities in the world. Today, millions of visitors come to admire its architecture, art, and history and to find peace in St. Peter's Basilica. It has not always been that way, though: once it was a miserable village! Explore the past in this exhibit of materials from the Vatican Library's most precious manuscripts, books, and maps. This exhibit was at the Library of Congress in 1993, but it lives on—on the Net.

http://sunsite.unc.edu/expo/vatican.exhibit/
   Vatican.exhibit.html

Vietnam Veteran's Memorial

The U.S. National Park Service administers this memorial site, which is in Washington, D.C. Over 58,000 American men and women died in the Vietnam War, a conflict so controversial it divided the generations as well as the country. All their names are engraved on a mirrorlike granite wall. People leave flowers, poems, military gear, and other objects around the wall. It is a very moving place to visit, and we guarantee you will never forget your experience there.

http://www.nps.gov/vive/

Virtually Boston: Walk Boston

It's only 2.5 miles long, but you'll be walking through years of Boston's history. Check out the Paul Revere House and the Old North Church ("one if by land, two if by sea..."). Don't miss the Boston Massacre site or the Bunker Hill Monument. Bring a cup of tea and take the virtual tour.

http://www.vboston.com/boswalks/index.html

White House for Kids

Let Socks, the First Cat, take you on a fascinating kid's-eye tour of the White House in Washington, D.C. You'll learn how the White House was built (bricks were made on the front lawn), tour the rooms, and find out the First Family pets that have lived there (don't miss President Harrison's goat or Caroline Kennedy's pony). We learned something we didn't know before: the president's desk was once part of a ship, abandoned north of the Arctic circle in 1854! The HMS *Resolute* was later found by the crew of an American whaling ship. It was repaired and refitted, then sent to Queen Victoria as a gesture of goodwill. Later, when the ship was taken out of service and dismantled, a desk was made from some of its timbers. Queen Victoria presented the desk to President Hayes in 1880. The desk has been used by most presidents since then. Socks never gets to sit on it, though. Well, maybe he does, late at night, when no one is around.

http://www.whitehouse.gov/WH/kids/html/
  kidshome.html

Did you know that although George Washington, the first President of the United States, directed the construction of the White House, he never got to live in it? It was our second President, John Adams, elected in 1796, who first lived there. His term was almost over by the time he moved in, and only six rooms had been finished. Take the tour, led by Socks, the First Cat, at the White House for Kids page.

Surf today, smart tomorrow.

MIDDLE AGES
Labyrinth Home Page

Welcome to the Labyrinth, a World Wide Web server for medieval studies, located at Georgetown University in Washington, D.C. The Middle Ages are those years after the fall of the Roman Empire and before the Renaissance, so think the years 500–1500 (some authorities say 1300 or 1400). You can navigate the Labyrinth by selecting a main menu item or by using the search engine to search all Labyrinth files. Sources available include bibliographies, text, images, and archives. Also offered are Daedalus's guides to the Net and Web. Find your own Ariadne's thread to hold onto as you surf the Labyrinth!

http://www.georgetown.edu/labyrinth/
  labyrinth-home.html

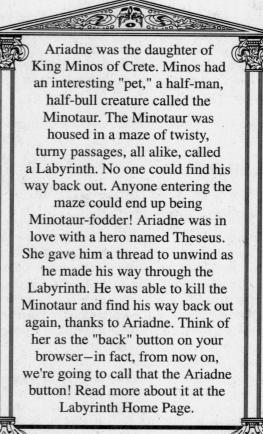

Ariadne was the daughter of King Minos of Crete. Minos had an interesting "pet," a half-man, half-bull creature called the Minotaur. The Minotaur was housed in a maze of twisty, turny passages, all alike, called a Labyrinth. No one could find his way back out. Anyone entering the maze could end up being Minotaur-fodder! Ariadne was in love with a hero named Theseus. She gave him a thread to unwind as he made his way through the Labyrinth. He was able to kill the Minotaur and find his way back out again, thanks to Ariadne. Think of her as the "back" button on your browser—in fact, from now on, we're going to call that the Ariadne button! Read more about it at the Labyrinth Home Page.

A
B
C
D
E
F
G
H
I
J
K
L
M
N
O
P
Q
R
S
T
U
V
W
X
Y
Z

TIME LINES

HyperHistory Online

Hey, your mom says you can have some friends over for lunch! She says to invite three people you admire from history—which heroes would you choose? You might get some ideas here. This site will teach you about important people from 1000 B.C. to the present. You'll find scientists, artists, musicians, authors, politicians, explorers, and many others. But that is not all: you can also trace events through history as well as look at important maps of time periods and the spread of civilizations.

http://www.hyperhistory.com/

Modernism Timeline, 1890-1940

This time line highlights significant events from 1890 to 1940. When you click on a year, you get a list of events that happened in that year, including political and literary events and social customs. For example, in 1917, bobbed hair was popular, the Senate rejected Wilson's suffrage bill, Freud's *Introduction to Psychoanalysis* was published, and there was a famine in Germany. The issue of what is significant is up for grabs here, and you can make suggestions for additions to the list.

http://weber.u.washington.edu/~eckman/timeline.html

U.S. HISTORY

Adventures of Wells Fargo - Original Information Superhighway

These days, you can hop on a jet plane and travel the width of the U.S. from coast to coast in five or six hours. In the 1800s, however, there were no planes, so people traveled as far as they could by rail, ship, and other transportation, then made the rest of the trip by a bouncy overland stagecoach pulled by a team of horses. They often began their stagecoach journey from places halfway across the country, such as St. Louis, Missouri. The trip from St. Louis to San Francisco, California, generally took about 24 days! Wells Fargo was one of the companies to offered this form of travel, and they present some maps, stories, and tall tales about it all here.

http://wellsfargo.com/ftr/ftrsty/ch11/

The African-American Mosaic

This exhibit is a sampler of materials found in the Library of Congress illuminating the last 500 years of the African American experience in the Western Hemisphere. This exhibit covers four areas—Colonization, Abolition, Migrations, and the WPA (Work Projects Administration) era. This is an excellent starting point to search for materials about African American history. Be sure to check the "African Americans" section of this book, too.

http://lcweb.loc.gov/exhibits/african/intro.html

America's West - Development and History

Return with us now to the days of yesteryear— of gold rush and ghost town, the heyday of cowboy and gunslinger. At this site, you'll discover links to information on America's westward expansion, famous Western trails, pioneers, trappers, and biographies of Kit Carson, Davy Crockett, Daniel Boone, Billy the Kid, Sitting Bull, Roy Rogers, and lots of famous folks in between. There are links to movies about the West as well as to Western theme parks and dude ranches. A caution to parents: Not all the outbound links have been reviewed.

http://www.AmericanWest.com/

American Memory from the Library of Congress

You have memories of your own life. Your parents have memories of their lives, and your grandparents have memories of theirs. Wouldn't it be great to find a place to archive all those memories, so they wouldn't be lost when someone died? You could call it the American Memory Project! Look no further. Browse through 25,000 turn-of-the-century postcards; maybe some are from your home town. Look in the Prints and Photographs Division under Detroit Publishing Company (show this to your parents, they will love it). Check old movies of New York City made by Edison himself in 1903. Look into the eyes of the immigrants coming to America—so much hope is expressed there. The historical periods covered are from the Civil War to World War II. Each collection is annotated, and broad topics are listed. This is an excellent source for students looking for nonprint sources to accompany an American history report. Don't forget to remember American Memory.

http://rs6.loc.gov/amhome.html

What happened on 23rd Street, during the summer of 1901, in New York City? Move over, Marilyn Monroe! Inventor Thomas A. Edison was experimenting with films that year. The film is now in the Library of Congress' American Memory collection, and it's also on the Internet. From a contemporary Edison film company catalog: "The scene as suggested by the title is made on 23rd Street, New York City. In front of one of the large newspaper offices on that thoroughfare is a hot air shaft through which immense volumes of air are forced by means of a blower. Ladies crossing these shafts often have their clothes slightly disarranged, (it may be said much to their discomfiture). As our picture was being made a young man escorting a young lady, to whom he was talking very earnestly, comes into view and walks slowly along until they stand directly over the air shaft. The young lady's [ankle-length] skirts are suddenly raised to, you might say an almost unreasonable height, greatly to her horror and much to the amusement of the newsboys, bootblacks and passersby This subject is a winner. Class B. 50 ft. $6.00." It should be noted that the dress blows up "almost" to her knees. It was shocking for those times! To see the film, go to *http://rs6.loc.gov/papr/paprquery.html* and search on the term "twenty-third" (don't forget the hyphen). For more, remember American Memory from the Library of Congress.

from Revolution to Reconstruction and what happened afterwards

The main body of this home page comes from the booklet "An Outline of American History," distributed by the United States Information Agency. The text is illustrated with stamps! It has very dense text, so you may want to look at this site for heavier research only. Additional original sources with hypertext links (which go all over the Net) have been added. This site covers American history from the Colonial period until World War I. Check it out; it's fun just to know there was a stamp with the Carolina charter on it!

http://grid.let.rug.nl/~welling/usa/

Library of Congress World Wide Web Home Page

The Library of Congress, founded in 1800, uses the World Wide Web to present materials from its collections so that people all over the world can see them without traveling to Washington, D.C. You can view exhibits, search and view documents in digitized historical collections, search the LC card catalog, and learn about Congress and the government by using the collection known as Thomas. This is an excellent starting point to find information about the United States government and history, both present and past.

http://lcweb.loc.gov/

Pioneer Spirit

In the 1800s, many settlers left the east coast and headed west to make better lives for themselves. Trying to carve out places of their own from wilderness prairie wasn't easy. This excellent site shows in pictures and words the struggles of the Dakota pioneers. You'll read a diary written by a physician in the 1870s Dakota territory. And you will be fascinated by a series of "then and now" photographs comparing photos of long ago to the same spot in photos from today. How things have changed!

http://www.gps.com/Pioneer_Spirit/Pioneer_Spirit.htm

**See what's shakin' in
EARTH SCIENCE
GEOLOGY-EARTHQUAKES.**

Become one with the Net.

A
B
C
D
E
F
G
H
I
J
K
L
M
N
O
P
Q
R
S
T
U
V
W
X
Y
Z

A
B
C
D
E
F
G
H
I
J
K
L
M
N
O
P
Q
R
S
T
U
V
W
X
Y
Z

Presidential Libraries IDEA Network

"PresidentS" is located at the University of North Carolina at Chapel Hill. Its mission is to help to bring presidential library materials to the Internet for improved public access and to link America's past to her future. Presidential libraries from Herbert Hoover through President Clinton and Vice President Gore are included. Some of the more recent libraries have their own home pages. The earlier presidential papers are available via Gopher. Photographs are also housed at the newer libraries. This is an excellent site for accessing info on the twentieth-century presidents and first ladies and links to their homes, libraries, and other resources.

http://sunsite.unc.edu/lia/president/pres.html

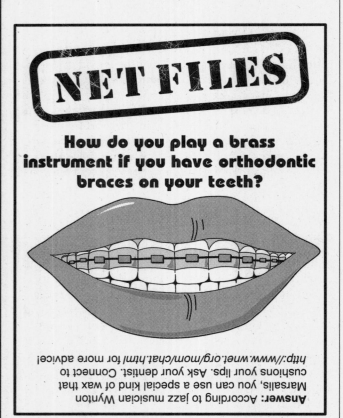

NET FILES

How do you play a brass instrument if you have orthodontic braces on your teeth?

Answer: According to jazz musician Wynton Marsalis, you can use a special kind of wax that cushions your lips. Ask your dentist. Connect to http://www.wnet.org/mom/chat.html for more advice!

You never lose the pieces to the online games in GAMES AND FUN!

Wm. Murray's Time Page

Murray categorizes the generations in American history based upon his reading of the book *Generations*. You can then trace his links by eras, generations, and the future. One of the most valuable aspects of this site is the collection of links to resources in American history, although his take on who the visionaries were in each era is also interesting.

http://www.seanet.com/Users/pamur/time.html

U.S. HISTORY—CIVIL WAR

The Battle of Gettysburg

It was the turning point of the Civil War: on July 1, 2, and 3, 1863, at Gettysburg, Pennsylvania, more men fought and died than in any other battle on North American soil. A total of 51,000 were killed and wounded. Today, the battlefield is a national military park, with over 1,000 monuments. Follow the maps of the battles and explore other Civil War links from this site.

http://www.gettysbg.com/battle.html

Old Abe the War Eagle

During the Civil War, many military units adopted an animal mascot. Usually it was a dog or a goat, but the Eighth Wisconsin Infantry Regiment had something really unique: a bald eagle, which they named "Old Abe," after President Abraham Lincoln. You can read about Old Abe's war stories and see pictures. Old Abe's legacy lives on in the logos of Wisconsin companies, in replicas at the Wisconsin State Assembly and elsewhere, and in the names of school sports teams. Additionally, the insignia patch of the U.S. Army's 101st Airborne Division, originally formed in Wisconsin during World War I, carries a graphic of Old Abe. According to this page, the "Screaming Eagles" saw extensive action in World War II and the Vietnam and Persian Gulf Wars.

http://badger.state.wi.us/agencies/dva/museum/cybergal/oa-main.html

Space Exploration is a blast. Check out ASTRONOMY.

U.S. Civil War Center — Index of Civil War Information

The Civil War is a fascinating event in American history. Many people have spent a great deal of time studying the war and collecting material on it. The "Civil War related Web Links Index" will lead you to hundreds of sites. Diaries, forts, miniatures, maps, music, and much more are all a click away. This is your starting point for any topic on the Civil War. Pictures? Oh yes, there are plenty of those, too!

http://www.cwc.lsu.edu/civlink.htm

WORLD HISTORY

Gateway to World History

The Gateway provides "Internet resources for the study of world history and in support of the struggle for social progress." Resources offered include an archival document collection, online resources, and searching tools for online resources. You can search by keyword or by subject. In addition, Internet discussion lists and pointers to history departments online are included. Reference works, resources about navigating the Internet, and other favorite places are offered by Haines Brown. This is a good launchpad for world history students. A caution to parents: We have not checked all these links.

http://library.ccsu.ctstateu.edu/~history/world_history/

World Cultures

Welcome to the Internet portion of a course taught by Richard Hooker at Washington State University! While this site is background for a college course, it also offers much information for the world history student. You can find a glossary of world cultures, including concepts, values, and terms, readings about the world, and Internet resources. This is a good supplement or starting point for world history students. A caution to parents: Not all links have been explored.

http://www.wsu.edu:8080/~dee/

World History to 1500

This excellent site contains links to resources on the Internet dealing with world history prior to 1500. This material was collected as a supplement to materials covered in a course at Brigham Young University (Hawaii). The information is mostly arranged geographically. Geographic regions covered include Mesopotamia, India, Rome, Europe, Egypt, China, Greece, Africa, Eurasia, and East Asia. Topics addressed include prehistory, cultural evolution, Islam, Christianity, Judaica, and cultural diffusion. This is a good beginning site for world history reports that cover the early years of civilization.

http://www.byuh.edu/coursework/hist201/

The World-Wide Web Virtual Library: History

This home page contains history indexes, conferences, world news, historical newsgroups and discussion lists, and Carrie: An Electronic Library. Kansas students will particularly like the Kansas sites! You can explore history by era, subject, or world region.

http://history.cc.ukans.edu:80/history/
    WWW_history_main.html

WORLD WAR II

D-Day

This archive of World War II facts, pictures, movies, and memories was built by students at Patch American High School, located at the United States European Command in Stuttgart, Germany. You'll find battle plans, newsreel footage, and famous speeches connected with D-Day and World War II.

http://192.253.114.31/D-Day/Table_of_contents.html

See the light in ARCHITECTURE, look for LIGHTHOUSES.

A
B
C
D
E
F
G
H
I
J
K
L
M
N
O
P
Q
R
S
T
U
V
W
X
Y
Z

Enola Gay Perspectives

War is an ugly thing, and it's hard to understand how people could want to harm other people. In 1945, the United States dropped an atomic bomb on the Japanese city of Hiroshima. This Web resource, developed by library school students as part of a project for the University of Maryland, tries to make sense of it all. You'll find out the reasons government leaders decided to drop the bomb. You'll learn about the crew of the plane *Enola Gay* and about the consequences of their mission. There is also a section on the controversy surrounding the *Enola Gay* exhibit at the Smithsonian Institution's National Air and Space Museum. For an objective look at the issue, try this site. Look in the "Peace" section of this book for more on this subject.

http://www.glue.umd.edu/~enola/welcome.html

HOLIDAYS

KIDPROJ'S Multi-Cultural Calendar

Around the world, every day is a holiday somewhere, and kids just like you are celebrating something. Now kids have a place to tell the rest of the world about their holiday foods, decorations, parades, songs, and other ways they make this day special from all the others. You can look at the holidays by month, by country, or by name. Do you have a special holiday you want to talk about? Add it here!

http://www.kidlink.org/KIDPROJ/MCC/

World Birthday Web

This site is kind of silly and cool at the same time. Whose birthday is today? Find out here. Enter your own name and birthday. You can also enter your e-mail address and your home page, if you want. The info gets added to the database immediately. When your birthday rolls around, you'll get e-mail greetings from all sorts of well-wishers. This year, we got one from the Klingon Language Institute!

http://www.boutell.com/birthday.cgi/

ASIAN HOLIDAYS
Annual Events in Japan

Did you know that May 5 is Children's Day in Japan? Learn a little more about it at *<http://www.wakhok.ac.jp/~nobuaki/japan.html>*. You'll also learn about the beautiful Star Festival (July 7), in which children tie their wishes to tree branches, and you'll hear an audio of the tolling New Year's bells. You can see photos of many festivals at a site offered by a Japanese newspaper, at *<http://www.mainichi.co.jp/photogallery/omatsuri/index-e.html>*. Learn even more about traditional festivals and holidays in Japan at *<http://fumi.eco.wakayama-u.ac.jp/English/Kishu/festival.html>* and at *<http://w3.lab.kdd.co.jp/japan/>*.

http://www.jnto.go.jp/08events/08frame.html

Chinese Holidays & Festivals

June 1 is when China celebrates its Children's Day. Kids are showered with presents, and their schools give them big parties. Sound like fun? Read about this and more Chinese traditions here. Another fascinating place to look is at *<http://198.111.253.141/festivals/chinese.html>*, where you'll find photos and descriptions of interesting holidays such as the Dragon Boat Festival, as well as learn about the Hungry Ghosts Festival.

http://www.chinascape.org/china/culture/holidays/hyuan/holiday.html

Chinese New Year

The Chinese calendar is based both on the Gregorian and a lunar-solar system. It divides a year into 12 months, each with 39 1/2 days. Twenty-four poetic solar terms describe seasonal changes, including the Beginning of Spring, the Waking of Insects, Grain in Ear, Frost's Descent, and Great Cold. There is also a system that names the years in a 12-year cycle: Rat, Ox, Tiger, Hare, Dragon, Snake, Horse, Sheep, Monkey, Rooster, Dog, and Boar. Find out how the Chinese New Year is celebrated, and remember, 1997 is the Year of the Ox! Check out *<http://www.cf.ac.uk/uwcc/suon/chinese/year.html>* for additional information.

http://harmony.wit.com/chinascape/ChineseNewYear/

Festivals & Culture (Keeping Faith With the Past)

Learn the traditions of the Taiwanese Dragon Boat Festival, the Birthday of the Goddess of the Sea, and the Lantern Festival, among many others. You'll also read a bit about Chinese knots, rice-dough figures and candy sculpture, and lion dances.

http://peacock.tnjc.edu.tw/ADD/TOUR/keep.html

Hawaii's Greeting of the Season

Many folks in Hawaii come from a Japanese, Chinese, or other Asian heritage. As in many countries, the coming of the New Year deserves a big celebration. One of the symbolic Japanese decorations you might see is the *kadomatsu* (gates of pine). These graceful arrangements of pine and bamboo, symbolizing good wishes for a long, prosperous life, are displayed for several days before January 1, then burned or tossed into flowing water. The Chinese celebrate New Year's Day according to another calendar system (see CalendarLand in the "Time—Calendars" section in this book); in 1997, the Year of the Ox begins in February. One of the exciting traditions is the lion dance, many of which are performed by martial arts clubs in Hawaii. The lion is a symbol of life, luck, and health. Colorfully costumed lion dancers parade down the streets accompanied by the sounds of gongs and drums. Merchants and others throw firecrackers at the feet of the "lions," symbolically chasing away bad luck. Read more about these joyous Asian celebrations here.

http://www.aloha-hawaii.com/c_greetings.shtml

Hong Kong Terminal - Chinese Festival

Arranged by moon, or lunar month, you can learn about everything from Chinese New Year to the Day the Kitchen God Visits Heaven. In between you'll find the Dragon Boat Festival, the Hungry Ghosts Festival, and a lot more in this fascinating peek into the culture of both traditional and modern China.

http://zero.com.hk/hkta/culture.html

Samir's india page

Click on any of the months, then see a text description of the festivals celebrated that month. We wish there were photos and multimedia—the descriptions are intriguing! November 14 is Children's Day in India. This site has many unchecked links to other cultural resources about India.

http://cse.unl.edu/~samir/india.html#Festival page

NET FILES

How many miles do the Cotter High School (Winona, Minnesota) marching band members march in a year? How many total bars of music are played by the Cotter band each year?

Answer: They march 95 miles, give or take a few, er, feet, and they play 21,434,058 musical bars. By the way, there are 250 members in the band. The number of hamburgers consumed by Cotter band members in an average summer is 6,324, and at least 12 T-shirts go unclaimed on the band bus after every road trip. Find more funny facts about this band at http://www.mps.org/~chsband/marching/HTML/facts2.html

Justice now! Free software from the archives in COMPUTERS!

A B C D E F G H I J K L M N O P Q R S T U V W X Y Z

A
B
C
D
E
F
G
H
I
J
K
L
M
N
O
P
Q
R
S
T
U
V
W
X
Y
Z

CHRISTMAS

Christmas Around The World

Here's a trip you can take without even packing your suitcase! Travel through cyberspace to countries in Asia, Eastern Europe, Latin America, and the United Kingdom to learn the different ways children celebrate Christmas. The spirit of the Christmas season, of giving and goodwill toward everyone, is shared by many countries worldwide, each with its own unique traditions and customs. You'll learn which countries have a Santa Claus or a Santa-like figure as part of the holiday celebration. Sometimes he is called a different name—such as St. Nicholas, Svaty Mikalas, Hotei Osho, Grandfather Frost, Lan Khoong-Khoong, or Father Christmas. When you return from your trip, you can even send e-mail to Santa Claus. Don't miss the X-MAS Files for those of you who wonder, "Is there really a Santa Claus?" We want to believe, and here's convincing evidence!

http://www.christmas.com/

Christmas Down Under

Here at Pollywood Farm, we celebrate Christmas with lots of snow, ice, and hot chocolate. But that is because we live in the northeastern U.S., in the Northern Hemisphere, where December is a winter month. In the Southern Hemisphere, the seasons are reversed. In Australia, for example, Christmas comes during the summer. Because we couldn't imagine it, we visited this site. Lots of families go on Christmas picnics, and it is a festive time for all! Some people are afraid Santa and the reindeer may suffer from the Aussie heat, so they are thinking of letting Swag Man deliver the presents in his four-wheel-drive truck. Read all about it at *<http://www.gil.com.au/ozkidz/Christmas/poppytra.html>*.

http://www.gil.com.au/ozkidz/Christmas/

The Christmas Page

It's the night before Christmas, and you need some new holiday stories. Here's a collection in the St. Nick of time! You'll find the complete text of L. Frank Baum's *The Life and Adventures of Santa Claus,* as well as lesser-known tales from European and other cultural traditions.

http://www.ucalgary.ca/~dkbrown/christmas.html

The Grinch Net

Do you remember the Grinch and how he "stole" Christmas from Whoville in *How The Grinch Stole Christmas*? If you are a Who fan, or even a Grinch fan, this site is for you! The *Grinch* song lyrics are here, as well as images from the book and the cartoon. If you just can't get enough of Dr. Seuss, jump to the Cyber-Seuss Page at *<http://www.afn.org/~afn15301/drseuss.html>*.

http://lamar.colostate.edu/~ddave/grinchnet.html

The Gospel of Luke 2:1-20

Do you know that Christmas really celebrates the birth of the baby Jesus? To read the traditional Bible story about Mary and Joseph and the birth of Jesus in Bethlehem, try this beautifully done site. First, pick the background music you want (we liked "What Child is This?"). Next, select the language you prefer (English, Spanish, Portuguese, or Danish). Then sit back and read the familiar story on the right, illustrated with artwork by medieval and Renaissance masters on the left.

http://north.pole.org/santa/

NET FILES

What do Bob Hope, Henry Aaron, the Apollo 12 astronauts, John Wayne, Frank Sinatra, Gerald Ford, Pele, Walt Disney, Shannon Miller, and Carl Lewis have in common?

Answer: *They have all served as grand marshals of the Tournament of Roses Parade! Read more about it at* http://www.citycent.com/tournamentroses/rosegm.htm

NET FILES

When was the first PEZ candy made?

mints

Answer: In 1927, Austrian candy executive Eduard Haas invented PEZ as a diversion for adults trying to quit smoking! The original little candy bricks were only peppermint and not the many different flavors they are now. The word PEZ is an abbreviation of the German word for peppermint (Pfefferminz). At http://www.best.com/~spectrum/pez/pezinfo.html you can read more about this collectible candy.

Santa's Workshop

"'Twas the night before Christmas, when all through the house..." Wait a minute, you don't have to wait until Christmas Eve to visit this site. It's fun any time of the year, especially if you enjoy reading this poem made famous by Clement Moore in the 1820s. This is a great place to find answers to lots of Santa Claus FAQ's (Frequently Asked Questions), as well as learn other holiday traditions and fun historical facts about Christmas. Have you ever wondered about the origins of Santa Claus? Dutch settlers in New Amsterdam (later renamed New York) brought the idea of Santa Claus, or Sint(e) Klass, to America. Even though Christmas songs date back to the fourth century, the lighter and more joyous Christmas songs that we know today as carols came from Renaissance times in Italy. The word "carol" comes from the French word *caroler*, meaning "to dance in a ring." And for the Scrooge in your family, you'll find that famous Charles Dickens story, *A Christmas Carol*. This site is available in English, Spanish, and Portuguese.

http://home1.gte.net/santa/

Don't be a stick-in-the-INTERNET MUD!

CINCO DE MAYO
Cinco de Mayo

Do you like a really good party? Well, every May 5, many Latino Americans and citizens of Mexico celebrate a grand event, and they have a party in the process. In 1862, on Cinco de Mayo (that's Spanish for the fifth of May), a handful of Mexican troops defeated a much larger and better-armed force of soldiers from France. This victory showed that a small group, strengthened by unity, can overcome overwhelming odds. Ever since, Cinco de Mayo is celebrated with music, tasty food, parades, and a party. Read about the history behind this celebration, and learn a little more at <*http://soundprint.brandywine. american.edu/~soundprt/more_info/nogales_history.html*>.

http://latino.sscnet.ucla.edu/cinco.html

DAY OF THE DEAD
The Day of the Dead

On November 2, Mexicans celebrate the annual Day of the Dead. It's not a sad occasion. They make special foods and prepare a feast to honor their ancestors. They have picnics on their relatives' graves so the dead can join in the festivities, too. One of the special foods is called "Bread of the Dead" (*pan de muerto*). The baker hides a plastic skeleton in each rounded loaf, and it's good luck to bite into the piece with the skeleton! People also give each other candy skeletons, skulls, and other treats with a death design. The holiday has complex social, religious, and cultural meanings. Learn more about this celebration here.

http://www.public.iastate.edu/~rjsalvad/scmfaq/muertos.html

There's some funny business going on in the CIRCUSES AND CLOWNS section!

A B C D E F G H I J K L M N O P Q R S T U V W X Y Z

Sidebar alphabet: A B C D E F G **H** I J K L M N O P Q R S T U V W X Y Z

EARTH DAY

EcoNet's Earth Day Resources

Do you worry about whether you will have clean streams to fish in 20 years from now, or whether fish will even be in the stream at all? If you are concerned about the environment and want to do something about it, then join the millions of people worldwide who celebrate Earth Day this year. Read about ways you and your family or classmates can help preserve the environment for years to come. The slogan for the 25th Earth Day in 1995 was "More than just a day—a way of life," and the promoters of Earth Day celebrations around the world want to encourage every individual and organization to make awareness of environmental issues part of their daily lives. This site provides great links to Earth Day information, state by state in the U.S. as well as in Canada and many foreign countries.

http://www.econet.apc.org/earthday/

Here's a fun way you and your school can celebrate Earth Day and raise environmental awareness in your community.

Check out Earth Day Groceries! to see what children in 115 schools in the U.S., Canada, and Australia did with paper bags, markers, a little imagination, and a lot of energy. Find out more at EcoNet's Earth Day Resources.

EASTER

Cathy's Picnic

After you've colored all your Easter eggs, what do you do with them? Do you put them in a bowl on the table? That looks pretty, but try something new—check the Easter Village! Just print out the pictures and color them. In fact, some of them are already in color. Then wrap the pictures around the eggs, set them up, and play with your beautiful creation. Six-year-old Cathy made this page with her family.

http://www.geocities.com/Heartland/7134/index.html

Easter Fun

Easter is a very *egg-citing* occasion! This site gives terrific ideas for making Easter crafts, including lots of ways to dye eggs and make your own candy. We made our own duck mask, some no-bake clay, and planted an Easter basket with wheat seeds to make our own Easter grass. We can hardly wait to try the other Easter links here.

http://www.ok.bc.ca/TEN/easter/easter.html

How to Make Ukrainian Easter Eggs

This page explains everything you need to know about the art of *Pysanky*, the Ukrainian Easter egg. You need an adult to help, because this process involves a candle and hot wax. First, you must decide on the designs you're going to use. Many geometric patterns have traditional meanings—for example, curlicues mean protection and diamonds signify knowledge. You'll find suggested beginner designs here, so get your equipment and get started (the page lists several sources for materials). Using a special stylus, called a *kistka*, apply wax to the egg wherever you want the shell to remain white. Then dip the egg in colored dyes. When completed, you melt the wax off. It takes a long time to make one of these, but in the end you'll have a true work of art. If handled carefully, you'll be able to give these eggs to your children and maybe even your grandchildren. This may be *eggs-actly* the hobby you've been looking for!

http://www.isisnet.com/amorash/ukregg.htm

Zia Easter

OK, Christmas is always on December 25, Valentine's Day is on February 14, and St. Patrick's Day is always celebrated on March 17, so what about Easter? Why is it on a different date each year? The answer is a long one, but here goes: Easter is observed on the first Sunday following the first full moon after the first day of spring (vernal equinox) in the Northern Hemisphere. This can occur any time between March 22 and April 25. Many of the Easter customs we practice today (such as Easter baskets filled with grass and the Easter bunny) are thought to come from activities related to the ancient goddess of spring, Eostre. The hare, a larger relative of the rabbit, was the animal sacred to Eostre. Find out more interesting facts about the history of Easter festivals at this site.

http://www.zia.com/holidays/easter/

GERMAN HOLIDAYS
German

This cultural gem originates at the Patch American School, on a U.S. military base in Germany. Because a lot of American kids, who live there with their military families, find some of the local customs unusual, this site attempts to explain them. For example, this site explains the differences between a German Christmas and an American one. You'll also learn all about St. Martin's Day, the witches of May, and the beautiful, candlelit traditions of the Advent season.

http://192.253.114.31/German/Ger_Home.html

> Ships are only hulls,
> high walls are nothing,
> When no life moves in
> the empty passageways.
>
> —Sophocles

GROUNDHOG DAY
Groundhog Day - February 2, 1997

Long before we had weather satellites, Doppler radar, and the Weather Channel, we got our winter weather forecasts from a rodent. Yes, it's part of what has made America great, and the tradition continues in Punxsutawney, Pennsylvania. Now you can get up close and personal with Punxsutawney Phil, groundhog extraordinaire. Some may call him a woodchuck, and some may call him a gopher. We call him a great publicity stunt, but we always pay attention to his predictions for an early or late spring. As the legend goes, if Phil comes up out of his hole on February 2 and sees his shadow, he'll be frightened back for six more weeks of winter; if, on the other hand, it's cloudy, we'll get an early spring. Will he see his shadow? Film at 11... If that is not enough, look for more Phil trivia at <http://www.csh.rit.edu/~jones/ghd.html> or check out the CNN investigation into a groundhog conspiracy at <http://www.cnn.com/US/9702/02/groundhog.conspiracy/index.html>.

http://www.groundhog.org/

"Groundhog Day—half your hay."

That's an old saying connected with February 2, Groundhog Day. New England farmers knew that despite how sunny or cloudy the day was, there was still a lot of winter to come. If less than half the year's store of hay was left in the hayloft, the cows were in for a stretch of rationing before spring rains brought the new grass. Discover the strange and fanciful traditions of this unusual holiday at the Groundhog Day—February 2, 1997 page, which celebrates the weather forecasting abilities of a rodent.

A B C D E F G H I J K L M N O P Q R S T U V W X Y Z

A
B
C
D
E
F
G
H
I
J
K
L
M
N
O
P
Q
R
S
T
U
V
W
X
Y
Z

Wiarton Willie's World Wide Website

Lest you think Canadians don't have a weather rodent (*en Français, météo marmotte*) of their own, meet Wiarton Willie, an albino marmot. "Born on the 45th parallel, exactly midway between the Equator and the North Pole, this white groundhog has the uncanny ability to signal the end of winter. Weather watchers around the world look to Willie's shadow and its 90 percent accuracy rate to see just how long winter is going to continue!" The statue of the critter is not to be missed, and Willie has fun games and mazes to play with, too. You can even send him e-mail (he must have a modem in his burrow). Come join the fun in southwestern Ontario on Lake Huron.

http://www.wiarton-willie.org/welcome.html

NET FILES

You've seen the U.S. flag, with its 50 stars. What other world flags display stars?

Answer: A whole sky-full of flags have stars on them! Flags with constellations on them include those of Australia, Brazil, and New Zealand. Flags with stars in other arrangements include those of China, Panama, and Somalia, among many others. At *http://www.adfa.oz.au/CS/flg/col/index.html* you can explore more on world flags.

Explore the past in ANCIENT CIVILIZATIONS AND ARCHAEOLOGY.

HALLOWEEN

The Penny Whistle Halloween Book

From bloodcurdling beverages (with insects in the ice cubes) to devilish desserts (with chocolate spiders), your Halloween party is sure to be ghoulish if you follow some of the ideas here. There are Halloween decorations and activities that any witch, wizard, or goblin will love. Don't forget to tiptoe through the pumpkin patch for design do's and don'ts about carving and lighting the best jack-o'-lantern ever!

http://family.starwave.com/funstuff/pwhistle/pwhallow/

Zia's Haunted House

Tricks and treats abound at this great Halloween site! Enter the haunted house if you dare, but watch out for the horrible jokes (Why does a witch ride on a broom? Because vacuum cleaners have to be plugged into the wall!). Stroll through the site (keep your eyes closed if you're scared) and get some tips on easy-to-make costumes, decorations, and party food. There are lots of links to other haunted Web sites, none of *witch* we have checked.

http://www.zia.com/holidays/halloween/

Did you know that the first carved jack-o'-lantern was not a pumpkin?

Find out what other large vegetable was used for this purpose during the Middle Ages, and learn about other Halloween lore and legend at Zia's Haunted House.

INDEPENDENCE DAY

4th of July - Independence Day

This patriotic site features a message from Vice President Al Gore, an audio file of the U.S. National Anthem, links to lots of government resources around the Net, and last but very important: fireworks safety tips!

http://banzai.neosoft.com/citylink/usa/

NATIONAL FOREIGN HOLIDAYS

The United States celebrates its birthday on July 4. There are parades, picnics, and at night—fireworks! Most countries celebrate national holidays that are their equivalents of the American Independence Day. You'll find a list of them here.

http://www.worldculture.com/holidays.htm

JEWISH HOLIDAYS

A - Z of Jewish & Israel Related Resources

Search the subject index or browse alphabetically to find interesting topics, such as "Hebrew children's songs for the holidays," "Choreographic descriptions of Israeli folk dances," and our personal favorite, "Uncle Eli's Special-for-Kids Most Fun Ever Under-the-Table Passover Haggadah."

http://www.ort.org/anjy/a-z/festival.htm

What is the sound of one cow mooing?

Answer: We're not sure, but you can hear what we mean at http://www.gl.umbc.edu/~dschmil/cows/sounds.html Besides solo cow sounds, you'll hear a cow duet, a cow chorus, and cacophony of cowbells. Mooove over, Garth, here comes Bossie!

Ben Uri Art Society

Here is a great site to learn about art, history, and the Jewish holidays, all rolled into one! The Ben Uri Art Gallery is a collection of over 700 paintings, drawings, prints, and sculpture by Jewish artists—selections from which are shown regularly in the gallery in London, England. The first two art selections show the *Shabbat,* the Hebrew word for Sabbath, which begins at sundown each Friday. Because the Jewish calendar is based on the lunar calendar (cycles of the moon), the new "day" begins at this time. *Rosh Hashanah,* the Hebrew phrase for the "Head of the Year," is the Jewish New Year celebration, and so our illustrated tour begins with this holiday in September. Continue through the Gallery and the months of the year, to learn more about the other Jewish holy days and festivals and the food, songs, and dances that are part of these traditional celebrations.

http://www.ort.org/links/benuri/home.htm

Calendar of Jewish Holidays

This resource, offered by B'nai B'rith, gives the dates for all important Jewish holidays through the year 2000. Mark your calendars in advance.

http://www.bus.miami.edu/~hillel/holiday.htm

Hanukkah—Festival Of Lights

It's the year 165 B.C., and after a three-year struggle, the Jews in Judea have successfully defeated the Syrian tyrant, Antiochus. Now they are ready to hold festivities and celebrate the reclaiming of their Temple, but only a very small bottle of oil is left with which to light all the holy lamps. Miraculously, this small amount of oil lasts for eight days. *Hanukkah,* the Jewish Festival of Lights, involves the lighting of candles each night for eight days during a special ceremony. Around December of every year, Jewish families celebrate Hanukkah by lighting candles held by a *menorah,* a candleholder with nine branches. And, just like the holiday celebrations of other cultures, there are special foods and music for Hannukah. It's all here: the history, the goodies, and three traditional Hanukkah songs with music and lyrics, in both English and Hebrew. You'll even find a pattern for making a *dreidel* (a four-sided spinning top), which is part of a traditional children's game of luck.

http://www.ort.org/ort/hanukkah/title.htm

A
B
C
D
E
F
G
H
I
J
K
L
M
N
O
P
Q
R
S
T
U
V
W
X
Y
Z

JOHN MUIR DAY
John Muir Day Study Guide

Every April 21, students in California celebrate the life of John Muir and his contribution to conservation and appreciation of the environment. He founded the Sierra Club and pushed the U.S. government to establish the national parks system. The first national park, designated in 1890, was Yosemite, located in California. You can visit it via this site, as well as an online Muir exhibit. There is also a biography of Muir and accounts of his travels around the world.

http://www.sierraclub.org/john_muir_exhibit/
　john_muir_day_study_guide/

JUNETEENTH
JUNETEENTH: Freedom Revisited

Celebrate freedom! African Americans recall June 19, 1865, as the date when many slaves in the state of Texas learned that they had been freed, over two years earlier, by President Abraham Lincoln. This celebration is known as Juneteenth, and it is usually marked by historical displays, feasts, songs, and dancing. Learn about the origins of Juneteenth at the Anacostia Museum in Washington, D.C.

http://www.si.edu/anacostia/june.htm

KWANZAA
Kwanzaa Information Center

The symbolic lighting of candles is associated with many holidays. And so it is with Kwanzaa, an African American spiritual holiday emphasizing the unity of the family and encouraging a festive celebration of the oneness and goodness of life. Learn how the seven candles, the *Mshumaa*, represent the seven principles of Nguzo Saba. Read about the history and meaning of the other symbols used in the celebration of this holiday. A list of children's books about Kwanzaa is also provided here.

http://www.melanet.com/kwanzaa/

Brother reading your diary again? Learn to encrypt in CODES AND CIPHERS.

The Meaning of Kwanzaa

In 1966, a man named Maulana Ron Karenga and the U.S. Organization invented a new American holiday based on harvest celebrations in Africa. They called this celebration *Kwanzaa*, a Swahili word meaning "first," signifying the first fruits of the harvest. Many Americans of African heritage celebrate this holiday each December.

http://www.si.edu/anacostia/kwanz.htm

NET FILES

How many flowers must honeybees visit to make one pound of honey?

Answer: *Two million flowers!* A hive of bees has to fly an average of 55,000 miles to visit that many flowers and bring you that sweet pound of honey. Find out more fun bee facts at http://www.billybee.com/infocenter.html

ST. PATRICK'S DAY
RCA Victor: I Am Irish

They say that on St. Patrick's Day everyone is Irish! Come join the parade as you *March* through this site to find answers to questions like: Are potatoes Irish? Why do people kiss the Blarney Stone? Which city boasts the very first St. Patrick's Day parade in North America? Learn more about the legend of St. Patrick, along with other Celtic lore. Yes, you'll find leprechauns here, too! If you're a history buff, there's even more here for you with a great list of famous Irish Americans throughout history. If you think the shamrock is the official emblem of Ireland, guess again—it's the harp, a favorite musical instrument in Ireland, dating back hundreds of years.

http://www.classicalmus.com/bmgclassics/
　promotions/irish/irish-stuff.html

A Wee Bit O' Fun

Have you ever wondered who St. Patrick really was and why we celebrate St. Patrick's Day? Is there really such a thing as a leprechaun? Americans have been celebrating this holiday for over 200 years. Read all about the history of St. Patrick's Day at this site. Also check out the list of other Web sites dominated by the color green, including one called 40 Tips To Go Green, which has ideas for saving the environment.

http://www.nando.net/toys/stpaddy/stpaddy.html

THANKSGIVING
THE FIRST THANKSGIVING

Would you like to fix the perfect Pilgrim-style Thanksgiving dinner? Check out this site to learn about the Pilgrims and the first Thanksgiving in 1621. Great recipe ideas will help you re-create that seventeenth-century harvest feast. The interpretive guides, dressed in historic period costumes, will take you on a virtual tour of "Plimoth Plantation," the first permanent European settlement. You'll also see Hobbamock's Homesite, a reconstructed Native American hamlet, complete with a wigwam and a bark-covered longhouse.

http://media3.com/plymouth/thanksgiving.htm

Zia Thanksgiving

This site has tasty recipes, directions for carving the turkey, and even instructions for making table decorations. If you've ever wondered how to make a cornhusk doll, look no further!

http://www.zia.com/thanks.htm

VALENTINE'S DAY
ZIA Valentines

At this site, you can send a fun or a sappy e-mail valentine to your friend or your true love. You can also find Valentine's Day party ideas, recipes, and crafts, and read all about the history of this *love*-ly holiday. This site is designed for kids.

http://www.zia.com/holidays/valentine/

DON'T want to eat your Brussels sprouts? What would you do if your Mom made you finish all your furmenty, a dish from colonial times? You'd probably be happy! Furmenty is a delicious dish containing cracked wheat, milk, and brown sugar. It's sort of like a sweet oatmeal. Find this recipe and others at THE FIRST THANKSGIVING.

HORSES AND EQUESTRIAN SPORTS

See also MAMMALS—HORSE FAMILY AND ZEBRAS

Aberdeen University Riding Club World Equestrian Information

This U.K. site is the most comprehensive collection of equine resources we've seen. There is a nice kids' pony page, with a horse glossary and hints on how to guess your horse's age! You'll find stories, clubs, newsletters, events, loads of personal pages, and more. We haven't checked all the links here, so parents, do your thing!

http://www.abdn.ac.uk/~src011/equine.html

Curl up with a good URL in BOOKS AND LITERATURE!

A B C D E F G H I J K L M N O P Q R S T U V W X Y Z

BLM Wild Horse and Burro Program- Home Page

Ever thought of adopting a wild horse? This site tells you all about what you have to do to adopt one from the U.S. Bureau of Land Management. There are requirements though, and remember, these are wild animals who have never been around people before, so folks sometimes have difficulty getting the horses tamed. This site has a schedule of adoption locations and dates and plenty of information for the potential adoptive family. For a nongovernmental opinion on this controversial program, try the original Wild Horse, Mustang, and Burro Page at <http://iquest.com/~jhines/mustang/>.

http://www.blm.gov/whb/

The Hay.net A comprehensive list of almost all the horse sites on the 'net

This site is the Internet equivalent of sweet feed for horse owners: all sorts of delicious grains, dripping with molasses, each crunchier than the last. Start with the Pick of the Week—maybe it's about x-raying large animals or an interactive guide to horse health care. Let's move into the barn and see all the different breeds: Arabians, quarter horses, thoroughbreds, sure; you'll also find Icelandic ponies, Halflingers, and all kinds of drafts. What's this little one here, not moving at all? Oh, it's a model horse—you'll find lots here on them, too. Check the Olympic events, the Denver Stock Show, and lots of racing and driving information. Pull up a hay bale and make yourself comfortable!

http://www.freerein.com/haynet/

Horse Country

This is the ultimate horse site for juniors! Horse history, care, stories, sounds, images, and associations are all here. Several fantasy games let you create your own dream stable, "buy and sell" virtual horses, "compete" in virtual horse shows, and share the results with your fellow dream stable owners. Other musts here are the Junior Riders Mailing Digest and an International Pen Pal List for horse lovers. This site is the best thing to happen to junior riders since Misty of Chincoteague.

http://www.horse-country.com/

International Museum of the Horse - Lexington, Kentucky

"Our history was written on his back," says this site, dedicated to the history of horses and horsemanship. Learn about horses in war, in sport, in work, and in recreation. There are also some fascinating online special exhibits: "The Draft Horse In America: Power for an Emerging Nation"; "The Buffalo Soldiers on the Western Frontier"; and the famous thoroughbreds at "Calumet Farm: Five Decades of Champions." Don't miss the fabulous online equine art gallery, as well as a comprehensive selection of links to horse farms, racetracks, breed clubs, and commercial sites all over the Web.

http://www.horseworld.com/imh/imhmain.html

Do you love horses?

Are you into rodeo or racing?

Did you know that the horse evolved from an animal no bigger than a modern-day fox? If horses are your thing, then this is your page. Everything from the history of horses to a gallery of breeds to horse sports will be found here. Gallop on over to the **International Museum of the Horse—Lexington, Kentucky.**

Extinction is forever, as ENDANGERED AND EXTINCT SPECIES know.

Janet's Horsin' Around on the Web Page

It's raining, and you hate to ride in the rain! It's a pain to clean the mud off your tack afterwards, to say nothing of making your horse look presentable again. Why not give your horse an apple and the day off, and ride the trails of this great Web site instead? Janet's pulled together a nice group of links, including breed home pages, horse health, sports, wild horses, and electronic horse magazines. The back issues of these e-zines alone will keep you busy for hours. Hey, it's stopped raining! Not all links have been reviewed from this site.

http://www.cowgirls.com/dream/jan/horse.htm#horse

The Model Horse Gallery Home Page

If you love horses, we mean *really* love horses, then chances are you have a model horse or two. Did you know there are horse shows for model horses, too? You can find out where they are and what classes you and your model horse can enter. You'll also get tips about painting and otherwise reworking your Breyer or other collectible horse models. You won't believe the photos of the detailed models here and at <http://www.freerein.com/haynet/model.html>.

http://www.astroarch.com/modelhorse/

FOXHUNTING
Horse Country Horse and Hound Pages

Nowadays, many hunts don't actually hunt foxes; instead, they follow a scent of fox urine that has been dragged over the ground hours before. Still, the sight of hounds running across a field with a herd of bold horses and riders galloping behind is pretty exciting! Here you'll find some interesting history about foxhunting and learn some of the special jargon you'll need to know in the hunt field. You can also hear some hunting horn fanfare and learn why those bright red hunting jackets are called "pink coats."

http://www.horse-country.com/hunt.html

It never rains in cyberspace.

HORSE RACING
Racing Memorabilia Page

Swaps, Man O' War, and Citation are some of racing history's most well-known horses. You can see color postcards of them here, as well as some of the racetracks and breeding farms they made famous. Don't miss the photo of the only three-way tie in stakes race history: at the Carter Handicap race at Aqueduct in 1944, Brownie, Bossuet, and Wait a Bit all finished first!

http://www.wsnet.com/~sysclp/postcard.html

POLO
PoloNet

Polo is a four-person, four-horse team sport, requiring a mallet and a ball about the size of a baseball. The object is to score points by hitting the ball to a goal. The outdoor variation of polo is played on a grass surface measuring 300 by 160 (or more) yards, about the size of six football fields! Learn about the tactics and strategy of the game, and link to polo clubs and other players around the world.

http://www.cts.com/browse/polonet/

NET FILES

Why would you want to play a medieval krummhorn with a blanket over your head?

Answer: According to "The strangest thing you have been asked to do at a gig," at Windplayer Online: It's impossible to play the krummhorn softly. The only way to quiet it down a little is to throw something over the player's head! Try http://www.windplayer.com/wp/strangest.html for more strange tales.

A
B
C
D
E
F
G
H
I
J
K
L
M
N
O
P
Q
R
S
T
U
V
W
X
Y
Z

INSECTS AND SPIDERS

See also INVERTEBRATES

Billy Bee Honey Products Limited - Canada's #1 Honey

To *bee* or not to *bee*...but the question is, what do you know about bees? Worker honeybees have many jobs in taking care of their hives. They do the feeding, cleaning, guarding, the long-distance and short-distance flying; they carry pollen, produce honey, and build the honeycomb. To learn more about beekeeping, visit this site, and *bee* careful! For still more bee facts, try the USDA bee pages at <*http://gears.tucson.ars.ag.gov/ic/index.html*>.

http://www.billybee.com/

The Butterfly WebSite

Do you know what the first butterflies of spring are? Here's a hint: they have a blue sparkle about them. Give up? The azure butterflies are the first, followed by the sulphurs, then the whites. But you don't have to wait for spring to see butterflies. There are hundreds of butterflies and moths waiting for your discovery year-round. Find out how to locate moths and butterflies any time of the year. Learn about butterfly gardening and which flowers and plants attract butterflies and encourage them to lay eggs.

http://mgfx.com/butterflies/

Entomology for beginners

This very basic page gives an introduction to insect anatomy and metamorphosis. Click on a part of the insect to find out what that part is called and what it's for. If you click on the mouth parts, you'll find that butterflies and moths have coiled tongues, while other insects have mouths that are good for chewing or sucking. In the metamorphosis section, you can see how a caterpillar changes from a crawler to a flier as it morphs into a moth.

http://www.bos.nl/homes/bijlmakers/ento/begin.html

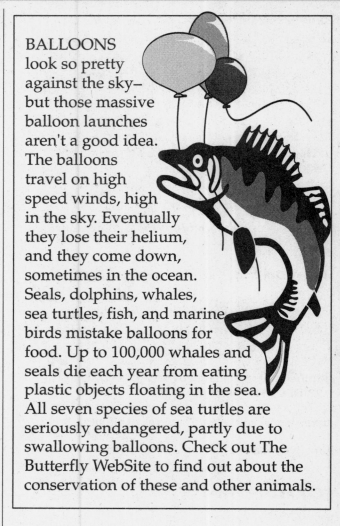

BALLOONS look so pretty against the sky— but those massive balloon launches aren't a good idea. The balloons travel on high speed winds, high in the sky. Eventually they lose their helium, and they come down, sometimes in the ocean. Seals, dolphins, whales, sea turtles, fish, and marine birds mistake balloons for food. Up to 100,000 whales and seals die each year from eating plastic objects floating in the sea. All seven species of sea turtles are seriously endangered, partly due to swallowing balloons. Check out The Butterfly WebSite to find out about the conservation of these and other animals.

Gordons Entomological Home Page

Did you know that insects were often used as medical treatment? Bedbugs were thought to be a cure for malaria, beetle grubs were used as a cure for toothaches, and acid from ants was often used as a cure for neurotic troubles. Others perceived insects as a delicious addition to their diet. In case you were wondering how to make banana worm bread or rootworm beetle dip, you can find the recipes at <*http://www.ent.iastate.edu/Misc/InsectsAsFood.html*>. On the other hand, insects make great pets! OK, so you may need to convince your mom and dad. Not only are insects small and less intrusive, but generally they are quieter and cheaper to feed. You can even learn how to care for your pet tarantula or cricket.

http://info.ex.ac.uk/~gjlramel/welcome.html

Minibeast Homepage

Question: Why was the inchworm angry? Answer: He had to convert to the metric system! For more insect jokes sure to *bug* you, try this site. You'll also find educational resources here, so you can learn fascinating bug trivia, bug care, and bug facts.

http://www.tesser.com/minibeast/

Spiders of the World

Help a real scientist in her research! Help Dr. Rosie Gillespie, a professor in the Department of Zoology at the University of Hawaii, answer this question: Why do the *Tetragnatha* and other families of spiders in Hawaii live in such diverse habitats, in comparison to families of spiders on the mainland? Look at various species of spiders and learn how to identify them. Then go on a spider hunt! Find out the kind and number of families of spiders in your neighborhood, then submit your spider data to Dr. Gillespie online. See your spider data graphed with other information from students and teachers worldwide.

http://seawifs.gsfc.nasa.gov/JASON/HTML/
SPIDERS_HOME.html

NET FILES

Where would you find a tiger's pug mark?

Answer: *On the ground—it's another word for a footprint or track. Its actual size is 5.5 inches (10.8 cm) by 4.5 inches (8.75 cm)! You can see a tiger's pug mark at http://www.5tigers.org/pug.htm*

Steve's Ant Farm - A T O M I C W E B . C O M

This is a happenin' place. In fact, it's a crawlin' place. Steve's got an ant farm, and he's got a camera pointed at it. Every five minutes, the camera posts a new picture to this Web site. You can watch ants build tunnels, construct bridges, and make molehills out of mountains.

http://sec.dgsys.com/antfarm.html

University of Kentucky Department of Entomology

Have you ever been to the Olympics? How about the insect Olympics? See a flea go for the gold in the high jump competition. Watch a bolus spider go for a "bolus-eye" in archery. Check out insect world records and discover which insects are the ugliest, have the longest legs, and have the smallest wings. Is your class looking for a mascot? How about an insect? Here you'll find some guidelines to help pick the best choice for your classroom. Interested in an insect treat? How about ants on a log? Come on, it's just a stalk of celery spread with peanut butter and sprinkled with raisins!

http://www.uky.edu/Agriculture/Entomology/
ythfacts/entyouth.htm

Welcome to Cockroach World

Betty the Bug Lady is the host of the yuckiest site on the Internet. You can ask her about cockroaches and other bug stuff. Take the Cockroach World quiz, or tell your cockroach story to the rest of the forum. Stop by Cockroach World's multimedia library for yucky sights and sounds. Hear the hiss of the Madagascar hissing cockroach or watch the "Smelly Roach" QuickTime movie. You'll also learn that cockroaches spend 75 percent of their time resting up for those late-night snack runs!

http://www.nj.com/yucky/roaches/

Things are purrfect in the CATS section!

A B C D E F G H I J K L M N O P Q R S T U V W X Y Z

A
B
C
D
E
F
G
H
I
J
K
L
M
N
O
P
Q
R
S
T
U
V
W
X
Y
Z

You Can - Spider Webs

Why doesn't a spider stick to its web? Try this experiment with Beakman and Jax to find out. Then look at the many different kinds of spider webs, and maybe even collect some using the method described here. But be sure to wait until Charlotte's done with hers before you take it home!

http://pomo.nbn.com/youcan/spider/spider.html

INTERNET

Hobbes' Internet World

Everything you need to know about the Internet is probably on this page. We haven't checked every possible link, but we're pretty sure everything is here. If you're looking for an Internet service provider, try the POCIA link. Want to control your own domain name? The forms are here. Curious about Internet organizations, including The Internet Society? Looking for beginner's guides, standards documents, or security alerts? Told you it was all here. Links galore and even more!

http://info.isoc.org/guest/zakon/Internet/

ILC Glossary of Internet Terms

Confused by all those new Internet terms? Can't tell an IMHO from a TTFN? Don't SLIP in the MUD, come on over to this terrific glossary, and all will be revealed.

http://www.matisse.net/files/glossary.html

Don't cave in!
Better spelunk a bit in
EARTH SCIENCE.

 in the can? No, SPAM on the Net! On the Internet, people sometimes send e-mail messages to many, many people on electronic conferences like listservs and Usenet. Usually these messages advertise some product or service, having nothing to do with the topic of the discussion. This is called SPAMming. This is just like junk mail, and you can throw it away. Read more new words at the ILC Glossary of Internet Terms.

The Scout Toolkit Homepage

The Internet Scout has put together a page that will help you. If not today, then tomorrow. Trust us when we say that you will need this page. All the tools you need are right here in the toolbox: browsers, search options, specialized applications like Real Audio (radio and other audio over the Net), and CU-SeeMe (video over the Net). There's also a great section on how to keep up with what's current on the Net. Remember, if you don't have the newest stuff in your toolkit, everything looks like a *This Old Net* rerun.

http://rs.internic.net/scout/toolkit/

The Unofficial Internet Book List

Obviously, you know that reading about the Internet is one way to learn about it, otherwise you wouldn't be holding this book. There are many other books about the Internet, and they cover a wide range of information. If you're eager to do more book reading, you can get a complete catalog of Internet books from Kevin Savetz's The Unofficial Internet Book List. Then go to your local public library to get the ones that interest you. If you read all of the books listed, you'll know as much about the Internet as anyone. That will take a while, though: there are 500 books on the list!

http://www.northcoast.com/~savetz/booklist/

BEGINNER'S GUIDES

A Beginner's Guide to URLs

From the inventors of Mosaic comes this brief guide to URLs, or uniform resource locators. If something's out there on the Internet, you can "point" to it using a URL and your favorite Net browser. This will give you the syntax for pointing at gopher servers, ftp archives, news, and of course Web resources!

http://www.ncsa.uiuc.edu/demoweb/url-primer.html

CyberU Internet Elective

This online tutorial aimed at high school kids explains how to use the Web, organize bookmarked resources, and use Net tools like telnet and ftp. It also goes into Internet history, netiquette, and more.

http://dune.srhs.k12.nj.us/WWW/contents.htm

EFF's (Extended) Guide to the Internet - Table of Contents

The EFF (Electronic Frontier Foundation) Guide to the Internet is very dated, but it still contains good information on Internet lore and legend. If you try the version of EFF at <http://www.eff.org/papers/eegtti/> you can get a copy in Japanese, Russian, Italian, and several other languages. A caution to parents: This site gives addresses, but does not link to, various resources that may be inappropriate for your family.

http://www.nova.edu/Inter-Links/
    bigdummy/bdg_toc.html

The Internet Companion, 2nd Edition

One of the best books ever written about the Internet is called *The Internet Companion,* by Tracy LaQuey. The entire book is available on the Internet for free! If you want to learn how the Internet came about, what you can do with the Internet, and how to become more familiar with the Internet in general, take a look here.

http://www.obs-us.com/obs/english/books/editinc/

InterNIC 15 Minute Series

These very short tutorials were developed to help people who need to train other people about the Net. The lessons are both on the Web and in a downloadable presentation software file. You'll find lots of useful basic info here in bite-size chunks. Recent additions include: What is a Web page? What is a Domain Name? What is an Internet Service Provider? What is a network? and more.

http://rs.internic.net/nic-support/15min/

Walking the Web: A Short Course in Getting Around

If your parents are hopelessly clueless about what the Web is and how to use it, just take them by the hand and lead them here. Then go away and have a sandwich. When you get back, they will know all about hypertext, inline graphics, and how to fill out an online form. Their eyes won't even be glazed over! This course is short, snappy, and simple.

http://www.edf.org/Earth2Kids/walking/contents.html

NET FILES

All dinosaurs are extinct . . . right?

(Hint: This involves the greatest fish story ever told!)

Answer: Maybe not. In 1938, fishermen off the coast of South Africa found the first living coelacanth in recent history; another was reported in 1952, off the Comoros Islands (to the northeast, in the Mozambique Channel). The coelacanth (pronounced "see-la-kanth") is a 400-million-year-old "living fossil" fish, once thought to have become extinct long ago. The account at http://www.dinofish.com/discoa.htm of its amazing discovery reads like a mystery story. Check the "dinofish" home page at http://www.dinofish.com/ for pictures and more amazing details.

A B C D E F G H I J K L M N O P Q R S T U V W X Y Z

A
B
C
D
E
F
G
H
I
J
K
L
M
N
O
P
Q
R
S
T
U
V
W
X
Y
Z

Your Internet Consultant

Kevin Savetz is one of Net-mom's favorite people, especially because he invented telling time with Foam Bath Fish Time at <http://www.northcoast.com/savetz/fish/fishtime.cgi>. Kevin's book, *Your Internet Consultant: The FAQs of Life Online,* is on his home page. It was originally published in 1994, but every so often Kevin updates it just a little bit more, and it's great for general info, like how the Net works and what you need to know about Net culture.

http://www.northcoast.com/~savetz/yic/

FINDING PEOPLE

As you use the Internet, you may start wondering if people you know have Internet accounts. Maybe you have a favorite uncle who lives on the other side of the country or a friend from a town where you used to live, and you'd like to communicate with them via the Net. Problem is, how can you determine if they are on the Internet? The surest way is to call or write the person and ask. There are a variety of experimental programs on the Internet, though, that you can use to track people down. Listed here are a few places you can look that provide links to different people-finding tools. Happy hunting, but be sure to read the instructions for these programs. Some are much easier to use than others.

Finding Internet People on the Internet

Here's a general introduction to the problem and some solutions. Try these ideas if WhoWhere? and Four11 (also listed in this book) don't help.

http://www.sil.org/internet/email.html

Four11 Directory Services

Similar to WhoWhere? (see separate entry), Four11 claims to be the largest directory of its kind, with over ten million e-mail address listings. If you don't find who you're looking for, they have a notification service. You'll get e-mail if your friend's name turns up in the directory. If you're looking for a phone number, they have over 100 million! There are also directories of celebrities and famous folks in sports, entertainment, business, and government. You'll find lots of other cool services, too, such as free Web-based e-mail accounts.

http://www.Four11.com/

Jean's People-Finding Internet Resources

Here's another general one to try as a last resort, with the added strategy of checking college Web phone books and more.

http://www.benoit.com/jean/find.html

WhoWhere? E-Mail Addresses

Finding addresses should always have been this easy. We don't just mean e-mail addresses. We mean street addresses and phone numbers! You can also find people's home pages with the search tools here. Another cool thing is to find other people interested in the same things you are—or people who went to the same school or summer camp. That's called the "Communities" feature, so check it out! You can also find business home pages, toll-free phone numbers, and more (we find something new every time we visit). There are English, French, and Spanish versions of this page. And if you didn't find who you were looking for, WhoWhere? will keep looking and e-mail you if your friend ever turns up in the database.

http://www.whowhere.com/

NET FILES

WHEN WAS THE FIRST CAMERA MADE AVAILABLE TO CONSUMERS?

Answer: The first consumer camera was marketed in 1888. The Kodak camera was priced at $25 and included film for 100 exposures. It was a little inconvenient to get your pictures developed, though: the whole camera had to be returned to Kodak in Rochester, New York for film processing! Click over to http://www.it.rit.edu:80/~gehouse/timeline/kodak1.html for more on the history of photography!

HISTORY

Hobbes' Internet Timeline

How did all this Internet stuff get started, anyway? The unofficial history of the Internet is here.

http://www.isoc.org/guest/zakon/Internet/
  History/HIT.html

WWW History

A big part of the Internet is the World Wide Web, or the WWW, or the Web. The World Wide Web makes it easier to use pictures (or graphics) and also helps to link information together on the Internet. To better understand the WWW and get a good dose of Internet history in the process, take a peek at this page.

http://k12.cnidr.org:90/web.history.html

MACHINES ON THE NET

Anthony's List of Internet Accessible Machines

For some time, various folks on the Internet have attached computers to all kinds of machines. With the machines hooked up, the owners are then able to give updates on those machines live on the Net. Soft drink vending machines, refrigerators, toasters, and cameras (with live pictures) are among the types of devices connected. For example, you can learn how many cans of soda are available in a machine and what the temperature in a refrigerator is; you can also see students live in a college dorm room. Why have people done this? It's probably better to ask, "Why ask why?" Take a look at this site to see what it's all about! Parents, not all remote links have been checked.

http://www.dsu.edu/~anderbea/machines.html

Why surf the Internet when you can sail it in BOATING AND SAILING?

MUDS, MOOS, AND IRC

MUDs and MOOs (you'll also hear of similar MUSHs and MUSEs) are programs that let you explore, and sometimes create, computer-generated, text-based worlds. For example, you can build a stream next to a mountain and maybe put a magical fish in it. You can talk live, via your computer keyboard, to kids from all over the world and learn about science, history, and computers. Best of all, these are a ton of fun! You'll also see one recommended IRC (Internet relay chat) in this section. It involves a multichannel real-time chat with kids all over.

KIDLINK Internet Relay Chat

Kidlink is one of the oldest kid-friendly sites on the Net. Internet relay chat (IRC) is a way for you to talk to kids all over the globe in real time. With IRC, when you type something, other kids can type right back! Some IRC channels are open to everyone and they are pretty wild. This one is just for kids, and you have to register before they will let you use it. It is carefully monitored. Don't pass by, give IRC a try!

http://www.kidlink.org/IRC/

MOO Central

A medley of MOOs, MUDs, and MUSHs, including a few in languages other than English. These are collected especially for the education community, and some are targeted towards kids.

http://www.pitt.edu/~jrgst7/MOOcentral.html

SchoolNet MOO

You've never seen a school like this. Housed in a computer in Canada (it's a multilingual system for French and English speakers), this is the place where you can build all sorts of things while interacting with kids from all over. To connect to this site, you'll need telnet capability, so ask your parents or teachers if you have that.

http://schoolnet2.carleton.ca/english/moo/

A
B
C
D
E
F
G
H
I
J
K
L
M
N
O
P
Q
R
S
T
U
V
W
X
Y
Z

A B C D E F G H I J K L M N O P Q R S T U V W X Y Z

Welcome to MOOSE Crossing!

Would you like to build your own world with other kids from around the planet? Would you like to work on special projects with kids age 13 and under? Would you like to work on a computer at MIT, the foremost center of computer innovation? Do you own or have access to a Macintosh computer? If you answered yes to these questions, then MOOSE Crossing is the place for you!

http://lcs.www.media.mit.edu/people/asb/
  moose-crossing/

NETIQUETTE, FOLKLORE, AND CUSTOMS

Electronic smiles won't shock your lips

When writing e-mail messages, sometimes it's hard to express what you are really feeling. This has been a problem for folks on the Internet for a long time, and to help express emotions better, smileys were created. For example, turn your head sideways to the left, and look at this —> :-). Do you see this makes a little smiley face? There are many variations of these smileys—to see more, take a peek at this page. A note to parents: There are lots of smiley lists on the Net that are more comprehensive, but this one is family-oriented.

http://www.clarku.edu/~scarlet/issues95/
  scarlet030295/electronic-smiles-won-t-.html

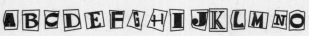

A smiley, or emoticon, is a way of expressing your feelings through typed characters. Look at this sideways :-D does that look like a really happy face?

Find more at the *Electronic smiles won't shock your lips* **page.**

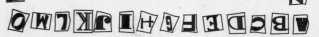

NET FILES

What are Moki Steps and where can you climb them?

Answer: In the 1200s was a flourishing culture of cliff dwellers called the Anasazi in southwestern Colorado, in a beautiful place called Mesa Verde, now a national park. To climb from their cliffside homes to the top of the mesa to get water and harvest crops, they used the Moki Steps, which are handholds and footholds built right into the vertical cliff faces—hundreds of feet above the canyon floor. The Anasazi carved these in the rock in such a way that anyone who started climbing down with the wrong foot would be stuck halfway down! Travel back in history to *http://artseek.com/anasazi/ MesaVerde.html* and read more about the Anasazi cliff dwellings and other mysterious places.

The Net: User Guidelines and Netiquette

Everybody knows that politeness and good etiquette make life easier. Waiting your turn in line, keeping your locker in order, or being nice to your friends helps you as much as the people around you. The same is true on the Internet. There are some basic rules of etiquette (on the Internet it's called *netiquette*) that help keep things running smoothly. Check out some of these basic rules of Internet good behavior. At *<http://rs6000.adm.fau.edu/rinaldi/net/trans.html>* you can find this document in many other languages!

http://rs6000.adm.fau.edu/rinaldi/net/

AMUSEMENT PARKS will amuse you!

PARENTAL CONTROL
Parental Control Product Review

The Internet is great: you can learn a lot, make new friends, and have a whole new world opened to you. However, there may be parts of the Internet your parents don't want you to see. As with some television programs, or books, or magazines, or parts of town, your parents decide what you can and cannot view. There are a variety of software products your parents can place on your computer to help you better use the Internet and to help them guide what you see. Show this page to your mom, dad, or another adult in charge. They'll see what is available and also get answers to questions about what they can do to make your Internet experiences great! We support these types of products because we believe that this type of guidance should come from the home and not be imposed by the government.

http://www.neosoft.com/parental-control/

What are Cybersitter, Cyberpatrol, Netnanny, and Surfwatch?

They are different pieces of software that parents or schools can use to help guide your Internet experience and make sure you're safe. Want to compare them? Read more at the **Parental Control Product Review** page.

PEDINFO Parental Control of Internet Access

There's been a lot of talk in the news about the Internet having stuff on it that is inappropriate for kids. The overwhelming majority of information is OK, but those news stories might make your parents and teachers nervous. Some people are even talking about keeping kids off the Net entirely, which would be terrible! We think that access to information is a good thing. But we also recognize that parents may want to participate in and guide your selection of information resources. There are ways for your parents, other adults, and your school to help you select the best of the Net, and this page is a good place for those folks to see what's available.

http://www.uab.edu/pedinfo/Control.html

SAFETY
OUDPS: Notes, Advice and Warnings for Kids

The Internet is a fun place to be. It is important, though, that you learn to use the Internet safely and wisely. What if someone asks for your phone number? What if someone asks for your password? What if you stumble into something that's "too old" for you? The University of Oklahoma Department of Public Safety gives loads of great tips on using the Internet in a good way.

http://www.uoknor.edu/oupd/kidsafe/warn_kid.htm

Rules for Kids on the Internet/ Information Highway

It's OK to keep a secret, especially when you meet people on the Internet. Never give anyone personal information about yourself, and never send a picture to someone or agree to meet someone without talking to your parents or your teacher about it first. To learn many other safety rules of the road on the Information Superhighway, view this site!

http://www.discribe.ca/childfind/educate/kidrule.hte

Keep on your toes in DANCE.

A B C D E F G H I J K L M N O P Q R S T U V W X Y Z

SEARCH ENGINES AND DIRECTORIES

Short on time? Just read "Net-mom's Seven Secrets of Internet Searching." For more details, continue and read "A Little More Information."

Net-mom's Seven Secrets of Internet Searching

When you look for something on the Internet, do you get the answers you want, or do you get 400,000 possible answers to wade through? A *hit* is an answer the computer sends back in response to your question. Sometimes a question is also called a *query*. Net-mom knows some secrets to cut down on the number of hits and focus on the resources that will help you find what you need. Remember these tips and tricks!

Secret Number 1: Think before you search.

You'd be surprised how many people forget this step! You need to think about what you want to find and how much information you need. Here are some questions you can ask yourself before beginning your search:

- Do you need a lot of background material, or are you looking for only a few resources?

- What words can you think of to describe the answers you want?

- Are you looking for text, audio, pictures, movies, or all of these?

- Are you looking for something specific or something more general? For example, you may be interested in overall information on endangered species, or you may want to know a specific fact, such as the exact number of cheetahs left on the planet.

Thinking about what kind of answers you want will help you decide how to ask your question.

Secret Number 2: Look in the right place.

You wouldn't look for your sneaker in the refrigerator, would you? Of course not! So you need to know a little bit about how Internet Web pages and other resources are discovered, sifted, and sorted so that you can figure out the best places to look for that sneaker!

You need to know about directories and search engines and how they are different. The next section ("A Little More Information") will explain more about

this difference and why it's important, but here's a brief summary:

Directories are created by humans who try to sort useful resources into logical subject categories. These are often better to use if you are looking for general information. *Search engine* indexes are machine-made, built of actual words used on Web pages and in other resources. This is good, because it means that search engines offer a huge amount of material for you to use. But it is sometimes bad, because having too much information is often worse than having none at all! People using search engines for the first time often get thousands of answers back, way more than they want. The good news is that you can learn how to ask a carefully crafted question so that the search engine is forced to give you just a few targeted answers. To find out how to do this, just go to Secret Number 3.

Secret Number 3: Check the HELP files to learn how to ask your question.

Each search engine has its own specific tricks, so be sure to read the HELP screens for the ones you want to use. For example, say you are looking for the lyrics to "Yellow Submarine" by your favorite group, The Beatles. One engine may want you to ask it this way:

```
+"Yellow Submarine" +lyrics +Beatles
```

But another one wants this:

```
"Yellow Submarine" AND lyrics AND Beatles
```

Search directories have their own rules, too, so take a minute to read those HELP files! And remember:

As we live a life of ease
Everyone of us has all we need
Sky of blue and sea of green
In our yellow submarine.

Secret Number 4: Check your spelling.

There are a lot of slippery fingers out there. In fact, the most frequently mistyped word is "the"! If your search words aren't spelled correctly, they won't match up with the words in the indexes, and you won't find what you want. Keep a dictionary close by, or use one of the online dictionaries listed in the "Reference Works" section of this book. Now go ahead and send in your search, then meet us at Secret Number 5.

Secret Number 5: Narrow your search.

Too many hits? Learn how to narrow your search by reading the search engine's HELP files. Often, you can better retrieve the answers you need by searching on a phrase rather than on individual words. To do this, you typically put quotation marks around the phrase in order to keep the words together. For example, a search on the phrase "Hubble Space Telescope" will find only resources containing that entire phrase. It will ignore resources on space and telescopes and people named Hubble. Occasionally, you may have the opposite problem, noted in the next Secret.

Secret Number 6: Broaden your search.

Not enough hits? Learn how to broaden your search. What words can you use that are more general? The wider the terms you can use, the more hits you will get back. Not enough hits when you searched on beagle AND training? Try searching on dog AND training instead.

In most cases, it is best to use lowercase, singular terms. Example: searching on dog will usually find both Dog and Dogs and dog and dogs. If you had searched on Dogs (uppercase, plural) the results would not contain dog (lowercase, singular). Strange, but true.

Secret Number 7: Evaluate your results.

Is it true? Is it old? Does it come from a source you, your parents, your teachers, or others trust? Don't forget to evaluate your results! It may well be the most important step of all.

A Little More Information

There is a lot of treasure out there on the Internet, but the problem is trying to find exactly the gold you want, hidden somewhere in the millions of grains of sand. Now you know a little about how search engines and Internet directories can help.

Still fuzzy on what the difference is? Maybe this example will help. Say you want a tuna fish sandwich for lunch. But there's a problem: you don't have any tuna fish! Think of a search engine as a way to go catch your own fish in the ocean. You hope to cast out your net and get a nice tuna. You may even catch one. But you may also catch some dolphins, some sea turtles, and maybe some floating sea trash.

A directory, on the other hand, is more like a grocery store, where you can just walk over to the canned goods aisle and pick out a can marked "Tuna." Someone has already caught the correct kind of fish for you, marked the can the right way, and put it in the right store aisle.

A search engine (the fishing net) is a computer program that will search through millions of resources looking for the appearance of the words you've used to describe your topic. But it won't search all those actual places while you wait. It's only looking through its own list of words, in its own index. Where does it get the words? Special software is always working in the background, combing the Net, looking for new sites (and words) to harvest. These harvests are used to create the search engine's word index. So, if a resource was put up on the Internet an hour ago, you probably won't be able to find it yet, whether you use a search engine or a directory. It won't turn up in an index until it's harvested by one of the search engine's robots. The exception to this rule is in the case of current events and breaking news. Some search engines now let you search recent press releases and news desk stories. One of these is Infoseek, which has its own listing in this section of the book.

Just because a word appears in a document doesn't mean the document will really be about the topic you want! Searching on the word "cat" will pull up

NET FILES

When is the best time of year to get your piano tuned?

Answer: According to the Piano Home Page, the best times are in the fall, after your furnace has been on for about a month, and again in summer, after the air conditioning has been on for about a month, so that the instrument has stabilized with the humidity changes the seasons bring. You should also never try to fix or tune a piano yourself. Get a real piano technician to do it. And remember, just because someone can tune a piano doesn't mean he or she can tune tuna fish. Check out http://www.unm.edu/~loritaf/pnobuying.html

thousands of hits. Asking for a search on CAT will return information on CAT and CATS, but also CATalog, CATapult, and CATacombs. (Remember the sea turtles and the dolphins? These are hits you don't need.) There are advanced ways of using search engines to pare down the number of unwanted hits and narrow the focus more towards what you want. The best way to learn how to do this is to read the searching tips each search engine offers. They are all different.

There have also been instances of people stuffing their Web resources with keywords that have nothing to do with their real topics, just so they will turn up as hits in more searches. One guy wanted to sell his new product. He reasoned that if more people saw his product, he'd sell more of it. So, he put his ad on an Internet Web page. Then, he padded the Web page with about a thousand extra keywords! The keywords had nothing to do with the product, but that trick did make his ad turn up in millions of searches (remember the floating sea trash we mentioned earlier?).

A directory (the grocery store), on the other hand, takes Internet information resources and puts them in some kind of logical subject order. In other words, a real person looks at the resources, then decides what they are about and where they should go on the directory's subject "shelves." A directory will return hits that should be generally on target. But, because the Internet is growing so fast and there are so many documents, most subject directories are not fully up to date. Some have Current Events shelves, though, for recent news, so look for them.

Another thing to notice is that some search engines and directories are concerned with only *part* of the Internet. Some deal with Web resources only. Some include Web, gopher, and maybe ftp or Usenet newsgroup information. Some include press releases. Some include e-mail addresses or telephone books. Some will index sounds, pictures, movies, and maps! Pay attention and know what region of the Internet you're really searching.

There is one more thing you need to know. Not everything on the Net is true. Some of the information is out of date. Some of it is just plain wrong. And some of it is put there as a way to mislead you. How do you tell the good stuff from the bad stuff? One of the ways is to use this book, which you're holding in your hands. We've found some of the good stuff for you. Other authorities in which to place your trust will vary. Ask your parents, a teacher, or a trusted

adult. They may help you to decide if the information you find on the Net is right for your purpose.

A good Internet searcher knows how to use lots of searching tools to advantage. Read on for some tips on using some of the best so far.

AltaVista Search: Main Page

AltaVista indexes 30 million Web pages plus four million articles from 14,000 Usenet newsgroups. Over 23 million searches a day are requested here! We use this search engine because it is easy, it is straightforward, and it doesn't try to distract us with a lot of extra stuff we don't want.

AltaVista allows special searches on URLs, images, and host names, among other things. Do you have a cool home page? Do you want to know if other pages around the Web have linked theirs to yours? Then type this into the AltaVista Simple Search form: **link:***your page name here*.

Did you ever search on something and get 400,000 hits? You need to narrow your search. Are you searching on a phrase, something more than one word? (For example, "Major League Baseball" is a phrase.) Then you should tell the computer to search on the phrase, not just single words. How? Say you are looking for something on the Hubble Space Telescope. If you just type **hubble space telescope**, then the search engine will look for all occurrences of hubble, add them to all occurrences of space, and add *them* to all occurrences of telescope. And then you *will* have 400,000 sites to look through!

Instead, type your search terms inside quotation marks, like this: "Hubble Space Telescope." Putting the words inside quotation marks tells AltaVista that the words must be right next to each other—you want to look for the phrase, not just the individual words. This one tip will help you focus in on the best resources to answer your question.

Use lowercase letters, not capitals. If you search on Dogs, AltaVista will be forced to look for Dogs that begin with a capital letter, ignoring dogs. Lowercase search terms will find *both* uppercase and lowercase hits.

Hint: Be sure you type the address just as we have it here. Do not try <*http://www.altavista.com*>. It *looks* like AltaVista, but it is not the real thing, so don't be fooled.

http://www.altavista.digital.com/

Excite Home

Excite combines the features of a search engine and a directory. Excite says it indexes 50 million Web pages, plus thousands of Usenet newsgroups. But there's more: sites in 16 categories, all of them reviewed; links to Big Yellow's address and telephone directory; and City.Net's mapping and travel information. Plus, there is an easy-to-use "design your own newspaper" tool!

This directory has something a little different. It gives you a "confidence" rating alongside your hits, and it gives you what it thinks are its "best" hits first. Do you agree? If not, look through the hit list until you find a site that you do like. To see similar resources, just click the "more sites like this" button.

Don't miss the Excite guided tours to the Net. They are called Exciteseeing Tours at <http://tours.excite.com/>. You may want to submit your own list of useful sites, based on a subject you know well.

To make your own designer view of the world's news, weather, sports, TV listings, best-seller lists, and more, try Excite Live! at <http://live.excite.com/>. You can bookmark this page or make it your browser's start-up page.

http://www.excite.com/

Infoseek

Infoseek is a search engine and directory, and it is Net-mom's favorite for searching. Look carefully, as there are two versions to choose from: Ultraseek and Ultrasmart. If you just want the sites index and not the added suggestions, go right to the streamlined version, Ultraseek.

The second version, Ultrasmart, is the engine that tries to be smarter than you are! If you search here, you will get results from Infoseek's index of over 50,000 URLs. Notice also that you can choose to search the Web, just FAQ files, or several other choices, including newswires (good for extremely current topics); use the drop-down menu to select one. You'll also get things Ultrasmart thinks might also interest you: items pulled from news stories, plus suggested links from Infoseek's subject directory.

Are you interested in finding photos, or do you have other special requests? Try a Special Search at <http://www.infoseek.com/Forms?pg=special.html> and fill in the blanks. Additional things you may want to explore are the mapping features, as well as the personalized news services and other toys. There are also two regionalized versions: Infoseek Japan and Infoseek U.K.

http://www.infoseek.com/

Welcome to Lycos

Lycos has been around a relatively long time, and now they have merged resources with The Point. It's easy to use, but we still like Infoseek and AltaVista better as search engines and Yahoo! better as a directory. Still, this is very useful for searching for pictures and sounds ("I need a picture of Mount Rushmore right now!"). The Top 5% collection is still as uneven as ever, but we use it occasionally, along with the other tools here. Try it—you are allowed to like it better than Net-mom does!

http://www.lycos.com/

NET FILES

What are *Gidzhaks* and *Tyuidyuks*?

a) Characters in a Dr. Seuss story

b) Musical instruments

c) Types of currency used in Mongolia

Answer: *The answer is b. A Gidzhak is a bowed instrument and a Tyuidyuk is a kind of flute, played by Turkmenis. Read about them at* http://www.kingrecords.co.jp/e51 75inst.html

**Know your alphabet?
Now try someone else's
in LANGUAGES AND
ALPHABETS.**

A
B
C
D
E
F
G
H
I
J
K
L
M
N
O
P
Q
R
S
T
U
V
W
X
Y
Z

Welcome to Magellan!

This directory of reviewed sites has another twist, called "green light" sites. If, at the time of review, "no objectionable material" was found, the site gets a green light (safe for kids) rating. Magellan is merging with Excite (see separate entry), so the biggest difference here is the green light feature. If this Web page disappears, look for green lights on Excite.

http://www.mckinley.com/

NET FILES

What is the world's largest kite?

Answer: As far as we know, it's Peter Lynn's Trilobite at 165 feet long, 72.5 feet wide, and about 30 feet high. In fact, it's so huge that kids can fly other kites inside it! The kite is made of 20,000 yards of fabric and is built in zippered sections, which makes it easier to carry around and repair. It has only a single line, and it can be flown by one person. See pictures of this awesome kite at http://www.comunlimited.com/tleblanc/closet/kite/large/large.html from the Cool Links area of http://www.kts.org/kites/cool.html, the Kite Flier's Site.

Feeling a bit bogged down? Check EARTH SCIENCE and get swampwise!

Yahoo! and Yahooligans!

Yahoo! is a directory. In other words, Yahoo! does not index the whole Internet but a selected view of it. However, it is allied with AltaVista (see separate entry), which does search the entire Net, so from this site you can have it all!

This directory is fun and easy to use. Browse 14 general categories, like science or education. Under those are smaller subdivisions, which branch into still smaller sub-subtopics, and on and on. Don't worry, it's simpler than it sounds! You can also choose to search the entire database or just a small part of it. Every so often you'll see a pair of sunglasses next to a listing. That means the folks who create Yahoo! thought the resource was way cool.

Yahoo! tries to organize resources into collections with a geographical focus. Try Yahoo! Canada, Germany, Japan, or Yahoo! Metro Boston, Chicago, Los Angeles, New York, or the San Francisco Bay Area. If you don't live in one of those areas, don't despair, "Get Local." Type in your U.S. ZIP code for links to your local TV stations, weather, and other news.

They also have a resource with "kid safe" listings, called Yahooligans! at *<http://www.yahooligans.com>*. Try it! We have found a lot of dead links there, so it is not as well maintained as we think it should be. Still, it may be improved by the time you read this.

We particularly like their My Yahoo! service. It creates a home page for you, based on your preferences. Want to follow the scores for just your favorite teams? Want to see the weather for your city and for someone you know in another state? Want to read news about computers but not news about entertainers? Set your news up *your* way at *<http://my.yahoo.com>*.

Yahoo! is experimenting with different ways to search through information, since people learn in different ways. Here are two:

- VRML (Virtual Reality Modeling Language) *<http://3d.yahoo.com/3d/docs/bridge.html>* This is a fly-through database, so far impossibly slow on a modem connection. It works with Netscape 3.0 or Microsoft's Internet Explorer 3.0, and you need the Live3D plug-in.

- HotSauce *<http://mcf.research.apple.com/>* If you like flight simulators and aren't prone to motion sickness, try Apple's HotSauce (formerly ProjectX). It simulates "flying" through the Yahoo! database.

It's available for Macintosh (PowerPC and 68K) or for Windows NT/95 systems.

http://www.yahoo.com/

WEBWEAVING AND HTML

How to write HTML files

Would you like to be a webweaving expert, a person who knows the ins and outs of HTML? Then this tutorial is for you. Soon, you'll be making the most rad pages ever! The author, Peter Flynn, will be your step-by-step guide.

http://kcgl1.eng.ohio-state.edu/www/doc/
htmldoc.html

NCSA—A Beginner's Guide to HTML Home Page

Itching to write your own cool home page? You may want to learn hypertext markup language (HTML), so you can write your own code to amaze the world with your Web creation. This is a very good place to learn HTML and how to weave your Web pages. Here you'll find step-by-step descriptions and instructions.

http://www.ncsa.uiuc.edu/General/Internet/WWW/
HTMLPrimer.html

Web66: Classroom Internet Server Cookbook

Wouldn't it be great to have your very own home page on the World Wide Web? You could write funny stories, talk about your pets, or discuss your favorite hobby. Creating a Web page is not too hard—especially if you have one of those newfangled programs that builds Web pages for you. If not, you'll need to learn a simple computer language called hypertext markup language (HTML). There are many free tutorials to help you learn HTML, and the Web 66: Cookbook is a good one (especially if you have a Macintosh). Now that you've got a home page, where are you going to put it? Did you know you can also run your own server? You'll want a direct line to the Internet to do that in the most effective way, and that can be pretty expensive. Maybe you can help your school create its own Web server, instead. The directions are here, for Macintosh, Windows 95, or Windows NT.

http://web66.coled.umn.edu/Cookbook/

INVENTIONS AND INVENTORS

Ball Run Sculptures

If we said, "Kinetic sculpture," you might say, "Huh?" How about marble runs—do you know what they are? No? OK, then how about those cool machines you see in museums, airports, and malls with the balls that travel around mazes of tracks, doing strange things like ringing bells, inflating balloons, traveling in elevators, only to get to the bottom and travel up to the beginning again? *Now* you know what we mean! This no-frills page is a collection of kinetic art resources that reside on the Web. You can also use it to plan your vacations around visiting these fun sculptures, since there is a checklist by city and state. Don't miss the audio-kinetic "Tower of Bauble" at the Vancouver Science World at <*http://www2.portal.ca/~raymondk/ Spider/QuickTime2/scienceWorld.html*> and be sure to listen for the gongs, xylophones, and cymbals. If you can wait long enough, you can see a QuickTime VR movie of the area, but alas, not the sculpture in action!

http://www.msen.com/~lemur/ball-runs.html

Internet 1996 World Exposition

You may have learned about all the world's fairs and expositions of the last century. The idea was to show people what new inventions—like railroads, telephones, lights, and cars—could do for them. Well, if you've been wondering what this new invention called the Internet could do for you, then welcome to this site. It's a world's fair for the Information Age. One of the most important parts of this expo is the Global Schoolhouse Pavilion, which links schools around the world, showcases young artists, and features activities to help kids learn (and like) the Internet.

http://park.org/

Trick roping secrets revealed in KNOTS.

A
B
C
D
E
F
G
H
I
J
K
L
M
N
O
P
Q
R
S
T
U
V
W
X
Y
Z

The Lemelson-MIT Prize Program and Invention Dimension

Would you like to win half a million dollars? All you have to do is invent something so cool, so unique, and so compelling that everyone says, "Wow!" That's the idea behind the Lemelson-MIT Prize, which is presented every year to an American inventor-innovator for outstanding creativity. You can find out about the prize and its past winners here, and you'll also find a collection of material about other great inventors and inventions. Check the Inventor of the Week archives, but be prepared for a lengthy wait: the page loads over 60 drawings of famous (and not-so-famous) inventors. Why they don't have a text-only option yet is unknown; perhaps they will by the time you read this. Don't miss the Links area for more inventions and resources.

http://web.mit.edu/afs/athena.mit.edu/org/i/invent/
www/invention_dimension.html

NET FILES

What is the Rosetta stone?

Answer: Ancient Egyptian hieroglyphics had been seen for years, but no one could decipher their meanings. In 1799, one year after Napoleon captured the Nile delta area of Egypt, a French soldier found a black basalt slab while working on a fort near the Rosetta branch of the Nile. It held a message in hieroglyphs but also held translations of the message into other known languages—and this cracked the "code." The message dated March 27, 196 B.C.! Nowadays, people often describe the key to any mystery as "the Rosetta stone." The original is in the British Museum. Check out http://www.clemusart.com/archive/pharaoh/exhibit/glyphs.html

National Geographic Society - Super Fun INVENTIONS!

You'll need Shockwave to play these inventing games, but if you don't have it, you can use the neat selection of links to other pages on inventions around the Web. There are five games; one is guessing the purpose of a wacky patent drawing. Hmmm, is it an automatic baby-patting machine or a mitten stretcher? If you guess right enough times, you'll get a token. Get five tokens, and you can operate the wackiest machine of them all back at the Lab: the Action Contraption!

http://www.nationalgeographic.com/modules/
inventions/index.html

NET FILES

What tiny critters can be found from 20 miles beneath Earth's surface to 20 miles overhead?

Answer: Microbes! You'll find they inhabit almost every friendly corner on Earth. Visit Dirt Land at http://commtechlab.msu.edu/CTLprojects/dlc-me/zoo/ and be sure to check out the snack bar.

PM TIME MACHINE MAIN PAGE

Popular Mechanics is *the* magazine for anyone interested in machines. They have built an Internet time machine to help you see how machines have improved over the last 90 or so years. See high-flying French balloons from the early 1900s and crazy car designs from 1960. It's a walk through history, and you won't even have to leave the chair in front of your computer! Your time machine comes with a lot of shiny buttons, and there's even an owner's manual. Let's see, what happens if we press this button right here?

http://popularmechanics.com/popmech/sci/time/
1HOMETIME.html

Rube Goldberg Home Page

Reuben Lucius Goldberg, better known as Rube Goldberg, was a cartoonist with a wacky sense of humor. He loved to draw machines that would perform simple tasks, like pouring a glass of milk. First he would draw a way to open the refrigerator, then a way to get the bottle, then a way to open it—before he would ever get the milk into the glass! He accomplished this easy job by using the most complex, roundabout methods possible, often using common household objects in uncommon ways. You can see some examples of this here. A contest is held every year to see which team of students can perform a simple assignment using the weirdest, wackiest, and most complex machine. This year, all they have to do is get a CD into a CD player and play it. Come here and find out what they invent. You can also find out how to get your school involved in the fun!

http://www.anl.gov/OPA/rube/index.html

NET FILES

Who are **Nahuelito, Champ, and Ogopogo?**

Hint: If you can find them at all, they will be in water.

Answer: Like Nessie of Loch Ness, they are all legendary lake monsters. Nahuelito supposedly inhabits Nahuel Huapi Lake (Argentina), while Champ is from Lake Champlain (between New York and Vermont). Ogopogo has been spotted in the waters of Lake Okanagan in British Columbia, Canada. Read more about them at http://www.cais.net/strangemag/nessie.home.html

Welcome to Invention!

Girl Tech will introduce you to some cool inventions by women throughout history. The first U.S. patent granted to a woman went to Mary Dixon Kies. In 1809, Kies got a patent for inventing a new way to process and weave straw with thread. But you may want to read about more recent inventions, such as the one by ten-year-old Becky Schroeder! She thought up a way to write in the dark, using a phosphorescent clipboard! She got a patent on her invention and became famous. Have you got a brilliant idea like that?

http://www.girltech.com/HTMLworksheets/
IN_menu.html

INVERTEBRATES

See also INSECTS AND SPIDERS

The Cephalopod Page

An octopus is more than just a tentacled cephalopod that squirts ink and runs. It is the smartest of the invertebrates, with both a long- and a short-term memory. It learns through experience and solves problems using trial and error. Check out this site about the octopus and its relatives, and you'll soon realize that these octopi are not just a bunch of *suckers*.

http://is.dal.ca/~ceph/wood.html

Let balloonists take you to new heights in AVIATION AND AIRPLANES.

A B C D E F G H I J K L M N O P Q R S T U V W X Y Z

A B C D E F G H I J K L M N O P Q R S T U V W X Y Z

Lobster Institute

Can lobsters bite? No, they may be able to pinch you with their claws, but their teeth are in their stomachs. Take the lobster quiz and learn more about this large shellfish. Then, if you want, join a lobster chat. But if you feel the only way to appreciate a lobster is to eat it, the Lobster Institute proudly presents their cookbook pages, with recipes and tips for choosing the perfect lobster.

http://inferno.asap.um.maine.edu/lobster/index.html

Sea Urchins Harvesters Association - California

Sea urchins may look spiky and threatening, but when you come right down to it they have no *backbone*. Harvested by divers, these colorful invertebrates are part of a growing industry, as they have become a popular food source. You can find out more about these creatures and how they saved the economy of the north coast of California, although urchins aren't particularly happy about it.

http://seaurchin.org/

NET FILES

In the famous painting by Leonardo Da Vinci, what color are Mona Lisa's eyes?

Answer: Brown. This painting is also known as La Gioconda, and you can read all about the woman in the picture at http://sunsite.unc.edu/wm/paint/auth/vinci/joconde/

WORMS
The Burrow

Just the dirt, please. This is the serious worm place, where worms are elevated to new heights, er, depths. Dig deep here, and you'll find something about worms of all ages, sizes, and squirms.

http://gnv.fdt.net/~windle/

NET FILES

Who was Senator Bob Dole's boyhood hero?

Answer: He liked Ike: General and President Dwight "Ike" Eisenhower. See some of Dole's childhood photos while you read more at http://www.usnews.com/usnews/wash/doleyth.htm

The Worm Page

Tractors and earthworms both plow the land, but you don't have to gas up worms. Just give them some garbage or organic material, and watch them go! Learn more about the different types of worms and how slimy, yet beneficial, they are. Then choose your side, as notable worm minds debate the greatest unsolved mystery of all: Why are there so many worms all over the pavement after it rains?

http://users.multiverse.com/~wibble/worm.html

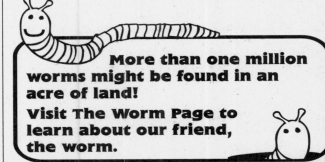

More than one million worms might be found in an acre of land!
Visit The Worm Page to learn about our friend, the worm.

JOKES AND RIDDLES

Fleabusters' Kids Fun Page - Jokes

Submit your own jokes here and see if you can top these:

Where does a general keep his armies?
In his sleevies!

Where do you put a noisy dog?
In a barking lot!

http://www.fleabuster.com/kids/kjokes.htm

NET FILES

What nation will welcome the new millennium first?

Answer: This is currently a huge dispute! Pacific Islanders are now arguing over which remote piece of land will be first to see the sunrise of that special new year. Whichever country is officially "first" stands to make lots of tourist dollars. Recently, the tiny nation of Kiribati (formerly the Gilbert, Phoenix, and Line Island groups) has angered its Pacific neighbors by moving part of the international date line to its eastern extremity, Caroline Island. Get the latest facts at http://www.earth.tohoku.ac.jp/kiribati/news_int.html#dateline

Gymster's Jokepage

Gymster has an awful collection of jokes here—awfully funny, that is. Real groaners. You'll be faced with humor like this:

Why did the rabbit go to the barber shop?
To get a hare-do!

And don't forget to iron your moose—if you don't, you may get a Bullwrinkle! (We learned that at this joke page.)

http://starcreations.com/stardreams/kidzweb/
kw-03.htm

NET FILES

Here's a knotty problem: What's the difference between a hitch and a bend?

Answer: Know the ropes! A *hitch* is a knot that ties a line onto something else, and a *bend* ties two lines together. If tying knots leaves you in a snarl, then be sure to drop in on http://www.pcmp.caltech.edu/~tobi/knots/ for a new twist in learning.

Kaitlyn's Knock Knock Jokes and Riddles

Kaitlyn's only seven, but she has dreams of being a children's doctor or maybe a figure skater! She's got some jokes and riddles here on her home page that may make you chuckle. Here's an example:

Why did it take the monster ten months to finish a book?
Because he wasn't very hungry!

You can also send Kaitlyn your jokes and riddles, and she'll add them, giving you credit!

http://www.usa.net/wolfBayne/kaitlyn/

Riddle du Jour

This site offers a new riddle or brainteaser every day and archives the last week's worth of riddles for your amusement. Other games on this site include a trivia contest, word games, a guess-the-GIF, and more!

http://www.dujour.com/riddle/

A
B
C
D
E
F
G
H
I
J
K
L
M
N
O
P
Q
R
S
T
U
V
W
X
Y
Z

A
B
C
D
E
F
G
H
I
J
K
L
M
N
O
P
Q
R
S
T
U
V
W
X
Y
Z

NET FILES

Your buddies (who like math as much as you do) invite you to the Pi Day celebration at the Exploratorium—but they've forgotten to tell you when it is and what time to show up!

What's your best guess?

Answer: *Pi Day is celebrated every year on March 14, at 1:59 in the afternoon. Third month? Fourteenth day? The value of pi to a few decimal places is 3.14159! This irrational celebration happens to coincide with Albert Einstein's birthday. Read about it at* http://www.exploratorium.edu/learning_studio/pi/

Science Definitions

"Most books now say our Sun is a star. But it still knows how to change back into a Sun in the daytime." This is a little collection of things kids have said on class exams, and you may think they are pretty funny. Don't use any of these on your next test, though!

http://aurora.carleton.ca/~cbulsara/pages/
   science.shtml

Tree and Forest Jokes - Hands On Children's Museum

The jokes here change all the time; you can even submit your own, and maybe the museum will use them! These are some of the jokes we liked when we visited:

How can you tell your dog is slow?
He brings you yesterday's newspaper!

How did the skunk call home?
With a smellular *phone!*

http://www.wln.com/~deltapac/treejokes.html

JUGGLING

See also CIRCUSES AND CLOWNS

How to Devil Stick

The first time we tried these juggling sticks, cats were running for cover in all directions. With a little practice, we got so we could do some simple flips, but what we really needed were the pictures and explanations at this Web page. You'll learn how to start the sticks into motion, plus how to do tricks we haven't mastered yet: the helicopter and the propeller spin! Even more tricks and info may be found at <http://www.juggling.org/help/circus-arts/devil-sticks/>.

http://infinite.pd.net/howto/dstick/

Juggling Information Service

Believe it or not, the first thing a new juggler learns is how to juggle only one ball! But it gets much harder after that. This site is for every juggler, from beginner to experienced. There are tips and tricks, links to jugglers' home pages, a photo gallery, and even a movie theater with great performances and demonstrations.

http://www.juggling.org/

Juggling Jukebox Home Page

The worlds of technology and entertainment really come together here. If you ever run into the Juggling Jukebox, put your money in the machine and then watch and listen. Depending on your selection, you see a variety of juggling routines, and the "wired" juggler makes high-tech music your ears won't believe. It's a fascinating real-life invention you can see and hear on the Net!

http://www.jamesjay.com/juggling/jukebox/hightech/

Feeling a bit bogged down?
Check EARTH SCIENCE
and get swampwise!

Kel Krosschell holds one of his tiny microkites.

"I was able to help kids on another continent have some kite building and flying fun!"

KITES

Kel's MicroKite Site

Webmaster: Kel Krosschell

http://www.millcomm.com/~kitenut/ index.html

Who came up with the idea for your page or project?

I had this crazy idea to see how small I could make a kite. I had to invent new ways to make them, and find smaller and smaller line on which to fly them. I thought I would call these tiny kites "MicroKites" because they were so small.

Finally I made a kite only one-sixteenth of a square inch! Line used for flying this tiny kite is so small it would take about 30 strands, twisted together, to be the width of a typical human hair. One gram of the line would be over 13 and one-half MILES long, and remember that there are over 28 grams in one ounce.

In September 1995, Disney World sponsored the "EPCOT World Festival of Kites" and featured noted kite builders and flyers from around the world. When I heard that Peter Lynn of Australia was bringing a new world's largest kite, I contacted the organizers and they invited me to display the world's smallest kite. I had so much fun showing kids of all ages that it truly does fly! I could have them close their eyes, then land it on their hands without them even feeling it, it was so light.

So when I finally got onto the Internet, I wanted to create a home for the microkites, as well as other kites, kiting fun, and even how to build some very simple kites. The result is "Kel's MicroKite Site."

You must hear from people all over the world! Can you think of an unusual request, question, or comment someone has sent to you?

I like to help with group projects. Recently, a teacher in South Africa was looking for plans for building kites with his students. I was able to help kids on another continent have some kite building and flying fun!

Do you have a family?

I have two children, 14 and 12. They are now building their own home pages. I'm sure they will eventually put pictures of their pet rabbits and gerbils there, as well as their other interests.

What are your hopes and fears for the future of the Internet?

I hope people continue to add things tailored to teaching simple things to kids around the world. My biggest fear is that the Internet will become a luxury item that some people will not be able to access. I hope libraries and communities will make sure that everyone can take advantage of the vast amount of information that can now be found in seconds from around the world.

When you're not using the Net, what do you like to do?

I like to fly a variety of kites. Another hobby: folding dollars into various animals and objects. I tinker with magic a bit. I work to improve our government and the laws that either exist or are in the making. I am a "ham" (amateur radio) operator. And I am fascinated by new technology that is being invented. That leaves about three minutes a day to sleep (just kidding).

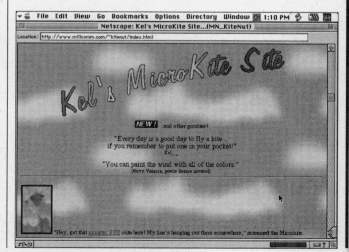

KARTING AND SOAP BOX DERBY

All American Soap Box Derby

No motorized vehicles are allowed on this page! Since 1934, kids have been hauling their gravity-powered racers up a hill in Ohio to see who has the fastest vehicle. World Championship finals are held each August, and kids from all over the United States and several foreign countries turn up to race their homebuilt beauties to victory. You can learn all about soap box derbies here, including how to get your community to sponsor a qualifying race!

http://pages.prodigy.com/SOAPBOX/

NET FILES

What animal is known as the "ship of the Andes" and why?

Answer: The cold and dry high-altitude climate of the Andes Mountains is home to a unique creature: the llama, an animal that can survive on the area's sparse grass vegetation and is more surefooted than a burro. Llamas are used as pack animals. They can carry as much as 125 pounds for up to 12 hours a day, up and down the rugged slopes and very high altitudes characteristic of the Andes Mountains in Peru, Bolivia, Chile, and northwestern Argentina. Stop by http://www.woolly.com/about.htm for some legends and fascinating facts about llamas.

Want a snack? Learn to make one in COOKING, FOOD, AND DRINK.

The Inside Track - America's Karting Newspaper

This magazine covers the karting scene in the U.S., and some of their articles are online here. You can also explore the links to manufacturers and parts suppliers, as well as participate in the bulletin board forums. Looking for an indoor track in San Antonio? Want to know what to look for when buying a used kart? Ask the experts here!

http://www.theinsidetrack.com/

THE Karting Web Site

Karting is a worldwide sport that hardly resembles the go-cart races of yesteryear. If you watch an old movie or TV show, you might see kids rolling down the hill in go-carts, which were homemade little "cars" put together by kids with their parents' help. Sometimes the wheels came from a baby stroller or an old wagon; other parts came from almost anywhere else. Well, times have changed! Today's karts are complicated, streamlined racing vehicles. Here, you'll find out all about the various forms of this racing hobby practiced all over the world. Latest news, track listings, organizations, and pictures are all here. A caution to parents: Not all links have been checked.

http://www.muller.net/karting/

KITES

Japan Close-up

Japanese kites have the most spectacular designs in the world. They are painted to look like fanciful birds, animals, insects, and fierce warriors. A kite isn't just a toy in Japan; it's closely tied to good luck and special occasions. Kites often have symbolic meaning, and they were once associated with prayer. See some beautiful kite pictures and learn all about the history of kites, including miniature kites that fit inside a clam shell!

http://www.sumitomocorp.co.jp/closer/index.html

A B C D E F G H I J **K** L M N O P Q R S T U V W X Y Z

Everyone enjoys the sight of cheerful kites against the sky, like confetti or willful fish pulling towards some bottomless sea. Did you know that at one time some kites were illegal? The *tsugaru*, a strong, heavy kite made in Japan, was actually banned during the Second World War. These kites are noisy: they have a slim bit of rice paper on them that produces a deep scream in flight, remarkably similar to that of an approaching aircraft engine. Find out more about kites at Japan Close-up!

Kel's MicroKite Site...(MN_KiteNut)

"Any day is a good day to fly a kite," says Kel, "if you remember to put one in your pocket!" At this site you'll see the world's smallest kite (1/16 square inch) and learn how to make microkites of your own. You can fly these sub-one-inch kites indoors, or fly them outside on windless days. Or tie one to your wheelchair, and take off!

http://www.millcomm.com/~kitenut/

Would you like to have a kite you can fly indoors? Find out how to make one at Kel's MicroKite Site...(MN_KiteNut)!

Sharpen your digital crayons for COLOR AND COLORING BOOKS!

Kite Aerial Photography - Title Page

Ever wonder what the view is like from your kite as it soars high above your head? Now there's a way for you to see it. Check the tools and techniques at this site, then go fly a kite!

http://www.ced.berkeley.edu/~cris/kap/

Kite Flier's Cool Links

Did you know that some people use kites for fishing? Or that you can make a tetrahedral kite from drinking straws? Maybe you want to attend a kite festival, or you just want to get some online tips for flying technique. This is the site you'll want to visit!

http://www.kfs.org/kites/cool.html

NET FILES

More than a millennium ago, letters in Southeast Asia were written on what commonly found objects?

Answer: People wrote on palm leaves and bamboo slats. Many people all over the world used leaves as writing paper. This is why a piece of paper bound in a book is properly called a leaf. A leaf has two pages, one on each side. Learn more at http://WWW.BIBINGKA.COM/dahon/

Ask not what the Net can do for you, ask what you can do for the Net.

Kites for Kids Only

You'll find links to lots of kite plans for kids, although some are easier to put together than others. At this site, you can go around the world on a kite: learn to make a box kite from Australia, a sled kite from England, or a Bermuda kite from—that's right—Bermuda! There is also a link to software that will help you design your kite. One level back, at *<http://www.sound.net/~kiteguy/ kites.html>*, are more kite ideas, including directions on how to make a paper clip kite to fly in a magnetic field!

http://www.sound.net/~kiteguy/kidspage/kidspage.htm

NET FILES

The Chinese inventor Pi-Cheng (1016–1076) is credited with inventing... what?

(Hint: It was a moving type of experience!)

Answer: According to HyperHistory Online, "Pi-Cheng is the inventor of printing with moveable types. Pi-Cheng cut characters into cubes of clay and put them into an iron frame. When it was full, the whole frame made one solid block of type ready to print." Find out more at http://www.hyperhistory.com/online_n2/History_n2/a.html

KNOTS

The Knotting Dictionary of Kännet

Clear black-and-white drawings and explanations of how each knot should be used (and not used) make this a must-see page for kids wanting to improve their rope skills. Besides common ones like reef knots, fisherman's knot, and the sheet bend, here you'll find the round turn, the prussick, and the jug sling hitch, among others. The page is also available in Swedish, and Jan Andersson (who put the page together) is looking for people to help translate to lots of other languages. Also look for a link to Swedish Scouting's Home Page here.

http://www.netg.se/~jan/knopar/english/index.htm

A lot of us learned to tie a bowline by thinking of the end of the rope as a rabbit, and making a loop to represent its burrow hole. We memorized this little speech by Elmer Fudd: "The wabbit goes up, out of his hole, 'wound the back of the twee, and back down into his buwwow." Visit **The Knotting Dictionary of Kännet** if you want to learn the ropes!

The Lasso: A Rational Guide to Trick Roping

We're always impressed when we see trick roping in old Western movies. The intricate patterns cowboys make with their twirling ropes take a lot of practice, and we always wished we could learn how to do it. Carey Bunks, holder of a Ph.D. from MIT, has written a book on this subject, and it's all online. Now we know our flat loops from our merry-go-rounds and our wedding rings from our Texas skips. All we need now is a really big cowboy hat and some of those furry chaps to wear!

http://www.juggling.org/books/lasso/

Some useful knots

Are you all thumbs when it comes to tying knots? Do you try to follow diagrams in books, but your fingers get tangled up like pretzels? Here's a site with some remarkably clear live-action MPEG movies that make the bowline, sheet bend, clove hitch, and tautline hitch knots seem as easy as tying a shoelace!

http://www.pcmp.caltech.edu/~tobi/knots/

YOUNG SAILOR ROPES AND KNOTS

Have you come to the end of your rope? If so, it's time to *whip* it. That means to tie a special thread around and around the end of the rope to keep it from fraying. "An untidy rope end is a sign of a careless sailor," says this site, which will teach you how to whip a rope as well as tie several useful knots for sailing and other uses. It's *knot* hard—give it a try!

http://www.yachtnet.com/journal/youngsailor/ ropesandknots.html

LANGUAGES AND ALPHABETS

ALPHABET SOUP

When you're eating alphabet soup, have you ever tried to spell your name on the edge of the soup bowl? Ever notice you never have the right assortment of letters? We're including this site as an example of two things: one, it's amazing the type of information you can find on the Net; and two, some people have way too much time on their hands if they can count the letters in a can of soup!

http://www.gigaplex.com/food/soup.htm

Ethnologue Database

What languages do they speak in Croatia? Did you know that in Kenya, at least 61 languages are spoken, including Kenyan Sign Language? You can select any country on this page and then discover which languages are spoken there. Also find out how different languages are related, using the language family tree. The Inuit language, Aleut, is related to the Russian Siberian language, Yupik. Do you know why that could be?

http://www.sil.org/ethnologue/

Foreign Languages for Travellers

Just select a language you already speak and then click on a language you'd like to learn. You'll find over 40 of them here, including Hindi, Mandarin, and Zulu. Then you can decide to learn basic words and phrases (How are you? What is your name? Where is the bathroom?) or other words or phrases in these categories: numbers, shopping/dining, travel, directions, places, or time/dates. You can read the phrase and hear it (just click on the underlined words). There are also useful links to grammars and translation dictionaries.

http://www.travlang.com/languages/index.html

Globalink Translation Service

Did you ever get e-mail from a pen pal, but it was in a language you couldn't read? This site will come to the rescue—they offer a free translation service! You can go from English to Spanish, French, or German, or the opposite way. The messages have to be short (only about 1,000 characters) and the translation is done by machine, so it won't always be exact. The translation is e-mailed to you within 24 hours. Give it a try!

http://www.globalink.com/home.html

The Human-Languages Page

Do you like to amaze people by saying things in a different language? Here's the place to get more vocabulary words in your favorite language. There are tons of links to every imaginable tongue. You'll also find lots of translating dictionaries, including a project called The Internet Dictionary, which is a multilingual dictionary created by Internet users!

http://www.june29.com/HLP/

NATIVE LANGUAGES PAGE

Would you like to learn a little Navajo or a smattering of Ojibwe? Maybe you'd like to try using a Cherokee font or learn something about Mayan hieroglyphs. This page offers links to all of this and more!

http://www.pitt.edu/~lmitten/natlang.html

Right to Left Software Home Page

What would happen if alien dinosaurs came to explore our planet? With all the languages spoken here, they would surely wonder how to communicate. If you are a Windows user, you can download the shareware version of "Earth Words" to see what the aliens recorded with their dino-flex movie camera!

http://rtlsoft.com/ewords/

Crack open CODES AND CIPHERS.

A B C D E F G H I J K L M N O P Q R S T U V W X Y Z

A B C D E F G H I J K **L** M N O P Q R S T U V W X Y Z

Yamada Language Guides

Wow! This is a set of guides to 115 languages, from Afrikaans to Yiddish (guess they don't have a language starting with Z). Let's say you wanted to learn some Italian. You could look up phrases that you would need to know if you were traveling to Italy, find information about Italian culture and history, get the daily news in Italian, and even dissect a frog in Italian (that last one is *really* useful!). Besides languages, this gives links to cultural and historical information about the people who speak these languages. Check the Lakota or the Inuit home pages, for example; there are even pages for Klingon and the languages from J. R. R. Tolkien's books!

http://babel.uoregon.edu/yamada/guides.html

BRAILLE
General Braille Information

Imagine reading words by the way they feel to your touch. That's one of the ways blind people read, by feeling the little bumps, which represent letters. This is Braille, and you can learn about it at this page. Included is a cool tutorial that shows how all the Braille letters look. You can also ask the Internet Braille Wizard at <http://www.access2020.com/> to translate your phrase into Braille, and you can learn a lot about the inventor of the system, Louis Braille.

http://disserv.stu.umn.edu/AltForm/brl-guide.html

CHINESE
SPEAKING CHINESE

This site offers three short lessons in Chinese and includes audio files. Learn some useful words and phrases to help you meet new Chinese friends. Don't think you'll ever need to know how to say hello in Chinese? Don't be too sure. Once we used CU-SeeMe's Internet video to meet students in China, and they were very impressed we could at least say "*Ni hao*"!

http://redgum.bendigo.latrobe.edu.au/~zhang/
speaking.htm

CYRILLIC
Cyrillic Text

The Russian alphabet is very different from the one we use in English (the Latin alphabet). To get a look at it and learn how to pronounce the letters, try this site. You'll also find links to Cyrillic fonts on the Net and instructions on how to view Web pages in Cyrillic. Also check <http://ASUdesign.eas.asu.edu/places/Bulgaria/cyr/> for more, as well as <http://solar.rtd.utk.edu/oldfriends/cyrillic/cyrillic.html> for the fonts.

http://solar.rtd.utk.edu/friends/cyrillic/
cyrillic.htmlopt-tables-mac-english-

NET FILES

What happens in London every night at exactly seven minutes before ten o'clock?

Answer: The Chief Warder of the Tower of London begins the Ceremony of the Keys, a ritual locking of the Tower gates that has continued every night, virtually unchanged, for 700 years. Look over his shoulder and know the passwords, which may be found at http://www.voicenet.com/~dravyk/toftour/keys.html where "Alf's well."

DAKOTA
The Dakota Language Homepage

As you were growing up, you learned your language. You heard other people speak, and then you imitated the sounds yourself. Here's a way to do just that while you learn the Dakota language, one of many Indian languages. Native speakers help you make the sounds of the Dakota language as you explore a color-coded language "keyboard."

http://www.geocities.com/Paris/9463/

ENGLISH

Aussie English

The kids at the Springwood Central State School in Australia want to explain how Australian English is just a little bit different from what you may be used to hearing. So they have created a fair dinkum glossary that's the best thing this side of the black stump. Don't winge, get in here and translate!

http://www.uq.oz.au/~zzlibrar/aussie.html

ESL Home Page - English as a Second Language

A new family has moved into your neighborhood. You and your sister decide to visit them and invite them to play. As you knock on the door, three kids race to greet you. They don't speak English, but they want to learn! Here's a page to help you teach them. One of the best ways to learn a language is to hang around other kids. Bet you'll pick up some of their language, too. You'll find links to lots of ESL-related info around the Web.

http://www.lang.uiuc.edu/r-li5/esl/

Grammar and Style Notes

Are you a little shaky on the parts of speech? Can you tell a preposition from a present participle? The names may be strange, but you use these elements in everyday conversation. A *preposition* usually describes the object of the sentence and its location in time, space, or relationship to the rest of the sentence. For example, in the next sentence, the prepositions are capitalized: BEFORE the alarm rang, the cat was ON the table. A *present participle* just adds "-ing" to the rest of the verb: singing, sitting, walking. This resource teaches the parts of speech in a fun and easy way. You'll also learn about punctuation, building sentences and paragraphs, and yes—even spelling! Knowing the correct names for these grammatical terms becomes very important when you begin to learn another language. You'll want to know what the teacher means when talking about French subjunctives and superlatives!

http://www.english.upenn.edu/~jlynch/grammar.html

FRENCH

French Lesson Home Page

A language can really come in handy. Sometimes it's hard to learn a foreign language if you can't hear a native speaker of the language. Here's a way to learn how to pronounce French without having to go to a foreign country. You'll also discover how to write common words. *Papa*? That's French for daddy. See, it's not so hard!

http://home.hkstar.com/~jleung/french/french.html

Who bought the first car?

Answer: Dr. Pfennig, from Chicago, bought the first car, which was sold by the Ford Motor Company in 1903. Back then, auto makers didn't name cars after fast animals and reptiles; they just started naming models of cars after the letters of the alphabet! Henry Ford started what is today one of the largest corporations, and his Model N was a big success, but the Model K, well....Find out all about the fascinating history of Ford at http://www.ford.com/archive/FordHistory.html#Beginning

What is the sound of one router flapping?

A
B
C
D
E
F
G
H
I
J
K
L
M
N
O
P
Q
R
S
T
U
V
W
X
Y
Z

GAELIC

Gaelic and Gaelic Culture

If you're interested in Irish or Scottish variants of Gaelic or other Celtic languages, check this site. You'll find lots on the various Gaelic languages, plus links to music, products, literature, and more. One of the links has a tutorial in Welsh.

http://sunsite.unc.edu/gaelic/gaelic.html

HAWAIIAN

Ernie's Learn to Speak a Little Hawaiian

Mahalo nui loa (thank you very much), Ernie, for this page, which teaches just a little Hawaiian. You'll find pronunciation notes and a little glossary.

http://www.mhpcc.edu/otherpages/ernie/ernie1.html

Native Tongue - Discover the Hawaiian Language

Learn about *petroglyphs*: ancient pictographs found on rocks all over the Hawaiian islands. What do they mean? Who left them there for us to discover? Listen to audio clips of Hawaiian vowels and many common words and phrases. Check out this site *wiki-wiki* (fast)!

http://www.aloha-hawaii.com/0common/
 speaking.shtml

HEBREW

Sounds Of Israel — The Hebrew Alphabet

You can see and hear pronunciations of the Hebrew alphabet letters at this site. There are pictures of what each letter looks like in its script and print forms. Check the links to Hebrew stories and other language notes and to the page for numbers and counting in Hebrew.

http://www.macom.co.il/hebrew/the.alphabet.html

ICELANDIC

Icelandic Alphabet

If you're wondering what those strange runes in Icelandic words are, check this page. There's also a handy pronunciation guide.

http://www.cs.cornell.edu/home/ulfar/
 IcelandicAlphabet.html

ITALIAN

Learn to Speak Italian

Ragu, maker of Italian sauces and foods, presents Mama to teach you a little useful Italian. Some are actually phrases your parents might use, such as *Hai già fatto il tuo compito per casa*? (Have you done your homework yet?) It's funny and entertaining, plus there are Real Audio files so you can hear the phrases. For more beginner's Italian, try Tyler Jones' site at <*http://www.hardlink.com/~chambers/Italian/*>.

http://www.eat.com/learn-italian/index.html

It appeared on the cover of Mad magazine back in 1965. It has been called the Poiuyt, the Devil's Fork, the Three Stick Clevis, the Widgit, the Blivit, even the Triple Encabulator Tuned Manifold. No, it is not Alfred E. Neuman. **What is it?**

Answer: It is an impossible drawing that looks like a pitchfork with three tines, but if you look closely, it has only two. Find out how this famous optical illusion appeared on the *Mad* cover at http://www.illusionworks.com/trident_fram.htm

JAPANESE

The Japanese Tutor

This extensive guide to Japanese culture and language will let you hear everyday words and phrases, spoken by a native speaker. You'll also learn the polite way to count on your fingers and how to use chopsticks!

http://www.missouri.edu/~c563382/

Kid's Window

This little window on things Japanese will bring a smile to your face. Learn several origami folded figures, select items from a Japanese restaurant menu, and hear some Japanese letters and words.

http://jw.nttam.com/KIDS/kids_home.html

MIDDLE EGYPTIAN

Middle Egyptian

Want to be Indiana Jones someday? Better learn about hieroglyphs so you can read the markings inside the pyramids! Hey, where's the exit sign? This is just the site for that, and you can even type in your name and get it back in hieroglyphs.

http://weblifac.ens-cachan.fr/Portraits/
  S.ROSMORDUC/EgyptienE.html

PIG LATIN

Pig Latin Converter.. or something

Now here's something to confuse your teacher. Go to this site and enter the location of a familiar Web page you've seen a million times. You'll get to the site, all right—but the whole thing will be in Pig Latin! "Oh, teacher, there's something wrong with my browser!" Worse, every link you follow from that site will be in Pig Latin, too. Your only hope is to open a new site. Ave-hay un-fay!

http://voyager.cns.ohiou.edu/~jrantane/menu/pig.html

O-day ou-yay et-gay a ick-kay out of eading-ray Ig-pay Atin-lay?

En-thay oint-pay our-yay rowser-bay o-tay Pig Latin Converter...or something. Ave-hay un-fay!

PORTUGUESE

Short Portuguese Lessons

Portuguese is spoken by almost 200 million people around the world, including not only the people of Portugal, but also the peoples of Brazil, Angola, and Mozambique, among others. Six short lessons here will help you learn the basics of this beautiful language. Don't miss the links to online Portuguese-English dictionaries and other useful information.

http://wwwAlu.ci.uminho.pt:8888/~si17836/
  portuguese/portlessons.html

RADIO ALPHABET AND MORSE CODE

Morse Code and other Phonetic Alphabets

In addition to Morse code, various United States and other military alphabets are here. Words are sometimes easier to understand than letters when broadcast over radios. For example, it's clearer for a listener to hear "Victor" instead of the letter *V*. *V* by itself sounds like *E* or *B* or *D* and may be misunderstood. So, many military and civilian radio broadcasters use an alphabet made of words rather than letters.

http://www.soton.ac.uk/~scp93ch/refer/alphabet.html

SIGN LANGUAGES

Interactive Finger Spelling & Braille Guide

Finger spelling is one way to communicate with folks who can't hear. Or it's a secret language you and your friend can use when the teacher says, "No talking!" Here's an interactive finger spelling guide and a quiz. See how fast you can "sign" your name! This site also has a Braille guide.

http://www.disserv.stu.umn.edu/AltForm/

Sign Language

Input any word, and see it spelled in the sign language finger alphabet. This works better for some words than others. Remember that finger spelling is done in three dimensions; sometimes the letters have associated hand motions. Maybe this site will put up QuickTime movies someday. Still, try it out!

http://www.wolfram.com/~mathart/signs/sign.html

A
B
C
D
E
F
G
H
I
J
K
L
M
N
O
P
Q
R
S
T
U
V
W
X
Y
Z

A B C D E F G H I J K L M N O P Q R S T U V W X Y Z

SPANISH

Spanish Alphabet

Do you know the alphabet? "Sure," you say, "I learned that in nursery school." However, every language has a different alphabet. Sometimes the letters are completely different from English, and other times the letters may be the same but are pronounced differently. With Spanish, the alphabet is the same as English, but the pronunciation is different. You can learn how a good part of the Spanish alphabet is pronounced by taking a glimpse at the Ralph Bunche School El Alphabeto Español page. Each letter also has a nice drawing.

http://mac94.ralphbunche.rbs.edu/spanish.html

Web Spanish Lessons, by Tyler Jones

Sometimes it's tough to learn a new language if you don't know how it sounds. Here are some Spanish lessons, complete with pronunciations that you can hear. This page will also test you on translations of written phrases. It's like having your own built-in Spanish teacher! There are links to similar pages teaching French and Italian.

http://www.hardlink.com/~chambers/Spanish/

NET FILES

When the 21st century arrives, Fiji will be one of the first places to welcome it.

Do you know why?

Answer: Fiji lies just west of the international date line. Thus, as the world turns to the first day of the new century, Fiji will enter that new day before most of the rest of the world. An 1879 ordinance moved all of Fiji west of the date line. People still like to stand on the "old" date line, with one foot in one day and the other in tomorrow. Kind of eerie, huh? Read about it at

http://www.en.com/users/laura8/tav.html

Webspañol

Did you know that English and Spanish share many similar-sounding and similar-meaning words? For example the English "delicious" sounds very like the Spanish word for "tastes good"—*delicioso*. Over a thousand of these are collected and explained at the Espanglés section of this page. You can hear pronunciation sound files, puzzle over some devilish verbs, try some lessons and links, and even get a Spanish-speaking key pal here.

http://www.geocities.com/Athens/Acropolis/7409/

LATINO

Art of Native Mexican Children

Kids everywhere like to paint and draw. True to form, kids in Mexico like to do artwork, and it's fantastic. See samples of drawings from Mayo, Tzeltal, and Mayan children at this Web page. The colors will grab you, and the world they paint is filled with animals, musicians, and festivals. Brighten your day and take a look now!

http://www.DocuWeb.ca/Mexico/1-engl/kids.html

The Azteca Web Page

Did you know many kids in the United States are of Mexican descent? They are proudly called *Chicanos y Chicanas*. Understanding what it means to be Chicano is about many things: music, history, culture, and language. To learn about this fascinating culture, this page is a good place to start.

http://www.azteca.net/aztec/

Conexión Latina Home Page

Hispanic culture is a vibrant combination of language, food, entertainment, sports, and on and on. This Web site provides a place where Hispanics from around the world can share their culture. Take a special look at Profiles, a Web page that lists distinguished Hispanics. Also check out Kid's World—this is a special portion of Conexión with *you* in mind!

http://www.conexionlatina.com/

Diego Rivera Web Museum

Diego Rivera was a famous painter originally from Mexico, but his paintings have been enjoyed throughout the world. You can sample some of this great artist's works here. You'll see fantastic murals, learn about Rivera's life, and enjoy Latino art at its best.

http://www.diegorivera.com/diego_home_eng.html

HISPANIC Online

This is the Web page for *HISPANIC*. Here you'll find tons of news for Latinos and Latinas: music, news, and links to dozens of Hispanic-related Web sites. If you want the latest and greatest on Hispanic news, this is the place to go!

http://www.hisp.com

karlacom

Check out Karla's world on the Internet. She lives in Mexico, and she has lots of links to great sites. The difference here is that her Web pages are written in Spanish. Even if you don't understand Spanish, you'll find Karla has pulled together some great information. Best yet, maybe you'll learn a thing or two in a new language!

http://www.internet.com.mx/egopage/
   karla/el_mundo.html

La Escuela Virtual

For many Latin American kids, surfing the Internet can be tough. Just about everything is in English, and for Spanish speakers, this can be difficult. Fortunately, this is a good starting point for Spanish-speaking kids learning to use the Internet. All instructions and descriptions of some great Internet sites are in Spanish. *Es cool*!

http://www.escuela_virtual.org.mx/escuela-virtual/

If you are a Spanish speaker or you are learning Spanish, take a look at La Escuela Virtual. It's a starting point for Spanish-speaking kids who want to explore the Internet.

LatinoWeb

Bienvenido! That's Spanish for "Welcome," one of the first things you'll see on LatinoWeb, one part of the Internet set aside for things Latino. If you want to see what's hot on the Internet, this site has much to offer: news, music, cool sites—they are all here. Parents, the extensive set of links from this page has not been checked.

http://www.catalog.com/favision/

The Ultimate Macarena Site

The Macarena is *the* dance of the nineties, and it is Latino all the way. Check out how to do the dance, learn its history, and even get a translation of the song. Get ready for a true Latin beat, and let's do the Macarena!

http://www.macarena.org/index.html

You know something the Net doesn't. Make your own home page!

A
B
C
D
E
F
G
H
I
J
K
L
M
N
O
P
Q
R
S
T
U
V
W
X
Y
Z

Zona Latina: Latin American Children Resource

What are the good sites for kids, with a Latino flair? You'll find them all listed at this page. With sites from the U.S., Brazil, Argentina, Chile, and Mexico, Zona Latina covers a wide territory. Some of the sites listed here may be familiar to you, but we bet you'll find at least a few that are unique and loads of fun! Parents—not all links have been checked.

http://www.zonalatina.com/Zlchild.htm

CULTURE
Chicano Mural Tour

Can you picture an art museum that's completely outside? Murals are paintings on buildings, and they turn the outdoors into an art gallery. Some of the best mural artists are Latino. In the past, many Latino artists couldn't get their work placed in art museums. Instead, they painted walls, hallways—all kinds of places—producing some beautiful murals. In Los Angeles, with its large Latino population, there are many, many murals. Take a tour of some of the best of these murals, and see what an outdoor art museum looks like!

http://latino.sscnet.ucla.edu/murals/Sparc/
    sparctour.html

NET FILES

What are *Goudse Stroopwafels*?

Molasses

Answer: They are treacle (molasses) pancake cookies found in the Dutch city of Gouda! Although considered a kids' treat, most adults like one with their morning coffee. You can see a picture of one at http://www.xs4all.nl/~eleede/prodniew.htm

Lotería: Mexican Bingo Games

Latinos like to play a fun game called *Lotería*. It's like Bingo, but it has colorful pictures with Spanish names instead of numbers and letters. Would you like to play the game? Go to the Lotería page on the World Wide Web. It's fun!

http://www.mercado.com/juventud/loteria/loteria.htm

HISTORY
Galvez

Who is Marshall Bernardo de Gálvez? Well, among other things, the city of Galveston, Texas, is named for him! He was a hero of the American Revolutionary War. This Web page says, "Between 1779 and 1785, Marshall Bernardo de Gálvez...defeated the British in Baton Rouge, Mobile, Pensacola, St. Louis, and Fort St. Joseph, Michigan. These victories relieved British pressure on General George Washington's armies and helped open supply lines for money and military goods from Spain, France, Cuba, and Mexico." There might not have been a United States of America if de Gálvez hadn't helped. Learn more about this American hero at the Hispanics in American History page.

http://www.clark.net/pub/jgbustam/galvez/galvez.html

Hispanos Famosos

What do Roman Emperor Hadrian, Nobel Prize-winning scientist Luis Leloir, and painter Pablo Picasso have in common? They are all famous Hispanics—people with a Spanish heritage. Throughout history, Hispanic people have been great scientists, soldiers, political leaders, artists, and musicians. Read about many famous and accomplished Hispanics here. This page is in both English and Spanish!

http://www.clark.net/pub/jgbustam/famosos.html

ARCHITECTURE, building blocks for grown-ups!

A
B
C
D
E
F
G
H
I
J
K
L
M
N
O
P
Q
R
S
T
U
V
W
X
Y
Z

Did you know that the longest held, confirmed POW (prisoner of war) in U.S. history was **Lieutenant Everett Alvarez**? During the Vietnam War, he flew a jet plane from an aircraft carrier and was shot down, but he somehow landed safely. He was then captured as a POW and held for eight and a half long years. Read about other famous folks by taking a peek at Hispanos Famosos.

LANDMARKS OF HISPANIC L.A.

What do you think of when you hear someone say Los Angeles, California? Maybe movie stars come to mind, or surfers, or rock musicians. Los Angeles, though, is a very old center of American Hispanic and Latino culture. To understand Los Angeles, you have to understand its Latin roots. This page is a good place to begin. Here you'll read about some of Los Angeles' earliest history and you'll see the landmarks where the history took place.

http://www.usc.edu/Library/Ref/LA/
la_landmarks_hispan.html

LIBRARIES

ALSC HOMEPAGE — AWARDS AND NOTABLES

There's no doubt that librarians know tons about books. Every year, children's librarians in the American Library Association give two awards to authors and illustrators of the best books for kids. The Caldecott Medal goes for the best illustrator of a children's book, and the Newbery Medal is given to the author of the finest kids' book. See the winners at these Web sites; you'll find some librarian-tested and approved books!

http://www.ala.org/alsc/awards.html

The CIC Electronic Journals Collection

You've got a tough school assignment, and you might be wondering if you can find an article in a publication that can help you. E-zines (electronic magazines) and journals are available on the Internet. The problem is—how to find these resources? A good place to start is the CIC Electronic Journals Collection (EJC). Here you'll find a number of quality electronic magazines and journals on a variety of subjects. Most of the material is written for college-level research, but it sure can't hurt to get the most current material available!

http://ejournals.cic.net/

IPL the Internet Public Library

Wouldn't it be great to have a public library available 24 hours a day? Well, you have one! The Internet Public Library is a project by the library school at the University of Michigan, and you'll find a whole host of material available to you for research projects. There are links to many useful resources on the Internet, guides to help you use the Internet, and librarians available to help you with your studies in a really cool MOO (a *MOO* is a type of software that lets you interact live with other people in a computer-created world).

http://ipl.sils.umich.edu/index.text.html

Kid's Place

The Internet is confusing to use; it's hard to figure where the good stuff is. (That's why you're reading this book!) For centuries, librarians have been organizing information, and they have gotten pretty good at it. One way librarians do this is with the Dewey decimal system: an easy-to-use system of numbers that correspond to subjects. At Nashville Public Library in Tennessee, the librarians select great Internet sites for kids, and they use Dewey decimal numbers to organize the sites by subject. Take a look—it's nice to see the Internet from an organized viewpoint.

http://www.nashv.lib.tn.us/kids.html

A B C D E F G H I J K L M N O P Q R S T U V W X Y Z

A B C D E F G H I J K L M N O P Q R S T U V W X Y Z

NET FILES

Is there really anyplace on Earth where "you can't get there from here"?

Answer: Our vote goes to tiny Pitcairn Island in the Pacific Ocean, former home to the HMS *Bounty* mutineers and one of the most remote and isolated spots on the face of the planet. To visit for more than 48 hours, you need permission from the local island government and from the British Consulate General in New Zealand (if you get one, you may not get the other!). Planes can't land there, and it has no harbor. Still, some people do manage to visit, and you can learn about it at
http://wavefront.wavefront.com/~pjlareau/pitvisit.html

Library of Congress World Wide Web Page

The U.S. Library of Congress is the world's largest single collection of library materials anywhere. It would be great if everything in the library were available to view on the Internet, but that hasn't happened yet. However, the folks at the Library of Congress have made a large amount of information available here. From their home page on the World Wide Web, you can view beautiful graphic images of exhibits, such as original photographs from the U.S. Civil War, or you can see replicas of documents from Columbus' voyages to America. You can also connect easily to the Library of Congress online catalog (if you have telnet software), and there are convenient links to many U.S. government sites.

http://lcweb.loc.gov/

Attention everyone. The Internet is closing. Please go play outside.

SJCPL's List of Public Libraries with Gopher/WWW Services

Public libraries all over the world are active on the Internet. Some have their library online catalogs available, others have gopher sites, and yet others have great World Wide Web home pages. To see a list of many public libraries with Internet services, take a look at this site. On most of the public library sites, you'll find links to great resources on the Internet. Maybe you'll see your own neighborhood library on the list!

http://sjcpl.lib.in.us/homepage/PublicLibraries/
PubLibSrvsGpherWWW.html#wwwsrv

Smithsonian Institution Libraries

The Smithsonian Institution Libraries in Washington, D.C., are among the world's best libraries. As part of the Smithsonian, these libraries are dedicated to spreading knowledge. Take a look at this home page and see outstanding online exhibits, browse through a huge library catalog, and read unique Smithsonian electronic publications.

http://silweb.sil.si.edu/

NET FILES

When was U.S. President Bill Clinton born?

Answer: He was born on August 19, 1946. You can find out more vital statistics and biographical information here at
http://www.giftcards.com/p000030.htm

LISTS

The List Server Page

In an attempt to make the whole discussion list subscription process easier, this site makes it as easy as point and click! So far, there are only about a thousand lists available here. New lists are being added all the time, though, so keep looking if you don't find one of interest the first time.

http://www.cuc.edu/cgi-bin/listservform.pl

NET FILES

Where is the Plimsoll Line, and why shouldn't you cross it?

Answer: These days, it's more of a pictograph than a line. It's painted on the hulls of merchant ships, showing the safe load limit for that ship. In 1870s England, Samuel Plimsoll, a member of Parliament, proposed this "line" to help halt the number of shipwrecks and casualties caused by overloading. If this line was under water, the ship was overloaded and was therefore unsafe. Calculating the placement of the line is not easy! It's dependent on the type of ship, cargo, season, and geographic area of operation. So there are really several Plimsoll lines painted on every merchant ship. See a picture of one at http://pacifier.com/~rboggs/PLIMSOLL.HTML.

Liszt: Searchable Directory of e-Mail Discussion Groups

Need a mailing list or a newsgroup? This site has over 23,000 lists and 13,000 newsgroups, all searchable by word or phrase. Just enter a word, such as "horse," and you'll get a list of items containing that word. For example, your "horse" search will pull up EQUINE-L and 14 others. To get more information on a particular list, follow the instructions on the screen. Your Internet service provider may not give you access to all these newsgroups, but at least you'll know they exist. Maybe you can ask your provider to carry it for you. A caution to parents: Many of these lists and newsgroups are not for children.

http://www.liszt.com/

Mailing List WWW Gateway

Have you ever recalled reading something on a discussion list months ago and wished you could search for and find that information again? Or maybe you want to search the archive library of a list, but you don't subscribe to it. This site makes that process fairly easy. Remember, though, not all lists archive old messages, and some do require that you be a subscriber before you can read the archives. The LWGate supports mailing lists provided by Listserv, ListProcessor 6, Majordomo, and SmartList servers.

http://www.netspace.org/cgi-bin/lwgate/

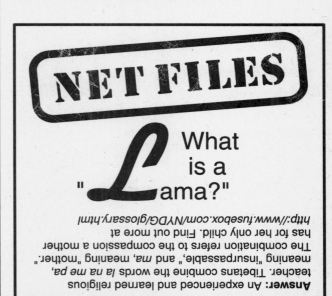

NET FILES

What is a "*L*ama?"

Answer: An experienced and learned religious teacher. Tibetans combine the words *la na me pa,* meaning "insurpassable," and *ma,* meaning "mother." The combination refers to the compassion a mother has for her only child. Find out more at http://www.fusebox.com/NYDG/glossary.html

A
B
C
D
E
F
G
H
I
J
K
L
M
N
O
P
Q
R
S
T
U
V
W
X
Y
Z

Publicly Accessible Mailing Lists

This mega-list of discussion groups is arranged by name and subject for your searching pleasure. Parental advisory: Many of these lists are not for children.

http://www.neosoft.com/internet/paml/

DISCUSSION AND NEWSGROUPS FOR CHILDREN

Discussion Lists: Mailing List Manager Commands

Your pen pal in Michigan says you should subscribe to a favorite discussion group mailing list on snakes. That's great, but how the heck do you subscribe? And does it cost money? You'll be glad to know that usually list discussion groups are free. To subscribe, you send a mail message to a computer running the mailing list software. Because the subscription process is done by that remote computer, you need to send your request in a way the computer can understand. This means you have to use certain common commands to tell the computer what you want to do. That wouldn't be too hard, except that discussion lists use different software packages to distribute mail—some popular ones are called Revised Listserv (also called BITNET Listserv), Unix ListProcessor (or Listproc), Mailbase, Mailserv, and Majordomo. And they all use different commands! James Milles has sorted it all out. Check this site to learn how to talk to all the major discussion group list mailers.

http://lawlib.slu.edu/training/mailser.htm

KIDLINK: Global Networking for Youth 10-15

You know the world's got some big problems: pollution, hunger, poverty. Why not talk to other kids and see if you can help solve some of them? Make new friendships, and have some fun with kids from 87 different countries on the KIDCAFE discussions. Take a look at the KIDLINK mailing list page, and start e-mailing new friends. Show this to your teacher and parents, too. They'll find lots of good information about how to share a project with a class in another country. Many of the discussions are held in languages other than English, too!

http://www.kidlink.org/home-txt.html

KIDZMAIL

How would you like to contact kids from around the world and share messages? You could ask them about life in their countries. Make a new *key pal* (that's like a pen pal, but one you send e-mail to, using a keyboard rather than a pen and paper in regular mail). KIDZMAIL is a good place to connect with kids from the world over.

List Address: kidzmail@asuvm.inre.asu.edu
Subscription Address: LISTSERV@ASUVM.INRE.ASU.EDU

Usenet Newsgroups for Kids

Usenet is like a huge e-mail party where people get together to exchange messages on all kinds of subjects. Part of Usenet is just for kids. However, it is IMPORTANT to remember the following: Even in areas set aside for kids, adults can send messages. You might even find adults pretending to be kids. Also, sometimes the kids in these discussion groups can say things you might not like. You never have to read, or believe, everything you see. Access to Usenet depends on your Internet service provider, and not all Usenet discussions (called *newsgroups*) are available through all providers. You can read newsgroups through many World Wide Web browsers, or you can use a separate application. Ask your provider for suggestions, and ask your parents or teacher for help.

To search for information contained in newsgroups or to find newsgroups of potential interest to you, we recommend DejaNews. You can find it at *<http://www.dejanews.com/>*.

Here are two Usenet groups for kids:

- *alt.kids-talk* This is another newsgroup for kids, but this area can include high schoolers and younger kids.

- *alt.tv.nickelodeon* This newsgroup is dedicated to the first TV network just for kids.

http://www.dejanews.com/

**See what's shakin' in
EARTH SCIENCE
GEOLOGY-EARTHQUAKES.**

David S. Carter, one of six people who work full-time on the Internet Public Library site.

"People have asked the Internet Public Library questions on all manner of topics, from leprechauns to elections in Mexico to the biodegradation of linear alkylbenzene sulfonate."

LIBRARIES
Internet Public Library
Webmaster: David S. Carter
http://www.ipl.org/

Who came up with the idea for your page or project? Was it you? How did the idea originate?

The IPL began in a graduate seminar in the School of Information and Library Studies at the University of Michigan, during the winter 1995 semester. The idea was twofold: (1) to ask some interesting and important questions about the interconnections of libraries, librarians, and librarianship within a distributed networked environment, and (2) to learn a lot about these issues by actually designing and building something called the Internet Public Library.

From a large pool of interested students, a group of 35 was selected to make up the class. Work began on January 5, 1995, and the Library opened on March 17, 70 days later.

How many people work on your pages? Does it take a lot of time? How many hits do you get a day?

There are six full-time staff, plus a host of volunteers and students. It takes an extraordinary amount of time! A typical weekday at the IPL sees over 100,000 hits (roughly 9,000-10,000 different people).

You must hear from people all over the world! Can you think of an unusual request, question, or comment someone has sent to you?

We receive so many, it's hard to choose just one. People have asked the IPL questions on all manner of topics, from leprechauns to elections in Mexico to the biodegradation of linear alkylbenzene sulfonate.

What is your favorite resource on the Net?

The Internet Movie Database <http://www.msstate.edu/Movies/>. One of the original content-rich sites on the Web, it shows what the Internet can accomplish as a community.

If this isn't your main job, what do you do, what is your training?

This is my job. I have degrees in electrical engineering and library science.

What's the one thing you'd really like to do on your page but have not yet implemented?

A fully integrated online database for distributed collection development. (Yes, that's a mouthful.)

Do you have a family? A Dog? A lizard?

I have yet to start a family of my own, but I have parents, a sister and brother-in-law, a grandmother, and plenty of aunts, uncles, and cousins to go around. No pets, sorry.

What are your hopes and fears for the future of the Internet?

Hopes: More bandwidth, more people connected. More useful content and less flash.

Fears: Commercialization, government regulation.

When you're not using the Net, what do you like to do?

Read, collect comic books, gaming, volleyball.

If you could invite three people throughout history to your house for dinner, who would they be?

Philip K. Dick (science fiction writer), Richard Feynman (physicist and drummer), Teddy Roosevelt (26th President of the United States).

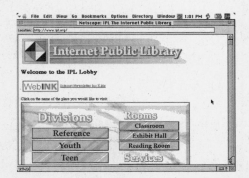

MAGIC TRICKS

David Copperfield

A lot of people think David Copperfield is the greatest magician and illusionist alive today. After all, he "vanished" the Statue of Liberty in front of a live audience (even its radar blip went away), and he walked through the Great Wall of China. We attended one of his stage shows, and it sure looked like he was flying around the stage to us. This page will tell you about David's childhood, his current schedule, and his illusions, but it does not give away any of his secrets!

http://www.digiweb.com/~dannyb/welcome.html

What is a Labradoodle?

Answer:
It's a Labrador-poodle cross, often used in Australia and Great Britain as a guide dog for the blind. Other commonly used service dogs are Labrador Retrievers, Golden Retrievers, and German Shepherds. Approximately 60 to 70 percent of all working guides in the U.S. are Labradors. Discover more about service dogs at http://www.zmall.com/pet_talk/title/pets/dog-tags/service.html

"Use the source, Luke!" and look it up in REFERENCE WORKS.

Hocus Pocus Palace

Dare to challenge The Great Mysto in a game of mind reading and clairvoyance. Through magical and as yet unexplainable Internet protocols, The Great Mysto will astound you with his long-distance feats. Doubters may scoff and say these are simple "magic square" tricks, but we're not so sure (how did he know we were thinking of Marge Simpson?). You'll laugh out loud at the catalog of old magic trick apparatus, revealed and explained. O Great Mysto, you have a truly fun site!

http://www.teleport.com/~jrolsen/

Magic Show

Abracadabra! The magic trick amazes the people in the audience, who whisper to each other, "That's impossible! How do they do it?" Everyone loves a magic show. The only thing better than watching a magic show is being the magician. This Web magazine has articles about professional magicians who amaze people, show after show. Each issue also contains the secrets of how to perform tricks yourself. There are even movie clips of tricks being performed. Whether you want to learn magic or you just enjoy it, this site has something for you. Don't forget the hat (and the rabbit)!

http://www.uelectric.com/magicshow/

Mathemagic Activities

Put one end of a rope in each of your friend's hands and ask her to tie a knot without dropping the rope. Or amaze your friends with card tricks and other stunts. It's not magic; it's math!

http://www.scri.fsu.edu/~dennisl/CMS/activity/math_magic.html

Get on board, little children, in RAILROADS AND TRAINS.

MAMMALS

Australian A to Z Animal Archive

Not every animal listed in this archive is a mammal. Do you know how the kangaroo got its name? When European explorers first saw a strange animal jumping around, they asked the Aborigines what it was. The Aborigines replied, "Kangaroo," which means "I don't understand," but the Europeans thought that was the strange animal's name. Check out this site and learn about other Australian animals.

http://www.aaa.com.au/A_Z/

California Department of Fish and Game

Look at that cute little dog—wait, that's not a dog, it's a San Joaquin kit fox! They look just like small dogs with big ears. This endangered animal is about 32 inches long, and 12 inches of that is its luxurious tail. You can see one at this site, along with great photos of lots of other mammals, such as bobcats, porcupines, and raccoons.

http://darkstar.delta.dfg.ca.gov/species/mammal.html

The Electronic Zoo

This page is the best place to start your search for animal info on the Web. For zoo animals and wildlife, check in the Exotics category under the Animals selection. Other mammals (dogs, cats, ferrets, pigs, cows, horses, and more) have their own sections.

http://netvet.wustl.edu/e-zoo.htm

Mammals Home Page

Mammals are divided into three subclasses. Placentalia is the subclass to which most mammals belong. The other two subclasses include pouched mammals (look, a kangaroo!), known as marsupials, and egg-laying mammals, such as the platypus and the spiny anteater. See pictures of these unusual mammals here.

http://edx1.educ.monash.edu.au/~juanda/vcm/
 mammals.htm

Sounds of the World's Animals

Everybody knows that a dog's bark is "woof-woof," right? Well, not everybody knows that! A French dog says "*ouah ouah*," while a Japanese dog says "*wanwan*." In Sweden, the dogs say "*vov vov*," and in the Ukraine, you'll find them saying "*gaf-gaf*." This is a Web page full of what the world thinks various animals sound like. There's an audio sound file for each animal, so you can hear and decide for yourself which language "says it best."

http://www.georgetown.edu/cball/animals/
 animals.html

BEARS
THE BEAR DEN Home Page

This page says: "For bears everywhere, and for those humans who are on their side." We don't know how many bears are actually using the Internet. For one thing, there is the problem of getting a telephone line installed in their dens. For another, there is the difficulty of hitting the right keys when they type with their big, furry paws. However, we are sure that when bears finally get all those problems solved, they will love this Web page. It has two sections, one for everyone and one just for "cubs," so check them both out! You'll learn about eight species of bears, catch up on current news in the world of bears, and discover some tips on what to do if you ever meet up with a wilderness bear who doesn't act like Yogi and Boo-Boo.

http://www.nature-net.com/bears/

North Cascaders National Park:Grizzly Bear

Think you can tell the difference between a grizzly and a black bear? Guess what—black bears are not always black, and grizzly bears are not always gray-grizzled, making it very difficult at times to tell which is which. Learn the distinguishing characteristics that set these highly intelligent animals apart. Discover what precautions you can take to avoid a confrontation when you are camping or hiking in the places they call home. Will you know what to do if an encounter becomes unavoidable? You will, if you stop in here.

http://www.halcyon.com/rdpayne/ncnp-grizzly.html

A
B
C
D
E
F
G
H
I
J
K
L
M
N
O
P
Q
R
S
T
U
V
W
X
Y
Z

A B C D E F G H I J K L **M** N O P Q R S T U V W X Y Z

NET FILES

It's a sunny winter day, about 10 degrees Fahrenheit outside. It's breezy, too, with the wind blowing about five miles per hour. Your mom says it's way too cold to go out and play. She keeps talking about something called "windchill"—what the heck is that?

Answer: Wind removes heat from your body. The windchill equivalent index measures the heat loss from any skin that's exposed to the air (where did you leave your mittens, anyway?). Heat loss is caused by a potentially dangerous combination of wind and low air temperature. Risk of frostbite from low windchill "temperatures" makes windchill a winter weather hazard. Show Mom the windchill chart on the Net. It indicates that at today's air temperature (10 degrees) and wind speed (5 mph), the apparent temperature will "feel like" 6 degrees Fahrenheit. It will be unpleasant, but not dangerous. Check http://www.weather.com/weather_whys/teachers_resources/charts.html#windchill and remember, the definition of a sweater is "what goes on a child when mom feels cold."

Polar Bears

Do polar bears really like winter? You bet they do! In fact, polar bears would rather live on ice than on land. Discover more about their chilly lifestyle, and learn why you can't sneak up on a polar bear (they can smell you coming up to 20 miles away).

http://www.bev.net/education/SeaWorld/polar_bears/
pbindex.html

Looking for the State Bird or the State Motto? It's in the UNITED STATES section.

CAT FAMILY
The BIGGER Big Cats Info Page

Have you ever known of a cat that swims? The fishing cat is the best swimmer of all cats. Not only that, as its name implies, it fishes, too! By using its long claws as fishhooks, it can catch fish, crayfish, mollusks, rodents, reptiles, and other small animals. To learn more about wild cats, visit this page and discover (among other things) what strange sleeping habits the margay has.

http://www.lam.mus.ca.us/~pcannon/cats.html

International Tiger Information Center

Why is this server's domain named "5tigers"? Because only five subspecies of tigers remain on Earth today. Three other subspecies have disappeared into extinction in the last 70 years. There are estimated to be only about 5,000 to 7,300 wild tigers left. This organization will teach you something about conservation efforts and how you can help. You can also take a quiz and see how much you already know about the natural history of tigers, play a fun adventure, and listen to tiger sounds, scratches, and growls.

http://www.5tigers.org/

*Tyger! Tyger! burning bright
In the forests of the night,*

So begins the poem by William Blake. Besides those forests of the night, tigers inhabit both the snowy woods of Siberia and the steamy jungles of Sumatra. Visit the **International Tiger Information Center** and see some tigers close-up.

ELEPHANTS
An Elephant HomePage

Can you tell the difference between an Asian and an African elephant? While Asian and African elephants have a lot in common, each species looks a bit different, and each faces different threats to its survival. Asian elephants are *endangered*, meaning they are in danger of extinction. African elephants are *threatened*, which means they are on their way to becoming endangered. Neither situation is a good one. Find out more about the different species and the efforts that are being taken to protect these precious pachyderms. There is also a recipe for Elephant Trunk oatmeal cookies!

http://raptor.csc.flint.umich.edu/~mcdonald/

Elephant Managers Association

Did you ever wonder what an elephant does all day in the zoo? Elephants demand instruction and guidance to flourish in a man-made environment. The Elephant Managers Association tries to help, and you can read about them here. In the Other Links area, you will find lots of additional info about elephants. For example, The Indianapolis Zoo strives hard to provide the psychological, physiological, and social fulfillment needed to keep elephants happy and healthy. Spend a virtual day with the elephants and the trainers as they go about their busy schedules at *<http://estel.uindy.edu/outReach/guestSchools/indyzoo/ema/old/emaday/>* or try the link off the Other Links page.

http://www.indyzoo.com/ema/

GIRAFFES
Giraffe Cam

You've got to see the giraffes at the Cheyenne Mountain Zoo in Colorado Springs, Colorado. Sometimes they are in, sometimes they are out, but keep tuning in and you're bound to see a giraffe or two eventually. We did! They are normally visible from 10 A.M. to 4 P.M. (mountain time). This zoo is famous for successfully breeding giraffes in captivity.

http://c.unclone.com/zoocam.html

Giraffes

Tall and majestic, giraffes cruise the grasslands of Africa with grace and style. But don't even think of messing with them! These 15-foot reticulated wonders are into neck wrestling and head banging, and if threatened, they can kill a predator with a single kick. You definitely want to keep on the good side of this 4,000-pound animal. Even the babies are six feet tall at birth.

http://www.wolfe.net/~ohwell/giraffe.html

HORSE FAMILY AND ZEBRAS
Animal Bytes: Grevy's zebra

Did you know that each zebra's stripe pattern is as unique as a fingerprint? Zebras help other plant-eaters on the grassland plains, since they eat off the coarse forage at the top of plants, leaving the tender new growth for other animals.

http://www.bev.net/education/SeaWorld/
   animal_bytes/grevysab.html

Equus burchelli

Meet some Damaraland zebras at Woodland Park Zoo in Seattle, Washington. They have not only black and white stripes but also brownish "shadow" stripes. This camouflage helps them disappear in the sun-on-shifting-grasslands habitat of their native Africa. Unfortunately, fewer than one-half million of these herd animals remain in the wild. You'll learn a lot about the natural history of zebras and also something you probably did not know about legendary rock star Jimi Hendrix and why a plaque in his honor is at the Seattle zoo. If you want more pictures of zebras, try Bexley's Zebra Page at *<http://www.wildfire.com/~ag/zebras.html>*.

http://www.zoo.org/science/animals/zebra.html

A B C D E F G H I J K L **M** N O P Q R S T U V W X Y Z

MARINE MAMMALS

Manatees

Have you ever heard of the manatee? Found in waters around Florida, throughout the Caribbean, and into South America, manatees are gentle vegetarians that are also called sea cows. They are, believe it or not, related to elephants, and some think the myth of mermaids may have come from sailors who saw these graceful creatures swimming. To learn more about manatees, take a look at this page.

http://www.dep.state.fl.us/psm/webpages/
   manatee.htm

THE MARINE MAMMAL CENTER

This San Francisco area wildlife rehabilitation center specializes in pinnipeds: California sea lions, northern elephant seals, and harbor seals. Do you know why elephant seals' eyes are so big? So they can see in low light levels when they dive deep. They get most of their food this way. They prefer to be offshore, up to 35 miles, diving to 4,000 feet and possibly even deeper! On land, because they have nonreversible rear flippers, elephant seals must slide, wriggle, and roll, using movements that resemble those of a caterpillar. To learn more about other marine mammals, visit this home page.

http://www.tmmc.org/

MARINE MAMMALS—WHALES

Whale Songs

Follow in the footsteps of Saucon Valley School District (Pennsylvania) bioethics teacher Lance Leonhardt as he joins the crew of the sailing yacht *Song of the Whale*. Before his journey, he had his students research the island of Dominica, in the Azores of the Caribbean. They learned about the climate, landscape, wildlife, and especially the marine mammals of the vicinity. Their findings on each whale are here, as well as their teacher's journals, which describe encounters with many kinds of dolphins and whales during the two-week voyage. The detailed entries include rich multimedia resources, such as links to photos, audio files, and a handy glossary.

http://whales.ot.com/

Whales

Have you ever heard of friendly whales? No, not Baby Beluga or Shamu. The term "friendly whale" usually refers to the gray whale. In the lagoons in Mexico, sometimes gray whales will approach small boats. Scientists are not sure why the whales do this, since most wild animals are too wary to approach people or allow people to approach them. Maybe they just want to be friendly! Is a whale a fish? No. Although they share the same environment, there are important differences between a fish and a whale. Visit this page to discover differences in the way fish and whales breathe, swim, and eat. This page is full of references for teachers, activities for students, and whale projects for all!

http://curry.edschool.Virginia.EDU/go/Whales/

Why do we have four seasons?

(Here at Pollywood Farm, we have only two seasons: four months of winter and eight months of bad skiing!)

Answer: Because of Earth's tilt in its orbit around the Sun, sometimes parts of Earth lean close to the Sun, and sometimes these parts lean farther away. Without the tilt of Earth's axis, we wouldn't have seasons at all! We would have about the same temperature year-round, according to the Missouri Botanical Gardens. Find more info and a drawing of how this all works at
http://www.mobot.org/MBGnet/vb/temp/4seasons.htm

You know something the Net doesn't. Make your own home page!

WHALETIMES

Did you ever look for a dolphin in a tree? If you're looking for *boutos,* or Amazon River dolphins, sometimes that's the place to look. They live in South America. During the rainy season, when the rivers flood and the water gets as deep as 40 or 50 feet, the dolphins and other animals in the river actually swim through the trees. Can you tell the difference between a shark and a whale? Many sharks have two dorsal fins; a whale has only one dorsal fin, if at all. Also, a shark's tail is vertical and a whale's tail is horizontal. If you're fishing for fishy facts, you can ask Jake the Sea Dog, who will answer questions online. You can even help write an ocean story! Take a swim to this Web page and see for yourself.

http://www.whaletimes.org/

MARSUPIALS (POUCHED MAMMALS)

Koala's page

What seldom drinks, has a big rubbery nose, large fluffy ears, and little or no tail, and looks like a cuddly toy? Why, a koala bear, of course! Koalas live in trees, eat eucalyptus leaves, and are categorized as marsupials because they nourish their young in abdominal pouches. A mother koala only has one baby at a time, and she carries it around in her pouch for seven months; after that, the baby clings to its mother's back until it is about one year old. An old Australian story tells how the first koala was created. Stop by this page and check it out.

http://www.geom.umn.edu/~jpeng/KOALA/koala.html

Lone Pine Koala Sanctuary Home Page

Visit a wildlife park near Brisbane, Australia! It is home to over 150 koalas and 100 species of unique Australian wildlife. Besides koalas, you'll meet kangaroos, Tasmanian devils, and wombats, among others. You can vote for the cutest koala, download some screen wallpaper, or follow some of the other animal links. This page is available in Chinese, Indonesian, Korean, Japanese, and Thai.

http://www.koala.net/

Ruth's Sugar Glider Page

Sugar glider? Do you eat it or fly it? Neither. It's only the cutest marsupial to come up from "down under." About the size and shape of a flying squirrel, these creatures are soft, striped, and captivatingly cute. Native to Australia, they are considered exotic to the U.S., so you need a license to buy and own one. But owners will tell you they make great pets and are well worth any paperwork hassle. Think twice before checking out this site—once you see one, you're going to want one!

http://www.rtis.com/nat/user/regrove/

MONKEYS AND PRIMATES

Jane Goodall Institute

Chimpanzees are biologically close to humans; there is only a 2 percent genetic difference. This is why they are frequently used in research. The Jane Goodall Institute is committed to improving the lives of chimpanzees both in the wild and in captivity. Goodall's wildlife research in Africa is internationally known and respected. You can get involved with her Roots and Shoots program or the Youth Summit sponsored by the Institute.

http://www.gsn.org/gsn/proj/jgi/

Orang Utan

The current number of orangutans left in the wild is estimated at between 20,000 and 27,000. They are an endangered species, and are the only big apes found in Asia. Unlike other primate species, they do not live in groups, preferring a solitary life. They feed on fruits, bark, leaves, and insects, such as ants, termites, and bees. Male orangutans feed at ground level; the females never leave the trees. Stop by this page and meet Grungy the Orangutan, and learn more about projects in support of orangutan rehabilitation and preservation around the world.

http://www.tourismindonesia.com/orang.htm

A
B
C
D
E
F
G
H
I
J
K
L
M
N
O
P
Q
R
S
T
U
V
W
X
Y
Z

A
B
C
D
E
F
G
H
I
J
K
L
M
N
O
P
Q
R
S
T
U
V
W
X
Y
Z

Primate Gallery

What's all the monkeying around? Why, it's the Primate Gallery Web site! You'll find information on over 200 living primate species, including links to images, animations, and primate audio files. Stop by and see which primate is being featured this week. This comprehensive site will lead you to other monkey business on the Net as well!

http://www.selu.com/~bio/PrimateGallery/

RHINOCEROS

Animal Bytes: Black Rhinoceros

Fewer than 2,500 of these animals exist on the planet today. Some people believe that the rhino "horn" has medicinal properties, and the animals are killed by poachers who want to harvest the horn. The rhino "horn" isn't attached to the skull, and it's made out of keratin (the same substance found in fingernails), so it is not a true horn at all. Some zoos, such as the San Diego Wild Animal Park, have had some success breeding these animals, but they will never return to the wild, since their habitat is mostly gone.

http://www.bev.net/education/SeaWorld/
animal_bytes/black_rhinocerosab.html

Save the Rhino Home Page

It may be a little thick-skinned, but its reputation for aggressiveness is totally overblown. Normally timid and with no natural enemies, a white rhino will charge only when confronted. Yet the loss of home and poaching of its horns has nearly destroyed its population. Here you can learn more about this rhino and its relatives and see how one organization is attempting to keep the 97 percent extinction rate from becoming 100 percent.

http://www.cm-net.com/rhino/

In the last 30 years, 97 percent of the world's rhinoceros population has been wiped out, and less than 10,000 are left!

What can kids do to make sure their kids get to see live rhinos?

Check the **Save the Rhino Home Page**.

RODENTS

The Capybara Page

What would you get if you crossed a guinea pig and a hippopotamus? Probably something that looks like a capybara. These large, friendly rodents are rather vocal, making a series of strange clicks, squeaks, and grunts. Although they adapt easily to captivity, mice and rodent collectors will have to pass this one by as a pet: capybaras are the largest living rodents on earth, weighing in at 100 pounds or more! Our great-grandma calls them "outdoor hamsters."

http://www.access.digex.net/~rboucher/capybara/

Guinea Pigs

In English, it's called a guinea pig or cavy. In German: *Meerschweinchen.* Spanish: *conejillos de Indias.* French: *Cobaye.* Italian: *Porcellino d'India.* Japanese: *Tenjiku nezumi, marumotto.* No matter how you say it, these little whistling guys are cute! Here you'll find a cavy care FAQ, plus loads of photos so you'll be able to tell a lemon agouti from a silver one.

http://www.mpiz-koeln.mpg.de/~stueber/cavia/
cavia.html

Bring your shovel and meet me in the TREASURE AND TREASURE-HUNTING section.

Guinea Pigs on the Net

We love this page, and not just because of the "surfing guinea pig" pictures. There is a pet cavy care FAQ, plus links to other guinea pig pages and loads of "family portraits" of beloved "pigs" everywhere. This pig page is on a server in Italy.

http://cezanne.ing.unico.it/carlo/cavie.html

RMCA Home Page

Move over, Mickey—it's the Rat and Mouse Club of America (RMCA)! These pages are absolutely stuffed with more information and resources about mice and rats than you can ever imagine. Show standards, photos, pet info—this site is a pack rat's dream come true.

http://www.rmca.org/

VARIOUS ANIMALS

Adam's Fox Box II

When Fox went out on a chilly night, it was probably heading to this home page. Learn to fox trot, view some great fox photos, and read stories, songs, and poems about foxes. Links off the "fox fringe" have not been checked, and the fox hunting section is not for the sensitive.

http://tavi.acomp.usf.edu/foxbox/

From another galaxy? Learn about Earth in the ASTRONOMY—SOLAR SYSTEM AND PLANETS area!

Bat Conservation International Top Page

Did you know that the world's smallest mammal is the bumblebee bat? It weighs less than a penny does. Nearly 1,000 different kinds of bats account for almost 25 percent of all mammal species. Most bats are very good to have around. One little brown bat can catch 600 mosquitoes in just one hour. Visit this site to learn more about bats and bat houses, or stop in at North America's largest urban bat colony at <http://www.batcon.org/congress.html>.

http://www.batcon.org/

Official House Rabbit Society Home Page

"Wanted: A patient human with a sense of humor who spends a lot of time at home and doesn't mind hanging out on the floor with me. I am a bunny rabbit in need of a good home. I am inquisitive, sociable, litterbox-trained, and would make a wonderful companion for the right person. I need to be protected from predators, poisons, temperature extremes, electrical cords, and rough handling. I may even purr when I am happy. Stop by to find out what life would be like if you adopted me. Please hurry, my friends and I need your help!" The House Rabbit Society has rabbits for adoption all over the U.S. You'll also find out a lot about rabbit care and handling, so hop on over!

http://www.rabbit.org/

The Wonderful Skunk and Opossum Page

What would you do if your dog got sprayed by a skunk? Does a tomato juice bath really work? Sort of, but it may turn your dog pink for a while! You can also try a newer remedy, involving hydrogen peroxide, baking soda, and liquid soap; the recipe is here. There's advice on keeping skunks as pets, plus loads of lore on both skunks and opossums. Opossums are marsupials, meaning they carry their babies in a pouch. Another little-known fact is that a possum has 50 teeth—more than any other North American mammal.

http://elvis.neep.wisc.edu/~firmiss/
   mephitis-didelphis.html

A B C D E F G H I J K L **M** N O P Q R S T U V W X Y Z

What causes the distinctive odor of skunks?

About a century ago, T.B. Aldritch published his analysis, which said that it was primarily 1-Butanethiol (also known as n-Butyl Mercaptan). Many books still think Aldritch got it right. However, a 1990 analysis of the volatile components of skunk musk reveals it's actually made of seven chemicals. The **Wonderful Skunk and Opossum Page** *reports: "One component had never before been seen in nature and another had never been reported anywhere (natural or man-made), yet none of them were 1-Butanethiol!"*

Did times change or did skunks?

The World Wide Raccoon Web

Who's that bandit prying off the lid of your garbage can? It's a family of raccoons! Their nimble paws, black masks, and long, ringed tails make them unmistakable. Visit this home page to meet a true fan of raccoons and their natural—and unnatural—history. You'll find lots of photos, legends, and links, and you can read the incredible story of how one raccoon saved a student's life at Cornell University!

http://www.loomcom.com/raccoons/

Well-informed lizards, snakes, and other herps read the REPTILES resources.

WOLVES AND DOG FAMILY

Desert Moon's Wolf Page

Wolves are large, powerful, wild canines that depend on large prey, such as deer, elk, moose, and bison, for survival. Some of their prey weigh more than 1,000 pounds! The wolf has powerful jaws, capable of exerting about 1,500 pounds per square inch, or about twice that of the domestic dog. It is a highly social animal, generally living within the same pack for most, if not all, of its life. To learn more about wolf natural history, lore, and legend, visit this page—and listen for the howling wolves.

http://www.scs.unr.edu/~timb/desertm.html

Welcome to the Wolf HomePage

Imagine this: You are on your way home, and you decide to take a shortcut through the woods. As you enter the forest, the night gets darker. You start hearing things. Suddenly, you hear an animal howling nearby. You're sure it's a wolf, and you're convinced it is getting closer. Should you be afraid of wolves? No! In fact, wolves are very shy around people and try very hard to avoid them. They do not eat people. Also, wolves will howl any time of the day, but they are most often heard at night, when they are most active. Wolves will howl to defend their territory or to reunite pack members. And they will howl whether the moon is full or not! Visit this page and learn more about wolf communication and how wolves live.

http://www.usa.net/WolfHome/

MATH AND ARITHMETIC

Brain Teasers

If you're looking for some cool puzzles to stretch your brain cells, try this site. Every week you'll find new brainteasers, arranged by grade level. Typical puzzles include map reading, word problems, and puzzles that require a genuinely different outlook. Stumped? If you need a clue, the solutions are provided.

http://www.hmco.com/hmco/school/math/brain/

Chapters of the MegaMath Book

Kids from 9 to 90 will have hours of fun playing the thinking games here, which involve flat and topological geometry as well as other math and logical concepts. Everything is presented in a colorful, simplified manner, so you may be surprised by the complexity of thought that is needed for some of these games. The Most Colorful Math of All, Games on Graphs (which can be played on a table or playground), Algorithms and Ice Cream for All, and The Hotel Infinity are some of the activities awaiting you here.

http://www.c3.lanl.gov/mega-math/workbk/
   contents.html

NET FILES

What are HOUSEBUN-L, EXOTIC-L, and SMLDOG-L?

Answer: Nope, not a new rap group! They are all mailing lists for animal lovers. One is about bunnies, one is about birds, and one's about small dogs. Can you guess which is which? You'll find the answers at http://netvet.wustl.edu/e-zoo.htm

CTC's Trigonometry Explorer

This site offers a few Java demos from a larger CD-ROM about trigonometry. The easy-to-use demos include a little game of measuring angles with a protractor as well as a brief introduction to angles and their functions and pi. There is a bit on sextants, navigation, and latitude and longitude, too.

http://www.cogtech.com/EXPLORER/

Math Forum: Student Center

Part of a larger forum devoted to geometry, this page focuses on links that could be useful or of interest to students. Lots of games, projects, and downloadable software can be found here. Most interesting is the High School/Elementary Partnership program, which allows high school kids to act as Math Mentors for younger kids. There is also a Problem of the Week and an Internet Hunt, where you can search for answers to math trivia on the Net. In addition, there is a whole archive of math tricks so you can beat a calculator anytime you want!

http://forum.swarthmore.edu/students/

The Math Forum - Ask Dr. Math

Mom and Dad don't understand your math homework; neither does your best friend. But you can ask Dr. Math! You'll enjoy finding out the answers to some of the questions that kids have already asked Dr. Math, for instance: Can one infinity be larger than another? Why can't you divide a number by zero?

http://forum.swarthmore.edu/dr.math/dr-math.html

COUNTING
The Abacus

As early as 500 B.C., the Chinese were using calculators! Not battery or solar ones, as we have today. An abacus has a graceful hardwood frame, divided into upper and lower decks. Within these decks are beads, representing numbers, which may be moved up and down thin bamboo rods. You can perform addition, subtraction, multiplication, and division on an abacus. To learn how to use one, try this site. There are also directions on how to make your own abacus out of Lego blocks.

http://www.ee.ryerson.ca:8080/~elf/abacus/

Surf, and you shall become empowered (or wet).

A B C D E F G H I J K L M N O P Q R S T U V W X Y Z

A
B
C
D
E
F
G
H
I
J
K
L
M
N
O
P
Q
R
S
T
U
V
W
X
Y
Z

Blue Dog Can Count

Painter George Rodrigue's famous character, Blue Dog, has appeared in paintings, books, and an animated film. Now she will solve simple math problems for you! Simply enter the problem on this page, then listen to Blue Dog bark out the answer. Actually, your browser will download and play a sound file of Blue Dog—the more barks, the longer it will take to load. Make sure your cat isn't around!

http://kao.ini.cmu.edu:5550/bdf.html

Print A Googolplex

Mathematician Edward Kasner's nine-year-old nephew coined the name for a very large number. That number—ten to the power of 100, otherwise written as a one with a hundred zeroes trailing it—was named a *googol*. While this was a very large number indeed, perfect for trotting out at parties to impress people, another mathematician was unimpressed and came up with something even more immense: *googolplex*, a 10 to the power of googol. This page examines exactly what this incredibly huge number is, and it explains why no computer of today could ever print out something that large. You'll find a downloadable program here that will store a much-abbreviated version of a googolplex in about ten hours on a 10-gigabyte hard drive. The program is only 1,235 bytes in size and is triple-zipped so your Web browser won't try to unpack it automatically. Be the first (and probably the last) on your block to have your very own pet googolplex!

http://www.uni-frankfurt.de/~fp/Tools/Googool.html

The world's smallest abacus

Consider this tiny abacus. It is made up of molecules of carbon moved across a copper surface one at a time. If you use a soccer ball to represent the size of one of these molecules, the pointer that moves them would have to be as tall as the Eiffel Tower! View a movie of this abacus in action here, and say you saw it on the Net.

http://www.zurich.ibm.com/News/Abacus/

FORMULAS AND CONSTANTS
Appendix F: Weights and Measures

You'll find a lot more about this topic in the "Reference Works" section of this book. Still, we thought you'd find some of this Central Intelligence Agency resource interesting. For example, you've heard of megabytes (1,000,000 bytes) of hard drive space, right? The next step is a gigabyte (1,000,000,000 bytes), but did you know the next largest threshold is a terabyte (1,000,000,000,000 bytes)? And after that, well, we can't count that high, but this site says it's a petabyte (1,000,000,000,000,000 bytes). A petabyte of hard disk storage: bliss!

http://www.odci.gov/cia/publications/95fact/
  appendf.html

MATHMANIA

Did you know there are a number of math problems that have never been solved? Paul Erdös, one of the greatest mathematical minds of the century, has challenged young people to help come up with the solutions! The areas include background information on the unsolved problems and the mathematicians who originally posed them.

http://www.csc.uvic.ca/~mmania/

Pi Mathematics

What good is pi anyway? This page answers that question and provides activities to help you learn about this most interesting mathematical constant. The Indiana legislature once voted to make the value of pi equal to 3.2. This was hailed as a "new mathematical truth." The Senate, however, indefinitely postponed its vote on the Act! You can get the full story at <http://www.ts.umu.se/~olletg/pi/indiana.html>.

http://www.ncsa.uiuc.edu/edu/RSE/RSEorange/
  buttons.html

For happy hedgehogs see PETS AND PET CARE.

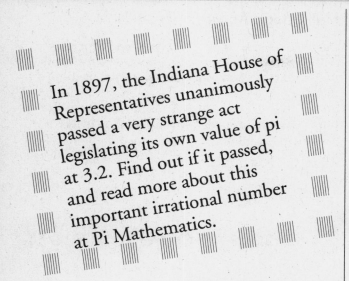

In 1897, the Indiana House of Representatives unanimously passed a very strange act legislating its own value of pi at 3.2. Find out if it passed, and read more about this important irrational number at Pi Mathematics.

The Ridiculously Enhanced Pi Page

Every March 14, at 1:59 P.M., the Exploratorium museum celebrates Pi Day. Get it? The value of Pi to a few decimal places is 3.14159! This irrational celebration happens to coincide with Albert Einstein's birthday. Read about the ceremonial addition of a pi bead to the strand (they are up to 1,600 decimal places) and other events that make San Francisco a unique place to live. There are also plenty of links to places where pi is elevated to new heights of acclaim by its many fans around the world.

http://www.exploratorium.edu/learning_studio/pi/

FRACTALS
The Fractal Microscope

This page explains the Fractal Microscope, a tool devised by the National Center for Supercomputing Applications, which enables schools to link to supercomputers via the Internet. This procedure allows schools to run fractal-generating programs much faster than can be done with a stand-alone desktop computer. The ideas behind fractals are clearly explained here, and a number of images are presented, including a group designed by students at an Illinois elementary school.

http://www.ncsa.uiuc.edu/Edu/Fractal/
  Fractal_Home.html

Sprott's Fractal Gallery

What is a "Julia set," a "strange attractor," or an "iterated function system"? They are all math equations that generate beautiful fractal images. A *fractal drawing* is the picture a computer makes as it maps out one of these equations. Sprott's Gallery includes sample programs to download and run on your computer so you can see fractals for yourself. There is an FAQ section and also lots of cool fractal pictures to download. Don't miss the animated GIF attractors!

http://sprott.physics.wisc.edu/fractals.htm

Is there order in chaos?
Discover the wonders of the Mandelbrot set.

Check out the fractals created daily using a program from the book Strange Attractors, and Quadratic Map Basins *at Sprott's Fractal Gallery.*

GEOMETRY
The Fibonacci Numbers and the Golden Section

Leonardo of Pisa, Italy, was known as Fibonacci, the son of Bonacci. He was the greatest European mathematician of his time. In 1202, he wrote a book introducing the Hindu-Arabic number system to Europe. That is the base ten number system we use today, including the decimal point and zero. He also wrote about a sequence of numbers that could be found over and over again in nature. These later became known as *Fibonacci numbers,* and they describe the spirals of pine cones and the leaf growth patterns of plants. You can learn more about Fibonacci and his numbers here as well as investigate where they appear in art, architecture, science, math, and nature. Closely related is The Golden Section, and you will see how it is used in everything from origami to flags of the world.

http://www.mcs.surrey.ac.uk/Personal/R.Knott/
  Fibonacci/fib.html

A
B
C
D
E
F
G
H
I
J
K
L
M
N
O
P
Q
R
S
T
U
V
W
X
Y
Z

A B C D E F G H I J K L **M** N O P Q R S T U V W X Y Z

The Geometry Center Welcome Page

If you're looking for interactive geometry, you've come to the right place. You can get the directions for building the world's largest 20-sided icosahedron for your room at <*http://www.geom.umn.edu/docs/ education/build-icos/*>. Or perhaps you'd prefer manipulating some of the Java or other Web-based geometric drawing programs. You can also download many of these to play on your own computer. One of our favorites is KaleidoTile for the Mac, which lets you create geometric figures you've never heard of before (fortunately, a voice tells you what they are). The interactive "math you can manipulate" programs have big names, but don't let that put you off. Get into them, and have fun with the unique drawing tools!

http://www.geom.umn.edu/

Math Tessellations

You may not know the word tessellation, but you've seen the results of it before. Ever seen those M. C. Escher drawings with repeating geometrical patterns, where a fish turns into a bird? That's tessellation! (If you have not seen these before, check Sky and Water I at <*http://www.texas.net/escher/gallery/exhbt1.html*>.) But what does it have to do with math? Look at the tessellation art done by students at Highland School; then you can download a Tesselmania demo and try it out yourself! These students live in Libertyville, Illinois.

http://www.mcs.net/~highland/tess/tess.html

MAGIC SQUARES AND TRICKS

Magic Squares

Magic squares are those pesky little grid puzzles that require you to fill in the boxes with numbers that add up the same in every direction. Visitors to this site not only will find out what a magic square is, and generate odd-numbered squares with a click, but also will find out the amazingly simple solution for creating and solving their own. With a little practice, you can mystify your friends by easily writing out magic squares with any odd number per side! Next, try a magic square word puzzle; the examples here are amazing.

http://www.auburn.edu/~harshec/WWW/ MagicSquare.html

Mathemagic Activities

Put one end of a rope in each hand and tie a knot without dropping the rope. Or amaze your friends with card tricks and other stunts. It's not magic; it's math!

http://www.scri.fsu.edu/~dennisl/CMS/activity/ math_magic.html

MODELS AND MINIATURES

Miniatures WWW Archive

Maybe you like war game miniatures. Maybe you like collecting and painting them. Maybe you even like playing with them. See the pictures of some very detailed models, check out the painting tips, and learn the moves for your favorite game. It's all here!

http://www.cabm.rutgers.edu/~hooper/miniatures/ miniatures.html

Scale Models: Front Page

Did you know that an old dental pick is great for cleaning up filler and carving plastic when you're building a model? It feels great to know you started with pieces, then put it together, painted it, and finished it off yourself. It doesn't matter if you like model ships, vehicles, figures, or fighter planes; it's all assembled here. Find out what new kits are available, and read reviews before you buy them. Learn how to build your model from the excellent online beginner's course. Get building!

http://www.clever.net/dfk/

Read any good Web sites lately?

NET FILES

How much water does the average Canadian use in a day?

Answer: The average Canadian uses 340 liters (about 90 gallons) of water per day. Think about how much water that is. It's about 1.5 bathtubs full! Imagine all the people in the world using that much water each and every day. That's a lot! What can you do to help? Read about some good water saving tips at http://www.cciw.ca/glimr/metadata/water-wise-pamphlets/intro.html

Welcome to the Testors Web Site!

When you're building a model, chances are you'll want to paint it. You'll need to stock up on forest green, chrome yellow, and metallic flake, or maybe olive drab, flat black, and candy apple red. And you may choose to use Testors paints. This site gives extensive tips and tricks for painting and cementing like a pro. There is also a gallery of superb models—finished using Testors materials, of course!

http://www.testors.com/

AIRPLANES
EAST COAST MODEL CENTER - Introduction to R/C Aircraft

Flying your own airplane might have to wait until you're just a little older—unless you have a radio-controlled model airplane. Then you can fly! Here you can find out how to get started in this fun hobby. Even if you already fly, there's so much information that you're bound to learn something new. It starts with practical material about the planes, and then covers everything from building them to flying them. There are extensive sections on the parts, the words that the hobbyists use, and the specialized accessories. So what are you waiting for? Prepare for takeoff!

http://www.peinet.pe.ca/ECMC/document/intair.html

All You hear is a faint buzzing.

Then, suddenly, a model airplane flies right over your head!

Models fly at anywhere between 20 and 150 mph, although the average speed is about 40 to 60 mph. You need space to fly these sleek planes, and you need expert advice to get started in the hobby. Come in for a landing at EAST COAST MODEL CENTER - Introduction to R/C Aircraft.

RAILROADS

Lionel Home Page

The Lionel Manufacturing Company was founded in New York on September 5, 1900. In 1901, they sold animated display trains called "The Electric Express" to draw customers to store windows. A year later, they published a 16-page catalog, but it wasn't until 1906 that their product line included steam locomotives, trolleys, passenger cars, freight cars, and a caboose. Since then, Lionel has become a name famous in model railroading. You can check out their history, catalogs, cool accessories (we liked the "Plutonium Purple" toxic tanker, but there is no accounting for taste), and tips for hobbyists.

http://www.lionel.com/

Expect a miracle in RELIGION!

A
B
C
D
E
F
G
H
I
J
K
L
M
N
O
P
Q
R
S
T
U
V
W
X
Y
Z

A
B
C
D
E
F
G
H
I
J
K
L
M
N
O
P
Q
R
S
T
U
V
W
X
Y
Z

Model Railroad Information

Everything from garden trains—larger than O scale (1:48) but smaller than the trains that are large enough to ride on—to tiny Z gauge (1:220) trains is collected here. Want a track layout that does more than go around a Christmas tree? It's here. Painting scenic backgrounds or sculpting your own figures to dress up the stations will be a breeze with these lessons. All aboard—the track's clear as far as you can see on the Net!

http://www.cse.ucsd.edu/users/bowdidge/railroad/
    rail-models.html

ROCKETRY

Irving Family Web Pages: Rocketry

Thinking about blasting off into the wide world of model rocketry? At this site, you can learn about it, see some rockets, and explore this exciting hobby. There's basic information on small, large, and high-powered rockets and some great picture samples to give you a look at what you can do. Now that you're this far, you may want more, so plenty of links to other rocketry resources are listed. Just consider this your launchpad to model rocketry!

http://www.irving.org/rocketry/

rec.models.rockets FAQ Table of Contents

Did you know that model rockets can actually take off? Here are the answers to many questions you might have about model rocketry, including basic questions such as: How do you do it? Where do you do it? Is it dangerous? Is it legal? Or, you may be experienced in model rocketry, and your questions are more like these: Where can I find engines that are discontinued? How can I prevent body tube damage from the shock cord? Should I invest in a piston launcher? Come on in, too! This site has categorized questions and answers for every level of rocket enthusiast. Now, should we use a thermalite fuse...?

http://www.dtm-corp.com/~sven/rockets/
    rmrfaq.toc.html

MONEY

The Buck Book

Klutz Press publishes lots of very cool books (which are described here in their catalog), and one of the most fun is *The Buck Book*. It teaches you fun things to do with a U.S. dollar bill. For example, would you like to know how to fold a dollar to make a ring you can wear on your finger? The directions are here!

http://www.klutz.com/treefort/buck.html

Currency Comparison

Can you believe there's a project on the Internet dedicated to finding out just how much food you can buy for five dollars? And they mean you! The idea is to compare the value of your five dollars to the same amount of money in other countries. It's fun, and the interactive currency conversion chart lets you compare different money from all over the globe. If you're not from Albania, you might still be interested in just how much lunch the *lek* (Albanian monetary unit) will buy!

http://www.wimmera.net.au/CurrComp/
    CurrComp.html

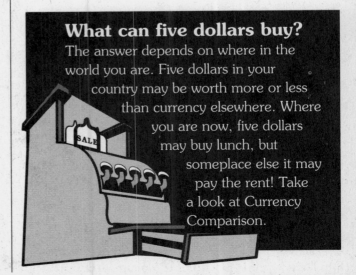

What can five dollars buy?
The answer depends on where in the world you are. Five dollars in your country may be worth more or less than currency elsewhere. Where you are now, five dollars may buy lunch, but someplace else it may pay the rent! Take a look at Currency Comparison.

Get Fiscal

How does a checkbook work? How do you buy stocks, and why would you want to? What is the stock market, anyway? What's a contract and why do professional sports teams always want one? And how do you convince your mom that just because she got a $5 a week allowance when she was a kid doesn't mean you should get the same amount? Five dollars today just doesn't have the same buying power it did back then. Learn about the consumer price index—it may help you raise your allowance!

http://www.ingenius.com/product/cyberhd/youth/
   fred/fred.htm

Money Curriculum Unit

Money: you see it every day. You probably have some in your pocket right now. But how much do you know about its history and how it's made? Recently, the government has made many changes in U.S. money to make it harder to be copied. See what the new tricks are to stop counterfeit cash. And if you don't know what all the symbols on U.S. bills mean and whose portrait is on each one, then you will by the time you finish *spending* some time at this site!

http://woodrow.mpls.frb.fed.us/econed/curric/
   money.htm

NOVA Online/Secrets of Making Money

This is a fascinating look at the new security features built into the U.S. $100 bill. You'll discover color-shifting ink made possible by metallic flakes mixed into it. Check the special engraving techniques used to foil counterfeiters, as well as the special items embedded into the paper the bill is printed on. These include the red and blue fibers, the microprinted security thread, and other items too secret to mention in a public book. But you can read about them on the Web! Then see if you can spot the bogus bill in the online quiz.

http://www.pbs.org/wgbh/pages/nova/moolah/

Olsen Currency Converter

When is a dollar not a dollar? Wait a minute! Where did you get that dollar? Is that a U.S. dollar, or an Australian dollar, or a Namibian dollar? If it's a Namibian dollar, then it is likely worth less than half the U.S. dollar. The Australian dollar is worth more than the Namibian dollar but is still not worth as much as the U.S. dollar. Confused yet? What about the German mark, the Japanese yen, or the Slovenian tolar? Whoa! This stuff can get confusing. Luckily, at this site, with just a couple of clicks you can compare 164 currencies all over the world. Try it!

http://www.olsen.ch/cgi-bin/exmenu

NET FILES

What do comedians, animals, lost articles, and snake bite victims all have in common?

Answer: They all have a patron saint! St. Vitus takes care of comedians, St. Francis of Assisi looks after animals, St. Anthony of Padua may be a help with lost articles, and St. Hilary comforts snake bite victims. Here's the page where you can find these saints and more

http://
www.catholic.org/
saints/patron.html

**OPTICAL ILLUSIONS:
now you see them,
now you don't!**

A
B
C
D
E
F
G
H
I
J
K
L
M
N
O
P
Q
R
S
T
U
V
W
X
Y
Z

A
B
C
D
E
F
G
H
I
J
K
L
M
N
O
P
Q
R
S
T
U
V
W
X
Y
Z

Printing money

It takes 65 distinct steps to print a U.S. dollar bill. You can follow the process here at *Newton's Apple* and also learn how to make and print your own "pretend" money!

http://ericir.syr.edu/Projects/Newton/12/Lessons/
money.html

Street Cents Online

Young people make money, save money, and spend money, just like everyone else! But sometimes there just isn't much advice for young people about handling their money. Do you spend money on entertainment, sports, music, and food? What's the deal on using horse shampoo on people? Does Duracell really outlast the Energizer bunny? All of these topics and more are covered by *Street Cents,* a popular Canadian television show. And now it's online in an informative and fun Web page. *Spend* some time here!

http://www.screen.com/streetcents.html

The part-time job in the newspaper sounds good, since you need way to make some spending money. The boss says "Let's try you out for one afternoon and see if if you can do the job." That sounds like a fair request, but should you be paid for the tryout? Does it depend on whether you get the job? What are your rights? Young people have money concerns too, and Street Cents Online is worth "spending" some time to visit. It makes "cents"!

U.S. National Debt Clock

Did you know that if you're an American citizen, you owe the government about $20,000? That is currently every citizen's share of the national debt, and that is a lot of weekly allowance money! What's the national debt? The U.S. government spends more money than it takes in. When this happens, it has to borrow money from someplace else. The amount it owes to other sources is called the *national debt.* This site explains more about how this happened and what the government is trying to do to pay off the debt and keep this from happening again. Canada's also got a national debt clock, which is linked here, too.

http://www.brillig.com/debt_clock/

MONSTERS

Alt.fan.dragons: information & files on dragons

There are real dragons, you know! The Komodo dragon is the world's largest lizard, and it lives (among other places) on Komodo Island, which is part of Indonesia. Other dragons live in the fantasy worlds of literature, lore, and legend. This home page celebrates all kinds of dragons. You'll find dragon art, stories, and riddles. Dragons love to ask people riddles. Here is one, from J. R. R. Tolkien's *The Hobbit*:

It cannot be seen, cannot be felt,
Cannot be heard, cannot be smelt,
It lies behind stars and under hills,
And empty holes it fills.
It comes first and follows after,
Ends life, kills laughter.

A parental advisory goes on this site because we haven't explored all the links, and some fantasy dragon art is graphic. (The riddle's answer: Darkness.)

http://icecube.acf-lab.alaska.edu/~fxdlk/

Become one with the Net.

Real surfers get their feet wet in OUTDOOR RECREATION.

Chupacabra Home Page

The rumors started in southern Texas, then in Puerto Rico, Miami, New Jersey, even Oregon. Word was out that farm animals were dying—all left with no blood and mysterious puncture wounds. Some claimed seeing a strange creature in the vicinity; they called it the Chupacabra. Fact or strange fiction? You decide. Take a look at this page.

http://www.princeton.edu/~accion/chupa.html

Nessie, the Loch Ness Monster

Mark Chorvinsky has put together a remarkable Web site exploring the controversies surrounding Scotland's world-famous Loch Ness Monster. Nessie, as the lake monster is affectionately known, has been the subject of numerous credible sightings over the past 60-plus years, even though extensive scientific efforts to track it down have been a lesson in frustration. This page presents well-researched and clearly written essays on the sightings, the searchers, and the debunkers, as well as investigations into other, lesser-known lake monsters from around the world, such as Canada's Ogopogo, spotted regularly since 1926 in Lake Okanagan in British Columbia.

http://www.cais.net/strangemag/nessie.home.html

You've heard of Nessie—the Loch Ness Monster. But have you ever heard of Champ? It was first spotted in July 1883 cavorting in New York's Lake Champlain. This was 50 years before Nessie was first seen! Since then, Champ has been sighted over 240 times. Read more about Champ and other lake monsters at **Nessie, the Loch Ness Monster** home page.

Western Bigfoot Society/Internet Virtual Bigfoot Conference

These folks take their Sasquatches seriously! Back issues of their newsletter, *The Track Record,* which include plenty of up-to-date Bigfoot sightings, are available here, as well as information about the ongoing Digital Bigfoot Conference. Links to other Bigfoot sites are also included. One of the best is The Bigfoot Research Project, which coordinates many of the efforts to gather solid evidence of the existence of this large, hairy, elusive creature. A caution to parents: Other links (in the "Skeptics" area) lead to places you may want to preview.

http://www.teleport.com/~caveman/wbs.shtml

A Yeti Tale: Introduction

The Abominable Snowman has been spotted high up in the Himalaya Mountains by a number of respectable mountaineers. To folks in Nepal and Tibet, he's known as Yeti, where he has been sighted countless times for hundreds of years. If Yeti does exist, chances are the creature is not possessed of magical powers, although legends about it persist. Read some of those legends here.

http://www.dzogchen.org/yeti/ytale1.html

MOVIES

AMPAS - The Academy of Motion Picture Arts and Sciences

If you're a movie fanatic, don't miss the Official Interactive Guide to the Academy Awards, designed to help you explore Oscar nominees and winners, past and present. There are pictures and lots of information on all of them. You may be surprised to find out that the Academy of Motion Picture Arts and Sciences does a lot more than just give out awards: they have an amazing movie history library and sponsor Student Academy Awards, designed to recognize excellence among college students enrolled in film courses throughout the United States.

http://www.ampas.org/ampas/

A B C D E F G H I J K L M N O P Q R S T U V W X Y Z

A
B
C
D
E
F
G
H
I
J
K
L
M
N
O
P
Q
R
S
T
U
V
W
X
Y
Z

Babe's World: Hoggett Farm

Babe is a pig who marches to the beat of a different drummer—he wants to be a sheepdog! Find out about the movie production and see some video clips from the film, which is based on Dick King-Smith's children's book, *The Sheep-Pig*. There is also a sheep-herding game, although we could not get it to work properly.

http://www.uip.com/babe/farm.html

Hollywood Online

Parental advisory: this site lists all movies, not just "G-rated" ones. This is the place for the latest on all the hottest movies. It's got all the video, sound bites, pictures, and production notes you could possibly want, but what makes it really special is the stuff you can download and keep to play around with later. For many movies, you can download an interactive multimedia kit—a complete package of goodies about the movie. Often, there are neat interactive games for Macintosh or Windows systems. The *Goldeneye* game, for example, challenges you to put an exploding pen's pieces back in their correct order. The game that comes with *The American President* kit has you try to figure out which gift will win the heart of the President's new love interest. Don't miss the Movietunes area for information and audio from recent soundtrack albums!

http://www.hollywood.com/

The Indian in the Cupboard

A toy comes to life after being put inside a magic cupboard, and amazing things begin to happen! How did this Iroquois youth from the 1800s get transported to a nine-year-old boy's room of today? Even more curious: how did they make a grown man look like he was only three inches tall? Find out how they did it, download clips from the movie, and learn about Native American lore.

http://www.paramount.com/Indian.html

lion king home page

Young lion cub Simba prepares to follow in his father's footsteps to become king of the vast African plain. After his father's death, Simba blames himself and runs away. Will he come back to the Pride Lands and take up his destiny in the "Circle of Life"? Find out at this site, with music and clips from the popular movie.

http://www2.disney.com/DisneyPictures/LionKing/

NET FILES

Has a bird ever won a military medal?

Answer: At least one has. Cher Ami, a carrier pigeon, served in World War I and was awarded the French Croix de Guerre with Palm for his heroic service between the forts of Verdun. He died in 1919 as a result of his battle wounds. He was one of 600 birds owned and flown by the U.S. Army Signal Corps in France during World War I. His body was mounted and preserved and is now part of the Smithsonian Institution collections in Washington, D.C. At http://www.si.edu/resource/faq/cherami.htm you can read more about the exploits of this brave bird and the final message he carried.

MovieLink | Home

Okay, let's go to the movies—but which one? And where's it playing? If you live in a major American city, the best place to find out is here at MovieLink, which calls itself "America's online source for movie information." Type in your city or ZIP code and find out what's playing near you and what the show times are. From there, you can read movie reviews and even let your family check out the Parents' Guide ("Look, Mom, it's rated PG!"), so they can put their stamp of approval on your choice. Once you've settled on a movie you'd like to see, you can reserve your tickets online. If you loved the movie, you can download posters and movie trailers as electronic souvenirs.

http://www.777film.com/

MOVIEWEB: Mighty Morphin Power Rangers

Power Rangers Tommy, Kimberly, Billy, Rocky, Aisha, and Adam have been busy practicing their martial art moves for their next battle with Ivan Ooze and the evil he is cooking up. This site is dated, but the movie stills and trailers are still there. The best Power Rangers page, at *<http://ic.www.media.mit.edu/Personal/manny/power/>*, is written up in the "Television" section of this book.

http://movieweb.com/movie/powrangr/

Pocahontas home

This is the story of an independent Native American girl and her relationship with Captain John Smith in Jamestown, Virginia, in 1607. Download the film clips and coloring pages. Don't forget to use your "Colors of the Wind" crayons!

http://www2.disney.com/DisneyPictures/Pocahontas/

The Sun never sets on the Internet.

Welcome to Toy Story

This is Disney's first completely computer-generated movie. What happens in Andy's room once he gets a new toy? This exciting adventure features the voices of Tim Allen as Buzz LightYear—Space Ranger, Annie Potts as Bo Peep, and Tom Hanks as Woody the Cowboy. Download coloring books, games, computer screen wallpaper, icons, film clips, and more!

http://www.disney.com/DisneyVideos/ToyStory/

REVIEWS

Dove Family Approved Movies and Videos

Free Willy 2: The Adventure Home, The Baby-Sitter's Club, and *Babe* are just three of the movies that have won the Dove Foundation's seal of approval for being "family friendly." So far, this group, whose motto is "Families everywhere deserve a choice," has approved over 1,400 movies. If you still can't decide what to see, just fill out a simple online form and search by viewer age group or type of movie, including action, adventure, classic, and lots more.

http://www.dove.org/dove/dove.htm

The Movie Mom's Guide to Family Movies and Videos

Nell Minow is an author and a critic, but most importantly she is a mom. She calls herself "Movie Mom" and gives lots of advice to kids and families on the best movies to see. According to Movie Mom, no one should grow up (or be a grown-up) without seeing *The Muppet Movie, Tom Thumb, The Absent-Minded Professor,* and *Captains Courageous,* among others. Take a look at this site to read her reviews and to find out other movies you must see. The authors of a new book called *The Practical Guide to Practically Everything* liked her opinions so much they included them in their book!

http://pages.prodigy.com/moviemom/moviemom.html

A
B
C
D
E
F
G
H
I
J
K
L
M
N
O
P
Q
R
S
T
U
V
W
X
Y
Z

A
B
C
D
E
F
G
H
I
J
K
L
M
N
O
P
Q
R
S
T
U
V
W
X
Y
Z

Welcome to the IMDb

Wow—this international volunteer effort covers over 95,000 movies! You can find info on the following: biographies of actors; plot summaries; character names; movie ratings; trivia; famous quotes from the movie; goofs and things that went wrong but didn't get cut out; sound tracks; filming locations; sequel/remake information; advertising tag lines; and Academy Award information. If the movie is based on a book, you'll get that information here too. Butter up some popcorn and enjoy this site!

http://us.imdb.com/welcome.html

Viewers around the world have voted *Star Wars* as their all-time favorite movie. Did you know part of it was filmed in Tunisia? The movie has a lot of famous mistakes in it, such as the scene in which a storm trooper hits his or her head on a door. To see famous quotes from the movie other than "Use the force, Luke!" and to learn lots of great trivia, be sure to check **Welcome to the IMDb**.

Mr. Spock agrees it is highly logical to want to know all about STAR TREK, STAR WARS, AND SPACE EPICS.

SOUNDS AND THEMES
IMDb Soundtracks Section Search

You loved a song you heard at the movies last night, but you have no idea what it's called or who sang it. Here's what you do: pop a word from the movie title into this searching machine to get all the details in a flash. You can do the same thing with your favorite group. We typed the word "Mozart" into the search box and found out his music has been in lots of movies, even *Operation Dumbo Drop!*

http://us.imdb.com/Search/soundtracks/

Newton's Apple: Movie Sound Effects.

Grab your rubber bands, sandpaper, popsicle sticks, and tape recorder and head over to this site to learn how to be a foley artist. *Foley artists* decide which movie sounds need to be fixed, replaced, or just improved a little. They even invent sounds nobody's ever heard before, like the sound of a dinosaur egg hatching. They're named after Jack Foley, a film sound pioneer from the days when talking pictures were first invented.

http://ericir.syr.edu/Projects/Newton/12/Lessons/ movisnd.html

Skywalker Sound

Learn how movie sound tracks are made from the pros at Skywalker Sound, where the famous sounds of the *Star Wars* movies, *Jurassic Park*, and *Toy Story* were made. One of Skywalker's specialties is creature sounds, like the ones made by Imperial Walkers, Chewbacca, and other aliens. To make these characters sound sad, happy, or scary, sound artists use everything from bicycle chains dropping on concrete to the voices of lots of different animals mixed together.

http://www.thx.com/thx/skywalker/skywalker.html

What TIME is it, anyway?

www.filmmusic.com: Music

Whether you're looking for movies with bagpipe music, the theme to *Jurassic Park* (watch out—it's 1.5 megabytes!), or music to shoot aliens by, this is the place. Movie music composers, collectors, and fans will find all the reviews, music clips, discussions, and guides they could ever possibly want at this site. External links have not been reviewed.

http://www.filmmusic.com/music/

STUDIOS AND PRODUCTION COMPANIES

MCA Home Entertainment Playroom

Kid's Playroom will keep your little sister entertained with lots of sights, sounds, and online games. She'll love the "Casper the Friendly Ghost" treasure hunt and the "Timmy the Tooth" interactive adventure. Make sure she doesn't find her way back into the movie previews section of this page without Mom or Dad, or another adult, to help guide her to other kid sites.

http://www.mca.com/home/playroom/

MUPPETS AND PUPPETS

MUPPET TREASURE ISLAND

The Muppets go on a treasure hunt. Join Jim Hawkins, Gonzo, Rizzo, Long John Silver, and, of course, Kermit as they travel the seas in their quest. Take the Statler and Waldorf tour that will (mis)guide you through movie clips and interviews. Read all about the puppeteers, production staff, crews, and filmmakers that make the story come alive. If you want to go on your own adventure, you can play the Muppet Treasure Island game and seek your own fortune. Click on the treasure map and check it out!

http://www.disney.com/DisneyVideos/
MuppetTreasure/

Muppets Home Page

Bill Sherman's unofficial page is about as close to an "official" site as there ever will be. All images, sounds, and scripts are here with permission from Jim Henson Productions, with episode guides for *The Muppet Show, Fraggle Rock, Dinosaurs,* and even *Sesame Street*! Look for press releases from Jim Henson Productions to be posted here and lots of lists and reviews.

http://www.ncsa.uiuc.edu/VR/BS/Muppets/
muppets.html

When Jim Henson started producing short television programs and commercials for a a local Washington, D.C. station back in the 1950s, he could not have dreamed what an international phenomenon his creations, the Muppets, would become. Visit the Muppets Home Page tribute to Kermit, Miss Piggy, Fozzie, and friends.

The Puppetry Home Page

Looking for a place to buy fake fur, foam rubber, and neoprene to build your own original puppets? Check the resources listed here. If your puppet-making aspirations are more along the old sock variety, you'll find links and patterns to help with that, too. Explore puppetry traditions around the world, from the Punch and Judy shows of France to the shadow puppetry of Asia. There are also links to ventriloquism resources on the Web, so you can learn to throw your voice in cyberspace, where no one can see your mouth move!

http://www-leland.stanford.edu/~rosesage/puppetry/
puppetry.html

Try actual reality.

A B C D E F G H I J K L **M** N O P Q R S T U V W X Y Z

A
B
C
D
E
F
G
H
I
J
K
L
M
N
O
P
Q
R
S
T
U
V
W
X
Y
Z

Stage Hand Puppets * Activity Page *

Puppet theater requires a stage, puppets, and a play. Read puppet plays other kids have written, or try writing your own and submitting it here. There are also lots of ideas and patterns for making puppets from scrap and other materials around your house. You'll find performance tips, hand-shadow directions, and even information on ventriloquism!

http://fox.nstn.ca/~puppets/activity.html

MUSIC AND MUSICIANS

CDnow : Main : Homepage

This is an online store, where you can get your parents to order cassettes and CDs. It's also the new home of the volunteer-built All Music Guide (AMG), which is a huge review archive for—guess what?—all music. You can search for albums by artist, title, or record label. This site also links to Real Audio files, so you can listen to some albums. A caution to parents: There are lots of artist home page and concert links.

http://cdnow.com/

The All Music Guide (AMG) will steer you to whatever music pleases you. Two hundred independent music and film writers evaluate albums and give short reviews. Whether you seek rap or rock, country or classical, you'll find it at CDnow : Main : Homepage.

Eyeneer Music Archives

Find links here to world music, contemporary classic, new jazz, and American music. Each link will keep you busy exploring. In the International Music Archive you'll find an abundance of photos, sound samples, and descriptions of instruments. You can see and hear a Chinese qin, or a Japanese shakahachi. Elsewhere, look for biographical information, photos, QuickTime videos, interviews, and information on new recordings.

http://www.eyeneer.com/

Instrumental Music Resource Page

Here's help for "students, parents, and teachers of Instrumental Music." It's a good gathering place for much musical information. Click on The Brass Page (Western Illinois University), and learn why it's not such a great idea to smile and play the trombone at the same time *<http://www.wiu.bgu.edu/users/mfham/ brass/tbnotes1.html>*. Try the Internet Resources for Brass Players. You'll find the French horn home page, as well as a site on Mahler Symphony recordings, the Classical Music Home Page, and others. Under "Instrumental Music Information" are a clickable trumpet, trombone, sax, clarinet, and flute. Each leads to a brief essay on instrument care, e-mail lists, embouchure, tips on technique, and links to home pages for the given instrument. The flute has an additional link to an extensive project on the history and practice of flute playing. And have you ever needed a great excuse for not practicing? Get inspiration from "Great Excuses" collected by music teachers over the years at *<http://www.fcasd.edu/ teachers/traugh/excuse.html>*.

http://www.fcasd.edu/teachers/traugh/imrp.html

> It's hard to remember, but mnemonic memory tricks are in WORDS.

K-12 Resources For Music Educators

You can show this page to your music teacher. Resources are collected in categories for band, orchestra, and choral music teachers, and there are links for classroom music teachers. The selection is really interesting for the rest of us, too. You'll find composer biographies, newsgroups, MIDI resources, and hints on how to really listen to music. There are also links to free piano lessons by Web, online sheet music, guitar tuning software, and lots more. We also liked one of the links from here, the Music Education Online page at <*http://www.geocities.com/Athens/2405/index.html*> for general excellence and being right on key!

http://www.isd77.k12.mn.us/resources/staffpages/
shirk/k12.music.html

NET FILES

If UFOs are real, how come no astronauts have ever reported seeing one?

Answer: Ah, but they have! Reports from 13 different astronauts are collected at http://ernie.bgsu.edu/~jzawodn/ufo/misc/astro-sightings.html
The truth is out there, and some of it may be at this page.

What's playing at the MOVIES?

Musi-Cal

So you want to go to a concert or a festival. You like acoustic music (or blues, or ska) and your dad is willing to travel up to ten miles from your home. Musi-Cal will pinpoint the very concert you seek. The site strives to provide easy access to current worldwide music information. They promise no weird pictures, no old information, no 200K graphics to download. Search by performer, city, venue, or event, or go to "Options" for a detailed search form. It includes artist(s), event, city, radius around city (up to 200 miles, or 400 kilometers), dates, venue, musical genres, and even keywords. You can also contribute concert information. There are sometimes links to performers' Web pages as well.

http://concerts.calendar.com

NARAS®: The National Academy of Recording Arts & Sciences, Inc.

Music is a universal language. Everybody likes music, whether it's pop sounds, rock and roll, rap, or R&B. Most music we listen to is recorded, either on tapes, CDs, the radio, or TV. The National Academy of Recording Arts & Sciences is an organization of recording specialists who vote on the best recordings each year. The winning recording artists receive an award called a Grammy. To see (and hear) who has won in the past and who is nominated for the upcoming awards, take a look at this page. It's the place to look if you like music!

http://www.grammy.com/index.html

San Francisco Symphony Index Page

This site has specific information about the San Francisco Symphony (tickets, concert hall, and so on), and it also has real Web value. You can meet some of the 106 musicians—you'll see what they look like, why they chose their instruments, who likes baseball, and what other kinds of music they like. The Web Links lead you to searchable archives of listservs, reference guides to composers, music, and recordings, and an array of other symphonic ensembles.

http://www.sfsymphony.org/

A
B
C
D
E
F
G
H
I
J
K
L
M
N
O
P
Q
R
S
T
U
V
W
X
Y
Z

A B C D E F G H I J K L **M** N O P Q R S T U V W X Y Z

VibeOnline - The Mammoth Music Meta-List

This site is like one of those nesting Russian dolls. Every link opens up a new world of music. Where else could you find Morris dancing, the San Francisco Symphony, and a sight and sound demo of different Renaissance consorts and instruments? The webmaster hopes to keep the site a relatively complete set of all music resources available. If you have an interest in Christian music—or Indian, or Russian, or reggae (pick your subject)—it's probably here. The pop/rock section is huge, with bands both well known and obscure. Also there are links to the home pages of specific bands and musicians, as well as reviews and "top 40" and other countdown charts. The links to specific instruments are very complete. For whatever information you need or want on any aspect of music, start here. A caution to parents: Outside links have not been viewed.

http://www.vibe.com/mmm/music.html

NET FILES

What do Julius Caeser, Annie Oakley, Betsy Ross, and Leonardo da Vinci have in common?

Answer: *According to the Chinese zodiac's 12-year cycle, these famous people were all born in the Year of the Monkey. The Chinese belief is that people born in the Year of the Monkey are very intelligent and are always well liked. Find out more at* http://pasture.ecn.purdue.edu/~agenhtml/agenmc/china/zmonkey.html

No lines at a virtual museum!

Welcome to Philomel Records!

You know what an optical illusion is: a picture that can look like several different things all at once. (If you don't know, check the "Optical Illusions" section in this book.) Are you ready for an audio illusion? Diana Deutsch's CD is called *Musical Illusions and Paradoxes*, and you can hear several samples at this Web site. Did you know that people hear sounds differently? Sometimes your brain can be tricked into hearing melodies that aren't really there. Sound impossible? Listen to the audio files here and see if you can identify the mystery tune.

http://www.philomel.com/

BRASS INSTRUMENTS

The Canadian Brass

A review in the *Columbus Dispatch* called this group "the best thing to happen to brass music since the invention of the spit valve" (Barbara Zuck). They play music from Bach to blues, and some say they put brass music on the map. Their witty arrangements, vast repertoire, and humorous commentary beguile their audiences. Here you'll find biographies of each member, a history of the group, and brass-related articles from the *New York Times* and other sources. You can read mostly glowing reviews, check out the popular, classical, and Christmas discographies, and find out about their line of brass instruments and arrangements.

http://www.canbrass.com/

The Home Page of the Trombone

A picture of the Three Stooges sets the stage nicely for this sometimes goofy page. Here you can explore the soul of the trombonist. Read about the 500 trombone players (over 6 times 76!) who descended upon Las Vegas for the 24th International Trombone Workshop in May 1995. Did you know there's an International Women's Trombone Choir? You'll find a picture here to prove it. There are also sound clips, a mouthpiece chart, and selected bibliographies. The Trombone-L listserv is a discussion list dedicated to "any aspect of the trombone"—even messy slide treatments. The archives are here, too. If you like what you read, sign on for daily reports from the Land of Trombone. The links include other brass Web sites, for example, trumpet, French horn, and euphonium.

http://www.missouri.edu/~cceric/

Trumpet Players' International Network

Trumpet players of the world, unite! At the TPIN site you'll find advice, lists of literature, facts about jazz and orchestral playing, and notes (so to speak) on improvisation. If you want a daily dose of trumpet lore, sign up on the e-mail Trumpet List. There's also an online chat server at this site. The graphics file includes pictures of performers such as Dizzy Gillespie as well as trumpets old and new. Go through the more than two dozen Web pages for individual trumpet players—some famous, some not. There's also a miscellaneous section on valve alignment, humor, performance anxiety, and trumpet myths. How do you get to Carnegie Hall? Practice, practice, practice—then stop, and read essays on practice routines you might try, written by famous performers and teachers. Even nontrumpeters can benefit from these specific ideas.

http://trumpet.dana.edu/~trumpet/

CHILDREN'S MUSIC

Children's Music List

Here you can find *mucho* info on children's performers, recordings, kids playing music, and where to order tapes and CDs. Run down all those links: Resources, Children's Musicians, Record Labels, Retail Outlets, Songbooks, and Children's Musical Theater. They'll lead you to yet more musical information!

http://www.cowboy.net/~mharper/Chmusiclist.html

Children's Music Web

Want to know when your favorite performer is coming to a town nearby? Looking for a radio station that just plays music for kids? Want to find some online songbooks? Check here for an extensive collection of links about all this and more.

http://www.childrensmusic.org/

"Use the source, Luke!" and look it up in REFERENCE WORKS.

The Judy and David Page

This Canadian duo started performing in 1993, and they recently had their first TV special. Are they the next Raffi(s)? Time will tell. In the meantime, they've put together a sweet home page. If you are in the audience when Judy and David perform, you'll find that every song they sing also has a part for you. Their online presence is similar. The Online Songbook includes the words (and some sound clips) of traditional children's songs and their original songs as well. After you listen to or sing "Alice the Camel," go to the coloring page, print out a picture of her, and color her to your liking.

http://judyanddavid.com/

CLASSICAL

BMG: Classics World

You know, there is a Beethoven other than the St. Bernard movie star (pant, pant, drool, drool). Here's where you find out when the other one lived and what he did. This is also the place to satisfy your raging curiosity about Early Music, the Romantic period, or what's happening today in classical music. "A Beginner's Guide to Classical Music" at <http://www.rcavictor.com/rca/hits/guide/cover.html> is an online music miniencyclopedia. It covers eras (no, not ears) and famous composers, with good graphics and solid information. You can get a little background on the composer of that new piece you're playing in orchestra this week.

http://www.classicalmus.com/

Classical Net Home Page

People new to classical music have two questions: Which pieces should I listen to? What are the best recordings of those pieces? This dense site answers both questions. The "List of Basic Repertoire" is a tutorial on styles and forms of music organized by period, from Medieval to Modern. You'll also learn about each composer. Then there are reviews of recommended CDs. There's even a "Composer Data" section, with birth dates, further links to home pages, lists of works, and more classical links. Classical music spans nearly a thousand years. This site will give you a good start at understanding it.

http://www.classical.net/

A B C D E F G H I J K L M N O P Q R S T U V W X Y Z

A
B
C
D
E
F
G
H
I
J
K
L
M
N
O
P
Q
R
S
T
U
V
W
X
Y
Z

Culturefinder: Composers' Biographies and Program Notes

If you're going to an orchestra or chamber music concert, take a look at this site. You'll find good biographical information on many famous classical composers, and maybe even the be able to read the story behind the piece you'll hear.

http://www.culturefinder.com/composers.htm

NET FILES

How deep in the ocean can fish live?

Answer: In 1960, two scientists in a submersible vehicle observed a foot-long type of flatfish swimming along. It was just taking a stroll at 35,800 feet deep—that's over six and a half miles down! Find out more fun fish facts at http://pathfinder.com/pathfinder/kidstuff/underwater/ and don't forget to bring your towel.

The J.S. Bach Home Page

The home page of J. S. Bach really does lead you to his home. Under "Biography," a clickable hypermap shows you the relatively limited geographical space he inhabited from 1685 to 1750. You can travel through time and space from Eisenach, Germany, where he was born, to Leipzig, Germany, where he died. Either click on the map or go from link to link in the right order. You'll see portraits of significant people and photos of buildings. Also, check the entry for his birth in the official birth registry in Eisenach. It's quite a time capsule! You'll also find directory information on his complete works here: by catalog number, category, instrument, and title. There is a similar listing for Bach recordings.

http://www.tile.net/tile/bach/

RCA: Idiot's Guide to Classical Music

Did you know that when you listen to the Elmer Fudd theme song ("Kill da wabbit! Kill da wabbit!") you're really tapping your foot to "Ride of the Valkyries" by Wagner? You probably recognize more classical music than you'd think! Take a listen to some of the sound bites at this site, and see which ones you know from TV commercials, shows, and movies. You'll also find a Beginner's Guide to Classical Music at this site.

http://www.rcavictor.com/rca/hits/idiots/cover.html

COUNTRY
COWPIE Bunkhouse

COWPIE stands for Country and Western Pickers of the Internet Electronic Newsletter. Look here to find country music songs: lyrics, tablature, and chords. They were gleaned from various newsgroups and other Net sources. Take a look at the archives of the newsletter. If you like it and you have an e-mail address, you can subscribe for free, and new issues will be e-mailed to you. The country music archives are worth a look, too. You'll find such gems as Jimmy Buffett's "Love in the Library" ("Surrounded by stories/Surreal and sublime/I fell in love in the library/Once upon a time").

http://www.roughstock.com/cowpie/

Great American Country Home Page

Fourteen-year-old LeeAnn Rimes is a country superstar! She won a Grammy award as the Best New Artist of the year in 1997. You can find out all about LeeAnn's life, including her musical influences, her favorite foods, and things she likes to do when she's got a day off. All your other favorite country stars are here too, many with video and audio clips.

http://www.countrystars.com/

Programs, reviews, theme songs, and more in TELEVISION.

FOLK

FolkBook: An Online Acoustic Music Establishment

This is the place to be if you're looking for info on acoustic music and musicians. There are artist biographies, collections, pictures, audio, lyrics, guitar tablature, tour schedules, and more! Want to see Mary-Chapin Carpenter in person? Try the festival and concert listings and information organized by date and by region. You'll also find pointers to other folk-related World Wide Web and Internet information. Parental advisory—we have not chased down all the links, so you should use this site with your kids.

http://www.cgrg.ohio-state.edu/folkbook/

NET FILES

What is a *Zampoña?*

(Hint: It's not that big machine the guy at the ice rink rides around on.)

Answer: It's a South American pan pipe (a wooden flute of sorts). Blow on over to *http://ekeko.rcp.net.pe/snd/snd_ingles.html* and hear what it sounds like! To see a picture of one, try Lark in the Morning's catalog at *http://www.mhs.mendocino.k12.ca.us/MenComNet/ Business/Retail/Larknet/LarknetAndes*

Computers are dumb, people are smart.

Richard Robinson's Tunebook

Haul out your fiddle (or flute, sax, or tuba) and try some of these great tunes. This is real sheet music! If you hang out with acoustic or traditional musicians, you'll recognize some of these tunes. Jigs, reels, polkas, schottisches, and more were selected from France, Finland, Turkey, and Cape Breton, as well as lots from the British Isles. There's bound to be some bourrée or other you've never played before. The real fun comes when you share the tunes with other players. Anybody can play them. If you've been taking Suzuki method lessons for a while, try something new. It's the 32-bar pause that refreshes!

http://www.leeds.ac.uk/music/Info/RRTuneBk/
     tunebook.html

Welcome to Arlonet!

Arlo Guthrie calls himself a "folkperson and part-time thinker." He made it big in the '60s with "Alice's Restaurant," a 20-minute song that eventually became a feature film. He's been around ever since, touring, writing songs, producing albums, and hanging out. Recently, he acquired the church that used to be Alice's Restaurant. Now it's home to the Guthrie Foundation (a charitable organization), the Guthrie Center, and Arlo's record label, Rising Son Records. The site has lots of lyrics, album covers, and some liner notes. You can link up to Pete Seeger, Bob Dylan, Bonnie Raitt, and other folk singers here. What does Alice Brock (of Alice's Restaurant fame) serve the night before Thanksgiving? "The Night Before Seafood Soup," of course! Get the recipe at <http://www.clark.net/pub/downin/cgi-bin/ rbr.html?rbr17>.

http://www.clark.net/pub/downin/cgi-bin/arlonet.html

Home schools are cool, study them in PARENTING AND FAMILIES—EDUCATION— HOMESCHOOLING.

A B C D E F G H I J K L M N O P Q R S T U V W X Y Z

A
B
C
D
E
F
G
H
I
J
K
L
M
N
O
P
Q
R
S
T
U
V
W
X
Y
Z

JAZZ
Jazz Improvisation

How does jazz work? This site can tell you. Not for performers only, these lessons on jazz theory and practice fill you in on history, fundamentals, and playing with others. You'll get new insights into the heart of jazz. Also take a look at the shorter "Jazz Improvisation Primer." The rest of this site is an entire jazz library. Other links are to Pop and Commercial Music, Jazz Education resources, and World Music, where you'll find Chinese, Russian, and Bulgarian sounds, and the Mbira Home Page! Also take a look at European jazz, more photos, and jazz literature. Bring a sandwich and spend the day here.

http://hum.lss.wisc.edu/jazz/

Marsalis on Music Online Home Page

Wynton Marsalis, the great jazz and classical trumpet player, says, "We play at music, we don't work at it." This site is a great place to play with music. It's an overview of the four-part PBS special, *Marsalis on Music*. Marsalis taped this show at Tanglewood, Massachusetts, in front of a live, young audience. Yo Yo Ma and Seiji Ozawa also appeared on the show. You'll get an idea of what each episode is about. "Why Toes Tap" introduces rhythm and meter. You'll get some background on wind bands and early jazz in "From Sousa to Satchmo." Marsalis also has advice on "taming the monster"—how to practice productively and enjoy it. You can take the interactive quizzes for each show. The Blow Your Horn link allows you to express yourself: ask a question, share a musical anecdote, or talk about your favorite performer. Musical Accompaniments has software you can download so you can listen to the audio examples. Ordering information for the video and book of the series is also included. On the Welcome page is the complete transcript of a live chat appearance in November 1995. Marsalis answers questions about the television series and his experiences, and he gives advice to aspiring musicians. As Wynton Marsalis says, "The world of music always accepts new citizens. It's never too early or too late."

http://www.wnet.org/mom/

WNUR-FM JazzWeb

Look in "The Styles of Jazz" at the clickable hypermap. It's a chart that somehow manages to place everything from blues to bebop in the proper perspective, both time- and place-wise. When you click on "ragtime," for example, you are given a fascinating article on the history and particulars of that style of jazz. You'll find artist biographies, discographies, and reviews in "Artists." In "Performance," you'll find out about festivals, venues, and regional jazz information. You can also pick an instrument, such as the guitar, organ, trombone, or violin, and find more information on resources and musicians. There are also links to media: radio stations on the Web, magazines, and a few books (remember books?).

http://www.nwu.edu/WNUR/jazz/

KEYBOARD INSTRUMENTS
The Piano Education Page

Having fun while practicing the piano—isn't that a contradiction in terms? Maybe not. The "Just for Kids" section of this page features piano-related advice from Taz, tips for practice fun (really!), and an interview each month with a famous (sometimes dead) composer. There's a section on how to choose a piano teacher, studio etiquette, and lots of MIDI piano files.

http://www.unm.edu/~loritaf/pnoedmn.html

Welcome to Piano on the Net '97

Would you like to learn how to play the piano or how to read music? You can! The first few lessons don't even require a piano, but for later lessons you will want a piano. Even a small portable keyboard will do. This easy, reassuring series of modules includes QuickTime movies, audio files, even online metronomes to keep you on time with the music.

http://www.artdsm.com/music.html

VIDEO AND SPY CAMS let you look in on interesting parts of the world.

LYRICS

Digital Tradition Folksong Database Search Page

What makes a song a folk song? Folks sing them, of course! The Digital Tradition Folk Song Database is a "not-for-profit, not-for-sale, not-for-glory" collection. The 5,000-plus (and growing) songs are searchable by keyword, title, and tune. If you're interested, look at the detailed notes on how to search and how songs get included in the database. A caution to parents: Not all songs are for children.

http://www.deltablues.com/dbsearch.html

Songs for Scouts

Gather 'round the campfire and share some singing—here are silly songs, lots of gross songs, and songs that are just plain fun. If you want the definitive version of "Greasy Grimy Gopher Guts," look no further.

http://www.macscouter.com/Songs/index.html

Welcome to the Tower Lyrics Archive!

At Tower Lyrics Archive, you'll discover lyrics to Broadway and Disney shows. Take a look at Andrew Lloyd Webber's *Cats*. Since it's based on T. S. Eliot's *Old Possum's Book of Practical Cats*, you'll find wonderful cat poetry here. The Disney archive has words to songs from *Aladdin*, *Beauty and the Beast*, *The Jungle Book*, and *The Little Mermaid*. For Gilbert and Sullivan fans, *The Pirates of Penzance* (with the song "Modern Major General") and three other entire plays, with dialogue as well as lyrics, are available. The rock opera *Tommy* and movies such as *The Nightmare Before Christmas* and *Grease* are also here.

http://www.ccs.neu.edu/home/tower/lyrics.html

The Web in Pig Latin? Make it so in LANGUAGES AND ALPHABETS.

MARCHING BANDS

Links to Marching Bands

Do you love a parade? If you're a fan of *The Music Man* or if you're in a band yourself, this is the site for you. Bands by the score, of every description, abound. You can see pictures, statistics, contest standings, and lots of homecoming celebrations from all over the U.S. You can download sound clips, too. "Professional" bands, like the Right Reverend Al's Screamin' Hypin' Revival Band ("dedicated to the production of camaraderie and volume") vie with the 60 or so college bands. You'll find great variety here, from the straight-laced traditional bands like Michigan State to the newer "scramble" bands of the Ivy League schools. Take a look at "The World's Worst Marching Band" or the international bands (especially if you read Norwegian). Even if you don't play the glockenspiel, these links are good fun. Links to instrument jokes for every instrument and musical style are fun (although a few may be mildly racy).

http://seclab.cs.ucdavis.edu/~wetmore/camb/other_bands.html

NET FILES

What tree, whose wood and flowers have been revered by the Chinese and Japanese for centuries, has recently been discovered growing in Washington, D.C.?

Answer: It's called the paulownia. According to Chinese legend, the tree means good luck because of its association with the mythical phoenix bird. The story told that the phoenix would only roost in the very best paulownia trees and only when a very excellent ruler was in power. See http://moneytree.scescape.net/history.html for more legends and stories associated with this tree.

A B C D E F G H I J K L M N O P Q R S T U V W X Y Z

A B C D E F G H I J K L **M** N O P Q R S T U V W X Y Z

MUSICAL THEATER
Annie

This play will come out
Tomorrow
Bet your bottom dollar
That tomorrow
There'll be an official Web page!

But for now, be satisfied with the links and lyrics here, as you enjoy the story of Little Orphan Annie and her new life with Daddy Warbucks, which is being revived on Broadway in spring 1997.

http://live.mit.edu/musicals/shows/Annie/

The Musicals Home Page

You are a talented kid! If you can't decide among singing, dancing, or acting, you can do all three in musical theater. Hey kids, let's put on a show! Let's find one we like, first. At this site you can explore the stories, songs, and productions of favorite musicals old and new—from *Annie* to *The Wiz*. There's lots of news and up-to-date info on all the current shows, too.

http://live.mit.edu/musicals/

On Broadway WWW Information Page

A live performance in a theater—there is nothing like it. Lights, stage props, music, and acting are all parts of what makes the theater great. If you've ever seen or participated in a play, you know it can be fantastic! Some of the best theatrical performances take place on Broadway in New York City. Want to know what's playing there right now, plus get reviews of the performances and maybe hear some sound clips? The Antoinette Perry (Tony) Award is presented annually for distinguished achievement in the professional theater. These are the best of the best, and if you like theater, take a look to see which plays have won.

http://artsnet.heinz.cmu.edu/OnBroadway/

Go climb a rock in OUTDOOR RECREATION.

The Phantom of the Opera

This page celebrates the popular musical about love between a singer and a ghost in the Paris Opera House. Or was he a ghost? Come experience the "Magic of the Night," but watch out for that chandelier! Lots of kids love the special effects in this production as much as they love the music. This page offers chat sessions about the musical as well as the story, sound clips, and an FAQ section.

http://phantom.skywalk.com/

NEW AGE
Music for a New Age

Just what is New Age music, you might ask? "What else can you call electronic synthesizers combined with the droning of the ancient Aboriginal didgeridoo?" says this site. All this, and more, can be found here. "Record Company Web Pages" starts with Windham Hill and has links to many more. In "Artists," you can find out about Kitaro, a Japanese "national living treasure." He once gave a free concert specifically for 2,000 pregnant women. Yanni, Ancient Future ("world fusion music"), Enya, Andreas Vollenweider, and many other artists have home pages. Other music sources include links to jazz sites, CD sources, a database of ambient musicians (including John Cage), and reviews of more than 100 artists.

http://www.his.com/~fjp/music.html

PERCUSSION INSTRUMENTS
The Bodhrán Page

Just what is a *bodhrán*? How do you even pronounce it? Find out here: it's "the heartbeat of Irish music," and it rhymes with "cow brawn." A large wooden round frame is loosely covered with goat skin (or donkey or greyhound skin!). The resulting large shallow drum is played with a double-headed stick. The head can be damped with the player's hand to make different tones. Look here for advice about making, buying, playing, and caring for the *bodhrán*. The usual assortment of tasteless musician jokes are also included (example: What do you call a *bodhrán* player with a broken wrist? A huge improvement!). Chieftains fans and Irish music lovers, check it out!

http://celtic.stanford.edu/instruments/bodhran/
  bodhran.html

Change Ringing Information

Have you ever heard the sound of bells from a church and thought how much fun it would be to pull the bell ropes and work the levers yourself? If a church has several bells, sometimes a group of people can perform what is called *change ringing*. The object is to ring the bells in succession, according to specific patterns, which are often complex and lengthy. A change ringer needs to be very aware of timing, to pull the bell through a ring and have it stop at the top of the arc, mouth up. If it stays there for a split second, the next bell in line becomes the "lead" bell and the "round" starts with that bell. Each bell takes a turn at being the lead bell, and the others switch positions in the order of ring. According to this page, "Twenty-four changes [is called] Plain Bob Minimus, and twenty-four changes are all the permutations possible on four bells. It takes less than a minute to ring. If you add a bell, you have Plain Bob Doubles: 120 different permutations are possible on five bells. Each new bell brought into the pattern multiplies the number of changes which can be rung without repetition. Six bells offer 720 changes; seven: 5,040, and a peal. A peal entails five thousand or more changes without break, without irretrievable errors, and (when seven or more bells are being rung), without repetition. It takes six or more people working together coordinating hand and eye, minding permutations and bells for three hours or more." You will learn all about the history of change ringing here and find out where you might be able to hear it, learn it, and participate in it!

http://web.mit.edu/bellringers/www/html/
  change_ringing_info.html

The Drums and Percussion Page

Is there a drumming circle near you? If so, this site will lead you to it. You'll also find specifics about drumming, like choosing and caring for drums, drum etiquette, and percussion folktales. The standard methods of drumming are included. And there are grooves—transcriptions and patterns, like paradiddle, Latin rhythms, and ska. Check out the hand drum grooves, from *Abakua* (Cuban) to *Zebolah* (Congolese). You'll find an illustrated encyclopedia of percussion instruments and lots of other drum-related sites linked here, too. Once you find one, you're on to them all.

http://www.cse.ogi.edu/Drum/

Kids, Percussion, and STOMP

Is pure rhythm really music, or is it just a cacophony of noise? If you go to a performance of STOMP, you will see and hear the cast members "play" Zippo lighters, push brooms, trash cans, newspapers, and other common objects. Visit this Web site to see and hear audio from the show and learn more about the science of rhythm.

http://www.usinteractive.com/stomp/studyguide/
  contents.htm

REGGAE

JAMMIN REGGAE ARCHIVES Home Page

Immerse yourself in this deep reggae site. You'll find: a huge archive of articles, including a sketch of Rastafarian history; .au and .wav audio; and books, graphics, interviews, and biographies of artists. Find reggae radio stations near you. Check out tour schedules. Look at all the Bob Marley Web pages, plus many other artists' home pages. And there are associated Web sites on ska and Jamaica. Not all links have been checked.

http://www.arrowweb.com/jammin/

ROCK GROUPS

The Internet Beatles Album

A splendid time is guaranteed for all! Look here for Beatles history, interviews (sometimes as audio files), lots of photos, and some gossip. The information is classified using Beatles song titles. For instance, the section called I Want to Tell You debunks (or verifies) certain Beatles rumors. Is "Lucy in the Sky with Diamonds" about drugs? No. Four-year-old Julian Lennon's drawing of the same name gave John the inspiration, and you can look at the picture here. Eight Days a Week tells you what happened today in Beatles history. Nowhere Man explains and updates the "Paul is dead" rumors.

http://www.primenet.com/~dhaber/beatles.html

Never give your name or address to a stranger.

A B C D E F G H I J K L M N O P Q R S T U V W X Y Z

A
B
C
D
E
F
G
H
I
J
K
L
M
N
O
P
Q
R
S
T
U
V
W
X
Y
Z

Rock & Roll Hall of Fame + Museum

Are these really the 500 songs that shaped rock and roll? Well, it's a start, and if you have other ideas, you can always vote in the Ballot Box for your personal choice. The Rock and Roll Hall of Fame and Museum is in Cleveland, Ohio, and it is a little bit like the Baseball Hall of Fame in Cooperstown, New York. Read profiles of the rock legends who have been inducted into the Hall of Fame and listen to their audio files. You can also read about and listen to the 500 songs. If you "Visit the Rock Hall of Fame" you'll see photos of the building and those paparazzi who have visited lately. In "Win Free Stuff" you can submit your best rock and roll memory (in 75 words or so); you may win a T-shirt. Even if you don't win, look at the sweet memories of previous winners. What rock star was born on your birthday? A file in "Rock News" will tell you. And there are searchable archives and articles (from the *Cleveland Plain Dealer*) about "Cities That Formed Rock & Roll," such as Detroit, Los Angeles, and Liverpool, England.

http://www.rockhall.com/

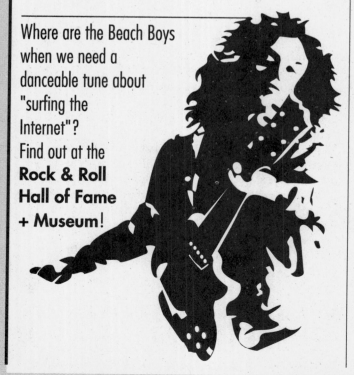

Where are the Beach Boys when we need a danceable tune about "surfing the Internet"? Find out at the **Rock & Roll Hall of Fame + Museum**!

SACRED
Christian Artists List

Maintained for a Christian radio station in Ohio, this site offers a great variety. Some of the pages are more official than others. The webmaster says these are not necessarily all Christian artists but defines them as "artists that have been found to be of interest to Christians." You'll also find a discussion area here, where you can talk about your favorite groups.

http://www.ccmusic.org/artists/

Christian Music Online Welcome Page

For rock and other popular music with a message, look here. You'll find album covers, long biographies, and lyrics to songs by artists such as Amy Grant and Guardian. You can browse the artists alphabetically. There's also a link to two Christian magazines: *Christian Calendar* magazine has sample interviews with William Bennett and others; *Release* is specifically about Christian entertainment.

http://www.cmo.com/cmo/

STRINGED INSTRUMENTS
The Classical Guitar Home Page

Suppose you've been playing classical guitar since three weeks ago last Tuesday. Is there anyplace you can find quality guitar music with fingerings? Try the Classical Guitar Beginner's Page on this site. Whether you're a beginning or experienced classical guitarist, you'll have fun browsing here. The Beginner's Page suggests recordings, books, and videos to get you off to a good start. Suggested Playing includes pieces by Carulli and Sor in GIF format, with MIDI files to go along with them. More complicated music is available in "Guitar Music," with pieces by Bach and Satie and a flamenco exercise. If you like the flamenco exercise, look at the Flamenco Guitar Home Page. There are links to guitar organizations, with reviews of concerts and recordings and guitar-related articles.

http://www.guitarist.com/cg/cg.htm

NET FILES

What country is home to the tallest freestanding structure, has the largest collection of tulips, and boasts having the oldest city in North America?

Answer: Canada! The CN Tower in Toronto, at 553.34 meters tall, is the tallest freestanding structure in the world. It took two-and-a-half years to build and cost 52 million dollars. The Tulip Festival in Ottawa features the largest collection of tulips in the world—four million at last count! Quebec City was founded in 1608 by Champlain and claims to be both the oldest and the only walled city in North America. Find out lots more interesting facts about the land and people of Canada at http://www.nais.ccm.NRCan.gc.ca/schoolnet/quiz2/english/html/quiz_a_human.html

The Internet Cello Society

Cellists young and old, amateur and pro, will love this site. Here's an introduction to the instrument, including an interactive multimedia presentation. You'll find out about repertoire, history, and famous artists and teachers. If you're a young cellist, there's a special section just for you on getting started and on picking what to play and what to listen to. In a photo tour, Baby Alec will introduce you to the parts of the cello. Don't miss the sound samples in the "Guide for the Clueless" (the harmonic bugle call would make a great start-up sound). The Tutor includes a few goofy exercises—hey, everyone, time to hug your cello!

http://www.cello.org/

May the forces be with you in PHYSICS.

TEJANO

Tejano Home Page

Tejano (you pronounce this word "tay-yawno") is a cool music style that is a combination of Mexican sounds, American rock and roll, and a little bit of country music. If you are a fan of Tejano, or if you'd like to see what all the excitement is about, take a look at this page. All the best groups and solo artists are here, as well as birthdays of the stars, some great pictures, and the latest news on the Tejano scene. Parents, not all links have been checked.

http://www.OndaNet.com:1995/tejano/tejano.html

WIND INSTRUMENTS

The Recorder: Instrument of Torture or Instrument of Music?

Nicholas Lander, webmaster of this site, ponders the above question. While mulling it over, he imparts information on history, technique, and repertoire of the recorder. His notes on fingerings and vibrato techniques are very complete. He also has links to recorder makers, catalogs (this is an Australian site), MIDI files, and references to journals and books.

http://www.iinet.net.au/~nickl/torture.html

NET FILES

There is a body of water called Pink Lake in Gatineau Park, in Ottawa, Canada. If you throw a yellow stone into it, what do you get?

Answer: A wet rock! The lake is actually green but is named after a family of settlers (the Pinks) who lived in this region in 1826. Find out more at http://www.iatech.com/tour/loc/loc/loc144.htm

A B C D E F G H I J K L **M** N O P Q R S T U V W X Y Z

A
B
C
D
E
F
G
H
I
J
K
L
M
N
O
P
Q
R
S
T
U
V
W
X
Y
Z

Renaissance Consort

Have you ever heard a shawm played? No? Well then, how about a crumhorn? A tabor? A bass viole? These were instruments of the hottest bands of the Medieval and Renaissance eras! You can see them and hear some rockin' audio files at this page from Japan.

http://www.hike.te.chiba-u.ac.jp:80/cons1/

Windplayer Online

Woodwind and brass musicians, take note. At this site, you'll find tips and advice from those in the know—professional musicians. The featured instruments are an unlikely quintet: trombone, trumpet, sax, clarinet, and flute. In each category you'll find player profiles (of artists like clarinetist Don Byron).Then you might take a master class from Herbie Mann on Brazilian flute playing. New products from many instrument makers are presented. And if you're in the market to buy or sell an instrument, check out the classified ads.

http://www.windplayer.com/

WORLD MUSIC

Ceolas celtic music archive

Celtic music can be defined rather loosely as music from Ireland, Scotland, Wales, Brittany (France), and Galacia (Spain), with U.S. and Canada also contributing. This site is truly a Celtic cornucopia. The Ceolas Archive includes radio stations, magazines, events, and local information. "What is Irish Music?" "Hearing Irish Music," "Learning Irish Music," and "Studying Irish Music" are some good pamphlets from the Irish Traditional Music Archive. Ceolas: Tunes has links to GIF and "abc notation" formatted music. There are more links to tunes, listservs, newsgroups and mailing lists, festivals, and concerts. And all those interesting Irish instruments, like Uilleann pipes, *bodhráns*, and tin whistles, have explanatory essays.

http://celtic.stanford.edu/ceolas.html

Be an angel and check what we've found in RELIGION.

Lark In The Morning

Where could you buy a hurdy-gurdy, or an Italian bagpipe, or an eighteenth-century oboe? This site specializes in hard-to-find musical instruments, music, and instructional materials. They also sell recordings from all over the world and have sound samples to entice you to buy. Their picture dictionary, describing music makers strange only to us, is complete and fascinating. Read the articles on instrument repair, the interviews with musicians, the essays on various unusual instruments, humor, and dance, and other resources. Lark in the Morning is truly more than a music store. If you don't happen to live in Mendocino, California, you can still visit via the Net!

http://www.mhs.mendocino.k12.ca.us/

MAUI MUSIC PAGES

Listen to beautiful classical and contemporary music from Hawaii at this site. Definitely check out traditional slack key guitar music from Keola Beamer as well as the best-selling hits from Keali'i Reichel, who *swept* the Hawaiian Music Awards in 1995.

http://www.maui.com/~sbdc/music/

NET FILES

NORTH POLE

What is Santa Claus's postal code?

Answer: In Canada, it's H0H 0H0. This is a special promotion used around the Christmas holidays. Try http://www.io.org/~djcl/postcd.txt for more information on postal codes of the world!

Julie Richer of CyberKids holds Sundance the cat;
Shara Karasic, CyberTeens editor, is on the right.

"My hope is that the Internet will reduce conflict by encouraging communication between people of different countries and cultures."

NEWS, NEWSPAPERS, AND MAGAZINES

CyberKids, CyberTeens

Webmaster: Julie Richer

http://www.cyberkids.com/
http://www.cyberteens.com/

How many people work on your pages?

Four. I manage CyberKids. Shara Karasic is the CyberTeens editor. Tiffany Tarin is responsible for public relations and helps format the stories and articles submitted by kids. My husband, Mark Richer, is a programmer who does the technical work. Every day, Shara checks the bulletin boards several times to delete any nasty messages on the Web sites. When young composers send me their music, I try to put it up within a few days.

Our hits are increasing very quickly. At the end of 1996 we were getting over 500,000 hits each week.

Can you think of an unusual request, question, or comment someone has sent to you?

We get e-mail and bulletin board messages from kids in the U.S., Canada, Australia, Singapore, South Africa, Mexico, Brazil, Norway, Sweden, Denmark, Italy, and many other countries. One of the features in CyberTeens is an advice column called "Ask Lola." Usually kids e-mail their questions to her, but one day a young man called our office and asked to talk to Lola. He said it was urgent, and the person who answered the phone thought he sounded depressed. We were afraid he might be thinking of hurting himself, so while he was on hold, we called the telephone operator in the city where he lived to get a phone number for the suicide hotline in his area. Then I picked up the phone to talk to him, because Lola wasn't there. I discovered that he just needed advice on how to talk to a girl that he was dating for the first time. Needless to say, we were very relieved to hear that.

Do you have a family?

I am married and have three daughters: 10-year-old Eve, and 7-year-olds Allison and Diana (twins). We also have an orange-striped cat named Sundance.

What are your hopes and fears for the future of the Internet?

My hope is that the Internet will reduce conflict by encouraging communication between people of different countries and cultures. My biggest fear is that people who hurt children can use the Internet to contact kids. That's why I hope kids will remember not to give out their home address to people they don't know and will tell their parents if unpleasant e-mail messages are directed to them.

If you could invite three people throughout history to your house for dinner, who would they be?

Jesus Christ, so that I could find out what He was really like. Harriet Tubman, because I've always admired her courage in going back to help other slaves, after she herself escaped slavery through the Underground Railroad. Felix Mendelssohn, because he's one of my favorite composers and I'd like to hear him personally play his Prelude and Fugue in E minor.

A
B
C
D
E
F
G
H
I
J
K
L
M
N
O
P
Q
R
S
T
U
V
W
X
Y
Z

NATIVE AMERICANS AND OTHER INDIGENOUS PEOPLES

Native American Indian PlentyStuff

Want to learn about astronomy, traditional foods, or read some stories written by kids at Indian schools? You'll find loads of annotated links to Mayan, aboriginal, and other resources. There's also an HTML tutorial for eight-year-olds! This page is a must for anyone interested in Native American issues and current events. Not all links have been viewed.

http://indy4.fdl.cc.mn.us/~isk/

Arvol Looking Horse is the nineteenth-generation Keeper of the Sacred White Buffalo Calf Pipe for the Lakota, Dakota, and Nakota Nations. Two thousand years ago, the pipe (or sacred bundle) was given to the People by White Buffalo Calf Woman. She taught seven sacred ceremonies, including the sweat lodge and sun dance ceremonies, before she left the nations. She made a prophecy that she would come back for the pipe someday and that a sign of her coming would be the birth of a white buffalo calf. In 1994, a white buffalo calf was born in Wisconsin. You can read about the cultural and spiritual significance of this event at **Native American Indian PlentyStuff.**

NATIVE LANGUAGES PAGE

Would you like to learn a little Navajo or a smattering of Ojibwe? Maybe you'd like to try using a Cherokee font or learn something about Mayan hieroglyphs. This page offers links to all of this, and more!

http://www.pitt.edu/~lmitten/natlang.html

NativeWeb Home Page

Did you know there are hundreds of federally recognized nations within the United States? Learn more about Native Americans at this site, which collects info on art, culture, government, languages, music, religious beliefs, and current tribal issues. You can read newsletters and see a calendar of upcoming events. Particularly interesting are the rules you should follow when attending a powwow, which is a ritual celebration including dance, singing, and drumming. To help find one near you, this site has event listings for the U.S., Canada, and Mexico.

http://web.maxwell.syr.edu/nativeweb/

NMAI Exhibitions

The Smithsonian's National Museum of the American Indian is in New York City, not Washington D.C. Most of the one million objects in its collection represent cultures in the United States and Canada, although there are also items from Mexico and Central and South America. You can see many artifacts of ancient and contemporary culture through the online exhibits of clothing, baskets, beadwork, and other objects. This museum displays sacred materials only with the permission of the various tribes and returns these materials on request. Chances are you've never seen things like this before! Imagine wearing a beautiful, eagle-feather costume as you dance. "When a Ponca singer sings, the singing and the music make you dance. Some singers don't move you, but a Ponca singer will move you in your heart and mind; they make it easy to dance longer. These eagle feathers are stripped so they can hang down and flutter in the wind, like the ribbons on our shirts." (Abe Conklin, Ponca-Osage)

http://www.si.edu/nmai/

What did grandma do when she was a kid? There is a list of questions to ask in GENEALOGY AND FAMILY HISTORY.

AUSTRALIAN ABORIGINES

Indigenous People

This site, created in support of Australian schools, is a collection of links about Aborigines, the native peoples of the Australian continent. This culture is one of the oldest on Earth, with an oral tradition going back about 40,000 years! Aborigines belong to various clans, each having a spiritual ancestor from long ago in the Dreamtime. An individual experiences a personal connection with the ancestor by something called a *dreaming*, which bridges the present to the past. At these sites you can read more about the spiritual and cultural life of Australian Aborigines, the first ecologists. Don't miss the link to the Yothu Yindi band's Web site. This band combines traditional instruments and music with Western pop music sounds. The audio files of *yidaki* (didgeridoo or hollow log) music are haunting.

http://www.gil.com.au/ozkidz/Indigenous/

NET FILES

What vegetable, nicknamed the "King of American Crops," has its own palace, complete with towers and Moorish minarets?

Answer: Corn. The Corn Palace, made out of 3,000 bushels of corn, is located in Mitchell, South Dakota. See it at http://www.state.sd.us/state/executive/tourism/20reason/corn.htm

People are the true treasures of the Net.

NATIVE AMERICANS

A Guide to the Great Sioux Nation

The people of the Sioux Nation prefer to be called Dakota, Lakota, or Nakota, depending on their language group. On this South Dakota home page, you can learn about the languages, legends, and rich cultural traditions of these proud peoples. You'll see beautiful costumes, and maybe you can attend one of the powwows. You'll find a calendar of annual events here, so go get yourself some fry bread and enjoy the music and dance!

http://www.state.sd.us/state/executive/tourism/sioux/sioux.htm

Chetro Ketl Great Kiva 3-D Model Home Page

Over a thousand years ago, there was a great civilization in what is now northwestern New Mexico, in the desert southwest of the United States. What remains now are cliff dwellings and other scattered hints about how these people lived and worked. One central part of their existence was the *kiva*, an underground enclosure used for sacred and other purposes. Young men would enter the kiva to learn secret languages and hidden lore of the tribe. The kiva was the central spiritual focus of the community. Large communities needed a Great Kiva, and this site reconstructs one for you to climb down in and visit virtually. It is based on the recently excavated Chetro Ketl Great Kiva, which is located in isolated Chaco Canyon, in northwestern New Mexico. You can choose the multimedia tour, with QuickTime VR, or you can try the less bandwidth-intensive version. The descendants of these ancient peoples now live in the various pueblos of the area. They also use kivas for ceremonies, and they are off-limits if you are a visitor to the pueblo.

http://www.sscf.ucsb.edu/anth/projects/great.kiva/

If you feel funny, think what we went through when we wrote the JOKES AND RIDDLES section!

A
B
C
D
E
F
G
H
I
J
K
L
M
N
O
P
Q
R
S
T
U
V
W
X
Y
Z

A
B
C
D
E
F
G
H
I
J
K
L
M
N
O
P
Q
R
S
T
U
V
W
X
Y
Z

Indian Lore Galore

The movie *The Indian in the Cupboard* is based on the culture of the Onondaga Nation, part of the federation of six eastern U.S. tribes known as the Iroquois or *Ho di no sion ni.* Jeanne Shenandoah, Turtle Clan Mother, shares Onondaga history, legend, and lifestyle. Read about the Great Law of Peace and how the Creator's messenger united the original five Iroquois nations to be of one mind and cease their conflicts.

http://www.paramount.com/ILore.html

Native Americans Home Pages

You have a report due on an Indian nation you've never heard of before. So you walk down to the public library to look for it. Trouble is, all the books on Native Americans have been checked out, and the reference books have just one paragraph on your topic! Now you can go straight to the source. Many nations have their own home pages, complete with historical and cultural information. They are listed here, at a site put together by a librarian who says she is "mixed-blood Mohawk urban Indian." You'll also find links to tribal organizations, colleges, businesses, powwows, singers, and more. This site is carefully tended and updated. We have not checked outside links.

w.pitt.edu/~lmitten/indians.html

NET FILES

The world's largest waterfall is 16 times the height of Niagara Falls! Where can it be found?

http://www.lonelyplanet.com/dest/sam/ven.htm

To find out more, visit wonders. To find out more, visit one of that country's numerous natural **Answer:** *Angel Falls is in Venezuela, and it is*

New Perspectives on THE WEST

This is a companion site to the eight-part PBS television series *The West.* It is a history of the expansion of the American West, and we are including it because of the rich biographical information about famous Native Americans: *<http://www.pbs.org/weta/thewest/ wpages/wpgs400/w400_001.htm>.* You'll find short biographies about Sitting Bull, Chief Joseph, Chief Seattle, Crazy Horse, Sacagawea, and more.

http://www.pbs.org/weta/thewest/

Oneida Indian Nation

The Oneida were the first Indian nation to put up a Web page and claim territory in cyberspace. The Oneida are located in central New York State, and they remain an unconquered nation. In fact, they were the only Indian tribe to fight on the side of the American colonists during the American Revolution. This fact, often left out of history books, is detailed on this page. In 1777–78, Washington's soldiers were enduring a hard winter at Valley Forge, Pennsylvania. Oneida people walked hundreds of miles south, carrying food and supplies, to come to their aid. Polly Cooper was an Oneida woman who helped the soldiers, and she taught them how to cook the corn and other foods the Oneida had brought with them. Although offered payment, she refused, saying it was her duty to help friends in need. She was thanked for her assistance by Martha Washington herself, who presented Polly with a fancy shawl and bonnet. The shawl has been a treasured Oneida relic since then, and you can see a photo of it here. You can also hear some Oneida words, take a tour of the cultural museum, read original treaties, and see some real wampum!

http://www.one-web.org/oneida/

Pocahontas Start Page

For a Native American perspective on the popular Disney movie, check this Web page. The true history of Pocahontas and Captain John Smith might make less of a story than the Disney version, since she was only about 11 or 12 years old when she begged for his life. See what some Native American kids and adults think about the cartoon and its look at their culture and history.

http://indy4.fdl.cc.mn.us/~isk/poca/pocahont.html

Pueblo Cultural Center

In the American Southwest desert in New Mexico, 19 Pueblo communities welcome visitors, both real and virtual. You can read descriptions of all of them here, as well as pick up maps to the pueblos, calendars of events, and even rules for attending dances (don't applaud—dance is a prayer, not a performance). Gaze at the stunning wall murals, with titles such as these: The One-Horned Buffalo Dance; The Sounds of Life and Earth as It Breathes; and Indian Maiden Feeding Deer. You can read biographies of the artists, too.

http://hanksville.phast.umass.edu/defs/independent/
   PCC/PCC.html

NATIVE ARCTIC PEOPLES

Arctic Circle: History & Culture

You'll find information here about many people who are native to the Arctic Circle region of the world. You'll learn not only about the Cree of northern Quebec and the Inupiat of Arctic Alaska, but also about the Nenets and Khanty of Yamal Peninsula, northwest Siberia, and the Sámi of far-northern Europe. Find out why the concept of "wilderness" is unknown to these people, who live in harmony with their natural surroundings.

http://www.lib.uconn.edu/ArcticCircle/
   HistoryCulture/

NATIVE HAWAIIANS

GODS AND MYTHS

Read about how the fire goddess, Pele, created the Hawaiian Islands, raising them with her volcanic power. If you visit Volcanoes National Park on the Big Island today, you will find flower leis and other offerings to this very powerful goddess. You'll also find out about the many other gods and goddesses of Hawaii, sacred sites like ancient *heiau*, and other traditional practices.

http://hawaii-shopping.com/~sammonet/gods.html

Something fishy going on? Try AQUARIUMS.

HAWAI'I - INDEPENDENT & SOVEREIGN NATION-STATE

In November 1993, President Bill Clinton signed into law U.S. Public Law 103-50, which is "To acknowledge the 100th anniversary of the January 17, 1893 overthrow of the Kingdom of Hawaii, and to offer an apology to Native Hawaiians on behalf of the United States for the overthrow of the Kingdom of Hawaii." Some native Hawaiians are trying to restore Hawaii to sovereign nation status. That means it would have its own leaders and could determine its own future. Read news about the Nation of Hawai'i, and find out about native island culture here.

http://hawaii-nation.org/nation/

NEWS, NEWSPAPERS, AND MAGAZINES

See also INTERNET—SEARCH ENGINES AND DIRECTORIES
Many of these offer customizable newspapers you can easily design yourself. One example is <http://my.yahoo.com> but almost all the search engines and directories have something similar.

AJR NewsLink

Wow—stop the presses! Check this site: over 4,000 links to newspapers, broadcast stations, magazines, plus other special links from all over the world. You ought to be able to get all the news here! Have you started wondering about which college is right for you? Maybe you've got a sister, brother, or friend who's already gone away to one. One of the best ways to find out about a college is to check out its newspaper. You can keep up with campus news by reading the online versions of college newspapers from the *Arizona Daily Wildcat* to *The Yale Daily News* at this site.

http://www.newslink.org/menu.html

A
B
C
D
E
F
G
H
I
J
K
L
M
N
O
P
Q
R
S
T
U
V
W
X
Y
Z

A
B
C
D
E
F
G
H
I
J
K
L
M
N
O
P
Q
R
S
T
U
V
W
X
Y
Z

CRAYON

Wouldn't it be great if you could design a newspaper with just the news *you* want to read? How about an all-sports newspaper or an all-music newspaper? How about adding the current weather map or the current stock price on a share of Toys 'R' Us? This interactive site lets you do just that and "publish" an updated paper anytime you want, to your very own Web browser.

http://crayon.net/

PointCast, Inc - Front Door

A new wave is out there on the Web, and it's called "push" technology. That means the information is being pushed at you rather than having you click on it to request it, or "pull" it. Sort of like television broadcasting, except you tell them what shows you want to watch. One of the cool uses of this is customized news, including weather and sports scores. You select the types of stories you want to read and the news resources you want to have checked. You can sometimes choose to have new information pushed to you every few minutes, every hour, or every day. You can even have floating news stories or weather maps as your screen saver! You can download software to try one version of it here, but ask your parents before installing it to make sure you have the right hardware.

http://www.pointcast.com/

Timecast

Now hear this! The news, that is. Yep, this site's for people who'd rather listen to the news than read it. You're going to want to grab your own version of the RealAudio player (it's free, courtesy of Progressive Networks) once you check out all the cool stuff you can hear. The RealAudio player software enables users to access RealAudio programming and play it back in an on-demand audio stream, which means you don't have to download those gigantic files first, which gets a little boring. Not to be missed is the news from French, Italian, and Japanese public broadcast networks (not to mention National Public Radio), political speeches from C-SPAN, the evening news from *ABC World News Tonight*, and broadcasts from Greenpeace ships around the world.

http://www.timecast.com/

Yahoo! Get Local

All this national and international news is sometimes overwhelming! If you just want to focus on your local community news, this is the place. You need to set up a profile the first time you use it. You have to type in the name of your city, and sometimes your ZIP code, but that's about it. Then, every time you go to this page, it will bring up your local news! This may include links to your local TV and newspaper's Web sites, local team scores, movie listings, special event calendars, weather, and lots more. If you ever want to change to another city, a button at the top of the page will let you do that. You can "get local" in the U.S. or in many other countries.

http://local.yahoo.com/

MAGAZINES

CyberKids Home

CyberKids magazine is chock-full of games, word searches, and crossword puzzles, but—watch out!—you could learn something before you know it. All the stories and artwork have been created by kids, of course. They've told about the first African American woman in space, how one family came from Vietnam to the United States, and about Egyptian gods. Also pretty great are the reviews of computer stuff, like software and printers. You can contribute your own stories, enter contests, and comment on other kids' ideas.

http://www.cyberkids.com/

MidLink Magazine

Design an alien or visit a virtual haunted house at *MidLink*, where kids ranging in age from 10 to 15 years gather to share news of their schools and cities. And speaking of cities, why not take a virtual tour of kids' homes around the world while you're there? Or join a virtual voyage with a weather research vessel. And don't miss the Cool-School Home Pages. There is always something fun happening at this site, which gets better and better every time we see it!

http://longwood.cs.ucf.edu/~MidLink/

NGS - WORLD Magazine

National Geographic has been a family favorite for decades. They also have a magazine just for kids, called *WORLD*, and this is its online version. The contents of the issues vary, but recently we found articles on the space station, pirates, and movies of an avalanche in action! There are links to challenging games, plus a way for you to get an international pen pal, too.

http://www.nationalgeographic.com/ngs/
   mags/world/world1.html

NWF's Ranger Rick

The National Wildlife Federation has a magazine for kids that's about nature, wildlife, and wilderness, and some of it is online. You can sample articles from past issues, such as "Ladybug Lore," "Elephant Jokes," or "Far-out Numbers." Check out Ranger Rick!

http://www.igc.apc.org/nwf/lib/rr/

OWLkids Online

These Canadian kids' magazines have online versions full of stories, jokes, puzzles, crafts, and of course, links! Kids age eight and up will love *Wired OWL*, while younger kids should try *Chickadee Net*. The Cybersurfer section in *Wired OWL* has a nice overview of the culture of the Net.

http://www.owl.on.ca/index.html

Pathfinder Latest News: Top News

Click on a headline in News Now, and instantly you'll be taken to the complete story, whether it's the latest from Washington, D.C., or the batting average of your favorite player. The news is updated hourly, and sports is updated even more often. In fact, the sports news here is awesome: you can get stats, schedules, box scores, game recaps and previews, and the very latest transactions. Since Time Warner, Inc.—the people who publish *Time, People, Sports Illustrated, Money, Fortune*, and lots of other famous magazines—runs this site, you can get the complete background on any subject right here.

http://pathfinder.com/news/latest/

Sports Illustrated for Kids

When was the last time you climbed a treacherous rock wall, shredded some ramps with the only pro female skateboarder in the country, or picked up some racing tips from the world's best BMX bicycle racer—all without leaving your computer? This online magazine is all about athletic challenges. If you've been wanting to try your hand at a new sport, this is where you can find out all about the moves, the lingo, and the equipment. Don't miss the interviews with sports heroes, hilarious comics, games, and a whole lot more.

http://pathfinder.com/SIFK/

Stone Soup, the magazine of writing and art by young people

Stone Soup is a well-known magazine of stories, poems, and artwork by kids, for kids. Here at their home page, you can peek at a sample issue, plus read some online stories and poems. Maybe you'll be able to send them some of your own work! There is nothing like seeing your name in print, next to something you wrote, whether it's printed in a magazine, a book, or on the Net!

http://www.stonesoup.com/

NET FILES

What carnivorous "bear" isn't really a bear after all and doesn't even eat meat?

Answer: The giant black and white panda in China. Pandas actually belong to a family of their own, closely related to raccoons. The panda has the digestive system of a carnivore but long ago adapted to a vegetarian diet and now feeds almost entirely on the stems and leaves of bamboo in the forests of southwestern China. Find out more at the Giant Panda Page at http://www.wwfcanada.org/facts/panda.html

A
B
C
D
E
F
G
H
I
J
K
L
M
N
O
P
Q
R
S
T
U
V
W
X
Y
Z

A
B
C
D
E
F
G
H
I
J
K
L
M
N
O
P
Q
R
S
T
U
V
W
X
Y
Z

U.S. News Online

Do we even need to mention that a magazine called *U.S. News* is going to bring you news, news, and more news every week? Want more than just the week's news? Click on "News You Can Use," a weekly feature, full of some really helpful tips, like how to order healthy food at a restaurant, how to buy a new computer, and which colleges are the very best in the country. Want to get into politics? Click on "Washington Infobank" to link to the White House or your own senators and representatives and to find out all about the people running for elective office.

http://www.usnews.com/usnews/main.htm

NET FILES

How much does it cost to rent the 100-inch Telescope at the Mount Wilson Observatory for a night of observing the stars?

Answer: Only $1,300 a night, and it includes the services of one telescope operator. Such a deal! Not only that, but you get use of two dorm rooms in the refurbished monastery and kitchen access for that late-night cookies and milk break. Check it out at http://www.mtwilson.edu/Services/Professional/100in.html

Never give your name or address to a stranger.

Welcome to FishNet

This site is an ever-changing gathering place for teens on the Web, and its goal is to have you spend "quality time" on the Internet. This bills itself as a "high-performance magazine for students." Learn how to handle stress before a test, how to buy a backpack, how to recognize bogus advertising claims, and more. Many of these articles are written by teenagers. You can send in your own story and earn money if your story's good enough to be published. You can also read what other kids think about different topics and post your own responses. Check out current slang at the Streetspeak area, and try the Shockwave games.

http://www.jayi.com/Open.html

Welcome to TIME.com

Okay, okay, we know this is a news magazine for adults, but we've got a helpful homework hint for you. Say it's 8:00 P.M. and you've got a report due tomorrow on how Russians and Americans are cooperating in space, or on hurricanes, or on computer hackers. Are you in big trouble or what? Well, here's what you can do. Go to this home page, where you can search through magazines for articles. And there's a whole lot more than just *Time* magazine. Don't forget, *Time* has a bunch of sister magazines, including *Fortune, Money,* and *People,* and they're all right here. Just type in a word or a phrase, and let this Web site do the walking for the stories you need.

http://pathfinder.com/time/

YES Science Magazine for Kids

Canada's science magazine for kids has an electronic version! It includes book and software reviews, in-depth articles, and science news and projects. We particularly liked the "How Does it Work?" section, where we learned lots about telescopes, cameras, submarines, and other inventions.

http://www.islandnet.com/~yesmag/

NEWSPAPERS

The Nando Times

What's a "Nando"? Are we talking about another planet? Nope, *Nando* refers to News and Observer—the newspaper of Raleigh, North Carolina. The online edition keeps news of the world, sports, and entertainment coming around the clock, with updates from the Associated Press and lots of other places. While you're here, make sure you link back to the paper's online service, Nando.net, and check out NandoNext at *<http://www2.nando.net/links/nandonext/next.html>*. It's a Web site created just for the interests and attitudes of the "next" generation, featuring stories and art from local high school students. Don't miss their music, movie, and concert reviews! If you need to take a break, try the games of skill in the Toybox (you will need Shockwave).

http://www2.nando.net/nt/nando.cgi

Tomorrow's Morning

When your family talks about what's going on in Washington or in the world, do you just sit there with a puzzled look on your face? After you've checked out *Tomorrow's Morning,* the first national weekly newspaper for kids from 8 to 14, you'll dazzle everyone with your knowledge of the news. What's really great is that the editors who put this paper together think being informed should be fun! Of course they've got the serious stuff, such as national and international news. But they throw in tons of fun stuff, too, like comic book news, Brainiac quizzes, science fiction updates, and news about kids from other parts of the country. Future business executives should be sure to take a look at Kid$tock$, to see how Coca-Cola, Nike, Toys 'R' Us, and lots of other stocks are doing.

http://morning.com/

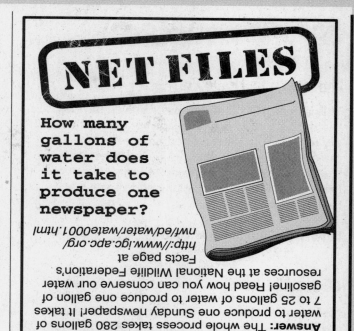

NET FILES

How many gallons of water does it take to produce one newspaper?

Answer: The whole process takes 280 gallons of water to produce one Sunday newspaper! It takes 7 to 25 gallons of water to produce one gallon of gasoline! Read how you can conserve our water resources at the National Wildlife Federation's Facts page at http://www.igc.apc.org/nwf/ed/water/wate0001.html

USA Today

"Your news when you want it" is *USA Today*'s motto, and you're going to get exactly that at this site. You can go right to the sections you want by clicking on the buttons for News, Sports, Money, Life, or Weather. And speaking of weather, there's a ton of forecasts, fun facts, and lots of other goodies here, from information on tornadoes and hurricanes to tips on weather forecasting. Everything's just as readable and colorful as the actual newspaper. It's a whole lot more than a newspaper, though, because the news is updated every day and sports scores are updated every two minutes. Impress your family by downloading the interactive crossword puzzle and a special puzzle viewer so you can work it out offline.

http://www.usatoday.com/usafront.htm

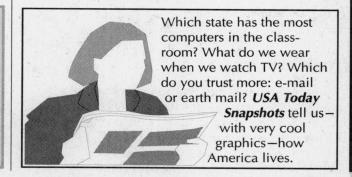

Which state has the most computers in the classroom? What do we wear when we watch TV? Which do you trust more: e-mail or earth mail? *USA Today Snapshots* tell us—with very cool graphics—how America lives.

A
B
C
D
E
F
G
H
I
J
K
L
M
N
O
P
Q
R
S
T
U
V
W
X
Y
Z

OPTICAL ILLUSIONS

IllusionWorks Home Page

This is the coolest optical illusion site on the Net. Discover not only sight illusions but sound illusions! Try to figure out the distorted puzzles or the camouflaged hidden pictures. Some of these require Shockwave or Java-enhanced browsers. A caution to parents: Not all links leading off this site have been checked.

http://www.illusionworks.com/

Optical Illusions

Now you see them, now you don't. Optical illusions are given wide representation here. Open up the doors of perception and come into this exhibit at the Cyberspace Middle School. Maybe you'll even be able to find your way back out!

http://www.scri.fsu.edu/~dennisl/CMS/activity/ optical.html

Welcome to Philomel Records!

You know what an optical illusion is: a picture that can look like several different things all at once. Are you ready for an audio illusion? Diana Deutsch's CD is called *Musical Illusions and Paradoxes,* and you can hear several samples at this Web site. Did you know that people hear sounds differently? Sometimes your brain can be tricked into hearing melodies that aren't really there. Sound impossible? Listen to the audio files here and see if you can identify the mystery tune.

http://www.philomel.com/

World of Escher

Waterfalls that flow up? Stairs that seem to keep going down, yet, suddenly, they're back on top of a building? These inexplicable drawings by M. C. Escher must be seen to be believed!

http://www.texas.net/escher/textonly.html

NET FILES

Where is the world's largest bell?

Answer: The Tsar Bell, weighing 210 tons, is in Moscow, Russia. It stands 20 feet high and has a diameter of 22 feet at the base. A fire swept Moscow in 1737, and it engulfed the Kremlin. When water was poured on the hot bell, it cracked, and a huge piece broke off. The bell now rests on a special granite stand at the foot of the Ivan the Great bell tower. See a picture of it at http://www.geom.umn.edu/~ipavlovs/Russia/Moscow/moscow.html

You Can Illusions

What you think you see is not always what's really there. Look at some famous optical illusions with Beakman and Jax, who explain things like whether that's a young lady wearing a hat or an old woman wearing a scarf.

http://pomo.nbn.com/youcan/illusion/illusions.html

ORGANIZATIONS

Children's Defense Fund

Being a kid in the 1990s can be tough. Poverty, abuse, and negligence are a few of the problems kids confront. The Children's Defense Fund (CDF) is an organization designed to help kids with some of the difficult problems they face. To learn more about how kids can get a Head Start, a Healthy Start, a Fair Start, a Safe Start, and a Moral Start—find out what the CDF is doing.

http://www.childrensdefense.org/

Make-A-Wish® Foundation of America

Founded in the belief that lives are measured by memories and not by years, the Make-A-Wish Foundation has granted more than 30,000 wishes to American children between the ages of 2 1/2 and 18 who have terminal illnesses or life-threatening medical conditions. Since the first wish (granted in 1980 for a seven-year-old boy with terminal leukemia who wanted to be a policeman), 81 chapters have sprung up around the U.S. With the family's participation, the Foundation is committed to providing a memorable and carefree experience for these children, whose wishes are limited only by their own imaginations. If you know someone who would like to make a special wish, check the Chapter Listing to find the Make-A-Wish chapter nearest you. One of the most frequently requested wishes is to travel to Disneyland or Disney World, but many unusual wishes have been granted, and you can read about them here. Also, be sure to check out the story of Craig Shergold. Long ago, he had a life-threatening brain tumor and asked that people send him greeting cards so that he could get into the *Guinness Book of World Records.* They did. Then he had surgery and (hooray!) fully recovered. Trouble is, those original requests are still floating around the Internet! You may receive a request from a friend; tell your friend the truth. The Shergold family is swimming in cards, and they want it to stop. Make-A-Wish was never involved with the original request, but you'll find the whole story explained here about this Net chain letter.

http://www.wish.org/

National 4-H Council

What does it mean to be involved in 4-H? It can mean learning how to give a great speech, helping save the environment, raising animals, or working on a project with friends. From country lanes to city streets, kids are involved in 4-H activities, and 4-H kids are having fun and learning much. To get the inside scoop on 4-H, take a peek at this home page.

http://www.fourhcouncil.edu/

Plugged In

Plugged In is an outreach program providing computer access to children and families in Palo Alto, California. Projects kids work on include fine arts, filmmaking, and storytelling, all via the computers. You can see the results here. This page describes Summer Drop-In Projects and directs you to Cool Spots on the Internet and other fun Web things. Plugged In is also learning about student-run enterprise by creating Web pages for individuals, businesses, and other nonprofits. Check their rates!

http://www.pluggedin.org/

YMCA's on the WEB

Why would you go to the "Y," the YMCA? You could go for all kinds of reasons. You could go for a game of B-Ball, swimming or judo lessons, or even classes in basketry. The "Y" is a fun place for everybody in the family, and there are many YMCAs all over the Internet. Take a look at YMCAs on the Web to see if a "Y" near you has a presence in cyberspace.

http://www2.interaccess.com/ymcaweb/

SCOUTING

The InterNETional Scouting Page

Scouting is *everywhere.* Girl Scouts, Boy Scouts, Explorers, the college fraternity Alpha Phi Omega— all are scouting organizations, and you can find them in just about every country in the world. Naturally, scouting groups are all over the Internet as well. To learn about scouting from A to Z, take a look at this page. You'll learn that scouting is more than tying knots and selling cookies! Download some of Baden-Powell's original scouting handbooks, or learn to use a compass or build backpacking equipment. Looking for camp songs and skits? They are collected here too, and many of them are wonderfully gross.

http://scout.strw.leidenuniv.nl/scout/

Feeling a bit bogged down? Check EARTH SCIENCE and get swampwise!

Wet or dry, give AMPHIBIANS a try!

A
B
C
D
E
F
G
H
I
J
K
L
M
N
O
P
Q
R
S
T
U
V
W
X
Y
Z

ScoutLinks On-Line Home Page

Your patrol is supposed to come up with a campfire skit or funny songs for Scout camp. No problem—just check some of the entertainment links here! You'll also find resources on international scouting, times and places for the next Jamboree or other scouting event, fund-raising ideas, discussion groups, and links to other pages for both Boy Scouts and Girl Scouts.

http://www.scouter.com/sl/

OUTDOOR RECREATION

See also AQUARIUMS; FISH

FISHING

Fishing Knots

Are you all thumbs when it comes to trilene? Do your hooks and sinkers fall off the line? You just need to know the moves when you're tying fishing knots. There are easy directions and pictures for a number of popular and useful knots here!

ftp://ftp.geo.mtu.edu/pub/fishing/from_nicb/knot.gif

GORP - Great Outdoor Recreation Pages - Fishing

Looking for the right *angle* on fishing? GORP is where they're biting! This is no *line*—you'll find everything from general fishing to fishing gear to information on fishing trips. There are lots of links to fishing hot spots in Scotland, Africa, and other places to cast your line. Stop by and catch your limit today.

http://www.gorp.com/gorp/activity/fishing.htm

J.P.'s Fishing Page

Something smells *fishy* here! That's because this page is full of fish-type information. Looking for places to go night fishing? Interested in learning about fly-fishing, or just want to talk with others interested in this art? This is the place to go. Hurry, before this one gets away!

http://www.geo.mtu.edu/~jsuchosk/fish/fishpage

GOLF AND MINIATURE GOLFING

Golfweb-Library-Fun and Games

There's no doubt about it: golf is fun! But sometimes just keeping score isn't enough. At this site, you can find the simple rules to dozens of different golf games. There are games for two, three, or four players, and there are team games for groups. And the best part is that they're all fun!

http://www.golfweb.com/glbb/index.htm

Putt-Putt Golf Courses of America Home Page

Net-mom loves to play miniature golf. Well, actually, Son of Net-mom really loves to play, because he usually *beats* Net-mom's score! (However, there was that one time, on Jekyll Island, Georgia...but then again, there were all those other times.) There are Putt-Putt mini golf courses in 34 states and seven other countries. The first course was built in North Carolina, in 1954, and the cost of a round of play was twenty-five cents! At this site, you can learn a little history and find a course nearby or near where you'll be on vacation.

http://putt-putt.com/index.html

HIKING, ORIENTEERING, AND BACKPACKING

Appalachian Trail Home Page

The Appalachian Trail stretches from Springer Mountain, Georgia, to Mount Katahdin, Maine, a distance of 2,160 miles. If you walked it straight through, it would take you between four and six months before you emerged on the other end. At this outstanding site, you will see a map of the trail and read hikers' journals about their travels. Don't miss the story about Bill Irwin, a blind man who completed the trail accompanied by his trusty guide dog, Orient. There are also links to Web sites about major trail systems, such as the Pacific Crest Trail, the Natchez Trace, and several others.

http://fred.net/kathy/at.html#top

DINOSAURS are prehistoric, but they are under "D."

GORP - Hiking

GORP stands for the hiker's staple food: good old raisins and peanuts! The hiking section of their extensive outdoor recreation site covers trails all over the world. You can find tips on hiking equipment as well as a multimedia collection of links, books, and videos. You can read other hikers' stories of the trails they have traveled or check the jawboning in the discussion areas. There is also a very interesting section on historic routes, such as the Oregon Trail, the Santa Fe Trail, and others.

http://www.gorp.com/gorp/activity/hiking.htm

Can you guess this riddle?

In a marble palace white as milk,
Lined with skin as soft as silk,
In a fountain crystal clear,
A golden apple does appear.
There are no doors to this stronghold,
Yet thieves break in to steal the gold.

Answer: It's an egg! Find more at http://www.dujour.com/riddle/ where you can compete for prizes with others around the world.

How to Use a Compass

On a hike, a compass will help you find your way, but first you have to learn to use one properly. You can learn in your own backyard, or in a park, or in a school playground. This site gives you a guided tour to a compass and its use. There are also tips on how to find your way in very difficult conditions, like fog or snow whiteouts.

http://www.uio.no/~kjetikj/compass/

Orienteering

Does this sound like fun? You and your friends use a very detailed map and a compass to visit various checkpoint flags hidden in the forest. When you reach a checkpoint, you use a special hole punch (usually hanging by the flag) to verify that you found the flag. The punches make differently shaped holes in your control card. This fast-growing sport can be enjoyed as a simple family walk in the woods or as a competitive team race. Learn about getting started in orienteering here, and don't miss the explanation of orienteering clue symbols. Remember: a big asterisk means look for an ANTHILL!

http://www.williams.edu:803/Biology/orienteering/o_index.html

LUMBERJACKS
The North American Guide to Lumberjack Entertainment and Sporting Events

Ever heard of timbersports? They include logrolling, crosscut sawing, and standing block chop. There are world records for lumberjack (or lumberjill) sporting events. If you haven't heard of this sport, you will. It's growing like crazy. On this page, you can see who holds the world record in a variety of timber competitions as well as see other information about this unusual sport, such as where to see a competition and where to buy the unusual equipment required.

http://www.starinfo.com/ljguide/lumberjack.html

MOUNTAIN AND ROCK CLIMBING
Go Climb a Rock!

Check the Climber's dictionary. They actually have an entry under "AAAAAAHHHHHHHH!!!" The definition is "a fall in progress!" Seriously, this is a site you need to traverse. Check climbing shoe ratings, technique tips, and a slew of links to climbing magazines and gear companies. There is also a listing of the top competitive climbers in the world. They have big plans for expanding this site; so far, they have an excellent start.

http://ic.net/~pokloehn/

A
B
C
D
E
F
G
H
I
J
K
L
M
N
O
P
Q
R
S
T
U
V
W
X
Y
Z

A
B
C
D
E
F
G
H
I
J
K
L
M
N
O
P
Q
R
S
T
U
V
W
X
Y
Z

ROLLER AND INLINE SKATING

CSC - In-Line Skater

Looking for pictures of basic fitness rollerblading? Or maybe you're an aggressive skater looking for the latest moves. It's here! As this page says, "Hey, these guys know what they are doing. These tricks are hard, so wear the gear. No one looks good wearing their brains on the outside." There's info on roller hockey here, too, as well as competition results and a whole lot more.

http://www.xcscx.com/SKATER/

Hockey Skating Tips

This site provides tips for ice skaters, rollerbladers, hockey players, roller hockey players, and others who strap blades or rollers on their feet. Try some of the speed and scoring drills described here, and explore the links off-site. Use your inside edge on your outside skate and shoot in here!

http://relay.cs.toronto.edu/~andria/skating_tips.html

Rollerblade: Site Menu

This is a commercial site, developed by the Rollerblade company. It has lots of info on how to get started in rollerblading and catch up with your friends (or your parents, as the case may be). You'll learn about the scenes, the moves, the equipment, even the lingo. There's lots on safety, too, because "asphalt bites"!

http://www.rollerblade.com/site_menu.html

SCUBA DIVING AND SNORKELING

Scuba Times Online's: Home Page

Swimming around for information on scuba diving? Dry off and sit down at the computer! This online magazine covers scuba from the serious diver's perspective. There is a treasure chest of information on scuba here. Online access to club listings worldwide, gear reviews, dive sites, and weather reports are always available. If you just can't get out on (and under) the water today, plenty of photographs will make you feel like you're there. But please, remove that gear and dry off before booting up your computer!

http://www.scubatimes.com/

Welcome to CyberDIVE!

An underwater adventure on land, in front of your computer? This must be some unusual way of scuba diving, if you don't even get wet. It is! You'll visit a database of great dive sites in Florida, read equipment reviews, and see underwater photos that must have been taken by fish! Confused about all the different types of certification courses you can take? Learn their differences here. Don't miss the info on snorkeling, either, or the live weather updates from marine buoys. Sure, there are the usual quizzes and win-free-stuff contests, since this is a site sponsored by commercial dive shops. But hey, who can't use a cool new T-shirt?

http://www.cyberdive.com/

NET FILES

You break a leg somewhere in the outback of Australia, but luckily, you remembered to bring a two-way radio. **Who do you call?**

Answer: Why, The Royal Flying Doctor Service of Australia, of course. For over 66 years, they have provided medical and health services to the remote locations of Australia's outback. The service uses a fleet of 38 aircraft and 27 doctors to cover 5,000 locations in an area of over six million square kilometers. They can be anywhere in Australia within 90 minutes! Read more about the service and its history at http://www.csu.edu.au/australia/detail/flydoc.html

I wonder what the QUEENS, KINGS, ROYALTY are doing tonight?

SKYDIVING
Canadian Sport Parachuting Association

Do you think that people who jump out of airplanes are just plain nuts? Or are you one of those who live to skydive off into the wild blue yonder? Skydiving may be the sport for you, and this page could be your jumping-off point. This bilingual (French and English) page includes information on how to get involved in skydiving, links to other skydiving Web sites, and an area for people to talk about their skydiving experiences. You'll find some pretty funny stories here!

http://www.islandnet.com/~murrays/cspa/

United States Parachute Association

This is the home page of the U.S. Parachute Association, and the first thing you need to know is that you can't skydive until you're 18 years old. Some drop zones will allow skydiving at 16 with parental consent, but keep in mind that this is an expensive sport. Expect to pay $150 to $300 for your first instruction. It does get cheaper after you've convinced an instructor that you know what you're doing. You should find an accredited teacher, too; there's a list here so you can find one near you.

http://www.USPA.org/

SNOWMOBILES
The Snowmobile Homepage

Snowmobiling is one of the great escapes during the cold and snow season. Beginning and experienced snowmobilers are always interested in the latest models from the major snowmobile makers, the coolest pictures of snowmobile action, and the facts on all the equipment. At this Swedish site, you can even submit your questions and have them answered by the experts. Or you can chat with other interested amateurs and compare the fine points of snow, machines, and brand loyalty!

http://www.sledding.com/

SNOWSHOEING
Welcome to L.L. Bean

Snowshoeing is a really cool (no pun intended) activity! It's a bit easier for most people than cross-country skiing, and it allows you to do a little more exploring. This page is where you can find out what you need and how to get started. After reading the helpful hints, maybe you still have a few more questions. Chances are the answers are only a mouse click away. For example, did you know you can make an emergency snowshoe repair with duct tape? (Is there anything you *can't* fix with duct tape?)

http://www.llbean.com/aos/snowshoeing/

NET FILES

What country "spans 11 time zones, 2 continents, and comes within 50 miles of North America"?

Answer: *Russia*, of course! *The Official Guide to Russia* ought to know, and it will show you more at
http://www.interknowledge.com/russia/

It's like wearing tennis racquets on your feet! How do you get down a hill in snowshoes, anyway? Whatever you do, don't jump down—that can damage the shoe and the webbing. There are specific techniques for snowshoeing, and things like going up and down hills or walking backwards can get a little tricky. Stop in at the **Welcome to L.L. Bean** page for the tips you need.

A
B
C
D
E
F
G
H
I
J
K
L
M
N
O
P
Q
R
S
T
U
V
W
X
Y
Z

"Bill Nye believes he can change the world, and his enthusiasm is infectious!"

PHYSICS

Bill Nye the Science Guy's Nye Labs Online

Webmaster: Bill Predmore

http://nyelabs.kcts.org/

Who came up with the idea for your page or project? Was it you? How did the idea originate?

Bill Nye the Science Guy's Nye Labs Online was conceived of and created by POP! Multimedia. A couple of current POP! staffers were among the crew of the hit PBS series, and when the show went on hiatus in the Spring of 1995, we had a vision: build a way-cool interactive version of Nye Labs!

How many people work on your pages? Does it take a lot of time? How many hits do you get a day?

Nye Labs Online is produced and maintained by POP! Multimedia. We make small adjustments to the pages every day, and receive up to 40,000 hits and 150 pieces of e-mail from the page each day.

You must hear from people all over the world! Can you think of an unusual request, question, or comment someone has sent to you?

We have received e-mail from around the globe. Although I won't comment on the weirdest requests, we generally receive a lot of support and encouragement for the work we do with the TV series and the Web site. Bill Nye believes he can change the world, and his enthusiasm is infectious!

What is your favorite resource on the Net?

Amazon.com's online bookstore <http://www.amazon.com>—perhaps the most useful site on the Internet.

What's the one thing you'd really like to do on your page but have not yet implemented?

We have always felt like Bill Nye was born to be on the Internet. As such, we are always dreaming up new ideas and plans for the site. Our long-term vision for the site includes bringing more video to the site, more frequent and extensive updates to the site, and a weekly newsletter which shares new science information with our audience.

What are your hopes and fears for the future of the Internet?

Because we feel that we have an important message which should be heard by the widest possible audience, we hope that the Internet eventually reaches every school and every home in the world. Education should be the highest priority of the United States, and the Internet should prove a useful tool for a lifetime of learning.

PARADES

The Great Circus Parade - Wisconsin's National Treasure

Hey, look at this poster! It says: "Come to the Great Circus Parade! A two-hour processional over a three-mile route, authentically re-creating turn-of-the-century circus street parades. Features 60 historic wagons, 700 horses, cavorting clowns, wild animals in cage wagons, and the fabulous 40-Horse Hitch." Sounds like fun! Look over there—isn't that Buffalo Bill Cody in that beaded buckskin jacket? You can learn something about circus history, including circus trains, at this colorful, animated site. If you have Java, you'll also hear vintage calliope music!

http://circus.compuware.com/

NEW ORLEANS .NET: CARNIVAL ON PARADE

Have you heard about Mardi Gras in New Orleans, Louisiana? The carnival season begins at the end of January and is celebrated right up until Fat Tuesday, the day before the Christian season of Lent begins. It's a series of parties, parades, and nonstop fun and foolishness! Over 70 parades are given by special clubs called *krewes*. Everyone dresses up in outlandish costumes and yells, "Throw me somethin', Mister!" Then they line the streets to catch "throws" tossed from the krewes on the floats. Popular throws include doubloons, beads, cups, and sometimes coconuts (get out of the way if you see a coconut hurled your way!). You can see some of the fun and learn about the history of this gala event at this site, created by the *Times-Picayune* newspaper.

http://www.neworleans.net/carnpages/parades.html

Tournament of Roses

Alas, you won't be able to take time to smell the roses at this Web site, because there aren't any! But all the info is here about this traditional New Year's Day parade, held in Pasadena, California. All the floats must be completely covered with flowers or other natural, organic material.

http://www.rosebowl.com/

Trooping the Colour

One of the largest military parades in the world, the Trooping of the Colour is held every June to celebrate the official birthday of Elizabeth II of England. It's not on her real birthday but on her "official" birthday. It's a grand show of heraldry, music, prancing horses, and dashing soldiers. The presentation of the flag ("the colour") to Her Majesty is the highlight of the event. The flag is weighty and cumbersome, but no one would turn down the honor of carrying it, and the soldier who carries the flag during the ceremony must train for months. The ceremony requires strict adherence to military regulations. Anyone falling from a horse could get three months in jail! Learn about one of the most stirring parades in the world at this Web site.

http://www.buckinghamgate.com/events/
    past_features/trooping/trooping.html

PEACE

1000 Cranes Project

Sadako and the story of the thousand cranes has touched hearts worldwide. An old Japanese legend says that anyone who folds 1,000 origami cranes can have a wish. Sadako was a survivor of the atomic bomb attack on Hiroshima, Japan, in 1945. The radiation made her very ill, and she died before completing all her cranes. Her friends completed them for her. Sadako's story is not forgotten. Her inspiring statue stands today in the Hiroshima Peace Park. The year 1995 marked 50 years of peace between the U.S. and Japan, and many people around the world decided to fold cranes and send them to the Peace Park to honor Sadako and her gentle message of peace. Read the story of how many children's hands made these cranes, which flutter today over the park of peace.

http://www.csi.ad.jp/suzuhari-es/1000cranes/

Computers are dumb, people are smart.

A
B
C
D
E
F
G
H
I
J
K
L
M
N
O
P
Q
R
S
T
U
V
W
X
Y
Z

"We are pleased to present nearly 20,000 paper cranes made by children in 42 states and one Canadian province. The children were linked to each other and to Japan through the Internet, and they were linked by love and a desire for peace," said teacher Sharon O'Connell. She had carried brilliantly colored origami cranes to Hiroshima, Japan for the 50th anniversary celebration of peace between the U.S. and Japan. Read about the program at the 1000 Cranes Project.

Declarations of Peace

"The key to peace starts with each of us. Many times peace is defined as not fighting. However broken feelings can be as painful as throwing a punch." This is one of the Peace Declarations published by an eighth-grade class at St. Julie Billiart School in Hamilton, Ohio. Go one level back, to <http://www.iac.net/~esimonds/julie.html> and choose to see what some seventh-graders say about peace.

http://www.iac.net/~esimonds/stjulie/eighthg.html

Find historic documents and spell-check them for fun in HISTORY.

Get Your ANGRIES Out!

Are you always yelling at your sister? Is there a bully bothering you at school? Are you mad and cranky a lot? This site gives you some useful ways to get your anger out in constructive ways. For example: "Check your tummy, jaws and your fists. See if the mads are coming. Breathe! Blow your mad out. Get your control. Feel good about getting your control. Stop and think; make a good choice. People are not to be hurt with your hands, feet or voice. Remember to use your firm words, not your fists." There are many more good ideas here, and don't forget to check the links about peace here while you're dealing with your angries!

http://members.aol.com/AngriesOut/index.htm

Kids 4 Peace

"What if for 1 DAY no gun were fired...
What if for 1 DAY we tried to get along...
Imagine what it could mean for us all...
Imagine how 1 DAY could change all the world...
1 DAY Of Peace, on January 1, in the Year 2000
Spread the word, the World has declared:
1 DAY Of PEACE, for all the world to share..."

Kids for Peace want to get everyone on the planet on board for this world day of peace. Learn how you can help!

http://members.aol.com/kidz4peace/index.htm

Line around the world

Here's something unusual, called a *Web Ring*. Its creator wants to draw a line around the world, linking Web page to Web page, to show how we're all connected to each other on this little blue planet of ours. Register your home page, and within a few days, you'll receive the "line" to place on your page. You link back to the last person in the line, and the next person after you will link to your home page. Thus, you're standing in line between two strangers, but, oddly enough, it feels pretty good. By linking your home page, or your school's, into this big virtual "hug," you've agreed to perform a good deed. How far has the line gone so far? Check this page to find out!

http://www.stairway.org/latw

Peace in Pictures

The project, located in Jerusalem, is both a contest and a collaboration. It invites kids to draw what they think "peace" looks like and share those drawings with other kids all over the world. You can mail, fax, or ftp your drawing to this site. There are prizes but no information yet on what they might be or details about when the contest ends. But you can enjoy some of the pictures already entered.

http://www.macom.co.il/peace/

PEN PALS

eMail Classroom Exchange - K-12 Education Resource

Would your whole class or home school like to write to another class of kids on the other side of the world? You can, just by adding your information to the database here! Search for kids by city, state, country, grade/age, or language. There are also some real-time conferencing facilities here.

http://www.iglou.com/xchange/ece/

NET FILES

How many people are on Earth?

Answer: Quite a few! For the latest estimate, check the world population clocks at http://sunsite.unc.edu/lunarbin/worldpop

Maddy Mayhem's PenPal List!

A part of the safe, fun Maddy Mayhem's Kids' Stuff site, the PenPal List is a good place to go to learn about others and the world around you as you exercise the art of writing. If you're 17 or under, fill out a form with information about yourself and your interests, click a button, and ZAP! you've just joined the group! Scan the list of correspondents or use your browser's find feature to look for that certain penpal that shares your interests. But remember, read Maddy's reminders about how to be safe while meeting people on the Net. Reach out and write someone!

http://nebula.on.ca/madbo/1penpal.htm

Pen Pal Planet - Friends by Mail from America

Do you live outside North America and want a pen pal in the U.S. or Canada? You can get one, free, by sending a letter to this site. U.S. and Canadian participants need to pay a small fee to join. This nonprofit group is not interested in matching up kids who want to send e-mail to each other, since most of the kids in the world don't have e-mail yet. But if you want to practice your writing or your English with a pen and paper pal, this might be a good place to find a friend. Be sure to read the tips for addressing letters in Arabic or Chinese, and please note that this site will not resell your name and address.

http://www.epix.net/~ppplanet/index.html

Pen Pal Request Form

There is a great service for kids called Schoolnet. The Schoolnet folks have set up a service to help kids in Canada and elsewhere find pen pals. If you think you'd be interested in making contact with kids from all over the world, take a look at this site. All you need is e-mail and a willingness to make new friends. The top level of this gopher is at <gopher://gopher.schoolnet.ca:419/1>. You can also search their Web page and listserv archives at <http://schoolnet2.carleton.ca/>.

gopher://gopher.schoolnet.ca:419/11/K6.dir/
  penpals.dir

A
B
C
D
E
F
G
H
I
J
K
L
M
N
O
P
Q
R
S
T
U
V
W
X
Y
Z

WKN Fun Clubs

If you want a quick way to find other kids who are interested in space, animals, computers, books, writing, volunteering, entertainers, and more, try this site. For example, if you're a fan of *Star Trek*, transport into the USS *Jaguar* and take the turbolift to any deck to learn about the various officers and their duties on the ship. Then become an officer yourself and write to other officers all over the world! At this site, kids rule.

http://www.worldkids.net/clubs/clubs.htm

PEOPLE AND BIOGRAPHIES

See also AFRICAN AMERICANS; ASIAN AMERICANS; INVENTIONS AND INVENTORS; LATINO; NATIVE AMERICANS AND OTHER INDIGENOUS PEOPLES; QUEENS, KINGS, ROYALTY; REFERENCE WORKS; U.S. PRESIDENTS AND FIRST LADIES

Albert Einstein Online

Lots of people think Albert Einstein was the greatest physicist ever. His famous theory of relativity includes the equation $e = mc^2$. He even had an element named after him! Einsteinium, element 99, was discovered in 1952. Einstein won the Nobel Prize for Physics in 1921. Although he urged President Roosevelt to consider making an atomic bomb (the letter is at this site), he believed in peace.

http://www.sas.upenn.edu/~smfriedm/einstein.html

America's West - Development and History

Return with us now to the days of yesteryear—of gold rush and ghost town, the heyday of cowboy and gunslinger. At this site, you'll discover links to information on America's westward expansion, famous Western trails, pioneers, trappers, and biographies of Kit Carson, Davy Crockett, Daniel Boone, Billy the Kid, Sitting Bull, Roy Rogers, and lots of other famous folks. There are links to movies about the West as well as to Western theme parks and dude ranches. A caution to parents: Not all the outbound links have been reviewed.

http://www.AmericanWest.com/

Biographical Dictionary

Sometimes you'll get an assignment in school about a famous person, or maybe you're curious and you'd like to know some quick facts about a famous person. This site is the place to go for this type of info, even if it is presented in "good old ASCII" text. Here you'll find 15,000 people listed, from both historical and current times. In this simple alphabetical list, you'll learn when the famous person was born, the year of death (if applicable), and a very brief explanation of why the person is famous. You won't find detailed information here, just the bare minimum of facts. Sometimes, though, even a little bit of info can be handy!

ftp://obi.std.com/obi/Biographical/

NET FILES

What are the Seven Wonders of the ancient world?

(Hint: The list does not include Sneezy or Dopey or have anything to do with Snow White.)

Answer: The list of the Seven Wonders of the ancient world was originally compiled around 2 B.C. In chronological order, they are: the Great Pyramid of Giza, the Hanging Gardens of Babylon, the Statue of Zeus at Olympia, the Temple of Artemis at Ephesus, the Mausoleum at Halicarnassus, the Colossus of Rhodes, and the Lighthouse of Alexandria. Immerse yourself in the history of these beautiful structures and then see if you can guess the Seven Wonders of the modern world at http://pharos.bu.edu/Egypt/Wonders/Home.html

Whooooooo will you find in BIRDS?

HyperHistory

Hey, your mom says you can have some friends over for lunch! She says to invite three people you admire from history—which heroes would you choose? You might get some ideas here. This site will teach you about important people from 1000 B.C. to the present. You'll find scientists, artists, musicians, authors, politicians, explorers, and many others. But that is not all. You can also trace events through history as well as look at important maps of time periods and the spread of civilizations.

http://www.hyperhistory.com/online_n2/
    History_n2/a.html

The Lemelson-MIT Prize Program and Invention Dimension

Would you like to win half a million dollars? All you have to do is invent something so cool, so unique, and so compelling that everyone says, "Wow!" That's the idea behind the Lemelson-MIT Prize, which is presented every year to an American inventor-innovator for outstanding creativity. You can find out about the prize and its past winners here, and you'll also find a collection of material about other great inventors and inventions. Check the Inventor of the Week archives, but be prepared for a lengthy wait. The page loads over 60 drawings of famous (and not-so-famous) inventors. Why they don't have a text-only option yet is unknown; perhaps they will by the time you read this. Don't miss the Links area for more inventions and resources.

http://web.mit.edu/afs/athena.mit.edu/org/i/invent/
    www/invention_dimension.html

Man of the Year Home Page

Need biographies of famous people? Cruise over to this page for information about the man, woman, or idea considered by *Time* magazine to be the biggest influence on events each year since 1927. In 1982, the computer was "Man of the Year." You may want to select the text-only version of this page, since the graphics take a long time to load.

http://pathfinder.com/time/special/moy/moy.html

Martin Luther King, Jr.

In a thoughtful and moving Web site, *The Seattle Times* commemorates the life and legacy of Dr. Martin Luther King, Jr. You'll find a timeline of his life, along with many photos and audio files. You'll be able to hear part of his famous "I Have a Dream" speech as well as others. Check the sections on the history of the civil rights movement, and read about how the Martin Luther King, Jr. Day national holiday was created in memory of this great leader, called "America's Gandhi."

http://www.seattletimes.com/mlk/

Dr. Martin Luther King, Jr. has been called "America's Gandhi" because of his commitment to nonviolent struggle.

Written on a plaque in the hotel room in which he was killed are these words: *"Behold here comes the dreamer. Let us slay him, and we shall see what becomes of his dream."* His dream lives on, despite the violent act that ended his life. Read about it at the Martin Luther King, Jr. page.

MSU Vincent Voice Library

Wouldn't it be great to be able to hear the voices of some famous people? At this site, you can! Listen to sound files of many U.S. presidents as well as brief conversations with people such as George Washington Carver, Babe Ruth, and Amelia Earhart. Test: Teddy Roosevelt has left the building...he has left the building!

http://web.msu.edu/vincent/index.html

A
B
C
D
E
F
G
H
I
J
K
L
M
N
O
P
Q
R
S
T
U
V
W
X
Y
Z

A
B
C
D
E
F
G
H
I
J
K
L
M
N
O
P
Q
R
S
T
U
V
W
X
Y
Z

Pirates at the City Art Center

"Shiver me timbers!" If you don't know a pirate from a buccaneer, better sail over to this page. You'll learn lots about famous pirates, legends, and perhaps locations of buried treasure!

http://www.efr.hw.ac.uk/EDC/CAC/pirates/pirates.htm

The World of Benjamin Franklin

Hey! Who's that guy on the one hundred dollar bill, the hippie with the long hair? It's Ben Franklin: famous American scientist, statesman, and inventor. You remember him—he's the guy who flew the kite in the thunderstorm to learn about electricity. Or did he? Here are some classroom activities to help you learn more about some of the things that interested Franklin. He was interested in lots of things, too. For example, he was one of the original signers of the Declaration of Independence. And you know where it was signed, right? At the bottom!

http://sln.fi.edu/franklin/rotten.html

BIRTHDAYS
Brittanica's Lives

Ever wonder who shares your birthday? Sure, it might be your mom or your dad or even your twin brother. But was anyone famous born on your birthday? (Besides you, of course!) Find out at this useful site. You can also discover which famous people in history share the same generation. For example, John McEnroe and Magic Johnson both turned 21 in 1980. Want to know more about each famous person? This site gives you short biographies.

http://www.eb.com/bio.html

WOMEN'S STUDIES
Biographies of Historical Women

Did you know a woman helped start the field of social work (Jane Addams)? Did you know a woman was one the best guides for slaves fleeing to freedom (Sojourner Truth)? Did you know a woman was one of the world's first great novelists (Charlotte Brontë)? You can read brief biographies of these and other women here.

http://www.inform.umd.edu:8080/EdRes/Topic/
  WomensStudies/ReadingRoom/History/Biographies/

Encyclopedia of Women's History

Some kids noticed that the Web didn't have a site that brought together a list of famous women and their contributions to math, science, and the arts. So they decided to make one! You can submit biographical reports about famous women in history and read what other kids have submitted so far. A lot of these reports were not spell-checked, but you'll get the idea.

http://www.teleport.com/~megaines/women.html

WIC - Biography Index

What are you going to do? Your next reading assignment is to read a biography, but you just don't know which book to pick—and whose life is really that interesting, anyway? Here's a series of short biographies of interesting women who've won either an International Humanitarian Award or a Living Legacy Award. Look at this site and then head back to your library for more information. You can even find out names of famous women who were born on your birth date at <http://www.wic.org/cal/idex_cal.htm>.

http://www.wic.org/bio/idex_bio.htm

Women in Canadian History

Women have always been an important part of Canada's history. Dr. Emily Jennings Stowe was the first woman to practice medicine in Canada. Lucy Maud Montgomery became known worldwide as the author of *Anne of Green Gables* and other books. Madeleine Jarrett Tarieu single-handedly defended an entire fort against invaders. And there are others. The stories here are very interesting! You'll also find quotes, trivia questions, and more.

http://www.niagara.com/~merrwill/

Women Mathematicians

These pages are an ongoing project by students in mathematics classes at Agnes Scott College in Decatur, Georgia. You'll find brief comments on over 50 women in mathematics and expanded biographies, photos, and more information on at least ten of them. There are also extensive links to pages about women scientists, computer scientists, and others.

http://www.scottlan.edu/lriddle/women/women.htm

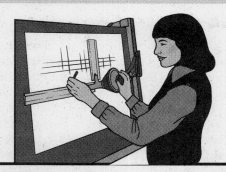

Ada Byron Lovelace is credited with the invention of programming for her work in explaining the details of how the "analytical engine" (a precursor to the computer) operated. The programming language Ada is named after her as a tribute to her work. Read more about Lovelace and other women's achievements at Women Mathematicians.

PETS AND PET CARE

See also AMPHIBIANS; AQUARIUMS; BIRDS; CATS; DOGS AND DOG SPORTS; HORSES AND EQUESTRIAN SPORTS; MAMMALS; REPTILES

Acme Pet—Your Guide to Pets on the Internet!

Pet enthusiasts, welcome! Here you'll find a current and complete source of pet information, discussion lists, and resources all over the Internet. Send in your facts, views, or opinions about pet-related topics on this home page. Whether you want to keep a pet gerbil or a pet prairie dog—check into it here first!

http://www.acmepet.com/

Flint River Ranch - Super Premium Health Food for Pets

Is your dog's coat looking a little ragged? Perhaps your cat seems a little pokey. Get a free sample of health food for your pet by calling an 800 number or by sending e-mail. Net-mom's cats endorse this product. They also eat it.

http://www.snni.com/ferguson/flint-rr.htm

Hedgehog Hollow

Hedgehogs: the trendy pet of the '90s! Have you been considering getting a hedgehog as a pet, or are you just wondering what all the interest in those hedgehog things is about? Either way, this page is the place to go. Contrary to popular belief, hedgehogs are not related to porcupines. They make great pets, but some kinds make better pets than others; find out here. Some hedgehogs can even be trained to use a litter box! They eat a variety of food, such as cat food, hard-boiled eggs, cottage cheese, oatmeal, fruit, mealworms, crickets, grasshoppers, earthworms...well, you get the picture.

http://www.pci.on.ca/~macnamar/hedgehogs/

Hedgehogs of steel!

These cute critters have an amazing immunity to most toxic things. Toxins that would kill a human hundreds or even thousands of times over often have no noticeable effect on a hedgehog. Scientific research has even confirmed this fact. Visit Hedgehog Hollow to learn more about these adorable little creatures.

Pet Index Homepage

Ferret, fish, feline, facts—you'll find them all here. Crazy over chinchillas? Silly over snakes? Raving over rabbits? There's surely something for you on this page, with animals, animals, everywhere!

http://www.zmall.com/pet_talk/pet-faqs/

A
B
C
D
E
F
G
H
I
J
K
L
M
N
O
P
Q
R
S
T
U
V
W
X
Y
Z

A B C D E F G H I J K L M N O **P** Q R S T U V W X Y Z

Pet Loss and Rainbow Bridge

It's so sad to lose a pet. This gentle site gives one beautiful idea of what happens when a beloved pet crosses the "Rainbow Bridge" and waits with the other pets for their human friends to join them someday. You'll find pictures, poems, and thoughts about pets on this touching page, which always makes Net-mom cry. There are also numerous links to dealing with grief over the loss of a companion animal. You can also submit a memorial for your own pet by leaving a message in the guest book.

http://www.primenet.com/~meggie/bridge.htm

Pets, Vets, You and Dr. Sue (Davis Virtual Market) vers 1.4

Did you know that a six-year-old dog or cat is equivalent to a 40-year-old human? This is based on tooth and bone growth and other items relating to maturity. This site offers additional interesting information, such as pig and raccoon fun facts and seasonal pet care tips. Future topics will include iguana care, llamas as companions, and more. Stop by and see what Dr. Sue has to say.

http://vme.net/dvm/DrSue/

Heat stress can be a big summertime problem for your furry friends. Your dog will enjoy a splash in a hard plastic wading pool instead of a walk on hot, burning pavement. Or, freeze water in a closed gallon jug and leave it for your pet to "snuggle up to." Keep your pets cool in the shade, give them plenty of water, and don't leave them in parked cars, even "for a minute"—summertime temperatures can soar in an enclosed space like your car. Know the signs and first aid tips for heat stress, located at Pets, Vets, You and Dr. Sue (Davis Virtual Market) vers 1.4. Be sure to call your own veterinarian in an emergency, though.

Racine County dot Com - Pets

For a brief guide to a lot of different kinds of dogs, cats, fish, and birds, you might explore this resource. What really sets it apart, though, is the pet's guide to selecting and caring for a human. For example, if a fish picks a human wearing a "power" tie, it is a safe bet that it'll get better-quality fish flakes in its tank; but if the fish chooses one that works too much, the person might forget to feed the fish at all, and that would be bad! Did you know that dogs and cats are really space aliens from the planet Kibble? Their mission is to enslave humans so that the planet can be colonized by animals. Does your cat control you? Ever notice how much the cat sits in the sun? That's because cats are really solar-powered. And when they get that really blank look in their eyes, cats are really communicating with their home planet about plans for the invasion!

http://rcc.webpoint.com/pets/

Virtual Pet Home Page

If you can't have a real pet, maybe you can own a virtual pet! The Tamagocchi "Lovable Egg" has become a real craze in Japan, and all signs point to overwhelming popularity when the little pastel-colored eggs are introduced to the U.S. this summer (as "Tamagotchi"). What are they? Net-mom's never seen one (Bandai, are you listening?) but according to the descriptions in the press releases, and the pictures on the Bandai site <http://www.bandai.com/theegg.html>, it looks something like a little game on a keychain or a necklace. There's a little chicken-like bird on the LCD screen, and you have to feed it, pet it, and clean up after it, or it gets sick and dies, leaving you feeling way guilty. But there are other virtual pets you can get, some of them as free demos, which live on your computer screen. Check the Virtual Pet Home Page for a collection of all known virtual pets. Hint: if this catches on, you may want to think about becoming a virtual veterinarian!

http://www.virtualpet.com/vp/

Take a ride on a Carousel in AMUSEMENT PARKS.

Welcome to NetVet

The doctor is in! You'll find information on animal care and behavior from breeders, vets, and researchers. This site features anything that walks, flies, hops, slithers, or swings through the trees. The NetVet resource contains some of the most respected and popular resources about pets on the Net.

http://netvet.wustl.edu/

PHOTOGRAPHY

Bob Miller's Light Walk

This site will really *illuminate* your knowledge of light and shadow. In fact, it's a *bright* idea to check it out if you have a science fair project due, since there are project directions for building your own pinhole camera, making your own "light walk," and performing more tricks of light. You'll find a whole spectrum of links here and a fascinating look into shadows. Don't be scared, just *lighten* up!

http://www.exploratorium.edu/light_walk/
lw_main.html

Center for Creative Photography Homepage

The University of Arizona maintains one of the largest and most accessible collections of fine photography in the world, with over 15,000 images. Renowned nature photographer Ansel Adams helped to found this institution, and his work, along with a who's who of other photographers, is well represented at this site. Along with rotating selections from its archives, the Center's home page also features information on its educational programs, library, research facilities, publications, and museum shop. Parental advisory: not all photos have been previewed.

http://www.library.arizona.edu/branches/
ccp/ccphome.html

Exposure - A Beginners Guide to Photography

Photography—is it technology or magic? Even if you have a nonadjustable camera, you can try some of these tips and tricks to jazz up your photos. If you do have a camera with a lot of controls on it, you can really change how the picture looks. You can learn how to set the camera so that the background blurs out of focus. This puts more emphasis on your main subjects in the foreground of the picture. On the other hand, you might want to make sure that as much of the scene as possible stays in focus. There is a special way to set the camera for that, too. You can try it all using Sim-Cam, a way-cool JavaScript applet that will teach you the mysteries of f-stops and aperture by letting you set a virtual camera, take a picture, and see immediate results!

http://www.88.com/exposure/lowrez_index.htm

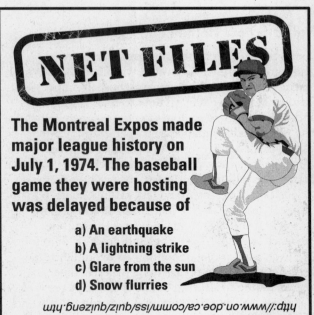

NET FILES

The Montreal Expos made major league history on July 1, 1974. The baseball game they were hosting was delayed because of

a) An earthquake
b) A lightning strike
c) Glare from the sun
d) Snow flurries

Answer: The answer is c. According to The Great Canadian Weather Quiz, "Blinding sunlight delayed the start of the game between the Expos and the Chicago Cubs for 20 minutes because the umpire couldn't see the pitches." Take the weather quiz and find out more fun facts at
http://www.on.doe.ca/comm/iss/quiz/quizeng.htm

Visit historic sites via the Net in HISTORY.

A B C D E F G H I J K L M N O **P** Q R S T U V W X Y Z

A
B
C
D
E
F
G
H
I
J
K
L
M
N
O
P
Q
R
S
T
U
V
W
X
Y
Z

George Eastman House

Explore the history of photography and view some very interesting early cameras and photographic experiments. George Eastman was the founder of the Eastman Kodak company. This is a tour to his house and gardens in Rochester, New York, which has been preserved as a photographic museum. There is also a handy guide to preserving your family's photo albums at *<http://www.it.rit.edu/~gehouse/exhibits/album/ album.html>*. One type of album to avoid is the "magic" or magnetic type, which has a heavy cardboard sheet with lines of adhesive on it. In these types of albums, you put the photo on the page and then fold a clear sheet over the photos; over time, the adhesive deteriorates and bleeds right through your photos! Get the facts on how to store photos so your great-grandchildren can enjoy them.

http://www.it.rit.edu/~gehouse/

Hoffer School Home Page

For over five years, the California Museum of Photography has collaborated with the students and teachers of Hoffer Elementary School in Banning, California. Students learn how to use photography and other multimedia tools to express themselves. The results are displayed in this engrossing Web page, which features pictures, voices, and written words of the student artists. They include a collection of their fun photos, montages, magazine collages, videos of motion toys, a collaborative e-mail "books project," and a history of the town of Banning in words and pictures. As more schools add their presence to the Internet, they would do well to follow this example. And as more high-powered graphic designers and ad agencies develop Web sites, it will be heartening to see that one of the best pages around was designed by third-graders! A caution to parents: The UCR/California Museum of Photography has other exhibits that contain adult subjects and may not be suitable for children; proceed to links off this page with caution.

http://www.cmp.ucr.edu/exhibitions/hoffer/
hoffer.homepage.html

Watch your step in DANCE.

Kodak Home Page

You would expect Kodak to have an active home page, and they do indeed. You can find all sorts of valuable information on photography here, whether your interests lie in producing professional-quality photographs or simple snapshots. A What's New section will keep you coming back regularly. One example is a section featuring the Top Ten Techniques for photographers to get good pictures.

http://www.kodak.com/

Want to take great pictures at the next ball game?

If you have a telephoto lens, use that; otherwise, move in as close as you can. Then, to freeze the sports action, use the fastest shutter speed your camera will allow. This will depend on the speed of the film you're using, so ask for some professional advice at the photo shop beforehand. It's also important to anticipate the peak of action, like when the bat cracks against the ball, when the runner jumps the hurdle, or when the basketball swishes through the hoop. Photos taken at the peak tend to be the most exciting! You can also freeze action by using a flash, but remember that your subject must be within about 15 feet of you for a flash to work. Get more great photo tips at the Kodak Home Page!

Do you know the way to San Jose? If not, check a map in GEOGRAPHY.

PHYSICS

Bill Nye the Science Guy's NYE LABS ONLINE

It's Bill Nye the Science Guy, and is he loaded with science goodies to show you! If the graphics are too much, stop the page after part of it loads and click the TEXT Menu option. There are photos, sounds, and movies (caution: these are big files) in the Goodies area. Check out Today's Demo or visit the U-Nye-Verse to see what's happening in Bill's world of science. Lots of experiments and lessons on things scientific can be found here, plenty of fodder for your next science fair project. TV listings are also available if you want to find out when he's on the tube. There is even a chat area where you can post comments and see if anyone replies.

http://nyelabs.kcts.org/

When you're giving an opinion, sometimes you say that's your "two cents' worth." Where did that phrase originate?

Answer: *According to Evan Morris, "Two cents or two-center has been a slang synonym for very cheap' since the middle of the 19th century, when the cheapest cigar available was literally a two-center. The U.S. Treasury Department actually issued a two-cent coin in 1864, which was, incidentally, the first U.S. coin to bear the motto 'In God We Trust.' The government, evidently feeling frisky in a monetary sort of way, also issued coins in three-cent and twenty-cent denominations during the same period." Read more at* http://www.word-detective.com/back-k.html#cents

Curl up with a good Internet site.

Little Shop of Physics Online

Welcome to the Little Shop of Physics; nothing here will harm you (well, you might want to stay away from that disreputable-looking plant over in the corner!). They have concocted some interesting demonstrations using everyday objects that might amuse you and teach you something about physics. There are optical and auditory illusions plus lots of special effects you can try right on your computer screen. Come closer!

http://129.82.166.181/Expframe.html

ELECTRICITY
Theater of Electricity

Did you ever get zapped by touching a metal doorknob at home? Where'd the electricity come from? Static electricity built up on your shoes as you walked across a carpet. Scientists who need a lot of static electricity for an experiment use a Van de Graaff generator, which makes electricity from a huge revolving belt inside one of its towers. Read about its history and construction and all about lightning and electricity. You can see the huge original generator, built by Dr. Robert J. Van de Graaff, in the Theater of Electricity at the Museum of Science in Cambridge, Massachusetts, and on this World Wide Web site. You probably won't have a generator like this at home, but here you'll find some experiments you can do with balloons, paper bunnies, and static electricity!

http://www.mos.org/sln/toe/toe.html

FORCES
Bill Nye Episode: MAGNETISM

Here's an experiment that explores the world of magnetism. Bill Nye the Science Guy guides you through a simple project that shows you how to make your own compass out of a needle and bowl of water. Did you know some animals use magnetism to find their way when they migrate? Is it magic? No, it's magnetism!

http://nyelabs.kcts.org/nyeverse/episode/e21.html

A
B
C
D
E
F
G
H
I
J
K
L
M
N
O
P
Q
R
S
T
U
V
W
X
Y
Z

A
B
C
D
E
F
G
H
I
J
K
L
M
N
O
P
Q
R
S
T
U
V
W
X
Y
Z

The Coriolis Effect Page

Because the Earth rotates, it has a special effect on the behavior of fluids on its surface. We see this when large low-pressure storms turn one way in the Northern Hemisphere and the other way in the Southern Hemisphere. This is known as the Coriolis effect. It has led to speculation that the same thing happens to water draining from a sink, bathtub, or toilet bowl. Physicists state at *<ftp://rtfm.mit.edu/pub/usenet-by-group/news.answers/physics-faq/part3>* that the Coriolis effect doesn't work in something as small as a drain. But people still believe it anyway! This page wants *you* to help answer the question once and for all. Take a look at water in your sink. Which way is the water turning: clockwise or counterclockwise? Now go to this Web site and register your observation for your area of the world. Check the online results to see what others have said so far! For another explanation of the Coriolis effect, see what *USA Today* has to say about it at *<http://www.usatoday.com/weather/wcorioli.htm>* and check how you can fake out your class into believing the equator runs right through your classroom at *<http://www.ems.psu.edu/~fraser/Bad/BadCoriolis.html>*.

http://chemlab.pc.maricopa.edu/drain.about.fcgi

How to Use a Compass

One use of magnetism is finding your way with a compass. On a wilderness hike, a compass is necessary, but first you have to learn to use one properly. You can learn in your own backyard, or in a park, or in a school playground. This site gives you a guided tour to a compass and its use. There are also tips on how to find your way in very difficult conditions, like fog or snow whiteouts.

http://www.uio.no/~kjetikj/compass/

Magnetism

What's the *attraction*? Magnetism helps us find our way with a compass. It's what makes electric motors run. Did you know it's also responsible for the northern lights? Read about the history of magnetism and how it works. Drawings show how magnetic fields are made up of invisible field lines. There are also facts about the contributions of Michael Faraday and James Maxwell to the "field" of magnetism. May the force be with you!

http://lepmp.gsfc.nasa.gov/Education/Imagnet.html

Professor Bubbles' Official Bubble Homepage

You don't need a lot of skills to learn to blow soap bubbles, right? So what is with this guy who calls himself "Professor"? Turns out he really is an expert. At his home page, he reveals the ultimate soap solution for making the most colorful, sturdy bubbles. He explains how to make your own bubble-blowing tools from soup cans and coat hangers (ask your parents for help). But you don't even need anything special—he teaches you how to blow bubbles using only your HANDS! But wait, there's more. Check the bubble FAQ, bubble games, and the other wonders of the Bubblesphere.

http://bubbles.org/

Rocket Principles

This isn't exactly rocket science, but then again, this is where it all starts. Read all about Newton's first, second, and third laws of motion and forces and how they relate to rocketry. These basic laws rule all motion, not just rocketry. They explain why a basketball bounces, why a baseball goes so far when you hit it with a bat, and why you go over the handlebars if you run into a tree with your bike (you don't have to try the last one—just take our word for it!). The top level of this page is at *<http://www.lerc.nasa.gov/Other_Groups/K-12/TRC_activities.html>* where you'll find some cool experiments to help you understand the laws of motion. Our personal favorite is the balloon-powered pinwheel!

http://www.lerc.nasa.gov/Other_Groups/K-12/TRC/Rockets/rocket_principles.html

Soap Bubbles

Have you ever noticed that bubbles are always round, no matter what shape the wand you blow through is? Is that because your breath is shaped like a circle as it comes out of your lips? No. A bubble is round because of physical forces you can learn about here. You'll also learn that when a bubble looks gray or black, it is about to pop. Why does it lose its pretty colors? Find out here, and don't miss the Internet Resources section for more good, clean fun.

http://www.exploratorium.edu/ronh/bubbles/bubbles.html

-- WaterWorks --

Oh, the magic of water fountains! Some are tall, some are wide, others squirt in many directions at once. Discover what makes a fountain work and the forces it takes to make water do its tricks. Pictures of different types of fountains are shown along with some that were made by students. There are even movies and sounds of the different fountains available (caution: the files are big!).

http://www.omsi.edu/sln/ww/waterworks.html

NET FILES

WHY DO BATTERS LOVE TO PLAY BASEBALL AT COORS STADIUM IN DENVER, COLORADO?

(Hint: Denver is known as the "Mile-High City.")

Answer: Batters can hit a ball farther at higher elevations than they can at lower elevations! Why? According to the experts at *USA Today*, "The air pressure at Denver and other high elevations is lower than the pressure at lower elevations, which means fewer air molecules occupy a given volume....The collision of air molecules with the baseball creates the 'drag,' or friction, that slows the ball down. Since more air molecules are packed into a given volume at New York City, more collisions occur...and as a result, the baseball slows down more quickly [there] than in Denver." Find out more at http://www.usatoday.com/weather/wbasebal.htm

SLIME is a polymer, as anyone who's read CHEMISTRY knows!

LASERS

The Internet Webseum of Holography

Lasers can do some pretty amazing things. Did you know they are used to make interesting 3-D pictures that allow you to "look inside" and see around objects? That's called *holography*. Although lasers are needed to make a hologram, you don't need a laser to view one. You can view laser shows and holograms right here if you have the right plug-in. If you don't, there are links to get you the free software, so don't worry. Think it's all too complicated? Not at the Holo-kids area, at *<http://www.enter.net/~holostudio/kids.html>*.

http://www.enter.net/~holostudio/

Laserium Home Page

The word "laser" is really an acronym, which stands for "light amplification by the stimulated emission of radiation." Lasers are used in many scientific and medical applications, but everyone agrees the most fun you can have with lasers is at a "laserium" show! Often held in planetarium buildings and performed to music, the laserist is a true artist, as he or she "plays" the laser controls to draw fabulous light effects on the domed ceiling. This page tells about the history of laser shows and explains the science behind the vibrant colors overhead.

http://www.laserium.com/

LIGHT

Bob Miller's Light Walk

This site will really *illuminate* your knowledge of light and shadow. In fact, it's a *bright* idea to check it out if you have a science fair project due, since there are project directions for building your own pinhole camera, making your own "light walk," and performing more tricks of light. You'll find a whole spectrum of stuff here and a fascinating look into shadows. Don't be scared, just *lighten* up!

http://www.exploratorium.edu/light_walk/lw_main.html

A B C D E F G H I J K L M N O P Q R S T U V W X Y Z

Bubbles

Bet you didn't know that soap bubbles can teach you a lot about light and optics, right? Check the Light and Optics Activities at <http://www.scri.fsu.edu/~dennisl/CMS/activity/lightoptics.html> to explore light, refraction, lenses, and lasers. Practice tricks with bubbles, including how to make a bubble within a bubble! You'll also find the secret to making long-lasting "tough" bubble mix here.

http://www.scri.fsu.edu/~dennisl/CMS/activity/bubbles.html

MACHINES

You Can & Levers

The basic principles of levers are explained nicely here by Beakman and Jax. All three classes of levers are shown in easy-to-understand diagrams. Did you know that many household devices are levers? Nail clippers, pliers, nutcrackers, and fly swatters are just a few. After reading this page, see if you can tell which class of levers each device belongs to.

http://www.nbn.com/youcan/lever/lever.html

NET FILES

What four languages are spoken in the African country of Cameroon?

Answer: *French, English, Sudanic, and Bantu. Learn more about the fascinating continent of Africa, where over 1,000 languages are spoken, at* http://www.africaonline.com/AfricaOnline/kidsonly/languages/cam.html

SOUND

Bill Nye Episode: SOUND

Bill Nye the Science Guy has a sound project for you. It's not just educationally sound, it's *about* sound! With the help of a few household objects, learn how to make a sound-detecting device. You'll love the links to auditory experiments and demos elsewhere on the Web, too. Put on your lab coat and get out the fire extinguisher (just kidding), then prepare to sound off.

http://nyelabs.kcts.org/nyeverse/episode/e12.html

Characteristics of Sound

We'll bet you didn't know that the standard A musical note has a length of 16.4 inches. Its wavelength, that is! The calculation to prove it is right here on this page. There are comparison diagrams of a simple sine wave and of Bart Simpson saying, "Wow, cool, man." There are also comparisons of different sound levels, a diagram of how the ear works, and a chart showing the range of human hearing. Sounds great, huh?

http://jcbmac.chem.brown.edu/scissorsHtml/sound/charOfSound.html

Interactive Experiments

Part of a larger site called Little Shop of Physics (see earlier entry under PHYSICS), this lets you experience two weird Shockwave demonstrations. The first is an illusion in sound—pure sound, that is. Do you hear the notes as going up or going down? Check the science behind this very strange auditory foolery! The second explains how they make that Emergency Broadcast signal sound so annoying. Check it out.

http://129.82.166.181/online.html

Kids, Percussion, and Stomp

Is pure rhythm really music, or is it just a cacophony of noise? If you go to a performance of STOMP, you will see and hear the cast members "play" Zippo lighters, push brooms, trash cans, newspapers, and other common objects. Visit this Web site to see and hear audio from the show, try some fun activities, and learn more about the science of sound.

http://www.usinteractive.com/stomp/studyguide/contents.htm

POLLUTION

Environmental Bill of Rights

Do you know your environmental bill of rights? You'll find five important points here that include controlling waste and pollution as well as preserving wildlife habitat. There are also links to the Sierra Club and The Wilderness Society. You may also want to check the Definition of Pollution Prevention at <http://www.snre.umich.edu/nppc/p2defined.html> for more information. Links off this page have not been viewed.

http://www.dtm-corp.com/~sven/bill_o_rights.html

AIR

Acid Rain Program's Home Page

Acid rain is a scientific puzzle that was not easy to solve. It takes years for acid rain to cause problems, so its existence remained unknown for years. It can cause acid levels in lakes to increase so that fish and plant life cannot survive. Acid rain can also slowly eat away at buildings and structures, causing long-term damage. Where does it come from? What can be done about it? Two major chemicals combine to cause acid rain: sulfur dioxide and nitrous oxide. Although there are many sources of these two chemicals, coal-burning plants, cars, and trucks are the major contributors. This page, from the Acid Rain Program of the Environmental Protection Agency, describes some of the things that are being done to stop acid rain and the destruction it causes. For handy student resources, go directly to <http://www.epa.gov/acidrain/student/student2.html>.

http://www.epa.gov/docs/acidrain/ardhome.html

Air Table of Contents

According to this site, "Americans make the equivalent of 3 million trips to the moon and back each year in cars, using up natural resources and polluting the air." Find out about the major kinds of air pollution and what you can do to help. There are lots of classroom activities, too—how about putting on a play about pollution? Maybe you can get the part of reporter Connie Lung!

http://www.nwf.org/nwf/ed/air/

Burning Issues

If you live in a snowbound part of the world, you may know that there's nothing like a nice, warm fire in the fireplace. It feels so cozy and is so relaxing to watch. Have you ever thought of how your wood smoke might be polluting the air? Particles from the smoke can drift far away before settling out of the air. Along the way, that smoke may be inhaled by anyone in the area. You have probably noticed the often pleasant-smelling smoke from a neighbor's fireplace yourself. Have you ever thought that your lungs may not think it's so pleasant? Read more about this issue here.

http://www.webcom.com/~bi/

NET FILES

What's the hottest-selling CD in Tokyo?

Answer: Maybe it's the same as the hottest-selling CD in your town! As a matter of fact, it often is. But sometimes what "catches fire" in Japan is different than what's hot in Europe or America. Find out what's selling big in Tokyo, as well as what's not so cool, at http://www.infojapan.com/JWAVE/, which is a radio station in Tokyo!

You Can & Acid Rain

Beakman and Jax answer the question "How can rain be acid?" They talk about acid rain and show you how to make an acid tester. Use the acid tester to check the rain in your town to see if your area's being affected. Oops, there's one small detail you should know: you need to boil some cabbage to make the tester. So what, you say? Well, we'll let you discover that one on your own. :-)

http://www.nbn.com/youcan/acid/acid.html

A
B
C
D
E
F
G
H
I
J
K
L
M
N
O
P
Q
R
S
T
U
V
W
X
Y
Z

A
B
C
D
E
F
G
H
I
J
K
L
M
N
O
P
Q
R
S
T
U
V
W
X
Y
Z

TOXIC WASTE

Ocean Planet:perils-toxic materials

Out of about 65,000 chemicals used by industry, do you know how many of them are toxic? No? No one else does, either! Only about 300 of them have been thoroughly tested to discover if they have a toxic effect on our environment. That leaves a whole lot of waste materials that could have an unknown effect on us and our future health. Read about how dredging harbors to make them deeper can stir up toxic problems that have long been "sleeping." There's also a success story about how oyster beds have recovered their vitality since a certain paint was banned from use on boats.

http://seawifs.gsfc.nasa.gov/OCEAN_PLANET/HTML/
    peril_toxins.html

WATER

NWF: Table of Contents

These fun K–8 activities teach the sources of pollution, the reach of a watershed, and the problems of discarded plastics in the sea. Can you solve the mystery of who is polluting the neighborhood's water? There's also a quick tutorial on water pollution. Sure sounds like a fun way of learning!

http://www.igc.apc.org/nwf/ed/water/wate0000.html

The water we have on Earth now is all we will ever have, so we'd better take care of it. Did you know that one quart of motor oil can contaminate up to two million gallons of drinking water? Find out about the types of water pollution at NWF: Table of Contents, which is a National Wildlife Federation site.

Take a closer look through the microscope in BIOLOGY.

Ocean Planet: Oceans in Peril

Did you know U.S. sewage treatment plants discharge more oil into the ocean than spills from oil tankers do? Medical waste, plastics, and other debris threaten not only water quality but also sea creatures' lives. You can learn more facts about pollution of the ocean and waterways by taking a look at this exhibit, presented by the Smithsonian Institution as part of a larger Internet exhibition on the ocean. You'll never think the same about water draining from your kitchen sink!

http://seawifs.gsfc.nasa.gov/OCEAN_PLANET/HTML/
    ocean_planet_oceans_in_peril.html

Water Quality

This is a collection of reports to Congress that define the quality of U.S. lake, river, and stream water. The reports reveal findings about the different types of pollutants, such as metals and pesticides. There are sections on the sources of water pollution, ocean waters, wetlands, and ground water. The information is presented in graphics and text and is good material for a school project on water pollution. You can also find out about water quality in your state, although you need the free PDF Reader to view it (you'll find a link here to obtain the free PDF software).

http://www.epa.gov/305b/

Ships are only hulls, high walls are nothing, When no life moves in the empty passageways.
— Sophocles

QUEENS, KINGS, ROYALTY

The 700 Years of Grimaldi

Monaco's Grimaldi dynasty has ruled this small principality for the past seven hundred years! Your grandparents may remember how exciting it was in 1956, when the dashing Prince Rainier III married the American film star Grace Kelly. You can read about the stirring history of the Grimaldis, including biographies of Rainier and Prince Albert, his son. Surprisingly, Monaco did not join the United Nations until 1993.

http://www.monaco.mc/monaco/700ans/index.html

Alexander Palace Time Machine

Once, a second-grade boy visited the library and found a book about the great tsars of Russia. He became fascinated with their stories and their palace lifestyle. As time went on, he read everything he could about the great palace, hoping someday to visit Russia to see it for himself. Incredibly, this boy grew up to do that very thing, and now he's written a comprehensive Web page all about it. This outstanding multimedia tour will give you a look into the past as you explore the life and times of Tsar Nicholas II and his family and friends.

http://www.travelogix.com/emp/batchison/
   BobHome.html

THE BELGIAN MONARCHY

To see the background of one king, take a look at the curriculum vitae (that's Latin for "life's work") of King Albert II of Belgium. You'll see it's not easy to become a king, but, then again, the perks of the job are probably really great! The Belgian monarch's position is well respected in Belgium, as he is responsible for keeping the country independent and free.

http://belgium.fgov.be/Engels/417/41709/41709.htm

Online LIBRARIES rock!

The British Monarchy

This is the official Web site of the British monarchy. Here you will learn about the monarchy as it exists today as well as how it was in the past. You'll visit the palaces, the Crown Jewels, even find out why Elizabeth II keeps corgis as pets! There is a section on a typical day in the life of Her Royal Highness, and you can find out about the many ceremonial duties she must perform. This site is very new, very popular, and very, very slow. If you're interested in exactly what was said, sung, and done back on June 2, 1953, when Elizabeth became an anointed sovereign, you can follow the complex procedure at <http://www.ely.anglican.org/~sjk/liturgy/cor1953.html>.

http://www.royal.gov.uk/

Czars Lobby

Royalty's rule of Russia started with the Romanov Dynasty in 1613 and ended tragically with the Bolshevik Revolution of 1917. At this site you can meet some of Russia's fascinating leaders, such as Peter Alexeevich. The 14th child out of a family of 21 children, he grew to a height of seven feet at a time when the average person's height was even shorter than it is today. He was a skilled diplomat and a talented leader. It was under his rule that Russia became an empire, and he was given the title Emperor of All Russia, Great Father of the Fatherland. You may know him as Peter "the Great."

http://www.times.st-pete.fl.us/Treasures/
   TC.Lobby.html/

Elizabeth I (1533-1603)

Her father was Henry VIII, and she didn't have a very nice childhood. When still a toddler, her father had her mother killed for crimes against the State. Elizabeth was raised by others. When she was 20 years old, Elizabeth was imprisoned and narrowly missed following in her mother's footsteps. While she was in jail, she scratched some lines of verse on the windowpane, using a diamond ring. You can read what she wrote here, plus learn about Gloriana, one of the most famous monarchs of history.

http://www.alchemyweb.com/~alchemy/englit/
   renlit/eliza.htm

A B C D E F G H I J K L M N O P Q R S T U V W X Y Z

A B C D E F G H I J K L M N O P Q R S T U V W X Y Z

Gail Dedrick's Guide to The Monarchs of England and Great Britain

Who said the English lead boring lives? William the Conqueror started on his claim to fame when he became Duke of Normandy at age seven. But even after spending grueling days out in the field conquering his enemies, he still had to keep his guard up when relaxing back at the castle. The desire to be king among the ruling family members often led to assassination attempts and fatal "accidents." Learn more about William and his "unruly" family at this illustrated site. A long list of links is also provided so you can find out what the rest of the royals were up to during their time of rule.

http://www.ingress.com/~gail/

NET FILES

They stay up all night, working in the freezing cold. They mix proteins into water and make "whales." Nothing pleases them more than the sight of fresh powder.

Who are they?

Answer: *They are the folks who run the snowmaking equipment at ski resorts! Did you know that water makes better snow than clean water? Check http://www.cyberski.com.au/features/snowmaking.html to find out about the snowmaking process.*

Visit the CHEMISTRY section periodically.

A Glossary of European Noble, Princely, Royal and Imperial Titles

Can you tell a baronet from a marquis? How about a duchess from a countess? This interesting site tries to make sense of it all across various European nobility systems. If you're confused about how to address a sovereign, check *<http://128.220.1.164/heraldry/topics/highness.htm>*. That way, you'll know if you should use Highness, Royal Highness, or Most Serene Highness.

http://128.220.1.164/heraldry/topics/odegard/
   titlefaq.htm

Hawai'i: Queen Liliuokalani

Did you know that Hawaii was once a sovereign nation with its own monarch? The last queen of Hawaii was Lydia Liliuokalani, who was illegally deposed in 1893 by the American "Committee of Safety." Though briefly restored, the monarchy was over by 1894, when the Queen was arrested and imprisoned inside the beautiful Iolani Palace. You can read about her life and history here. Although President Clinton has officially apologized to the Hawaiians, there is a movement to restore sovereignty to the Islands. You can read more about that at *<http://hawaii-nation.org/nation/>*.

http://hawaii-shopping.com/~sammonet/
   liliuokalani.html

The Monarchs of England

They are all here: the monarchs of England, from the Anglo-Saxon kings to Her Majesty Elizabeth II. This site is lavishly illustrated with portraits and photos.

http://www.britannia.com/history/h6.html

Royal Residences and Stately Homes

A queen has got to have someplace to hang her hat. Oops, we mean her crown. Most people of royal rank choose to do it in a castle or palace, and many of them have a whole collection of stately homes in which to kick back and chill out from a hard day at the monarchy. This page provides links to wonderful places where queens, kings, royalty, and other important people have lived in the past. Some, like Windsor Castle, are still occupied by royalty today.

http://walden.mo.net/~landrum/homes.htm

Thailand: His Majesty King Bhumibol Adulyadej's Golden Jubilee Home Page

His Majesty King Bhumibol Adulyadej of Thailand was born in Cambridge, Massachusetts. He became King in 1946, and in 1996 he celebrated his Golden Jubilee—50 years as monarch. According to the information presented here, he is very popular among his subjects. He is involved in making technology and other scientific advances available to his people. Read about his agricultural and other reforms, and get a glimpse of the beautiful Jubilee celebration and its royal regalia.

http://kanchanapisek.or.th/index.en.html

Trooping the Colour

One of the largest military parades in the world, the Trooping of the Colour is held every June to celebrate the official birthday of Elizabeth II of England. It's not on her real birthday but on her "official" birthday. It's a grand show of heraldry, music, prancing horses, and dashing soldiers. The presentation of the flag ("the colour") to Her Majesty is the highlight of the event. The flag is weighty and cumbersome, but no one would turn down the honor of carrying it, and the soldier who carries the flag during the ceremony must train for months. The ceremony requires strict adherence to military regulations. Anyone falling from a horse could get three months in jail! Learn about one of the most stirring parades in the world at this Web site.

http://www.buckinghamgate.com/events/
    past_features/trooping/trooping.html

Welcome to the Royal Court of Sweden

This is the official Web site of the Swedish monarchy. Carl XVI Gustaf, who ascended the throne in 1973, is the 74th King of Sweden. The monarchy goes back over a thousand years. You will learn about the King, Queen Silvia, and the rest of the royal family here. Check the information on the palace and why it has a different architectural style on each of its four sides.

http://www.royalcourt.se/eng/index.html

Who is Who in Norway - KING HARALD

His Majesty King Harald and Queen Sonja have the beginnings of a home page here. You can learn biographical facts about the King of Norway, including his sailing victories and involvement with the Olympics.

http://www.norway-info.com/history/people/
    kingharald.html

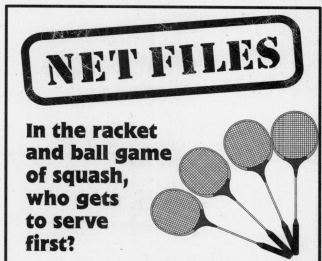

NET FILES

In the racket and ball game of squash, who gets to serve first?

Answer: The players spin a racket on the smooth floor, and whoever it points to serves first. According to the singles rule 4.1 of the World Squash Federation, "The right to serve first is decided by the spin of a racket. Thereafter, the server continues to serve until losing a stroke, whereupon the opponent becomes the server, and this procedure continues throughout the match. At the commencement of the second and each subsequent game the winner of the previous game serves first." Look at http://www.squash.org/Rules/singles.html for the rest of the rules.

A
B
C
D
E
F
G
H
I
J
K
L
M
N
O
P
Q
R
S
T
U
V
W
X
Y
Z

QUOTATIONS

Bartlett, John. 1901 Familiar Quotations

Project Bartleby, from Columbia University in New York, is an easy way to look for "phrases, proverbs, and passages" from works of literature. Keep in mind that you won't find anything contemporary here, just things prior to 1901. You can search for specific words or for entries from various authors. Want to know some famous Ben Franklin sayings? Just click on his name. Hmmm—"Early to bed and early to rise, makes a man healthy, wealthy and wise." And you thought your dad made that up! According to the notes, Franklin didn't make it up, either, but he helped popularize it.

http://www.columbia.edu/acis/bartleby/bartlett/

"The web of our life is of a mingled yarn, good and ill together."

Was Shakespeare a psychic? Did he predict the growth of the Internet, almost 400 years ago? Check more of his quotes at the Bartlett, John. 1901 Familiar Quotations home page and decide for yourself!

KITES big and small, this section has them all.

Murphy's Laws

Have you ever heard a saying and wondered who said it or where it came from? For example, did you know that "When all else fails, read the instructions" is known as Cann's Axiom? How about "A clean tie attracts the soup of the day"? These quotes and sayings are fun to read and are sometimes more fun to try to figure out. Remember: "Experience is something you don't get until just after you need it."

http://www-und.ida.liu.se/~c94niker/
murphys.laws.html

Quotations Home Page

"A child of five could understand this. Fetch me a child of five." The comedian Groucho Marx said that. To find all kinds of quotes, from long ago and just yesterday, be sure to try this page. You'll find quotes from Miss Piggy to David Letterman here. There's a collection of the world's most annoying proverbs ("Haste makes waste") as well as student bloopers ("The Egyptians built the Pyramids in the shape of a huge triangular cube"). Don't miss "The Best of Anonymous" either ("Remember, a day without sunshine is like night"). You may want to download some of the inspirational color posters, too, for example, the photo of the cute kids with the text, "We all smile in the same language." This site is highly recommended!

http://www.lexmark.com/data/quote.html

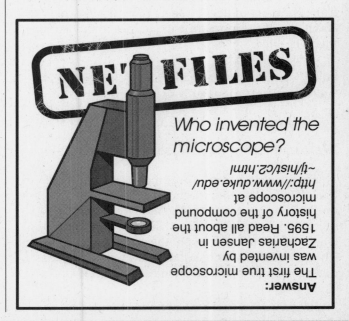

NET FILES

Who invented the microscope?

Answer: The first true microscope was invented by Zacharias Jansen in 1595. Read all about the history of the compound microscope at http://www.duke.edu/~tj/hist/hist2.html

RADIO

100 TEARS OF RADIO - HOME PAGE -

Today, we think nothing of turning on the TV and seeing events happen, live, on the other side of the world. This was not always the case. Before the development of fast communication technologies, news often took months to work its way across the globe. One of these great technological breakthroughs was radio—wireless communications. The year 1995 marked the 100th anniversary of its invention by Guglielmo Marconi. His first test radio experiments took place in Italy, in 1895. At first, radio communication was limited to a distance of about 100 miles from point to point. To make the invention a commercial success, long-distance communication had to take place. The first stations that Marconi built to meet this goal were in Poldhu, Cornwall, England, and on Cape Cod, Massachusetts. According to this page: "Unfortunately, gales in the autumn of 1901 blew down the antennas of both stations, so Marconi had to improvise for his first transatlantic experiment with a temporary antenna at Poldhu and portable receiving equipment at St. John's, Newfoundland. In December, 1901, the first radio signals were transmitted across the Atlantic Ocean from Poldhu, and were received by Marconi at St. John's. This proved to Marconi (but not to everyone else!) that transatlantic radio communications were possible." The signal sent was the letter *S* in Morse code: "click-click-click." Marconi set out to build his permanent stations, and he settled on Nova Scotia as his western Atlantic radio terminus. On December 15, 1902, Marconi sent the first wireless transatlantic message to Cornwall, England, thus making Glace Bay, on Cape Breton Island, Nova Scotia, the birthplace of transoceanic wireless communication. Read more and see historic photos of the stations and the original equipment at this most interesting site.

http://www.alpcom.it/hamradio/

You won't believe how the GARDENS AND GARDENING section grew!

Broadcasting History

Can you imagine riding in a car without hearing tunes on the radio? Car radios weren't introduced until 1930. Radios were expensive back then, and not every home had one. In 1929, home radios were $120 each, which was a fortune! Before 1935, most radios broadcast only live music. After that, stations got record players and began spinning 33 1/3 or 78 rpm records. You say you don't remember records? Ask your parents about them! Radio plays were big, too: one of the biggest early successes was a western called *The Lone Ranger,* and one of its sponsors was Cheerios. Follow the amazing history of broadcast radio from the 1920s through the 1950s at this site.

http://www.people.memphis.edu/~mbensman/ history1.html

Original Old Time Radio (OTR) WWW Pages

Many years ago, before cable TV, even before any TV, there was radio. Not just talk and music on the radio, like today, but radio "shows." Radio shows were like today's TV shows, without the pictures. People enjoyed listening to comedies, dramas, mystery thrillers, and variety shows. It was a whole different kind of radio, at a whole different time, and now it is known as "old time radio." This page is entertainment and history all rolled into one, and it is packed with information, pictures, and sounds. Hear clips from such radio greats as *The Lone Ranger.* (What kind of Indian was Tonto, anyway? You'll find theories about that here.) You can also take a fascinating virtual tour of the old NBC radio studios in Chicago's Merchandise Mart. Don't turn that dial!

http://www.old-time.com/

AMATEUR RADIO
Amateur Radio Beginners Information page

Amateur radio has long been an exciting hobby for people of all ages all over the world. Would you like to set up your own equipment and broadcast from your home? Do you need to organize a team to provide mobile communications at special events and festivals? The "ham" is always ready to be "on the air." Absolutely anyone can do it in most countries, so find out how. Even if you're already a ham, find out more from this up-to-date FAQ.

http://www.acs.ncsu.edu/HamRadio/FAQ/

A B C D E F G H I J K L M N O P Q R S T U V W X Y Z

A
B
C
D
E
F
G
H
I
J
K
L
M
N
O
P
Q
R
S
T
U
V
W
X
Y
Z

Ham Radio Online Magazine

Licensed ham radio operators use high-tech radios for communications with others (it's sort of like using a cellular phone, but without the cost of airtime charges). Hams meet new friends and "visit" with hams in countries all over the globe. Hams have even talked with astronauts orbiting Earth! Many U.S. and Russian astronauts are also licensed hams, and they make contacts from space for educational uses and sometimes just for fun. If you're not already a ham, get in on this. If you are a ham, here's where you'll keep up on all the newest amateur radio news and latest technological developments. Since hams often provide emergency communications in the event of a disaster (some systems even have 911 emergency access), this site also has real-time links to earthquake and other disaster monitoring sites all over the globe. Other unusual features are real-time forecasts for auroral, solar, and meteor shower activity. Don't forget to bring an umbrella if you're going out in a meteor shower!

http://www.hamradio-online.com/

NET FILES

What sport uses the following apparatus:

a ball,
a rope,
some
clubs,
and a
ribbon?

Answer: Rhythmic gymnastics combines flexibility and ballet movements with these pieces of equipment. Visit http://www.sd68.nanaimo.bc.ca/schools/wdls/homepages/students/jford/subpage1.htm to see the beautiful results!

Welcome to the Amateur Radio Web Server

You knew "ham radio" was another name for amateur radio, didn't you? You didn't imagine knobs and buttons and an antenna sticking out of a ham, did you? Ham radio is fun and exciting, and people of all ages have found it to be a useful hobby as well. This site is a great home base to check up on the latest news and events in the world of amateur radio. You can also take a sample amateur radio licensing exam. How did you do?

http://www.acs.ncsu.edu/HamRadio/

RADIO STATIONS

AAHS New Home Page

Maybe you've heard of Radio AAHS, the 24-hour radio network for kids. There are lots of terrific tunes, from vintage rock and roll to soft rock hits of today, plus tunes from your favorite movies, like *The Lion King.* They broadcast from interesting places, too, such as Universal Studios Florida. You can also hear a talk show done for kids, by a kid—and he broadcasts from his room! If there is no Radio AAHS affiliate in your area, you can listen over the Net, right from the link on this home page. You can listen even while you're doing other things with your computer. This is a new page, and it is under construction, but it's worth it for the live music alone.

http://www.netradioaahs.net/

J-WAVE Home Page

Japan has its share of rock music artists and fans, too. In fact, many of the most popular performers in the U.S. and Europe are just as big in Japan! There are English and Japanese versions of this page right at your fingertips. So tune in J-WAVE on the Web and learn about Japanese performers in pop music as well as all the rockers. You can also find out what the top 100 CDs are in Tokyo. How many are also your favorites?

http://www.infojapan.com/JWAVE/

DISNEY: a man, a plan, a land!

KISS FM

Who's hot in music? What's the latest news on your favorite artists? Where can you "jump off" to the best music sites on the web? KISS FM in Boston, Massachusetts, has all the answers! This station plays the hottest music on the air and gives you the weekly hit charts and music news you're looking for. The Jump Station in the Music section takes you to everything from album covers to concert tickets. So stop spinning the dial and find the answers here!

http://www.kissfm.com/kiss/index.shtml

The MIT List of Radio Stations on the Internet

Is your favorite radio station on the Internet? How about that great station you listen to when you visit your cousin in Boston? This is the place to find out. This site lists radio stations all over the world that have home pages on the Web. So whether it's that country music station in Nashville or that hot rocker on the dial in the Netherlands, you can get there from here!

http://wmbr.mit.edu/stations/

NetRadio Home Page

NetRadio was the first "radio station" just for the Internet. You can go to NetRadio and listen to music on your computer even while you surf somewhere else. There's lots of good music news to read about while you listen. You can get the latest concert information, enter contests, win prizes, and vote in a monthly poll. It's all the fun stuff about radio right at your fingertips! Parental advisory: links from this site have not all been reviewed.

http://opus.netradio.net/

What did grandma do when she was a kid? There is a list of questions to ask in GENEALOGY AND FAMILY HISTORY.

Radio Sweden's Virtual North

Radio Sweden broadcasts in several languages, including English. Luckily, the Web pages are available in these languages too, because this site has a lot of fascinating information. Click on "Our Programs" and read about (or listen to) the latest sports, media, money, science, and even environmental news. Hey, what's important in Sweden is important to everyone! Radio Sweden has useful current information on the air and on the Internet. A recorded daily broadcast is available via Real Audio streaming, or you can ftp the entire file. A live broadcast occurs daily using Streamworks technology. Find out more here, and don't miss the Moose Gallery.

http://www.sr.se/rs/

Welcome to NPR

Many people think that National Public Radio (NPR) gives us the best news, feature stories, and music on the radio. This site certainly gives you a lot of all these and lets you know where you can find NPR locally. Like PBS on television, NPR is federally and privately funded programming. It's also commercial-free. This Web site has the same "Breaking News" and "Story of the Day" as the NPR radio broadcasts. Yes, you can actually listen to the most recent NPR news report right on your computer. Tune in and see what public radio has to offer. You'll also want to check out Ira Flatow's NPR Science Friday Kids Connection at <http://www.npr.org/sfkids/index.html>. You'll find study guides to some of Science Friday's cool topics: the physics of *Star Trek*, scientific toys, ocean acoustics, backyard astronomy, and more!

http://www.npr.org /

Welcome to Vatican Radio

Staff from 50 countries prepare 400 hours of broadcast material every week in 37 different languages. Radio Vatican broadcasts on short wave, medium wave, FM, satellite, and the Internet. You can download Real Audio files or ftp features in several languages. As they say: "Listen, for heaven's sake!"

http://www.wrn.org/vatican-radio/

A
B
C
D
E
F
G
H
I
J
K
L
M
N
O
P
Q
R
S
T
U
V
W
X
Y
Z

A
B
C
D
E
F
G
H
I
J
K
L
M
N
O
P
Q
R
S
T
U
V
W
X
Y
Z

Welcome to WCBS NEWSRADIO 88

In New York City, WCBS is the all-news radio station. On the Web, WCBS is also up to the minute with top news, sports, and weather stories. The feature series "Boot Camp" reports on the newest developments regarding computers and technology, and "Lifestyle" highlights travel and dining. The WCBS archives are all online, so if you missed a technology report, you can scan the archives for a computer topic that interests you!

http://www.newsradio88.com/

WNUR-FM JazzWeb

Hey, jazz-lovin' cats out there! This site is real cool, so breeze on in and chill awhile. The JazzWeb has a treasure chest of information for those who get into jazz music. There are sections on different jazz styles, individual musicians, musical instruments, and performances. Finding the info on jazz art, education, and resources is also a smooth ride. Linking up to jazz labels and retail sellers on the Net is a simple note. Brought to you by Northwestern University's radio station, if it's jazz, it's here.

http://www.nwu.edu/jazz/

SHORTWAVE
Amateur Radio FAQ (Shortwave subsection)

What is shortwave radio? Technically, that's the name for radio frequencies between 3 and 30 MHz. Shortwave broadcasts can be received over long distances, making it possible to communicate internationally—yes, without the Internet! You can tune in radio broadcasts from around the world. Questions, anyone? The answers are here.

http://www.acs.ncsu.edu/HamRadio/FAQ/
FAQ_Shortwave.html

You are your own network.

Numbers Stations on Shortwave

"So this is a shortwave radio. What do you guys listen to on these things? Wait, turn the knob the other way, slowly. Right there—stop! What in the world is THAT? It sounds like counting in a foreign language. What is that?" Could it be a math lesson in Russian? A language class in the U.K.? A spy sending secret code from some remote island? Or maybe someone in the U.S. is giving someone in Germany a company e-mail address? Hmmm, the spy answer is definitely the most fun—and it just might be the right one! The so-called "numbers stations" heard on shortwave radio make a fascinating topic. For many years, listeners came across them now and again, never really sure of their purpose. Even today, their origin and meaning are mysterious. Can you find the signals? What might they really be? This page helps you track them down and uncover the truth. Listen in!

http://itre.ncsu.edu/radio/numbers.html

Shortwave/Radio Catalog

Shortwave radio enthusiasts can find lots of new information in each new issue of this page. There are always links to basic information and resources that the radio hobbyist will use again and again. Hardware, software, and radio services are covered in depth. Many familiar radio-related topics are reviewed in each issue, but new ideas are being introduced all the time. You'll find plenty of quality links to all kinds of radio information from all corners of the globe. This really is a one-stop radio information catalog for the Internet!

http://itre.uncecs.edu/radio/

The wonderful world of worms may be admired in the section called INVERTEBRATES.

RAILROADS AND TRAINS

See also MODELS AND MINIATURES—RAILROADS

Corey's Choo-Choo CAD

Thinking of building your own model railroad? If you have Java on your browser, you can start here by building your own railroad track and running your own little cybertrain. This program won't let you derail your train when you remove a piece of track, but you can make it turn angles that real trains can't. It is simple but entertaining fun, and it doesn't take up any space in the family room or basement.

http://kidshealth.org/kid/games/choo_choo/

Cyberspace World Railroad Home Page

This sites has all the bells and whistles that train lovers adore. Hang out in the lounge car and check out the travel stories. Listen to an actual recording of a train crew member's transmission as he is trapped on a runaway train. Download train typefaces for your computer. Brush up on the General Code of Operating Rules. And if all the monthly articles about trains and transportation issues are still not enough, you can always switch tracks to one of the over 900 railroad links that will have you riding the rail all over the globe.

http://www.mcs.com/~dsdawdy/cyberoad.html

Interactive Model Railroad - MAIN

Wow, that's a cool model train—too bad it's in Germany. Bet you'd love to play with it. Guess what? You can! Through the magic of forms and server-push technology, you can select one of two trains to control. Then select which platform the train should travel to. Then press GO and watch your train speed along past the miniature Bavarian town. Watch out for that alp!

http://rr-vs.informatik.uni-ulm.de/rr/

**Strike up the bandwidth
in MUSIC.**

Jeremiah L. Toth Railroads Page

This site features information about Maryland railroad stations, Washington, D.C.'s colossal and historic Union Station, railroading in Delaware, Pennsylvania, New York, and Connecticut, and trolley, interurban, and heavy rail resources. This is a good, fact-driven resource center for railroad buffs looking for on-track information.

http://www.clark.net/pub/jltoth/trains.html

North American Steam Locomotives

While a rarity today, steam trains have not entirely vanished from the American landscape. This page provides information about steamers of the past and today's survivors, including schedules of currently running steam excursions, specifications of steam trains, and sections on trains that are "Lost Forever (but not forgotten)." There is also information on rail fairs, rail museums, and a special piece on the annual reenactment of the Golden Spike ceremony in Utah, featuring some terrific photographs. Look for it in the Virtual Tours area.

http://www.arc.umn.edu/~wes/steam.html

The Golden Spike was "driven" at Promontory, Utah, in 1869, completing the railroad track that would join the East and West coasts of the North American continent for the first time. There were really several ceremonial spikes, some silver and some gold. Now there is an annual reenactment of this event. For a full-color report on it and other steam locomotive events, run on over to the North American Steam Locomotives page.

A
B
C
D
E
F
G
H
I
J
K
L
M
N
O
P
Q
R
S
T
U
V
W
X
Y
Z

A B C D E F G H I J K L M N O P Q R S T U V W X Y Z

NET FILES

When was the planet Uranus discovered?

Answer: Uranus was discovered on March 13, 1781 by William Herschel. Check out the Chronology of Solar System Discovery at http://seds.lpl.arizona.edu/billa/tnp/history.html for an astronomical list of facts.

Operation Lifesaver, Inc.

Trains are fascinating but dangerous. Did you know that a big, 150-car freight train traveling at 50 mph can take up to 1.5 miles to come to a complete stop? In the U.S., about 6,000 deaths and injuries per year involve trains and cars or pedestrians walking on the tracks. Most train accidents occur when the train is traveling 30 mph or slower. Even at 30 mph, the approximate stopping distance is 3,500 feet, or two-thirds of a mile! Operation Lifesaver educates adults and kids on trains and train safety. Make tracks to visit here soon.

http://www.oli.org/oli/

READING AND LITERACY

Children's Literature Web Guide

"If my cunning plan works, you will find yourself tempted away from the Internet and back to the books themselves!" says David K. Brown, children's librarian. He's collected links to many outstanding reading experiences. You can find information on fictional people and places in children's books. Play Virtual Poohsticks at the 100 Acre Wood. Look at the links to Arthurian legend. Book series, such as Nancy Drew, Hardy Boys, and Goosebumps, also have their own pages. If you have a favorite author, like C. S. Lewis, or Dr. Seuss, look here for links to their pages. There are online children's stories and lists of award-winning books. And you'll find a whole section called Children's Writings and Drawings. If you want to put your work on the Net for the world to see, start here. Check the "Books and Literature" section of this book for more!

http://www.ucalgary.ca/~dkbrown/

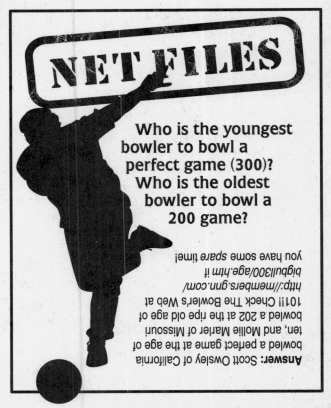

NET FILES

Who is the youngest bowler to bowl a perfect game (300)? Who is the oldest bowler to bowl a 200 game?

Answer: Scott Owsley of California bowled a perfect game at the age of ten, and Mollie Marler of Missouri bowled a 202 at the ripe old age of 101!! Check The Bowler's Web at http://members.gnn.com/bigbull300/age.htm if you have some spare time!

CyberKids Home

This "cool place for kids to learn and have fun" is a free online magazine. Kids create the stories, articles, reviews, and artwork. A Young Composers section has music written by kids! This creative site also has puzzles and games to play.

http://www.cyberkids.com/

IPL Youth Division

Some kids really like to go to the library and spend time there: reading and rereading favorites, listening to CDs in the audiovisual (AV) department, maybe even doing a little homework. Here's another library to explore, with guides to help you. Like any good public library, the Internet Public Library, or IPL, has a vibrant children's room. There are lots of things to read, a story time (with illustrated folktales), homework help, and an Authors' Corner. If you go to the Story Hour, some stories have audio or animations; most of them are illustrated. If you like science, Dr. Internet will direct you to interesting sites on the Internet, where you can explore dinosaurs, earthquakes, geology, volcanoes, and weather. In the Authors' Corner, Matt Christopher, Jane Yolen, Avi, and Lois Lowry, among others, share their life stories and talk about their books. You can ask them questions, too. If you like contests, you'll find links to many Internet contests. And the hours are great—this library is always open.

http://www.ipl.org/youth/

KidPub WWW Publishing

Here's a great place to share your stories, poems, and news about where you live. Kids from all over the world have their writing published on this Web page. You'll find stories mostly from the U.S., but some are also from places such as Tasmania, West Malaysia, Germany, and Singapore. Most of the young authors include their e-mail addresses, so you can write back to them. Writers also write a little bit about themselves. Contributors range in age from 4 to 15. Write on!

http://www.kidpub.org/kidpub/

Parents and Children Together Online

Part of the fun of reading and writing can be the sharing of it. This site is fun to explore with your mom or dad or with a younger sister or brother. There are illustrated stories and articles for sixth grade and under. Some of the stories and articles have links to resources on the Internet. You can follow the links to find information on koalas, cats, or Scottish terrier dogs. The Scottie article even has a link to a site about U.S. President Franklin Delano Roosevelt, who had one! If you like to write stories, hunker down around The Global Campfire, where you can contribute your part to an ongoing story (science fiction, adventure, a family story, or a mystery). And if you want a key pal, look here. There are requests from like-minded sorts, from Alaska to Zanzibar.

http://www.indiana.edu/~eric_rec/fl/pcto/menu.html

RECYCLING

The Consumer Recycling Guide: Common Recycled Materials

You recycle, right? But maybe you have questions about some things, like those cryptic markings on the bottoms of plastic containers—what do they mean? You'll find a description of them here. Also, you can learn what to do with items such as used motor oil or spent NiCad batteries. This is the one-stop answer place for recycling questions.

http://www.best.com/~dillon/recycle/guides/
common.html

**Your family
has a history—
write it down!
Hints in GENEALOGY
AND FAMILY HISTORY.**

A
B
C
D
E
F
G
H
I
J
K
L
M
N
O
P
Q
R
S
T
U
V
W
X
Y
Z

Your mom says this new juice is good for you, but you're not so sure you want to drink it. After all, the bottle has some other kid's name on it. There's this triangle with a "1" in it, and below that it says "PETE." Not to worry. That's a recycling symbol. It means the container is made out of polyethylene terephthalate (PET). Lots of soda and water containers and some other waterproof packaging have the same symbol. These markings help us know which plastics are recyclable and which are, well, trash. Find out more at The Consumer Recycling Guide: Common Recycled Materials.

Rot Web Home Composting Information Site

This is the lowdown on dirt (for those of you who have a sense of *humus*). It gives basic information about home composting. You can find out how to build compost heaps of every description, some even including worms. If you want to see a heap in action, there's a nationwide list of Composting Demo Sites. It's a *rotten* Web site, and that's why we've included it!

http://net.indra.com/~topsoil/Compost_Menu.html

You Can Make Paper

This site will give you directions on making your own paper out of recycled materials. Making paper is fun, but it is pretty messy, so make sure an adult helps you!

http://www.nbn.com/youcan/paper/paper.html

We like the INVERTEBRATES best. —The Nields

REFERENCE WORKS

Learn2.com—the ability utility

Do you know how to use chopsticks or clean a freshly caught fish? Could you use a lesson in putting a golf ball or breaking in a new baseball mitt? How about tips on folding a shirt or cleaning up a stain? This truly great site will teach you all of the above and more!

http://www.learn2.com/

The Scholes Library Electronic Reference Desk

Groan...your paperback dictionary has disappeared. Hmmm, well, here's the *A*s in the middle of the kitchen, and there are *B* through *F* down the basement stairs. Maybe it was the dog? Don't despair. You can use dictionaries online! This site also has encyclopedias, a thesaurus, maps, current news, historical documents, time zones, area codes, and more!

http://scholes.alfred.edu/Ref.html

ALMANACS AND GAZETTEERS
Events for ...

Ho hum, today is just another day, right? It seems there are so few special days—like Christmas, your birthday, and the Fourth of July. Actually, every single day has been important in history: some momentous event is taking place somewhere, or someone great was born. To see why today is important, take a look here. Maybe you can use the information here as a good excuse for a party!

http://astro.uchicago.edu/home/web/copi/events.html

How Far Is It?

In the not-too-distant past, finding the distance from one part of the globe to another took a fair amount of work. It involved using complicated tables and converting map scales. Now, we have an alternative! On this page, all you need to know is the name of two locations, and the distance between the two is calculated for you. This service provides distance for almost all places in the United States and a good number of major cities elsewhere.

http://www.indo.com/distance/

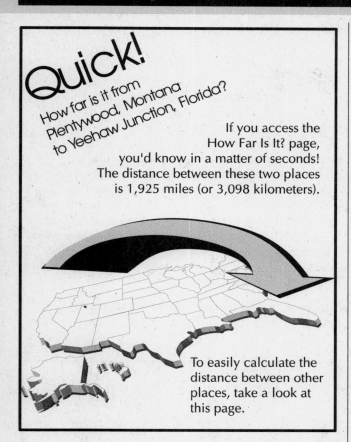

Quick!

How far is it from Plentywood, Montana to Yeehaw Junction, Florida?

If you access the How Far Is It? page, you'd know in a matter of seconds! The distance between these two places is 1,925 miles (or 3,098 kilometers).

To easily calculate the distance between other places, take a look at this page.

U.S. Gazetteer

A quick way to find the county, state, area code, ZIP code, and latitude and longitude of a place in the United States is to check this resource. It is linked to the XEROX PARC Map Viewer, so once you find out that Prague, Arkansas, is in Grant County, ZIP code 05053, latitude 34 17 12 N, longitude 92 16 50 W, you can click on those coordinates to view the map.

http://www.census.gov/cgi-bin/gazetteer/

Did the groundhog see his shadow? Find out if it will be an early spring in HOLIDAYS.

Welcome to Almanac.com

The *Old Farmer's Almanac* has been published ever since George Washington was President. This almanac gives the best time to plant crops, helps to determine the weather long in advance, and has lots of cool old sayings (these are called *aphorisms*). People have used and enjoyed the *Old Farmer's Almanac* throughout history. Now, parts of this publication are available on the Internet. You can see weather predictions, read some old-timey quotes, and find a great history of the almanac. Whether you live on a farm or in a city high-rise apartment, you'll like this site!

http://www.almanac.com/

The World Factbook Master Home Page

Did you know that Kenya (569,250 square kilometers) is twice the size of Nevada? Did you know that the people of Denmark can speak four languages (Danish, Faroese, Greenlandic, and German)? If you ever wanted to know facts like these about countries around the world, this is the place to look. You'll also find a section on oceans of the world. By the way, did you know there are 193 million TV sets in the United States? A 1994 gopher version is also available at <*gopher://hoshi.cic.sfu.ca/11/dlam/cia*>.

http://www.odci.gov/cia/publications/nsolo/wfb-all.htm

AWARDS
Academy of Television Arts & Sciences

Have you ever heard the song by Bruce Springsteen, "Fifty-Seven Channels and Nothin' On"? Sometimes nothing good seems to be on TV, but many good shows are available. An organization called the Academy of Television Arts and Sciences selects some of the best programs and gives the winning shows and actors an award called an Emmy. To see who the most current winners are, check out this Web page. You'll learn television history, see who is being nominated, and get a behind-the-scenes look at the annual Emmy awards show.

http://www.emmys.org/tindex.html

A
B
C
D
E
F
G
H
I
J
K
L
M
N
O
P
Q
R
S
T
U
V
W
X
Y
Z

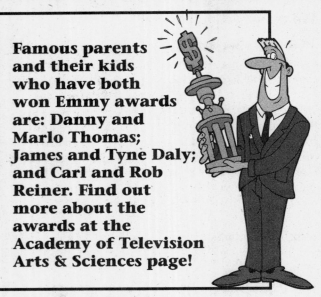

Famous parents and their kids who have both won Emmy awards are: Danny and Marlo Thomas; James and Tyne Daly; and Carl and Rob Reiner. Find out more about the awards at the Academy of Television Arts & Sciences page!

ALSC HOMEPAGE — AWARDS AND NOTABLES

There's no doubt that librarians know tons about books. Every year, children's librarians in the American Library Association give two awards to authors and illustrators of the best books for kids. The Caldecott Medal goes for the best illustrator of a children's book, and the Newbery Medal is given to the author of the finest kids' book. See the winners at these Web sites; you'll find some librarian-tested and approved books!

http://www.ala.org/alsc/awards.html

AMPAS - The Academy of Motion Picture Arts and Sciences

If you're a movie fanatic, don't miss the Official Interactive Guide to the Academy Awards, designed to help you explore Oscar nominees and winners, past and present. There are pictures and lots of information on all of them. You may be surprised to find out that the Academy of Motion Picture Arts and Sciences does a lot more than just give out awards: they have an amazing movie history library and sponsor Student Academy Awards, designed to recognize excellence among college students enrolled in film courses throughout the United States.

http://www.ampas.org/ampas/

Children's Book Awards

Every year, thousands of books are written for kids. Most of the books are good, but trying to decide which books to borrow from the library can be difficult. Fortunately, several organizations pick the finest books for children each year. These books are judged by a variety of criteria, including best for young children, best for elementary school kids, and so on. Some of the awards for the best children's books are listed on the Internet, and you can find convenient links to many of those lists here. Besides the Caldecott and the Newbery Awards, you'll find the Coretta Scott King Award and the Laura Ingalls Wilder Medal winners. This year, there are also many international awards, plus awards given to books selected by kids! If you're looking for a good book to read, take a glance here.

http://www.ucalgary.ca/~dkbrown/awards.html

You are bored.

There's nothing good on TV. You've played all the video games a million times, and none of your friends are around. What to do? You can find a really great book to read! On the Children's Book Awards page, you'll find links to lists of some of the best books for kids of all time.

Get to know some famous AFRICAN AMERICANS.

A
B
C
D
E
F
G
H
I
J
K
L
M
N
O
P
Q
R
S
T
U
V
W
X
Y
Z

NARAS®: The National Academy of Recording Arts & Sciences, Inc.

Music is a universal language. Everybody likes music, whether it's pop sounds, rock and roll, rap, or R&B. Most music we listen to is recorded, either on tapes, CDs, the radio, or TV. The National Academy of Recording Arts and Sciences is an organization of recording specialists who vote on the best recordings each year. The winning recording artists receive an award called a Grammy. To see (and hear) who has won in the past and who is nominated for the upcoming awards, take a look at this page. It's the place to look if you like music, and who doesn't!

http://www.grammy.com/index.html

NET FILES

What are "Storm Chasers"?

Answer: Storm Chasers are people who chase tornadoes! Not that they want to catch them, you understand. They just want to record information about them and study them. Meteorologists, college professors, students, and curious citizens can all be storm chasers! Training is strongly encouraged, and you can find out how to get it at http:// www.weather.com/ weather_why/teachers_ resources/all_about_meteo /start.html#chase

People are the true treasures of the Net.

The Nobel Foundation

Alfred Nobel was a Swedish-born inventor and international industrialist, most famous for the invention of dynamite. He died in 1896. His will founded the Nobel Prizes in the fields of physics, chemistry, physiology/medicine, literature, and peace. Since 1901, they have been presented to the winners (called Nobel laureates) at ceremonies on December 10, the anniversary of Alfred Nobel's death. Most of the prizes are awarded in Stockholm, Sweden, while the Nobel Peace Prize is awarded in Oslo, Norway. Since 1969, the Sveriges Riksbank (Bank of Sweden) Prize in Economic Sciences in memory of Alfred Nobel has been awarded in Stockholm at the same time. You can get a list of all the winners, pictures of the medals awarded, plus a biography of Nobel and a history of his prizes at this site.

http://www.nobel.se/

On Broadway WWW Information Page

A live performance in a theater—there is nothing like it. Lights, stage props, music, and acting are all parts of what makes the theater great. If you've ever seen or participated in a play, you know it can be fantastic! Some of the best theatrical performances take place on Broadway in New York City. Want to know what's playing there right now, plus get reviews of the performances and maybe hear some sound clips? The Antoinette Perry (Tony) Award is presented annually for distinguished achievement in the professional theater. These are the best of the best, and if you like theater, take a look to see which plays have won.

http://artsnet.heinz.cmu.edu/OnBroadway/

If you feel funny, think what we went through when we wrote the JOKES AND RIDDLES section!

A B C D E F G H I J K L M N O P Q R S T U V W X Y Z

A
B
C
D
E
F
G
H
I
J
K
L
M
N
O
P
Q
R
S
T
U
V
W
X
Y
Z

Pulitzer Prizes presented by CJR

Joseph Pulitzer was an American newspaper publisher known for his innovative ideas and bold reporting style. When he died, his will established the Pulitzer Prizes. The first ones were awarded in 1917. Each year, achievements in American journalism, letters, drama, and music are recognized. Fourteen prizes are given in journalism. The prizes in letters are for fiction, history, poetry, biography or autobiography, and general nonfiction. There are also prizes for drama and music. At this site, you can read about the 1995 and 1996 winners; perhaps in the future the site will expand to include past years.

http://www.pulitzer.org/

DICTIONARIES

Acronym and abbreviation list

Do you know what an *acronym* is? It's a word that is formed by the letters or syllables of other words. For example, let's say we created an organization called American Children Reading Online Notes for Young Mothers—its acronym could be ACRONYM! If you want to look up and see what some real acronyms stand for (try UNESCO or PTA for fun), take a glimpse at this site.

http://www.ucc.ie/info/net/acronyms/acro.html

BREWER: Dictionary of Phrase and Fable

Are you forever forgetting the Riddle of the Sphinx? Want to know who Apollo was? Can't wait to find out what the Seven Wonders of the ancient and modern worlds were? The current printed edition of this classic book is one of Net-mom's favorites, but the 1894 edition is online and searchable!

http://www.bibliomania.com/Reference/
    PhraseAndFable/

Something fishy going on?
Try AQUARIUMS.

Casey's Snow Day Reverse Dictionary (and Guru)

Casey's a 12-year-old girl who lives in Los Alamos, New Mexico. One day, there was a lot of snow and her school closed, so she went to work with her dad. While she was there, she got this great idea. Sometimes, people know what a word means, but they just can't think of the word—so how about a reverse dictionary? The programmers thought Casey's idea was great, so they came up with a way to do it. All you do is type in the definition, then you see a list of choices that match it. The programmers were so happy with it that they named it after Casey. If words have a habit of escaping you, a reverse dictionary might be just what you need!

http://www.c3.lanl.gov:8064/

English-Estonian Dictionary

Estonia is a recently independent Baltic country with a very long and wonderful history. This well-designed dictionary can help you translate over 17,000 words from English to Estonian. You'll be one of about a million speakers of Estonian around the world!

http://www.ibs.ee/dict/

English Estonian Dictionary

You're sitting in class one day, and your teacher introduces a new exchange student from Estonia. You'd love to impress the student by saying hello in Estonian, but you don't have a clue where to begin to find the word. Not to worry! All you have to do is take a look at the English-Estonian Dictionary, and you see that hello in Estonian is "halloo." Now, you'll never be at a loss for words when you meet an Estonian!

The Internet Dictionary Project: Search the IDP

This site lets you convert English words to French, Spanish, Italian, Portuguese, and German, and back again. The catch is, the dictionary isn't very big, so often the word you want won't be found. If you know one of these languages, you can help the dictionary to grow!

http://www.hardlink.com/~chambers/IDP/
IDPsearch.html

NET FILES

"Watch him barney this jump! I wish he'd get a case of Kodak courage!"

Huh? Where might you hear these comments?

Answer: A rough translation is: "I hate it when he goes over the jump too slowly and flattens it! Maybe he'll get braver if a camera is around!" You might hear these expressions from snowboarders on the ski slope. Snowboarders have just about created their own language. Meanwhile, the sport of snowboarding is growing, and it's gaining in recognition. Find out how to do it and how to "speak" it, at http://www.snwbrd.com/snoukkaslang.html

Never give your name or address to a stranger.

Jeffrey's Japanese<->English Dictionary - Gateway

About 126 million people speak Japanese. Many more know a few words, such as "karaoke" or "sushi." Those are Anglicized versions of the actual Japanese words, because Japanese doesn't use the same alphabet that English does. Since your computer is designed to display the letters in English and other Western languages, you have to obtain special software just to display Japanese characters (Japanese words have characters instead of letters). If you would like to translate some Japanese, take a look here. You'll find software to view Japanese characters as well as a well-designed translation dictionary.

http://enterprise.ic.gc.ca/cgi-bin/j-e/

OneLook Dictionaries, The Faster Finder

Did you know that a lot of specialized online dictionaries are scattered all over the Net? There are dictionaries for medicine, sports, religion, art, music, and more. This site has cobbled together 85 of them to create a huge dictionary you can search with just one look (can you guess what it is called?). Be sure to check out the survey, too. It will ask you how you pronounce certain Net-related words. Past surveys have sampled world opinion on the correct way to say "GIF," "URL," and "FAQ." Vote for your favorite audio file and let your voice be counted!

http://www.onelook.com/

ENCYCLOPEDIAS
Encyclopedia Smithsonian

For 150 years, the Smithsonian Institution collections have been a treasure trove. They house many wonders of history, science, and the natural world. Thousands of people visit the museums of the Smithsonian Institution in Washington, D.C., where the staff hears the same questions over and over. The Smithsonian folks took the answers to many of those questions and put them in an encyclopedia format on the Internet. You can get information on the history of the U.S. flag, great lists of books on animals, the inside scoop on the *Titanic*, and loads of other info!

http://www.si.edu/resource/faq/start.htm

A
B
C
D
E
F
G
H
I
J
K
L
M
N
O
P
Q
R
S
T
U
V
W
X
Y
Z

A
B
C
D
E
F
G
H
I
J
K
L
M
N
O
P
Q
R
S
T
U
V
W
X
Y
Z

Kidopedia, Version 0.20

Lots of schools are starting their own *kidopedias*, which are encyclopedias written by kids, for kids. The creators of this one pull together the best entries from all the other kidopedias they know about. Housed on a computer in Canada, this kidopedia is part of a worldwide effort to get kids not only to read great information but also to contribute. See what other kids from all over the world are writing, and maybe you'll be inspired to write something yourself!

http://www.kidlib.org/kidopedia/

Vose Kidopedia Index

Imagine an encyclopedia written by kids, for kids. Each article in the encyclopedia would feature the things kids are interested in, and kids could easily understand what's written. Well, you don't have to imagine this, because kidopedia is here! The Vose School in Beaverton, Oregon, presents a nice encyclopedia with tons of articles on animals, famous people, space, and other topics. Every single word is written by elementary school students. Hey kids—this is *your* encyclopedia.

http://www.icon.portland.or.us/education/vose/
    kidopedia/kidindex.html

Welcome to Britannica Online

The *Encyclopedia Britannica* is available on the Internet. All those great articles on science, history, and geography are obtainable by point and click—the whole enchilada is here! However (and this is a big however), it costs money to subscribe to this service. You can, though, sample the Britannica Online to see if you want to purchase access. Use the Sample Search area to get partial information in answer to any question; sometimes that's enough. Also, all the details for cost and other subscription information are available. If you think you might be interested, take a look.

http://www.eb.com/

Not everything on the Net is true.

POPULATION
POPClock Projection

The current estimated U.S. population is found at this site. The U.S. Census Bureau starts with the 1990 census and add the births and subtract the deaths. Then they factor in their best guesses about trends and come up with this estimated result. In case you wondered, only residents in the U.S. and the District of Columbia are counted and not families of military serving overseas or others living abroad.

http://www.census.gov/cgi-bin/popclock

PRB Home Page

The Population Reference Bureau has been providing the public with solid information on trends in world and U.S. population and demographics since 1929. This nonprofit organization has put together a useful and lively home page, which enables visitors to query the extensive World Population Data Sheet and read current and back issues of the magazine *Population Today*. There are also links to many other online population resources and a nifty game called Demographic Challenge: World Food Facts.

http://www.prb.org/prb/

U.S. Census Bureau Home Page

Do you know what Obi-wan Kenobi said to Luke Skywalker in *Star Wars*, when he had a question about the population of the United States? "Use the Source, Luke!" For such questions, go right to the source: the U.S. Census Bureau. How do they count the number of people in the U.S.? Find out here, plus learn lots of statistical info on jobs, housing, health, crime, income, education, marriage and family, race and ethnicity, aging, transportation and travel, and recreation. You might think that statistics are boring, but try this: of the U.S. population, 26 percent are under the age of 18! And if you don't have cable TV, tell your dad to get with the program, because 61 percent of American households have it.

http://www.census.gov/

W3C/ANU - Demography & Population Studies WWW VL

The world is a mighty big place, and this is a mighty big Web page. From here, the intrepid Internaut gathering data on population and demographics can click on over 150 links around the world, covering every aspect of the field. From tiny little sites dealing with local matters all the way up to massive data banks at major colleges and government institutions, this site has it all.

http://coombs.anu.edu.au/ResFacilities/
DemographyPage.html

How do we know what time it is?

http://tycho.usno.navy.mil/history.html

Answer: In the U.S., we ask the U.S. Naval Observatory. They have been keeping the Nation's time since the 1800s. In 1845, they installed a time ball atop their telescope dome. According to their Web site, "the time ball was dropped every day precisely at Noon, enabling the inhabitants of Washington to set their timepieces. Ships in the Potomac River could also set their clocks before putting to sea." Times have changed since then. Now hydrogen maser clocks are used, which keep atomic time. There is a good correlation of atomic time to more traditional celestial observations, but every now and again the atomic clock has to be given a whack, known as a "leap second," to bring it into alignment with the heavens. If you have time, read more about it at

World POPClock

Quick! If you wanted to send a letter to everyone in the world, how many stamps would you need? See an estimate of the world's current population at this site. You'll also find out how many births and deaths occur each minute.

http://www.census.gov/cgi-bin/ipc/popclockw

World Population

Every 30 seconds, the world population clock at this site clicks to the latest figures. If you have Netscape 1.x or greater, you can have the clock animated as well. From here, you can check out the U.S. Census Bureau's national and world POPClocks with just a click and link to other related sites.

http://sunsite.unc.edu/lunarbin/worldpop

World Population Trends

Check this site for United Nations world population statistics and trends. Included are population figures for countries and a brief list of historical milestones in world population. For example, the estimated world's population was one billion people in 1804. It took 123 years for it to double to two billion, in 1927. By 1974, 47 years later, it had doubled again to four billion. Estimates are that the world's population will double again, to eight billion, by 2021. Right now, it's just under six billion people. You'll also find a link here to world abortion policies as it applies to population trends.

gopher://gopher.undp.org:70/11/ungophers/popin/
wdtrends

Want a snack?
Learn to make one
in COOKING,
FOOD, AND DRINK.

A B C D E F G H I J K L M N O P Q R S T U V W X Y Z

A
B
C
D
E
F
G
H
I
J
K
L
M
N
O
P
Q

R
S
T
U
V
W
X
Y
Z

SUN AND MOON RISE CALCULATION
Sunrise/Sunset Computation

Sometimes you have to get up awfully early to watch the sun rise. Exactly when the sun or moon rises or sets depends on where you live and the time of year. You can take the mystery out of when old Sol (that's another name for the sun) takes off in the morning by using this U.S. Naval Observatory's page. All you have to do is plug in a date and a place, and through the magic of computers, the time of sun (and moon) rise and set is provided. For fun, enter your birthday and birthplace or pick an interesting date, like December 31, 1999.

http://tycho.usno.navy.mil/srss.html

THESAURI
ARTFL Project: ROGET Thesaurus Search Form

Sometimes words can be so frustrating. Have you ever had a homework assignment and found you were using the same word over and over again? To solve this problem, a guy named Peter Roget came up with a list that grouped similar words together. This list of similar words is called a *thesaurus*, and Roget's is considered one of the best. All you have to do is type in a word. Now you'll be able to impress your teachers with your growing—expanding, increasing, enlarging—vocabulary. Keep in mind that this is the edition from 1911, so newer words will not appear.

http://humanities.uchicago.edu/forms_unrest/
  ROGET.html

WEIGHTS AND MEASURES
The Beaufort Scale

Your kite instructions say that you need a 10-knot wind before you can launch. How do you know? The Beaufort scale is a way to estimate wind speed without the use of instruments. For example, the description of Beaufort force 3 is this: "Leaves and small twigs in constant motion; wind extends light flag." That translates to a wind speed of 7 to 10 knots (8 to 12 mph, or 12 to 19 kph, or 3.4 to 5.4 mps). Find out the other indicators here.

http://www.anbg.gov.au/jrc/kayak/beaufort.html

Conversion of Units / Umrechnung von Einheiten

This is another HUGE measurement converter. Written in English and German, at this site you'll be able to get the formulas to convert just about anything. Included are electronic measures, such as amperage and watts. Remember, this one doesn't convert—it just gives the formula.

http://www.chemie.fu-berlin.de/chemistry/general/
  units.html

Martindale's 'The Reference Desk: Calculators On-Line'

Hotlist this one now. First off, find out what time it is, not only where you live but all over the world. You'll learn what the weather is, where the earthquakes are, and where the surf's up. Then move on to the calculators. Sure, you get the usual converted units: feet to meters, Celsius to Fahrenheit, and more. But then you go from the commonplace to the exotic: automotive, loan and budget, math and engineering, medical, and even fabulous miscellaneous calculators (calculate the size of the fish tank you need). There are guitar tuners, card games, even translation services to get your name in Hawaiian or Japanese. You can definitely *count* on this Web site!

http://sun2.lib.uci.edu/~martindale/
  RefCalculators.html

Scales of Measurement 1.7

Have you ever compared small things to bigger things, or hot things to colder things? This site lists various types of comparisons in orders of magnitude. For example, people are listed at about 1.8 meters tall, or long. On the smaller side of people, we find an "unraveled human DNA strand" with a length of 0.068 meters. On the other side, we have a blue whale, with a length of 30 meters. Your backyard's grass grows at a faster rate than the seafloor spreads, but that's still not as fast as the typical rate a glacier advances. Maybe they are checking the wrong grass; we seem to mow ours a lot around here!

http://physics.hallym.ac.kr/reference/scales/
  scales1p.html

NET FILES

How do you say, "Where is the bathroom?" in Klingon?

Answer: "nuqDaq 'oH puchpa'e'?"
*Say that six times fast! If you need help
with your pronunciation, go to*
http://www.kli.org/kli/phrases.html

Unit Conversion Form Selector

Provided by the University of Southampton in
England, this great resource will convert distance (such
as miles to kilometers), mass (or weights, including
pounds to kilograms), temperature (for example,
Celsius to Fahrenheit,) speed (such as kilometers per
hour to miles per hour), and other types of
measurements.

http://www.soton.ac.uk/~scp93ch/refer/
  convform.html

WORLD RECORDS

See name of sport or subject under SPORTS

ZIP AND POSTAL CODES

Les codes postaux des villes francaises

In France, postal codes are called *Les Codes Postaux*. At
this page, you'll see which postal codes are assigned
to various towns in France. For anyone mailing letters
to France, this is great, but be advised, the site is in
French!

http://www.unice.fr/html/French/codePostal.html

Danske Postnumre

In Denmark, the postal codes are called *Postnumre*. If
you're sending a letter to Denmark, get the right code
first by checking out this site. It's a Great Dane page,
but be advised: it's in Danish!

http://www.dk.net/misc/postnumre

Italian Zip Codes

You can easily find Italian postal codes on this page.
All you have to do is type in a city or province, and
you'll see the codes. Keep in mind, though, that this
computer understands Italian only; for example,
Rome is *Roma*!

http://www.crs4.it/~france/CAP/cap.html

PLZ Request Form (English)

Germany changed its system of postal codes a few
years ago. This means if you want to send a letter
to Germany and you have an old code, it is best
to convert from the old code to the new one.
Fortunately, your old number can be converted
via the magic of the Web.

http://www.uni-frankfurt.de/plz/plzrequest.uk.html

Postal Code Formats of the World

Ever wonder what all the letters and numbers mean
in a Canadian postal code? Turns out that the first
letter identifies the province or region of a province.
The rest of the letters and numbers have specific
meanings, too. If you're interested in what postal
codes might look like for Singapore, Estonia, and
Vatican City, as well as many other countries, stop
in here!

http://www.io.org/~djcl/postcd.txt

Postal Code Lookup

If you need to send a message to Canada (or if
you're in Canada and you need postal code info),
take a look here. A neat graphic shows you exactly
where everything goes when you address an
envelope. Toll-free 800 numbers are provided for
assistance, and all sorts of info on the Canadian
postal code system is available at this site.

http://www.mailposte.ca/english/pclookup/
  pclookup.html

A
B
C
D
E
F
G
H
I
J
K
L
M
N
O
P
Q
R
S
T
U
V
W
X
Y
Z

USPS ZIP+4 Code Lookup

This is another U.S. ZIP code lookup service. Just like the National Address Service at <http://www.semaphorecorp.com/> this site will provide, in most instances, a ZIP code for a street and town address you provide. The difference is this service is provided by the U.S. Postal Service. So you have two sites available to find ZIP codes for all the important letters you have to send! If you don't know your nine-digit ZIP code, this site will tell you, based on your address.

http://www.usps.gov/ncsc/lookups/lookup_zip+4.html

RELIGION

APS Research Guide - Theology and Religion

This jumpstation contains briefly annotated links to resources on religious subjects, from Gregorian chant to the Anglican Church (including a link to Archbishop Desmond Tutu's texts in South Africa) to Buddhist, Islamic, and other texts and links. It is heavy on Christian resources but lists resources on other religions that we have not mentioned elsewhere in this book.

http://www.utoronto.ca/stmikes/theobook.htm#TOP

Ontario Centre for Religious Tolerance

This site does not promote a specific faith or religious view. Instead, you get a fair-minded presentation of religious issues and beliefs designed to help you make your own decisions. Their goal is to increase the understanding and tolerance of minority religions by supplying information on various religions, "from Asatru to Zoastrianism." They expose religious hatred and misinformation and supply information on religious conflicts with today's current issues.

http://web.canlink.com/ocrt/ocrt_hp.htm

NET FILES

How many footballs are used in each NFL game?

Answer: According to the NFL Digest of Rules, 36 are used outdoors and 24 are used for indoor games. Visit the NFL's online library at http://www.nfl.com/fans/rules/fieldbal.html to find out more.

Religious and Sacred Texts

If you go to church or temple services, you probably know a lot about your own religion. But have you ever wondered about other people's beliefs? This site contains electronic versions of texts sacred to followers of many of the world's major religions, including Judaism, Islam, and Hinduism. Also explore links to early Christian texts, Zen gardens, and a thematic guide to world scripture.

http://webpages.marshall.edu/~wiley6/

A B C D E F G H I J K L M N O P Q R S T U V W X Y Z

ANGELS

Angels on the Net - The most informed source on the net

Many people believe that angels, while invisible to the human eye, may be felt by the human heart. Did you know that there are nine different kinds of angels? This is the place to learn about angels and share stories about how they have touched people's lives. The monthly newsletter will keep you up to date on new angel sightings. This site has added a lot of advertising since last year. The stories section is still the best.

http://www.netangel.com/

Mb's Angel Page

Have you ever had a close call? Did you wonder if you had a guardian angel who saved you from a mishap? This angel page has beautiful graphics and poems about angels and lots of angelic links.

http://www.cs.iastate.edu/~gurski/Angels/angel.html

APPARITIONS AND MIRACLES
CATHOLIC APPARITIONS OF JESUS AND MARY

An *apparition* is a supernatural sight. People have made various claims about apparitions all over the world. Did you ever wonder about which ones might have really occurred? Here's a list of reported apparitions, some of which are still ongoing! Some sites have been disproved by the Catholic Church, but others have been verified. This resource provides a code so that you can tell which is which. Decide for yourself whether you are a skeptic or a believer in these happenings. There is also information about some saints, and you can download a current calendar with the saint's important dates.

http://web.frontier.net/Apparitions/apparitions.html

> **Ask not what the Net can do for you, ask what you can do for the Net.**

Miracles Page

Crosses of light, weeping statues, healing waters, Hindu milk miracle, crop circles—are these events hoaxes or real? One thing is sure: it's next to impossible to find information about them in a book, since so many of them are new and facts are sketchy. Check the info here and see if you can make up your own mind from the information as it is presented. You might want to ask a parent or other trusted adult what he or she thinks about it all.

http://www.mcn.org/1/miracles/default.html

Shroud of Turin Home Page

In a cathedral in Turin, Italy, sits a silver chest. Inside the chest is the mysterious Turin Shroud, which many believe to be the burial cloth that covered Jesus Christ. You'll view amazing photographs and research about the famous shroud. Examining the evidence, what do you see? There are links to many Catholic sites on the Net as well as a link to a Fatima Home Page.

http://www.cais.net/npacheco/shroud/turin.html

BAHÁ'Í
A Bahá'í Faith Page

One of the world's fastest-growing religions, Bahá'í was founded in the mid-nineteenth century by Bahá'u'lláh, a Persian nobleman from Teheran. He gave up a comfortable and secure lifestyle for a life of persecution and deprivation. Learn more about his life and teachings here, in many different languages.

http://www.bcca.org/~glittle/

Soc.Religion.Bahai

Could many of the world religions be rolled into one? The Bahá'í believe that there have been many messengers from God, each one arriving during a different age. This online archive will show you other teachings, texts, sacred sites, and where to find more on the Bahá'í faith.

http://www.bcca.org/srb/

A B C D E F G H I J K L M N O P Q R S T U V W X Y Z

Which flag, with vertical bands of blue, yellow, and red, was flown with a hole cut out of its center?

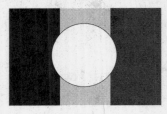

Answer: The Romanian flag. During the years of Communist rule, a coat of arms was added to the flag. In 1989, Romanians fighting for democracy cut it out in protest, making the flag with the hole a symbol of Romania's revolution. Read about it at http://students.missouri.edu/~romsa/romania.html

BUDDHISM
On-line Resources

Buddhism is a philosophy of life taught by Gautama Buddha, who lived and taught in northern India in the sixth century B.C. The Buddha was not a god—*Buddha* means "enlightened one." The teachings of Buddhism are aimed solely to relieve beings from suffering. This meta-resource includes art, philosophy, meditation, and many fascinating links. Parental advisory: all links have not been checked.

http://www.psu.edu/jbe/resource.html

**Little Bo Peep
lost her sheep,
but she found them
again in FARMING AND
AGRICULTURE.**

The White Path Temple

Visit a virtual Shin Buddhist Temple. You'll see intricate mandalas and other contemplative art. Learn about this religion by reading the beginner's guide, checking the online Buddhist dictionary, and visiting temples in Kyoto, Japan. To further investigate this religion, you'll find an extensive collection of links at W3C/ANU—Buddhist Studies WWW VL at <http://coombs.anu.edu.au/WWWVL-Buddhism.html>. See the art, read the literature, and find out about the four great vows of Buddhism.

http://www.mew.com/shin/

CHRISTIANITY
Distinctive Church Collection!

Many churches have their own parishes in cyberspace these days. This site is trying to collect them all and selects "distinctive" ones to highlight each month. Churches from eight countries are represented so far. It's interesting to drop in on many congregations and see what's happening. There are also (what else?) lots of links. Don't miss the Christian clip art or the "Six Days of Creation" screen saver at <http://www.gospelcom.net/gf/gallery/>.

http://www.rwf2000.com/church.html

Kingdom Surf

This site changes every week, so we won't even bother to describe what's on it! Here's your chance, though, to see what the Christian religion has to do with *you*. Look here first if you want a lift, because it's a timely, upbeat place that'll keep you on your toes. Other recent items have been Christian jokes, sermon clip art, readings from the Bible, and pen pal lists. You don't have to be a Christian to enjoy this site.

http://www.crusade.org/surf/

What is the sound of one router flapping?

Virtual Church (SM)

This virtual church has a youth room just for kids. You'll find Bible stories with colorful graphics to go along with them. If you want to read an exciting one, try "The Men in the Fiery Furnace." If you're a younger kid, you can ask a parent to download coloring pages, and then send them back after you've colored them on your computer. Explore the other rooms in this church, too. The library, for instance, contains crossword puzzles, trivia quizzes, and word jumbles. Don't miss a peek at the skeletons in the closet! There is also an award-winning area all about Biblical angels.

http://www.virtualchurch.org/

CHRISTIANITY—AMISH, MENNONITE

The Amish And "The Plain People"

If you've ever been curious about the Amish, Mennonites, the Brethren, or the other "Plain People" of the Pennsylvania Dutch country, visit this page. You'll learn a little about their beliefs, their mode of dress, and their customs. Did you know that an Amish bride wears a blue wedding dress, or that kids attend school only through the eighth grade? You can also "Ask the Amish" and submit your own questions.

http://www.800padutch.com/amish.html

CHRISTIANITY—CATHOLIC

Catholic Kiosk

The archdiocese of Cincinnati, Ohio, has an extensive collection here. You can read the entire catechism of the Catholic Church as well as tour the Vatican and other Catholic art and architecture resources. You can also see a list of all the members of the College of Cardinals around the world, with links to their home pages, if they have them. Many religious orders have opened up abbeys and cloisters on the Web, and you can visit them here. There are links to saints' lives, Marian resources, and sources of Catholic news. Many "right-to-life" links are included.

http://www.erinet.com/aquinas/arch/dio.html

The Holy See

The Vatican has established an official and attractive Web site under its own top-level country domain, ".va." The content is still being built, but you can get press releases about the Pope's daily activities and official appearances. The definitive Vatican site is Christus Rex at <http://christusrex.org/www1/icons/>. You'll find an annotation for it in the "Splendors of Christiandom" entry in the ART—MUSEUMS section of this book. It contains not only pictures of the Vatican museums but many more documents, and these items are in many languages. You may also want to check out Vatican Radio: "65 years of serving the unity of the Church and the peace in the world, night and day, every day, all over the world, in 37 languages... broadcasting on short wave, medium wave, FM, satellite, and the Internet." It's located at <http://www.wrn.org/vatican-radio/welcome.html>.

http://www.vatican.va/

The Marian Hour

Many Catholics around the world pray using a special set of beads called a *rosary*. They use the beads to count the various prayers they have said. You can learn about the Mysteries of the Rosary at this well-designed site as well as hear the various prayers for yourself. The organization will send a free rosary to anyone who wants one. This site has audio files in French as well as English and text files in many languages.

http://netpage.bc.ca/marianhr/

CHRISTIANITY—SAINTS

The Blessed Virgin Mary: Catholic Cincinnati Info Web

Mary, the mother of Jesus: what is the history of this woman who has been revered by so many? How did the prophets know that a virgin would bear a son, long before it happened? Find out about the miraculous events and what some people think they mean. Here, too, you'll find the Little Internet Library of the Blessed Virgin Mary and links to all over. You'll also want to visit The Mary Page at <http://www.udayton.edu/mary/> for answers to frequently asked questions about Mary.

http://www.erinet.com/aquinas/arch/marian.html

A B C D E F G H I J K L M N O P Q R S T U V W X Y Z

The Saints: Catholic Cincinnati Info Web

At this site, you can read various saints' lives and check the calendar to see whose feast day it is. Check Nicholas of Myra, the patron saint of children—whom you may know better as Santa Claus! Here's your chance to look up Saint Nick, Saint Valentine, Saint Patrick, and other Catholic saints. Still more information on saints is at Catholic Online Patron Saints Page at *<http://www.catholic.org/saints/patron.html>*.

http://www.erinet.com/aquinas/arch/saints.html

CHRISTIANITY—THE CHURCH OF JESUS CHRIST OF LATTER-DAY SAINTS

World Wide Web 1st Ward

At this site, you'll find a lively discussion of many topics of interest to Mormons, including what to do when your kids are disappointed they can't celebrate Halloween. Be inspired by the Daily Devotional and the scripture class for Sunday school teachers and interested others. There is a ton of genealogy resources, Church news, and sacred texts and resources. Don't miss the Salt Lake City, Utah, Temple Square tour. Somewhat inexplicably, the "What Mormons Believe" resources are filed at the end of the tour, where you can also send e-mail to have a free Book of Mormon delivered to your house. For still more links to LDS information resources, try *<http://www.ldsworld.com/links/>* for links to sacred texts and commentary, family activities, clip art, and more.

http://www.uvol.com/www1st/

Utah's state bird is the seagull, even though Utah is miles from any coastline! Seagull Monument stands in Temple Square, in Salt Lake City, as a reminder of a miracle that occurred there during the time of the Mormon pioneers. In the spring of 1848, their newly planted fields were being devoured by crickets. Without those crops, the settlers were sure to starve. However, seagulls appeared, gobbled up all the crickets, and saved the settlement. Read more about early Mormon history at the World Wide Web 1st Ward.

HINDUISM

Nine Questions about Hinduism

On July 4, 1990, the youth meeting of the Hindu Temple of Greater Chicago had a special visitor: Gurudeva, Sivaya Subramuniyaswami. He was asked to give "official" answers to nine questions, ranging from "Are Hindus idol worshippers?" to "What's this reincarnation thing?" to "Why do Hindu women wear the dot on the forehead?" It's a revealing look at what kids want to know about Hinduism. Hindu gods are explained and illustrated in one link from this page, and the top level at *<http://www.spiritweb.org/Spirit/Veda/Overview.html>* includes numerous outside links. Parental advisory: links from this page have not been checked.

http://www.spiritweb.org/Spirit/Veda/nine-questions.html

You know something the Net doesn't. Make your own home page!

If you can read this, good! Now check BOOKS AND LITERATURE.

Spirituality/Yoga/Hinduism Home Page

One of the first things you will learn in yoga class, besides where to take off your shoes, is the word namasté. Your instructor will say it to you, and you're expected to say it back. Namasté is derived from the Sanskrit word, Namaskaar, meaning "I bow to the divine in you." Yoga is from the Sanskrit word "Yug," meaning union with the Divine. This site is a great overview of major yogic disciplines, although it's kind of wordy. You'll also get an introduction to Hinduism and tips on learning Sanskrit.

http://www.geocities.com/RodeoDrive/1415/

ISLAM
FAQ on Islam

This is a very easy-to-understand look at Islam and "Who's a Muslim?" Find out what Muslims believe, and read about their sacred text, the Quran. You'll also find answers to questions like "What do Muslims think about Jesus?" and "What about Muslim women?"

http://darkwing.uoregon.edu/~kbatarfi/islam_1.html

Masjid of the Ether: A Place of Prayer and Fellowship in Community

Devout Muslims pray several times a day at specific times. You can use the Prayer Calculator and a ZIP code or city to find out the correct times and the correct direction to face. See if your answers can be found in the FAQ area, and make a small visit to the Digital Tekke, a Sufi lodge in Web space. Parental advisory: links off this site have not been checked.

http://www.uoknor.edu:80/cybermuslim/
cy_masjid.html

USC Muslim Students Association Islamic Server

Explore the sacred pillars of this religion, its texts, and its practice. One interesting article states that the "Nation of Islam," among others, should not be calling itself that, based on its writings.

http://www.usc.edu/dept/MSA/

JUDAISM
Josh's Bar Mitzvah Web Site

The bar/bat mitzvah ceremony (bar mitzvah for boys, bat mitzvah for girls) is celebrated when a Jewish boy turns 13 or a Jewish girl turns 12. The child embraces the Jewish tradition and assumes adult responsibility for fulfilling Jewish law. This site was created by Josh from Lawrenceville, New Jersey, as part of his bar mitzvah project. He relates his bar mitzvah requirements and offers suggestions on planning the reception, which is often as elaborate as a grown-up wedding.

http://www.geocities.com/TelevisionCity/1333/

NET FILES

THE FOIL, THE ÉPÉE, AND THE SABRE REFER TO WHAT?

a) Essential items for your next barbecue
b) Those little bones in your ear
c) The three weapons of fencing

Answer: C. Fencing is that sport where the players engage in, well, swordplay. You've seen them, with those cagelike masks on their faces. Fencing is a sport and, to many, an art. Concentration, quickness, and agility are all very important to the fencer. At http://architecture.ubc.ca:8080/vds96/gymnasium/whatis.htm, find out how fencing started and how it is done, scored, and won. It's not just for swashbucklers!

HAY! Gallop over to HORSES AND EQUESTRIAN SPORTS.

A B C D E F G H I J K L M N O P Q R S T U V W X Y Z

A
B
C
D
E
F
G
H
I
J
K
L
M
N
O
P
Q
R
S
T
U
V
W
X
Y
Z

The Judaica Web World

This is a terrific archive of spiritual and cultural Jewish knowledge. First off, we'll say we have not checked all these links. But there is a lot to like about these pages. For one thing, there is judaism.com.kids *<http://www.nauticom.net/users/judaica/jdckids.html>* special stories, games, key pals, and more for Jewish kids. You'll also find kosher Asian recipes, a Judaic calendar, GIFs of famous rabbis, "the ultimate Jewish link-launcher," and a service that faxes (or e-mails) you a little daily Torah teaching.

http://www.nauticom.net/users/rafie/judaicaworld.html

REPTILES

See also PETS AND PET CARE

Mike's Herpetocultural Home Page

Here's a herp, there's a herp, everywhere's a herp, herp. It's not Old MacDonald and it's not a farm, but this page is the place to go for information about reptiles. You'll learn about *herpetoculture*, the keeping and breeding of amphibians and reptiles. You'll find links to other herp home pages, research organizations, herp FAQs, journals and magazines, and much more.

http://gto.ncsa.uiuc.edu/pingleto/herp.html

Trendy's House of Herpetology

Everything you need to know about snakes, amphibians, lizards, turtles, and iguanas is here, including lots of great photos. Learn how to treat your turtle and how to coddle your chameleon. Whether you want to soothe your snakes or animate your amphibians, this page will surely be of use. Parental advisory: There are two versions of this page; the URL listed here is the K–12 version, but not all links off it have been checked.

http://fovea.retina.net/~gecko/herps/

CROCODILES AND ALLIGATORS
The Gator Hole

Much-maligned and misunderstood, alligators have existed since the time of the dinosaurs. Hunted almost to extinction, they have made an astounding comeback. You will find an amazing collection of gator myth and fact lying around this virtual gator hole. Find out here if the stories you hear about alligators are true, or if it's just a "croc."

http://magicnet.net/~mgodwin/

St. Augustine's Alligator Farm

Chomp, chomp! Be careful, don't get too close. Gomek is eating, and you wouldn't want to become part of his dinner, would you? Gomek is the world's largest known reptile on exhibit. He's almost 18 feet long and weighs over 1,700 pounds! Gomek wouldn't hurt us, would he? He certainly could! In the wild, alligators eat fish, turtles, and small mammals, but because Gomek has been fed by his innkeepers, he could be very dangerous to humans. Alligators that have been fed by humans lose their fear of people. They become bold and aggressive and they expect more food. Visit Gomek and his other friends at the St. Augustine Alligator Farm, and remember: you should never feed wild animals. Don't forget to pick up your discount admission ticket at this Web site, too, should you ever visit the real zoological park in Florida.

http://www.alligatorfarm.com/gator2.html

LIZARDS
Heatherk's Gecko Page

Are you a "herper"? Perhaps you should stop by this site, just to be sure. Ask yourself the following questions, and be careful how you answer them. Do you carry a moisture-mister and spray yourself three times a day? Do you lick your lips and curl out your tongue when a bug lands near you? Is your house a field trip destination for the school's science classes? This page also has links to other herp interest sites, herp home pages, and care sheets for other lizards, not just geckos.

http://www.geckoworld.com/~gecko/

Iguana iguana

You really want to raise a reptile, but you can't stomach the thought of having to feed it icky insects. Then maybe you wanna iguana. These lovely lizards are very vegetarian, but they will swiftly snarf your pepperoni pizza if left alone all night. Find out what makes these captivating creatures the most popular pet from the reptile race.

http://fovea.retina.net/~gecko/herps/iguanas/

NET FILES

What's "short track"?

http://web.mit.edu/jeffrey/speedskating/intro.html

Answer: Nope, it's not track and field for little kids! This is a sport kids can participate in, though. It's speed skating, usually skated on indoor hockey rinks. Long-track skating is the older sport, skated on huge ovals, usually outdoors. These two sports are fast and they take hard work, but they're lots of fun and terrific exercise. Find out more at

Tricia's Water Dragon Page

Looking for a new pet? How about a dragon? Water dragons, also known as *Physignathus cocincinus*, are easier to take care of than iguanas. Tricia's Web page shows that she certainly knows her dragons. She presents information on everything you could possibly need to know about selecting and caring for these two- to three-foot lizards, including tips on how to travel with your dragon if you can't bear to leave it home when the family goes on vacation.

http://www.icomm.ca/dragon/

True Chameleons

That little statue-like lizard never moves, but you could swear those eyes follow you wherever you go. They do. Chameleons have globular independent eyes that can do almost a complete 360-degree turn without ever moving their heads. The fascinating behavior, unusual body shapes, and changing color of these creatures have kept collectors intrigued for decades. However, they often face one major challenge: delicate by nature, these critters tend to die easily. But the availability of quality information on raising chameleons and new restrictions on importing them has led to captive-bred lizards that are healthier and better adapted, increasing their chances of survival. Did you know you should buy food-quality crickets for your lizard and not bait cricks, which are often fed growth hormones? You'll find lots of great info here for general lizard care, too!

http://www.skypoint.com/members/mikefry/
    chams2.html

SNAKES

An Interactive Guide to Massachusetts Snakes

You've found a snake you don't recognize sunning itself on your deck, and you want to know if it's safe to move it. Answer a series of questions at this interactive site, and you can quickly identify that suspect snake. If you already know the snake's name and want to know more about its lifestyle and habits, you can also find that here. But once you make an identification, remember: usually it's best to let a sleeping snake lie.

http://klaatu.oit.umass.edu/umext/snake/

Jason's Snakes and Reptiles

Do you have questions on housing your snakes, feeding them, or what diseases they can get? This page has the answers. Check out the care sheet for snakes, or get information on other snake sites, snake newsgroups, and gopher (the Net protocol, not the rodent) sites.

http://www.shadeslanding.com/jas/

A
B
C
D
E
F
G
H
I
J
K
L
M
N
O
P
Q
R
S
T
U
V
W
X
Y
Z

A B C D E F G H I J K L M N O P Q **R** S T U V W X Y Z

TURTLES

Turtle Trax - A Sea Turtle Page

Did you know that *all* species of marine turtles are either threatened or endangered? That's right, and a major reason for this is danger to their nests. These dangers include increased numbers of people on the beaches where the turtles dig their nests. Also, some people dig up the nests and sell or eat turtle eggs. Another problem is artificial lighting around beaches, which has a disorienting effect on little turtles—they can't find the safety of the sea. In addition to the nesting threats, don't forget about the environmental threats to turtles, which include water pollution and getting stuck in floating trash. These are just some of the most serious threats. For more information about marine turtles, their environment, and ways you can help, visit this page. Don't miss the series of pictures from the Amazing Way Cool Bogus Cam (hint: keep loading them—you'll get a surprise!).

http://www.turtles.org/

NET FILES

What do you get if you walk the dog correctly on your first try?

Answer: Five points when competing in the American Yo-Yo Association Competition. Find out more at http://www.pd.net/yoyo/list.html

ACLU American Civil Liberties Union

Who defends your right to read this sentence? The American Civil Liberties Union (ACLU) is the nation's foremost protector of individual rights and personal freedoms. They cover the full spectrum: students' rights, women's rights, workplace rights—and of course, free speech. And their new Web site is timely, as they have stepped to the front to defend cyber-rights.

http://www.aclu.org/

The Human Rights Web Home Page

Certain human rights are guaranteed to everyone by United Nations declarations and other international agreements. But people in some countries have had to struggle to make those rights a reality. The very existence of the Internet has made it easier for those folks to communicate with the rest of the world. This page clearly and thoroughly spells out what human rights are, how they are abused, and what you can do. The resources section features links to groups like Amnesty International, PEN International Writer's Union, and Physicians for Human Rights, among dozens of others. Middle school and high school kids will find this page an endless source of thought-provoking information.

http://shell3.ba.best.com/~hrweb/

National Child Rights Alliance

It is startling that as we enter the twenty-first century, children have little more legal rights and status than they did in the nineteenth century. The National Child Rights Alliance (NCRA) has a simple point of view: they feel that children have to be protected from abuse. Abuse includes the overt physical acts that are reported in the newspapers every day and the more subtle forms, such as deprivation of safety, food, shelter, medical care, and dignity. Check out the NCRA's proposed Youth Bill of Rights. Kids should explore this site with their parents.

http://www.ai.mit.edu/people/ellens/NCRA/ncra.html

Reebok and Human Rights

This well-designed page shines as an example of how corporations can become involved with more than just a ledger sheet. Since 1988, Reebok has been actively involved in the worldwide human rights movement. This isn't just a publicity stunt, either. They have given their Human Rights Awards to four young people so far and include a major cash donation to each recipient's organization of choice. They also have been promoting their Witness Program, which provides mass communications tools such as computers, video cameras, and fax machines to human rights groups, and their Project America has been responsible for getting thousands of people involved in community service organizations. Although sports shoe and other apparel manufacturing has come under scrutiny for poor labor practices in Asia and elsewhere, Reebok seems to be doing something positive about a situation that has existed in the industry for a long time.

http://www.reebok.com/humanrights/

The Religious Freedom Home Page

Beginning with the U.S. Bill of Rights and continuing onward through the United Nations Universal Declaration of Human Rights, religious freedom has been a cornerstone of progressive government worldwide. This well-designed, nondenominational Web site, sponsored by the Christian Science Committee on Publication, explores what religious freedom really means and looks at the phenomenon both nationally and globally. It includes conflicting thoughts on controversial issues but always takes the viewpoint that individuals should be informed and educated about their right to worship freely.

http://northshore.shore.net/rf/

From another galaxy? Learn about Earth in the ASTRONOMY— SOLAR SYSTEM AND PLANETS area!

U.S. House of Representatives - Internet Law Library - Civil Liberties and Civil Rights

Human rights may be inalienable, but it takes a lot of documentation to put them into law. This page includes literally hundreds of important documents pertaining to human rights from nations in every corner of the globe and throughout history. If you're looking for the complete text of Thomas Paine's "Rights of Man" or the International Covenant on Civil and Political Rights, you'll find them only a click away here.

http://law.house.gov/93.htm

Y-Rights

Kids have rights, too! The question is, what rights do they have? Y-Rights is an electronic mailing list where discussion of the rights of kids and teenagers is front and center. Parents, teachers, kids, and others talk about the give-and-take of minors and their legal status. Younger children may have a hard time keeping up with the conversation, but teens may find this very interesting. For parents, keeping tabs and providing input on the rights of kids is essential.

List Address: y-rights@sjuvm.stjohns.edu
Subscription Address: listserv@sjuvm.stjohns.edu

NET FILES

In the latest *Star Trek* series, what class of ship is the **U.S.S. Voyager**, and how many like it have been built? (You need to be a real trekker to answer this one!)

Answer: *Voyager* is an Intrepid-class ship; it is the second of four such ships in Starfleet. It was launched stardate 48038.5 (the year 2371). Find more *Star Trek* trivia at http://lausd.k12.ca.us/~png1/www/startrek/voy.html

A
B
C
D
E
F
G
H
I
J
K
L
M
N
O
P
Q
R
S
T
U
V
W
X
Y
Z

ROBOTS

Cog, the Robot

Back in 1921, playwright Karel Čapek coined the word "robot," and since then, books, movies, and television programs have all speculated about the form these mechanical creatures will take. Now a group of researchers at the Massachusetts Institute of Technology's Artificial Intelligence Lab are actually attempting this feat. *Artificial intelligence* is the process in which a computer takes in information and uses it to create new knowledge—a simulation of human thinking. Cog the Robot is a collection of sensors and motors that attempt to duplicate the sensory and manipulative functions of the human body. Coupled with artificial intelligence programming, Cog may eventually succeed in bringing science fiction's fantasies to reality. Move over Data, here comes Cog!

http://www.ai.mit.edu/projects/cog/Text/
    cog-robot.html

NET FILES

How did the term "computer bug" originate?

past-women-cs.html#Grace Hopper
Learn more at http://www.cs.yale.edu/homes/tap/
among many other honors in the computer field.
the Distinguished Service Medal from the Navy,
mathematician and programmer and received
of it here! Admiral Hopper was a distinguished
pasted into the UNIVAC I logbook. See a picture
first computer "bug." It was a real moth, which she
Answer: In 1951, Grace Hopper discovered the

Info on Hobby Robots (from comp.robotics.)

Why wait for George Jetson and Spacely Sprockets to build you a robot, when plenty of folks are building their own right now? This page gives you the lowdown on where to pick up inexpensive hobby kits for assembling your own robot! It also includes links to places where you can download hints and plans, information on building sensors, and the entire "6.270 Robot Builder's Guide," which is also available in hard copy from the Massachusetts Institute of Technology.

http://www.cs.uwa.edu.au/~mafm/robot/

Lego Robot Info

You know those cute little Lego blocks that you keep finding under your sofa cushions? Those odd-shaped things are actually capable of being constructed into computer-driven, sophisticated robots! In 1994, the Boston Museum of Science had a robot design workshop and contest for seventh- through tenth-grade students using Legos and Lego Dacta kits. The kids designed incredible machines, some using computerized interfaces, and this page has full-color photographs of their creations as well as lots of information on how to build them yourself. Even if you don't particularly want to build a robot, you may want to drop in here and marvel at the kids who did.

http://legowww.homepages.com/robots/

Xavier

Where in the world is Xavier the Robot? Exploring the classrooms and halls of Carnegie Mellon University, of course! Check in at this Web site and find out where he is, plus see what he's "seeing" as he wanders around. You can even control his movements if you visit during certain times (check the schedule). See if you can think up some new jokes for him to tell when he encounters people; the ones on the list right now are real groaners: "I'm a screen Xavier." For more interactive robots, check the Computer Museum's Hotlist at <*http://www.tcm.org/info/education/programs/interact/robotonl.html*>.

http://www.cs.cmu.edu/People/Xavier/

A caricature of Ron Hipschman, webmaster of the Exploratorium's site.

"My favorite question was, 'A thermos keeps hot things hot and cold things cold. How does it know?'"

SCIENCE—SCIENCE MUSEUMS
The Exploratorium's ExploraNet
Webmaster: Ron Hipschman
http://www.exploratorium.edu/

Who came up with the idea for your page or project? Was it you? How did the idea originate?

The Web was this brand-new and extremely cool way to distribute information on the Internet. I decided that we absolutely had to be part of this and put up a server.

Oh, yep, it was me...

How many people work on your pages? Does it take a lot of time? How many hits do you get a day?

Nowadays, we follow the American Ideal and have 2.3 people working on our pages.

You must hear from people all over the world! Can you think of an unusual request, question, or comment someone has sent to you?

Well, hundreds of people have asked us interesting science questions and hundreds more students have learned how to dissect a cow's eye from our site...

My favorite question was, "A thermos keeps hot things hot and cold things cold. How does it know?"

If this isn't your main job, what do you do, what is your training?

It's my main job along with taking care of our network and UNIX systems.

What's the one thing you'd really like to do on your page but have not yet implemented?

A good redesign, and some really good interactive exhibits that will let people really manipulate an experiment online.

Do you have a family? A dog? A lizard?

I have the first, but not the latter two.

What are your hopes and fears for the future of the Internet?

I hope that we will have the bandwidth to do all the really cool stuff that everyone wants to do. I also fear that the Internet will fall under some sort of governmental regulation.

When you're not using the Net, what do you like to do?

What? There's something else? Actually I run a laser light show, Laserium, at Morrison Planetarium here in San Francisco. You can see my Web pages for Laserium at <http://www.laserium.com> and my pages for the planetarium at <http://www.laserium.com/planetarium>.

If you could invite three people throughout history to your house for dinner, who would they be?

Let's see... Galileo (astronomer and mathematician), Samuel Clemens (author "Mark Twain"), and Douglas Adams (author) or Robin Williams (actor, comedian) might make an interesting party. Can I have it catered? I'm not a very good cook...

A
B
C
D
E
F
G
H
I
J
K
L
M
N
O
P
Q
R
S
T
U
V
W
X
Y
Z

SCHOOLS AND EDUCATION

See also separate PARENTING AND FAMILIES section at the end of the book

Access Excellence

Focusing on the biological sciences, the activities collection is truly excellent. Online "seminars" put you in touch with scientists and science teachers. Offerings include "Local Habitats," "Science of Amber," and "Emerging Diseases." Collaborative classroom projects like "Fossils Across America" help in sharing resources.

http://www.gene.com/ae/

NET FILES

SOUTH POLE →

Is there really a striped pole stuck in the ice at the South Pole?

Answer: According to astronomer Chris Bero, "There is the ceremonial pole, which is several yards away from the actual South Pole. It is striped red and white like a barber's pole with a metallic mirror ball on top. The real geographic South Pole is marked by a metal rod with a U.S. Geological surveyor marker on top." You'll see a little picture at *http://205.174.118.254/nsp/question/question.htm* but be sure to read his hilarious FAQ on life in Antarctica at *http://205.174.118.254/nsp/question/christaq.htm*

Little Bo Peep lost her sheep, but she found them again in FARMING AND AGRICULTURE.

ARTSEDGE: The National Arts and Education Information Network

This site aims to teach and learn what technology can do for education and the arts. The "arts" doesn't just mean drawing and painting; it also includes performing arts, such as music, dance, and theater. Since technology and the arts is a relatively new area of learning, think of this site as sort of an experimental lab. You'll find discussion areas for students and teachers, news flashes, and even showcases of art by kids; teachers will also find curriculum guides. There's a section for online exhibits, museums, and galleries, plus links to other Web arts sites.

http://artsedge.kennedy-center.org/

Cisco Educational Archive and Resources Catalog

OK, you've got this great new computer sitting in front of you, with a super-fast modem. Now, how do you actually use it for your day-to-day homework? Are you looking for information about the dilophosaurus? Or perhaps you want to find out more about civil rights. Don't waste any time—go right to the door of the Virtual Schoolhouse! Investigate your questions here and "CEARCH" using a very fast search engine. Cisco's done an excellent job of collecting great resources for kids, teachers, and parents. You'll also find a list of online schools and links to their home pages. You may never have heard of Cisco, but your Internet service provider has, and chances are good that much of your Internet traffic travels through Cisco equipment. A note to teachers: Cisco often announces special grants and other opportunities for schools here, so check often.

http://sunsite.unc.edu/cisco/edu-arch.html

Classroom Connect

Classroom Connect is one of our favorite magazines. Their Web site doesn't disappoint, either. Check it out for info on upcoming conferences, a jumpstation to great Web links, newsgroups, ftp sites, a Web toolkit, and more. This is a commercial publisher, but they know their market, so stop in and browse!

http://www.wentworth.com/

The Cyberspace Middle School

"It's not just a school, it's an adventure." This is one of the best places on the Net for sixth- to ninth-grade students. Looking for excitement? Take a wild virtual bus ride to hook up with other schools. Or, you can get ideas for the science fair, research your projects, and ask questions of a real scientist. Are you an author or artist? Contribute to *MidLink* magazine and see your work published for the whole world to see. Best of all, the Cyberspace Middle School is free!

http://www.scri.fsu.edu/~dennisl/CMS.html

Global SchoolNet Foundation Home Page

"Where in the World Is Roger?," "Roots and Shoots with Jane Goodall," "International CyberFair," "Global Schoolhouse Videoconferencing"—any of that sound interesting? The folks in charge of GSN just keep collecting and coming up with more terrific ideas all the time. Always fresh and exciting, this is where K–12 innovation lives on the Net!

http://www.gsn.org/

Global Show-N-Tell Museum Wings

You know how you can't find your refrigerator door anymore because your mom has put your pictures, paintings, and other stuff there? How about displaying your artwork on an electronic refrigerator door for a while? This site showcases the artwork of students worldwide. Visit the current exhibit, explore past ones, or search other kids' art sites on the Internet. The directions to enter your work are right here. Some of the drawings are linked back to kid's personal home pages.

http://www.telenaut.com/gst/

Kathy Schrock's Guide for Educators - Home Page

The links in this guide are organized according to subject area. In World History, for instance, you'll get a breakdown of Web pages, from "Ancient World Web" to "World War II: The World Remembers." A list of new pages each month will point you to the latest and greatest.

http://www.capecod.net/schrockguide/

KIDLINK: Global Networking for Youth 10-15

Wow! Kids from more than 87 countries have answered these four questions: Who am I? What do I want to be when I grow up? How do I want the world to be better when I grow up? What can I do now to make this happen? Once you've answered those questions to introduce yourself, you can take part in any of the KIDLINK projects. You can even have a dialogue in the KIDCAFE in languages such as Spanish, Japanese, and Portuguese. Make the world a better place through KIDLINK! This site is available in 14 different languages.

http://www.kidlink.org/

Kids Web - A World Wide Web Digital Library for Schoolkids

What's your assignment? Here you'll find a short list of links arranged by subject category: arts, sciences, social studies, reference, sports, and some fun and games, too. Syracuse University's Living Schoolbook Project did a nice job in compiling this short list.

http://www.npac.syr.edu/textbook/kidsweb/

Quest: NASA K-12 Internet Initiative

OK, everybody at your school wants to get hooked up to the Net, but not even the teachers know everything about how to do it! NASA will help you get started with all the ins and outs of getting online. Then they've got links to online interactive projects—new ones every year! Past projects have included "Live from Antarctica," "Online Jupiter 1997," and "Earth to Mars Activities." Ask the scientists questions, order interesting materials, and help NASA decide what they will do next.

http://quest.arc.nasa.gov/

TEACHERS HELPING TEACHERS

Don't you just hate to read "advice" from someone who has never set foot in the classroom? Instead, here are your teachers' peers, who know *exactly* what they are going through and how to help. Show this one to your teachers!

http://www.pacificnet.net/~mandel/

A
B
C
D
E
F
G
H
I
J
K
L
M
N
O
P
Q
R
S
T
U
V
W
X
Y
Z

Web Sites And Resources For Teachers

All subject areas are covered here, but let's take math as an example. Your teacher will get not only lesson plans but also online math applications, like a calorie calculator and even a magic square checker. Online board games such as Mancala (the great strategy game that teaches critical thinking) and dozens of puzzles will challenge you to go beyond worksheet math.

http://www.csun.edu/~vceed009/

Web66 Home Page

If your school has its own Web server, it should be linked here. It's the largest collection of all the schools with Web sites in the world! If your school doesn't have a Web site yet, a cookbook here will give your school the recipe to create one: where to get the software, how to write the HTML, and more. Teachers: Can't tell a LAN from a WAN? You say you just found out administration wants the fifth grade to run ethernet around the building? No fear, stop here. You'll find technical info anyone can understand, plus acceptable use policies as well as other technology planning musts. You want links on top of all that? No surprise, they got 'em.

http://web66.coled.umn.edu/

Check the "International Registry of K12 Schools on the Web" at the Web66 Home Page for a comprehensive list of schools with home pages. If your school starts its own home page, you'll want to get it listed here, too.

NET FILES

Here is the same sound described in several languages. What sound is it?

Arabic (Algeria): couak couak
Chinese (Mandarin): gua gua
Finnish: kvaak kvaak
Japanese: gaagaa
Russian: krya-krya
Turkish: vak, vak

Answer: It's the sound of a duck quacking! Hear the duck for yourself and see what language you think says it best at http://www.georgetown.edu/cball/animals/duck.html

ELEMENTARY

Aloha! from Lanikai School

Visit Oahu in the Hawaiian Islands to see Lanikai School's page. You can even get a taste of their spot of heaven *from* heaven—see a space shuttle photo of their location! Learn about Hawaiian culture here.

http://www.doe.hawaii.edu/~lanikai/

Hartsfield School's Home Page

This school is located in Tallahassee, Florida, and was one of the very first schools to have a page on the Web! You'll also find links here to other fantastic sites in Tallahassee; try DeSoto Trail and The Academic Resource Center for sure bets.

http://www.hartsfield.leon.k12.fl.us/
  hartsfieldhome.html

Sister MacNamara School

Located in the heart of Winnipeg, Manitoba, Canada, this is a multicultural school. Check out the Monet reproductions by Miss Wallis' fourth-graders!

http://hal9000.wsd1.winnipeg.mb.ca/nnl/sister_m/
sismac.htm

Vose School General Information

The students at Vose School in Beaverton, Oregon, are actually writing their own encyclopedia! Click on the Vose Kidopedia button at the bottom of the page to check out their work in progress. They've already covered a lot of topics, with more to come in the future.

http://www.teleport.com/~vincer/info.html

Wangaratta Primary School

Wangaratta Primary School is in a rural city in North East Victoria, Australia. The school has 250 students, ranging in age from five to twelve years. Wow, is this page fun! Be sure to check the Aussie Activities. While you are learning about Australian animals, you can listen to a kookaburra laugh, search for the hidden Aussie animals in a word search puzzle, and learn how to make a kite that looks like a sugar glider (that's a squirrel-like creature in Australia). You can also meet Michael, a cool kid with cerebral palsy; he has an Internet address, so be sure to write and say hi!

http://www.ozemail.com.au/~wprimary/wps.htm

Washington Magnet and Gifted School of Communication - Web Site

Wow—the graphics on this site will jump off the page at you! Find out what a "magnet" school is and how kids learn in this school in Rockford, Illinois. There is also a For Kids Only area with cool links.

http://shoga.wwa.com/~desktop/washschl.htm

MIDDLE SCHOOL
Cool School Pages

If you want to find still more middle schools on the Web, here's a listing of sites pronounced "cool" by *MidLink* magazine.

http://longwood.cs.ucf.edu/~MidLink/
middle.home.html

First Colony Middle School Home Page

These middle-schoolers in Sugar Land, Texas, invite you to become an official migration-watcher. They are collecting data on the movements of birds and butterflies! You'll also want to have a look at their 'Netting The Butterfly project and their reports about animal migrations in Texas.

http://chico.rice.edu/armadillo/Ftbend/fcms.html

Highland Home Page

You may not know the word "tessellation," but you've seen the results of it before: for example, those M. C. Escher drawings with repeating geometrical patterns, where a fish turns into a bird. But what does it have to do with math? Look at the tessellation art done by students at Highland School, then download a Tesselmania Demo and try it out yourself! These students live in Libertyville, Illinois.

http://www.mcs.net/~highland/

Marion Cross School

The kids at this school in Norwich, Vermont, will show you how to make your own home page. Go to their MCS Easy Home Page Guide for the scoop. Also check out the recommended reading lists, Web resources for schools and families, and much more!

http://picard.dartmouth.edu/~cam/MCS.html

Monroe Middle School

Take a tour of the historic Oregon Trail as it travels through Wyoming. Enjoy the scenery and read the students' fictional journals, describing what life would have been like along the trail. You'll also see lots of Wyoming wildlife, described by the kids in Green River, Wyoming, where Monroe Middle School is located.

http://monhome.sw2.k12.wy.us/

A B C D E F G H I J K L M N O P Q R S T U V W X Y Z

A
B
C
D
E
F
G
H
I
J
K
L
M
N
O
P
Q
R
S
T
U
V
W
X
Y
Z

Vista Middle School Home Page

Join up with the students of Vista Middle School in Las Cruces, New Mexico, to become a Knight in Space. They aren't real astronauts, but their school has the next best thing: a life-size space shuttle cargo bay! They go on "missions" to work and learn about space and about cooperation, too. Sometimes they have electrical problems (the teacher shuts off the lights) or a rough ride if they are not secured when one of the hydraulic jack thrusters fires. Learn about their scientific experiments "in space." They've also got a great English As a Second Language program. In fact, you can get to a Spanish/English dictionary right from their home page.

http://taipan.nmsu.edu/vista/vista_home.html

STUDY AND HOMEWORK

B.J. Pinchbeck's Homework Helper

"Beege" is ten years old and has collected over 350 resources that he uses with his school homework. Maybe they will work for you, too! You'll find everything from biographical dictionaries to flags of the world. We just wish they weren't all on one page, since it takes so long to load and reload.

http://tristate.pgh.net/~pinch13/

CalRen Home Page

Something's clanking in the dryer. The dog is barking at a bike rider going by outside. You can smell dinner cooking, and you feel hungry. All of a sudden, a football whizzes by your bedroom window. So many distractions make it hard to study! Here are some tips to help you study better, listen, take notes, and take tests.

http://www-slc.uga.berkeley.edu/CalRENHP.html

HomeWorkHelper! Welcome!

Kids, got a question? Your answer may be just a click away! Here you can submit your question, select any or all of the six source types, and GO. For older students, there is also a link to the Electric Library and Researchpaper.com, the Internet's largest collection of topics, ideas, and assistance for school-related research projects.

http://www.homeworkhelper.com/

How to be a Successful Student

Being a successful student isn't just about doing your homework. You have to learn about your own learning style and find out how to avoid putting things off. You'll find a few tips here that will get you started. For more techniques on how to conquer procrastination, go directly to <http://128.32.89.153/CalREN/procrastechniques.html> without waiting another minute! Here is one tip: "Break the task down into little pieces. Not: There's so much to do, and it's so complicated. I'm overwhelmed by my English term paper. Instead: I don't have to do the whole project at once. There are separate small steps I can take one at a time to begin researching and drafting my paper."

http://marin.cc.ca.us/~don/Study/Hcontents.html

IPL Citing Electronic Resources

Using the Net to find information for research projects is great, but how do you cite all those electronic resources? This useful list from the Internet Public Library will show you the way.

http://www.ipl.org/classroom/userdocs/internet/citing.html

SCIENCE

See also under name of specific subject throughout the book

IN Jersey: ION Science: Science and nature news and information

Keep current with what's happening in the world of science. Once a week, this site updates its collection of late-breaking science news stories. When we first reviewed this site, one of the new stories was about the ruffe in the Great Lakes. This fish was a stowaway that escaped to the lakes from a European freighter. It's now a possible threat to the fish that naturally live there. Apparently, ruffe doesn't taste very good and has no natural predators to keep it under control. Time will tell if the ruffe will become an eco-disaster. There's other interesting news for inquiring minds: read the story on the thermodynamics of pizza. Also, check out their archive of older news stories.

http://www.injersey.com/Media/IonSci/

The MAD Scientist Network

Do you have a question about science that is stumping everyone you ask? Or maybe you have a really simple question you're too embarrassed to bring up in class. Look no further. You have just stumbled onto the solution. This site is a collaboration of scientists around the world gathered to answer your questions. You can search the archives and see if your question, or one like it, has already been answered.

http://medinfo.wustl.edu/~ysp/MSN/

NCAM/Captioning and Audio Description on the Web

This is a demonstration of how QuickTime movies can be captioned so that deaf kids know what is happening in the film. That's interesting, and we also found the scientific questions that are answered in the short films really fascinating! For example, why are manhole covers round instead of some other shape? And how do traffic lights seem to know your car is there? And why are some potato chips green? Check out these and other puzzling questions (and their answers) here.

http://www.boston.com/wgbh/pages/ncam/
    captionedmovies.html

Newton's Apple Index

This is the *Newton's Apple* home page. This site is full of science-related lessons and experiments from the TV show. The lesson on "Arctic Nutrition" explains why Arctic explorers need a carbohydrate-rich diet to maintain their strength. Another lesson explains why you don't get a strong smell from garlic until it is cut or crushed. You'll find lots more here to learn and experiment with. Have fun!

http://ericir.syr.edu/Projects/Newton/

Quest: NASA K-12 Internet Initiative

OK, everybody at your school wants to get hooked up to the Net, but not even the teachers know everything about how to do it! NASA will help you get started, with all the ins and outs of getting online. Then they've got links to online interactive projects—new ones every year! Past projects have included "Live from Antarctica," "Online Jupiter 1997," and "Earth to Mars Activities." Ask the scientists questions, order interesting materials, and help NASA decide what they will do next.

http://quest.arc.nasa.gov/

Science Friday Kids Connection

Every Friday, science guru Ira Flatow hosts a radio show on National Public Radio, called (what else?) "Science Friday." The companion Web site for kids is a real treasure for all listeners! Interested in the show topic? Find study questions, links, and resources to find out more about it. Recent topics have included comets, identifying smashed bugs on your car windshield, and HAL, the robot from the movie *2001: A Space Odyssey*. A close-up look at the creators of this Web site appears in the Postcards from the Net section of this book.

http://www.npr.org/programs/sfkids

NET FILES

As the story goes, the governor got headaches from the sun's glare off all the white houses, so he required the citizens to paint their houses in soft pastels. (Maybe sunglasses hadn't been invented yet.) Where in the world was this?

Answer: Willemstad, on the island of Curaçao. Maybe it's a legend, maybe not. Find out this and more about the group of five islands in the Caribbean Sea called the Netherlands Antilles. Go to http://caribbe.an/islands/an/curacao/curacao.pht and get the scoop.

ARCHITECTURE: building blocks for grown-ups!

A B C D E F G H I J K L M N O P Q R S T U V W X Y Z

A
B
C
D
E
F
G
H
I
J
K
L
M
N
O
P
Q
R
S
T
U
V
W
X
Y
Z

Science, Technology - Dr. Bob's Home Page

Dr. Bob is a scientist who also directs a Sylvan Learning Center and this Web page! He hopes to get kids ten years old and up really hooked on science. Mysterious lights at the thermal vents on the bottom of the ocean, or the case of the sliding boulders in the desert—do these topics sound interesting to you? How about the guy who lived for 13 years with a metal pipe stuck through his head (a photo of his skull is here, and it's very gross anatomy). If that is just too weird, skip it and read about the space shuttle or insects, or try some of the neat science links.

http://ny.frontiercomm.net/~bjenkin/science.htm

NET FILES

What famous event occurred in 1989 and marked the end of the Cold War?

(Hint: It attracted a huge flock of "wall woodpeckers.")

Answer: The demolition of the Berlin Wall, which had divided East and West Germany. Many people chiseled off pieces as souvenirs. With all their tapping, they were called "wall woodpeckers"! See the before and after photos at http://www.users.dircon.co.uk/~chrisx/

Attention everyone. The Internet is closing. Please go play outside.

The Why Files

Your coach has really gone crazy this time, somehow getting up to the top of the backboard and dropping a round basketball and a flat basketball (with no air in it) at the same time. Which one will hit the floor first? Everybody guesses one or the other, but the answer is that they will strike the floor at the same time. Why? The answer is at this site, which is funded by the National Science Foundation. You'll also find current science news for kids, as well as archives of past whys (and wise) answers!

http://whyfiles.news.wisc.edu/

Yahoo! - Science

This is Yahoo's science list. It's big! There are lots of different subcategories to browse through, from acoustics to zoology. Use the search function to get a list of things quickly. Hint: The default for the search is to search all of Yahoo. To narrow down the area for the search, click on the "Search only in Science" button. This limiting feature is available throughout Yahoo, so use it to your advantage.

http://www.yahoo.com/Science/

You Can With Beakman and Jax

Why do feet smell? What's Jell-O really made of? What direction is down? Where are the latest Hubble Space Telescope photos? If it has something to do with science, you may find it collected here. Look for more Beakman information at the *Beakman's World* TV show home page at <*http://www.spe.sony.com/Pictures/tv/beakman/beakman.html*>.

http://pomo.nbn.com/youcan/

SCIENCE FAIRS
CMS Science Fair 97

Are you stumped trying to think of an interesting project for the science fair at school? The Cyberspace Middle School's resource page will give you a great start! Lots of science fair ideas, projects, and tips are collected here. If your school doesn't have a science fair and you'd like to start one, several suggested books contain everything you'll need to know.

http://www.scri.fsu.edu/~dennisl/CMS/sf/sf.html

Helping Your Child Learn Science

OK, it's really a brochure for parents, but you should check out the experiments here, because some of them would make neat science fair projects. You'll find lots of kitchen chemistry tricks and fun with static electricity, and don't miss "celery stalks at midnight"!

http://www.ed.gov/pubs/parents/Science/

Science and Math Carnival

How about organizing a math and science carnival for your school? This site gives you a complete how-to manual. There is a list of all the equipment and materials you'll need, although the first thing you need to assemble is a long list of volunteers to help! Your ten hands-on exhibits will be fun for kids of all ages, but you need adults to help, because some of the exhibits involve electricity, liquid nitrogen, and other similar materials.

http://www.ca.sandia.gov/outreach/
     carnival-cover.html

SCIENCE HOBBYIST

Are you into amateur science? If so, you've just found a great place to bookmark! This site has lots of science links. Sites are grouped in categories, such as amateur science, science projects, kids asking scientists, science suppliers/stores, and others. If you're looking for a place to browse for science stuff, be sure to experiment with this one, but get an adult to help you.

http://www.eskimo.com/~billb/

Zia Kid's Experiments Page

If you're looking for a way to dazzle the rest of the class with your science fair know-how, put your safety goggles on and take a look here! You'll learn how to make raisins dance, grow crystal cubes and needles, and examine the attraction of magnetic breakfast cereal. Most of these kitchen chemistry experiments are based on a series from the American Chemical Society, so you know it's not just science, it's GOOD science!

http://www.zia.com/tech/exp/default.htm

SCIENCE MUSEUMS
Exploratorium: ExploraNet

Do you know what makes a fruit fly grow legs out of its head? How would you like to take a light walk and explore the world of shadows? The Exploratorium, in San Francisco, California, is a huge hands-on science laboratory for kids of all ages. Discover the many interesting wonders that they have ported to the Web!

http://www.exploratorium.edu/

The Lost Museum of Sciences

No, they didn't lose the museum—the idea here is for you to get lost. No, we don't mean GET LOST, just lose yourself amidst all the stuff you'll find here. Now you're starting to get the picture. By the time you do find your way back, if you find your way back, you're sure to have learned something. No, we don't mean you'll learn how to find your way back, we mean you'll learn something scientific. Oops! If you like to be challenged, you can always play "Find The Exhibit." The first one to find it gets his or her name displayed here for all to see!

http://www.netaxs.com/people/aca3/ATRIUM.HTM

SHARKS

See also FISH

Beyond Jaws

Sharks have terrible eyesight, right? Wrong. OK, but aren't sharks just brainless eating machines? Wrong again. Discover what is fact and what is fiction about these great ocean dwellers and learn shark no-no's when swimming in potentially shark-infested waters.

http://hockey.plaidworks.com/sharks/great-white.html

A B C D E F G H I J K L M N O P Q R S T U V W X Y Z

A
B
C
D
E
F
G
H
I
J
K
L
M
N
O
P
Q
R
S
T
U
V
W
X
Y
Z

Fiona's Shark Mania

Shark! Good thing you're just surfing the Net and not the ocean. Actually, sharks do live in the ocean, but they can also be found in rivers, lakes, and other freshwater bodies. Sharks are saltwater fish, but they can live in fresh water for several days. This page celebrates "all things sharky." At this site, you'll find sharks in literature, shark info, shark photos, even shark clip art and graphics.

http://www.oceanstar.com/shark/

The Great White Shark

Carcharodon carcharias is the scientific name of the great white shark. It comes from the Greek *carcharos*, meaning "ragged," and *odon*, meaning "tooth." *Jaws* was a pretty scary movie, but it was just a story, after all. Discover the truth about great white sharks!

http://www.cybervault.com/users/D/dgrgich/
    shark.html

SHIPS AND SHIPWRECKS

See also TREASURE AND TREASURE-HUNTING

Chesapeake Bay Maritime Museum

Although the museum is located in Maryland, the Chesapeake Bay's estuary runs 190 miles and touches several states, from the mighty Susquehanna River in Pennsylvania to Virginia's capes. At its widest point, the bay is 30 miles across, and its greatest depth is 174 feet. An interesting array of boats has developed around the bay's main occupations: crabbing, oystering, and waterfowling. Take the online museum tour to get a look at some of these sleek maritime beauties, and learn a lot about the Chesapeake Bay as you explore.

http://www.cbmm.org/

Edmund Fitzgerald Bell Restoration Project

You may have heard the Gordon Lightfoot song commemorating the wreck of the *Edmund Fitzgerald*. On November 10, 1975, the 729-foot freighter was hauling a heavy cargo of iron ore pellets across Lake Superior and was caught in a severe storm that sent the ship suddenly to the bottom, killing its 29 crew members. This page describes the search for the wreck, the salvage effort, and the restoration of the ship's bell. Surviving family members asked that the bell be recovered as a memorial to the sailors who gave their lives in the maritime accident. A duplicate bell, inscribed with the names of the sailors, was left in the pilot house of the ship. The original bell was brought to the surface and dedicated on July 7, 1995. At the ceremony, the bell was rung 30 times: once for each of the 29 *Fitzgerald* crew members, and once for all mariners who have lost their lives at sea.

http://web.msu.edu/bell/

*The legend lives on from the Chippewa on down
Of the big lake they called 'Gitche Gumee'
The lake, it is said, never gives up her dead
When the skies of November turn gloomy
With a load of iron ore twenty-six thousand tons more
Than the Edmund Fitzgerald weighed empty.
That good ship and true was a bone to be chewed
When the gales of November came early.*

Read about the history of this famous shipwreck at the **Edmund Fitzgerald Bell Restoration Project** page.

Visit the BRIDGES of Internet County in ARCHITECTURE!

Hawaii's Living History - Voyaging into New Horizons

Hawai'i was first discovered by some very smart and courageous people, over 2,000 years ago. They navigated across the ocean—without special instruments—in small boats. You can learn about these ancient watercraft and Polynesian navigation techniques at this site. Replicas of some of these voyaging canoes sail today; find out more at the Polynesian Voyaging Society Home Page at <*http://leahi.kcc.hawaii.edu/org/pvs/*> where you can see the double-hulled sailing canoes *Hokule'a* and *Hawai'iloa.*

http://www.aloha-hawaii.com/hawaii_magazine/
polynesia/index.shtml

The La Salle Shipwreck Project

The Texas Historical Commission has quite a find on their hands! They are excavating a shipwreck believed to be that of the *Belle,* one of the ships brought by the French explorer René Robert Cavelier, sieur de La Salle. La Salle was the explorer who claimed the Mississippi and all its tributaries for France. His ship was lost in 1686. It lies in about 12 feet of water in a bay about halfway between Galveston and Corpus Christi. Archaeologists built a special double-walled coffer dam around the wreck, then pumped out the water in the middle of this "doughnut." They were then free to explore and carefully record their findings. You can read about La Salle and the recovery of his ship and its artifacts at this very special site!

http://www.thc.state.tx.us/belle/

NET FILES

What's the next number after a **zillion**?

Answer: *Actually, the number zillion doesn't exist—it is a slang word, meaning "a great many." But there are names for big numbers. According to Dr. Math, "Here's how the sequence starts (in the United States; British use different names):*

1,000,000 million
1,000,000,000 billion
1,000,000,000,000 trillion
1,000,000,000,000,000 quadrillion
1,000,000,000,000,000,000 quintillion
and so on. 'Vigintillion' is 1 with 63 zeroes after it. Some people use the word 'googol' to mean the number 1 with 100 zeroes after it. And a 'googol-plex' is a 1 with a googol zeroes after it—a VERY large number." Count on
http://forum.swarthmore.edu/dr.math/problems/

MERCHANT MARINE AND MARITIME PAGES

Have you ever wondered what it takes to pass the Coast Guard exam for a marine engineer license? Here's your chance to take a quiz! Examine many kinds of ship engines and ship designs. Maritime poems are interspersed with drawings and photos of all kinds of freighters in many world ports. Don't miss the Russian vessel in Kobe, Japan, "exporting" souvenir cars for each crew member. They sprout all over the deck, sticking out like porcupine quills! You'll find links to lots of other maritime sites around the Web, including virtual port authorities and research fleets. This Web site, written by a real merchant marine engineer, is a real winner.

http://pacifier.com/~rboggs/

Surf, and you shall become empowered (or wet).

**Nothing to do?
Check CRAFTS AND HOBBIES
for some ideas.**

A
B
C
D
E
F
G
H
I
J
K
L
M
N
O
P
Q
R
S
T
U
V
W
X
Y
Z

A
B
C
D
E
F
G
H
I
J
K
L
M
N
O
P
Q
R
S
T
U
V
W
X
Y
Z

VNP Exhibit of the Titanic

For many years, the sinking of the *Titanic* was thought to be a disaster in "modern" times. Now, the year 1912 seems long ago in the past. It has even become a distant memory for the dwindling number of people who were alive both then and now. Web sites such as this become excellent depositories for a great deal of information that could easily become lost. This page not only gives the hard facts of the sinking of the *Titanic* but also explores (through contemporary newspaper headlines, articles, and cartoons) how the average person of that time found out what was happening in the world—there was no cable TV satellite news back then! You'll also find information at another Titanic home page, at *<http://gil.ipswichcity.qld.gov.au/~dalgarry/>*.

http://www.lib.virginia.edu/cataloging/vnp/titanic/
titanic1.html

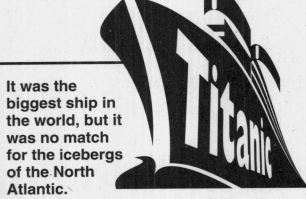

It was the biggest ship in the world, but it was no match for the icebergs of the North Atlantic.
On April 15, 1912, the *Titanic* struck an iceberg that caused enough damage to sink the ship off the coast of Halifax, Nova Scotia. Read about it at the VNP Exhibit of the Titanic.

ART is more than crayons and finger paint!

Welcome to the Mary Rose

July 19, 1545: On the flagship, the Tudor king Henry VIII was having a lavish dinner. The *Mary Rose*, a four-masted warship built between 1510 and 1511, sailed nearby. French ships appeared and fired on the fleet. A little while later, the *Mary Rose* was lying at the bottom of the Solent, a body of water between Portsmouth, England, and the Isle of Wight. Most of the 500-person crew drowned. The ship was rediscovered in 1971 and was raised to the surface in 1982. This site takes you on a tour of the museum artifacts found on board as well as a dry dock containing what is left of the ship itself. You'll be fascinated at the technology used to raise the ship and the stories of shipboard life during those times.

http://www.maryrose.org/

SPORTS

The AudioNet Sports Guide

You missed the big game? Check here to see if an audio broadcast is available. Some are live; others are here whenever you tune in. You'll also catch online shows with coaches and players, as well as special reports.

http://www.audionet.com/sports/

CNN - Sports

Get the top stories in the world of sports from CNN. From auto racing to rugby to yachting—even the more unusual sports get attention here.

http://www.cnn.com/SPORTS/

College Nicknames

Teams usually pick a nickname to describe themselves, like the Wolverines or the Wildcats. Which names go with which U.S. colleges? Find out here! Did you know there's even a team nicknamed the White Mules? They're at Colby College, in Waterville, Maine.

http://www.afn.org/~recycler/sports.html

You've picked a really cool name for your new team:

The Banana Slugs.

You figure that no one will have thought of that name before. But you'd be wrong. It's the nickname for teams from the University of California at Santa Cruz! Try College Nicknames to find out more about team nicknames.

ESPNET SportsZone

Get the latest in up-to-the-minute sports reporting, including scores, from this site. There are also columns and feature stories, too. Want to track Michael Jordan's progress since he came back to the NBA? Just do it. Or maybe you want to play Fantasy Football or get some industry insider information. If so, then this site is for you, from the folks who bring you ESPN, the all-sports cable TV network. To get all the features of this site, you must be a paid subscriber, but much is available for free.

http://espnet.sportszone.com/

SI Online from Sports Illustrated

Have you ever wondered how *Sports Illustrated* picks people for its "Faces in the Crowd" section? Do you know a local high-school athlete or amateur athlete who deserves to be listed? Nominate him or her online! This site lets you read many of the magazine's articles, including special features like the college basketball preview or the NBA preview. Also, visit the Sports Illustrated for Kids site at <http://pathfinder.com/SIFK/> for a kids version. (There's a listing for this site in the NEWS, NEWSPAPERS, AND MAGAZINES—MAGAZINES section of this book.) Parental alert: the swimsuit issue is also online.

http://pathfinder.com/si/simagazine.html

Sports Spectrum Magazine

Who was the first NHL goalie to wear a mask? Jacques Plante, of the Montreal Canadiens, began wearing one in the late 1950s after getting a head injury. Which teams in the NFL have had record single-season scoring leaders who were *not* placekickers? Seven NFL teams have had such record scorers: the Packers, 49ers, Bills, Cowboys, Vikings, Browns, and Colts. These are examples of the questions that are answered in the Web edition of *Sports Spectrum* magazine. You can search for articles on lots of topics here!

http://www.gospelcom.net/rbc/ss/ssm/

ARCHERY

Angus Duggan: Archery

Archery is hard! Making an arrow go where it's supposed to may seem easy, but it isn't. At the World Target Archery Records, you'll see who is the best in bending bows and slinging arrows. You'll also learn something about the history of archery and its equipment.

http://www.dcs.ed.ac.uk/home/ajcd/archery/

Many common phrases originated in the sport of archery: "point blank," "high strung," "straight as an arrow," "bolt from the blue," and "wide of the mark" are a few. Shoot over to the **Angus Duggan: Archery page** *to learn more!*

A
B
C
D
E
F
G
H
I
J
K
L
M
N
O
P
Q
R
S
T
U
V
W
X
Y
Z

A
B
C
D
E
F
G
H
I
J
K
L
M
N
O
P
Q
R
S
T
U
V
W
X
Y
Z

National Archery Association

Ever since Justin Huish won two Olympic gold medals (individual and team) in Atlanta for his archery skills, there has been renewed interest in this family sport. The National Archery Association governs the U.S. Olympic archery team, and you can read about the team members here. A handy spectator's guide will tell you what it means when the arrow hits various places on the target. You'll also learn about the different kinds of bows and other equipment. There is an online publication for youth archery, called The Edge, and its archives are available.

http://www.USArchery.org/

BADMINTON

Anita's Badminton Homepage

What's the world's fastest and oldest racket sport? Badminton! The "bird," or shuttlecock, has been clocked traveling up to 200 miles per hour. And although the sport goes back to the fifth century B.C., badminton only recently became an Olympic sport—first appearing at the 1992 Olympics in Barcelona. Current world rankings, results from major badminton tournaments, photos, and links to other major badminton sites are collected here. Rules and regulations are here, too. If you want to organize your own tournament, why not use the Swiss Ladder System—the details are in the Programs area, where a computer program is available to do the calculations for you. There is a mirror site in the U.S. at <http://WWW.Zmall.Com/sports/badminton/anita/badmint.html>.

http://huizen.dds.nl/~anita/badmint.html

BASEBALL

Black Baseball's Negro Baseball Leagues

Among the many great African American baseball players were Satchel Paige and Josh Gibson. Did you know there was a time in American history when major league teams didn't allow African American players on the same team with white players? It seems impossible to believe now. These fantastic players competed in what was called the Negro Baseball Leagues. You can find out all about their history and greatest athletes at this excellent site.

http://www.blackbaseball.com/

Fastball

Do you love major league baseball and hate when the season is over? Then this is the site for you. It is devoted to covering baseball during the off-season and has discussion areas and the latest news for each team. If you are hooked on baseball, this is one site that will make it easier for you to wait for spring training!

http://www.fastball.com/

Major League Baseball MLB@BAT

All the information you'd ever need to settle any World Series argument is here: all the stats, all the teams, everything but the hot dogs. You'll need to hotlist this site right away, because you'll need it all season. Here, you'll find official information on all the major league teams, expanded box scores for all the games, and a great photo gallery! A baseball team shop is here, too, as well as contests for kids and others.

http://www.majorleaguebaseball.com/

Mudball

Austin "Mudball" Taylor's dream is to play baseball in the major leagues. At his Web site, you can follow his personal stats and his training progress through Little League. Check his secret training weapon—but make sure you have your parents' and coach's approval before you try it, and always remember to stretch and warm up first!

http://www.halcyon.com/kat/mudball.htm

The National Baseball Hall of Fame and Museum

Visit the Baseball Hall of Fame in Cooperstown, New York! Get information on exhibits and tours, and read Around the Horn, the Hall of Fame newsletter. You'll read about Babe Ruth's bat, Mickey Mantle's locker, and Abbott and Costello's famous routine, "Who's On First?" Unfortunately, the text to that routine isn't here, but you can get it at <http://www.ece.uc.edu/~pbaraona/stories/abbott_costello.txt> if you want to hear one of the funniest routines about baseball.

http://www.enews.com/bas_hall_fame/

Official Site of Little League Baseball International Headquarters

Do you play Little League baseball? Did you know that the Little League baseball organization has a Web site? This site gives you answers to frequently asked questions about Little League and its history. You'll also find summer camp information, Little League World Series news, and access to the Little League Gift Shop. No Little League near you? Talk Mom and Dad into starting one for you and your friends—contact names for starting the procedure are here!

http://www.littleleague.org/

Professional Baseball in Japan

Let's go, Yakult Swallows! Look out for the Hiroshima Toyo Carp! Baseball is huge in Japan, and this page is the place for information and stats on Japanese baseball. You'll also find a search engine to look up Japanese and non-Japanese baseball stars. (Remember former New York Yankee Mell Hall? He's now a "hit" in Japan.)

http://www.inter.co.jp/Baseball/

YPN: Sports: Baseball

This is a neat, annotated collection of Web sites, newsgroups, and graphics from all over the Net. You'll find links to baseball history, stats, Little League, coaching, and lots more here. How about softball, whiffleball, and the Irish and Swedish baseball teams? Yes, they are here, too, as well as a link to the U.S. Olympic baseball team's home page. Bring some peanuts and hot dogs—you'll be here all day!

http://www.ypn.com/topics/1033.html

BASKETBALL

College Hoops

This site gives news, scores, and stats about men's and women's college basketball, as well as info on TV schedules, rules changes, recruiting, team nicknames, and college basketball rankings. You'll find links to other basketball sites around the Web, too.

http://www.onlysports.com/bball/

The Harlem Globetrotters

One sports team has played before more people and has won more consecutive games over the last 70 years than any other: the Harlem Globetrotters, of course! Check out these funny athletes at their Web site, and play some neat basketball trivia games while you're here.

http://www.harlemglobetrotters.com/

NET FILES

How did the chipmunk get her stripes?

Answer: A Native American tale has the answer. Because the winters were cold and people were starving, Coyote went to the mountains to steal fire from the Fire Beings. As he was returning with it, the easily annoyed Fire Beings ran after him. One of the Fire Beings reached out to grab her, but the rodent was too fast, and she got away. However, the clawed white burn marks can be seen on Chipmunk's fur to this day. Read more about this story at http://www.ece.ucdavis.edu/~darsie/hcst.html

See what's shakin' in
**EARTH SCIENCE—
GEOLOGY-EARTHQUAKES.**

A
B
C
D
E
F
G
H
I
J
K
L
M
N
O
P
Q
R
S
T
U
V
W
X
Y
Z

A
B
C
D
E
F
G
H
I
J
K
L
M
N
O
P
Q
R
S
T
U
V
W
X
Y
Z

NBA.com: The Official Site of the National Basketball Association

The official NBA Web site really lets you interact with the players and teams. You can't go one-on-one (yet), but they do have live chat sessions with all your favorite players, which are saved, so if you miss one you can go back and read the transcript! This site also gives you the latest news, schedules, results, and links to the home pages of your favorite NBA teams. You can also read reports in Spanish and French, as well as follow international hoop tournaments.

http://www.nba.com/

The Unofficial Australian National Basketball League Page

It's not enough just to follow the NBA and the NCAA if you're a real basketball nut. You have to follow the sport wherever it's played! Head for this site and get the latest information on all the Australian teams, including schedules, standings, statistics, rumors, results, and box scores from the most recent NBL playoff series.

http://www.ozsports.com.au/basketball/nbl.html

The Unofficial Michael Jordan Picture Gallery

Normally we wouldn't concentrate on just one sports figure. But for Michael Jordan...well, we just had to make an exception. See Michael dunking the ball. See Michael shooting a free throw. See Michael soaring through the air. See Michael driving around an opponent. See Michael smiling. You've got to love this guy!

http://rossby.metr.uoknor.edu/~jbasara/mike/
jordan.html

**It's not a fable
that kids love
the stories in FOLKLORE
AND MYTHOLOGY.**

BICYCLES AND BICYCLING
Mountain Biking

Let's say you live in Kansas but go on family vacations to California, and you love to go mountain biking there. Then you see on the news that there are wildfires in Point Reyes, and you wonder what might have happened to your favorite seaside trails. Your local newspapers and bike shops don't have any info on trails that far away, so what do you do? You connect to this Web site and read updates about the trail damage, of course! Here you'll find news, race information, and advice on riding and taking care of your mountain bike. You can also get information about cool mountain bike trails in the United States, Canada, Europe, Latin America, Asia, and Africa.

http://xenon.stanford.edu/~rsf/mtn-bike.html

The Stolen Bike Registry

It's too bad, but plenty of bikes are stolen every year. You can preregister your bike's description here, before it gets stolen. Or look for your bike in the database—maybe it's been found in the next city. You should know your bike's serial number, colors, decorations, and any other identifying equipment, dents, or markings. It is even interesting to browse the directory and read how peoples' bikes were stolen, how much they miss their bikes, and more.

http://www.nashville.net/cycling/stolen.html

BOWLING
The Bowler's Web!

At this site, you can get bowling news from around the world, tournament dates and results, plus links to other bowling sites. But there's so much more: consider the moan and groan archives of bowling horror stories, the lists of bowling organizations (including those for the disabled), and the history of bowling. You'll also find a link to information about the National Bowling Hall of Fame and Museum in St. Louis, Missouri. What is the probability of bowling a perfect game? Find out here!

http://members.gnn.com/bigbull300/index.htm

Bowling has been popular longer than you'd think. Artifacts from a game similar to bowling have been found in the tomb of an ancient Egyptian teen who died in approximately 5200 B.C. Find more interesting bowling facts and milestones at The Bowlers Web!

Professional Bowler Association

You're going to love this Web site. Are you having a hard time finding the latest news stories and results from the PBA tour? At this site, you can get the latest results, tour schedules, and the history of the PBA. The PBA is popular all over the world: tournaments have been held in Canada, Puerto Rico, Japan, South America, France, and England. Chat with other bowling enthusiasts in the real-time chat emporium. Maybe you'll even get to talk to a pro!

http://www.pba.org/

**Origami:
the fold to behold!
Check out CRAFTS AND
HOBBIES.**

BOXING
EPPN SportsZone: Boxing

If you want up-to-the-minute information on boxing, try this page full of boxing news. You can see how your favorite boxer did in a recent fight and see the schedules for future fights. You'll find information on fights and about boxing, including items like a list of the top ten heavyweight boxers.

http://web1.starwave.com/box/

CANOEING AND KAYAKING
See also BOATING AND SAILING

Bruce's Paddling Page

Paddling is a fun and exciting adventure for the "real outdoors type." This site is from Delaware, and there's some information of local interest, including some neat information on Chesapeake Bay; you can even get the local sea buoy meteorological readings. However, this site also has extensive material for paddlers everywhere. Answers to frequently asked questions, a list of resources, and a checklist of gear you really ought to have are all included. There's even a recipe page full of good "outdoor" eating. Paddle on over!

http://ssnet.com/~bef/BrucesPaddlingPage.html

CHEERLEADING
WorldWide Cheerleading Homepage

"Hold that line, push 'em back, waaay back!" Sometimes it really helps to have someone cheering a team on. Family and friends are always good at that, but it's also great to have a whole cheerleading squad yelling and screaming for the team. If you are a cheerleader, you'll find some great cheerleading tips here.

http://www.telepath.com/gdj1146/jenn/

COACHING
Coaching Tips

You ask your mother to coach your basketball team this year. She says yes. As the season gets closer, she starts wondering about what she should do. How can you help? Check out this site, which offers some basic tips about coaching kids in sports.

http://www.reebok.com/spfit/coachingtip.html

A B C D E F G H I J K L M N O P Q R S T U V W X Y Z

A
B
C
D
E
F
G
H
I
J
K
L
M
N
O
P
Q
R
S
T
U
V
W
X
Y
Z

CRICKET

CricInfo - The Home of Cricket on the Internet

This site is a gold mine of all things related to the sport of cricket, which has thousands of players and fans around the world. Here you'll find statistics, player profiles, news, match results, and even humor and history!

http://www.cricket.org:8003/

An Explanation of Cricket

What do rabbits, golden ducks, ferrets, and night watchmen have in common? No, we're not talking about Grimm's fairy tales or the night shift at the local zoo. They are all terms used in the sport of cricket. This site provides a good starting point for learning about cricket, the distant cousin of baseball.

http://www.ozsports.com.au/cricket/cricket_exp.html

Rick Eyre's Cricket Page

If you're curious about what happened in the history of cricket on your birthday, you'll want to check this site. There are also lots of interesting links to other cricket info, including one to *The Hindu*, India's national newspaper, where you can check up on Indian cricket news!

http://www.ozemail.com.au/~reyre/cricket.html

CURLING

Curling at Brown University

What sport uses a 42-pound granite rock and a broom? No, it's not a Flintstones version of stickball—it's curling. How is it played? You bowl a highly polished stone down an ice runway, you see, and try to knock your opponent's stone out of the house, and your teammates run in front of the hurtling stone and sweep ice crystals out of its way, and…well, maybe you'd be better off going to this site for an explanation. You'll find a history of curling stones and info about the sport, including video clips of curling technique. It also gives links to other curling sites around the Net.

http://www.brown.edu/Students/Brown_Curling_Club/

International Curling Information Network Group (ICING)

Curling is a game played on ice only in northern countries, right? Wrong! Curling is also played in the Southern Hemisphere. In fact, Australia participates in the World Curling Championships! This site offers information about curling history, rules, and equipment, as well as links to organizations and clubs around the world. This is the best site yet for information on the sport of curling.

http://www.netaccess.on.ca/~psmith/icing/
icehome.htm

EXTREME SPORTS

Eco-Challenge

It's a 24-hour-a-day, 300-mile race for teams over extremely demanding territory. It may involve running, hiking, scaling cliffs, canoeing, swimming, bicycling, or riding horseback. One of the unusual parts of this competition is that the entire team must finish together. If one team member can't go on because of injury or fatigue, the entire team is disqualified. This grueling race attracts worldwide media attention for environmental concerns, which are highlighted for each region where the race is held. In August 1997, Australia hosts the Eco-Challenge. Be there, or be here to find out more.

http://www.ecochallenge.com/

Ultramarathon World

What is an ultramarathon? Imagine people running races of 50 miles, 100 miles, even more! Consider the Sri Chimnoy ultramarathon: 1,300 laps around a one-mile loop. Or how about the Trans America Footrace, from Los Angeles to New York? Find out all this and more at this site.

http://fox.nstn.ca/~dblaikie/

Pony up to HORSES AND EQUESTRIAN SPORTS.

The Comrades Marathon, in South Africa, may be the greatest ultramarathon in the world. It was first run in 1921 and now more than 10,000 runners annually participate. The route varies, but the distance is 55.89 miles (90 kilometers), and there is an elevation change of 2,500 feet (762 meters) along the course. Read more about it at Ultramarathon World.

FENCING
Fencing Home

Everyone likes a great swordfight in the movies: Peter Pan, Zorro, a party of pirates, or a platoon of shiny knights, all jumping here and there, swiping at the opponent, all the while avoiding the other person's sharp sword. Sometimes it's scary, but it's always exciting. The sport of fencing is exciting, too. Fencing is an Olympic sport that is practiced almost everywhere. There may even be a fencing club near you. Find out!

http://www.architecture.ubc.ca:8080/vds96/
    gymnasium/fencing.htm

FIELD HOCKEY
United States Field Hockey Association

In 1997, the United States Field Hockey Association (USFHA) will celebrate its 75th year of constitutional history. The USFHA has over 11,000 members nationwide and promotes programs such as junior hockey, Olympic development, festivals, and educational programs. Read about some of the key players in field hockey here, and learn about the rules of the game.

http://inovatec.com/USFHA/

FOOTBALL
NFL.COM: Front Page

The official NFL site provides the latest headlines and league statistics and even offers an opportunity to chat with the players. In the Fan area, you'll also find a complete digest of NFL rules (in English, Thai, Chinese, and Malay), the Pro Football Hall of Fame, and a library of historical facts and timelines.

http://www.nfl.com/

FOOTBALL—AUSTRALIAN RULES
Frequently Asked Questions (FAQ) for rec.sport.football.australian

What is the oldest form of "football"? Australian rules football dates back to the 1850s and predates American football, rugby, soccer, and Gaelic football. This site provides an overview of Australian rules football and lets you take a look at Australian football trading cards. It also answers a burning question: what is the Australian equivalent of the hot dogs that are eaten at American football games? The answer is Aussie meat pies!

http://www.footy.com.au/dags/FAQ1v1-4.html

Ultimate AFL

This game resembles rugby. There are 18 people on a side, they use an oval ball, and they score by kicking the ball. This site is a virtual photo scrapbook of your favorite Australian rules football players in action! You can get dozens and dozens of pictures and links to other Aussie rules sites.

http://www.odyssey.com.au/sports/afl.html

FOOTBALL—CANADIAN RULES
OFFICIAL CFL WEB SITE HOME PAGE

Visit the official Web site for the Canadian Football League! Read the rules, the latest CFL news, and a history of the CFL. You can also look at a list of CFL records and awards and see the CFL Hall of Fame. There are also links to other sites about the CFL.

http://www.cfl.ca/

A
B
C
D
E
F
G
H
I
J
K
L
M
N
O
P
Q
R
S
T
U
V
W
X
Y
Z

A
B
C
D
E
F
G
H
I
J
K
L
M
N
O
P
Q
R
S
T
U
V
W
X
Y
Z

GYMNASTICS

Gymn Forum: The Gymn Forum!

Know the results of the gymnastics world championships and other current events by tumbling over to this site! Do you like to read articles about gymnasts? Would you like a list of gymnastics magazines with order forms? Find them here. You can take gymnastics trivia tests, too. Did you ever wonder about the "chalk" you see gymnasts rub on their hands? It's magnesium carbonate, and they use it to absorb sweat so that they won't lose their grips on the equipment.

http://gymn.digiweb.com/gymn/

Welcome to USA Gymnastics Online!

When the U.S. women's gymnastics team appeared at the 1996 Summer Olympics, it was truly a magical event! Their skill and courage inspired many kids. Where are they now? Keep up with the U.S. teams and other events in gymnastics at this site. Fan mail addresses for the team are at <http://www.usa-gymnastics.org/events/1996/olympics/fan-mail.html> and individual fan home pages for many of the members of the women's team are at <http://152.157.16.3/WWWSchools/MidSchools/MGM/Sports/Gym/gym.html>.

http://www.usa-gymnastics.org/

GYMNASTICS—RHYTHMIC GYMNASTICS

Rhythmic Sportive Gymnastics

Do you have trouble spelling "rhythmic gymnastics," but you love the sport anyway? Would you like to get pictures of your favorites in action? For current results from World Cup and European Cup competition, start here. All the pages here are packed with pictures and information and links to other interesting sites. This site is in English and German.

http://www.uni-karlsruhe.de/~uk4w/rsg/

ICE AND SPEED SKATING

Amateur Speedskating Union of the United States - ASU Page

When you take up the sport of speed skating, you are guaranteed to be hanging out with some "cool" people! Is it fast? You'd have to be crazy to go this fast. How crazy? Well, let's see—ice, blades, power, speed—sounds just crazy enough to be fun. And it is fun, for everyone from kids to seniors. If you're just thinking about starting, this page fills you in; if you're already a die-hard skater, you'll get advanced details on clubs and special events. It's great exercise, and it makes those long winters (and you) go really fast!

http://web.mit.edu/jeffrey/speedskating/asu.html

NET FILES

True or false: Most cartoons we see on TV these days are created completely on computers.

Answer: False. Computer animation is still rare in the world of television cartoons. In fact, while you might assume that the pictures are the first things to "go digital," it's sound that is usually stored and played back on computers and special keyboards. Cool, huh? There's lots of info on how cartoons are made at http://www.wbanimation.com/cmp/ani_04if.htm

Figure Skating: The Insider's Guide with Debbi Wilkes

Join Olympic silver medalist Debbi Wilkes for an insider's guide to figure skating news. Whether you're looking for info on commercial ice shows or biographical skater profiles or you want to find a good skating school, this is a good place to start. We keep looking for info on driving the Zamboni ice-making machine, but, alas, we found nothing here (yet)!

http://www.debbiwilkes.com/

Hockey Skating Tips

This site provides tips for ice skaters, rollerbladers, hockey players, roller hockey players, and others who strap blades or rollers on their feet. Try some of the speed and scoring drills described here, and explore the links off-site. Use your inside edge on your outside skate and shoot in here!

http://relay.cs.toronto.edu/~andria/skating_tips.html

NET FILES

Why are rainbows so frequently seen during summer and not so frequently during winter?

Answer: *To see a rainbow, you've got to have both rain and sunshine. In the winter, water droplets freeze into ice particles that do not produce a rainbow but scatter light in other very interesting patterns. Learn more at* http://www.unidata.ucar.edu/staff/blynds/rnbw.html

Recreational Figure Skating FAQ

What's the difference between a crossover and a progressive? Do you need to know how to execute a closed mohawk? How do you know when your skates need sharpening? At this site, you'll find the answers to these questions. In fact, chances are you'll find answers to most of your skating questions here.

http://www.cyberus.ca/~karen/recskate/

ICE HOCKEY

See entry Hockey Skating Tips *under* SPORTS—ICE AND SPEED SKATING

NHLPA

You and a friend are talking hockey, but you disagree on the number of goals your favorite player has scored this season. Where do you go for the answer? The NHLPA site provides player stats for each NHL player, and these stats are updated each day! You can find pictures, personal information, stats for this season, and stats from past seasons—just like online hockey trading cards. And there's more. Check this site for the weekly hockey trivia challenge. Answer the questions correctly, and you may win an autographed NHLPA replica jersey.

http://www.nhlpa.com/

WWW Hockey Guide

This site pulls together information about hockey from all over the Web, linking to over 1,100 other hockey sites. Would you like a list of all Stanley Cup finalists since the Stanley Cup started in 1893? How about a visit to the Hockey Hall of Fame? You'll find that here, as well as all official and unofficial home pages for your favorite National Hockey League teams. You can see the latest hockey news from ESPN or *USA Today,* too. If you can't get enough information about hockey, start with this site!

http://www.hockeyguide.com/

A B C D E F G H I J K L M N O P Q R **S** T U V W X Y Z

A
B
C
D
E
F
G
H
I
J
K
L
M
N
O
P
Q
R
S
T
U
V
W
X
Y
Z

MARTIAL ARTS

Black Belt Magazine Home Page

Brought to you by the publishers of *Black Belt* magazine, *Karate Kung-fu Illustrated* magazine, and *Martial Arts Training* magazine, this site has interesting articles, schedules of events, lists of martial arts schools, and links to other sites. They even have a Black Belt for Kids page. Remember, though, that the empty-handed master defeats another warrior with the most powerful weapon: the mind. Warning: This page is very graphics-heavy, so you may want to turn off automatic image loading.

http://www.blackbeltmag.com/

Judo—Judo Information Site

Are you interested in judo? If you'd like to learn more about its history or see the results of tournaments like the World Judo Championships, then this site is for you! You'll find links to dojos and judo schools and e-mail addresses of other people who are interested in judo. There are also interesting links to Zen koans and other sources of martial arts inspiration.

http://www.rain.org/~ssa/judo.htm

MARS - Martial Arts Resource Site

Are you interested in martial arts, but you don't know where to start? Then head for this site. They may not have everything, but they come close! You'll find links to martial arts books and articles, online magazines like *Black Belt* Magazine Online, information on how to choose a martial art, and links to many other good martial arts sites.

http://www.floor6.com/MARS/MARS.html

THE MARTIAL ARTS MENU PAGE

Parental advisory: this site has hundreds of links to other martial arts sites on the Web, and you should explore this with your child. This is a very comprehensive starting point to information about martial arts around the world. You'll find sites for judo, karate, aikido, jujutsu, ninpo, wing chun, tai chi, and much more!

http://www.mindspring.com/~mamcgee/
   martial.arts.html

TKD Reporter Home Page

Would you like to read articles about tae kwon do, karate, hapkido, and other martial arts? The Tae Kwon Do Reporter is an online magazine that has martial arts news from around the world, a list of martial arts schools, and articles on training and techniques.

http://www.taekwondoreporter.com/

NETBALL

NETBALL AT THE AUSTRALIAN INSTITUTE OF SPORT

The most popular women's sport in Australia is netball. The sport started in England way back in 1898. It's like basketball, except it's played with something more like a soccer ball. It can be played on wood floors, grass, cement, or artificial surfaces, which may be either indoors or outdoors. Today there are more than two million netball players in the world. Australia has won six world championships, more than any other country. Find out the history and rules of netball here!

http://www.ausport.gov.au/aisnet.html

OLYMPICS

2002 Winter Olympics

Did you go to the 1996 Olympics in Atlanta? Did you enjoy the experience? Are you wondering when the Olympics will come again to North America? The XIX Olympic Winter Games will be held in Salt Lake City, Utah, February 8–22, 2002! This site gives information on where the events will be held and where the Olympic Village will be located. If you live in the Salt Lake City area, there is information on how to join the volunteer program for the 2002 Olympics.

http://www.slc2002.org/

Britannica Sporting Record: The Olympic Games

"Faster! Stronger! Higher!" The Olympic Games motto says it all. Athletes from all corners of the world gather to test their skills and courage against those of others. Read all about the history of the ancient and modern Olympics, the events, the athletes, and more at this outstanding Web resource.

http://sports.eb.com/

Official 1998 Olympic Web Site - 1998 Olympic games Home Page

Seems like a long wait for the next Winter Olympics, doesn't it? It will be in Nagano, Japan. They have already picked the official mascots for the games—Snowlets! These four birds represent the owls found in the forests of Nagano. Owls are found throughout much of the world, and they are a Greek symbol of wisdom. There is a new special area just for kids, where you can play online games and send in stories about—what else?—snow, so look for it! Read more plans and ideas about the 1998 Winter Games here, and keep watching this site, which is available in English and Japanese.

http://www.nagano.olympic.org/

OLYMPICS Home Page

The Olympics roll around every few years, so there's always something to look forward to or highlights from the past to look back on. NBC's official site has special moments, results, athlete profiles, and fun facts.

http://www.olympic.nbc.com/

NET FILES

In Morocco, should you eat, drink, or wear the *meshwee, tagines, and couscous?*

Answer: You should eat them, but be careful so you won't wear them, too! Not only are they all delicious foods, but in Morocco, one is expected to eat some from each dish served. About silverware: leave it home. In Morocco, the thumb and first three fingers are used when eating. Find out other interesting facts about this north African country when you take the guided tour at http://www.dsg.ki.se/morocco/cuisine/about/

Sydney 2000 Olympic Games

Well, the 1996 Summer Olympic Games in Atlanta are over, so what's next? In the year 2000, athletes will gather in Sydney, Australia! The official Sydney Olympics 2000 site is the place to go for early information. Approximately 5.5 million tickets will go on sale in 1999, and this site will be the first to provide information about ordering tickets. You'll find a lot of info here now, including an explanation of what the logo means.

http://www.sydney.olympic.org/

RACQUETBALL

United States Professional Racquetball Association

You've wanted a racquetball racquet for a long time, and finally you spot one at a garage sale. It needs new strings, but you're not sure if it can be restrung or if it's junk. What do you do? The USPRA Web site provides handy tips on restringing racquets and offers links to information about Olympic racquetball, official rules, and the schedules for televised racquetball on ESPN. You'll also find tips on improving your backhand stroke, and you can ask a certified referee all your tricky rule questions.

http://www.uspra.com/

ROWING AND SCULLING

See also BOATING AND SAILING

Rowing Frequently Asked Questions

"Stroke! Stroke! Stroke!" That's the call of the coxswain as the rowers propel the *shell* (that's what those sleek racing vessels are called) ahead in a race for the finish line. Rowing is a sport particularly enjoyed by colleges and university teams around the world, with many amateur clubs as well. There are several variations on the sport, and the boats, equipment, and rowers are different in many cases. Did you know that rowers are grouped in heavyweight and lightweight classes? Learn all about the sport of rowing here.

http://riceinfo.rice.edu/~hofer/Rowingfaq.html

A
B
C
D
E
F
G
H
I
J
K
L
M
N
O
P
Q
R
S
T
U
V
W
X
Y
Z

A
B
C
D
E
F
G
H
I
J
K
L
M
N
O
P
Q
R
S
T
U
V
W
X
Y
Z

RUGBY

The Unofficial Official Rugby Webpage

If you don't know anything about rugby, then this site is a good place to start. It gives you basic information about rugby, a short history of the sport, and a little bit about rugby in the U.S., as well as a link to the official World Cup site. Rugby is a fast-moving team sport played with a ball that looks like a football, only slightly larger. You also can't pass forward. And don't forget, it's not a scrimmage, it's a scrummage!

http://icarus.uic.edu/~jgrzes1/rugby/rugby.html

Women's Rugby

Learn all about international women's rugby at this site. All the rules of rugby are here in an easy-to-use format, as well as links to other sites on the Web that have information about rugby. There's a great GIF of the dimensions of a rugby playing field, too. You'll find some off-site links that address other women's issues.

http://vail.al.arizona.edu/rugby/

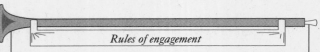

Rules of engagement

Get in position for your next scrummage! Everyone should read the rules of engagement at the Women's Rugby home page.

SKIING

A Resort Sports Network Home Page

You want to hit the slopes—but there's no snow. You can at least dream about it and see how much snow is on the ground at ski resorts across the U.S. and Europe. This site offers pictures taken daily at ski resorts, as well as weather forecasts. Come in out of the cold and ski the Net!

http://www.rsn.com/

The SkiCentral - Skiing and Snowboarding Index

They stay up all night, working in the freezing cold. They mix proteins into water and make "whales." Nothing pleases them more than the sight of fresh powder. Who are they? They are the folks who run the snow-making equipment at ski resorts! Did you know that dirty water makes better snow than clean water? Check <http://www.cyberski.com.au/features/snowmaking.html> to find out about the snow-making process. When you've satisfied your curiosity about that, look around at SkiCentral. This site is packed with information and articles about skiing, snowboarding, racing, clothing, and equipment, plus links to hundreds of other skiing and snowboarding sites.

http://skicentral.com/

SkiNet

Get the latest in skiing techniques, reports on snow conditions, and skiing news from the editors of *Ski* magazine and *Skiing* magazine. You can even read articles from the pages of these magazines and join the SkiNet mailing list. In the Technique area at <http://www.skinet.com/technique/index.html> is a list of the top 100 ski instructors in the U.S. There are also online beginner tutorials for kids, teens, and tots.

http://www.skinet.com/

Surface Conditions

You're reading the ski reports for your favorite slopes, and the descriptions just don't make any sense! What is frozen granular? What is corn snow? Is it even worth getting out your equipment? If you check that report against the definitions provided at this site, you'll learn that *corn snow,* typical in spring conditions, is made up of large ice granules, which are loose when the temperature is above freezing but freeze together if the temperature gets any colder.

http://www.travelbase.com/skiing/peek-n-peak/
    surface-term.html

**Space Exploration is a blast.
Check out ASTRONOMY.**

SKIING—ALPINE SKIING AND SKI JUMPING

Jump

Welcome to this site, created by a ski jumper. Get up-to-date information on the World Cup and other ski jumping competitions, and check out the links to other ski jumping sites. There are four phases to the ski jump (no, they are not approaching the jump, looking at the jump, screaming, and running away): you have the inrun, the takeoff, the flight, and the telemark landing (one foot in front of the other). If you doubt that humans can fly, look at the photos at this site!

http://www.cdnsport.ca/jump/

SKIING—FREESTYLE

Owens Corning World Cup Freestyle

Imagine ballet on a tilted stage that's almost three football fields long, where the dancers turn cartwheels and do handsprings wearing skis and ski poles! Welcome to the strange world of freestyle, or acro/ballet, skiing. This site gives a good description of this winter sport, which now includes water pools at the bottom of the run—hard to believe, but true.

http://www.freestyleski.com/

U.S. Ski Team Online - Freestyle Home Page

Which sport has back scratchers, double uprights, helicopters, mule kicks, twisters, and zudniks? Mogul skiing! That's when the only thing between you and the bottom of the hill is a steep, frozen landscape of bumps, jumps, and tricky twists. But these days, freestyle skiing also includes aerials and acro (formerly called ballet) competition. Learn from the pros here. Do you want to approach your first mogul and not fall down? You'll find a great tutorial called Fall-line Mogul Skiing at <http://easyweb.easynet.co.uk/~michaell/skier/ch15/index.htm> (especially the How to Cope with Moguls section).

http://www.sportsline.com/u/usskiteam/skisport/freestyle/

SKIING—NORDIC SKIING

Cross Country Ski World

Are you interested in cross-country skiing but don't know how to start? This site is packed with information on the world's oldest skiing sport, including a special section just for junior skiers. You'll find out how to choose equipment, how to wax for various conditions, and how to handle "botanical brakes," also known as trees!

http://www.weblab.com/xcski/

If you don't know your klister from your kick wax, better glide on over to Cross Country Ski World! There are lots of tips for skiing families about waxing and ski technique.

SNOWBOARDING

Snwbrdr's Snowboarding Page

Snowboarding just keeps getting more popular and more respected by athletes. It's fun but not easy, and advanced boarders can do some amazing tricks. Find out who's ruling, where, and how, at this great site in Finland. And check out these sweet action photos!

http://www.snwbrdr.com/

SOCCER

INTERNATIONAL SOCCER NET

Stay fit with stretching and conditioning tips. Read interviews with soccer greats. Get news about the World Cup. Link to college, pro, and international teams. What a kick!

http://207.67.226.117/soccernet/

A B C D E F G H I J K L M N O P Q R S T U V W X Y Z

A B C D E F G H I J K L M N O P Q R S T U V W X Y Z

The Soccer Home Page *

Why is the sport called "soccer" in some countries and "football" in others? The sport started as football in England. By the time it became popular in other parts of the world, some countries already had sports known as football: the U.S. had American football, and Australia had Australian rules football. In countries where football was already played, the sport became known as soccer, short for "association football," the original name for the sport in England. This site also has links to the Olympics soccer page, World Cup soccer facts and records, soccer camps, and soccer rules.

http://www.distrib.com/soccer/

Soccer— The International Soccer Cybertour

This soccer cybertour was created for kids, by a kid! Use the Soccer Worldwide Penpal Connection and read soccer tips and ideas from kids in other countries. Send in your own soccer photos and illustrations, and find a pen pal of your own. See what interests kids when it comes to soccer, and link to news of lots of international soccer teams.

http://www.cybergoal.com/soccer/

SPECIAL OLYMPICS
Massachusetts Special Olympics

"Let me win, but if I cannot win, let me be brave in the attempt." This is the oath of the Special Olympics. What great inspiration this is for all athletes, not just "special" kids with physical, mental, or other challenges! The first International Special Olympic Games was held in 1968, at Soldier Field in Chicago, Illinois. It was organized by Eunice Kennedy Shriver. Since then, the Special Olympics have become the world's largest year-round program of physical fitness, sports training, and athletic competition. In the U.S., games at the local and chapter levels are held every year, with special summer and winter events held every four years. Check out SPECIAL OLYMPICS INTERNATIONAL at <http://www.specialolympics.org/> and <http://meer.net/users/taylor/specolym.htm> for more information.

http://www.gran-net.com/olympics/mso_home.htm

SQUASH
THE INTERNET SQUASH FEDERATION

Do you love squash? Yum: Hubbard, summer, acorn—even zucchini! But we're not talking veggies here, we're talking about the fast-paced game of squash ball, sort of like racquetball, except the court, equipment, and rules are different. All the rules are here, including those governing clothing, equipment, and more. Player profiles, tournament schedules, even satellite broadcast schedules are here. Also, you can keep up with the latest news on the campaign to make this an Olympic sport.

http://www.squash.org/

The World Squash Federation

Squash has been played for over 130 years. You'll find a neat history of the game here, which explains that the name derives from the way the ball "squashes" against the wall as it hits! You'll also find the rules of the game as well as rankings.

http://www.squash.org/WSF/

SURFING
Global Oceanic Surf Links

This is the real thing, not this waterless digital surfing we've all gotten used to. Big surf, land surfing, swells—it's all here. See a live picture of Sunset Beach on Oahu, or check wave conditions in Australia. See some gnarly GIFs or check some equipment reviews. Keep scrolling—there are surf cams and beach reports from surfing culture all over the world! A caution to parents: Not all links have been checked.

http://magna.com.au/~prfbrown/tubelink.html

Surfrider Foundation USA

This organization is working to protect our coastlines. In addition to information on the group and its mission, you'll get numerous resources for surfers and some nice pictures and music clips. You can even take a look at today's waves on the Southern California coast. The resource list of links can send you coast to coast (USA), off to Hawaii, and all over the world. It's awesome, dude, hang ten!

http://www.surfrider.org/

SWIMMING AND DIVING
Open Water Swimming Tips

OK, you like to go swimming. The school pool is good, when that kid in the other class isn't there to do cannonball dives on your head. The backyard pool is nice, when the filter works. And you love the open water at the lake. But better yet, there's the ocean: the sand, the sun, and the surf. All of these are great, but open water swimming is not the same as swimming in a pool. For one thing, sometimes you can't even see the bottom under you! And there are other things to deal with, like the choppy water, the current, and those green, slimy things floating by. Here's the page that tells you all about swimming in the open sea. You'll find tips on everything from getting ready to swim to racing, plus good commonsense information on how to deal with hazards. The number one rule is never swim alone (but you can visit this site alone).

http://rs733.gsfc.nasa.gov/~jntjw/swim/openwater.html

SWIMNEWS ONLINE

Do you swim? We're not talking about an occasional wade through the baby pool. We're talking about competitive swimming. You know: pruny looking fingers, webbed toes, red eyes, and gills. If that's you, then you need to see this online magazine! Virtually every major swim meet in the world is here, and the results are updated regularly. You'll find features on the world's best swimmers, and all the world records are here, too. Links? You bet. This is the diving platform for your lane.

http://www.swimnews.com/

Alexander Popov, of Russia, swam the 100-meter freestyle in 46.74 seconds, on March 19, 1994. Will the record be broken soon? Who's favored in the next world championships? The only real news is up-to-date information. Get the latest at SWIMNEWS ONLINE.

The Yellow Pages of Swimming

Are you a swimmer? Would you like to go to other swimmers' sites? Then this is the place for you: over 220 links to Web sites related to swimming and diving! You'll find governing bodies for swim competitions, college and high school swim team pages, swim club news, and more. Look for water polo, coaching, rankings, and triathlete links here, too.

http://www.tcd.net/~jj/swimlinx.html

TABLE TENNIS
INTERNATIONAL TABLE TENNIS FEDERATION

At this official site, you will find official rules, championship and rankings information, and lots of table tennis links. This game has been around a long time. Around 1900, it was also called gossimar and whiff-whaff. By the way—did you know there's a way to fix dented ping pong balls? Put the balls in a pan, cover with a towel, pour hot water over them, and let them sit for about an hour. There, good as new!

http://www.ittf.com/

TENNIS
The Tennis Server Home Page

Would you like free tips from a tennis pro? Would you like to know how to avoid tennis elbow? Would you like information on tournaments, players, rankings, and equipment? How about links to other tennis sites? You get all this and more when you go to the Net for the WWW Tennis Server.

http://www.tennisserver.com/

See the light in ARCHITECTURE, look for LIGHTHOUSES.

A B C D E F G H I J K L M N O P Q R S T U V W X Y Z

A
B
C
D
E
F
G
H
I
J
K
L
M
N
O
P
Q
R
S
T
U
V
W
X
Y
Z

How did a spaceborne spider's web influence the design of earthly tennis racquets? Find out at The Tennis Server Home Page, under Equipment Tips.

TENNIS WORLDWIDE

This Net magazine offers a world of information on tennis. Television schedules for tournaments, sources of supplies, and rankings are all here, plus feature articles, like how hard a junior player should practice! You'll also find info on wheelchair tennis, tennis camps, racquet repair, jokes about tennis, and more.

http://www.tennisw.com/

TRACK AND FIELD
Athletics Home Page

Who is the world's fastest Norwegian? Who is the best overall Italian athlete? What's the Moroccan record in the high jump? If you are a track and field statistics nut, then this is the site for you. It lists world's records, indoor and outdoor, for men and for women, as well as track and field records for many nations.

http://www.hkkk.fi/~niininen/athl.html

The Official Boston Marathon Web Site

What is the world's most well-known race? A lot of folks would argue it's the Boston Marathon. Learn its history and facts about the next race at this official site. You'll view video clips, see a map of the 26.2 mile course, and more! The first race was in 1897, and since then runners have only been able to improve on the winning time by 48 minutes, despite all the high-tech shoes and training methods they have now.

http://www.bostonmarathon.org/

Road Runners Club of America

Runners can find a mile and a half of track at this site! Online articles and magazines about running are appearing all over the Internet. This site links you to them and also gives you a list of other resources, too, including their own publications at <http://www.rrca.org/~rrca/publicat/publicat.html>. The club is involved in a wide range of activities. There is general information on the club, their services, and an interactive map to let you find the local clubs and events in your own area. If you enjoy running and you want to stay current on running and amateur sports news, then jog on over!

http://www.rrca.org/~rrca/

How about a fun run? Sounds great, but leave the tunes at home. Don't wear headphones when you run—you need to rely on all your senses to be safe. Another rule is to tell someone where you'll be running and when you'll be back. Sprint over to the **Road Runners Club of America** for more tips about running, including how to run safely in hot or cold weather.

The Running Page

Running can be a sport, a hobby, or an exercise. This is a nicely organized page for all kinds of runners, from casual to serious. There are many links to a wide variety of running sources, and even one to a chat site for runners. Serious runners can find race results, columns geared toward their level of interest, and lists of publications, frequently asked questions, and clubs. You'll also find articles and links on ultramarathons as well as running injuries. Basically, you can run in here to see what's new "out there." It's another way of getting from where you are to where you want to be!

http://sunsite.unc.edu/drears/running/running.html

USA Track & Field

USA Track and Field is the governing body for track and field in the United States. This site gives you news on the latest happenings in track and field, with links to other track and field sites. You'll really enjoy seeing the U.S. Track and Field Hall of Fame and reading about record performances and the athletes who made them! This is a great source for short sports biographies, too.

http://www.usatf.org/index.shtml

NET FILES

Who (or **what**) is a **"haw-eater"**?

Answer: *Haw-eaters* are what Canadians born and raised on Manitoulin Island, in Lake Huron, call themselves. They like hawberries, the dark-red fruits of hawthorn species common in northern Ontario. Haws make delicious pies, tarts, and strudels. Find colorful tidbits of Canadian language trivia at
http://www.cangeo.ca/ND96Tongue.htm

TRACK AND FIELD—POLE VAULT

VaultWorld USA Track and Field Pole Vault Page

What is the single most important thing in pole vaulting, besides getting over the top of the bar? Pole vaulters and coaches answer this and other questions at this site. You can even give your own answers to these questions. By the way, not all vaulters agree on the most important thing, but most of them agree that it is speed. You'll also find the top 100 vaulters, some great animations, and a place to trade used poles!

http://www.vaultworld.com/

VOLLEYBALL

NCAA women's volleyball

The *USA Today* women's volleyball page provides the latest information on the sport. Want to know the latest National Collegiate Athletic Association (NCAA) volleyball rankings? How about information on volleyball win streaks? Check the sports stats and tournament schedules—it's all here!

http://www.usatoday.com/sports/volleyba/svcw/ svcwd1.htm

Volleyball Worldwide

Is beach volleyball an Olympic sport? Yes, it was, for the first time, in the 1996 Atlanta Olympics. What is wallyball? Where can you find information on international volleyball? What teams will play in the volleyball World Cup? If you love volleyball, start with this site, which has general volleyball info, including TV schedules, and links to organizations like USA Volleyball, Federation Internationale de Volleyball, and professional and college volleyball.

http://www.volleyball.org/

BOOKS AND LITERATURE give us Goosebumps!

A B C D E F G H I J K L M N O P Q R **S** T U V W X Y Z

A B C D E F G H I J K L M N O P Q R S T U V W X Y Z

WATER POLO

United States Water Polo

Water polo is your favorite game and you love to watch a local college game every week. But mom says you're moving, and you're worried there won't be a water polo club where you're going. What do you do? Check this site, and find one. This official page offers rules and regulations, links to college and club teams, and other resources. Don't get in over your head with all the water polo info here!

http://WWW.EWPRA.Org/uswp/

WATER SKIING

Canadian Water Ski WWW Page

Remember when water skiing was just a boat, two skis, and a lake? Oh yeah, and a skier, too. You might be surprised to see all there is to water skiing these days. Luckily, this page covers many different aspects of water skiing and answers many questions. Sure, you'll find plenty of material on traditional skiing, including slalom and jumping, and also links to barefoot and kneeboard sites. Did you think they would forget wakeboarding? It's here, too. You'll also find pictures here, and they are pretty exciting. You can even submit your own picture. (Hint: Don't take a picture of yourself while you're holding that tow rope. Get someone else to do it!)

http://www.utoronto.ca:80/ski/water/

WIND SURFING

windsurfer.com

If you're interested in boardsailing, you need to see this site, which has the expected tips on sailing, race schedules, world rankings, and links to other Web pages on this topic. But you'll also find a list of user reviews of various boards and user recommendations on the hottest travel destinations. Maps and other regional information will help you decide on where to beg your parents to take the next family vacation. You'll also find a handy calculator, which will convert knots to miles per hour, pounds to kilograms, feet to meters, and several other measurements. And if you're new to this sport, check the Beginner's Guide at <http://www.windsurfer.com/Beginners/index.html>.

http://www.windsurfer.com/

WRESTLING

InterMat: The Ultimate Amateur Wrestling Resource

You know, you don't have to look like Hulk Hogan to wrestle. Lots of people participate in this sport, in all different weight classes. For the latest in international, collegiate, and high school wrestling, including rankings, try this site!

http://www.intermatwrestle.com/

The Mat, the home page of Amateur Wrestling!

This site will get a *hold* on you, if you're into wrestling. Find info on the international, collegiate, high school, and youth wrestling scenes, including current results and news. Check the Wrestling Mall for info on books, equipment, videos, and links to photo archives.

http://wrestling.xnn.com/

STAR TREK, STAR WARS, AND SPACE EPICS

The 2001 Internet Resource Archive

"Good afternoon, gentlemen. I am a HAL 9000 computer. I became operational at the H.A.L. lab in Urbana, Illinois, on the 12th of January, 1992." Long before we had Picard and Kirk and before we had Luke Skywalker and Princess Leia, we had HAL, the killer computer on the spaceship in *2001: A Space Odyssey*. This movie was released in 1968, and it explored the differences between humanity and technology. The story is told in a free-form kaleidoscope of images and sounds, and years later, people are still arguing about what it all means. This site gives you a lot of famous audio clips from the movie, as well as pictures and links to other resources about the film, including a HAL birthday Web site at <http://www.HALbday.com> featuring the book's author, Arthur C. Clarke.

http://www.design.no/2001/

The Klingon Language Institute

How many languages do you speak? Have you checked the batteries in your universal translator? If you saw a snarling Klingon warrior, what would you say? Are you worried that your opportunities on the Klingon homeworld are limited because of the language barrier? If so, then this site is the place for you!

http://www.kli.org/KLIhome.html

PEOPLE Online - 30 Years of Star Trek

In September 1996, the original *Star Trek* crew got back together for a 30th year anniversary party. *People* magazine was there to cover the event, and you can read some of the interviews and see how everyone looks now that they have retired from Starfleet service. Try the trivia quiz to see how good you are, and remember, Vulcans have green blood!

http://pathfinder.com/people/sp/trek/

Star Trek

Resistance is futile. The Microsoft Network has swallowed up most of the great *Star Trek* info that Paramount used to offer for free. You may still be able to get to it if you are a subscriber to the Microsoft Network and have a password there. If you do, you will be able to login to the MSN Continuum from this Web site. The rest of us can look at brief histories of all the series and look at what's coming up on future shows. This is the official site, but since it's not available to all, it's no longer the best site.

http://startrek.msn.com/

Star Trek: Deep Space Nine

Are you a *Star Trek: Deep Space Nine* fan? Who's your favorite character? Check out Paramount's official DS9 page, which has now been assimilated into the Microsoft Network's Star Trek pages. It offers a brief description of the next episode, with a cast photo and a list of actors in the episode. You can also download a QuickTime video preview of the episode to play on your computer.

http://startrek.msn.com/UpcomingDS9.asp

Star Trek Nexus: Welcome

This is the ultimate collection of *Star Trek* links on the Net—well over 1,400, the last time we checked. You can beam over to official pages and fan pages and, along the way, perhaps discover some intelligent life. Watch out—links to the Borg Continuum are here, too!

http://users.aol.com/ksc1/startrek.htm

Star Wars Trilogy: Special Edition

Who is your favorite character in the *Star Wars* saga? Is it Jedi Knight Luke Skywalker, or do you prefer that scoundrel Han Solo? Maybe you'd like to be like courageous Princess Leia and have a couple of happy-go-lucky droids like C-3P0 or R2-D2 to give you a hand. Whether you like the old or the new digital version of these sci-fi classics, you're really going to like this Web site!

http://www.starwars.com/

NET FILES

What country is considered to have the most skilled labor force in the world?

Answer: According to the Belgian Embassy, "Belgium has the most skilled labor force in the world and the most productive in Western Europe, having held this record for the last 15 years." Read much more about Belgium and its list of accomplishments at http://www.belgium-emb.org/usa/geninfos/didyknow.html#economy

Don't be a stick-in-the-INTERNET MUD!

A
B
C
D
E
F
G
H
I
J
K
L
M
N
O
P
Q
R
S
T
U
V
W
X
Y
Z

A B C D E F G H I J K L M N O P Q R S T U V W X Y Z

Starbase 907 — Starfleet Ship Registry Database

Can't tell a Galaxy-class ship from a Miranda-class ship? Have you always wondered where the USS *Bozeman* went for 80 years? This site lists over 18 classes of Starfleet ships. Within the classes, you'll find descriptions, Starfleet ship registration numbers in that class, and some ship histories. Also check out photos of the new *Enterprise-E* from the movie *Star Trek: First Contact.*

http://hpserv.utulsa.edu/sb907/ships.html

SUMMER CAMPS

National Computer Camps

Back in 1977, Dr. Michael Zabinski established the first "computer camp" in an effort to familiarize young people with the use and workings of computers. Soon after, the nation was awash with them, but as the fad wore off, Dr. Zabinski continued to develop the concept and curriculum of these summer camps to encompass all aspects of computer literacy. Today, the camps are held in California, Connecticut, Ohio, and Georgia. Students are given the option of an all-computer agenda or half computer/half sports. This page contains information on the entire program, schedules, staff, locations, and dates.

http://www.corpcenter.com/ncc/

What extremely well-known science fiction movie was partially filmed in a place where it is so hot that people live underground?

Answer: The movie was *Star Wars,* and Tunisia was the site of Luke Skywalker's uncle's moisture farm on Tatooine. Find out more at http://us.imdb.com/M/title-more?locations+Star%20Wars%20%281977%29

Peterson's Education Center: Summer Programs for Kids and Teens

Get your older brother or sister to apply for a job at camp! Peterson's (the educational directory publisher) posts lists of summer jobs here, mostly at summer camps, for both older teenagers and young adults. Phone numbers and e-mail contact addresses are included, making this a good place to look for that first-time job. Your parents may want to explore the rest of the items at this comprehensive educational directory. They will find everything from K–12 schools to colleges, from studying abroad to career information.

http://www.petersons.com/summerop/

U.S. Space Camp

It's light years away from any other camp experience! You can visit Space Camp here on the Web and see pictures of some of the things kids (and adults) get to do there. How would you like to ride a space shuttle simulator or build your own satellite? Beam yourself up to this site; you'll definitely find intelligent life here!

http://www.spacecamp.com/

United Camps, Conferences & Retreats Camp & Conference Homepage

Any search of the Web will bring up well over a thousand summer camp home pages in the U.S. and elsewhere. What's nice about this site is that they feature a highly organized listing of many top-notch camps, organized by region or type or even alphabetically. You might be looking for a performing arts camp in Northern California, a ranch camp for girls in Texas, a space camp in Florida, or a listing of dozens of Boy Scout camps in Virginia. Whatever kind of summer camp experience interests you, you'll find detailed listings for each of the camps, including phone numbers, addresses, and sometimes even photographs. A "Camp-O'-The-Week" is featured here every seven days, plus links to environmental and outdoor educational centers, retreats, associations, online magazines, and a detailed calendar.

http://www.camping.org/

Chris Rywalt, the originator of the Virtual Mr. Spud Head site, along with his wife.

"One person wanted me to make a combination Bob Dole-pineapple head in honor of the American presidential election. I settled for making a plain Bob Dole head."

GAMES AND FUN

Virtual Mr. Spud Head

Webmaster: Chris Rywalt

http://www.westnet.com/~crywalt/ pothead/pothead.html

Who came up with the idea for your page or project? Was it you? How did the idea originate?

A coworker showed me a programming library that made it possible to make graphic files from a program. He asked me if I thought I could do anything with it, and Virtual Mr. Spud Head was the first thing I thought of. Then it was just a matter of writing the program and drawing the art.

How many people work on your pages? Does it take a lot of time? How many hits do you get a day?

I work alone—everything on my pages is done entirely by me. About 600 games of Spud Head are played a day, but the number of hits is much higher than that—maybe 10,000 hits a day total.

You must hear from people all over the world! Can you think of an unusual request, question, or comment someone has sent to you?

One person wanted me to make a combination Bob Dole-pineapple head in honor of the American presidential election. I settled for making a plain Bob Dole head.

What is your favorite resource on the Net?

I spend a lot of time looking things up on MapQuest <http://www.mapquest.com/> because I never know how to get anywhere.

If this isn't your main job, what do you do, what is your training?

I have a bachelor of science in computer science and I'm a computer programmer by trade.

Do you have a family? A dog? A lizard?

I have a wife and a baby on the way (who will arrive in April or May of 1997). I have no dogs, but I do have a plastic iguana named Iggy sitting on my television.

What are your hopes and fears for the future of the Internet?

I hope the Internet continues to be fun. I'm afraid it will become boring and filled with advertising.

If you could invite three people throughout history to your house for dinner, who would they be?

R. Buckminster Fuller (designer of the geodesic dome), Frank Zappa (rock musician), and Lord Omar Khayyam Ravenhurst (cofounder of the Discordian Society and the Legion of Dynamic Discord thereof and coauthor of Principia Discordia and Grand Ballyhoo of Egypt of the Orthodox Discordian Society).

A B C D E F G H I J K L M N O P Q R **S** T U V W X Y Z

TELEPHONE

AT&T TalkingPower - Anatomy of a Telephone Call

Ever wonder how your telephone works? Why do the lights on your phone dial usually keep working even when the power goes out? What happens if you press two Touch-Tone keys at the same time? This site answers these questions and more, giving you an overview of what takes place when you make that call to your great-grandparents in Cleveland. You did remember to thank them for sending those cool handkerchiefs for your birthday, right?

http://www.att.com/talkingpower/anatcall.html

Telephony History

The name of this page is pronounced "tel-LEPH-ony." If you're like most people, all you know about how a telephone works is that you talk in one part and listen through another. The rest of it is magic. When you're through checking out everything on this page, you'll know more than you ever dreamed there was to know about the telephone! This page contains links to the Alexander Graham Bell Home Page, the history of the telephone page, and an antique phone page. You'll find sites on telephone and communication technology from Sweden and France plus the Smithsonian Information Age exhibit page. Home pages for virtually all of the long-distance carriers and the big "baby bells" are collected here at the Media History Project.

http://www.mediahistory.com/phone.html

TELEPHONE BOOKS

AT&T Internet Toll Free 800 Directory

You have a suggestion for a new toy, so you want to call the new products division at Mattel. How do you get the number? No problem. Fire up this Web site and search for the name Mattel, or look in the Toys and Games category. While not quite as thorough as AT&T's voice directory assistance, this handy Web tool features an easy-to-use interface. Search for toll-free numbers by category or name with a simple click.

http://www.tollfree.att.net/

Toll-free phone numbers can be very useful, but did you know that one 800 number is not free?

It's the Information number for getting the listings in the first place! Now you can dig up these listings yourself, from the **AT&T Internet Toll Free 800 Directory** page.

BigYellow

Do you need to look up a business somewhere? Why drag out that hefty telephone book, when this Web page is available? Let your mouse do the walking as you scour through millions of business listings in the U.S., organized by company names, categories, and even phone numbers.

http://s6.bigyellow.com/

Federal and State Government Information

Bell Atlantic is the local phone company for the Washington, D.C. area, and that makes it the company of choice for most of the United States federal government. This Web page offers every listed federal phone number in the D.C. area, and if a listed agency or department has a Web page, you can click on the listing to get there. This is a very handy page! If you want to see the entire resource, the top level is at <http://yellowpages.badg.com/>.

http://yellowpages.badg.com/high/govt/
   governmentpage_us.html

Four11 Directory Services

The name of this site is pronounced "Four-One-One." From the main menu, click on the Telephone area. If you're looking for a phone number, they have over 100 million! There are also directories of celebrities and famous folks in sports, entertainment, business, and government. You'll find lots of other cool services, too, such as free Web-based e-mail accounts.

http://www.Four11.com/

National Telephone and Communication

Do you need an area code for a city or a city for an area code? This page not only lets you find one with the other but also will narrow searches down to three-number phone prefixes as well. The directory now includes Mexico, Canada, and the Caribbean in addition to the U.S. If you want another country's dialing code (or vice versa), this is the place to look.

http://www.natltele.com/form.html

NET FILES

A junior is an athlete who is less than 20 years old on December 31 in the year of the performance. Who remains the holder of the U.S. junior record for the mile, more than 30 years after the race?

Answer: Jim Ryun of Lawrence, Kansas, still holds the U.S. junior record for his blistering pace of 3 minutes, 51.3 seconds on July 17, 1966. He was 19 years old at the time. He went on to become an Olympic medalist, and held many world records in his career. There are more junior records listed at http://www.hkkk.fi/~niininen/wjm.html

WhoWhere? Phone Numbers & Addresses

Finding addresses and phone numbers should always have been this easy. You can also find people's e-mail addresses and home pages with the search tools here. Another cool thing is to find other people interested in the same things you are—or people who went to the same school, or summer camp. That's called the "Communities" feature, so check it out! You can also find business home pages, toll-free phone numbers, and more (we find something new every time we visit). There are also English, French, and Spanish versions of this page. And if you didn't find who you were looking for, WhoWhere will keep looking and e-mail you if your friend ever turns up in the database.

http://www.whowhere.com/wwphone/phone.html

TELEVISION

Academy of Television Arts & Sciences

Have you ever heard the song by Bruce Springsteen, "Fifty-Seven Channels and Nothin' On"? Sometimes nothing good seems to be on TV, but many good shows are available. An organization called the Academy of Television Arts and Sciences selects some of the best programs and gives the winning shows and actors an award called an Emmy. To see who the most current winners are, check out this Web page. You'll learn television history, see who is being nominated, and get a behind-the-scenes look at the annual Emmy awards show.

http://www.emmys.org/tindex.html

Television History

Whether you're looking for the inventions that led to the development of television or the technologies that make direct satellite TV broadcast possible, you'll get a series of excellent links here. There are resources on general broadcasting technology as well as thoughtful essays on what we all have gained, and lost, through the spread of TV culture.

http://www.mediahistory.com/teevee.html

A
B
C
D
E
F
G
H
I
J
K
L
M
N
O
P
Q
R
S
T
U
V
W
X
Y
Z

NETWORKS AND CHANNELS

CNN Interactive

CNN, the 24-hour news channel, has made it easy and fast to get the news of the moment over the Internet. And it's in a multimedia format that brings you lots more than words. You'll find that QuickTime movies and sound turn up in the most amazing places! Look for them in stories about belly-flop contests as well as space shuttle dockings. And if you want to know more about the news CNN is covering, you can link to thousands of newspapers, magazines, and broadcasts from all over the world. Don't forget that CNN covers entertainment, sports, style, and other fun stuff. Check out Billboard's weekly Top Ten list, featuring sound clips of each song.

http://www.cnn.com/

For breaking news, we can't steer you anywhere else but to CNN Interactive. Check here for updates on news as it happens. You can also look over a Video Vault of cool QuickTime movies. You can see a virtual flyover of Bosnia, or you can view a demo of that hot Web application, Java, or maybe you'd prefer some video about the Great Pyramid, or elephants, or a sports event. It's here!

Discovery Online

You'd expect to find background articles on many of the Discovery Channel's programs here, and you'd be right. There are stories and pictures from shows on history, nature, science, and people. Here are some examples: You can visit a baseball factory in Costa Rica at <*http://www.discovery.com/area/skinnyon/ skinnyon970326/skinny1.html*>. Take a close-up look at elephants at <*http://www.discovery.com/area/nature/ elephants/elephants.html*>. There is even a Keiko-cam to let you keep an eye on the *Free Willy* whale at <*http://www.discovery.com/area/keiko/whale1.4.html*>. And there's more: links to The Learning Channel and Animal Planet programming and a way to search the archives of past fascinating stories!

http://www.discovery.com/

Will Keiko, the Free Willy whale, go free again?

Animal experts hope so. Keiko is now in a more spacious aquarium in Oregon. Trainers there will teach him skills a wild orca needs to survive. If Keiko's native pod (family of whales) can be found and his skills are relearned, Keiko may someday be released. Read regular updates on Keiko at **Discovery Online**.

Where is the world's largest colony of bats?

http://www.batcon.org/congress.html

Answer: The largest known colony is at Bracken Cave, Texas. The 20 million Mexican free-tails eat 250 tons of insects nightly. The largest known colony in a city is in Austin, Texas, under the Congress Avenue bridge. The Austin bats eat 10,000 to 30,000 pounds of insects per night, including mosquitoes and numerous agricultural pests. According to Bat Conservation International, "This is the largest urban bat colony in North America. With up to 1.5 million bats spiraling into the summer sunset, Austin now has one of the most unusual and fascinating tourist attractions anywhere." See the bats at

ESPNET SportsZone

Hey, sports fans! If you're really into sports, then you probably already know about ESPN, the all-sports cable TV network. They do the same great job on their home page as they do on their network. This site offers the latest, up-to-the-minute sports news, scores, and game summaries. Let's say your favorite team is in Seattle and you live all the way across the country on the other coast. Chances are, it's a pain in the neck to get the latest news, stats, and player profiles on your favorite team. Hey, relax. Tune in to the "zone" and get it all right here: college, amateur, pro. They cover it all, and they let you talk back. After all, you have to make your opinion known, right?

http://espnet.sportszone.com/

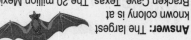

Curl up with a good URL in BOOKS AND LITERATURE!

Who won last night?
What was the score?
How did your favorite player do?

Do you want up-to-the-minute sports?
Then you want ESPNET SportsZone.

History for Kids

Do you say, "History? Yes!" or do you say, "History? Oh, no!"? Well, either way, sooner or later you have to know what happened when, where, and why. This is history that's made for your entertainment. Yes, history can be interesting. Color a few national landmarks. Find out what happened on your birthday. Learn fun historical facts. If you like history, or if you are writing a report, this is a great place to get started. Besides, where else can you learn while entering contests for free prizes? And if you're a person who can't get enough history, then you'll find lots more on the History Channel main pages at *<http://www.historychannel.com>*. Take a break from that history book and tune in!

http://www.historychannel.com/kids/kids.html

NASA Television on CU-SeeMe

Did you know there is a NASA channel, where you can watch broadcasts from the space shuttle mission or whatever else NASA is broadcasting today? If you have the right kind of Internet connection, you can watch this stuff right on your computer screen! All you need to know is right here on this home page, where you'll also get a programming schedule.

http://btree.lerc.nasa.gov/NASA_TV/NASA_TV.html

A
B
C
D
E
F
G
H
I
J
K
L
M
N
O
P
Q
R
S
T
U
V
W
X
Y
Z

A
B
C
D
E
F
G
H
I
J
K
L
M
N
O
P
Q
R
S
T
U
V
W
X
Y
Z

NICK-AT-NITE'S TV LAND

Everyone loves this stuff: *The Munsters, The Mary Tyler Moore Show, Bewitched, I Dream of Jeannie*...good ol' classic TV. Download the clever and funny ads used on the network. View the surfing horse on the *Mister Ed* download page. It's fun TV you can watch at night, and now you can visit those wacky characters on the Web. Lucy, I'm home!

http://nick-at-nite.com/

PBS Online®: Welcome!

If it's on PBS, it's educational, entertaining, excellent, or all three. Viewers support their local public stations, and these stations provide quality local programs as well as programs from PBS (Public Broadcasting Service). From Muppets to money, PBS brings us important issues and delightful special events. The Web site invites you to investigate what's on the schedule, what's going on inside the network, and what to try on in the network store. The online news reports keep you up to date, and links to your local station keep you in touch. A new kids site has just launched, at *<http://www.pbs.org/kids/>*. Did you know that you're the public? So it's your network!

http://www.pbs.org/Welcome.html

Sci-Fi Channel: The Dominion

If it's not of this world, then it must be from the sci-fi zone: UFOs, monsters, and vampires, *Star Wars*, Buck Rogers, *The Twilight Zone*, and all that cool stuff. It's far out—it's waaaaayyyy far out—and it's all out there on the Web. Can you get there? Can you get program schedules, highlights, and series information? Affirmative! Are there pictures, landscapes, sounds, and science fiction video clips? The sky isn't even the limit. There's a Schedulebot that knows what's on the Sci-Fi Channel right now; just look under the animated broadcasting tower and click on your area of the country. You'll also find a live chat area, where you can talk to actors, such as James Doohan, from the original *Star Trek* TV series. Explore the site beyond all others, Set your coordinates. Warp factor nine. Engage!

http://www.scifi.com/

TV LAND

This could be one of the most unusual (and fun) sites on the Web. It's a home page. It's a television museum. It's an amusement park! It's the best of classic television presented in a fun and interactive way. Wait for the first page to load all the way to the bottom; it takes a long time. Turn the channel (ask a parent or other "old" person why you "turn" the channel) and then (only if you use Microsoft Internet Explorer) play a wacky game based on a classic TV show, such as *Bewitched* and *I Dream of Jeannie*. The games don't work right under Netscape, alas. Take the time tunnel to the history of American television. Look at the classic old toys, and check out the ads: ask your parents if they ate this cereal, then pass the Quisp, since it's just hit the market again!

http://www.tvland.com/

UltimateTV — US TV — Broadcast Networks

A collection of all U.S. broadcast networks is here. If the network has a home page, you'll find a link to that. If the network has e-mail, you'll find that as well as fax and voice phone numbers and addresses. The cable broadcast channels are all collected at *<http://tvnet.com/tv/us/cable.html>* but you should peruse this list with your parents.

http://tvnet.com/tv/us/networks.html

The Weather Channel

How's the weather where you are, or anywhere else, for that matter? Actually, anyone can find out just by visiting this page. Sure, you'll find up-to-date weather information from around the world, but that's only the beginning. This site has more weather stuff than anyone could imagine. It includes shareware to download, maps, video clips, tips on getting started as a meteorologist, and special forecasts for sports fans. This site is really cool (in the north) and hot (down south)!

http://www.weather.com/

It never rains in cyberspace.

Welcome to Fox Kids

This network is a favorite for Saturday morning and after-school entertainment. Here you'll find the latest info on your favorite shows, with schedules, summaries, and the "kids countdown." What shows? How about *Carmen Sandiego*, *X-Men*, and *Mighty Morphin Power Rangers*? Heard of any of those? Don't forget our personal favorite, *The Tick*. And it keeps on going, gang! There are contests, games, and tips on getting the most out of the Internet. Here, the links are for kids only, not grown-ups (unless you supervise them). This sounds like just the place for you!

http://www.foxkids.com/

Welcome to the C-SPAN Networks

If you want to see the U.S. government at work, you'll see it here. Hearings, meetings, legislative sessions: this site will tell you what C-SPAN will be showing, and when. There are also classroom activities and lesson plans for the teachers among you. And aren't we all teachers, really? All you kids are teachers, and every truly great adult teacher knows that.

http://www.c-span.org/

Welcome to Warner Bros. Animation!

It seems like Warner Brothers has been making cartoons forever! Here's where you'll find their latest shows, the schedules, and even a historical look at some of the most famous cartoons of all time. But that's only part of this site. You'll find games to play and download, and you'll get a fascinating look at how cartoons are made. Stop in whenever you want to see, hear, or watch your favorite cartoon characters online, because the pictures, sounds, and video clips are right here. Shows included are: *Animaniacs*, *Freakazoid!*, *Pinky & The Brain*, *The Sylvester & Tweety Mysteries*, *and Earthworm Jim*, among others. Don't miss the karaoke songs!

http://www.wbanimation.com/

PROGRAMS

The Barney Plus Theme and Other Pro-Barney Stuff

It's finally here: a site that celebrates Barney and all his pals! You'll find photos, merchandise, fan page links, audio, and more.

http://www.geocities.com/Heartland/Plains/
    3041/barney.htm

Beakman's World Home Page

Beakman is a kid's personal scientist. He answers questions that kids can't get the answers to in school, like stuff about embarrassing body functions or why cats purr. The show has lots of zany characters; you can learn about your favorite cast member here! For answers to some of your science questions, try the companion home page, You Can With Beakman and Jax at <*http://pomo.nbn.com/youcan/*>.

http://www.spe.sony.com/Pictures/tv/beakman/
    beakman.html

NET FILES

What fruit, also called a "Chinese gooseberry," is sometimes used to patch bicycle tires?

(Hint: You probably know it under a more common name.)

Answer: It's New Zealand's most famous fruit, the kiwi. Eat it, fix a puncture, make it into a pillowcase. But whatever you do, point your browser to *http://www.lonelyplanet.com.au/dest/aust/nz.htm* and read all about it!

Extinction is forever, as ENDANGERED AND EXTINCT SPECIES know.

A B C D E F G H I J K L M N O P Q R S T U V W X Y Z

A
B
C
D
E
F
G
H
I
J
K
L
M
N
O
P
Q
R
S
T
U
V
W
X
Y
Z

Clarissa Explains it All

We love to listen to Clarissa explain her rather strange life. It sounds more and more like ours all the time! They only made 65 episodes of this show at Nickelodeon, but we never tire of watching them. We've even been to the set complex at Universal Studios in Florida—OK, so we're fans, but we think perhaps you are, too.

http://www.ee.surrey.ac.uk/Contrib/Entertainment/
    Clarissa/

CTW The Official Home of Sesame Street

Home to the *Sesame Street* Web site, here you'll also find a link to CTW's (Children's Television Workshop) new preschool series, *Big Bag*. Numerous activities are here: an interactive storybook, online games, and coloring pages. Be sure to click on the topics button to go to a list of advice and tips from experts. This site has laughs for parents, too!

http://www.ctw.org/

NET FILES

You are very hip to the latest fashions: Your front teeth have inlaid pyrite, obsidian, or jade gemstones, and you wear a lot of quetzal feathers and a big hat. You can't wear jaguar sandals, though, since they are reserved for the chief only. You're a member of an ancient civilization. Who are you?

Answer: You're a Mayan. Discover more classic Mayan beauty tips at http://www.halfmoon.org/beauty.html

Encyclopedia Brady

The Brady Bunch is one of those TV shows that just seems to go on forever. Just about everybody has seen at least a few of the original episodes, featuring Marcia ("Marcia, Marcia, Marcia!"), Greg, and all the rest as they struggle through life in suburbia. If you're a Brady Bunch fan, this site is just for you. Included here are details about the Brady Bunch that would inform even the most dedicated Brady follower! For example, although the series was filmed on a sound stage, the exterior shots are of a real house. The address (near Los Angeles) is here, along with real Brady trivia, like the mysterious connection between the show and *Gilligan's Island*, another popular show.

http://www.primenet.com/~dbrady/

Ghostwriter - Welcome Page

What is Ghostwriter, anyway? The kids don't really know, but Ghostwriter "talks" to them by rearranging whatever printed words happen to be around or by using the computer keyboard. Naturally, the next jump is to get a Web page. Here, you can meet the rest of the Ghostwriter team and learn how they solve mysteries! Descriptions of the shows are included (teachers will like the classroom activity suggestions that correspond to the shows). You'll also find a complete list of all the Ghostwriter books and videos. The only surprise is that Ghostwriter doesn't have an e-mail account. You have to send snail mail, and the address is here.

http://www.pbs.org/ghostwriter/welcomepage.html

I come from the 'net

Reboot lives inside Mainframe with all the other subroutines and sprites. Outside, there's something called User, and Reboot is trying to find who the mysterious "User" is. The cartoon is way cool, and so is this site. Download some fun games, and explore your computer from the inside. Feel what a program feels! Where do you want to click today?

http://alliance.idirect.com/reboot/title.html

Lamb Chop's Play-Along

Shari Lewis, "the lady who works for Lamb Chop," has a sweet home page here, with suggestions on how to help kids get the most out of the show, which is aimed at three- to seven-year-olds. You'll find knock-knock jokes, coloring pages, and classroom activities. Don't miss those; they have very silly jokes in them, such as the following. Shari: "Did you know it takes three sheep to make a sweater?" Lamb Chop: "I didn't know sheep could knit!"

http://www.pbs.org/lambchop/

Mister Rogers' Neighborhood

This beloved TV show has entertained three generations of neighborhood visitors and has won every broadcast award there is. Kids have fears, dreams, hopes, and feelings—just like everyone else. Fred Rogers has always understood that, and his Web site shows that care and detail. He has everything from play activities (just right for your preschooler brother) to his favorite song lyrics to an annotated book list. Read Rogers' biography and hear a message from him. Don't miss the history of the show, and learn what happened when viewers were invited to the studio to celebrate Daniel Striped Tiger's birthday.

http://www.pbs.org/rogers/

The Morphing Grid — Unofficial Power Rangers WWW Homepage

Who do you think is the best Power Ranger? According to the survey here, it's Tommy the White Ranger. Now the leader of the Power Rangers, Tommy stands for all things good and true. Did you know he started as a Green Ranger, lost all his power, and was reincarnated? Of course you knew that, because you love the show and really loved the movie! Who do you think is the best monster? Kids here have voted for Rito Revolto, younger brother of Rita Repulsa, who is married to Lord Zedd, of course. And the best villain is Lord Zedd himself, followed by Ivan Ooze. Learn all about the shows, discover powerful links, and discuss morph technology and other cool stuff with fans of the series.

http://ic.www.media.mit.edu/Personal/manny/power/

Newton's Apple Index

This insanely great science program covers everything from earthquakes to garlic, from the Hubble Space Telescope to the redwoods. We wish they listed the programs by topic so that all the Astronomy topics, for example, were together. Maybe they will, if they read this. You'll love the Science Try-it section, where you can learn to make your own barometer, and have fun with a Möbius strip.

http://ericir.syr.edu/Projects/Newton/

Shining Time Station- Introduction

Do you know *Thomas the Tank Engine & Friends*? If you're a fan of *Shining Time Station*, then you'll love the coloring book pictures and information on Thomas and the whole gang. You'll find lots of home activities here to go with the popular series.

http://www.pbs.org/shiningtime/intro.html

The UltimateTV Show List from UltimateTV

Are you a big fan of *Bewitched* or *Lost in Space*? Maybe you just love TV! If only you could find a Web site listing all the TV shows from the old days, and all the TV shows from today, and all the Web pages that are dedicated to them, and—STOP! That would have to be the grandest TV list of all. That would have to be the ultimate TV list, which this is! This list has over 3,000 links for over 600 TV shows. Wondering if there's a Web page, FAQ, or newsgroup devoted to your favorite show? If there is, you can get there from here. Parental advisory: Just as you guide what your kids watch on TV, guide them in using this site; not all shows are appropriate, and not all links have been checked.

http://www.ultimatetv.com/UTVL/utvl.html

Things are purrfect in the CATS section!

A B C D E F G H I J K L M N O P Q R S T U V W X Y Z

A
B
C
D
E
F
G
H
I
J
K
L
M
N
O
P
Q
R
S
T
U
V
W
X
Y
Z

The Web Site of Pete & Pete

What could be crazier than two brothers, both named Pete? Their surreal adventures! This unofficial fan page has everything you've always wanted to know about the Wrigley family, including speculation on where they live. Don't miss the quotes from superhero Artie, the Strongest Man in the World, fond of such words of wisdom as "Physics makes me strong!"

http://www.cs.indiana.edu/entertainment/
    pete-and-pete/

Where in Time is Carmen Sandiego?

It was late, on an evening with snow coming down like caramel corn. Shaking the stuff off of my mukluks, I headed over to warm my hands by the hot computer. Yes, Acme Crimenet was still booted up from this morning. It seemed so long ago. Like so many times before, I wanted to check the latest online contests. Later, gumshoes...

http://www.boston.com/wgbh/pages/carmensandiego/

NET FILES

Including the bull's-eye, how many rings are on an archery target?

http://www.USArchery.org/~imagemap/naa741,322
a score of zero. Learn more archery rules at
and so on. Missing the target entirely results in
nine if it hits the next circle, eight for the next,
You get ten points if your arrow hits the center,
Answer: The target has ten concentric circles.

Wishbone

How can a little dog know so much about literature? This new PBS series features a Jack Russell terrier with a big imagination. You'll find descriptions of all the shows, the classic literature on which they are based, and suggested activities.

http://www.pbs.org/wishbone/introduction.html

The X-Files

Are UFOs and extraterrestrials for real? *The X-Files* is a make-believe TV show about two FBI agents trying to answer that question. Join Special Agents Fox Mulder and Dana Scully as they investigate UFOs, extraterrestrial sightings, and many other bizarre cases. This Web site has in-depth character sketches, episode descriptions, and information about the show. A caution to parents: Some of the show descriptions are graphic.

http://www.TheX-Files.com/

SOUNDS AND THEMES

The Ultimate TV & Movie MIDI Page

If it's been on TV in the last 30 years or more, then the theme song is probably here. This collection is so extensive, it's impossible to describe. Themes for shows are categorized by comedy, drama, action-adventure, action-sci-fi, westerns, children's shows, cartoons, other shows, and even commercials. Why argue over the words to *Gilligan's Island* when you can listen to them? If you want to see your mom and dad act nostalgic, just play some tunes, such as the theme song from *Captain Kangaroo* or *The Mickey Mouse Club*. Are you looking for a great TV sound bite for your computer's start-up sound? Then get here and start browsing! Guess which TV show has a theme song that starts, "Here's the story..."

http://www.primenet.com/~mrdata/midi.htm

Don't cave in! Better spelunk a bit in EARTH SCIENCE.

STATIONS

UltimateTV — US Television Online

Is your favorite local television station on the Internet? Maybe you can e-mail them with your complaints and your compliments. Maybe they have a Web page full of information on their news team. Maybe you can find out what's on tonight. Never mind maybe—this is the place to find out if they are on the Net! This site lists U.S. television stations that have Internet addresses. In many cases, mail addresses, fax and voice phone numbers and Web pages are included. TV stations are there to entertain and serve you, so keep in touch!

http://www.ultimatetv.com/tv/us/stations1.html

NET FILES

What are Phobos and Deimos?

Answer: Phobos and Deimos are the moons of Mars. Get the inside scoop on all planets and their moons, the Sun, comets, and asteroids at

http://seds.lpl.arizona.edu/nineplanets/nine planets/nineplanets.html

UltimateTV — World Television

Where in the world can you find a television station that has an Internet address? Right here! A growing number of television stations and resources around the world are joining the Internet and "logging in." Some have e-mail capabilities and even Web pages. Find your favorite station, or just look around for someplace interesting. What's on TV in Iceland? You could find out here.

http://www.ultimatetv.com/WORLDtv/worldtv.html

You've just found out that your family's going to visit Great-Auntie Gwen in Great Britain! You're pretty excited, but then you realize you're going to miss two weeks of your favorite shows on Nickelodeon.

Before you get too depressed, check the UltimateTV--World Television page. This page will tell you what TV stations and networks are available all over the world. Nickelodeon is broadcast on cable channels in the United Kingdom, so hope that your great-aunt has cable. But, you know, you should get out more.

TIME

CALENDARS

@ February 29 LEAP DAY

Were you born on the leap year day, February 29? Your birthday only comes around every four years! When it isn't a leap year, do you celebrate your birthday on February 28 or March 1? Find other people facing the same dilemma. There are also fascinating resources from the Royal Greenwich Observatory about leap years and calendars in general.

http://www.clark.net/pub/stroh/leap.html

Why surf the Internet when you can sail it in BOATING AND SAILING?

A
B
C
D
E
F
G
H
I
J
K
L
M
N
O
P
Q
R
S
T
U
V
W
X
Y
Z

A B C D E F G H I J K L M N O P Q R S **T** U V W X Y Z

Calendar

If you've ever needed a quick calendar, for, say, the year 1753, or maybe the year 3000, or anything in between, you'll love this site in Norway. Key in the year you want (try the year you were born), and like magic, a calendar is generated. Be sure to read the technical information on how the calendar program works.

http://www.stud.unit.no/USERBIN/steffent/kalender.pl

CalendarLand

Are you looking for a new calendar, or maybe an old one? This page has calendars that will calculate moon phases, holidays, and many other types of date-watching delights. You'll also find Islamic, Hebrew, Chinese, and other cultural or religious calendars. There is downloadable software, links to pages of interest (lots on the year 2000), including one on Calendar Reform at *<http://ecuvax.cis.ecu.edu/ ~pymccart/calendar-reform.html>*. Did you know that some people think we should have 13 months in the year? Others propose 12 equal months, with "blank days" that don't belong to any month at all and are celebrated as world holidays. One result of this idea is that you wouldn't need a new calendar every year, because the dates would always fall on the same days of the week. Calendar manufacturers are probably not happy with the idea.

http://www.juneau.com/home/janice/calendarland/

NET FILES

**What are
Mancos milk-vetch,
clay-loving wild-buckwheat,
Dudley Bluffs bladderpod,
and Penland beardtongue?**

at http://www.fws.gov/~r9endspp/endspp.html

Answer: Well, they are not the names of new rock groups! They are all plants on the endangered species list for Colorado. Find out more about endangered and threatened species

Countdown to year 2000

Everybody's excited about the year 2000. The guy who wrote this Web page just can't wait: he's counting down the days, hours, and seconds until we can all say "Happy New Year, 2000!" People think that we'll be celebrating a new millennium that night, but that won't be until 2001. See the reason why at *<http://riemann.usno.navy.mil/AA/faq/docs/faq2.html>*. Many computers will have problems when the last two digits of the year roll around to "00," and you can find out the latest news on that at The Year 2000 Information Center at *<http://www.year2000.com/ cgi-bin/y2k/year2000.cgi>* along with some other useful links on timekeeping. For a clearinghouse of millennium plans, the Millennium Institute is the place to go at *<http://www.igc.org/millennium/ links/millen.html>* (a caution to parents: we have not checked all links).

http://www.stud.unit.no/USERBIN/steffent/aar2000.pl

Mesoamerican Calendars

The Mayans had two different calendars: one for sacred uses and one for everyday purposes. The sacred year had 260 days, while the "regular" year had 365. Think of that—you could have two different birthdays a year! Learn more about early Mesoamerican calendars here, and translate today's date or your birthday into a Mayan date.

http://www.mexico-virtual.com/~nagual/calendar/

Today Date and Time

"Today is Tuesday, April 1,1997 EST is 12:24 PM This is the 13 week of the year This is the 91st day of the year Year 222 of American independence 46th year of H.M. Elizabeth II, Queen of Canada 4th year of the 694th Olympiad Buddhist Year 2540 Atomic Era 56 Saturday, March 30 in the World Calendar Solar Cycle 18..." There is more. Did anything interesting happen today in history, movies, or literary history? What's the current population of the world? What's the total national debt? Know about the moon phase? How about tidal charts? How much time until the next space shuttle launch? It's all collected for you here.

http://www.panix.com/~wlinden/calendar.shtml

VNLich - Vietnamese Calendar

The Windows software found at this site will generate a Vietnamese calendar entirely in that language, with all important holidays noted. It indicates the lunar months as long, short, or leap. The documentation is in Vietnamese.

http://www.webcom.com/~hcgvn/software/win/
  vnlich.html

You Can Calendar

Check this cool calendar by Beakman and Jax. Click on any month and find out how it got its name. Look up the interesting things that happened in each month throughout history, and more! Did you know that August is the only month that doesn't have any U.S. national holidays? Can you think of a holiday we could celebrate then?

http://pomo.nbn.com/youcan/calendar/calendar.html

CLOCKS

Earth and Moon Viewer

This isn't really a clock, but it will show you where it's day and where it's night—right now—all over the planet. Besides, this is one of our favorite places on the Internet. We hope you think so, too!

http://www.fourmilab.ch/earthview/vplanet.html

Foam Bath Fish Time

Kevin Savetz plays with bathtub foam fish toys. You will, too, at this site, which will tell you the time in several time zones—using FISH. Just get in here and see one of Net-mom's all-time favorite Internet toys!

http://www1.nhttp://www.northcoast.com/savetz/
  fish/fishtime.cgi

Make a Two-Potato Clock

We just can't resist putting this page in the book. It gives you complete directions to make a clock powered by two potatoes. Be sure to have an adult help you with this, though. Will it work with other vegetables or fruits?

gopher://gopher.schoolnet.ca:419/00/K6.dir/
  trycool.dir/clock

Time Service Dept.

The U.S. Naval Observatory in Washington, D.C., is the official timekeeper for the United States. This site is tied into the official clock—clocks, actually. U. S. Naval Observatory timekeeping is based on several unusual clocks: cesium beam and hydrogen maser atomic clocks. You can find out more about these at this site. They also use a network of radio telescopes to make sure they are always right on time. Why is that so important? Well, if a rocket engine burns a second too long, the rocket may end up miles from where it should be. Or if one computer sends a message but the other computer isn't "on" to receive it yet, that's a problem. These clocks are correct to the nanosecond level, which is a billionth of a second! At this site, you can also calculate the sunrise, sunset, twilight, moon rise, moon set, and moon phase percentages and times for a U.S. location.

http://tycho.usno.navy.mil/time.html

The World Clock

Hey, what time is it, anyway? Are you curious about the clocks in Copenhagen? Or maybe you want to make inquiries in Istanbul. This page gives you the current time in over 100 locations on the globe! If you keep watching it, the page will automatically update every minute.

http://www.stud.unit.no/USERBIN/steffent/
  verdensur.pl

If you wonder whether tomorrow will ever come, just check The World Clock. You can find out where it's already tomorrow, in time zones all around the world!

A
B
C
D
E
F
G
H
I
J
K
L
M
N
O
P
Q
R
S
T
U
V
W
X
Y
Z

A
B
C
D
E
F
G
H
I
J
K
L
M
N
O
P
Q
R
S
T
U
V
W
X
Y
Z

GEOLOGIC TIME

Geology Entrance

Just when was the Paleozoic era? Find out here as you learn about how geologic time is measured and how the science of geology began. Remember, the oldest rocks are on the bottom!

http://www.ucmp.berkeley.edu/exhibit/geology.html

TIME MACHINES

PM TIME MACHINE MAIN PAGE

Popular Mechanics is *the* magazine for anyone interested in machines. They have built an Internet time machine to help you see how machines have improved over the last 90 or so years. See high-flying French balloons from the early 1900s and crazy car designs from 1960. It's a walk through history, and you won't even have to leave the chair in front of your computer! Your time machine comes with a lot of shiny buttons, and there's even an owner's manual. Let's see, what happens if we press this button right here?

http://popularmechanics.com/popmech/sci/time/
    1HOMETIME.html

The Time Machine by H. G. Wells

Probably the best story about time machines is one of the first—it was written by H. G. Wells, in 1898. This story, titled *The Time Machine,* has inspired a countless number of books, movies, and articles on time travel. Read a no-frills copy of the story right here on the Internet, and maybe you'll decide to write your own time travel tale!

http://www3.hmc.edu/~jwolkin/hum1/
    TimeMachine.html

AMUSEMENT PARKS will amuse you!

TOYS

The Kaleidoscope Collector - How Kaleidoscopes Work

Turn onto kaleidoscopes and watch things change before your eyes. Everything created inside those tubes is done with simple mirrors. It is the number of mirrors and how they are positioned that create all the different patterns that you see. Scope out the different types of kaleidoscopes and their mirror configurations here. The next time people say they're seeing double, ask if they have a Twin Two Mirror in their kaleidoscope.

http://www.kaleidoscopesusa.com/how.htm

Kids Health Toy & Game Reviews

Are Toobers and Zots a good gift for a four-year-old? How much fun are Zolos? What about that Brew Your Own Root Beer kit? Let Kyle, the KidsHealth train conductor, help you out. He rates games, toys, activities, even back-to-school stuff. First he finds out how much fun it is, using the Fun O Meter, and judges it from fair to awesome. Then he rates it on whether a kid would need lots, some, a little, or no skill to like the toy. If a toy has exceptional special qualities that make it stand out from all the others and gets a high rating, it is awarded the KidsHealth Best Toy Award. By the way, Toobers and Zots *are* good for four-year-olds, and Zolos are awesome. Check it out!

http://kidshealth.org/kid/games/review/

Matchbox Action Central | Garage

What should we do for fun today? Hey, Matchbox cars are always fun. Blast off your Zero G car toward the vertical stretch, get caught by a 180-degree U-turn, and be propelled into a free-fall jump leading to the Gyro Spiral. Why not? Oops, feeling a little light-headed? All systems are go here at Matchbox Action Central! Maybe you should change lanes and go off-road exploring. Check out the huge contest, a timeline of Matchbox history, and tons of cool info, including the hottest models of the year.

http://www.matchboxtoys.com/garage/

Minifig Generator

This neat interactive site uses Lego body parts and JavaScript so you can have fun picking heads, torsos, and legs to create your own mini figure. How about a pirate's head on a doctor's lab coat, with skeleton legs? You can make your own choices or let the computer randomly pick its own. You can then name your creation and build it so that you can print out a copy. Cool, huh?

http://www.legopolis.com/minifig/

MX Boomerang Home

Net-mom is always looking for the definitive boomerang, one that won't just come back and hit her in the head. If we had only had this page! It wasn't the boomerang at all, you see, it was a Net-mom throwing problem. For many happy returns, check the boomerang tips, tricks, and competitive advice here.

http://www.jcn.com/mx/home.html

NET FILES

Where is the Rainbow Bridge?

Answer: Some people believe it is a very special place "just this side of heaven." It is where beloved pets go when they die, and it's a wonderful happy place. There is always enough to eat and drink, and the pets play together and have a lot of fun. They wait at Rainbow Bridge until one day their owners follow them. There is a rush of barks and meows and waving tails! Then owner and pet cross Rainbow Bridge together. Read the story at http://www.primenet.com/~meggie/bridge.htm

Official Homepage of the Beanie Babies

If you know the birthday of Chocolate the moose or know that Sting the ray is retired, then you must be bonkers for Beanie Babies. Now you can find out the latest Beanie Baby scoop from the mouths (or bills) of the Beanie Babies themselves. Every month there is a spotlight on an individual Beanie Baby's personal Web page as well as an Internet diary. They have also collected some fun games they think you will enjoy. Collectors can check on the newest Beanie Babies and the ones that have been retired from the official list. Use the guest book to get in touch with other Beanie Baby collectors. In fact, about the only thing you can't get here is an actual Beanie Baby. Sorry, but you'll have to go to the mall for that—that is, if any are left.

http://www.ty.com/

The Official TMNT Home Page

Cowabunga, dudes! It's the official Teenage Mutant Ninja Turtle page, and it's totally awesome! Michelangelo, Leonardo, Raphael, and Donatello want you dudes and dudettes to send them some fabuloso mail with your thoughts and opinions, so they can have the coolest place on the Net. Check in frequently to see what happens with the next mutation.

http://www.ninjaturtles.com/

Steve's Place the Toy Zone

Do you go to McDonald's and buy their Happy Meals just to get the toy? Come on, admit it! You probably need to check out this site. It lists many of the Happy Meal promotions that McDonald's has done in the past and is doing now—and not just in the United States but also in countries like Germany and Australia. If you are interested in selling your Nerdlucks or just trading them for Monstar Blanko, you can post it in the Happy Stuff section. A McFAQ will answer questions about Happy Meal toys and provide more official McDonald's information and history. Enjoy this site, and happy meals to you.

http://www.ionet.net/~saylor/toyzone.shtml

A B C D E F G H I J K L M N O P Q R S **T** U V W X Y Z

Welcome to the official LEGO World Wide Web

Your dog chewed all the little pieces, and now you need some new ideas for other Lego projects to make with what's left! On the LEGO Information page, you can see pictures of other people's creations and discover how to make and play Lego games. You'll also find fun online games, screen savers, and other things to download for Lego-maniacs everywhere.

http://www.lego.com/

DOLLS AND DOLLHOUSES
Colleen Moore's Fairy Castle

The ultimate dollhouse is in the Chicago Museum of Science and Industry. It was created by Colleen Moore, a star of 1920s silent films, who decorated the interior with antiquities, real gold, jewels, and other precious items. The dollhouse is located in a magic garden, with a weeping willow tree that really weeps! Who is to say fairies don't really live there? You'll see the Rock-a-Bye Baby cradle, Santa Claus' sleigh, and lots of other objects familiar from nursery rhyme lore and legend. The table is set in King Arthur's dining hall, and the Bluebird of Happiness sings in the princess' bedroom. Don't miss the attic—Rumplestiltskin's spinning wheel hangs from the rafters.

http://www.msichicago.org/exhibit/fairy_castle/ fchome.html

Dollhouse Central

You finally own the house of your dreams, built with your own two hands. You don't plan to sell it, or live in it, for that matter. Use this site to get ideas on furnishings and wallpaper and to meet other people in similar situations. You do want your dollhouse to be the best-looking dollhouse in the neighborhood, don't you?

http://www.primenet.com/~meggie/dollcent.htm

Keep on your toes in DANCE.

Dolls of Every Description

Do you or someone you know look like your Barbie doll? Of course not—Barbie doesn't look like a normal human! If you'd like to get a doll that does, check this site. Browse through the catalog and click on a boy or girl doll that looks friendly. You can pick skin color, hair color, age, and so many other things. For example, you can customize your doll to wear glasses, a hearing aid, or to use a wheelchair. You'll also find dolls with special medical conditions here.

http://www.teleport.com/~people/

Pleasant Company for American Girls

The American Girls Collection is about five lovable dolls—Felicity, Kirsten, Addy, Samantha, and Molly—each from a different period of American history. Each doll is beautifully dressed in the historical clothes and accessories of her times. Their accompanying books invite you into their exciting times and show you that although their lives were very different, many of the traditions of girlhood (such as family, friends, and feelings) are still alive today. You can get the American Girl catalog here and also sign up for clubs and fun activities that focus on the interests and activities of American girls today.

http://www.pleasantco.com/

ZIA Corn Husk Dolls

Have you ever wanted to make a cornhusk doll but didn't know how to get started? This site doesn't have pictures or illustrations, but if you've ever looked at a cornhusk doll you can see they are not hard to make. It only takes a few simple materials, which are listed here along with the easy-to-follow directions. Then, get creative in decorating your dolls—you'll be surprised at how quickly and easily you can grow your own personal cornhusk doll collection.

http://www.zia.com/tcorn.htm

TEDDY BEARS
Bear Page

Germany and the United States each have laid claim to the fame of originating the teddy bear, back in 1903. Check out both stories and decide for yourself which one was *bear* first.

http://www.bucknell.edu/~thuber/bear.html

Second Canadian Parabear Squadron

Is it a bird, a plane, or a weather balloon? It's parabears! These daring and courageous bears thrill the masses at kite festivals with their exploits: they parachute jump from kites. You can meet the crew, view their home movies, and gather tips and techniques for forming your own parabear squadron. It's very uplifting!

http://www.interlog.com/~mgraves/parabear/ pb_menu.htm

YO-YOS

American Yo-Yo Association

What should you say to your friends if they tell you that last night they walked the dog, rocked the baby, hopped the fence, went around the corner, saw a flying saucer and a tidal wave, and entered into a time warp? Congratulate them for performing great yo-yo tricks, then check out this site. Maybe you'll find yourself reaching for the moon and perfecting a warp drive.

http://www.pd.net/yoyo/

NET FILES

They say that coffee was discovered in this country first. Which one?

Answer: Ethiopia. Legend has it that a shepherd noticed that his goats (some say camels) stayed awake after they had eaten the coffee berries, which contain the caffeine-rich coffee beans! Read more about this story at http://www.coffees.com/cofhist.htm

Tomer's Page of Exotic Yo-Yo

Is your favorite yo-yo a looper or a sleeper? You should also know if it's a butterfly or an imperial. If you have trouble doing some yo-yo tricks, you may be using the wrong type of yo-yo for that particular trick! Should you ever wax your string? How do you untie those pesky knots? And what do you do when you feel like your finger is about to fall off? Find out here.

http://pages.nyu.edu/~tqm3413/yoyo/

TRAVEL

See also UNITED STATES—STATES; *and* COUNTRIES OF THE WORLD *and* PARENTING AND FAMILIES *special sections*

City.Net

If your family wants to travel and is looking for a fun place, then surf to this site, which is a well-organized list of great places to go. Use the random destination link if you don't know where you want to go or if you want to find out about someplace new. You might even find information about what's happening in your own home town.

http://www.city.net/

DOS/CA: TRAVEL WARNINGS & CONSULAR INFO SHEETS

Have you ever fantasized you were an international spy? This site has links to all sorts of cool stuff! There are travel advisories and maps of all of the different countries. Check out the Central Intelligence Agency (CIA) publications and handbooks. Look at what's going on in different countries, what is necessary to get across the border, and what to take with you to be safe (besides your passport and your parents, that is).

http://travel.state.gov/travel_warnings.html

A B C D E F G H I J K L M N O P Q R S T U V W X Y Z

A
B
C
D
E
F
G
H
I
J
K
L
M
N
O
P
Q
R
S
T
U
V
W
X
Y
Z

European International Road Signs And Conventions

OK, you and your folks have a great trip planned in Europe. That's great, but the adults on your trip insist on a road trip, and they want to do their own driving. Problem is, the rules of the road in European countries are different than in North America: signs are different, traffic lights vary, and so on. That's where this site comes to the rescue! Show your folks this page so they'll know how to turn, when to stop, and, most important, get you safely to all the fun places you want to see.

http://www.travlang.com/signs/

GORP - Great Outdoor Recreation Pages

Do you love to play in the great outdoors? Is there anything more fun than hiking, camping, climbing, or seeing wildlife? GORP has it all. Check out the sections on places to go, things to do, good food to take, and staying healthy while traveling. If you are trying to get in the mood to go camping, enjoy the outdoor art, photography, cartoons, and, best of all, traveler's tales. Parental advisory: links off this page have not been checked.

http://www.gorp.com/

Klutz Press: Kid's Travel

You are on a 1,000-mile cross-country trip to visit Aunt Mabel. Your kid brother is singing "Do Your Ears Hang Low" for the umpteenth time, and your dad keeps going on and on about how he walked through the snow barefoot to school. In other words, you're bored out of your skull. Fight road boredom with some great travel games from this site. See license plates from around North America so you can quickly recognize which state cars are from (before anyone else). Learn a simple game called NIM that'll kill many road miles, and print off some matching games that'll keep your brother quiet and give you both fun times. You may even look forward to going to Aunt Mabel's now!

http://www.klutz.com/treefort/travel.html

The Penny Whistle Traveling With Kids Book

If you could go anywhere in the world, where would you go? How would you get there? What will you need to take with you? There's a lot of stuff that you want to take but not enough room to pack it all. How do you decide what to bring and what to leave? This site has tons of great ideas for you and your parents. For example, how about making your own "passport" to keep track of your travels? Or maybe you'd like to try some of the take-along snacks and recipes—there's even a handy recipe conversion chart. Or try some of the backseat travel games to pass the time. Are you there yet?

http://family.starwave.com/funstuff/pwhistle/pwtravel/
   pwttoc.html

Rec.Travel Library

Where in the world can you go to have fun? If you are asking yourself this question, check out this site, which is a collection of posted articles from the Usenet News section called rec.travel. You'll find recommendations for places to go, how to get there, what to do there, and much more! A caution to parents: Not all links off this page have been checked.

http://www.remcan.ca/rec-travel/

TREASURE AND TREASURE-HUNTING

See also SHIPS AND SHIPWRECKS

International Treasure Hunters Exchange

Do you think the days of digging up buried treasure are over? Does the idea of stumbling onto a chest of pirate gold or digging up Genghis Khan's fabled lost tomb seem like something from storybooks? It doesn't happen daily, but many people are looking for fabulous treasures, and they are finding them more often than you'd think! This site covers the worldwide treasure hunting scene with a thoroughness that makes dropping in on their site a true joy for anyone who has ever fantasized about carrying armloads of pieces of eight. If you want to go out and hunt up some treasure, then this page is a must for you. Some solid information can be found here on metal detecting, shipwrecks, and online research sources. The Treasure Hunting Shopping Mall is an virtual paradise for folks looking to equip their hunt, and there is online messaging and a regularly published newsletter. Perhaps most interesting is the Treasure Hunting in the News section, which features incredible stories of treasure hunters around the world.

http://www.treasure.com/

Oak Island

Did you ever dig a hole? What if you dug a hole and found beams of wood? What if you then found a buried shaft? You'd probably be excited! That's exactly what happened to a young man years ago on Oak Island, just off the coast of Nova Scotia, in Eastern Canada. What's really intriguing is that many people have dug deeper into the shaft since then and found inscribed stones, coconut fiber, an iron plate, and oak wood, just as might be found in treasure chests. Problem is, the shaft is booby-trapped to flood with water, and no one has made it to the bottom. Is there treasure? No one knows. See more about this mystery at this Web page.

http://www.activemind.com/Mysterious/Topics/
    OakIsland/

The On-Line Treasure Hunter

This site has exciting stories of real treasure finds. Sometimes the best place to look for treasure is where others have already looked. With today's modern computerized, electronic equipment, treasure hunters can often revisit sites that were "cleaned out" many years ago and walk off with riches! This site offers plenty of detailed information for folks who would like to find wealth in the ground or the ocean, as well as solid equipment data, classified ads, question and answers, and links to other related pages. Some of the articles are written by kids.

http://www.onlinether.com/

Pirates at the City Art Center

"Shiver me timbers!" If you don't know a pirate from a buccaneer, better sail over to this page. You'll learn lots about famous pirates, legends, and perhaps locations of buried treasure!

http://www.efr.hw.ac.uk/EDC/CAC/pirates/pirates.htm

Treasure Island

It's a tale of adventure, pirates, tropical islands, and murder! "If this don't fetch the kids, why, they have gone rotten since my day," said Robert Louis Stevenson, when he wrote this book in 1881. The book is available online at this site. Besides a biography of the author, you'll find links to sites about pirates, islands, and buried treasure. This finely designed site also has some rainy-day suggestions for things to do—besides reading, of course.

http://www.ukoln.ac.uk/treasure/

Treasure Net

With so much treasure hunting activity on the Web these days, it must seem like a gold rush is going on. As a matter of fact, there is! This site has all the usual resources for equipment and advice, plus a nice assortment of maps and historical photos. There are also links to sources of old state and county maps, which could be a bonanza for treasure hunters. It's especially useful, though, for the message forums, where you can discuss treasure sites and technical tips with others interested in this hobby.

http://www.treasurenet.com/

A B C D E F G H I J K L M N O P Q R S **T** U V W X Y Z

A
B
C
D
E
F
G
H
I
J
K
L
M
N
O
P
Q
R
S
T
U
V
W
X
Y
Z

Worldwide Treasure Links

Treasure—everybody wants to find coins, jewelry, or other valuables hidden or lost. Finding treasure, though, takes skill, the right equipment, good clues, and maybe a bit of luck. If you want to be a treasure hunter, then this Web page is a good place to start. You'll find links to dozens of treasure-related resources on the Internet. Learn about the latest equipment, find tips from treasure hunters, and read about treasure sites around the world. Start mining for valuables now right on the Net!

http://www.iwl.net/customers/norman/linksog1.htm

TRUCKS AND HEAVY MACHINERY

EMERGENCY - Emergency Service Vehicles

This comprehensive Australian site offers over 150 images of fire trucks, ambulances, rescue aircraft and boats, and other emergency equipment. Parental advisory: If you stay on this page, you should be OK; if you go back to the top level of the home page, do not choose the Action Photos. There are accident photos that may be disturbing for sensitive children and adults, so use with care. The top level does have links to many fire companies on the Web, some shoulder patch pictures, and information on fire safety. The Safety area has some coloring pages for kids, as well as printed and audio safety information.

http://www.catt.citri.edu.au/emergency/equip/
   es-vehicles.html

The Firehouse Museum's Home Page

Did you ever wonder how fires were fought in your grandparents' day? They didn't have the sleek, powerful fire trucks we have now! See some historic photos and memorabilia from this museum in San Diego, California, dedicated to firefighters all over the world. Check the steam fire engines and old fire extinguishers, and don't miss old La Jolla #1, a hand-drawn chemical fire truck. See more contemporary machinery at The FireWeb Apparatus Museum at <http://fireweb.com/nav/apparmus.html>.

http://www.globalinfo.com/noncomm/firehouse/
   Firehouse.HTML

George Hall/Code Red - Calendar Image Galleria

This photographer is trying to sell you his calendar, and what exciting fire truck photos he has! You almost need sunglasses to look at some of these shiny trucks. And the action photos—you'll want to step back from the heat and smoke. Parental advisory: The fire links from this page have not been checked.

http://www.code-red.com/calendar.html

Sam's Backhoe Links

Sam is crazy for pictures of backhoes, bulldozers, and trucks. He's got a list of sites in which he has found some; see what you think of his collection! There are also links to the Peterbilt and Kenworth Truck companies. One site he hasn't found yet is The Construction Site: Equipment for the Kids at <http://www.constr.com/kidloadr.htm>.

http://www.wolfe.net/~mcrosby/gackhoes.html

Know your alphabet? Now try someone else's in LANGUAGES AND ALPHABETS.

Feeling a bit bogged down? Check EARTH SCIENCE and get swampwise!

U.S. PRESIDENTS AND FIRST LADIES

A Day In The Life Of A President

Did you ever think about growing up to be president of the United States? If you think you have a busy schedule now—with school and sports and errands and homework—you should check this out! Taken directly from former President Gerald Ford's daily diary, read what a typical day in the life of the president is really like. The day is Monday, April 28, 1975. The day begins with breakfast at 6:50 A.M. and goes nonstop from there with staff meetings, press conferences, and various other meetings with important people from all over the world. At 9:15 P.M., the President and First Lady have dinner (hey, whatever happened to lunch?). Then, phone calls and more phone calls, and some pretty serious decision making in the Situation Room. At 12:05 A.M., the President finally returns to his second-floor bedroom so he can catch a few hours of sleep and then do it all over again.

http://sunsite.unc.edu/sullivan/ford/DayInTheLife.html

NET FILES

I like to keep track of all the different kinds of birds I've seen. Where can I find the rules I have to follow for counting birds on my life list? I was on the U.S. side of the Rio Grande and I saw a new bird across the river on the Mexican side. Can I count this on my American Birding Association Area list?

Answer: *No, the bird may be counted on your Mexican list, but not on your American Birding Association Area list. Go to the Geographical Birding Guide Page and learn about the other listing rules.*

http://www-astronomy.mps.ohio-state.edu/~ignaz/birds/ABA/ABA-listing-rules.html

Dear Mr. Lincoln...

How'd you like to take a trip back in history? More precisely, how about traveling back through the years to visit with Abraham Lincoln himself? That's right, Honest Abe, president number 16, is available for your questions. Through the magic of the Internet and a very knowledgeable actor who portrays Lincoln, you can send messages to a man many consider one of the greatest presidents of the U.S.

http://www.gettysbg.com/dearmr.html

Hillary Rodham Clinton, First Lady of the United States

Bet you didn't know that Mrs. Clinton is a serious baseball fan! Her father used to take her to all the Cubs games at Wrigley Field in Chicago when she was young. She was even invited to throw out the first ball of the Cubs' 1994 season. Check out this official site for more interesting facts about the First Lady of the United States. Her speeches are also included here.

http://www.whitehouse.gov/WH/EOP/
First_Lady/html/HILLARY_Home.html

Inaugural Addresses of the Presidents of the United States

George Washington's second-term inaugural speech remains the shortest on record, requiring only 135 words. William Henry Harrison delivered one of the longest, speaking for an hour and 45 minutes in a blinding snowstorm. He then stood in the cold and greeted well-wishers all day; he died a month later, of pneumonia. Read the speech here, but make sure you keep your hat on! Project Bartleby, at Columbia University in New York, houses a home page containing the inaugural addresses of the presidents. Also included is an article about presidents sworn in but not inaugurated and the Oath of Office itself. This is a good site for finding inaugural factoids, such as the revelation that Geronimo, the great Apache, attended the inauguration of Teddy Roosevelt and that attendees at Grover Cleveland's second inaugural ball were all agog at the new invention: electric lights!

http://www.columbia.edu/acis/bartleby/inaugural/

A B C D E F G H I J K L M N O P Q R S T U V W X Y Z

Sidebar letters: A B C D E F G H I J K L M N O P Q R S T U V W X Y Z

National Geographic's Inside the White House

Imagine, you've just been elected president of the United States! What would your first decision be? What can people expect of your presidency? You can let your imagination soar and get an idea of what it's like to sit in the president's Oval Office right here at this Web page. Best yet, you'll learn loads about presidents and U.S. history while having fun. Be careful of those pesky newspaper reporters and radio talk show hosts!

http://www.nationalgeographic.com/modules/
   whitehouse/ovalfrm.htm

NET FILES

Why do tropical cyclone winds rotate counter-clockwise in the Northern Hemisphere but clockwise in the Southern Hemisphere?

Answer: The Earth's rotation sets up a force—called the *Coriolis force*—that pulls the winds to the right in the Northern Hemisphere and to the left in the Southern Hemisphere. So when a low pressure area starts to form north of the equator, the surface winds will flow inward trying to fill in the low pressure area and will be deflected to the right. A counterclockwise rotation will start. The opposite will occur south of the equator. Find out more at the hurricanes, typhoons, and tropical cyclones FAQ at *ftp://downdraft.atmos.colostate.edu/pub/TCfaq/*

It never rains on the PARADES in cyberspace.

PresidentS

No, that is not a typo. This site really is called PresidentS, but we don't know why! You know that old story about George Washington chopping down the cherry tree? Did you ever wonder if that really happened, and if it did, where it happened? Find out at this site, which is loaded with information about many of the U.S. presidents. Take a tour of Woodrow Wilson's historic home in Washington, D.C. The Presidential Portrait Gallery provides links to each presidential library, beginning with Herbert Hoover and continuing through to President Bill Clinton. And, in recognition of the significant contribution to American history made by many of the presidents' wives, the First Ladies Web site is also under construction at *<http://sunsite.unc.edu/lia/president/FirstLadies/>*.

http://sunsite.unc.edu/lia/president/pressites/

The U. S. Presidents: Welcome Page

What a great way to learn American history and master presidential trivia all at once! Which U.S. president said, "The only thing we have to fear is fear itself"? (Franklin Roosevelt) Which president was responsible for starting the National Park Service in 1916? (Woodrow Wilson) Who initiated the United Nations? (Harry Truman) How about the Peace Corps? (John F. Kennedy) You can find answers to these questions and much more as you zip through more than 200 years of American history. Read the brief biographies of each U.S. president. The entry for each president includes a description of his administration, its chief concerns, highlights of his years in office, and links to his inaugural speeches. There is an Australian mirror of this site at *<http://www.nepean.uws.edu.au/library/SLR/uspres1.html>*.

http://funnelweb.utcc.utk.edu/~slras/uspres1.html

WIC Biography - Hillary Rodham Clinton

From her close-knit family in Park Ridge, Illinois, to Yale Law School to First Lady of Arkansas to the White House, Hillary Rodham Clinton has expressed her special concerns for protecting children and their families. Read about her many activities and the programs she has pioneered.

http://www.wic.org/bio/hclinton.htm

UFOS AND EXTRATERRESTRIALS

The Bermuda Triangle

There are two sides to every story, and this page takes the skeptic's side of the mysteries of the Bermuda Triangle. This page explains, in factual terms, why many of the mysterious events attributed to the Bermuda Triangle may be no more than products of "over-active imaginations."

http://orion.it.luc.edu/~tgibson/triangle/tri.html

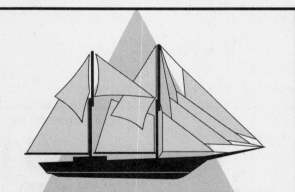

Would you sail a boat in the Bermuda Triangle? Wouldn't you be scared, because of all the mysterious boat and plane disappearances in that area of the Caribbean? The Salty Dog says there's no truth to all the rumors. Learn the facts he presents at The Bermuda Triangle page!

Home schools are cool, study them in PARENTING AND FAMILIES—EDUCATION—HOMESCHOOLING.

The World-Wide Web Virtual Library: Unidentified Flying Objects (UFOs)

You'll find loads of UFO-related links here! In the UFO Sightings by Astronauts area, you can read what 13 astronauts have to say about UFOs. These people aren't just average citizens with unbelievable stories. They are trained astronauts who have reported seeing various UFOs while in flight. Transcripts of their "live" reports are included, so that you can read what they actually said when they first spotted the strange sights. Were they being checked out by aliens while making their historic flights? Were they "warned off" the moon by aliens? You be the judge.

http://ernie.bgsu.edu/~jzawodn/ufo/

UNITED STATES

CITIES, COMMUNITIES, REGIONS

City.Net United States

City.Net combines the features of an atlas, gazetteer, and almanac, plus the best material from local guidebooks and newspapers. This page starts with a list of all the states and territories. Within each state, you'll find links sorted by city, county, or subject. Subjects include arts and entertainment, education, events, government, and more. Use the search function to find out if anything is available for a specific city or town. This is great for probing through local community Web pages to help you with that history or geography homework. Check it out!

http://www.city.net/countries/united_states/

USA CityLink Home Page

Homework can be fun with a resource like this to help! This is a nicely organized site, sorted by state. Within each state are links to general state pages, city, and regional pages. So, if you needed to find information on places of interest in Syracuse, New York, for example, you could click on New York and select one of the Syracuse links for more info. You can also search the Lycos index from the CityLink home page for even more Net links on that city.

http://banzai.neosoft.com/citylink/

A B C D E F G H I J K L M N O P Q R S **T** U V W X Y Z

A
B
C
D
E
F
G
H
I
J
K
L
M
N
O
P
Q
R
S
T
U
V
W
X
Y
Z

USA United States of America Community Page Index

This site specializes in collecting local community pages. Check out the index and find out if your town is on the Net. It's a great way to keep up with your local events and organizations. Take a trip to Anytown, U.S.A. and see what's happening in their neck of the woods. Look up your next vacation spot and find out what's fun to do there! Since each community publishes its own pages, the information you'll find will vary, but a lot of valuable local info is out there.

http://www1.shore.net/~nsbol//comindex/
us_index.htm

FEDERAL GOVERNMENT

Congress.Org

Did you know that you have representatives in Washington? They are supposed to be working for you, but they are so far away, how can you check up on them? One way is across the Internet. Type in your ZIP code and find out how your representatives voted on recent legislation. You'll also find address books here so you can write to your congresspeople and express your opinions! If you're a little hazy about how all this government stuff works, this site will get you up to speed. A similar site is Vote Smart, at <http://www.vote-smart.org/>.

http://congress.org/

Federal Court's Home Page

Order in the court! Hmmm, but which court? Supreme Court, Court of Appeals, bankruptcy court—more courts than a tennis tournament! This site is a clearinghouse of information on the U.S. federal judiciary system, and the hypertext links will give you a brief overview plus contact information for more in-depth help.

http://www.uscourts.gov/

VIDEO AND SPY CAMS let you look in on interesting parts of the world.

FedWorld Information Network Home Page

This is your one-stop location for finding information that's available online from the U.S. government. It's a master list of all the Net servers and resources, bulletin boards, and electronic documents the government has to offer. For example, check the new design and the new "security features" of the 1996 $100 bill. You'll find GIFs and a press release at the U.S. Treasury server. You can find lots of cool stuff here, if you take time to look. If you want to look something up by keyword, try a search from the National Technical Information Service (NTIS) area of FEDWORLD. You can also browse by subject area, such as Health Care or Space Technology. Download (or order) a number of free catalogs, ranging from *Environmental Highlights* to *Occupational Safety & Health Multimedia Training Programs*. Government documents are a gold mine of information; "pick" some today!

http://www.fedworld.gov/

NET FILES

What planet would float if you could find a big enough pond to put it in?

Answer: Saturn is the lightest of all the planets. Since it's mostly made up of gas, it's actually lighter than water, and would float just like a beach ball. Read more at
http://seds.lpl.arizona.edu/nineplanets/
nineplanets/saturn.html

Legal Information Institute — Supreme Court Decisions

Prepared by the Cornell University Law School in New York, these hypertext Supreme Court decisions date from 1991. Also included are a few famous historical cases that took place before this time.

http://supct.law.cornell.edu/supct/

Library of Congress Home Page

Did you know that the first American "postcards" were souvenir mailing cards sold at the Columbian Exposition in Chicago, all the way back in 1893? They didn't become popular, partly because you couldn't write on the back. What did people mail to their friends back home when they went on vacation? Luckily, on May 19, 1898, Congress passed a law that allowed private printers to publish and sell cards. The postage rate was one cent back then. This began the postcard era in the United States. This information was found in the American Memory Collection of the Library of Congress World Wide Web. This site has access to newspapers around the world and thousands of historical postcards, photographs, motion pictures, manuscripts, and sound recordings. Many Library of Congress exhibits are also available for viewing online.

http://lcweb.loc.gov/homepage/lchp.html

There's some funny business going on in the CIRCUSES AND CLOWNS section!

THOMAS — U.S. Congress on the Internet

It's Congress at your fingertips—you'll find lots of information here! Read a detailed account about how laws are made, find out what happened at the last Congress, or get the scoop on the hot bills now under consideration at this Congress. The full text of the Constitution of the United States is also available here, as well as other important documents.

http://thomas.loc.gov/

Welcome to the White House

Besides a tour of the White House, you can learn a lot about President Bill Clinton and the First Family. You can even hear Socks, the First Cat, meow! This is also a gateway to information about the executive branch of the U.S. government, its cabinet offices, and independent agencies.

http://www.whitehouse.gov/WH/Welcome.html

NATIONAL PARKS
PARKNET: The National Park Service Place on the Web

This site, hosted by the U.S. National Park Service, is loaded with facts! It includes visitor information, statistics, conservation practices, and park history. You can find information on a specific park or historic site in a variety of ways. Try the alphabetical list, or use a clickable map to select from a list of sites for that state. A selection sorted by theme or keyword is also available. They even include a list of keywords to use to make the selection easier.

http://www.nps.gov/

USDA Forest Service Recreation Home Page

America's national forests belong to you, but when was the last time you visited one? To find out where they are and how to visit them, check the USDA Forest Service graphical guide, a map showing every national forest, grassland, and park in the country. Click on any one of them to learn all about the area, including what kind of wildlife you can see and what there is to do, whether it's fishing, skiing, biking, kayaking, or camping. Once you've decided where you'd like to go, reserve your spot by downloading a reservation application.

http://www.fs.fed.us/recreation/welcome.htm

A B C D E F G H I J K L M N O P Q R S T U V W X Y Z

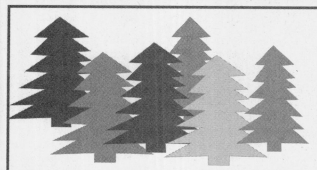

What good is a national forest, anyway? Quite a lot! America's national forests include more than two million acres of lakes, ponds, and reservoirs, 200,000 miles of perennial streams, and 16,500 miles of coastline. They also provide half the spawning and rearing habitat in the lower 48 states for salmon and steelhead trout and 80 percent of the nation's habitat for elk, wild sheep, and mountain goats. The nearly 22 million acres of habitat support more than 350,000 wild turkeys and lots and lots of migrating birds. Learn more at the USDA Forest Service Recreation Home Page!

POLITICS

CNN/Time AllPolitics

No matter where you live, your life is affected by these people. They are everywhere! Politicians make laws about a lot of different things every day. CNN, one of the world's most trusted news sources, offers these pages dedicated to political news. From the federal budget to the 1996 presidential elections, look here for great leads on today's top stories.

http://allpolitics.com/

Election '96

Do you want to be president? What would you tell voters to get them to elect you? What things would you change if you got the job? This is *U.S. News & World Report* magazine's online page dedicated to the candidates and the results of the 1996 presidential election. Each page lists a short biography and has a link to the candidate's Web page. Find out who won, and why.

http://www.usnews.com/usnews/wash/electemp.htm

The Life of a Bill in Mississippi

Governments have lots of laws and rules for people and businesses to follow. When a new law is needed, it goes through a maze of committees and meetings. The proposed new law is called a *bill*. This page contains a nice chart that shows all the steps necessary for a bill to become a law in Mississippi.

http://www.peer.state.ms.us/LifeOfBill.html

Project Vote Smart

Have you ever wondered how the U.S. government works? Politicians are everywhere, and they are constantly making important decisions. Vote Smart keeps track of what politicians are doing. If you are writing a paper about a candidate, a political issue, or even a project that requires a cartoon or an audio clip, try this site. It has links to campaigns, educational material, and a political humor section. If you don't know who your elected officials are, just type in your ZIP code, and Vote Smart will tell you! You'll also learn about their voting records and how to contact them to tell them they are doing a good job or complain if you don't agree with their stand on the issues so far.

http://www.vote-smart.org/

STATES

Do you need information about a U.S. state? We've found it for you! The "official" home pages of each state's government are included. General information about each state can usually be found at the other sites we've picked. Common resources may also include travel, historical, cultural, and statistical data.

A Brief Guide to State Facts

This page contains a list of all the states along with a short list of facts for each one. Here you'll find the state's capital, nickname, motto, flower, bird, tree, and song. The date the state entered the Union and its rank according to its acceptance as a state can also be found here. For more, look in this book under the individual state listings. You will find in-depth facts, including pictures of the symbols, history, and sounds, whenever available.

http://phoenix.ans.se/freeweb/holly/state.html

State and Local Government on the Net

Hear ye, hear ye! Citizens that be among you wishing to partake of information from the category of state and tribal governments, assemble freely here. Delve ye deep within divers agencies and departments. What ye find may astound you. Here be thy taxes at work.

http://www.piperinfo.com/state/states.html

Yahoo! - Regional:U.S. States

Yahoo has just about everything available when it comes to U.S. states. If you don't mind wading through lots of links to find just what you're looking for, try here. To your advantage, though, each state's links are also sorted by category. You can ask for just the links on education, sports, outdoors, cities, government, and more. There's also a search field that you can use to narrow down your selection.

http://www.yahoo.com/Regional/U_S__States/

ALABAMA

Located in the Deep South, Alabama is the 22nd state. Alabama is an Indian name for "tribal town." The state bird is the yellowhammer, and the flower is the camellia.

Official State Home Page:
AlaWeb Home Page
http://alaweb.asc.edu/

State Symbols:
Emblems and Symbols
http://www.asc.edu/archives/emblems.html

State Tourism:
AlaWeb - Tourism Welcome
http://alaweb.asc.edu/ala_tours/tours.html

ALASKA

Alaska is the largest state, in area, and is home to the tallest mountain, Mount McKinley (20,320 feet). It's both the westernmost and easternmost state at the same time! This curiosity is possible because, technically, part of the Aleutian Island chain of Alaska is located in the Eastern Hemisphere, while the rest of Alaska is in the Western Hemisphere. Alaska gets its name from an Inuit word for "great lands." It is the 49th state, and some of it lies above the Arctic Circle.

Official State Home Page:
State of Alaska's Home Page
http://www.state.ak.us/

State Symbols:
Student Information
http://www.state.ak.us/tourism/stubro.htm

State Tourism:
Official Homepage of the Alaska Division of Tourism
http://www.state.ak.us/local/akpages/COMMERCE/
    tourtran.htm

ARIZONA

The 48th state, Arizona, is home to the largest gorge in the U.S.: the Grand Canyon. It is 277 miles long and one mile deep. The name is from the Aztec word *arizuma,* meaning "silver bearing." The official state bird is the cactus wren and the flower is the saguaro cactus. This western desert state has lots of cactus!

Official State Home Page:
State of Arizona WWW
http://www.state.az.us/

State Symbols:
Arizona Tidbits
http://www.syspac.com/~thorne/amy3.htm

State Tourism:
*Key Attractions: National Marketing Division, Arizona
    Department of Commerce*
http://www.state.az.us/ep/natmrk/attrac.shtml

A
B
C
D
E
F
G
H
I
J
K
L
M
N
O
P
Q
R
S
T
U
V
W
X
Y
Z

**Go climb a rock in
OUTDOOR RECREATION.**

**Never give your name or
address to a stranger.**

ARKANSAS

Rice grows in much of the lowlands of the 25th state. Midlands Arkansas is home to Hot Springs National Park, where people come from miles around to relax and soothe their tired muscles in the hot mineral baths. The name is from the Quapaw language and means "downstream people." The official state bird is the mockingbird.

Official State Home Page:
Arkansas Home Page
http://www.state.ar.us/

State Symbols:
Welcome to the State of Arkansas
http://www.arkansasusa.com/Arkansas.html

State Tourism:
Arkansas Parks and Tourism Page
http://www.state.ar.us/html/ark_parks.html

CALIFORNIA

California, the 31st state, was once part of Mexico. It is known for its national park, Yosemite. Also, the lowest point of land in the United States is Death Valley, at 282 feet below sea level. Located on the west coast, California is known as the Golden State. The state tree is the California redwood, and its flower is the golden poppy.

Official State Home Page:
California State Home Page
http://www.state.ca.us/

State Symbols:
California Insignia
http://library.ca.gov/california/cahinsig.html

State Tourism:
Traveling & Vacationing in the Golden State
http://www.ca.gov/gov/tourism.html

COLORADO

One of the Rocky Mountain states, Colorado has the highest average elevation of all the states, and over 50 of the highest mountain peaks in the U.S. are found there. Yes, skiing is popular in Colorado! The 38th state has had over 20,000 years of human habitation. Its state flower is the graceful Rocky Mountain columbine.

Official State Home Page:
State of Colorado Home Page
http://www.state.co.us/

State Symbols:
Colorado State Information
http://www.gloriod.com/coloinfo.html

State Tourism:
Visitor's Guide to Colorado
http://www.state.co.us/visit_dir/visitormenu.html

NET FILES

What are the historical origins of the Frisbee toy?

Answer: It depends if you go with the "Pie Plate" theory or the "Cookie Tin" theory. But everyone agrees that the Frisbie Pie Company, operating in New Haven, Connecticut, in the early 1870s, had a lot to do with the origin of the game. Yale college students had a lot to do with it, too. You can learn about the history of the disc at http://www.upa.org/~upa/upa/frisbee/frisbee-hist.html

MOVIES are reel-y entertaining!

May the forces be with you in PHYSICS.

CONNECTICUT

Settled by the Dutch in the early 1600s, Connecticut was one of the original 13 colonies. It is the fifth state. The name of this East Coast state comes from a Mohican word meaning "long river place." The official state song is "Yankee Doodle."

Official State Home Page:
State of Connecticut Home Page
http://www.state.ct.us/

State Symbols:
State of Connecticut EMBLEMS of the State
http://www.state.ct.us/emblems.htm

State Tourism:
Connecticut Tourism
http://www.connecticut.com/tourism/

DELAWARE

Delaware was the first state, becoming one in 1787. It's the second smallest state in area, ahead of only Rhode Island. Delaware was named after Lord De La Warr, a governor of Virginia. The motto of this eastern seaboard state is "Liberty and independence."

Official State Home Page:
State of Delaware
http://www.state.de.us/

State Symbols:
Delaware Facts
http://www.state.de.us/facts/history/delfact.htm

State Tourism:
Delaware Tourism
http://www.state.de.us/tourism/intro.htm

> ## Be an angel
> ## and check what
> ## we've found
> ## in RELIGION.

DISTRICT OF COLUMBIA

Although it's not a state at all, the District of Columbia is well known for its city of Washington, D.C. It's the special place where the United States government buildings and leaders are. The president of the U.S. lives there, and you can visit the White House and other historic buildings either in person or over the Net. The District of Columbia has its own "state" motto, "Justice for all," as well as an official flower (American beauty rose), tree (scarlet oak), and bird (wood thrush).

Official Home Page:
D.C. Home Page
http://www.ci.washington.dc.us/

D.C. History:
Capitol Hill's Historic Sites
http://www.capitolhill.org/history.html

D.C. Tourism:
Washington DC Fun and Recreation Page
http://www.his.com/~matson/

FLORIDA

Florida has the distinction of being the flattest state. It is also home to the southernmost spot in the continental United States. Its peninsula divides the Atlantic Ocean from the Gulf of Mexico. Florida was named by Ponce de León in 1513; it means "flowery Easter." Lots of oranges and grapefruit grow here due to the mild, sunny climate. The 27th state's official flower is the orange blossom!

Official State Home Page:
Florida Communities Network - Welcome!
http://www.state.fl.us/

State Symbols:
Fact Sheet
http://hammock.ifas.ufl.edu/tmp/facts.html

State Tourism:
Communities of Interests
http://fcn.state.fl.us/oraweb/owa/www_index.
  show?p_searchkey=168&pframe=1

> ## It's time to go play.

A
B
C
D
E
F
G
H
I
J
K
L
M
N
O
P
Q
R
S
T
U
V
W
X
Y
Z

A
B
C
D
E
F
G
H
I
J
K
L
M
N
O
P
Q
R
S
T
U
V
W
X
Y
Z

GEORGIA

Georgia is named after King George II of England. The Cumberland Island National Seashore is a coastal wilderness area located in Georgia, also famous for its sea islands. The 1996 Summer Olympics were held in Atlanta. The fourth state's official tree is the live oak.

Official State Home Page:
State of Georgia Home Page - GO Network
http://www.state.ga.us/

State Symbols:
Georgia Secretary of State Department of Archives and History
http://www.state.ga.us/SOS/DOAH/

State Tourism:
Tourism
http://www.georgia-on-my-mind.org/code/tour.html

HAWAII

Hawaii's Mount Waialeale, on the island of Kauai, is the rainiest place in the world, with an average rainfall of over 460 inches a year. Also within this tropical state is the southernmost spot in the U.S., at Ka Lae on the Big Island of Hawaii. Hawaii comprises over 130 Pacific islands, but there are eight main islands. Its name is believed to have come from the native word *Hawaiki,* meaning "homeland." It is the 50th state, and its state tree is the candlenut. Some people in Hawaii are trying to return the state to sovereign nationhood. Please see the entry for the Nation of Hawai'i in the "Native Americans and Other Indigenous Peoples: Native Hawaiians" section.

Official State Home Page:
Hawaii State Government Home Page
http://www.hawaii.gov/

State Symbols:
Hawai'i Overview
http://www2.hawaii.edu/visitors/overview.html

State Tourism:
The Hawaii Visitors & Convention Bureau
http://www.visit.hawaii.org/

IDAHO

Idaho is known for its farming and its most famous crop, the Idaho potato. The deepest gorge in North America is in Hells Canyon, along the Idaho-Oregon border, measuring 7,900 feet deep. This Rocky Mountain state's official bird is the mountain bluebird. It is the 43rd state.

Official State Home Page:
The State of Idaho's Home Page
http://www.state.id.us/

State Symbols:
Other Idaho Information
http://www.state.id.us/other.html

State Tourism:
Visitor Information
http://www.idoc.state.id.us/Pages/SEEPAGE.html

ILLINOIS

Illinois is the Algonquin word for "warriors." The 21st state is the birthplace of Abraham Lincoln. The tallest building in the United States is the Sears Tower in Chicago, Illinois. The official bird of this Midwest state is the red cardinal.

Official State Home Page:
State of Illinois
http://www.state.il.us/

State Symbols:
State Symbols of Illinois
http://www.museum.state.il.us/exhibits/symbols/

State Tourism:
Illinois Tourism
http://www.state.il.us/CMS/HP0060.HTM

INDIANA

The 19th state, Indiana means "land of the Indians." Indianapolis, its capital and largest city, is where the Indianapolis 500 auto race is held every year. This Midwest state's official tree is the tulip tree.

Official State Home Page:
Access Indiana Information Network
http://www.state.in.us/

State Symbols:
Some Emblems of the State of Indiana
http://www.ai.org/sic/emblems/

State Tourism:
Travel Information
http://www.ai.org/tourism/

IOWA

A major producer of corn and soybeans, Midwest state Iowa is a Native American name for "beautiful land." It is the 29th state. Its state bird is the colorful and jaunty eastern goldfinch.

Official State Home Page:
State of Iowa Home Page
http://www.state.ia.us/

State Symbols:
Table of Contents for Iowa State Symbols
http://www2.legis.state.ia.us/Pubinfo/StateSymbols/

State Tourism:
Iowa Tourism
http://www.state.ia.us/tourism/

KANSAS

The geographical center of the lower 48 states is located near Lebanon, Kansas. Kansas is a Sioux word meaning "south wind people." Famous for farming and wheat fields, the 34th state is also known as the mythical home of Dorothy and Toto of *The Wizard of Oz*.

Official State Home Page:
State of Kansas (INK)
http://www.state.ks.us/

State Symbols:
Kansas State Symbols
http://skyways.lib.ks.us/kansas/KSL/Ref/GovDocs/
   Kan/symbols.html

State Tourism:
KANSAS SIGHTS
http://www.ukans.edu/heritage/kssights/

NET FILES

What are "utilidors"?

Answer: When Walt Disney World's Magic Kingdom was built in Florida, special "utility corridors," or utilidors, were built. These allow vehicle and pedestrian deliveries to the various "lands" throughout the park; they also allow cast members to travel to various areas of the park without being seen by visitors, who might be disconcerted to see a Frontierland cowboy walking through Tomorrowland. Learn more about this "tunnel system" at http://www.otic.com/Disney/WDW/MagicKingdom/Secrets/General.html

Beanie Babies rule in TOYS.

"Use the source, Luke!"
and look it up in
REFERENCE WORKS.

A B C D E F G H I J K L M N O P Q R S T **U** V W X Y Z

KENTUCKY

Kentucky, the "land of tomorrow," has possibly the largest cave system in the world, Mammoth Caves. The 15th state is also known for its many thoroughbred horse farms. Its state flower is the goldenrod.

Official State Home Page:
Commonwealth of Kentucky Web Server
http://www.state.ky.us/

State Symbols:
Commonwealth of Kentucky - Web Server - Ky. Facts
http://www.state.ky.us/kyfacts/history.htm

State Tourism:
Official Kentucky Vacation Guide
http://www.state.ky.us/tour/tour.htm

LOUISIANA

This southern state is where the mighty Mississippi River enters the Gulf of Mexico. Its largest city, New Orleans, is famous for its Mardi Gras celebration, held every year on the last day before Lent. The 18th state's bird is the brown pelican, which also appears on the state flag.

Official State Home Page:
Welcome to INFO Louisiana
http://www.state.la.us/

State Symbols:
Louisiana Symbols
http://www.crt.state.la.us/crt/symbols.htm

State Tourism:
Louisiana Office of Tourism
http://www.crt.state.la.us/crt/tourism.htm

> **Programs, reviews, theme songs, and more in TELEVISION.**

MAINE

This is the state where the lobster rules. It's also the easternmost point of the U.S. mainland. The 23rd state is also famous for Acadia National Park and its rugged coastline. The state bird is the playful black-capped chickadee, and the official tree is the eastern white pine.

Official State Home Page:
Maine State Government (WWW) Home Page
http://www.state.me.us/

State Symbols:
Visitmaine.com - State Facts & Information
http://www.visitmaine.com/facts.html

State Tourism:
Visitmaine.com and The Main Office of Tourism Welcome You
http://www.visitmaine.com/

MARYLAND

East coast Maryland is near where the District of Columbia, the capital of the United States, is located. The national anthem, "The Star Spangled Banner," by Sir Francis Scott Key, was inspired by a battle in 1814 at historic Fort McHenry. Surrounding the Chesapeake Bay, much of eastern Maryland is known for its fishing industries, particularly for soft-shelled crabs. You may have read the horse story, *Misty of Chincoteague*, by Marguerite Henry. These stories were set at the Assateague National Seashore, which Maryland shares with neighboring Virginia. The seventh state, Maryland's state bird is the northern oriole.

Official State Home Page:
Maryland Electronic Capital
http://www.mec.state.md.us/

State Symbols:
Maryland POGs
http://www.inform.umd.edu:8080/UMS+State/UMD-Projects/MCTP/Technology/School_WWW_Pages/pogs/

State Tourism:
Tourism in the State of Maryland
http://www.inform.umd.edu:8080/UMS+State/MD_Resources/Tourism/

MASSACHUSETTS

The Pilgrims landed at Plymouth Rock, near Boston, on December 21, 1620. They started one of the most traditional American feasts, Thanksgiving. Native Americans helped them to survive. Famous folks from Massachusetts include John F. Kennedy and Louisa May Alcott. The sixth state's official flower is the mayflower.

Official State Home Page:
Commonwealth of Massachusetts
http://www.state.ma.us/

State Symbols:
Massachusetts Facts
http://www.state.ma.us/sec/cis/cismaf/mafidx.htm

State Tourism:
Massachusetts Office of Travel and Tourism
http://www.mass-vacation.com/

MICHIGAN

Henry Ford's Detroit auto factory began an industry that has made Michigan the center of U.S. car manufacturing. Michigan gets its name from *mici gama*, the Chippewa words meaning "great water." Michigan is in two parts, the Upper and Lower Peninsulas. It has shoreline on four of the Great Lakes: Lake Michigan, Lake Huron, Lake Erie, and Lake Superior. The 26th state's official bird is the robin.

Official State Home Page:
Michigan State Government
http://www.migov.state.mi.us/

State Symbols:
Michigan Facts
http://www.travel-michigan.state.mi.us/mi-facts.html

State Tourism:
Tr@vel Michigan!
http://www.travel-michigan.state.mi.us/

MINNESOTA

The Mississippi River starts here! Minnesota is from the Sioux word meaning "cloudy water," but it referred to the Minnesota River. This northern border state has over 15,000 lakes, left there by glaciers. The 32nd state's official bird is the common loon, and its flower is the pink and white lady's slipper.

Official State Home Page:
North Star Main Menu
http://www.state.mn.us/mainmenu.html

State Symbols:
All About Minnesota Page 5
http://www.state.mn.us/aam/aamp5-6.html

State Tourism:
Minnesota Office of Tourism
http://tccn.com/mn.tourism/mnhome.html

MISSISSIPPI

Southern state Mississippi's history dates back to the 1500s, when Spanish explorers visited the area. The French were first to settle it, however, in 1699. The 20th state was a center of attention in the 1960s with the activities of the civil rights movement. The state flower is the sweetly scented magnolia.

Official State Home Page:
State Of Mississippi
http://www.state.ms.us/

State Symbols:
U.S Senator Thad Cochran — Mississippi Facts
http://www.senate.gov/member/ms/cochran/general/facts.html

State Tourism:
The CoastGuide
http://www.intconcepts.com/

Computers are dumb, people are smart.

What is the sound of one router flapping?

A B C D E F G H I J K L M N O P Q R S T **U** V W X Y Z

A B C D E F G H I J K L M N O P Q R S T U V W X Y Z

MISSOURI

Two major rivers, the Missouri and the Mississippi, meet in the 24th state. Samuel Clemens, also known as Mark Twain, lived in Hannibal, Missouri, on the Mississippi River. The Ozark Mountains in this state contain more than four hundred caves. A dam on the Osage River holds back the Lake of the Ozarks, one of the largest man-made lakes in the world. The official state tree is the hawthorn.

Official State Home Page:
Missouri State Government Home Page
http://www.state.mo.us/

State Symbols:
Missouri Facts & Figures
http://www.ecodev.state.mo.us/tourism/facts/

State Tourism:
Missouri Tourism Online
http://www.ecodev.state.mo.us/tourism/

MONTANA

Montana is "Big Sky Country," a nickname that came from the wide-open spaces that dominate the eastern grasslands. However, the Rocky Mountains in the west are responsible for its name, the Spanish word for "mountains." The 41st state's official tree is the ponderosa pine.

Official State Home Page:
Montana Online: Homepage For The STATE OF MONTANA
http://www.mt.gov/

State Symbols:
Montana
http://www.mt.net/~sftk/montana.htm

State Tourism:
Travel Montana
http://travel.mt.gov/

Wolves are a howl in MAMMALS.

NEBRASKA

Nebraska's name is from the Omaha word meaning "broad water," referring to the Platte River. The Agate Fossil Beds National Monument contains bones from animals over 22 million years old. This Great Plains state is known for farming and grazing land. The official tree of the 37th state is the cottonwood.

Official State Home Page:
Nebraska State Government
http://www.state.ne.us/

State Symbols:
Nebraska's State Symbols
http://www.ded.state.ne.us/tourism/report/symbols.html

State Tourism:
Nebraska Travel & Tourism
http://www.ded.state.ne.us/tourism.html

NET FILES

On May 18, 1980, Mount St. Helens erupted! Huge mud slides traveled at up to 30 mph, carrying boulders measuring 20 feet across. Wait—volcanoes erupt lava, don't they? So, where did all the water and mud come from?

Answer: Mount St. Helens did erupt hot lava and volcanic gases, as well as rocks, ash, and other debris. These combined to trigger enormous avalanches. Most of the water that poured across the surface of the mountain came from the debris itself. This included water that had been trapped inside the volcano and melting blocks of ice that had been glaciers before the mountain erupted. Find out more at http://volcano.und.nodak.edu/vwdocs/msh/msh.html

MOVIES are reel-y entertaining!

NEVADA

Nevada's Hoover Dam on the Colorado River is one of the tallest dams in the world. Tourists from around the world visit Las Vegas for its gambling and entertainment. The official flower of the 36th state is the pungent sagebrush.

Official State Home Page:
State of Nevada Home Page
http://www.state.nv.us/

State Symbols:
Nevada Facts & Info
http://www.travelnevada.com/facts.html

State Tourism:
Welcome to Nevada
http://www.travelnevada.com/

NEW HAMPSHIRE

This state's motto is "Live free or die." Although New Hampshire was the ninth state to be admitted into the United States, it was the first colony to declare its independence from Britain. Its state flower is the sweetly scented purple lilac.

Official State Home Page:
WEBSTER: The New Hampshire State Government Online Information Center
http://www.state.nh.us/

State Symbols:
New Hampshire at a Glance
http://www.nh.com/politics/firstntn/nhglance/

State Tourism:
NH Access Internet - Vacation & Tourism
http://www.nh.com/tourism/

NEW JERSEY

The third state admitted to the Union was New Jersey. Northeastern New Jersey is densely populated, with close ties to New York City. It is also known for Atlantic City, a popular seaside resort. The state flower is the purple violet.

Official State Home Page:
State of New Jersey
http://www.state.nj.us/

State Symbols:
Official Symbols of the State of New Jersey
http://www.state.nj.us/njfacts/njsymbol.htm

State Tourism:
New Jersey Travel and Tourism
http://www.state.nj.us/travel/

NEW MEXICO

The 47th state has many natural wonders. Carlsbad Caverns National Park has caves that are over 11,000 feet deep and 20 miles long. This western desert state claims the yucca as its official flower and the roadrunner as its bird.

Official State Home Page:
State of New Mexico Government Information
http://www.state.nm.us/

State Symbols:
More New Mexico Facts
http://stoper.nmt.edu/facts.htm

State Tourism:
New Mexico Department of Tourism
http://www.newmexico.org/

You know something the Net doesn't. Make your own home page!

Bring your shovel and meet me in the TREASURE AND TREASURE-HUNTING section.

A
B
C
D
E
F
G
H
I
J
K
L
M
N
O
P
Q
R
S
T
U
V
W
X
Y
Z

A
B
C
D
E
F
G
H
I
J
K
L
M
N
O
P
Q
R
S
T
U
V
W
X
Y
Z

NEW YORK

From New York City to the Adirondack Mountains to Niagara Falls, New York has a diverse array of sights. Its history dates back to the 1620s, when the Dutch colonized Manhattan Island. The Baseball Hall of Fame is located in Cooperstown. The 11th state's official tree is the sugar maple. This state also has an official muffin!

Official State Home Page:
Welcome to New York
http://www.state.ny.us/

State Symbols:
I LOVE NY - THE EMPIRE STATE
http://iloveny.state.ny.us/emblems.html

State Tourism:
I LOVE NY - TOURISM IN NEW YORK STATE
http://www.iloveny.state.ny.us/

NET FILES

If you took all the salt out of the ocean and piled it up on land, how much would you have?

Answer: *According to the U.S. Geologic Survey, 50 quadrillion (50 million billion) tons of dissolved salts are in the sea. If you could get them out, the resulting pile would form a layer more than 500 feet thick, about the height of a 40-story office building! Read why the ocean is salty at*
http://www.ci.pacifica.ca.us/NATURAL/SALTY/salty.html

NORTH CAROLINA

Orville Wright made his historic first flight at coastal Kitty Hawk, North Carolina. The first English settlement in the Americas was made on Roanoke Island in 1587, but three years later, the village was found abandoned and in ruins. What happened to these people remains a mystery to this day. The 12th state's official tree is the long-leafed pine.

Official State Home Page:
North Carolina Information Server
http://www.state.nc.us/

State Symbols:
Official State Symbols of North Carolina
http://hal.dcr.state.nc.us/NC/SYMBOLS/SYMBOLS.HTM

State Tourism:
North Carolina Travel and Tourism
http://www.visitnc.com/

NORTH DAKOTA

This state is famous for its uneven territory known as the Badlands. The Badlands were justly named by early travelers, because they are almost impossible to cross. Dakota is a Sioux word, meaning "friend." A 2,063-foot TV tower in Blanchard, North Dakota, is the tallest man-made structure in the country. North Dakota's official flower is the wild prairie rose. It is the 39th state.

Official State Home Page:
The State of North Dakota
http://www.state.nd.us/

State Symbols:
Facts & Info
http://www.glness.com/tourism/html/Facts.html

State Tourism:
North Dakota Travel & Tourism
http://www.glness.com/tourism/

Have an order of pi in MATH AND ARITHMETIC.

Attention everyone. The Internet is closing. Please go play outside.

OHIO

Ohio is an Iroquois word, meaning "good river." This was one of the ancient homes of the Mound Builders, who built thousands of earthen burial and ceremonial mounds, many of which can be seen today. The Pro Football Hall of Fame is located in Canton. The 17th state's official tree is the buckeye.

Official State Home Page:
State of Ohio Front Page
http://www.state.oh.us/

State Symbols:
Ohio Citizen's Journal
http://www.oplin.lib.oh.us/OHIO/OCJ/

State Tourism:
Welcome to Tr@vel.Ohio
http://www.travel.state.oh.us/

OKLAHOMA

The deepest well in the U.S. is located in Washita County. This gas well is 31,441 feet deep! Oklahoma gets its name from a Choctaw word, meaning "red man." The 46th state's official tree is the redbud. Yahoo! The National Cowboy Hall of Fame is in Oklahoma City.

Official State Home Page:
Oklahoma Home Page
http://www.oklaosf.state.ok.us/

State Symbols:
State of Oklahoma, Statistics
http://www.oklaosf.state.ok.us/osfdocs/genfacts.html

State Tourism:
Welcome to the Oklahoma Tourism and Recreation Department
http://www.otrd.state.ok.us/

Olympics and Special Olympics info is found in SPORTS.

OREGON

The deepest lake in the United States is Crater Lake, in Crater Lake National Park, with depths to 1,932 feet. This lake is located inside an ancient volcano and has no water flowing in or out. West coast Oregon is known for its dense woods and beautiful, mountainous scenery. Its state tree is the Douglas fir. It is the 33rd state.

Official State Home Page:
Welcome to Oregon On-Line
http://www.state.or.us/

State Symbols:
Oregon State Trivia
http://www.state.or.us/trivia.htm

State Tourism:
Official Oregon Tourism Web Site: Planning An Oregon Vacation
http://www.traveloregon.com/

PENNSYLVANIA

Pennsylvania was settled by Quakers from Great Britain in the 1680s. In 1863, during the Civil War, a famous battle was fought in Gettysburg. You'll also find the Liberty Bell in Philadelphia. Pennsylvania, which is the second state, has a small border on one of the Great Lakes, Lake Erie. Its official bird is the ruffed grouse.

Official State Home Page:
Pennsylvania Main Homepage
http://www.state.pa.us/

State Symbols:
PENNSYLVANIA STATE HISTORY
http://www.state.pa.us/PA_History/symbols.htm

State Tourism:
Pennsylvania - 1996 Visitor's Guide
http://www.state.pa.us/Visit/

Well-informed lizards, snakes, and other herps read the REPTILES resources.

A
B
C
D
E
F
G
H
I
J
K
L
M
N
O
P
Q
R
S
T
U
V
W
X
Y
Z

A
B
C
D
E
F
G
H
I
J
K
L
M
N
O
P
Q
R
S
T
U
V
W
X
Y
Z

RHODE ISLAND

Rhode Island is the smallest state in the U.S. It is also the 13th of the original 13 colonies and the 13th state. The first factory in the U.S. was built there in the 1790s. This East Coast state's official bird is the Rhode Island red chicken.

Official State Home Page:
Rhode Island State Government
http://www.info.state.ri.us/

State Symbols:
Rhode Island State Emblems
http://www.state.ri.us/rihist/riemb.htm

State Tourism:
Welcome to Rhode Island
http://www.brown.edu/Student_Services/
   Rhode_Island/welcome.html

SOUTH CAROLINA

The Civil War started in South Carolina, at Fort Sumter, in Charleston harbor. This historic East Coast city is very well-preserved. Hilton Head and Myrtle Beach are well-known and popular seaside vacation sites. The eighth state's official bird is the Carolina wren.

Official State Home Page:
State of South Carolina-Public Information Home Page
http://www.state.sc.us/

State Symbols:
SOUTH CAROLINA GENERAL ASSEMBLY-LPITR-
   Symbols & Emblems
http://www.lpitr.state.sc.us/symbols.htm

State Tourism:
South Carolina
http://www.sccsi.com/sc/

SOUTH DAKOTA

Famous Mount Rushmore is located in the Black Hills of South Dakota. Four 60-foot heads of U.S. presidents have been sculpted on the side of a mountain. The Black Hills look "black" from a distance because they are covered with dense pine forests. The 40th state's official bird is the ring-necked pheasant.

Official State Home Page:
State of South Dakota
http://www.state.sd.us/

State Symbols:
Signs and Symbols of South Dakota
http://www.state.sd.us/state/sdsym.htm

State Tourism:
Department of Tourism
http://www.state.sd.us/state/executive/tourism/
   tourism.html

NET FILES

WHO WAS GUSTAVE-GASPARD CORIOLIS?

Answer: In 1835, he provided a mathematical explanation for the behavior of fluids on the Earth's surface when large low-pressure storms turn one way in the Northern Hemisphere and the other way in the Southern Hemisphere. This is known as the Coriolis effect. It has led to speculation that the same thing happens to water draining from a sink; even though physicists say it has no effect, people still believe it! Find out more at http://www.usatoday.com/weather/wcoriol1.htm then check how you can take out your class into believing the equator runs right through your classroom at http://www.ems.psu.edu/~fraser/Bad/BadCoriolis.html

Surf, and you shall become empowered (or wet).

TENNESSEE

Tennessee, the 16th state, is known for the Great Smoky Mountains National Park. Nashville is famous as a world center for country music. The official state flower is the iris.

Official State Home Page:
Tennessee Sounds Good to Me
http://www.state.tn.us/governor/

State Symbols:
Tennessee Symbols and Honors
http://www.state.tn.us/sos/symbols.htm

State Tourism:
Department of Tourist Development Vacation Guide
http://www.state.tn.us/tourdev/vacguide.html

TEXAS

Cattle and oil dominate the economy of Texas. It's the largest state in area, except for Alaska. A famous battle in 1836, between thousands of Mexicans and a few hundred Texans, took place at an old Spanish mission called the Alamo, located in San Antonio. "Remember the Alamo" is a famous battle cry. Texas is the 28th state, and its flower is the bluebonnet.

Official State Home Page:
State of Texas Government World Wide Web Server
http://www.state.tx.us/

State Symbols:
Texas, the Lone Star State
http://www.main.org/boyscout/texas.htm

State Tourism:
TravelTex
http://www.traveltex.com/

For happy hedgehogs see PETS AND PET CARE.

UTAH

Utah comes from a Navajo word, meaning "upper." Salt Lake City is the center of the Church of Jesus Christ of Latter-Day Saints (Mormon) religion. The Great Salt Lake in Utah is eight times saltier than the ocean. Utah is the 45th state, and its official bird is the seagull.

Official State Home Page:
Official Web Site for the State of Utah
http://www.state.ut.us/

State Symbols:
Utah Stuff
http://www.state.ut.us/html/utah_stuff.htm

State Tourism:
Utah Travel and Adventure Online
http://www.utah.com/

VERMONT

Vert and *mont* are French for "green " and "mountain," respectively. The Green Mountains are located in Vermont. One interesting fact about Vermont is that it has no major cities. This makes it the most rural state in the country. Its official flower is the red clover, and it is the 14th state.

Official State Home Page:
State of Vermont Home Page
http://www.cit.state.vt.us/

State Symbols:
State of Vermont: State Treasures
http://mole.uvm.edu/Vermont/vttres.html

State Tourism:
A Traveler's Resource & Information Guide to Visiting Vermont
http://travel-vermont.com/tourism/vermont1.htm

Read any good Web sites lately?

A
B
C
D
E
F
G
H
I
J
K
L
M
N
O
P
Q
R
S
T
U
V
W
X
Y
Z

A
B
C
D
E
F
G
H
I
J
K
L
M
N
O
P
Q
R
S
T
U
V
W
X
Y
Z

VIRGINIA

Virginia has been home to both George Washington and Thomas Jefferson, and you can tour their homes today. Jamestown became the first permanent English settlement in 1607. Virginia is the tenth state, and the dogwood is both its official tree and flower.

Official State Home Page:
Welcome to Virginia
http://www.state.va.us/

State Symbols:
Virginia
http://chesapeake.skyline.net/va/

State Tourism:
Fun in the Kids corner of Virginia
http://www.thevirginiawaterfront.com/wfkids.html

WASHINGTON

Coastal Washington state is known for its many natural features. The Cascade Range is where Mount St. Helens erupted in 1980. Olympic National Park contains vast sections of ancient rain forest. It is the 42nd state, and the rhododendron is the official flower.

Official State Home Page:
Home Page Washington—Home
http://www.wa.gov/

State Symbols:
The Symbols of Washington State
http://www.leg.wa.gov/www/admin/legis/symbols.htm

State Tourism:
Washington State Tourism Home Page
http://www.tourism.wa.gov/

WEST VIRGINIA

West Virginia's natural features are dominated by the Appalachian Mountains. Mining in these mountains is a major industry, and coal is the main product. The 35th state's official bird is the brilliantly colored cardinal.

Official State Home Page:
WV State Main Page
http://www.state.wv.us/

State Symbols:
West Virginia State Symbols
http://www.wvauditor.com/wvinfo/wvinfo2.html

State Tourism:
West Virginia Travel/Recreation and Tourism
http://wvweb.com/www/travel_recreation/
     Tourism_Home_Page2.html

WISCONSIN

Wisconsin is a state with over eight thousand lakes, carved out by glaciers long ago. This state has more dairy cows than any other state, so it's no wonder that milk and cheese are its major products. Bordered by two Great Lakes, Lake Superior and Lake Michigan, Wisconsin is the 30th state. Its official flower is the wood violet.

Official State Home Page:
State of Wisconsin Web Page
http://www.state.wi.us/

State Symbols:
Forward Wisconsin - Wisconsin Symbols
http://www.jcw.com/forward/wisym.htm

State Tourism:
Wisconsin Department of Tourism
http://tourism.state.wi.us/

Explore underwater archaeology in SHIPS AND SHIPWRECKS.

OPTICAL ILLUSIONS: now you see them, now you don't!

WYOMING

Wyoming means "large prairie place" in Algonquin. Yellowstone National Park is famous for its geysers and hot springs (fictional "Jellystone Park" is where Yogi Bear and Boo-Boo live). This rugged Rocky Mountain state was the 44th to be admitted to the Union. Its official flower is the Indian paintbrush.

Official State Home Page:
Welcome to the State of Wyoming
http://www.state.wy.us/

State Symbols:
General Wyoming Information
http://www.state.wy.us/state/wyoming_news/
   general/general.html

State Tourism:
Wyoming Tourism Information
http://www.state.wy.us/state/tourism/tourism.html

TERRITORIES AND FREE ASSOCIATION NATIONS
AMERICAN SAMOA

American Samoa

This 76-square-mile island group sits in the middle of the South Pacific Ocean, 2,600 miles from Hawaii. Many American Samoans live in Hawaii. Its citizens are considered U.S. nationals and can freely enter the United States. American Samoa has a large tuna fishery; other exports include coconuts, taro, yams, bananas, and breadfruit. You can't make a sandwich out of breadfruit, by the way. Well, maybe you can in the Sandwich Islands, but not on American Samoa! If you go to this site, you'll hear a greeting in Samoan. You may want to check *<http://www.odci.gov/cia/publications/95fact/aq.html>* for further details.

http://prel-oahu-1.prel.hawaii.edu/pacific_region/
   am_samoa/

Real surfers get their feet wet in OUTDOOR RECREATION.

BAKER ISLAND

The World Factbook page on Baker Island

This is a teeny, low-lying atoll in the North Pacific Ocean, about one-half of the way from Hawaii to Australia. It was mined for its guano deposits until 1891. The birds are still there, the guano is still there, but you'll need a permit to visit. Only offshore anchorage is possible, and be advised that there are no malls or fast-food restaurants. This island is also a National Wildlife Refuge.

http://www.odci.gov/cia/publications/nsolo/
   factbook/fq.htm

GUAM

Welcome to Guam

Guam, located near the international date line, is "where America's Day Begins." This island is in the West Pacific, 3,700 miles from Hawaii. Guamanians are U.S. citizens. You can find more information at *<http://www.odci.gov/cia/publications/95fact/gq.html>* or at *<http://prel-oahu-1.prel.hawaii.edu/pacific_region/guam/>*.

http://www.gov.gu/

Sirena loved to swim in the sea.

One day, she forgot her chores and spent the day swimming. When she did not come home, her angry mother said she should just become a fish if she loved the sea so much. Sirena's god-mother quickly said, "But let the part of her that belongs to me remain." Sirena, still swimming, suddenly felt strange. She looked down and realized the lower part of her body had become a fish! The legend of Sirena is from Guam. Read more about the story and see a statue of Sirena at the **Welcome to Guam** home page, in the LEGENDS area.

A B C D E F G H I J K L M N O P Q R S T **U** V W X Y Z

A
B
C
D
E
F
G
H
I
J
K
L
M
N
O
P
Q
R
S
T
U
V
W
X
Y
Z

HOWLAND ISLAND

The World Factbook page on Howland Island

This tiny, sandy island is in the North Pacific Ocean, about one-half of the way from Hawaii to Australia. It's a National Wildlife Refuge, and you need permission from the U.S. Department of the Interior to visit it. The island is famous because of someone who never made it there. In 1937, an airstrip was constructed there as a refueling stop on the round-the-world flight attempt of Amelia Earhart and Fred Noonan. They had left Lae, New Guinea, for Howland Island, but something happened, and they were never seen again. Their disappearance is truly one of the world's great unsolved mysteries. Earhart Light, on the island's west coast, is a day beacon built in memory of the lost aviatrix. The airfield is no longer serviceable. For a possible solution to the mystery, see <http://msowww.anu.edu.au/~dfk/magazine/mpi/july95/tighar.html> about recent expeditions and findings on Nikumaroro. If you want to read the lyrics to a folk song about Earhart, try <http://www.asksam.com/cgi-bin/as_web.exe?October+D+153733>, and you can download a 540K audio file of Earhart discussing technology's impact on women at <gopher://gopher.msu.edu:70/ss/libraries/collections/main/voice/sounds/Amelia_Earhart.au>. A nice illustrated biography is at <http://www.dot.state.mn.us/aeronautics/amelia.html>.

http://www.odci.gov/cia/publications/nsolo/
    factbook/hq.htm

JARVIS ISLAND

The World Factbook page on Jarvis Island

This tiny coral island is in the South Pacific Ocean, about one-half of the way from Hawaii to the Cook Islands. It is a favorite nesting and roosting area for seabirds, and until the late 1880s, guano was mined there. Bird droppings are a rich source of fertilizer, but it seems like a long way to go to get some. You can't visit Jarvis Island without permission of the U.S. Department of the Interior, since it is considered a National Wildlife Refuge.

http://www.odci.gov/cia/publications/nsolo/
    factbook/dq.htm

JOHNSTON ATOLL

The World Factbook page on Johnston Atoll

This strategically located atoll group is in the North Pacific Ocean, about one-third of the way from Hawaii to the Marshall Islands. It's closed to the public and has been used for testing nuclear weapons. About 300 people work there on military and other projects. All food and other equipment has to be imported, but they do have excellent communications through an underwater cable link. Maybe they will get a home page on their own server soon!

http://www.odci.gov/cia/publications/nsolo/
    factbook/jq.htm

NET FILES

What was Michelangelo's last name?

(The artist, not the teenage turtle!)

Answer: Buonarroti. In 1508, he was commissioned by Pope Julius II della Rovere to paint the Sistine Chapel's ceiling; the work was completed between 1508 and 1512. He also painted The Last Judgment, over the altar, between 1535 and 1541.
http://www.christusrex.org/www1/sistine/0-Tour.html

I wonder what the QUEENS, KINGS, ROYALTY are doing tonight?

KINGMAN REEF

The World Factbook page on Kingman Reef

We're talking very tiny: only one square kilometer of land area. This reef is in the North Pacific Ocean, about one-half of the way from Hawaii to American Samoa. It's only about one meter in elevation, so it's often awash with waves! If you go, bring your boots, but you'll need permission from the U.S. Navy. This reef was used as a way station by Pan American flying boats in 1937 and 1938. Now, it's basically known as a maritime hazard.

http://www.odci.gov/cia/publications/nsolo/
   factbook/kq.htm

MARSHALL ISLANDS

The World Factbook page on Marshall Islands

This group of atolls and reefs is in the North Pacific Ocean, about one-half of the way from Hawaii to Papua New Guinea. The group has a population of over 56,000 people. It has had a free association agreement with the U.S. since 1990 and became an independent nation in 1991. One of the atolls is Bikini, famous for the first military atomic bomb tests. You can read an account of these tests and see a photo at <http://magic.geol.ucsb.edu/~fisher/ bikini.htm>. The bikini swimsuit, a very explosive new fashion, was invented about the same time as the weapon, and it was named for this atoll. Nearby islands with indigenous people were evacuated in 1948; some of them, and their descendants, are asking to be repatriated to their homelands. This is difficult, due to residual radiation in the soil and food sources. You can read a report about that at <http://www.nas.edu/onpi/pr/marshall/>. More information about the Marshalls is at <http://prel-oahu-1.prel.hawaii.edu/pacific_region/ marshalls/index.html>.

http://www.odci.gov/cia/publications/nsolo/
   factbook/rm.htm

**Expect a miracle
in RELIGION!**

MICRONESIA

The World Factbook page on Micronesia, Federated States of

This island group, called the Federated States of Micronesia, is in the North Pacific Ocean, about three-quarters of the way from Hawaii to Indonesia. Its landscape varies from low coral atolls to high forested mountains. About 123,000 people live on these islands, which achieved independent nation status in 1991. It has a Compact of Free Association with the U.S., which means that the nation is fully responsible for its internal government while the U.S. retains responsibility for external affairs. The Island of Yap has a home page at <http://prel-oahu-1.prel.hawaii.edu/ pacific_region/yap/>. The Island of Chuuk is a famous destination for scuba divers who want to explore a sunken Japanese fleet. Its home page is at <http://prel-oahu-1.prel.hawaii.edu/pacific_region/chuuk/>. Rural Kosrae's map and home page are at <http://prel-oahu-1.prel.hawaii.edu/pacific_region/kosrae/>, while Pohnpei—famous for gourmet pepper—has a home page at <http://prel-oahu-1.prel.hawaii.edu/ pacific_region/pohnpei/>.

http://www.odci.gov/cia/publications/nsolo/
   factbook/fm.htm

MIDWAY ISLANDS

The World Factbook page on Midway Islands

This is an atoll group in the North Pacific Ocean, about one-third of the way from Hawaii to Tokyo, Japan. Over 400 U.S. military personnel are stationed there, and the area is closed to the public. This is a famous WWII battle site.

http://www.odci.gov/cia/publications/nsolo/
   factbook/mq.htm

NAVASSA

The World Factbook page on Navassa Island

This Caribbean island is strategically located, about one-fourth of the way from Haiti to Jamaica, south of Cuba. Haiti disputes the U.S. claim to the territory. Haitians fishing there often camp on the island, which has steep cliffs and is populated by goats and cactus.

http://www.odci.gov/cia/publications/nsolo/
   factbook/bq.htm

A
B
C
D
E
F
G
H
I
J
K
L
M
N
O
P
Q
R
S
T
U
V
W
X
Y
Z

A B C D E F G H I J K L M N O P Q R S T U V W X Y Z

NORTHERN MARIANA ISLANDS

Commonwealth of the Northern Mariana Islands

Between Guam and the Tropic of Cancer lie the 17 volcanic islands that make up this commonwealth. Its inhabitants are U.S. citizens, and tourism is becoming a major industry. For more information about the people and culture, see <http://www.odci.gov/cia/publications/95fact/cq.html>.

http://prel-oahu-1.prel.hawaii.edu/pacific_region/ cnmi/

PALAU

Republic of Palau

This island, and its 16,000 people, is less than 500 miles from the Philippines. It consists of several hundred volcanic islands and a few coral atolls, but only eight islands are inhabited. It has mineral resources, including gold, but its main industry is tourism. This republic entered into a free association relationship with the United States in 1994.

http://prel-oahu-1.prel.hawaii.edu/pacific_region/ palau/

PALMYRA ATOLL

The World Factbook page on Palmyra Atoll

Administered by the U.S. Department of the Interior, this atoll group lies in the North Pacific Ocean, about one-half of the way from Hawaii to American Samoa. It has only 12 square kilometers in land area, and its many tiny islets are densely covered with vegetation and coconut palms.

http://www.odci.gov/cia/publications/nsolo/ factbook/lq.htm

PUERTO RICO

Welcome to Puerto Rico!

The island of Puerto Rico is the smallest and the most eastern island of the Greater Antilles, in the Caribbean. Puerto Rico is Spanish for "rich port." Puerto Ricans are U.S. citizens. You may have heard of these famous Puerto Ricans: musician Pablo Casals, sports figure Roberto Clemente, and actress Rita Moreno. Even more facts about Puerto Rico are located at <http://www.odci.gov/cia/publications/95fact/rq.html>.

http://welcome.2puertorico.org/

VIRGIN ISLANDS

American Caribbean Paradise: United States Virgin Islands

The Caribbean islands of St. Thomas, St. John, and St. Croix are known as the U.S. Virgin Islands, and residents are U.S. citizens. Columbus stopped there in 1493. Tourism has become a huge industry. Still more can be found at <http://www.odci.gov/cia/publications/ 95fact/vq.html>.

http://www.usvi.net/

WAKE ISLAND

The World Factbook page on Wake Island

This almost flat volcanic island group is in the North Pacific Ocean, about two-thirds of the way from Hawaii to the Northern Mariana Islands. About 300 people live there, and a U.S. military base is located there. It is also used as an emergency stopover for transpacific commercial aviation.

http://www.odci.gov/cia/publications/nsolo/ factbook/wq.htm

NET FILES

Look for the next Winter Olympics February 7–22, 1998, in Nagano, Japan. You'll see merchandise of all kinds bearing the special Olympic logo mascots. What are they?

Answer: The four mascots are called Snowlets, and they represent baby owls from the forests of Japan. Each has a different quality: passion (fire), curiosity (wind), calmness and wisdom (earth), and romance (water). Find out more at http://www.nagano.olympic.org/kids/stories/submit/ ksto5_e.shtml#top

Ira Flatow, executive producer and host of Science Friday (Photo by Carl Flatow)

"While it's great that more and more schools and homes gain access daily, it's important that we not leave any sector of society behind. My greatest fear is that this wonderful resource won't be accessible to everyone."— Chuck Alexander

SCIENCE

Science Friday Kids Connection

Webmasters: Lauren Brownstein and Chuck Alexander

http://www.npr.org/programs/sfkids

Who came up with the idea for your page or project?

National Public Radio (NPR), Science Friday, and KIDSNET, the computerized clearinghouse for children's television, radio, and multimedia, launched Science Friday Kids Connection (SFKC) in October, 1995. The idea for the project grew out of a series of focus groups. In those focus groups, educators and parents communicated a need for instant access to science teaching information. To help maximize the educational impact of Science Friday (NPR's two-hour weekly science call-in show), and provide an interactive multimedia science learning resource for students and teachers, Science Friday Kids Connection was developed.

How many people work on your pages? Does it take a lot of time? How many hits do you get a day?

SFKC is a very collaborative effort. At least five people work on the page every week, and sometimes more are involved. Editors, educators, writers, and technicians work on the page, and it takes about 20 hours per week to put together. During the 1995-1996 school year, we had up to 50,000 hits per month.

You must hear from people all over the world! Can you think of an unusual request, question, or comment someone has sent to you?

We do hear from students and teachers all the time. Many of them have important questions about science issues. Some, however, have questions about everyday objects and occurrences. For instance, one science enthusiast once asked us who invented the paper clip.

If this isn't your main job, what do you do, what is your training?

A number of people work on SFKC. Most of us have backgrounds in education, educational media, or science. All of us have varied responsibilities beyond SFKC responsibilities. For instance, Chuck Alexander at NPR is developing new aspects of SFKC and works with partner schools and public radio stations. But he also helps train public radio stations in how to do outreach, develops outreach brochures and tapes, and works on other projects at National Public Radio. Lauren Brownstein at KIDSNET works with broadcasters (mostly TV broadcasters and cable companies) to produce educational materials that accompany children's television, radio, and multimedia programming.

What's the one thing you'd really like to do on your page but have not yet implemented?

We plan to initiate a more interactive forum for information exchange between science mentors and visitors to SFKC. We also want to build an online area where we can really spotlight individual class and school projects.

What are your hopes and fears for the future of the Internet?

Chuck Alexander responds: My hopes and fears for the Internet are really centered around one issue—accessibility. I hope that some day soon, we'll find a way to make access to the Internet easy and affordable for everyone. While it's great that more and more schools and homes gain access daily, it's important that we not leave any sector of society behind. My greatest fear is that this wonderful resource won't be accessible to everyone.

A B C D E F G H I J K L M N O P Q R S T U V W X Y Z

VIDEO AND SPY CAMS

31 Online Guide to Better Home Video

This site was created by a professional photojournalist for a TV station in Huntsville, Alabama, and he has some great tips to improve your home video movies. According to this site, the biggest mistake amateurs make is panning and zooming the camera too much. He suggests we learn to think visually, and take a wide shot to establish the story, move in closer for a medium shot to focus interest, then use close-ups for detail. You should think of this as three separate shots that together tell a story, not one continuous zoom from far away to up close. You'll find some great tips here!

http://spider.waaytv.com/waay/31_video.html

A T O M I C W E B . C O M

Every time we visit this site showing an ant farm, the view reminds us of Auntie Em's farm in *The Wizard of Oz*. The cyclone's just struck, carrying Dorothy off, and everyone else is hiding in the root cellar. Yet, below the ground, the ants go on, industriously making molehills out of mountains. Check their activity, or lack of it, but keep an eye on the weather!

http://sec.dgsys.com/AntFarm.html

The Amazing Fish-Cam!

Yes, from wherever you are on the Web, you can watch fish swim around a tank in someone's office. These fish can be viewed by two different cameras (you get to pick), or you can choose the Continuously Refreshing Fish-Cam if you have Netscape 1.1. Ah, a nice, salty glass of refreshing fish-cam—there's nothing quite like it!

http://www1.netscape.com/fishcam/

The Sun never sets on the Internet.

Big Brother is Watching

From this one site, you can watch an observatory being built in Hawaii, check out the traffic in Hong Kong, or watch the planes at airports in San Diego and Denver. Are indoor cams more your style? OK, how about spying on the employees at Berkeley Systems? Watch them eat lunch or go down the slide. That's right, they have a slide in the employee lunchroom—sounds like a fun place to work! (This one is hard to find in the list; it's at <http://www.berksys.com/www/funtour/takepic.html>.) If you want to watch someone else's pets, try the piranha fish tank (especially entertaining when they clean it—any volunteers?). You can also monitor satellite weather and other forecasting models. Be sure to check real-time traffic reports for many cities, too! This is a very useful site, with thoughtful and current reviews.

http://www.pitt.edu/~sbrst4/html.camtitle

NET FILES

What would you be looking at if you were holding a copy of the "Dunlap Broadside"?

Answer: You'd be looking at one of only 24 known surviving copies of the first printing of the Declaration of Independence, printed by a Philadelphia printer John Dunlap on July 4, 1776. Read more interesting facts surrounding the creation of this famous document at http://lcweb.loc.gov/exhibits/declara/declara4.html

Discovery Online, Keiko — Keiko Cam

Did you ever see the *Free Willy* movies about the whale that was rescued from a small display aquarium? Did you know that "Willy" is really named Keiko, and he now lives in a two-million-gallon aquarium in Oregon? You can look at him every day. The text explains why Keiko, a boy, has a name that is usually a girl's name. You're right—it was a mistake!

http://www.discovery.com/area/keiko/whale1.4.html

Finnra, border traffic at Vaalimaa

There's something satisfying about watching traffic waiting to cross the Finnish border into Russia. Check the map to see where this particular crossing is located. What's in that truck? Hey, that lady in the car—she looks just like Carmen Sandiego! What stories can you make up about the people and vehicles you see? This picture is only updated twice an hour, so don't hang around—someone might ask to see your passport!

http://www.tieh.fi/evideo.htm

Giraffe Cam

Check out the giraffes at the Cheyenne Mountain Zoo in Colorado Springs, Colorado. You can view the giraffe entrance to their giraffe house. They are normally visible from 10 A.M. to 4 P.M. (mountain time). This zoo is famous for successfully breeding giraffes in captivity!

http://c.unclone.com/zoocam.html

You can always count on the info in MATH AND ARITHMETIC.

images.com WebCam Theater (Live Cams!)

Hey! Would you like to see a live picture from Antarctica? Oops, must be nighttime there. Well, how about Hawaii? Hmm, seems to be the middle of the night there, too. What about that office where they have the employee slide? (See the Big Brother is Watching entry previously in this section.) Gosh, they seem to have closed for the weekend. Sometimes you want to show someone a live video picture from somewhere exciting, but all your favorite spy cams are dark! This site takes care of that little problem. It has them all in a database, which knows where it's daylight (in the case of outdoor views) or where activity is likely to be taking place (in the case of nondaylight-dependent cams). You can look up cams by subject. For example, try landscapes, animals, or cities and see which ones are likely to have a live picture right at the moment. This is also a good way to visit a lot of webcams at once, using the video jukebox feature.

http://wct.images.com/

Interactive Model Railroad - MAIN

This one is pretty cool. You get to give commands to an actual model train at the University of Ulm in Germany! You pick the train you want to control, tell it which station to go to, and if you're quick (and lucky) enough, you're in charge. A box on the page gives the domain name of whoever happens to be controlling the train at the time.

http://rr-vs.informatik.uni-ulm.de/rr/

Live Iguana Cam

Check out Dupree the green iguana as he lazes the day away. The best time to visit is between about 9 A.M. and 6 P.M. (Pacific time), Monday through Friday. Otherwise, he's out partying, and you'll just see a typical image, not a live one.

http://iguana.images.com/dupecam.html

It never rains in cyberspace.

A B C D E F G H I J K L M N O P Q R S T U V W X Y Z

A B C D E F G H I J K L M N O P Q R S T U V W X Y Z

Mawson Station, Antarctica

It's extremely "cool" to get a live image of Antarctica. This picture is usually updated automatically each hour. The date/time on the picture shows local Mawson time, which is six hours ahead of Universal Coordinated Time, or UCT (previously known as Greenwich Mean Time or GMT). Gee, it's 1 A.M. there and the sky's pretty bright! Also, it's extremely depressing to find out that it's warmer at Mawson Station than it is outside our window. :-) To find out how your local temperatures compare, use the Celsius/Fahrenheit conversion entries listed in this book in the "Reference Works: Weights and Measures" section.

http://www.antdiv.gov.au/aad/exop/sfo/mawson/
    video.html

Pikes Peak Cam

Lieutenant Zebulon Montgomery Pike discovered the mountain in 1806, but he never climbed it—seems the snow was too deep. This page shows a live image of Pikes Peak, elevation 14,110 feet, near Colorado Springs, Colorado. The tourist info here says the best viewing time is from sunrise to noon. They say the sunsets are magnificent, too, and if you want to see the most spectacular lightning storms in the world, view the mountain between 3 P.M. and 5 P.M. (mountain time) in July and August.

http://www.softronics.com/peak_cam.html

Visit Pikes Peak, Colorado!

In 1893, Katherine Lee Bates did. An author and teacher from Massachusetts, she was so inspired by the view that she composed the lyrics to "America the Beautiful," one of the most beloved patriotic songs.

You remember it: spacious skies, amber waves of grain, purple mountains' majesties, and so on. You can see a live view of the mountain behind the song at the Pikes Peak Cam.

Room 100, Buckman Elementary School

What are the kids doing in Room 100 of the Buckman Elementary School in Portland, Oregon? What are they looking at under their video-equipped microscope? This spy cam will show you a recent view of the classroom, and maybe you'll get a picture of "the bee that just stung Ted" or something equally interesting.

http://buckman.pps.k12.or.us/room100/room100.html

San Francisco CityCam

Ah, the City by the Bay, where every nightclub crooner always manages to leave his or her heart. Now you can visit San Francisco over the Net and see a new view every five minutes. Station KPIX has a camera high atop the Fairmont Hotel on Nob Hill. Since the camera pans from the Golden Gate Bridge to the Bay Bridge, you may be able to catch video of both bridges, plus views of downtown, the famous Coit Tower, Fisherman's Wharf, the Marina district, and other attractions. Better hold onto your heart, though! If you miss the sunset, don't worry: you can view a series of time-lapse photos and relive the whole thing. And they have a new feature: the Monterey cam. See the beach, the waves, and sometimes kayakers.

http://www.kpix.com/live/

VIDEO GAMES

Electric Playground Home Page

Do you want the scoop on your favorite game? Click on the late-breaking news area to find out all that is hot in the world of gaming and all that is not! You can click on your computer or console platform and read reviews of new games. We prefer the other two sites reviewed in this section, but try this one if the others are busy.

http://www.elecplay.com/

Games Domain Review

Are you stumped deciding which computer or video game you want next? Do you wish you could find out about the games available for your system? This online magazine covers reviews, news, previews, and an opinion section for games on PC and Macintosh computers, as well as dedicated console game systems. Add to the review database!

http://www.gamesdomain.com/gdreview/

Happy Puppy's Front Porch

Happy Puppy brings you a list of computer gaming software and home pages of many of the video and computer game software companies on the Net. You'll find lists for Mac and PC games and info on new versions of your favorite games as they are announced. Other software archives listed here have cheat codes, shareware, demos, and upgrades available for those in need of too much fun!

http://happypuppy.com/

Sega Online

It's SEGA, home to the world's only blue hedgehog: Sonic. You'll find Sonic's fascinating biography here, in case you need to write a school report on a famous personality! You might also download hedgehog wallpaper for your computer screen. Check the latest news on all of SEGA's games, and get game hints! Do you need to know how to get extra air in Ecco the Dolphin? We'll "clam" up about it for now, but you can find out here.

http://www.sega.com

Sony PlayStation Homepage

Bandicoots are the coolest thing to come out of Australia since kangaroos! Take a "crash" visit to the Bandicoot's island to get the idea. You can also play other online games and find out about the latest titles for the Sony PlayStation.

http://www.sepc.sony.com/SCEA/index.html

Virtual Pet Home Page

If you can't have a real pet, maybe you can own a virtual pet! The Tamagocchi Lovable Egg has become a real craze in Japan, and all signs point to overwhelming popularity when the little pastel-colored eggs are introduced to the U.S. this summer (as Tamagotchi). What are they? Net-mom's never seen one (Bandai, are you listening?), but according to the descriptions in the press releases and the pictures on the Bandai site at <http://www.bandai.com/theegg.html> it looks something like a little game on a key chain or a necklace. A little chicken-like bird is on the LCD screen, and you have to feed it, pet it, and clean up after it, or it gets sick and dies, leaving you feeling way guilty. But there are other virtual pets you can get, some of them as free demos, which live on your computer screen. Check this site for a collection of all known virtual pets. Hint: If this catches on, you may want to think about becoming a virtual veterinarian!

http://www.virtualpet.com/vp/

Welcome to Computer Gaming World

How much do you know about video games? Do you know it all, or do you want to know more? *Computer Gaming World* has a very well-written collection of information about home computer video games. They have in-depth reviews, cheat codes, hints, tips, and previews of beta-release versions of games. You can never have enough great sources of gaming information. There are also links to almost every game manufacturer's home page. This site also features a text-only mode.

http://www.zdnet.com/gaming/

Welcome to www.nintendo.com

Everybody loves Mario (although they may get tired of his theme song). That crazy plumber has appeared on computer screens everywhere for years. If you can get into this site, you'll find the latest games, news, and inside information on dozens of Nintendo games. This popular site is very busy, though, so keep trying.

http://www.nintendo.com

A
B
C
D
E
F
G
H
I
J
K
L
M
N
O
P
Q
R
S
T
U
V
W
X
Y
Z

Sachiko Oba started the Kids' Space site after dreaming of good digital/international relationships.

"One boy wrote: 'I'd like to go to N.Y. and see the Statue of Liberty, the Empire State Building, and Kids' Space!' (The fact is Kids' Space is here in my small apartment. I am hoping to make Kids' Space a place worthy to visit!)"

FAMILY HOME PAGES

Kids' Space
Kids' Space Connection

Webmaster: Sachiko Oba

http://www.kids-space.org
http://www.KS-connection.com

Who came up with the idea for your page or project?

I did. I wanted children to have a safe, fun, and inspiring place on the Net, dreaming that if they would establish good digital/international relationships, the future of this planet would be little different.

How many people work on your pages? Does it take a lot of time? How many hits do you get a day?

For scanning and collecting data: four volunteer members (about 1-3 hours per week per person). For final scanning and updating: two—my friend and myself. My friend is working on many sections (about 12-15 hours per day per person). For developing the content, fixing bugs, creating pictures, scripting, answering questions: one—myself (about 5-6 hours per day). For proofreading: one—one of the volunteer members who also works on scanning and collecting data (about 2-3 hours per a day). Server maintenance: one (whenever I ask). Hits depend on seasonal and school events. So far around 50,000 to 100,000 per day. Readers are from 117 countries (as of 12/96).

You must hear from people all over the world! Can you think of an unusual request, question, or comment someone has sent to you?

The best one was sent from a boy: "I'd like to go to N.Y. and see the Statue of Liberty, the Empire State Building, and Kids' Space!" (The fact is Kids' Space is here in my small apartment. I am hoping to make Kids' Space a place worthy to visit!)

What is your favorite resource on the Net?

I don't have time to surf the Net...I should!

If this isn't your main job, what do you do, what is your training?

Educational background: MA, Ed.M in music education at Columbia U. Teachers' College. This is not my job. I'm supporting myself by writing books (in Japanese).

What's the one thing you'd really like to do on your page but have not yet implemented?

A very safe and meaningful forum where children can discuss many issues. I want to distinguish this from a chat room.

Do you have a family? A dog? A lizard?

I have a father, mother, brother, sister-in-law, nephews, and a niece in Japan. I see them once every year or two.

What are your hopes and fears for the future of the Internet?

It is the greatest tool we have ever gained in our history. Our responsibility is to use it for realizing a better world. If we do so, there would be no fears.

When you're not using the Net, what do you like to do?

If I could, I would want to have a day to lay down under the warm sun in a very comfortable cloth, with my favorite books and snacks.

If you could invite three people throughout history to your house for dinner, who would they be?

Musicians and composers: Bach, Beethoven, and Chopin!

WEATHER AND METEOROLOGY

DAN'S WILD WEATHER PAGE

Do you want to know how clouds are formed or what to do if you are caught in a lightning storm? Just see Dan! He has info on almost any weather occurrence. From hurricanes to air pressure, Dan has it covered with colorful diagrams and graphics. Teachers and parents might learn a thing or two, as well.

http://www.whnt19.com/kidwx/

Natural Disasters

This site is brought to you by a high school class on Canada's Prince Edward Island—the first ever to use the Internet there! They point you to some great natural disaster links, full of activities, pictures, and trivia on earthquakes, tornadoes, floods, and hurricanes. You could click around here for days, whether taking a virtual reality tour of Mount St. Helens at Volcano World or watching movies of hurricanes, clouds, or a space shuttle launch at NASA's Flood Management Page.

http://www.gov.pe.ca/educ/themes/disasters/
   disaster.html

NCDC Climate Visualization

Was this the rainiest April ever in your city? What was the weather like the day you were born? You're just a few clicks away from finding out, when you cruise over to the National Climatic Data Center (NCDC), the world's biggest collection of weather information. In seconds, you can create graphs showing what the weather's been like just about anytime or anywhere in the world. Some of the weather statistics go all the way back to the late 1600s.

http://www.ncdc.noaa.gov/onlineprod/drought/
   xmgr.html

USA Today WEATHER

This site is the best-kept secret on the Net for weather information! You'll find a ton of special articles, fun facts, and lots of other goodies here, from information on tornadoes and hurricanes to tips on weather forecasting. Check the index. If you have a weather-related report due or if you're just interested in things meteorological, do not miss this excellent site.

http://www.usatoday.com/weather/wfront.htm

The Weather Channel

Serious weather watchers and meteorologist wannabes should head over to the Weather Channel Home Page. Grab your own heat index or windchill charts from the Weather Whys and Teacher Resource areas at >http://www.weather.com/weather_whys/ teachers_resources/>. Find out how to become a meteorologist, a storm chaser for the National Weather Service, or even just a backyard observer. If you've still got questions about the weather, you can ask the Weather Channel meteorologists. They pick the best questions to answer online.

http://www.weather.com/

Weather Dude

"Weather Dude" Nick Walker, a weathercaster for KSTW-TV in Seattle, Washington, specializes in making weather fun for kids. Our favorite part of this site is Weather Resources for Kids, where you can download audio clips and sing along with songs from Nick's "Weather Dude: A Musical Guide to the Atmosphere." Don't miss his tips on how to get free stuff, like the Winter Survival Coloring Book and hurricane tracking charts.

http://www.nwlink.com/~wxdude/

WeatherNet

Are you tired of surfing the Internet? OK, then is it a good day for surfing in Maui? What's the latest view from above that hurricane swirling around in the Gulf of Mexico? And how does the weather look—right now—on the slopes of your favorite ski resort or on the streets of Hollywood? The answers can be found right here, along with links to over 200 great meteorology sites.

http://cirrus.sprl.umich.edu/wxnet/

A
B
C
D
E
F
G
H
I
J
K
L
M
N
O
P
Q
R
S
T
U
V
W
X
Y
Z

A
B
C
D
E
F
G
H
I
J
K
L
M
N
O
P
Q
R
S
T
U
V
W
X
Y
Z

CLOUDS
UIUC Cloud Catalog

If you can say "cumulonimbus" or "cirrostratus" and point out these kinds of clouds in the sky, you can call yourself a cloud expert! If you'd like to be one, check out the University of Illinois Cloud Catalog. There are some really great pictures to go along with all these huge words. You may be surprised to find out how much difference there is between clouds close to the ground and clouds much higher in the sky.

http://covis.atmos.uiuc.edu/guide/clouds/

NET FILES

What is the most easterly point in North America?

Answer: Cape Spear in Newfoundland, Canada. It is the site of one of Newfoundland's more than 200 lighthouses, built in the early 1800s to help transatlantic mariners and local fishermen navigate the treacherous coastline. The keeper's house at Cape Spear was constructed on top of a 300-foot sandstone cliff with a stone light tower built at its center, which anchored the house to the rock. Come visit this and other historic Newfoundland lighthouses at http://www.ucs.mun.ca/~dmolloy/lighthouse.html

HURRICANES
1997 Atlantic Tropical Season

Print out this site's handy tracking chart map and keep an eye on this year's 'canes in the Atlantic, Caribbean, Gulf of Mexico, and the eastern Pacific. See up-to-the-minute satellite pictures of tropical storms or even full-blown hurricanes. Maps of hurricane tracks are available for the past 100 years. What was happening the year you were born? This site is available in English and Spanish.

http://www.met.fsu.edu/explores/tropical.html

Miami Museum of Science - Hurricane Main Menu

During Florida's Hurricane Andrew in 1992, the Benitez family huddled together in a closet while their whole farm was destroyed in 150-mile-per-hour winds. "The part I thought was the worst was when we heard the windows break," says 11-year-old Patrick, whose family had nothing to eat for two days! Read this family's story and find out how they survived. Or maybe you'd like to try flying into the eye of a hurricane with a special, storm hunting plane. Check out Hurricane Andrew with 3-D glasses you can make, or learn how to create a model of a hurricane spiral.

http://www.miamisci.org/hurricane/

RAINBOWS
About Rainbows

The spectacular light shows known as rainbows are really just spread-out sunlight. People have been wondering about rainbows for a long time, but the first scientist to study them was René Descartes, over 350 years ago. He found out about rainbows by looking at just one drop of water and observing what happened when light fell on it. Learn all about the optics behind the magic of rainbows at this page, along with some fascinating facts. Did you know that no two people see the same rainbow? In fact, each of your two eyes sees its own rainbow!

http://www.unidata.ucar.edu/staff/blynds/rnbw.html

The Rainbow Maker Web Site Welcome to the Rainbow Maker

Meet rainbow maker Fred Stern, an artist who paints the sky! Using fire trucks or fire boats to pump water into the air, Fred only has to add sunlight to make rainbows of up to 2,000 feet across. He says if our planet had a flag it should be the rainbow, since it stands for peace and unity. To show how he feels, he recently created a rainbow over the United Nations Building that flew higher than the flags of all the nations. Want to stage a rainbow-making event in your town? Check out Fred's Web site to learn how.

http://www.zianet.com/rainbow/

SNOW

Current Snow Cover

So you think you're sick of shoveling the snow out of your parents' driveway? See where kids have it worse than you do! Check out how deep the snow is all over the U.S. today with this snow cover map. Hint: This map is very boring in the summer.

http://wxp.atms.purdue.edu/maps/surface/
  snow_cover.gif

Kids Snow Page

If you lived in the frozen North, you might have as many different words for snow as the Inuit do. There are words that mean falling snow, ground snow, smoky snow, and wind-beaten snow. Do you live in a snowy climate? Use the list of all the different kinds of snow and see how many you can find where you live. If you'd like to keep your snowflake finds, learn how you can do it with a piece of glass and some hair spray. Make an edible glacier, cut and fold paper snowflakes, and learn that soap bubbles won't pop if you blow them outside when it's –40 degrees Fahrenheit, as it is pretty often where the Teel family kids live—in Alaska.

http://www.teelfamily.com/activities/snow/

THUNDERSTORMS AND LIGHTNING

Exploring: Weather

San Francisco's Exploratorium brings you the story of lightning, chock-full of trivia that will amaze you. Did you know that a lightning bolt has enough energy to lift a 2,000-pound car 62 miles high into the air? Or that a lightning flash jumps from the ground up to a cloud at 61,000 miles per second? You won't want to miss the story of Roy "Dooms" Sullivan, a former park ranger who holds the world's record for being zapped by lightning more than any other person: seven times. Now that's an electrifying personality!

http://www.exploratorium.edu/ronh/weather/
  weather.html

NASA/MSFC/ESSD - Shuttle Observations of Lightning

Everybody's seen lightning from down here on Earth, but not many people get to see it from outer space. Lightning bounces around in some very weird ways out there. For a long time, pilots had been saying that they saw lightning that started at the tops of clouds and shot out into space, but nobody believed them. In 1989, space shuttle astronauts helped solve this mystery when they took pictures of this "vertical lightning." Check out their pictures and movies of some wild storms as seen from space.

http://wwwghcc.msfc.nasa.gov/skeets.html

NGS - Lightning: The Shocking Story

National Geographic brings you the whole shocking story of how lightning strikes the earth 100 times a second. Read the electrifying stories of what it's like to be hit by lightning from people who survived. And, when you've found out everything you've always wanted to know about lightning, take a quiz and win the hottest prize in cyberspace.

http://www.nationalgeographic.com/modules/
  lightning/1.html

Storm Chaser Warren Faidley's Homepage

Thunderstorms, monsoons, and waterspouts are all just part of the incredible day's work of photographer Warren Faidley, the world's only full-time, professional storm chaser. His storm pictures have appeared in *National Geographic* and *USA Today*, in commercials and music videos, and even in Michael Jordan's latest sports video. His severe weather slide show will amaze you!

http://www.indirect.com/www/storm5/

You Can & Thunder

Wow! That was a LOUD storm! You can come out now. Let Beakman and Jax answer your questions about thunder. What's it made of, anyway? Is it hot? Is it cold? If we could see this event, what would it look like? Try these simple experiments to help you learn more about thunder.

http://pomo.nbn.com/youcan/thunder/thunder.html

A B C D E F G H I J K L M N O P Q R S T U V W X Y Z

A
B
C
D
E
F
G
H
I
J
K
L
M
N
O
P
Q
R
S
T
U
V
W
X
Y
Z

TORNADOES

NWSFO Norman WWW Home Page - Spotter Guide

See what happens to a car during a tornado and why it's a bad idea to stay in one when these violent storms—some of them have winds of up to 300 miles per hour—come around. (Hint: The car left the ground and never came back!) The Storm Spotter's Guide explains how these long-lasting storms, called "supercell" thunderstorms, cause most of our really bad weather, including tornadoes and big hail. Learn how you can stay safe during all the different kinds of bad storms.

http://www.nssl.uoknor.edu/~nws/spotterguide.html

TSUNAMIS

Tsunamis

Tsunamis—walls of water, sometimes more than 100 feet high—are caused by earthquakes or big storms at sea. When you check out this collection of tsunami pictures, you'll see huge boats that have been thrown onto the shore like toys and amazing before-and-after pictures. See what happened to a five-story lighthouse that sat 40 feet above the sea when a tsunami came crashing ashore. Read a definition of a tsunami about one-third of the way down at >*http://www.ngdc.noaa.gov/cgi-bin/ seg/men2html?/usr/online/html/seg/menus/ slide2.men+MAIN+MENU*>. There is also a Tsunami Center at >*http://tsunami.ce.washington.edu/ tsunami/intro.html*>.

http://www.ngdc.noaa.gov/cgi-bin/seg/men2html?/
   usr/online/html/seg/menus/slide2.men+Tsunamis

WEATHER FORECASTING

Lighthouse Weather

Your picnic basket's packed, and you've got your Frisbee, but your mom's trying to make you wear your raincoat. Will it rain or not? Fast and reliable weather forecast service for 250 U.S. cities and summary data from many locations around the world are at this site. You'll need to know the airport code for the city you're interested in, but don't worry, this site has a button to locate that for you.

http://the-tech.mit.edu/Weather/

WORDS

Fake Out!

OK, give this multiple-choice quiz a try. The word "bleb" means: a) A Takis word for "blabbermouth"; b) A yellow fish with five fins and a long, blue tail; or c) The first movie that was ever on the big screen. If you said none of these, you'd be right, and you'll be a winner at this definition guessing game. The object of the game is to come up with word definitions so believable you fool other players into picking the wrong one.

http://www.hmco.com/hmco/school/dictionary/

GRY Words

Have you heard this puzzle? Quick—name three words that end in "-gry." Having a hard time? Here are a list of -gry words, but the solution to the puzzle may be that the question is just phrased the wrong way! Don't miss some possible solutions to the puzzle at Gry, Gry Everywhere and Not a Clue in Sight at >*http://www.word-detective.com/gry.html*>.

http://www.cruzio.com/~sclibs/internet/gry.html

Secret Language

Psssst! Want to send a secret message to a friend, one that nobody else can possibly decipher? Head on over to this page at San Francisco's Exploratorium, where you can print out a copy of some substitution cipher wheels. Put one inside the other, twirl them around a little bit, and you're in the spy biz!

http://www.exploratorium.edu/ronh/secret/secret.html

RAILROADS AND TRAINS are on track.

The Word Detective

This syndicated newspaper column has been running since 1953. William Morris started it, and now his son Evan does the honors. A short while after the columns run in newspapers, he posts them on this page. Morris answers readers' questions about the English language and its odd words and phrases, such as "busting chops," "lame duck," or "eyes peeled," and he does this cleverly, with wit and humor. He also has a sampling of *The Word Detective,* a newsletter that "aims for the large grey area between the *Oxford English Dictionary* and Monty Python."

http://www.word-detective.com/

Word.Net's Ambigram.Matic

It's a flipped out, backwards world at this site, the world's only ambigram generator. *Ambigrams* are words or phrases that can be read in at least two different ways, such as right side up and upside down. To find out how, cruise over to this silly site and try typing in your name.

http://ambigram.matic.com/ambigram.htm

ANAGRAMS

I, Rearrangement Servant

Do you know what an *anagram* is? Take all the letters in a word or phrase, scramble them, and come up with a new word or phrase! For example, "Inert Net Grave Near Mars" is an anagram for "Internet Anagram Server." Type in ten or less letters and see what mysterious phrase you'll get. For anagrams of more than ten letters, use the "anagram by email" service.

http://www.wordsmith.org/anagram/

Mr. Spock agrees it is highly logical to want to know all about STAR TREK, STAR WARS, AND SPACE EPICS.

MNEMONICS

The Mnemonic Number Alphabet

Mnemonics are handy little devices for jogging our memories. For example, the first letters of "My Very Educated Mother Just Served Us Nine Pickles" gives the initials, in order, of the nine planets. "Lucy Can't Drink Milk" provides the Roman numerals in order for 50, 100, 500, and 1,000. Some of these mnemonics have been helping students breeze through tests for years; now it's your turn to use them! Do you have trouble remembering dates in history class? Try the mnemonic alphabet system, which replaces numbers with consonants. Maybe you can make up some of your own, too.

http://www.curbet.com/speedlearn/chap10.html

TONGUE TWISTERS

Tongue Twisters

You'll find a couple dozen or so of these here, from the banal "How much wood could..." to the short and clever "Unique New York" and "Truly Plural." Go ahead—say them a few times.

http://www.geocities.com/Athens/8136/
   tonguetwisters.html

WRITING

For Young Writers

If you dream about writing, or if you write and you want your writing to be better or published or just appreciated by others, it's all here! Get advice from professional writers and editors. Participate in chat sessions and discussions with other young writers. Find links to other useful writing sites. Submit your work to the Young Writer's Collection for Web publication. You may even get your first, paying writing gig by visiting the Paying Markets page. Capital!

http://www.inkspot.com/~ohi/inkspot/young.html

A B C D E F G H I J K L M N O P Q R S T U V W X Y Z

A B C D E F G H I J K L M N O P Q R S T U V **W** X Y Z

Grammar and Style Notes

Are you a little shaky on the parts of speech? Can you tell a preposition from a present participle? The names may be strange, but you use these elements in everyday conversation. A *preposition* usually describes the object of the sentence and its location in time, space, or relationship to the rest of the sentence. For example, in the next sentence, the prepositions are capitalized: BEFORE the alarm rang, the cat was ON the table. A *present participle* just adds "-ing" to the rest of the verb: singing, sitting, walking. This resource teaches the parts of speech in a fun and easy way. You'll also learn about punctuation, building sentences and paragraphs, and yes—even spelling! Knowing the correct names for these grammatical terms becomes very important when you begin to learn another language. You'll want to know what the teacher means when talking about French subjunctives and superlatives!

http://www.english.upenn.edu/~jlynch/grammar.html

NET FILES

Here comes a 150-car freight train traveling at 50 mph! If the engineer suddenly slams on the brakes, how far does the train travel before it comes to a complete stop?

Answer: It can take up to 1.5 miles to stop! Even at 30 mph, the approximate stopping distance is 3,500 feet, or two-thirds of a mile! Operation Lifesaver educates adults and kids on trains and train safety. Make tracks to visit http://www.oli.org/oli/hf/factsterms.html soon.

Hop Pop Town

Precious musical games let preschoolers record a song or experiment with notes and instruments. Here's a writing activity that makes a cute, illustrated story. It's easy to use, with a little adult and kid help—the kiddos learn about music and the mouse, and the adults learn how to think more creatively!

http://www.95.interport.net/

KidPub WWW Publishing

Have you got the itch to get published? Here are 10,000 poems, stories, and more from kids your age! New stories appear every day, and yours can be one of them. The last time we checked, we saw titles such as "Great Excuses for Not Cleaning Your Room," "Being the New Kid," and "The Revenge of the Slime Monsters." This site also has a story to which you can add—it's called a collaboration!

http://www.kidpub.org/kidpub/

Kids' Space

This is every kid's home page! Do you want other kids to see your paintings? Do you want them to be able to hear you play your trombone? How about letting kids all over the world read your story or poem? Send your multimedia to this site for publication. Also, you can look for a pen pal to write to on the Internet; if you don't have a mailbox, use the bulletin board feature to let other kids know what you're thinking about, looking for, or dreaming about. Menus are in both Japanese and English.

http://www.kids-space.org/

Purdue University On-Line Writing Lab

Are those commas confusing? How about nouns, verbs, and adjectives—do they puzzle you? Are apostrophes getting you mixed up every time? And what's a preposition, anyway? Come to this writing lab to figure out how you should use all these things. Your reports, letters, and tests will look impressive!

http://owl.english.purdue.edu/

Study WEB: Punctuation and Spelling

To colon or semicolon, that is the question. For the answer, dash over here and capitalize on the grammar tips and tricks that punctuate this site. A variety of sources will help you organize your paragraphs, straighten your sentences, check your spelling, and keep those too-common commas and rogue apostrophes from running amok across the pages of your next assignment.

http://www.the-acr.com/studyweb/lit/punc.htm

Web.Kids Adventure

Write a science fiction story with up to 50 other kids. Get in on the start of a story, and you might even be the one to give it a title. Or, see how creative you can get in the actual story writing. Help to weave a tale of adventure!

http://www.hoofbeats.com/

NET FILES

What's the most visited national park in the U.S.?

(Hint: We mean national park, not national recreation area or national monument.)

Answer: *Nope, it's not the Grand Canyon in Arizona (a mere 4.5 million visitors a year). It's not Yosemite in California (a sparse 4 million tourists). And Yellowstone in Montana, Idaho, and Wyoming is way down the list (3 million), behind Olympic National Park in Washington (3.4 million). The winner is: the Great Smoky Mountains National Park in Tennessee. Nine million people a year come to see its beautiful forests and mountain vistas! Find out more parks trivia at* http://www.nps.gov/pub_aff/faqs.html

GREETING CARDS
Build a Card

Picture this: You're at school and suddenly realize today is your mom's birthday. No problemo. Just web over to this site and create a card online. Select a background, a font, and type your own message. Then mail the card to your mom's e-mail account—it will be there the next time she reads her mail. To keep your creation forever, download it as a GIF file from your browser; the directions are included on the page.

http://buildacard.com/

The Electric Postcard

Hey, it won't even cost you the price of a stamp, and you won't get writer's cramp. Instead, you can send a postcard to anyone who has an Internet address and access to the Web. First, choose a piece of art or a graphic for the front of your postcard. Then fill in your message (even links, if you want!). Type in the e-mail address where you want to send the postcard. The recipient will get a message by electronic mail, giving a code number and instructions to go to the Web site pickup window. Imagine your friends' surprise when they pick up their postcards from you!

http://postcards.www.media.mit.edu/postcards/

JOURNALS AND DIARIES
The Diary Project

Do you have fears that you don't want to discuss with anyone? Or maybe you have a secret dream that you'd like to see come true one day. You can write about these in your diary or journal; it is your personal and private business. But here at this site, kids from all over the world have decided to share their journals with you! Contribute an entry from your diary (only your first name will be used, if you wish, or you can write anonymously). Parental advisory: not all entries have been read.

http://www.well.com/user/diary/

A B C D E F G H I J K L M N O P Q R S T U V W X Y Z

A
B
C
D
E
F
G
H
I
J
K
L
M
N
O
P
Q
R
S
T
U
V
W
X
Y
Z

X-RAYS

Virtual Physics in Radiology Tutorials

Most of us have had our teeth x-rayed. That's so the dentist can "look inside" our teeth to see if any cavities are hiding there. X-rays are also used by doctors to look inside us to see if we are healthy. Did you know that x-rays are also used to check mechanical parts, such as airplane engines? Technicians can see if there are any cracks that might cause problems later on! Check out this site to discover what makes x-rays work and read about the different types of x-ray machines.

http://www.mcw.edu/medphys/html/
   virtual_learning.htm

X-Ray Tomographic Microscopy

Here's a 3-D x-ray technology that doctors and scientists use to help them look inside objects in a special way. In x-ray tomography, a series of x-rays are taken of an object. The object is moved a tiny bit between each picture. All the images are stored in a computer. The pictures from the computer can show the object from different angles. Also, it can show various depths inside the object. This can often reveal hidden information that would normally go undetected. This page describes the process in more detail and has some pictures that help show how it all works.

http://www.llnl.gov/IPandC/opportunities93/
   08-NDE/X_Ray_Tomo.shtml

> It's hard to remember, but mnemonic memory tricks are in WORDS.

YOGA

Spirituality/Yoga/Hinduism Home Page

One of the first things you will learn in yoga class, besides where to take off your shoes, is the word "namasté." Your instructor will say it to you, and you're expected to say it back. Namasté is derived from the Sanskrit word *Namaskaar*, meaning "I bow to the divine in you." Yoga is from the Sanskrit word *Yug*, meaning "union with the divine." This site is a great overview of major yogic disciplines, although it's kind of wordy. You'll also get an introduction to Hinduism and tips on learning Sanskrit.

http://www.geocities.com/RodeoDrive/1415/

Yoga Paths

Parental advisory: this site covers many spiritual topics besides yoga; you should explore this site with your child. When you think of yoga, do you think of impossible body postures and unusual breathing patterns? Maybe you think of burning incense or chanting Sanskrit mantras over and over. But yoga is less, and more, than that. Did you know there are many kinds of yoga, and the physical postures, or asanas, are only one small part? This site explains many yogic paths and provides links to Web sites that will help you choose a yoga center, if you're interested in learning more.

http://www.spiritweb.org/Spirit/Yoga/Overview.html

NET FILES

At what event were these famous firsts?

☐ George Ferris built the first Ferris wheel.

☐ The U.S. Postal Service produced the first picture postcards.

☐ Cracker Jacks were introduced.

☐ The hamburger became America's favorite fast food.

Answer: The 1893 Columbian Exposition, in Chicago, Illinois. Read more at http://users.vnet.net/schulman/Columbian/columbian.html

ZOOLOGY

Australian A to Z Animal Archive

Do you know how the kangaroo got its name? When European explorers first saw a strange animal jumping around, they asked the Aborigines what it was. The Aborigines replied, "Kangaroo," which means "I don't understand," but the Europeans thought that was the strange animal's name. Check out this site and learn about other Australian animals.

http://www.aaa.com.au/A_Z/

Internet Resource Guide for Zoology - Guide by animal group

Did you know that you're a *Homo sapiens*? That's the scientific classification name for humans. All life can be organized and classified this way, using a system of scientific naming or nomenclature. Visit the Zoological Record Home Page, where you'll find information on the ordering of organisms into groups based on their relationships. You'll find the order, class, and kingdom for everything here, from people to dinosaurs. In addition, you'll find reports containing the symbol, scientific name, common name, and family for each member of the animal kingdom.

http://www.york.biosis.org/zrdocs/zoolinfo/
     gp_index.htm

NATIONAL WILDLIFE FEDERATION

What's for lunch at the National Wildlife Federation home page? Flamingos eat algae, and that's how they get their beautiful pink coloring. Even though algae is green, it has a special chemical that turns the birds' feathers pink! Koala bears are very picky eaters. They eat only one kind of food: eucalyptus leaves. Tree squirrels eat nuts, pine cones, and other foods that they bury for winter storage. When winter arrives, they search for the food they have buried. Squirrels have an excellent sense of smell and can sniff out food that has been buried in a foot of snow! Did you know that up to 100 species become extinct every day? You can help. Visit this site and find out how you can get involved in a project or organization working to help endangered species. You may even be able to "adopt" an endangered animal.

http://www.nwf.org/nwf/

Phylum Level Index

You may know a sponge as something you use to wash your family's car, but do you know about the sponge sea animal? That's right, though it may look like a plant, the sea sponge is really an animal. Check out this site to learn all about sponges and other sea animals, such as flatworms and comb jellies. You'll also make your way to sea life with backbones, including various types of fish.

http://www.mbl.edu/html/MRC/HTML/phylum.html

MIGRATION

Journey North 1997

Can you imagine a hummingbird flying 600 miles, nonstop, in a matter of hours? It takes ships days to travel that far! These tiny birds can burn up to half their body mass making this kind of trip. Migration occurs every year with all kinds of animals (even some grandparents like to go south for the winter). Visit this site and learn about wildlife migration sightings from schoolkids around the globe.

http://www.learner.org/content/k12/jnorth/

ZOOS

The Birmingham Zoo

Look at the kudu antelope with that pair of oxpecker birds on its back. They're eating ticks and other "bugs" off of the antelope, bringing relief from an irritating source of discomfort. What's that black spot in the corner of that dik-dik's eye? It's a gland with black, sticky stuff that dik-dik antelopes rub on tree branches to mark their territory. Have you ever been on an African safari? These are some of the things you will see while taking a virtual safari through the Birmingham Zoo home page in Alabama. Have fun, and watch out for the leopards hiding in the rocks and trees!

http://www.bhm.tis.net/zoo/

A B C D E F G H I J K L M N O P Q R S T U V W X Y Z

A B C D E F G H I J K L M N O P Q R S T U V W X Y Z

DLC-ME | The Microbe Zoo

Did you know that you have a fabulous microbe zoo running wild in your yard, in your food, even on your clothes? Microbes are so small, you can't see them without a microscope, but they affect your life daily, in a big way. Zoom in on the invisible world of these small creatures and learn how they interact with the larger world around them. And don't forget to thank them for that last chocolate bar you ate or root beer you drank—they helped make it!

http://commtechlab.msu.edu/CTLprojects/dlc-me/zoo/

The Electronic Zoo

Let a veterinarian loose on the Internet, and what do you get? A Web site filled with information on all kinds of animals, plus resources on veterinary medicine, agriculture, biology, environment, and ecology—and the list goes on and on. Do you think this guy loves his job and knows his stuff? You bet!

http://netvet.wustl.edu/e-zoo.htm

Giraffe Cam

Check out the giraffes at the Cheyenne Mountain Zoo in Colorado Springs, Colorado. You can view the giraffe entrance to their giraffe house. They are normally visible from 10 A.M. to 4 P.M. (mountain time). This zoo is famous for successfully breeding giraffes in captivity!

http://c.unclone.com/zoocam.html

National Zoological Park Home Page

Admission is free. The only rule is: Don't feed the animals—and don't smudge the computer screen with your nose! Have you ever wondered what goes on behind the scenes at the National Zoo in Washington, D.C.? People, animals, and plants all play a part! How do cheetahs get their exercise at the zoo? Cheetah calisthenics! Yes, the cats actually warm up by playing ball, and then they run through a ropes course. Visit your favorite animal at the National Zoo home page, and get a behind-the-scenes look at this Web page in a "Postcards From the Net" story in this book.

http://www.si.edu/natzoo/

Rhinos and Tigers and Bears — Oh My!

What's that hippo doing with a watermelon? And why is that tiger rolling a barrel? Those are special toys and enrichment activities for the zoo animals. Find out more about animal toys and learn lots of other interesting information about the diet and conservation of the animals at the Knoxville, Tennessee Zoo.

http://loki.ur.utk.edu/ut2kids/zoo/zoo.html

ZooNet - All about Zoos!

ZooNet doesn't collect animals, they collect zoos! Their goal is to link to every zoo in the world, and so far they're doing a great job. They can link you to official home pages for private and specialized zoos or to zoo-related organizations. They also provide the latest stories on zoos in the news. Don't forget to download some animal screen savers while you're here. The animal galleries offer herds of animal photos and images for your pleasure. Also, check the endangered species info and the links to many animal pages across the Net.

http://www.mindspring.com/~zoonet/

Your report on giraffes is just about complete. It still needs some finishing touches, though. For example, it would be nice to have a picture! Hike over to the animal galleries at **ZooNet - All about Zoos!** and download or print your choice!

Marc Bretzfelder, webmaster of the National Zoo's site, all dressed up and ready to impress the animals.

"I have gone from scanning newspaper articles written by others, to setting up my own Web cam on our newborn rhino—all in a little over a year-and-a-half."

ZOOS

National Zoo Homepage
Webmaster: Marc Bretzfelder
http://www.si.edu/natzoo/

Who came up with the idea for your page or project?

I decided to start developing the zoo's Web pages early in 1995. I have gone from scanning newspaper articles written by others, to setting up my own Web cam on our newborn rhino—all in a little over a year-and-a-half.

How many people work on your pages?

Initially I was the only person working on Web pages at the zoo. Today there are five sections of the zoo's pages that are maintained by researchers and keepers: The Cheetah Conservation Station, The Migratory Bird Center, The Malaysian Elephant Satellite Tracking Project, The Golden Lion Tamarin Reintroduction Project, and The Conservation and Research Center. I get new converts all the time.

About 6,000 people come through our Web page's front door in a month.

You must hear from people all over the world! Can you think of an unusual request, question, or comment someone has sent to you?

The zoo is in Washington, D.C. The farthest location I have received mail from is New Zealand. As it worked out, two college students at Wanganui Polytechnic University are now working on graphics that will allow you to navigate the zoo's Web site from a map. This has long been a goal of mine, but I don't have the artistic ability. The Web is allowing me to collaborate with these students.

What's the one thing you'd really like to do on your page but have not yet implemented?

I want to make the site more accessible to the disabled. I want people with visual impairments to be able to hear descriptions of all of the pictures while they browse.

Do you have a family?

I don't have any pets, but I have the whole zoo to visit everyday! My wife has fish, and I will feed them when she asks me to, but I always have to bring the food to her and let her tell me how much of each type to use. It is all so confusing.

What are your hopes and fears for the future of the Internet?

My hope is that the Net will become a good medium for delivering video to everyone. My fear is that all those people trying to watch videos and other media-rich content will bring the Web grinding to a halt. Whenever I start editing a video to place on my Web site I have to remind myself that there are people with 14.4 kilobaud (and lower speed) modems out there.

If you could invite three people throughout history to your house for dinner, who would they be?

Frederick Douglass (orator and activist), Malcolm X (political leader and activist), and Albert Einstein (physicist). These men all went through terrible hardship and broke through societal and personal barriers, but still ended up changing the world with their words, thoughts, and deeds.

COUNTRIES OF THE WORLD

See also TRAVEL

Welcome to the Countries of the World!

We've found some educational, entertaining, interesting, and fun Web pages about countries of the world. Some countries have many great Web resources, while others have only brief mentions in networked reference sources.

In all cases, we thought of you at home, doing your homework and needing to find out what the flag of Latvia looks like, or the words to the national anthem of South Africa, or the major exports of Australia. So we found resources to provide that information to you. Along the way, we also found some fascinating facts and bits of trivia. Check out some of the annotations for any country, and you'll see what we mean.

We didn't look for resources on uninhabited places, such as small islands. If you're looking for the Arctic or the Antarctic, also check the "Earth Science—Land Features—Polar Regions" section of this book. If you still can't find the place you need, check some of the general resources we have listed just below, before the individual countries. The ones to check first are Yahoo! -Regional:Countries and The World Factbook Master Home Page.

Arab Countries' WWW Sites

Web pages from 21 Arab countries have been assembled here for those of you looking for information on this part of the world. Each country page has a list of links to servers around the world housing information related to that country. This site is available in English and Arabic.

http://www.liii.com/~hajeri/arab.html

ArabNet

If you need information on a country in the Middle East or North Africa, check this clearinghouse site. There are 22 countries represented and over 1,900 sites. You'll find maps and political and cultural information, plus links. They don't call this site a "magic carpet" without a reason!

http://www.arab.net/

City.Net Countries & Territories

World geography homework never had it so good! Enjoy touring the world, looking for interesting places for that class project. Inside each country page are links sorted by categories, such as country information, culture and language, maps, and travel. At the bottom of each country page is an additional choice that lists links to all the countries in the same region or continent. Happy trails.

http://www.city.net/countries/

Country Studies / Area Handbooks

Country Studies is part of a continuing series of books prepared by the Federal Research Division of the Library of Congress under the Country Studies / Area Handbook Program. This series presently contains studies of 71 countries. If you're looking for "bells and whistles," you won't find them here. What you will find is accurate and detailed historical information. Find out about the people who make up each country's society, their origins, dominant beliefs and values, and their common interests and the issues on which they are divided.

http://lcweb2.loc.gov/frd/cs/cshome.html

The Embassy Page

Countries that are friendly towards each other often set up embassies in each other's countries, to help continue their good relationships. The embassies provide a place for businesses and individuals to get accurate and authoritative information about the other country. Embassies also provide a place for their own citizens to get help when they are away from home and for travelers to get visas (entry permits, not the credit cards) to the other country. Since embassies are in the information business, they can also be a valuable resource for researching facts about their countries.

http://www.embpage.org/

Feeling a bit bogged down? Check EARTH SCIENCE and get swampwise!

K-12 Africa Guide

If you're trying to gather information for a homework assignment or a project about an African country, take a good look at this site. Find information about Africa's languages, customs, governments, environment, and people. You'll discover and learn about the heritage of the different African countries and their rich history. The Multimedia Archives offer maps, images of animals, flags, satellite images, and pictures of African face masks. This site is sure to give that extra something you need for an A in your next project.

http://www.sas.upenn.edu/African_Studies/
Home_Page/AFR_GIDE.html

Lonely Planet Online

Although this is a tourist-oriented service, Lonely Planet can be an excellent source of information about a country. They publish some of the most popular travel books in the world. You'll find facts on the environment, history, culture, and more about each of the world's countries here. Of course, since it's for tourists, there's even info on getting there, attractions, events, and travelers' reports. All this adds up to some of the best stuff for reports and homework assignments, not to mention interesting reading for that virtual trip.

http://www.lonelyplanet.com/

Multicultural Home Page

This site offers just what it says: a sampling of different cultures from all around the world. Hear Chinese folk music, or learn more about the history of the Canadian fur trade or details about historic Canadian women. How about a recipe for *brigadeiro* (a delicious Brazilian dessert) or a visit to the Taj Mahal in India? Not every country is listed here, but you'll find a good selection of diverse cultures from around the world, each listed with a color picture of the country's flag. If you haven't found the information you are looking for somewhere else, check out this site compiled by Purdue University.

http://pasture.ecn.purdue.edu/~agenhtml/agenmc/

The United Nations CyberSchoolBus: Educational Resources for Students and Teachers

It won't take you 80 days to go around the world at this site, but you'd find plenty here to keep you busy if you wanted to take that long! Besides learning all about the United Nations and how and why it began, you could learn about special celebration activities for days that are relevant to the entire world, such as World Telecommunication Day (May 17, 1997) and World Environment Day (June 5, 1997). Test your knowledge of flags with the Flag Tag game or take quizzes from Doctor Data. The City Profile section includes descriptions of 20 cities around the world and an urban fact game. The Country At A Glance section contains information about all 185 member countries of the United Nations. The Professor's global quizzes on UNESCO's World Heritage site are lots of fun, too. Periodically, the Professor goes on a seven-week tour of historically and culturally significant sites around the world. Based on the hints from the postcards, you have to figure out where the professor has been. If you uncover all seven destinations, you'll win a prize and get your name listed on the Photo Quiz site. You'll also find lots of info on Model U.N. activities here. You should also check the PBS Electronic Field Trip to the United Nations at *<http://www.pbs.org/tal/un/>*.

http://www.un.org/Pubs/CyberSchoolBus/

Virtual Tourist World Map

Virtual Tourist is a map-server front end for the WWW Consortium (W3C) Web server directory. You're first presented with a clickable world map. Pick a continent or region and zoom in to a more detailed map showing the countries. Click once more on a country, and you're off to W3C with a list of Web servers located in that country. The server may have information about that country along with other subject matter.

http://www.vtourist.com/webmap/

Wet or dry, give AMPHIBIANS a try!

W3C/ANU - Asian Studies WWW VL

The Asian branch of the World Wide Web Virtual Library at the Australian National University has, at last count, rated resources on 60 countries to search through. Links to and about all the Asian countries, from Turkey to Japan, are waiting here to be discovered. If you don't have a project that needs any of this information, browse around anyway and discover some of the exciting marvels to be found.

http://coombs.anu.edu.au/WWWVL-AsianStudies.html

WashingtonPost.com: International

Try the Search the World database to find news, reference materials, and Internet resources for more than 220 countries and territories. This is a great place to look if you need the very latest information on a country! You can type in the name of a specific country or territory or just browse the countries alphabetically. Regional sections are updated weekly, with news and features from six different regions of the world.

http://www.washingtonpost.com/
  wp-srv/inatl/front.htm

Welcome To The Environmental Atlas

Are you interested in the environment and concerned about conservation and resource depletion? So is the Green Plan Center of the Resource Renewal Institute. They have treated this environmental atlas as an Internet-based tool for researching environmental policy worldwide. The map-based atlas lets you view information about a country's environmental policies—just click on the appropriate continent. Or, you can search a text-based atlas by continent or alphabetically by country. Stop at this site for a profile of your country's major environmental problems, a brief chronology of its environmental history, and any recent policy developments. Learn if global conditions are affecting your country's environment and how it is cooperating on environmental issues with neighboring countries and the world community. Preserving our world's natural resources is a global issue.

http://www.rri.org/envatlas/

The World Clock

As you eat your breakfast cereal, you wonder what your pen pal is doing right now. What time is it where your pen pal lives, hundreds or thousands of miles away? Is it morning or is it the middle of the night? Here is a site that will answer this question for you. For more, try the Time Service Department, U.S. Naval Observatory at <http://tycho.usno.navy.mil/>. You'll find general information about time zones and telling time, and the FAQ area even has information on how to make a sundial (talk about retro!). This is one site you'll definitely want to refer to periodically.

http://www.stud.unit.no/USERBIN/steffent/
  verdensur.pl

The World Factbook Master Home Page

It's the job of the Central Intelligence Agency (CIA) to know what's going on in the world. This involves gathering information about each country's government, its people, economy, and transportation facilities, including maps of each country. They have recently redesigned their home page, and it's a winner! There is also a text-only option.

http://www.odci.gov/cia/publications/nsolo/
  wfb-all.htm

World Heritage

What do the Grand Canyon, the Galápagos Islands, Moenjodaro, Völklingen Ironworks, the Island of Gorée, and the Citadel of Haiti all have in common? Though each of these sites is located in a different part of the world, they share a common heritage as unique treasures. If environmental or political situations cause them to disappear, it would be a loss for each and every one of us. UNESCO (United Nations Educational, Scientific, and Cultural Organization) believes that preservation of this common heritage concerns us all. They have established a list of these sites, recognized as exhibiting "outstanding universal value." As of January 1, 1997, the World Heritage List included 506 cultural and natural sites. Find out if your country has any special sites on this list. Maybe your school can become part of the World Heritage Youth Project. If you want more information about UNESCO's other educational projects, try their home page at <http://www.unesco.org>.

http://www.unesco.org/whc/

Yahoo! - Regional:Countries

Brazil has its rain forests, Morocco has its desert, Chile has its mountains, and Yahoo has them all. Browse the world's countries here to your heart's content. Each country's links are sorted by up to 36 categories, such as government, health, libraries, culture, and more. Indices are also listed separately.

http://www.yahoo.com/Regional/Countries/

AFGHANISTAN

Online Concise "Encyclopedia" of Afghanistan

Civilization in Afghanistan dates back as far as 4000 B.C., and many empires have controlled this region throughout the centuries. Afghanistan became a republic in 1973, after being ruled by monarchs for over 2000 years. At this site you can check the latest news, learn about Afghan music, find information on cultural ceremonies, read historical facts, dream about some savory foods, and more!

http://frankenstein.worldweb.net/afghan/

ALBANIA

Albanian Home Page

Albania's rugged mountains have earned it a reputation as a remote and mysterious country. The Albanian language is one of the oldest original languages in Europe. Albania was home to Mother Teresa, a nun who became famous throughout the world for her humanitarian efforts towards the poor and was awarded the Nobel Peace Prize. At this site, you can learn all sorts of facts about Albania, the country, and Albanians, the people.

http://www.albanian.com/main/

ALGERIA

Miftah Shamali- Algeria

Algeria's earliest known inhabitants were Berber ancestors. France controlled the country from 1830 until 1962. The government and economy have been struggling to stabilize since its independence. Today, Algeria is a country of curfews and unrest, and foreigners are advised against travel there. Still, you can learn a lot about this North African country.

http://i-cias.com/m.s/algeria/

NET FILES

Dad says I can eat dessert first "once in a blue moon." What's a blue moon, and when is the next one?

Answer: Calendar months are either 30 or 31 days long; the lunar month is 29 1/2 days. So every now and again, there are two full moons in the same month. The second full moon in the same month is called a blue moon. Go to http://www.ast.cam.ac.uk/~adh/astro/bluemoon.html to calculate blue moons in a given year (there will be two blue moons in 1999, and none before then). But remember to correct for time zones—this site is in the United Kingdom. According to them, there was a blue moon in 1996 (full moons on July 1 and 30); but in the U.S., the two full moons were on June 1 and 30! See the time zone explanation at http://www.earthsky.com/1996/es960630.html

Ships are only hulls, high walls are nothing, When no life moves in the empty passageways. —Sophocles

ANDORRA

Andorra Central - All About Andorra

The principality of Andorra is a small country situated between France and Spain, in the Pyrenees Mountains. Its size is about half that of New York City! Skiing is by far the most popular industry there, and the abundant wildlife and natural beauty make it an outdoor enthusiast's paradise. At this page you will also find links to the official government Web pages and others, but many did not have English versions when we checked. This page is available in English, Castellano, Català, and French.

http://www.xmission.com/~dderhak/andorra.htm

ANGOLA

Welcome to the Official Home Page of the Republic of Angola

A colony of Portugal for 400 years, Angola gained its independence in 1975. Situated in equatorial Africa, Angola is rich in oil, gold, and other resources. Portuguese is the official business and international language, but Angola also has six national languages: Kikongo, Kimbundo, Umbundu, Chokwe, Mbunda, and Oxikuanyama. Political unrest has prevented development; according to the information here, the humanitarian crisis is still acute in Angola, and the United Nations and Red Cross relief efforts continue to help. In February 1997, Princess Diana of Great Britain visited Angola as a Red Cross volunteer. She focused world attention on the deadly legacy of years of military activity in the region: buried and forgotten land mines. Children and adults step on these hidden explosive mines and are sometimes killed or horribly maimed. A movement to demine the landscape is in progress, but the process is slow and the number of hidden mines is unknown.

http://www.angola.org/

DINOSAURS are prehistoric, but they are under "D."

ANGUILLA

Anguilla's Home Page

This small British dependency is located at the northern end of the Leeward Islands in the Caribbean Sea. It was discovered by Christopher Columbus in 1493 and was formerly the British colony administered as Saint Kitts-Nevis-Anguilla. In 1982, Anguilla became a separate British dependent territory. Anguilla has beautiful island scenery with lots of beaches and coral reefs that are great for snorkeling. Stay away from the manchineel trees (the ones with the green apples). The sap can burn and irritate the skin. Check the cool sound samples of Anguilla's country, rap, and reggae stars!

http://galaxy.cau.edu/Anguilla/anguilla.html

ANTARCTICA

See EARTH SCIENCE—LAND FEATURES—POLAR REGIONS

ANTIGUA AND BARBUDA

Antigua & Barbuda Official Travel Guide

These two West Indies islands are located about 400 kilometers southeast of Puerto Rico. Barbuda is known for its fantastic scuba diving, among other things. Most Antiguans are of African heritage, descendants of slaves brought to the island centuries ago to work the sugarcane fields owned by a British developer. According to the information on this page, "Antigua's history of habitation extends as far back as two and a half millenia before Christ. The first settlements...were those of the Siboney (an Arawak word meaning 'stone-people')...whose beautifully crafted shell and stone tools have been found at dozens of sites around the island."

http://www.interknowledge.com/antigua-barbuda/

Don't be irrational; check on the numbers in MATH AND ARITHMETIC.

ARGENTINA

Argentina!

At this site, you'll get facts on Argentina, nicely presented, and links to other regions, cities, and Internet resources. You might also like the virtual tour and other information presented at the official Secretaria de Turismo site at <*http://turismo.gov.ar/g/menu.htm*>. One of the interesting tidbits concerns the origin of the name Argentina. It comes from the Latin *argentum,* which means "silver." According to this page, "The origin of the name goes back to the voyages made by the first Spanish *conquistadores* (conquerors) to the Río de la Plata (Silver River). The shipwrecked survivors of the expedition mounted by Juan Díaz de Solís discovered Indians in the region who presented them with silver objects. The news about the legendary Sierra del Plata, a mountain rich in silver, reached Spain around 1524."

http://www.middlebury.edu/~leparc/htm/argent2.htm

Lonely Planet - Destination Argentina

This South American country is home to *los Gauchos*—Argentinian cowboys. Argentinians eat a lot of beef per person compared to the rest of the world, so they have many ranches to raise lots of cattle. Argentina is also known for the famous Latin dance, the tango! At this site, you can learn about the history, culture, music, and people of Argentina.

http://www.lonelyplanet.com/dest/sam/argie.htm

ARMENIA

Armenian Sites

This is a nicely designed jumpstation to many Armenian links on the Net, most of which we have not checked. You'll find a pilaf of information here, including an online Armenian songbook with MIDI audio files, a link to the Armenian national figure skating team, and even how to plan a memorable Armenian wedding! Traditionally, after the wedding, the bride was led to the groom's family's house: "At the door of the house, sweets, candles, and small coins were showered over the heads of the newlyweds from the roof to bring them a sweet life. At times, wheat was thrown to bestow fertility and prosperity. On the threshold, the couple was met by the groom's mother, who danced around them three times and offered a pot of butter, so that by her arrival in the house, butter in the household should always increase. The bride dropped a coin in the pot and slightly oiled her mother-in-law's hair with butter as a sign of her willingness to always obey her. She declined to cross the threshold until her mother gave her a present, and then broke a clay plate with one kick. Then, the bride was considered to have entered the house for good."

http://www1.shore.net/~narbey/armen/armen.html

NET FILES

Can you really hear dawn break or listen to the Aurora Borealis?

Answer: Sure, you can. You can download these unusual .wav files at http://www-pw.physics.uiowa.edu/mcgreevy/ *The sounds we are most familiar with vibrate air molecules, which in turn set our eardrums in motion so that we can hear. But natural radio waves are vibrations of electric and magnetic energy instead of air, so they cannot be "heard" without an audio-frequency ELF-VLF radio receiver to convert them. Some of these "natural radio" sounds are collected here.* To learn how to set up a Dawn Chorus Patrol listening team in your school, travel to http://www.gsfc.nasa.gov/education/inspire/listening_program.html

ARUBA

Aruba - Official Travel Guide

Aruba is a small, desertlike island just off the coast of Venezuela. Aruba is part of the Dutch realm. Formerly part of the Netherlands Antilles, Aruba was on its way to independence. However, in 1990, Aruba requested and received cancellation of the Netherlands' agreement to give independence to the island in 1996. Aruba's official language is Dutch. Its 85-degree weather and white sand beaches make it a favorite vacation spot. If you like sailing, scuba diving, or windsurfing, you'll love Aruba.

http://www.interknowledge.com/aruba/

AUSTRALIA

Cocos Island2

A giant palm tree welcomes you to this Australian tropical paradise in the Indian Ocean. Residents voted to become part of Australia's Northern Territory in 1984. Cocos Islands (sometimes called the Keeling Islands) are two atoll groups containing 27 islands. Details about seven of the islands are included at this site. West Island (Pulu Panjang) is the largest island in the territory and features the only airstrip. Direction Island (Pulu Tikus) was once the communications base for the linking of an undersea telegraphic cable linking Cocos with Cottesloe in Western Australia, Singapore, and South Africa. Watch out for the shipwrecks on the shark-infested reef around Horsburgh Island (Pulu Luar), and find out why North Keeling (Pulu Kiling) is the only island in the Cocos group that is in its original condition (just as it was when it was discovered in 1609), and why women are not allowed to visit it.

http://www.bs.ac.cowan.edu.au/IOTO/
    IOTO_COCOS/Cocos.htm

Guide to Australia

This is your jumpstation to facts on Australia and all its regions. Australia is the smallest continent but the sixth largest country. Australia's coat of arms features a shield containing the badges of the six Australian states. Supporting the shield on either side are a kangaroo and an emu. In the foreground are the yellow flowers of Australia's native wattle, also called acacia. Many unusual animals inhabit Australia, including the koala and platypus.

http://www.csu.edu.au/education/australia.html

Lonely Planet -- Destination Australia

Lonely Planet, which publishes a travel book series, is based in Australia. So you might guess that they would create a terrific page about their home country—and they have! Here you will find photos and general information on Aussie government, culture, environment, and tourist destinations.

http://www.lonelyplanet.com/dest/aust/aus.htm

Ships On Stamps (Ayesha)

Here is a short bit of history illustrated by a souvenir sheet of stamps issued by the Cocos Islands (part of Australia's Northern Territory) in 1989. The *Ayesha* was a three-masted schooner commandeered by German soldiers from Port Refuge after their ship, *Emden,* was attacked and captured by the Australian cruiser *Sydney* during World War I. It's a great story; read about it here. If you are a stamp collector or you have a passion for ships and boats of all kinds, be sure to try the top level site at <*http://saturn.sron.ruu.nl/ ~erikp/stamps.html*> to see how "the history of water transport mirrors that of mankind itself." This site's really cool!

http://www.sron.ruu.nl/~erikp/ayesha.html

Find historic documents and spell-check them for fun in HISTORY.

Whooooooo will you find in BIRDS?

AUSTRIA
Austrian National Tourist Office

This site is the Austrian National Tourist Board's North American edition. If you want to see another edition, just follow the handy link they have provided. Austria is rich with tradition. It was the home of Mozart, who created his first symphony when he was a boy. Austria is well known as the setting for the movie *The Sound of Music,* and the Austrian Alps are a famous place for skiing and outdoors adventure. This site has tourist-type info, as you might imagine. If you're looking for facts for your report, try the World Factbook page on Austria at <http://www.odci.gov/cia/publications/nsolo/factbook/au.htm>.

http://www.anto.com/

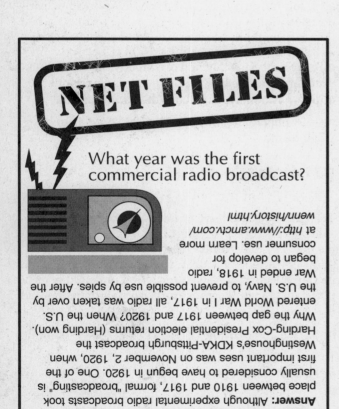

NET FILES

What year was the first commercial radio broadcast?

Answer: Although experimental radio broadcasts took place between 1910 and 1917, formal "broadcasting" is usually considered to have begun in 1920. One of the first important uses was on November 2, 1920, when Westinghouse's KDKA-Pittsburgh broadcast the Harding-Cox Presidential election returns (Harding won). Why the gap between 1917 and 1920? When the U.S. entered World War I in 1917, all radio was taken over by the U.S. Navy, to prevent possible use by spies. After the War ended in 1918, radio began to develop for consumer use. Learn more at http://www.amctv.com/wenn/history.html.

AZERBAIJAN
The AZERBAIJAN Pages

Once part of the Roman Empire and later conquered by the Turks, Azerbaijan became part of the Soviet Union in 1922. It became an independent country in 1991 when the Soviet Union broke up, but the country is torn by political unrest. The World Factbook page of Azerbaijan is at <http://www.odci.gov/cia/publications/nsolo/factbook/aj.htm>.

http://www.friends-partners.org/oldfriends/azerbaijan/

BAHAMAS
Bahamas On-Line

The Bahamas refers to a group of 700 islands located off the peninsula of Florida. Of these, only 40 are inhabited! The Bahamas boasts the world's third largest barrier reef, built up from thousands of years of coral deposits. And there's more: you'll even find pine forests and limestone caves on some islands. The Morton Salt Company operates a salt factory on Inagua, producing over a million pounds of salt a year. Check out Abaco, where Disney is building a "fantasy island" for its new cruise ships to visit. If you want to learn how to take a vacation without impacting Mother Earth very much, look at the Eco-Bahamas area of this site for ecotourism ideas.

http://www2.bahamasnet.com/bn/bnhome.html

BAHRAIN
BAHRAIN

Bahrain is a group of 33 islands on the west side of the Persian Gulf. Of these islands, most are uninhabited except for the largest, also called Bahrain. Bahrain, once known as Dilmun, was a popular regional trading center as far back as 2000 B.C. Today, it's a well-developed country with a low crime rate and stable economy.

http://copper.ucs.indiana.edu/~hqasem/bahrain/

Take a ride on a Carousel in AMUSEMENT PARKS.

Lost your marbles? Find them in GAMES AND FUN.

BANGLADESH
Bangladesh: Bangladesh

Bangladesh is a tropical country of hot, humid summers. This is the "Land of Bengal Tiger." A major feature of this country is a large delta into which the Brahmaputra, Ganges, and Meghna Rivers empty into the sea. The delta forms a large, fertile area that is rich in farmland. The heavy rains that fall during the monsoon season make this country one of the rainiest locations on Earth. In 1971, there was a war for independence between the Bengalis and the Pakistanis; over 10,000 Bengalis were killed (this site has disturbing photos in the Holocaust Museum). On the lighter side, you can try some online Bangla language lessons and get recipes for Bangladeshi Egg Haloa (a dessert) and Sandesh (it means "good news"), which is prepared by many Bengali families to celebrate good news or festivals.

http://axe.asel.udel.edu/~kazi/bangladesh/bd.html

BARBADOS
Barbados Tourism Encyclopedia

The Portuguese and Spanish traveled to this island as early as the 1500s in search of gold. However, no permanent settlements were there until the English arrived in 1625. Sugar production became the island's main industry. The work was done by slaves, starting in the 1630s, and the first slaves were white indentured servants who had somehow displeased the Crown and were "Barbadoed" from Britain. Barbados gained its independence from England in 1966. Read the story of various "landslips" that have occurred there, when movements of the earth have swallowed up houses and windmills: <http://www.mtt.net/axses/diduknow.htm>.

http://www.barbados.org/

The wonderful world of worms may be admired in the section called INVERTEBRATES.

BELARUS
Belarus

Belarus is an ancient country situated between Poland and Russia. Its western border is about 300 miles east of Moscow. The region was occupied by Slavic tribes back as far as the first century. According to this site's history area, "The name Belarus means 'white Rus,' and there's still no exact version of its origin. Some historians believe that 'white' in old Slavic languages meant 'free,' pointing to the fact that Belarus was never invaded by the Tatars or under their control, unlike the other principalities later in the 13-15th centuries. Others think that this name is older and served as a difference between Kievan Rus—Black Rus—a small territory in the western part of modern Belarus, and the territory known as White Rus." You'll also find information here on the Chernobyl nuclear disaster. Although Chernobyl is in the Ukraine, when the plant exploded on April 26, 1986, the winds took 70 percent of the radioactive dust over Belarus, causing problems that still exist today. Note that this is not an official page, and many strong opinions are expressed by the scientists who maintain it.

http://freedom.ncsa.uiuc.edu/~zelenko/belarus/
   Belarus.html

BELGIUM
THE BELGIAN MONARCHY

Take a look at the curriculum vitae (that's Latin for "life's work") of King Albert II of Belgium. You'll see it's not easy to become a king, but, then again, the perks of the job are probably really great! The Belgian monarch's position is well respected in Belgium, as he is responsible for keeping the country independent and free.

http://belgium.fgov.be/Engels/417/41709/41709.htm

Belgium: Overview

Belgium has the world's finest lace and the world's l4th largest port, Antwerp, which is called the diamond capital of the world. Belgium is the largest producer of azalea plants, cobalt, radium, and cotton thread and has one of the largest glass industries in the world. Its capital, Brussels, is also the headquarters of the European Commission and therefore is the administrative capital of Europe.

http://pespmc1.vub.ac.be/Belgcul.html

BELIZE

Lonely Planet - Destination Belize

Belize was once part of the 4,000-year-old Mayan empire. It was taken over by the Spanish in the sixteenth century and then by Britain in the nineteenth century. Belize gained its independence from Britain in 1981. Along Belize's coast are numerous cays, islands, atolls, beaches, and the longest barrier reef in the Western Hemisphere. What this really means is that there are more water-related activities available than you can imagine. You'll find more information at The Belize Virtual Guide Home Page at <http://www.belizenet.com/guide.html>.

http://www.lonelyplanet.com.au/dest/cam/belize.htm

NET FILES

Who can become a ham?

Do you copy?
http://www.acs.ncsu.edu/HamRadio/FAQ/
your questions about amateur radio, tune in to
even from your home. To find out the answers to all
That's right, you can broadcast your own radio signals,
commonly used to refer to an amateur radio operator.
in the pen, of course. But you can too! "Ham" is a word
Answer: Well, Penelope Pig and all of her friends out

BENIN

Benin Page

Benin is a small country on the west coast of Africa and is about the size of the state of Pennsylvania. It has undergone many changes in government since the French colonized it in the early 1700s. Previously known as Dahomey, it was also once part of French West Africa. Dahomey gained its independence from France in August 1960, and it has since changed its name to the People's Republic of Benin. Although the official language is French, over half the 4.5 million people speak Fon. Learn to say "good morning" in Fon: *AH-FON Ghan-Jee-Ah*. You'll find more handy phrases at this site!

http://www.sas.upenn.edu/African_Studies/
    Country_Specific/Benin.html

BERMUDA

Bermuda Background: Index of all Bermuda Online's files

Bermuda is a group of islands almost 600 miles east of North Carolina and 700 miles south of Nova Scotia. It was discovered by accident in 1503 by Juan de Bermudez, a Spanish navigator. However, Bermuda wasn't colonized until the British Admiral Sir George Somers wrecked his ship there in 1609. This became the first permanent settlement. One of the "castaways" from the wreck was John Rolfe, who later became the husband of Pocahontas. Today, the islands officially have the dual name of Somers Isles and Bermuda. This page is changing providers, so if it is not working, try the Bermuda Pages at <http://www.fes.uwaterloo.ca/u/kmayall/Bermuda/>. The Bermuda Pages have recipes and a PG-rated "Bermewjun Vurds Dicshunairy," among other things.

http://www.bermuda-online.com/

Salute the nations of cyberspace in FLAGS.

Visit historic sites via the Net in HISTORY.

BHUTAN

Bhutan homepage

Bhutan means "Land of the Thunder Dragon." It gets its name from the severe storms that come down from the Himalayas at the northern part of the country. Bhutan is a monarchy that gained its independence from India in 1949. It is an isolated country that tends to resist influences from the outside world; in fact, it limits the number of tourists to only 4,000 per year to help keep itself separated from the rest of the world. More Bhutan links are collected at <http://www.poi.net/~bhutan/bhutan.htm> and there is a nice map at <http://www.wellmet.or.jp/~mi_koba/bhutan_e.html>.

http://www.justnet.or.jp/ebf/uhdsppag/benjamin/
   BHUTAN_E.HTM

BOLIVIA

The Bolivian Home Page in South Africa

The Andes Mountains dominate the western part of Bolivia. They contain three of the highest mountain peaks in South America. Lake Titicaca, on the western border, is the highest commercially navigable lake in the world, at 12,506 feet above sea level. The 12,000-foot central plateau puts a large portion of this country higher than many of the rest of the world's mountains! This Web page has some info of its own and links to other pages about Bolivia, including a quick guide to Quechua, language of the Incas. For example, *K-MartMAN riyku* means "We have gone to K-Mart"!

http://ufrmsa1.olivetti.za/~ivan/bolivia.html

Lonely Planet - Destination Bolivia

Visit Bolivia, the "Tibet of the Americas"! It's also a great place to see wildlife. Some of the animals you might see there include the spectacled bear, jaguar, vicuña, llama, alpaca, anteater, tapir, capybara, turtle, alligator, rhea, and condor. Bolivia's La Paz is the highest capital city in the world (11,929 feet). Did you ever wonder about the bowler hats the Bolivian women wear? According to this source, the hats are worn on the side if they're single and on top if they're married.

http://www.lonelyplanet.com.au/dest/sam/bolivia.htm

BOSNIA AND HERZEGOVINA

The Bosnian Virtual Fieldtrip

Take this multimedia tour and learn a lot more about the country and why it is split along ethnic lines. This is more of a tutorial than a field trip, since they keep asking you to write paragraphs and answer questions, but it is a good way to learn about the history of the conflicts and the hope for their peaceful resolution.

http://geog.gmu.edu/gess/jwc/bosnia/bosnia.html

Information on History of Bosnia-Herzegovina

Once ruled by Croatian kings, Hungary, the Turks, Austria-Hungary, and Yugoslavia, Bosnia has undergone a long history of change. In recent years, Muslims, Croats, and Serbs have sought to gain control of the country. This continues today with clashes between the Serbs and Muslim-Croat confederation. This site puts the country's history at your fingertips.

http://www.cco.caltech.edu/~bosnia/history/
   history.html

BOTSWANA

Botswana Page

This southern African country is about the size of Texas. Botswana's early inhabitants were Bushmen and Bantus. It became the British protectorate of Bechuanaland in 1886, but the name Botswana was adopted when it gained its independence in 1966. There's some good information about Botswana's national parks and natural features at <http://www.africa.com/~venture/africa/south/btsw/btsw.htm> and don't miss *National Geographic*'s virtual visit to the Okavango River delta to see animals of swamp and savannah at <http://www.nationalgeographic.com/modules/okavango/index.html>.

http://www.sas.upenn.edu/African_Studies/
   Country_Specific/Botswana.html

Watch your step in DANCE.

BRAZIL

BRAZIL - EMBRATUR - Brazilian Tourist Web

Brazil is the fifth largest country in the world. Within its borders lies the Amazon jungle, the largest tropical rain forest in the world. The Amazon's trees are the world's largest source of oxygen. São Paulo and Rio de Janeiro are two of the ten most populated cities in the world. Rio was a candidate to host the Summer Olympics in 2004 but did not make it to the list of finalists (Athens, Buenos Aires, Cape Town, Rome, and Stockholm); read more at <http://www.rio2004.br/>. You can look at Rio's wonderful plans, their logo and pin designs, and more, should their bid be successful in 2001 for the 2008 games!

http://www.embratur.gov.br/

Meu Brasil by Sergio Koreisha

This is a lovingly crafted page about a country that is so large it touches almost all the other countries in South America. This site has tons of unchecked links! If you just want Brazil in a nutshell, go to <http://darkwing.uoregon.edu/~sergiok/brasilnutshell.html>; you'll love the collection of facts here.

http://darkwing.uoregon.edu/~sergiok/brasil.html

Welcome to Brazil.Web

This is another jumpstation to info on Brazilian culture, history, and education. Learn about Capoeira, a ritualized martial art combined with dance and music, as well as samba schools and their eagerly awaited thematic parades at Carnival.

http://www.escape.com/~jvgkny/Brasil.Web.html

BRITISH VIRGIN ISLANDS

The British Virgin Islands Welcome On-line Tourist Guide

This group of about 50 islands is located about 60 miles east of Puerto Rico. Its subtropical climate and island environment make the British Virgin Islands a popular tourist resort. All the islands are volcanic except Anegada, which is a coral and limestone atoll. Read about the history, the shipwrecks, the snorkeling, and all the fun you can have if you go! You might also like The British Virgin Islands' Home Page at <http://www.britishvirginislands.com/>.

http://bviwelcome.com/

BRUNEI

Lonely Planet -- Destination: Brunei

Brunei was once a powerful country, with Borneo and part of the Philippines under its control. The British were largely responsible for shrinking Brunei's territory since their arrival in the seventeenth century. Oil was discovered there in 1929. A revolt in 1962 eventually led to its independence in 1984. Today, this Muslim country (properly called Negara Brunei Darussalam), although rich from its oil exports, is isolated and underdeveloped.

http://www.lonelyplanet.com/dest/sea/brunei.htm

BULGARIA

Frequently Asked Questions about Bulgaria

Bulgaria is located south of Romania on the Black Sea. Its early ancestry started with the Slavs in the sixth century. In the seventh century, the Turkic Bulgars began their influence in the region and founded empires through the twelfth century. The Ottomans ruled for 500 years beginning in the late 1300s. Bulgaria became independent in 1908, but the Communists took power in the 1940s and abolished the monarchy. Since 1990, the Communist party has lost control of the government. This site offers everything from history to music, from how to make delicious baklava to Bulgarian holidays.

http://www.cs.columbia.edu/~radev/cgi-bin/bgfaq.cgi

BURKINA FASO

Burkina Faso Page

The Mossi tribe were the earliest settlers in this West African country as early as the eleventh century. After changing control with the Mali and Songhai empires over the centuries, France took control of the area in 1896. The region became known as Upper Volta in 1947 and gained its independence in 1960. It was renamed Burkina Faso in 1984. Most workers today are farmers, and many of them migrate to neighboring Ghana and Côte d'Ivoire every year to find additional work because of the poor farming conditions in their own country, due to drought.

http://www.sas.upenn.edu/African_Studies/
 Country_Specific/Burkina.html

BURMA

See MYANMAR (BURMA)

BURUNDI

Burundi Page

Burundi is a small country in central Africa on the northeast shore of Lake Tanganyika, the second deepest lake in the world. Coffee is Burundi's major export, so its economy is largely dependent on good weather and the international coffee market.

http://www.sas.upenn.edu/African_Studies/
Country_Specific/Burundi.html

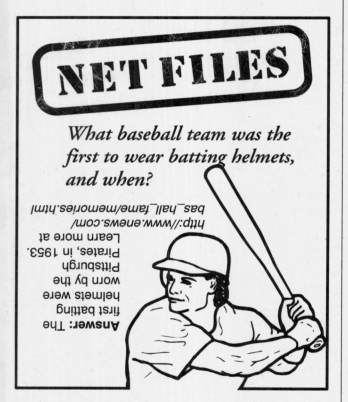

NET FILES

What baseball team was the first to wear batting helmets, and when?

Answer: The first batting helmets were worn by the Pittsburgh Pirates, in 1953. Learn more at http://www.enews.com/bas_hall_fame/memories.html

Do you know the way to San Jose? If not, check a map in GEOGRAPHY.

CAMBODIA

.asiatour / Welcome To Cambodia

This site offers fun and interesting information about the country of Cambodia and its climate, geography, and people. The photo gallery is a great way to learn the history of the country. You'll see Cambodian houses on stilts at Lake Tonle Sap—similar to those built by ancient civilizations dating back to 4000 B.C. Learn about ancient temples, royal palaces, and examples of how the French colonists influenced Cambodian architecture and culture. This site is available in English and German.

http://www.asiatour.com/cambodia/content1.htm

Lonely Planet -- Destination: Cambodia

Imagine being a teenager with the responsibility of ruling a whole country. That is what happened in 1941, when the French installed 19-year-old Prince Sihanouk on the Cambodian throne. King Sihanouk ruled this war-torn country up through 1995 and is now referred to as the Father of Cambodia. This is a great place to look for quick facts-at-a-glance about the history, culture, economy, and environment of Cambodia, along with a photo slide show. The map of the country clearly shows the major mountain ranges surrounding Cambodia on three sides, its only major port of Kampot in the south, and the dominant influence of the waters of the Mekong and Tonle Sap Rivers. You can go to the Royal Palace in Phnom Penh or to the Khmer temples of Angkor Wat with just one click of your mouse. Then be sure to read the nation's daily online newspaper, Cambodian Times, at *<http://www.jaring.my/at-asia/camb_at_asia/camb_times/ct_list.html>* for the latest news and current happenings.

http://www.lonelyplanet.com.au/dest/sea/camb.htm

Curl up with a good Internet site.

CAMEROON
The Home Page of the Republic of Cameroon

Cameroon is sometimes referred to as the hinge point of West and East Africa, since historically it has been a meeting place for diverse people and civilizations. Go to this page for information from Cameroonians about the Republic of Cameroon, its geography, its people and their warmth and friendliness, its government, its economy, its cultures and traditions, and its diversity of folklore. Listen to a MIDI version of the Cameroon national anthem. Be sure to check the Stepping Disks for some interesting links to other related sites, including a great large-scale map of Cameroon and sound clips of Cameroon music. You'll also find pictures of Cameroon's active volcano and its six national parks, where tourists can take pictures of Derby elan, rhinos, giraffes, and elephants in their natural habitat.

http://www.compufix.demon.co.uk/camweb/

CANADA
1996 Virtual Explorers Guide

This site takes you to Canada's Northwest Territories, which encompasses one-third of the land mass of Canada, about 1.3 million square miles. It is a land firmly rooted in the cultural past and old traditions of the Inuit, Inuvialuit, Dene, and Metis; it is a land of adventure and exploration, where some of the wildlife and scenery is like nowhere else on earth.

http://www.edt.gov.nt.ca/guide/index.html

Alberta's Endangered Species

Logging, oil and gas exploration, and other human activities have endangered many animal and plant species in Canada. The province of Alberta is passing legislation that will set aside portions of its six diverse natural regions (mountain, foothill, boreal, shield, parkland, and grassland) in order to protect endangered species. Each of these six habitats is mapped out and explained, with a fact file and photo of the 12 Alberta species that are most in danger of becoming extinct. There are links to articles that define the difference between the terms extinct, extirpated, endangered, threatened, and vulnerable. Be sure to follow the link to the World Wildlife Fund of Canada, where you can search by province for fact sheets with lots more information on other Canadian and international endangered species.

http://www.afternet.com/~teal/species.html

The British Columbia Wilderness - BC Adventure Network

Here you can venture into the beautiful and fascinating wilderness areas of British Columbia and learn about the creatures that inhabit its forests and coasts. From badgers to wolverines, bald eagles to wood ducks, from Alpine fir to yellow cedar, practically everything you might want to know about the animals, birds, fish, forests, and wildflowers of this Canadian province is all right here. You can learn how to tell the difference between a bobcat and its larger cousin, the lynx. Peer into the eyes of the great horned owl. Wade right in and take a look at some weird-looking fish that you may never have seen before. If you're more of a land rover, learn to identify the wildflowers and plants that paint this Canadian province with such spectacular color.

http://bcadventure.com/adventure/wilderness/

The Canada Flag

The beaver is the largest rodent in Canada. Beavers have played a significant role in the country's history and economic development. Hudson's Bay Company honored the furry little animal by putting it on the shield of its coat of arms in 1678. The beaver did attain official status as an emblem of Canada on March 24, 1975, but it didn't make it as the preferred symbol for Canada's distinct national flag (the maple leaf won out). This site presents a complete history of the first Canadian flags representing the alternating French and British colonization of Canada, right up through the lengthy debate and final selection of the single maple leaf design of the present national flag. Be sure to look at the National Archives to see sample drawings and flag suggestions that didn't get selected: <*http://www.archives.ca/www/ex/flag/ examp_e.htm*>. In About Canada, you'll also find flag etiquette rules and information about the origin of the name Canada and other national symbols.

http://canada.gc.ca/canadiana/flag_e.html

> **SLIME is a polymer, as anyone who's read CHEMISTRY knows!**

First Nations in Canada

Imagine yourself living thousands of years ago. You're traveling across a land bridge from Asia to North America and coming into the vast wilderness we now know as Canada. Maybe you would have hunted buffalo, moving your tipi and following the herds as they crossed the plains. Maybe you would have established a permanent village along the Pacific coast and fished for salmon and whales. Read all about the six distinct Canadian Indian cultures and the main tribes in each. Find out how they lived and hunted, what their dwellings looked like, and what they wore. This site takes you through the centuries of change the native populations have experienced, including progress in the last 30 years. This site is available in English and French.

http://www.inac.gc.ca/pubs/indian/

GHOSTS OF THE KLONDIKE GOLD RUSH - Home Page

It's 1898, and we're going to join the 100,000 others stampeding toward Canada's mysterious Yukon hoping to fulfill their dreams. We've survived avalanches and beat starvation, and we've made it as far as Dawson City. Now we're ready to pan for gold and strike it rich! You may not find "real" gold here, but you'll pick up nuggets of fact and fiction about this memorable time in history. Find out what motivated some of these prospectors by hearing what the grandchildren of a Klondike stampeder have to say.

http://www.gold-rush.org/

Take a closer look through the microscope in BIOLOGY.

Hinterland Who's Who index

Lemmings—those are cute little computer game characters who run up and down hills and in and out of caves, right? Better check out this site! Real lemmings are mouselike rodents that live in the treeless areas of northern Canada. They are a very important species in Arctic ecosystems. The curious thing is that lemming populations fluctuate drastically, peaking about every four years and then crashing almost to extinction. One of the Inuit names for the collared lemming is *kilangmiutak*, which means "one who comes from the sky." Read about this Indian legend and the various theories on the rise and fall of the lemming population as well as interesting information about more than 80 other animals native to Canada's hinterlands. Put on your snowshoes and follow the animal tracks across northern Canada.

http://www.ec.gc.ca/envcan/eng_ind.html

Leo Ussak Elementary School

These kids go to a cool school—we really mean it's cool there. This school is way up north. They live in the Northwest Territories, above the 60th parallel. At this site, you can learn about Inuktitut, the language of the Inuit people, and you can get a lot of information about what life is like in an Arctic village. Although the school is very Net-savvy (read about how they videoconference with a school in Hawaii) and modern, they honor the elders and their traditional ways; you'll find a good deal of cultural information here. For example, what kinds of foods do kids eat there? "Here in Rankin Inlet you can eat caribou (a lean, nutritious, delicious meat), delectable arctic char, lake trout, or grayling. In the fall you can pick ripe, juicy berries growing all over the tundra. You can sample seal, mukta (yes it's true, Inuit do consider it a delicacy to eat whale blubber!) and goose. You can also have a Pizza Hut pizza or Kentucky Fried Chicken if you want!" And how do people sleep when the sun stays above the horizon all "night"? "On June 21st, it is light almost all of the time. People sometimes put cardboard, plastic garbage bags or aluminum foil on their windows to help make it dark enough to sleep. It is darkest on December 21st when the sun rises at 9:45 in the morning and goes down at 2:45 in the afternoon. Sleeping is no problem then!"

http://www.arctic.ca/LUS/

The National Anthem of Canada

This resource is a music and history lover's delight. Not only do you get the official lyrics and sheet music for "O, Canada," Canada's national anthem, but you can also listen to the music, too. Then you can read the full history of this anthem, from its beginnings as a patriotic poem written by Sir Adolphe-Basile Routhier to when it was put to music by Calixa Lavallée in 1880. "O, Canada" was rewritten in 1908 by Robert Stanley Weir, in honor of the 300th anniversary of the founding of Quebec City. Despite the many English versions that have appeared over the years, the French lyrics have remained unaltered.

http://canada.gc.ca/canadiana/anthm_e.html

National Atlas on Schoolnet

You'll find maps of all kinds at this interactive learning site about the geography of Canada—in both English and French. You can Make-a-Map by defining map layer attributes from a preselected database, such as birds at risk or wetlands, or follow the link to Our Home: Atlas of Canadian Communities. Also in English and French, Notre Foyer lets you select a Canadian community and read what the kids who live there have written about it. Try your hand at the Interactive Geography Quiz, but don't think you have mastered it all just yet. Make sure you don't overlook the Canadian Geographical Names section—the ultimate Canadian trivia test—to find weird and wonderful answers to questions you never knew you wanted to know!

http://www-nais.ccm.emr.ca/schoolnet/

AMPHIBIANS!
Visit the Froggy Page
before you croak.

Nunavut Implementation Commission

Right now, Canada has ten provinces and two territories—the Yukon Territory and the Northwest Territories. These two territories together make up more than one-third of the entire country's land area. On April 1, 1999, the northern and eastern portion of the Northwest Territories will become Nunavut, Canada's third northern territory. Read the NIC's first report, "Footprints in New Snow," issued May 1995, for all the background details of the establishment of Nunavut. Find out all kinds of facts about the Northwest Territories as a whole, its three regions, and its communities. Link to *Nunatsiaq News,* the weekly Nunavut newspaper. Coming soon will be a section just for students.

http://www.nunanet.com/~nic/

Ontario: History

Do you need to know about the Indian tribes that make up Ontario's First Nations? What about the specific kinds of trees in the forests that cover three-quarters of this province? Early settlements? Upper and lower Canada? This government site lets you time-travel through 400 years of Ontario history at a glance.

http://www.gov.on.ca/MBS/english/its_ontario/
 ont-hist/

Ottawa Tourist

Being an Ottawa tourist is fun and educational. Here you can take a walking tour of the "Mile of History" in downtown Ottawa, the national capital region of Canada in the province of Ontario. Stroll through the famous Byward Market and learn about the Bytown Locks. Make sure to bring your sweater for ice skating on the Rideau Canal. And when you get too cold, you can take a virtual tour of some of Ottawa's historic museums: the Canadian Museum of Civilization, the Canadian War Museum, the National Library, and the National Aviation Museum, just to name a few. If you're not a history buff, there are also links to three of Canada's professional sports teams as well as Canada FAQs and weather and restaurant guides for all you real tourists.

http://www.iatech.com/tour/tour.htm

Prince Edward Island Visitors Guide: Main Page

What do Avonlea, Kindred Spirits, and Lover's Lane all have in common? You can find them all on Prince Edward Island, the birthplace of Lucy Maud Montgomery, who wrote the universally beloved book, *Anne of Green Gables,* first published in 1908. Her story was inspired by the land, the sea, and the people around her. *Anne of Green Gables* is so popular with young (and old) readers that it has been translated into 15 different languages and put on film. You'll enjoy all the stops on the "Anne" tour at this site, especially the Green Gables Farmhouse in Cavendish, which is preserved as a national museum. Check out the L. M. Montgomery literature links, and before you leave, don't forget to look through the IslandCam, Prince Edward Island's mobile digital camera located in Charlottetown, and enter the Island Trivia Challenge.

http://www.gov.pe.ca/vg/

Québec Maple Syrup Producers' Federation

Maple syrup is only produced in the northeastern part of North America, and the Canadian province of Quebec leads the region—it provides 70 percent of the world's production. In 1995, Quebec packed over 13.7 million liters of maple syrup. That's 3.5 million gallons, enough for more than 224 million servings of pancakes! This site will tell you about the history and techniques of maple syrup production in Quebec. As a good source of three essential elements (calcium, iron, and thiamin), maple syrup is really good for you, too, so be sure to try some of the great recipes listed here. This site is available in English, French, Spanish, German, and Japanese.

http://www.vir.com/~maplesyrup/sirop.htm

Welcome To Alberta, Canada

If you love outdoor recreation and the thrill of caving, hang gliding, white-water rafting, or downhill skiing in the Rockies, then here is a place you won't want to miss. Banff National Park, Canada's oldest national park, was established in 1855. Jasper National Park is home of the Columbia Icefields, the largest chunk of ice in the Rocky Mountains. The glacier itself is 16 kilometers wide and 24 kilometers long and straddles the Great Divide between Alberta and British Columbia. Find out even more about Alberta's national parks from the clickable map and the link to the official Banff National Park Home Page. It is no wonder that the motto of this Canadian province is *"Fortis et Liber"* ("Strong and Free"). No time to explore a glacier? You can also stop here for quick facts, a little history, and a tour of Edmonton, the capital city.

http://www.cuug.ab.ca:8001/VT/

Welcome to the Canadian Museum of Civilization (CMC)

If you think museums are b-o-r-i-n-g, this one will change your mind! Be sure to register as a visitor, then hop the elevator to Level 2 to see the displays of folk art and fine crafts. Visit the Treasures Gallery to see why Canada is truly a cultural mosaic. Canada Hall is on Level 3. An interactive map lets you explore 1,900 years of Canadian history. Or take the voyage through all the regions of Canada and see a prairie curling rink, an Alberta oil rig, and lots more. Take a snack break if you need to, but don't leave the museum before venturing up to Level 5 to see the History in a Box Exhibit and find out what the colors and symbols on a mailbox can tell about the history of a country. Cool! Learning history was never so much fun.

http://www.cmcc.muse.digital.ca/cmc/cmceng/
  welcmeng.html

Dinos rule in DINOSAURS AND PREHISTORIC TIMES.

Online LIBRARIES rock!

CAPE VERDE

Cape Verde Home Page (UNOFFICIAL)

The ten islands of Cabo Verde originated from volcanoes. The volcano on the island of Fogo burned almost continuously from 1500 to 1760 and served as something of a natural "lighthouse" to early sailors. Over hundreds of years, Fogo has developed as one massive volcanic cone, with an eight-kilometer-wide caldera that opens out to the east and offers some of the best farmland on the island. Naturally, the people who lived on the floor of this volcano were surprised by the most recent eruption of Fogo in April 1995. Find out about it at <*http://volcano.und.nodak.edu/vwdocs/current_volcs/fogo/fogo.html*> Read about all the volcanic activity in these islands, as well as their history and culture. You may even want to try one of the popular Cape Verdian recipes, but you'd better love to eat fish!

http://www.umassd.edu/SpecialPrograms/caboverde/
   capeverdean.html

Embassy of Cape Verde

Cape Verde, officially known as the Republic of Cape Verde (in Portuguese, it's Republica de Cabo Verde), is a chain of islands, or archipelago, in the Atlantic Ocean, off the northwest coast of Africa. Start your tour of this small and interesting country by clicking on the country flag. Sing along with the national anthem in English and Portuguese. You'll find a good Fact Sheet here. There is also information about Cape Verde's history and culture, from its discovery and colonization in the mid-1400s by the Portuguese to the wonderful blending of Christian and African traditions, art, and cuisine.

http://www.capeverdeusembassy.org/

Visit the CHEMISTRY section periodically.

CAYMAN ISLANDS

Class 5M - Red Bay Primary School

The kids here want you to know all about how they live and work in their beautiful Cayman Island communities. Take a look at how they celebrate Pirate's Week and Christmas in this tropical land. White beach sand is usually brought inside homes to be "pretend snow." Although these kids have never seen real snow, they know what it's like, and you can read their poems about it! You can also learn about the special programs to protect and support marine turtles.

http://www.monmouth.com/~bmeekings/5m.html

History of the Cayman Islands

The Cayman Islands motto is "He hath founded it upon the seas." The sea has definitely played a major role in the history of these three small islands in the Caribbean. Cayman's historical beginning (officially at least) was on May 10, 1503, when Christopher Columbus encountered the then-uninhabited islands of Little Cayman and Cayman Brac. You may have also heard of the notorious Edward Teach (or Thatch), better known as Blackbeard the pirate, who lived in the Caymans and offered refuge to other buccaneers and their stolen treasures. Today, tourists come from all over the world to enjoy Cayman's beautiful beaches and the natural wonders of the islands' waters.

http://cayman.com.ky/history.htm

Online Guide to the Cayman Islands: Welcome

Pirates, iguana, sea turtles, coral—you'll find them all on the Cayman Islands. Well, all but the pirates, unless you come to visit the last week of October and join in the annual Pirate's Week Festival. Any week of the year, you can see the other popular sights in Cayman, such as the endangered blue iguana in Queen Elizabeth II Botanic Park or green sea turtles at the Cayman Turtle Farm. Maybe you'd like to explore the mysteries of the ocean—take a dive and experience the spectacular Cayman Wall and the fascinating undersea world of sponges and coral. You can't beat the year-round temperatures here; just remember to bring your sun lotion!

http://cs.fit.edu/~jgoddar/cayman.html

CENTRAL AFRICAN REPUBLIC

The World Factbook page on Central African Republic

The Central African Republic was a part of French Equatorial Africa known as Ubangi-Shari-Chad. It became an autonomous republic within the French community in 1958 and fully independent in 1960. This site will give you some basic facts and figures about the geography, people, government, and economy of the Central African Republic. Try <http://www.lib.utexas.edu/Libs/PCL/Map_collection/ africa/Central_African_Republic.GIF> for a nicely detailed map of this landlocked country. For a good color picture of the country's flag, try <http://www.adfa.oz.au/CS/flg/col/none/cf.html>.

http://www.odci.gov/cia/publications/nsolo/ factbook/ct.htm

NET FILES

How does plain old air turn into a cloud, anyway?

Answer: Those magical, fluffy castles in the sky are caused by a process of air rising, expanding, and cooling to its saturation point, which then becomes visible as a cloud. Find out more and see some great cloud photos at http://covis.atmos.uiuc.edu/guide/clouds/ cloud_lifting/html/lifting_home.html

---

KITES big and small, this section has them all.

CHAD

Chad Page

If you need facts and figures about the geography, people, government, and economy of Chad, this is a good place to look. There is a color picture of the flag, too, as well as a link to Languages of Chad, part of the *Ethnologue* world languages website.

http://www.sas.upenn.edu/African_Studies/ Country_Specific/Chad.html

The World Factbook page on Chad

With 495,755 square miles of land area, Chad is the fifth largest country in Africa and Africa's largest landlocked state. By comparison, Chad is slightly more than three times the size of the state of California, but with only one-fifth the population. This site gives you basic information about Chad, but for a more detailed country map, be sure to visit <http://hif.org/hif1996/africa/chad.html>.

http://www.odci.gov/cia/publications/nsolo/ factbook/cd.htm

CHILE

Chile's Volcanoes

Of the 2,085 volcanoes in Chile, 55 are active. This site gives all the information you may ever want to know about seven of them, including great aerial photos. Two of these volcanoes, located in the Lake Country region of Chile, are continuously smoking today. Based on the eruptive history detailed here, Volcan Villarrica has had an "event" about once every ten years. As its last major eruption was in 1984, Villarrica may be due for another big one any time soon. During the summer season, it is estimated that as many as 150 tourists a day climb this volcano, despite the potential danger at the active crater (maybe they forgot to read this Web site!).

http://www.geo.mtu.edu/~boris/Chilehome.html

Take time to smell the virtual flowers in GARDENS AND GARDENING.

Easter Island Home Page

The inhabitants of the island call their land Rapa Nui, but Dutch Admiral Roggeveen called this lonely, South Pacific island Easter Island, in honor of the day he encountered it in 1722. How people first found this small, volcanic island is only one of its mysteries. Rapa Nui is 2,485 miles (4,000 kilometers) from South America and 1,243 miles from the nearest neighboring island. Even more curious are the peculiar stone statues, or *moais*. These 10- to 20-feet-tall giants all face inward toward the island. They have short bodies with long heads and ears and are made of a yellow-gray volcanic rock, topped with red rock hats. Despite the island's annexation by Chile in 1888, the people of Rapa Nui continue to preserve their Polynesian culture and identity. Come visit this unique island, learn its history, and meet its friendly people!

http://www.netaxs.com/~trance/rapanui.html

Educator's Guide to Chile

Explore the diversity that is Chile! More than 95 percent of Chile's population is made up of people who can trace some of their ancestry back to the 1800s. Learn why the culture of its Spanish ancestors is deeply imprinted on the Chilean character, and why German cuisine and architecture characterize so much of the Lake Country region of central Chile. Wherever you live and work in Chile, you are never more than about 150 miles from the coastline. Find out how the ocean controls the climate of Chile. Read about Punta Arenas, "the city at the end of the world," and Alexander Selkirk, the real Robinson Crusoe, at *<http://www.connectchile.com/eguide/c5.html>*.

http://www.connectchile.com/eguide/intro2.html

Lonely Planet -- Destination Chile

Described by some as an extravaganza of "crazy geography," Chile is characterized by a little bit of everything, from fertile river basins to snowcapped volcanoes to some of the driest desert on Earth. Zoom in and out of the interactive map. Read facts about Chile's climate, history, and culture. Or just flip through the photo album to view some of the most spectacular mountain peaks you'll ever see. If you're planning on more than a virtual visit to Chile, be sure to bring warm- and cold-weather gear! Are you still looking for more adventure? Take a detour to Rapa Nui (Easter Island), the world's most remote inhabited island.

http://www.lonelyplanet.com/dest/sam/chile.htm

Virtual World Jamboree '99

"Building Peace Together"—what could be a better theme? In 1999, thousands of young people from more than a hundred countries will meet at a hacienda just outside Chile's capital city of Santiago. These youngsters will be wearing colorful uniforms, and many of them will have kerchiefs around their necks. Welcome to the Virtual World Scouting Jamboree! This site is designed to provide information, multimedia presentations, and lots of images from the Jamboree site before, during, and after the actual event. Images and files will also be available at the Global ScoutNet Network for download. In addition to the Jamboree information, you'll find facts about the geography, history, people, and economy of Chile. Plus, there is an interesting map showing flying times and the different land regions of Chile from north to south. Did you know it takes more than five hours to fly from the northernmost city of Arica to Chile's southernmost city of Punta Arenas?

http://scoutnet.ch/events/jam99/

"Use the source, Luke!"
and look it up
in REFERENCE WORKS.

Programs, reviews, theme
songs, and more in
TELEVISION.

CHINA

China: Beyond the Great Wall

See some of China's most spectacular landmarks, including the Great Wall of China, Gugong: The Forbidden City, magnificent Mount Huang-shan, and breathtaking Jiuzhaigou Falls. Follow the link to Focus on China for even more fascinating details about this country's history, land, people, and culture. China has a recorded history of nearly 4,000 years! The Qinghai-Tibet Plateau is home to Mount Qomolangma on the Sino-Nepalese border. You may know it by another name: Mount Everest. It soars 29,028 feet (8,848 meters) above sea level and is the highest mountain peak in the world. China also boasts the highest population in the world, with more than 1.2 billion people. You'll even find a brief history of Chinese cooking, but unfortunately, there is no taste test!

http://www.uncletai.com/china/china.html

China Home Page

Each of China's 31 provinces/cities/autonomous regions are represented here. Find general information about the geography, climate, economy, and culture of each province, along with interesting facts about some of China's major cities. Find out more about the Dragon-Boat Festival, a holiday the Chinese have been celebrating for over 2,000 years. The descriptions of some of China's gourmet dishes can sure make you hungry. Too bad you can't smell things on the Internet! The pictures of Chinese folk art, including woodblock pictures, paper cuts, weaving, and ceramics also give you a real sense of the history and culture of this country.

http://www.edu.cn/www/china.html

China Maps

It's a lot harder to study the country of China if you don't know how to pronounce the names of all its provinces! Here is a great place to start. This is a clear and simple political map, and all the way at the bottom is a chart that shows the Chinese characters, Chinese name, and a pronunciation guide for each of China's provinces, autonomous (self-governing) regions, and special municipalities. Select "China: Administration 1991 (278K)" from the list on this page.

http://www.lib.utexas.edu/Libs/PCL/Map_collection/
   china.html

China the Beautiful - Chinese Art and Literature

Calligraphy is as much beautiful abstract art as it is a way of writing. It dates back to the earliest days of Chinese history and is still widely practiced. Even after 2,000 years, the five major styles of calligraphy (seal script, clerical script, standard script, semicursive script, and cursive script) are still in use today. This site is also filled with Chinese history. The outline of Chinese chronology and timeline included here is especially useful because it includes a listing of events happening outside China at the same time. And if you need more maps of historic and present-day China, this is a good place to look. This site even includes a set of flash cards for learning Chinese words and links to museums around the world that have Chinese art collections on their Web pages.

http://www.chinapage.com/china.html

China Today

China is *really* big—640 cities, 32 of them with a population of over one million people! These folks have loved music and art for a long time: as early as the first century B.C., more than 80 different kinds of musical instruments were already in use. Want more facts? Some Asians believe jade will bring them good luck and good health and can help them to get rid of bad luck. Did you know that the Chinese people love football (what Americans call soccer)? This is a comprehensive site with lots of information.

http://www.chinatoday.com/

Condensed China: Chinese History for Beginners

If you're dazzled by dynasties, confused by Qing, muddled by Ming, or even hazy on the facts about the People's Republic of China, come to this site. The author says it is more like "Chinese History: the Cliff Notes version" or "Chinese History's Greatest Hits" than a full-fledged history. For the highlights, visit here!

http://www.hk.super.net/~paulf/china.html

The Hong Kong Children's Choir

OK, on the count of three, everybody sing! This children's choir travels all around the world. At their site, you can even hear sound samples of their singing (these are quite large, so they will take time to come through your modem). Some are in English and some are in Chinese (the two official languages of Hong Kong). The boys and girls also learn to play instruments, dance, and paint. So it's much more than just a choir.

http://www.hkcchoir.org.hk/

Hong Kong Home Screen

Kids who have been to Hong Kong will often tell you that their favorite part is the boat rides! Some people even live on their boats, in large groups that form a type of community. Adults will probably mention the shopping or the food in Hong Kong. This is a crowded, bustling place full of excitement! A British Crown colony for years, in July 1997 it will return to China as a special administrative region. What will change?

http://expedia.msn.com/wg/places/HongKong/
    HSFS.htm

Hong Kong Lonely Planet -- Destination: Hong Kong

Hong Kong harbor has lots of junks. No, silly, not the trashy kind of junk. A *junk* is a type of boat. People can steer them with a long pole. A small slide show gives you an idea of how it's done. Wow! Hong Kong at night is like fireworks in the sky; it's very spectacular. You'll get a kick out of some of the customs, for example, you should never leave any rice uneaten at a meal (be a member of the "Clean Plate Club" here!) and be sure not to place your chopsticks vertically in your bowl; we'll leave it up to you to find out why.

http://www.lonelyplanet.com.au/dest/sea/hong.htm

Hong Kong Tourist Association: WONDER NET

Festivals are the best in Hong Kong! Start with the Chinese New Year. Keep going until the Chung Yeung Festival. There's always an excuse to have a party! This site has videos of the people, city, and even the food. Be sure to click on "The Wonder of the Day" for something new. Speaking about what's new, in 1997 Hong Kong's sovereignty will revert to China. What changes will come? You'll find answers at *<http://www.hkta.org/1997/index.html>* as well as links to special events surrounding the transition.

http://www.hkta.org/

Hong Kong Travel Guide

Cute little cartoon guys will guide you around Hong Kong. There are islands to explore, with lots of photos. You can even teach yourself Chinese! Hear a few of the common phrases, and then say them out loud. Then you'll be able to find your way to all of the attractions for kids. Hong Kong has lots of them: beaches, parks, and amusement centers. Don't forget to visit the Great Buddha. It's the tallest bronze sculpture in the world.

http://www.goasia.com/

Imperial Tombs of China

Long ago, when a Chinese emperor died, he was buried with fabulous treasures. One was buried with thousands of life-size terra-cotta soldiers and horses. One was buried in a special garment made of thousands of jade pieces held together by gold thread. Two hundred fifty objects from tombs spanning 2,500 years of Chinese history have been touring the world's museums. This Web page is from Denver, Colorado. You can find another description of the exhibits from the Museum of Art at Brigham Young University in Provo, Utah at *<http://advance.byu.edu/pc/china/China.html>*. "If you think the emperors of China lived like kings, wait till you see how they died!"

http://www.denverpost.com/china/china.htm

It never rains on the PARADES in cyberspace.

Never give your name or address to a stranger.

SILK ROAD

Imagine it is the year 1271. The Venetian traveler, Marco Polo, is packing a caravan for his first long expedition to a country called Cathay. He travels across the deserts and mountains of Asia and finally comes to a country filled with beautiful riches he has never seen before: silk, ivory, spices, and rare jewels. He brings these treasures back to Europe, as well as knowledge of new cultures, customs, and inventions such as the compass. The historical trade route Polo followed was given its name, The Silk Road, by a French historian in 1887. Silk, however, was only one of the many items in the exchange between inland China, its western border, India, and the Middle East. Travel along this ancient passageway—through the province of Xinjiang in the west and across into Gansu and Xi'an in the east—and see some of China's historical sites along the way.

http://www.xanet.edu.cn/xjtu/silk1/eng/silk.html

Tibetan Government's official web site

China calls Tibet an autonomous region, but others say China is taking away Tibetan culture and spiritual practices and abuses the human rights of the Tibetan people. The spiritual leader of Tibet, Tenzin Gyatso, His Holiness the Dalai Lama, leads a "government in exile" in India. This official Web site gives a lot of information about the Dalai Lama, who received the Nobel Peace Prize in 1989. The citation reads, in part: "The Dalai Lama has developed his philosophy of peace from a great reverence for all things living and upon the concept of universal responsibility embracing all mankind as well as nature." This Web site outlines Tibetan Buddhist beliefs, culture, medicine, astrology, and more. It also details the charges against China, and many of them are disturbing and contain adult subject material.

http://www.gn.apc.org/tibetlondon/

Tour in China

China is the world's third largest country (after Russia and Canada). At this site, you will really get a sense of China's diverse climates and land regions as well as the culture and history of its people. For example, Xinjiang, the largest region in China, covers one-sixth of its total land area. This large province is the source of both the Huang He (Yellow River) and the Yangtze River. You'll also learn about Qinghai Lake, China's biggest saltwater lake. And check out Snake Island, near the port of Dalian in Liaoning province, which is home to more than 13,000 pit vipers!

http://solar.rtd.utk.edu/~china/tour/china_tour.html

Virtual China '97

Here's something different. The seventh graders at the Hong Kong International School were offered a choice of two trips: a one-week biking trip in rural southern China or a week-long trip to Xi'an, home of the famous terra-cotta soldiers. Ninety of them went on one or the other. You can follow along in their diaries and read their impressions. When these kids made the trips, Hong Kong was still a British colony. In 1997, Hong Kong returns to the control of China. Based on these kids' observations, life will be very different under the Chinese government. Some of the "perspectives" are hilarious—you read a description of a hotel lobby from the point of view of the couch, for example. Virtual China '96 files (which include the couch) are at *<http://www.kidlink.org:80/KIDPROJ/VChina/>*. For a fabulous illustrated diary of a trip to China written by an adult, don't miss the descriptions, funny stories, and photos at China Experience: *<http://zinnia.umfacad.maine.edu/~mshea/China/china.html>*.

http://www.kidlink.org/KIDPROJ/VChina97/

VIDEO AND SPY CAMS let you look in on interesting parts of the world.

Everyone's flocking to BIRDS!

COLOMBIA

Lonely Planet -- Destination: Colombia

Like the other Lonely Planet sites, you will find a map of Colombia and just the basics here. But you'll learn about the country's geography, history, population, and culture. Be sure to check the photo journal for some great shots of the Andes Mountains, a pre-Columbian stone statue, beautiful Spanish architecture, and more. Need some trivia tidbits to pique your interest? The jungle of Colombia's Pacific coast holds the record for the highest rainfall. There are more than 1,550 recorded species of birds (more than in the whole of Europe and North America combined), ranging from the huge Andean condor to the tiny hummingbird. Colombian author Gabriel García Márquez won the Nobel Prize for Literature in 1982 for his book, *One Hundred Years of Solitude.* And if you think you're an adventurous eater, you might want to try Hormiga Culona, a "sophisticated Colombian dish." You'll have to visit this site to find out the main ingredient, but here is a hint: it has six legs.

http://www.lonelyplanet.com.au/dest/sam/col.htm

COMOROS ISLANDS

Action Comores Home Page

Have you ever seen a Livingstone's flying fox? Probably not, unless you have been to the Comoros Islands. Livingstone's flying fox is one of the rarest fruit bats in the world and is native there. Rapid population growth on these islands in the western Indian Ocean has caused the destruction of much of the upland forest habitat of these fruit bats. There may only be around 400 of this species left in the wild. Find out why the slogan for the Action Comores conservation organization is "People Need Forests Need Fruit Bats!" Be sure to follow the link to <*http://www.sas.upenn.edu/African_Studies/Country_Specific/Comoros.html*> for a great map showing the four main islands and information from the 1995 *World Factbook.*

http://ibis.nott.ac.uk/Action-Comores/

The Comoros Home Page

The Comoros Islands resulted from volcanic activity along a crack in the seabed that runs between mainland Africa and the country of Madagascar in the Mozambique Channel. Today, three of the islands—Ngazidja (Grande Comore), Mwali, and Nzwani—make up the Federal Islamic Republic of the Comoro Islands. The fourth major island of the archipelago, Mayotte (Maore), continues to be administered by France even though it is claimed by the Republic of the Comoros. Get a sense of the geography, economy, and people of these islands and then visit each of the four main islands separately to learn its own special story. Hear a sample of music, which is a blend of cultural and musical influences from East Africa, the Middle East, Madagascar, and southern India. The Comoros Islands provide a unique habitat for several endangered species. Follow some of the extra links here to read more about the mysterious coelacanth fish living in the caves along the west coast of Grand Comore island.

http://www.ksu.edu/sasw/comoros/comoros.html

CONGO

City.Net Map of Congo

Here is a great color map of the Congo. Produced by Magellan Geographix, it shows all the major cities and rivers in this African country.

http://city.net/countries/congo/maps/congo.html

Congo Page

In addition to the 1995 *World Fact Book* entry for the Congo, which gives you basic facts about the economy, geography, government, and people of the Congo, you'll find a small color picture of the flag and a nice map of the Congo.

http://www.sas.upenn.edu/African_Studies/
  Country_Specific/Congo.html

Go climb a rock in OUTDOOR RECREATION.

Never give your name or address to a stranger.

COOK ISLANDS

A best kept secret in the Pacific - The Cook Islands

Put on your *rito*, a hat made from the uncurled fiber of the coconut palm. We are going to meet with Cook Islands women to make a *tivaevae. Tivaevae*, the making of patchwork quilts by hand, is a major art form peculiar to the Cook Islands. It was originally brought to these Polynesian islands by the Europeans, but the patterns and techniques used for these quilts have evolved over time into styles distinct to the Cooks. The *tivaevae* represent the native surroundings of the islands with designs of flowers, leaves, birds, fish, insects, and animals. Imagine the rhythmic drumming on the *pate* as you read about the art of dance in the Cooks. The name Cook Islands was actually given to the group by the Russians in the early 1800s, in honor of the great English navigator Captain James Cook. But this nation of 15 islands, which spreads over 850,000 square miles in the middle of the South Pacific, has a rich and interesting history that dates back hundreds of years before then. Read about each island as you visit "the heart of Polynesia." This site is available in English and French.

http://www.ck/

COSTA RICA

Adventure! Costa Rica Home Pages

With 130 species of freshwater fish, 160 species of amphibians, 208 species of mammals, 220 species of reptiles, 850 species of birds (one-tenth of the world's total), 1,000 species of butterflies, 1,200 varieties of orchids, 9,000 species of plants, and 34,000 species of insects, Costa Rica is considered to have the greatest biodiversity of any country in the world. Check out this site for more fun facts and figures about this small country, called the "Coast of Plenty." Follow the Destinations section to go bird watching or visit an active volcano. The main site also provides links to the 1995 *World Fact Book* and the U.S. State Department Background Notes country info about Costa Rica.

http://www.amerisol.com/costarica.html

May the forces be with you in PHYSICS.

COCORI Complete Costa Rica Homepage

Costa Rica is located on the isthmus between North and South America. With a land area of less than 20,00 square miles, it is only about the size of the state of West Virginia. A lot of history and culture are packed into this small Central American country. Find out why this country is sometimes referred to as the "Switzerland of the Americas." Be sure to stop into the Library to read more about Costa Rica's traditions and holiday celebrations. Christmas in Costa Rica means eating tamales for breakfast, lunch, dinner, and even coffee breaks. This delicious dish is prepared almost exclusively in December to eat during the year-end parties and celebrations, and it has been a country tradition for thousands of years. Visit Iguana Park, take a ride through a mangrove forest, or learn more about Costa Rica's tropical rain forests, sometimes referred to as "nature's crumbling cathedral."

http://www.cocori.com/

NET FILES

Who were the world's first air passengers?

(Hint: They flew in a hot-air balloon.)

Answer: In 1783, the Montgolfier brothers flew the first hot-air balloon in Versailles, France, safely landing a duck, a rooster, and a sheep. Although there was no in-flight movie, the flight must have been very entertaining! Read more at http://www.metlife.com/Blimp/Docs/index.cgi

General Information

The Central American country of Costa Rica is one of the oldest democracies in America, as well as being a free and independent republic. In fact, this country is often described as an oasis of peace. The Costa Rican people are friendly to visitors and are anxious to show off their country's rich natural heritage. Costa Rica is a real paradise for nature lovers, volcano enthusiasts, and water sports fans, too. This small tropical country, situated between two oceans, offers the Canales of Tortuguero, a network of more than 100 kilometers of navigable canals and lagoons on the Caribbean side. If surfing is your thing, Playa Pavones on the Pacific Ocean side is internationally famous for having the longest waves in the world.

http://www.ticonet.co.cr/costa_rica/general.html

An Introduction to Costa Rica

In 1502, Christopher Columbus became the first European explorer to encounter Costa Rica. Later, a Spaniard named Gil Gonzalez Davila gave the country its name, meaning "rich coast" because of the gold jewelry worn by the Costa Rican inhabitants. Learn about the civilization that existed there thousands of years before Columbus, and then get to know the Costa Ricans of today. They are a people who really care about their environment. They have set aside one-quarter of their land as protected areas and national parks. Besides the basic geography and history facts you'll find here, you'll get the chance to explore some of these national parks. In Braulio Carrillio National Park, one of the best features is the *Teleferico del Bosque Lluvioso*, or "rain forest tram." It is the only vehicle of its kind in the world, and unless you want to climb the trees, it is the only way to view the canopy, or life in the treetops. Drive up to the edge of an active volcanic crater in Poas National Park. Corcovado National Park on the Osa Peninsula is home to jaguars, crocodiles, and hammerhead sharks. Tortuguero National Park boasts the largest breeding population of green sea turtles in the world.

http://www.interknowledge.com/costa-rica/

Be an angel and check what we've found in RELIGION.

CÔTE D'IVOIRE

City.Net Map of Côte d'Ivoire

If you need a clear map of Côte d'Ivoire, here's where to look. The map shows the capital city of Abidjan in the south, along the coast of the Gulf of Guinea, plus the other major cities, lakes, and rivers.

http://city.net/countries/cote_divoire/maps/civoir.html

Côte d'Ivoire: Tourism and Business Pages - Main Menu

Côte d'Ivoire, formerly called the Ivory Coast, is a West African nation located on the Gulf of Guinea. The country achieved independence from France in 1960, but because of the more than 60 ethnic groups and great number of local dialects, French was selected as the official language. Côte d'Ivoire is the world's largest producer of cocoa and the third largest producer of coffee, after Brazil and Colombia. After you've read the facts-at-a-glance, be sure to follow the link to read more about Félix Houphouët-Boigny, who was President of the country from 1960–80. During his tenure as President of Côte d'Ivoire, the country achieved a tremendous economic growth. The replica of St. Peter's Basilica of Rome, Our Lady of Peace, built in Yamoussoukro, was his inspiration. For more details about the cities of Abidjan, Yamoussoukro, Korhogo, Man, and Abengourou, visit the Côte d'Ivoire la belle Page at *<http://www.webperfect.com/afrinet/ivory/profile.html>*.

http://webperfect.com/ivory/cotivoir.html

United in Majesty

Here is a picture of The Basilica of Our Lady of Peace, one of the largest churches in the world. It was the vision of one man, Félix Houphouët-Boigny, President of the Ivory Coast. The marble was imported from Italy and the stained glass was from France.

http://www.allenorgan.com.au/majesty.htm

Lose yourself in a Museum. SCIENCE has them all.

CROATIA

1700 Anniversary of the City of Split

Because of its central position on the eastern coast of the Adriatic Sea, the country of Croatia, and specifically the district of Split and Dalmatia, have always had an important cultural and historical role. The Roman emperor Diocletian built his spectacular limestone palace in the year 295, near Salona (present day Solin), which was then the capital of the Roman province of Dalmatia. During the Middle Ages, Diocletian's palace became the center of the medieval town of Split. The palace has been recognized and preserved as a famous architectural and cultural monument, and today it is on UNESCO's World Cutural Heritage list. Jump back in time and brush up on your Roman history with this brief entry about the life of Emperor Diocletian. Enter the huge courtyard, or peristyle, of the palace. You will think you have been transplanted back in time as you look at the carved door frames or parts of Diocletian's mausoleum, which in later centuries became the site of a Christian cathedral.

http://www.st.carnet.hr/split/

Republic of Croatia home page

Imagine you are in an airplane. You are flying low over the coast of Croatia. When you look down, you see the magnificent blue of the Adriatic Sea set off by steep cliffs, dark green trees, and white stone buildings of cities like Dubrovnik and Zadar. Then you visit the eastern border town of Slavonski Brod and the Serbian-occupied city of Vukovar. This sensitive map lets you click on many of the Croatian cities to see aerial photos, get historical chronologies, and learn about famous personalities. What stories do the ancient Roman ruins and archeological items reveal about Croatia's historical heritage? The Croatian people are also dedicated to the preservation of their musical folklore. You may want to take a quick detour to learn about the stringed *tamburitza*, the most popular and most common Croatian folk instrument. A caution to parents: Some of the offsite war links and associated reportage include disturbing adult subject matter.

http://tjev.tel.etf.hr/hrvatska/HR.html

The Thousand Islands of the Croatian Adriatic

Croatia is a country with a thousand-year-old history. This horseshoe-shaped country has 1,777 kilometers of mainland Adriatic shoreline and no fewer than 1,185 islands, islets, and reefs. These islands are known for their natural beauty and also for the hundreds of years of history and legend they represent. The famous feast of Our Lady of Snows is still celebrated every August on the island of Kukljica. Every summer, the people of Korcula Island re-create the old knight's dance of Moreska, which dates back to the fifteenth century, and they re-create the battles with the Moors. The ancient island of Zadar is dominated by its Roman monuments. Brac Island is known all over the world for its white stone, which was used in ancient times to build the Palace of Diocletian in the Croatian coastal city of Split and in the late 1700s to build parts of the White House in Washington, D.C.

http://islands.zems.fer.hr/

CUBA

Cuban Postcards

Here's a quick way to look at some of the history of this island country in the West Indies. Cubans call it the "Pearl of the Antilles" because of its towering mountains, magnificent coastline, sandy beaches, beautiful coral reefs, and historical architecture. See for yourself from these historical postcards, old-time cigar box labels, stamps, and magazine covers. Another photo portrait of Cuba is at *<http://www.netpoint.net/~cubanet/fotoindex.html>*.

http://www.cc.gatech.edu/computing/SW_Eng/
   people/Phd/cuba.html

CubaWeb

Bienvenidos al CubaWeb! Here's a different way to learn a country's history—from a culinary perspective! Did you know that pineapples are a symbol of hospitality? That custom was originally practiced by the indigenous Tainos living in Cuba. There is a brief history of the Cuban flag. This site has interesting information, divided into a Business Library and a Culture Library. You'll find history, news, and maps in the Business Library. Check out art, literature, music, food, and sports in the Culture Library. A caution to parents: There is a link to a Cuban cigar manufacturer's home page.

http://www.cubaweb.com/eng/

CYPRUS

THE **CYPRUS** HOME PAGE

The small island of Cyprus, located in the northeast corner of the Mediterranean Sea, is a place rich in Greek heritage and legend and fabulous weather: it is estimated that the people of Cyprus enjoy 300 sunny days each year! But the ongoing political tension between the 608,300 Greek-Cypriots (well over three-quarters of the island's population) and the 93,000 Turkish-Cypriots is a darkness that continues to plague the island. Since the Turkish invasion of July 1974, the northern 37 percent of the Cypriot Republic's territory has been under Turkish military occupation. Learn about present-day Cyprus from the maps, country profiles, and chronology of events, then step back into the history of this country at the crossroads of Europe and the Middle East. See the ancient Greek temples where Aphrodite, the Greek goddess of love and beauty, was worshipped. You'll find songs, folk art, lots of color pictures of Cyprus, and interesting facts and folklore about the birds of Cyprus, too. You might also want to check out Kypros-Net at <http://www.kypros.org/> for more information and links.

http://www.wam.umd.edu/~cyprus/

POLLUTION stinks.

Cyprus Main Page

If you like sweet potatoes, you'll love *kolokasi*. This root vegetable (*Colocasia esculanta*) is a specialty of Cyprus. How about eliopitta, lountza, kefalotiri, kaskavali, sfyrida, or loukoumades? You'll have to visit this Web page, or any outdoor market on Cyprus, to find out about these other delicious foods! If you're eating Vasilopitta, it must be New Year's Day. The Cyprus food calendar is lots of fun, as you find out which special foods are associated with different celebrations throughout the year. After sampling some of the taste treats of Cyprus, be sure to tour the 143 photos included here. You can really see why people love to visit this unique island. A caution to parents: The "Cyprus Problem" links are disturbing.

http://www.cosmosnet.net/azias/cyprus/c-main.html

CZECH REPUBLIC

Czech Open Information Project

This site introduces Czech culture, music, art, history, and more. Travel through the countryside of the Czech Republic, visiting centuries-old châteaux and castles. Are you more into science than history? Read all about the founder of genetics, Johann Gregor Mendel, Czech's environmental concerns, and lots of other country information, too.

http://www.open.cz/

HISTORY AND VIRTUAL VISIT

Today, kids go to the movie theaters and cinemas at the mall. But what did kids do for entertainment in the 1800s? At the end of the eighteenth century, national theaters were built in many of Europe's capital cities and cultural centers. The Theatre of the Estates in Czech's capital city of Prague is one of the most beautiful historic theaters in Europe, and it is one of the few to have been preserved almost in its original condition. Take a virtual tour of the Theatre of the Estates, which first opened in 1783, and the National Theatre of Prague, which first opened in 1862, and get a sense of the Italian opera, German drama, and classical ballet that is still performed in these grand old theaters.

http://www.anet.cz/nd/english/history.html

Welcome to the Czech Republic

The Czech Republic contains beautiful cities, rugged mountains, rolling hills, and dense forests. Historically, the Czech Republic can be divided into three Czech lands: Bohemia in the west, and Moravia and Slovakia in the east. Lakes in the Czech Republic are usually artificial ponds for growing fish, mostly in south Bohemia, one of the least industrialized parts of the Czech lands. If you need business, news, and government information, this is your place to look.

http://www.czech.cz/

DENMARK
Copenhagen Home Screen

Copenhagen is the largest city in Scandinavia. The beloved statue of The Little Mermaid is in the harbor of this capital city, but it's not Disney's Ariel, it's the original, from the fairy tale of the same name. The red brick homes are very close to the water, too. Some people can step right out of their homes and into a boat! Even more fun might be Tivoli Gardens, an amusement park. The story goes that Walt Disney was so impressed by the place that he hurried back to the U.S. to begin plans for a similar facility: Disneyland. How about a visit to the palace of the royal family? Amalienborg Palace is actually four different buildings, and if the Queen is in residence, you can watch the Changing of the Guard every day at noon. It is a city custom for spectators to follow the bearskin-capped guards from their barracks all the way to the palace.

http://expedia.msn.com/wg/places/Denmark/
Copenhagen/HSFS.htm

Dansk for turister (English)

You can use Danish in either Denmark or Greenland (which has ties to Denmark). At this site are some words and phrases to learn, and it's easy because you can hear a sound file of the words and phrases. *Hvad er klokken?* ("What time is it?") It's time to call your travel agent!

http://www.travlang.com/languages/cgi-bin/
langchoice.cgi?page=main&lang1=english&lang2
=danish

Embassy of Denmark, Washington D.C.

Amazing fact: no one in Denmark is more than 52 kilometers from the sea. That's only 32 miles! But you might want to hop on a bike instead of a boat. You can bounce along the cobblestone streets. Amazing fact #2: the Danish line of 52 kings and queens is unbroken since its start. That's a world record. Queen Margrethe II's picture is on the site. She is a very well-educated woman who loves to ballet dance and create artworks. In fact, she was a great fan of J. R. R. Tolkien, author of *The Hobbit* and *The Lord of the Rings*. In 1977, *The Lord of the Rings* was published with illustrations by Ingahild Grathmer, a "pen name" which the Queen used for her first works. She now uses her own name. You'll find a fascinating biography of her here.

http://www.globescope.com/denmark/

Explore Denmark

Wow. Denmark—the land of the Vikings, the home of castles and queens, famed for fishing, furniture, and...Lego. Denmark's history is filled with names like Gorm the Old and Harald Bluetooth. Really! The seafaring people of Denmark's past and present are a strong bunch. Come and look at all that they've accomplished.

http://www.geocities.com/TheTropics/4597/

Fishing Denmark

Do you like fly-fishing? How about saltwater fly-fishing? Then Denmark is the place for you, and this is the page for you. Learn all about the parts of the feather and how to tie flies. Who would ever think that fishing lures could be so pretty? Learn the fine points of casting into the waves, which will make you an expert. We're not exactly sure what float-tubing is, but it appears to be a great way to get out in the water without a boat. Don't miss the photos of the float-tubing dogs!

http://www.idg.dk/mj/

Beanie Babies rule in TOYS.

H.C.Andersen

Hans Christian Andersen (1805–75) was a "Great Dane." No, he wasn't a dog! He often didn't attend school, and he left home at the young age of 14. He tried a lot of careers, but nothing clicked for him until he recognized that his imagination was his best quality. Later, he wrote some of the most delightful children's stories of all time (and you thought that Disney wrote *The Little Mermaid*). Check out this page; how many of his more than 160 fairy tales do you know?

http://www.geocities.com/WallStreet/2575/hcand.html

DJIBOUTI

The World Factbook page on Djibouti

We know it's a country in East Africa and that it was formerly known as the French Territory of the Afars and Issas and also as French Somaliland. It gained its independence in 1977. It's a mostly Muslim country, and the land is largely desert. You can also try the entry at *<http://www.sas.upenn.edu/African_Studies/ Country_Specific/Djibouti.html>*. There isn't much info about Djibouti on the Web. If you are an expert on Djibouti, you've got a chance to write your own Djibouti page! Lots of places give away free home page space; one you can try is *<http://www.geocities.com>*.

http://www.odci.gov/cia/publications/nsolo/ factbook/dj.htm

DOMINICA

Dominica: Essential Information on the Caribbean's prime eco-tourism island

Are you wondering how on earth to pronounce Dominica? (We were pronouncing it wrong!) You can find out this and a whole lot more. Here's a fact for you: there are 365 rivers on this island—one for each day of the year. But there is only one stoplight. Parrot watching is popular, as are hiking, snorkeling, and other outdoor activities. See some photos and maps at this lovely site.

http://www.delphis.dm/basics.htm

Dominica Home Screen

Dominica is a Caribbean island; don't get it confused with the Dominican Republic, which is elsewhere. You'll find lots of natural attractions here, but you don't want to step in the Boiling Lake! The reason it's bubbling is because it's HOT. Since this is a volcanic island, you'll find other hot spots, too. Here's some trivia: most of the beaches have a certain color of sand. Knowing it's a volcanic area, can you guess what color? You'll also find beautiful waterfalls in the mountainous rain forest. The "mountain chicken" on the menu is really something else.

http://expedia.msn.com/wg/Places/Dominica/ HSFS.htm

DOMINICAN REPUBLIC

Dominican Republic Home Screen

Check the entry in this book for Haiti, which shares the island of Hispaniola with the country of the Dominican Republic. Christopher Columbus wasn't the only member of his family who landed here. According to this site, "Christopher Columbus dropped anchor here on his first voyage in 1492; four years later, his brother Bartolomeo founded the colony of Santo Domingo; 13 years after that, Christopher's son became the colony's governor!"

http://expedia.msn.com/wg/Places/ DominicanRepublic/HSFS.htm

www.hispaniola.com: Dominican Republic

The Dominican Republic is the hot spot for windsurfing these days. On these pages you can learn about that, plus what other attractions await you if you get a chance to visit. Also, there are no poisonous snakes or spiders on the island! You might also like the collection of links at *<http://www.dr1.com/>*.

http://www.hispaniola.com/DR/

Looking for the State Bird or the State Motto? It's in the UNITED STATES section.

ECUADOR

Dorn Moore's Ecuador Page

Ecuador sits right on the equator, in South America. Would you like to be a student in Ecuador for seven months? This guy did just that: he lived with a host family and had many adventures. He even visited a tribe in the rain forest! Sail your mouse on over to his site to look at the great pictures he took and the terrific links he has collected on Ecuador, the Galápagos Islands, the Mayans, and Incas.

http://www.u.arizona.edu/~dmoore/ecuador.html

Virtual Galápagos

The Galápagos are islands off the coast of Ecuador. Some unusual plants and animals here aren't found anywhere else on Earth. Movies show a giant tortoise eating (what an appetite!) or lizards doing push-ups (lizard aerobics?). As you journey through the islands in virtual reality movies, you can even walk among the tortoises!

http://www.terraquest.com/galapagos/

EGYPT

Cleveland Museum of Art Pharaohs Exhibition

See kings and queens, pharaohs, and their treasures. See statues and carvings from long ago. Learn some fun facts about the pharaohs. Did you know that some of them were women? Construct a paper model of one of their death masks (the pattern is printable). Hut, hut, go King Tut!

http://www.clemusart.com/archive/pharaoh/

EGYPT has it all !!

From the Red Sea coast to the oases in the interior, Egypt really does have it all. You might want to visit a city like Luxor first. It has statues, carvings, and paintings. Perhaps you'd like to hop over to the Sinai. Its mountains tower above the sea, where you can snorkel. Check out the two-mile-long High Dam at Aswan, which supplies electricity for all of Egypt. Or maybe you'd rather sit back and see an automatic slide show of the whole tour.

http://its-idsc.gov.eg/tourism/

Guardian's Egypt - Main Gate

Venture through the ruins of a real pyramid. Can you figure out its mysteries? The Sphinx has clues about its past, too. But what on earth happened to its nose? Hint: it didn't fall off as a result of erosion or weather! This site is a complete guide to links on both ancient and modern Egypt and includes info about music and art, language lessons in Arabic, and more. One of the best is the official Egyptian Information Highway site at <http://www.idsc.gov.eg/> with a lot of background information on Egypt plus carefully sorted and arranged links to other pages.

http://pages.prodigy.com/guardian/egypt.htm

Odyssey in Egypt

Join archaeologists in a real dig at this award-winning resource. You can tour the dig site and move around it in virtual reality. But Egypt is much more than old stuff. Get to know kids who live there. One weaves carpets in a store. Another helps on the farm with his family. How would you study and preserve a wall painting? Where would you dig for archaeological ruins next? Your ideas are valuable! You can help by solving problems in the SOS section of each week's material.

http://www.scriptorium.org./odyssey/

EL SALVADOR

El Salvador

Did you think that the only pyramids were in Egypt? Guess again! There are ruins of ancient pyramids in El Salvador, too. Take a look at these Central American designs and compare them to those in Egypt. Volcanoes, lakes, and beaches are a part of the landscape of El Salvador. The people are creative, and you can see it in their crafts. Colorful sombreros, furniture made of twigs, ceramics, and hammocks are just a few of the things they make. You'll find lots of background info on the country here!

http://alpha.netaccess.on.ca/~biron/ElSalvador/
 salvdr-1.htm

ENGLAND

See UNITED KINGDOM—ENGLAND

EQUATORIAL GUINEA

Equitorial.Guinea Page

One clue about where this country is located is in its name. Here's another: it's on a large continent shared with the countries of Egypt, Uganda, and Zaire, among others. An island off its coast has two volcanoes. If you know Spanish, you'll feel right at home in Equatorial Guinea. Spanish is the official language, since the country was formerly owned by Spain. Careful—this country has a lot of political unrest.

http://www.sas.upenn.edu/African_Studies/
    Country_Specific/Eq_Guinea.html

ERITREA

Eritrea Network Information Center

This country has been torn by war for many years. But if you look around, you'll see the potential for many good things there. Many farmers share their land, because it is owned by all of them. Gold mines abound. Located on the Red Sea and formerly a colony of Ethiopia, Eritrea got its name from the Greek word for just that—Red Sea. You can also get more info and links at the Eritrea Community Online Network at <http://diglib.stanford.edu/dehai/>.

http://eritrea.org/

ESTONIA

Estonia Country Guide

When the glaciers left this area, they also left behind—Estonia! It still is very cold in the winter, with a permanent snow cover for months. Estonia used to be part of the Soviet Union. In 1991, it broke off and became independent. You'll find lots of political and cultural links here to music, museums, and stamps. Would you like to visit some Estonian school home pages? Check the Estonian Schoolserver at <http://www.edu.ee/index_en.html>.

http://www.ciesin.ee/ESTCG/

ETHIOPIA

EthioWeb.com, Your Guide to Ethiopia

See Ethiopia in pictures, from a waterfall on the Blue Nile to people in native dress, from modern buildings to ancient obelisks. Ethiopians also excel in sports; they have had an incredible number of Olympic runners. Why do you suppose this is so? Find out about the history of this African land at the link called "Ethiopia, the cradle of civilization."

http://www.ethioweb.com/

FALKLAND ISLANDS

Showcase - Falkland Islands

The Falklands, or Islas Malvinas, are claimed as part of the United Kingdom, which went to war to prove it when Argentina thought otherwise. You can learn a little about the history of the islands and the people, animals, and birds that inhabit them. Check the penguins. You'll see pictures and read about the different species. Isn't that rockhopper cute, with its tuft of feathers on top? You can get a good idea of how close the Falklands are to both Argentina and Antarctica at <http://www.tbc.gov.bc.ca/cwgames/country/Falklands/falkland.html>.

http://www.vni.net/~kwelch/penguins/showcase/
    showcase_Falklands.shtml

FAROE ISLANDS

Faroe Islands Travel Guide

The Faroe Islanders have home rule, but they are part of the kingdom of Denmark. In the summer, the sun never sets for three months! It gets low on the horizon, but it doesn't set. Photos of the villages are one of the best parts of this site, and they're picturesque. Many of the buildings have colorful roofs and siding. The green hills will entice you to hike around. Some footpaths are from olden times, before roads were built, but be sure to take a raincoat. It's foggy and drizzly there much of the time. The Faroese music will pick you up; a sample is available for you to hear. The map is in the Different Parts of the Islands section.

http://www.ozemail.com.au/~skuvadal/

Lonely Planet -- Detour Faroe Islands

About halfway between Norway and Iceland, the Faroes are volcanic islands. Lots of birds and sheep live there, but not many people. On one tiny island is a school with only one student! A great way to stay cheaply in some countries is to find a youth hostel. There's one here, just as in many European nations. What types of food do you suppose they eat there? (Hint: The growing season is quite short because of the cold climate, and some say this is the most vertical landscape in the world.)

http://www.lonelyplanet.com.au/detours/faroes.htm

NET FILES

How many cubic feet of helium does it take to fly the MetLife Snoopy blimp?

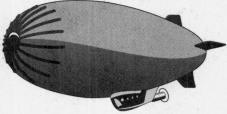

Answer: It takes 68,000 cubic feet. The envelope part of the blimp is 140 feet long and 45 feet tall. The blimp carries three passengers plus the pilot, and its top speed is 57 mph. You can read more at the MetLife Blimp page
http://www.metlife.com/Blimp/blimp-toc.html

If you forgot the words to "gopher guts" try lyrics in MUSIC AND MUSICIANS.

FIJI
ROB KAY'S FIJI ISLANDS GUIDE

Fiji consists of over 300 islands of various sizes. If you visit, you'll find all sorts of fun things to do: kayaking, hiking to a volcano, sliding down a watery slope, bird watching, scuba diving, and surfing. The main attraction, though, according to this Web site's author, is the people of Fiji. He says, "Fijian customs reflect an utmost dignity and courtesy toward the visitor. There are ceremonies for every occasion, which may include the presentation of tabua (whale's teeth), food or other gifts, or more commonly the drinking of yaqona (kava), the national beverage."

http://www.fijiguide.com/

Scrapbook of Fiji

This journalist's site is subtitled "A scrapbook of six months in paradise." Take a virtual vacation with the author, and you'll see that the customs in Fiji are unique. You'll get a feel for their ceremonies, clothing, homes, and special events by looking at the pictures and text. It's fun to attend a village wedding, a 21st birthday party, and the installation of a new tribal chief. You'll find a good collection of links here, too.

http://www.en.com/users/laura8/

FINLAND
A blast through SW Finland by Greg Rubidge

This fellow took a trip through Finland, and now he shares it on the Web. It's sort of a "What I Did on My Vacation" report, and it gets kind of wordy, but the stories are fabulous. He says it all boils down to the people, the places, and the food. One of the experiences he had was taking a "smoke sauna." They have 4.5 saunas for every one person in Finland! As for the food, he'll have you drooling with his description of the sweets.

http://www.hype.com/finnart/

The truth is out there in UFOS AND EXTRATERRESTRIALS. Maybe.

The Finnish Sauna

OK, here are directions for taking a sauna bath. Hop in the sauna room. It's about 175 to 210 degrees Fahrenheit. When you're good and hot, get out of there and run to the river, lake, or snowbank. Jump in. When you're good and freezing, run back to the sauna. Actually, there are better instructions at this site. Learn how to take a sauna the way the Finns really do. Along the way, you'll find out the history behind this thousand-year-old tradition and learn the vocabulary.

http://www.hut.fi/~icankar/sauna/

Suomea Matkailijoille (English)

Audio files will teach you Finnish. Listen carefully to a few of the words. Each one has the accent on a certain syllable, and it's always the same syllable! Can you tell which one? It makes the spoken language have a lilting rhythm. Could you recognize a Finn this way, even if you didn't know the language? You'll also find a nice collection of links here.

http://www.travlang.com/languages/cgi-bin/
   langchoice.cgi?page=main&lang1=english&lang2
   =finnish

Travel in Finland

From the reindeer in northern Lapland to Helsinki in the south, there's lots to see in Finland. Would you like to take a canoe out on the lake or have an adventure with a snowmobile? How about swimming in ten pools under one roof? If you strap on your skis, and your courage, you can learn to ski jump!

http://www.travel.fi/int/

Virtual Finland - Information about Finland - Facts about Finland

This is a super-complete site, with the lowdown on everything about Finland. A multimedia show awaits you in The Four Seasons of Finland. It has beautiful pictures taken during the year, along with the sounds of nature and poetic text. Is that a woodpecker you hear in the distance? Finland has six national nature symbols. See if you can figure out what they might be. The Finnish Way of Life section will tell you about the people's festivities, origins, sayings, food, and more. Arts and Entertainment has pictures of men and women in the national costume.

http://virtual.finland.fi/finfo/findeng.html

FRANCE

Cats in Paris

Cats that travel around and pose in front of landmarks in Paris? Why do they look suspiciously the same in every photo? There they are at the Eiffel Tower. Look—they got to go to Disneyland Paris! My, they look sophisticated in front of the Louvre. Check some landmarks of Paris with your tour guides, *les chats formidables*. These cats really get around; if you go to their main page at *<http://www.designltd.com/cats/>* you can see them in Boston and Houston.

http://www.neosoft.com/~dscarb/paris/france.htm

Discovery of a Palaeolithic painted cave at Vallon - Pont-d'Arc (Ardèche)

You're about to explore a cave in France. Crawl down. As you clear a narrow passageway, you head further into a previously untouched cavern. Wait, what's that on the ground? Cave bear skeletons! Shine your headlamp over there on the wall. You can just make out some things. They are paintings of animals, all over the walls. Discover more about these ancient cave drawings at this site.

http://www.culture.fr/culture/gvpda-en.htm

Wolves are a howl in MAMMALS.

What is the sound of one router flapping?

France - Travel - Tourism - Tours - Festivals - Studies - Ski

If you ski or snowboard, then you'll want to head to the French Alps for some of the best snow in the world. You're not a cold-weather fan? Find a coastal town and enjoy the beach life. You can discover the other regions of France, too, or learn about the many cultural festivals. The site is in both French and English. If you want to learn French, this would be one way to start.

http://www.france.com/francescape/top.html

Les Pages de Paris / The Paris Pages

Here's a more serious look at Paris. It's bilingual, with both French and English versions. The city, its culture, its tourist sites, train stations, museums, monuments—it's all here. In the Culture section are special expositions featuring historic postcards, including a photo history of the August 1944 liberation of Paris during World War II.

http://www.paris.org/

Louvre W3

This museum was originally designed as a palace. In medieval times, it was a fortress. Now you can walk in what used to be the moats, but now your feet will stay dry! The collections include not just French art but also paintings, sculpture, and works of art from many countries and times. To jump right to the paintings, go to <http://mistral.culture.fr/louvre/anglais/musee/collec/peinture.htm>. Whose eyes are those peering out at you? Click on them to find out.

http://mistral.culture.fr/louvre/louvrea.htm

> ## You know something the Net doesn't. Make your own home page!

Welcome Official Government Page of the President and the Prime Minister of France

Learn about the various duties of the President and the Prime Minister of France, how they are chosen, and how their jobs are similar, yet different. In the Quick Facts section, you know what you'll find! In the National Symbols area, you can find out about the history of the tricolor flag and discover how the rooster came to be an unofficial symbol of the French people. For more solid information, try the French Embassy in the US Page at <http://www.info-france-usa.org/>.

http://www.premier-ministre.gouv.fr/ENG/SOM.HTM

FRENCH GUIANA

Lonely Planet -- Destination: French Guiana

This South American country is about the size of the state of Indiana. It is an overseas department of France. This page includes basic tourist information, but there isn't much! You might also check the World Factbook page at <http://www.odci.gov/cia/publications/nsolo/factbook/fg.htm>.

http://www.lonelyplanet.com.au/dest/sam/fgu.htm

FRENCH POLYNESIA

Tahiti Explorer

Maybe you've heard of Tahiti. It's the largest of the 115 islands that make up French Polynesia, an overseas territory of France. If you were going to imagine a perfect South Pacific island, this would be it: volcanoes in the background, lush plants and huts in the foreground. Ocean life all around includes sharks, dolphins, and coral reefs. This page has info about many of the French Polynesian islands, including the Marquesas, Moorea, Bora Bora, and more. Other good pages on the area are at <http://www.fix.net/~wdavis/fp_home.html> and <http://www.wtgonline.com/country/pf/gen.html>.

http://www.tahiti-explorer.com/

> ## Have an order of pi in MATH AND ARITHMETIC.

GABON
Gabon

Albert Schweitzer did his humanitarian work in Gabon. Now there's a museum and hospital in the city where he lived. Gabon is also the land of the African pygmy tribes; you can reach some areas of the jungle only by canoe. If you have any mahogany furniture in your home, it may have come from Gabon. Most of the trees there are red mahogany, a beautiful hardwood. If you thought that Florida was the only place where manatees lived, guess again. They live off the coast of this country, too. The lowland gorilla is another inhabitant. Are you studying them, or is it the other way around? There is also a little more information at the Gabon General page: <http://www.wtgonline.com/country/ga/gen.html>.

http://www.sas.upenn.edu/African_Studies/
  Country_Specific/Gabon.html

GAMBIA
The Republic of The Gambia's Web Page

This snake-shaped country follows the river Gambia. If you take a boat upriver, you'll see all kinds of wildlife, including hippos. With your jungle hat and some tropical clothing, you'll be set to explore. Since the climate is pleasant compared to much of West Africa, it should be an enjoyable trip! What do you suppose it was like, though, back in the days of the slave ships? Learn about the history of this land here at the official government page.

http://www.gambia.com/

GEORGIA
Sakartvelo - former Republic of Georgia

Just about everything about Georgia must be on this page! You can listen to a Georgian folk song. See lots of art. Read about the history (it used to be part of the Soviet Union). Uncover old relics, like temples and feudal fortresses. See the Caucasus mountains—one of them is called the "Pyramid of Ice." Learn the language. Caution: This page has huge graphics and takes a long time to load, and there is a text-only option; the photos of the icons and paintings are wonderful, though.

http://www.missouri.edu/~c676747/sakartvelo.shtml

GERMANY
Chris De Witt's Berlin Wall Web Page

If Net-mom had written this book in 1989, it would have had two entries for Germany: one for East Germany and one for West Germany. In fact, the city of Berlin was divided by a huge wall, separating the western, Democratic side from the eastern, Communist side. Travel was very restricted between East and West. Border guards were always on the lookout for people trying to escape to the West. Some people were killed. But all that is over now, and the two sides are reunited into one Germany. Read about the history of the wall here.

http://www.users.dircon.co.uk/~chrisx/

Convention & Visitors Bureau Heidelberg - Home Page

Heidelberg is an historic German city with a famous university, which was founded in 1386! Don't miss the sight-seeing section of this page. Check the Student's Prison, which was sort of like detention in the 1700s. If a student played a trick on a teacher or participated in a duel with another student or was too loud or disorderly, then that student was sent off to "prison" for a few days. Supposedly, the prisoners were let out to go to class, but the rest of the time they had to stay there. You can still see the "artwork" on the walls! Don't miss the outstanding views of castles and other old buildings. This site is available in English, German, and Japanese.

http://www.germany.eu.net/shop/Heidelberg.info.cvb/
  english/

Deutsch für Reisende (English)

What do you say in Germany when you need to pass someone on a crowded bus? *Entschuldigen Sie.* OK, you're excused. But you'll want to be able to say lots more in German. You'll like these sound files, which teach you how to say the necessities, such as "swimming pool" and "ice cream"!

http://www.travlang.com/languages/cgi-bin/
  langchoice.cgi?page=main&lang1
  =english&lang2=german

Facts about Germany

This official site features a clickable map that lets you visit all 16 of Germany's states and find out info about them. The Country and People section will teach you about German national symbols, the flag, and the German national anthem—which you can also hear!

http://www.bundesregierung.de/ausland/index_e3.html

Germany Home Screen

Germany was one of the founding countries in the European Union. Here are facts and super photos of some of the more famous German sights. Hint: If you want to see a larger picture, click on any photo. You can then print it to include in a report or letter or scrapbook. Maps and travel tips for three German cities will help if you want to see them in person!

http://expedia.msn.com/wg/places/
   Germany/HSFS.htm

Lonely Planet -- Destination: Germany

From the industrial north to the alpine forests of the Bavarian south, Germany will charm you! It's true that the designers of the Disney World castle used Neuschwanstein Castle as their model; see it at <http://www.majesty.org/europe/germany1.html>. It is also true that there is no such thing as too much apple strudel! Why look at just any old map when you can click your way around this interactive map of Germany? A slide show and facts about the country will bring Germany to your desktop.

http://www.lonelyplanet.com.au/dest/eur/ger.htm

> ## Bring your shovel and meet me in the TREASURE AND TREASURE-HUNTING section.

GHANA

Ghana

Traveling to this African coastal country would be an adventure. Here's a woman who actually did it to take a drumming class, although she had never played the drums before. She really gives you a glimpse into what daily life is like. Learning to dance the native way, playing the drums, and eating *fou fou* (check it out) were all new things to try in this country. Wherever you are, you can learn how to make and tie a *lapa*, a long garment worn by women. There is also lots of information about kente cloth, batik, and other types of African textiles. And she suggests women splurge and get their hair braided! She kept her hair extensions in for seven weeks when she got home—they still looked great, but she got tired of them after that.

http://www.bpe.com/travel/africa/ghana/

The Republic of Ghana Home Page

Since this is the official site of Ghana, you'll get loads of accurate info, maps, and more. For example, you can see pictures of Ghanaian money. Can you spot a precious stone on the money? It's a diamond, an important export.

http://www.ghana.com/republic/

GIBRALTAR

Gibraltar Home Page

What a rock! You've seen it in commercials and logos. It's the Rock of Gibraltar in the Mediterranean Sea. Can you imagine wild apes roaming around on it? They are the only wild primates in Europe, and legend says that something will happen if the apes leave—find out here! The history of Gibraltar shows how it has been ruled by many different countries in the past. It has been a British colony since 1704 and has its own internal self-rule. A good, close-up map is at <http://www.lib.utexas.edu/Libs/PCL/Map_collection/europe/Gibraltar.jpg>.

http://www.gibraltar.gi/(plain)/home.html

GREECE
Greece Home Screen

Every country has its customs and manners. In Greece, it is impolite to leave any food on your plate. Of course, with all that wonderful Greek food, you won't want to quit eating! So get out your drachmas (Greek money) for some great meals. If you visit Athens, you'll be walking the same streets as Socrates and many other famous Greeks. The marathon (a 26-mile, 385-yard race) also started in Greece, when a runner was sent to tell others of a victory in battle. Aren't you glad we have telephones, radio, and the Net now?

http://expedia.msn.com/wg/places/Greece/HSFS.htm

Hellas On Line - Greek Pages

Hellas is another name for Greece. The interactive map here will show you a photo of each city as you click on it. There sure are a lot of islands! Now let's go back in time. The Mythology & History section is great to help you keep track of all those Greek gods, Fates, Muses, and semigods. A family tree and other info will help you get them straight. Another jumpstation site we like is called GoGreece, at <http://www.gogreece.com/> and from there you can take your pick of links on cooking, music, culture, and current events. One of the links we found through that site is called the Traveling Classroom at <http://www.gogreece.com/classroom/index.htm> where you join teacher Cheryl and her elementary students on a virtual tour to Greece.

http://www.hol.gr/greece/

THE HISTORY OF GREEK COSTUME

Do you only think of togas when you think of ancient Greek costume? Actually, their clothing changed through the centuries. They used a lot of cloth in their flowing dresses, and it must have cost a lot to weave threads of silver and gold into the costumes. You'll see many designs here, but parents, early ones are very revealing. How do you suppose we know what they wore if they didn't have photos back then? Find out here.

http://www.firstnethou.com/annam/costhist.html/

The Olympic Games in the Ancient Hellenic World

Click on a room of this virtual museum to find out about the ancient Greek Olympics. Read about the history of the games. (Did you know that they were held every four years, even back then?) Wander around Zeus' temple in virtual reality. A slide show of the ruins and modern-day cities gives you a look at Greece then and now. They didn't have as many different sports back then as we have now. How many are the same now as then? Visit this site and see!

http://devlab.dartmouth.edu/olympic/

Tourist Guide of Greece - Plus S.A.

This is a whole lot more than just a tourist guide. Sure, you get great pictures of the 9,000 miles of Greek coast; you can click on the regions and find more photos and information. You also get Greece's history, starting with the Stone Age.

http://www.vacation.forthnet.gr/

NET FILES

When you touch something **hot***, your brain makes you say "OUCH!" right away. How fast does information travel within the human nervous system?*

Answer: It depends on which type of neuron is sending the message. According to the Neuroscience Resources for Kids page, "Transmission can be as slow as 0.5 meters per second or as fast as 120 meters per second. That's the same as going 250 miles per hour!!! Check the math out yourself." Speed over to http://weber.u.washington.edu/~chudler/what.html for more fun facts from the world of neuroscience.

WebAcropol : Welcome !!

Take this virtual tour of the Acropolis, which is a famous monument in Athens, Greece. The temples are linked to the Greek gods and goddesses. As you take this tour, you'll unearth the ruins right along with the history. Many of the columns and marble slabs are still standing, after more than 24 centuries!

http://www.mechan.ntua.gr/webacropol/

GREENLAND
Greenland Guide Index

Lemmings, those furry, cute little creatures, are on the stamps of Greenland. Other animals, famous people, plants, and scenes are on the stamps, too. Be sure to send away for a free brochure and booklet about the wonderful world of Greenland. In the northern part of this cold country, the ground stays frozen all year! Here are just a few of the unusual sights in Greenland, home to the Inuit people: icebergs, whales, reindeer, dog sleds, the northern lights, the midnight sun, kayaks, musk oxen, and the fjords. If you don't know what some of these are, just visit the site to find out. Greenland is part of the kingdom of Denmark, but it has home rule and its own parliament, which you can find out about here. You can also look at Santa Claus' page, too! We thought he lived at the North Pole, but it turns out he has a place in Greenland, too.

http://www.greenland-guide.dk/

GRENADA
Grenada Home Screen

Grenada is also known as the Caribbean "spice island." Lots of spices are grown here, including nutmeg, allspice, and cinnamon. A nutmeg pod even appears on its flag! Perhaps you'd like a hike through the rain forest? Bring your machete along, because you'll need it to hack away the plants. Or, if you'd rather snorkel, the reefs are beautiful. Watch out for the jellyfish and other critters, though.

http://expedia.msn.com/wg/places/Grenada/HSFS.htm

Grenada - Official Travel Guide

Escaping to a tropical island can sound pretty good sometimes. Grenada is in the Caribbean. It's lush as can be, and no building may be taller than a coconut palm. Plus, it has an extinct volcano! The waterfalls will make you want to splash around underneath them. When Christopher Columbus sailed by this island, he named it something else. To find out this little tidbit and other history about Grenada, you'll need to go to the site. The World Factbook page on Grenada is at <http://www.odci.gov/cia/publications/nsolo/factbook/gj.htm>.

http://www.interknowledge.com/grenada/

GUADELOUPE
Guadeloupe Home Screen

Chris Columbus landed here too, like so many other places. He gave it its name. Today, it's nicknamed "the butterfly," because it's shaped like one. It's also known as the "Island of Beautiful Waters" because of its waterfalls. The people who live there love music. Can you hear that Caribbean beat? There are still wooden huts right alongside the big hotels. Where would you rather stay? If you like to bike, you'll be able to get around Guadeloupe just fine. It's the craze there, besides diving. Guadeloupe is an overseas department of France. Its World Factbook page is at <http://www.odci.gov/cia/publications/nsolo/factbook/gp.htm>.

http://expedia.msn.com/wg/Places/Guadeloupe/HSFS.htm

GUATEMALA
About Guatemala

In this land of volcanoes, caves, and the ancestors of the Mayan people, you'll see amazing sights. Check out the toucans or the green and red quetzal (the national bird), which appears on the flag. You'll also see photos of the ancient Mayan ruins. Guatemala's World Factbook page is at <http://www.odci.gov/cia/publications/nsolo/factbook/gt.htm>.

http://www.ualr.edu/~degonzalez/Guatemala.html

GUERNSEY

Welcome to the Official Guernsey Tourism WWW Site

Tucked right between England and France, this Channel Island is famous for its cows. Yes, Guernsey cows. You're just as likely to see one of them on the beach as in a pasture. Did pirates sail past Guernsey or did they land there with their loot? See these pages to find out. Another reminder of history is the Castle Cornet. They still fire a cannon there each day at noon. And look at the new stamps in the post office: cats, flowers, and movie detectives! Guernsey is a British Crown dependency; see its World Factbook page at <http://www.odci.gov/cia/publications/nsolo/factbook/gk.htm>.

http://www.guernsey.net/~tourism/

GUINEA

Guinea Republic General

Waterfalls, rain forests, and wildlife are special sights. Street musicians will share their talents with you in the city. If you like spicy food, then the dishes of Guinea will suit you just fine (pass the water, please—quickly!). We pointed out an error in the History section to the webmaster; perhaps it will be corrected by the time you visit. The error was that the history of Guinea-Bissau was in the Republic of Guinea page. Oops. Still more info is located at <http://www.sas.upenn.edu/African_Studies/Country_Specific/Guinea.html>.

http://www.wtgonline.com/country/gn/gen.html

GUINEA-BISSAU

Guinea-Bissau General

Another West African country, this one sits right near Guinea. It used to belong to Portugal, and the official language is still Portuguese. If you like to eat nuts, you'll go nuts in Guinea-Bissau! They are one of the main exports. The businessmen don't wear suits and ties. Instead, they wear safari suits to work (and we thought business casual was invented in the U.S.). There is a little more info at <http://www.sas.upenn.edu/African_Studies/Country_Specific/G_Bissau.html>.

http://www.wtgonline.com/country/gw/gen.html

GUYANA

The Guyana World Wide Web Handbook

Did you think that the Netherlands was the only low-lying country protected by a seawall? Nope. Guyana's capital city also sits below sea level. Hey, there's a jaguar in the forest! Jaguars are on the national coat of arms, too, along with sugarcane and rice. Many races live in this South American country. If you explore the history, you'll understand why.

http://www.guyana.org/Handbook/handbook.htm

HAITI

Haiti MC Page

Click! Each spot on the map will take you to the history of that area of Haiti. This country shares the Caribbean island of Hispaniola with another country. Can you find out which one? The style of paintings from Haiti really makes you feel like you're right there in the tropics. You'll see lots of colors, green being the main one. And the music! It will have you moving with the beat. Would you like to try a taste of pumpkin soup or fried plantain (banana)? Along with the happier part of this island country, though, is the darkness of poverty and unrest. You should also try The Unofficial Haitian Home Page at <http://www.PrimeNet.Com:80/~rafreid/index.html>. You'll find voodoo links at both sites, since, according to the World Factbook at <http://www.odci.gov/cia/publications/nsolo/factbook/ha.htm>, the majority of Haitians practice it.

http://pasture.ecn.purdue.edu/~agenhtml/agenmc/haiti/haiti.html

**Attention everyone.
The Internet is closing.
Please go play
outside.**

HOLY SEE

See VATICAN CITY

HONDURAS

Honduras WebExplorer

Do you know Spanish and have a love of adventure? Then you might want to visit this country in Central America. There are still primitive tribes living in some areas of the rain forest. Paddle a wooden dugout canoe downriver to see them! Or maybe a visit to the ancient Mayan city of Copán would suit you. There are more questions about the Mayan people than there are answers. Maybe you could unearth a piece of their history. You can also check the Lonely Planet pages on Honduras for more information, at <*http://www.lonelyplanet.com/dest/cam/hon.htm*>.

http://www.hondurasweb.com/

HONG KONG

See CHINA

HUNGARY

HUNGARIAN IMAGES AND HISTORICAL BACKGROUND

The Hungarian national anthem and other music are here for your enjoyment. Our favorite is Beethoven's "King Stephen Overture." This first King of Hungary later became a saint. You'll get to look at his royal crown and jewels here. The national costumes are beautiful, with fancy hats, aprons, and embroidery. And there is an interesting section on Transylvania, which was part of the kingdom of Hungary until 1921 and is now part of Romania.

http://www.msstate.edu/Archives/History/hungary/
   hungary.html

HUNGARY - Introduction

Right smack in the middle of Europe—that's where you'll find Hungary. In this decade, we've seen the Communists give up their power. Now, Hungary is a democracy. The best part of this site is the tour of Budapest, the capital. It used to be three towns. One was named "Pest," and one was named "Obuda." Can you guess what the other town was?

http://www.fsz.bme.hu/hungary/intro.html

The Hungary Page

Hungary was first formed over 1,100 years ago, in the year 896. This page has more on its history, along with maps at different times. Be sure to check out all the famous Hungarians in our century. See pictures and biographies of famous Hungarian scientists and Olympians. It's amazing that so many come from such a small country! This is a jumpstation for many sites with information on Hungary, and not all links have been viewed.

http://mason.gmu.edu/~achassel/

Lonely Planet -- Destination: Hungary

Hungary is a mixture: old and new, Islam and Christianity, mosques and cathedrals, water and land, city and country. The slide show at this site will show you the contrasts.

http://www.lonelyplanet.com.au/dest/eur/hun.htm

ICELAND

DAILY NEWS FROM ICELAND

Daily news out of Iceland is free on the Net. When we opened an issue, they were talking about the record fish catch. Another headline showed that one-quarter of all Icelanders use the Internet. One writer told the story of how he woke up to complete darkness and got lost in a broom closet. Sunrise that morning was at 11:10 A.M.!

http://www.centrum.is/icerev/daily1.html

Eruption 96 - Iceland

That volcano is blowing its top! There are a lot of "hot spots" in Iceland. They include volcanoes, hot springs, and geysers. For a close-up look at a recent eruption of a volcano, check here.

http://geo.princeton.edu/~rallen/eruption96/

IGI Iceland General Information

The Nordic wool sweaters look warm. But the real gems of this site are the pictures: winter photos of kids playing in the snow; trees covered with crystals of ice; summer pictures of the countryside and the fjords; even the midnight sun! Santa Claus comes to Iceland, and his helpers have some mighty crazy names. Gully-guy? Keyhole-sniffer? What will Santa think of next? Find out in the IGI Where, what, how, who section at <http://www.zocalo.net/iceland/ice1.html#1_12>.

http://www.zocalo.net/iceland/

Islandia - Your Guide to Iceland

Iceland used to be called "Thule" long ago in history. This land that the Vikings settled was a great stepping-stone to the discovery of North America. Then why did the Vikings leave the island? Maybe you can be a detective and figure out the answer to this mystery. Along the way, learn some words in the Icelandic language. Visit the famous sites of the country. The geothermal areas are hot!

http://www.arctic.is/islandia/

Reykjavik

The Icelandic word for the capital, Reykjavik, means "smoky bay." But the explorers who discovered it weren't really seeing smoke. They were seeing steam from the hot springs! Residents even heat their homes with the hot water from these springs. You can swim in heated pools right next to the snow and ice. This site is almost as attractive as the city. You'll love the icy-looking colors.

http://www.rvk.is/

Virtually Virtual Iceland

You could spend days at this site, written by an Icelandic man. The section on Norse mythology is illustrated. Other goodies jump out at you. Make your own pair of Viking shoes from the patterns and instructions. Or, learn some Icelandic words from original sounds. Or you can figure out what your name would be if you went by their naming customs. Interactive maps link you to photos and stamps of the country.

http://www.itn.is/~gunnsi/gardar1.htm

INDIA
Hello, India! Home Page

Head right to the Kids World section, because it's the best part. You'll read illustrated stories from Indian folklore. One is about a bedbug (yes, a bedbug) that lives in the king's mattress. What do you think happened when the king let his feet poke out from under the covers? The story about a lion might remind you of another fable.

http://www.helloindia.com/

Indian Culture

This site will teach you about Indian clothing, art, dance, music, festivals, foods, films, and more. For example, did you know that 15 national languages are recognized by the Indian constitution? These languages together have over 1,600 variations or dialects!

http://www.indiagov.org/culture/overview.htm

An Introduction to India

Hop on board a camel and take a trek through India. You'll go to the Taj Mahal and the Himalayas. Maybe you can convince your camel to take a detour back in time. Some of the most advanced civilizations lived in ancient India. Moving into more modern times, you meet Mahatma Gandhi. He was a peaceful leader. This site is very, very wordy, but the information is good. Hey, why is your camel spitting? Tell him that's not nice.

http://www.interknowledge.com/india/

Khazana: India Arts Online - Bronze Castings, Paintings, Indian Music, Apparel, Musical Instruments, Collectables

Sitar, sarode, tabla, santur—what are those? They are just a few of the musical instruments of India. Some are stringed instruments, and others are drums. Hear the unusual sounds coming right out of your computer. You'll also get to see folk paintings in two different styles, bronze castings, and clothing designs. Explanations tell you about the traditions behind the art.

http://khazana.com/

Lonely Planet -- Destination: India

Go to each one of the regions of India with a clickable map. Photos, maps, and slide shows will give you a taste of this busy, crowded country. But hey, don't fall off that mountaintop! Some of the tallest peaks in the world are in India, and it's a long way down. There is a lot more to see. The temples are colorful, and see if you can find out why so many flags are flying in the wind.

http://www.lonelyplanet.com.au/dest/ind/ind.htm

Welcome to Indiahorizons

In 1997, India celebrates it 50th year of independence. To celebrate, AT&T has started this site. You can send a cybercard to a friend. Choose from all sorts of Indian designs for your greeting card. An art gallery features Indian artists. Submit your best work, too! Try out an Indian recipe, song, or even a sport. Go on a scavenger hunt called the "Secret of the Tijori." The virtual tour from a guy named "Cool Russ" is another treat.

http://www.att.com./indiahorizons/home.html

Welcome to the Non-violence Home Page

Mohandas K. Gandhi was a great leader of India who believed in nonviolence. His family has formed the Gandhi Institute to carry on his beliefs. You'll find quotes from Gandhi, such as "Your character must be above suspicion, and you must be truthful and self-controlled" and "Truth is what the voice within tells you." He also gave us his Seven Blunders of the World, and his grandson has added an eighth. What would the world be like if everyone lived as Gandhi did?

http://www.cbu.edu/Gandhi/

Olympics and Special Olympics info is found in SPORTS.

INDONESIA

BEAUTIFUL INDONESIA ONLINE - Home Page

The Indonesian archipelago (that means island group) consists of 17,500 islands and spans more than 3,000 miles from east to west, 1,200 miles from north to south. About 3,000 islands have people living on them. Indonesia has a total population of more than 190 million, making it the fourth most populous nation in the world! This site has lots to see. Wander around the largest Buddhist temple in the world. It's kind of like a pyramid, built of stone and fitted just right. This site also has a lot of photos and info on the art, culture, nature, and history of Indonesia. You've never heard of an animal called the *anoa*? That's because it's only found on the island of Sulawesi. You've never heard of Sulawesi? Time to hop over to this Web page: <http://www.travel-indonesia.com/indonesi/ind_faun.htm>.

http://www.travel-indonesia.com/

NET FILES

Does the word "vexillology" leave you vexed? What does it mean anyway?

Answer: Vexillology is the study of flags. Find out more about it at http://flags.cesi.it/flags/vexilla.html

The Country of Indonesia

Get the facts about Indonesia, its people, and places to see. Tour the rain forest and mountains. The photos are wonderful: take your choice of the bird, flora (plants), or fauna (birds and animals) tours. Wow—there's a Komodo dragon!

http://www.indonesiatoday.com/home.html

Home Page Indonesia Online

Indonesia doesn't have an autumn or winter. But it's sure got a rainy season! Find out more about the climate, geography, and history of this tropical region. From primitive tribes to advanced cities, each island has a slightly different culture.

http://ourworld.compuserve.com/homepages/
   arno_winarno/indolink.htm

Lonely Planet -- Destination: Indonesia

Active volcanoes, hot springs, tribal masks, and an island way of life. That's Indonesia, a country of many islands. They are home to unusual exotic plant and animal species. Not only that, but also people speak over 300 languages there!

http://www.lonelyplanet.com/dest/sea/indo.htm

Tourism Indonesia Homepage

This official government tourism page is where you can learn about the traditional gamelan orchestra, batik textiles, and native Orang Utan primates! You might also like the Holiday In Indonesia page at <http://www.asia1.com.sg/travel/indonesia/indo.html> even though it is pretty commercial and opinionated.

http://www.tourismindonesia.com/

Travelling in Indonesia Home Page

"I want to go there!" That is what you'll be saying when you see the beaches of Bali, the houses built on stilts in Sulawesi, the lakes of Sumatra, and the floating markets of South Kalimantan. And wait till you see the snowcapped mountains of Irian Jaya. What will you say when you see the Java tiger?

http://www.travel2indonesia.com/

**MOVIES are reel-y
entertaining!**

IRAN
IRAN: An Introduction

So many things are done differently in Iran! For example, the Persian alphabet has 32 letters, compared to 26 in English. A pronunciation guide will help you here. Persian is written left to right, and it's very beautiful. This site also looks at the history, cities, pilgrimage centers, behavior rules, and literature of the culture.

http://knight3.cit.ics.saitama-u.ac.jp/
   hobbies/iran/farsi.html

Welcome To NetIran

Visit this historic land with a virtual tour of the capital city, Tehran. You'll see landmarks, the bazaar, forms of recreation, and religious sites. The Persian rugs are often used as art instead of flooring. Some of them tell a story about ancient times. The Culture section has a good explanation of the changes brought by the Islamic cultural revolution.

http://www.netiran.com/

IRAQ
ArabNet -- Iraq, Contents

Iraq is sometimes called the "Cradle of Civilization." The earliest cultures lived between its two great rivers, the Tigris and the Euphrates. Many of the Bible's ancient cities (Nineveh, Ur, and Babylon) were in the area we now know as Iraq. This site gives a virtual tour and information on culture, history, and the government of Iraq. There is also information on the Gulf War and the invasion of Kuwait by Iraq's Saddam Hussein.

http://www.arab.net/iraq/iraq_contents.html

**Well-informed lizards,
snakes, and other herps
read the REPTILES
resources.**

IRELAND

Eolas ar Sátt na hÉirwann - Information on the Irish State

The official site for the government of Ireland is filled with facts and information about Ireland and its government. You can read speeches by the current president and biographies of all the past presidents. How about a tour of the public reception areas, state dining rooms, and meeting rooms of Áras an Uachtaráin, the official residence of the president. Look at those Waterford crystal chandeliers—beautiful!

http://www.irlgov.ie/

Irish Tourist Board

This official site will get you in the mood for a trip to Ireland! Learn about Irish scenery (it's not always green!), places to visit, food and drink, and more. You might also like the Interactive Travel Guide to the best of Ireland at <http://www.iol.ie/~discover/welcome.htm>. Don't miss its tour to Blarney Castle, where you can kiss the Blarney Stone, if you are athletic!

http://www.ireland.travel.ie/

Lonely Planet -- Destination: IRELAND

This is a brief overview of travel in Ireland, as well as short facts on its history and culture. Did you know that Ireland is called "The Emerald Isle"? That's because its landscape is said to have 50 shades of green!

http://www.lonelyplanet.com/dest/eur/ire.htm

A Wee Bit O' Fun

Leprechaun followers finally have a Web site on Saint Patrick's Day and everything that goes along with it. Here, you can learn how Saint Patrick was kidnapped by pirates at the age of 16. Read how he eventually became the patron saint of Ireland. Check out the section of lucky things to do on Saint Patrick's Day!

http://www.nando.net/toys/stpaddy/stpaddy.html

ISLE OF MAN

Welcome to the Isle of Man

Legend has it that two fierce warriors battled between England and Ireland. In the course of the battle a large chunk of Ireland was hurled, but it missed its target and fell into the North Irish Sea. And that is how the Isle of Man was created! Well, believe what you like, but know for certain that this Web site contains a good overview of this historical island country, a British Crown dependency. Its history (wow, Vikings), its geography and climate (not too hot or cold), and its people (Irish and English settlers) are all explored briefly here. And there are great pictures, too! Check out the Basking Shark project and the Home for Old Horses. And what is the story behind the national symbol: three running legs connected in the center? Find out here. There is a little more at Manxman's Page at <http://ourworld.compuserve.com/homepages/manxman/>.

http://www.isle-of-man.com/

ISRAEL

Israel Ministry of Tourism

What part of Israel would you like to visit first? Perhaps the historic Galilee area to the north? Or maybe Jerusalem, with sites holy to three different religions: Christianity, Judaism, and Islam. This official government tourism site will give you lots of ideas, pictures, and even a brief QuickTime movie! Other great tourism sites, with lots of virtual tours, are at the (almost) Complete Guide to WWW in Israel at <http://gauss.technion.ac.il/~nyh/israel/english/34.html> and the Infotour at <http://www.infotour.co.il/main.html>.

http://www.travelnet.co.il/tnet/mtoursm/

Maven - More than 4,500 Jewish/Israel Links!

There are two words to describe this site: neat and complete. As the title says, there are thousands of links to sites with Jewish or Israeli stuff in them. Topic sections include Youth & Students, Sports & Hobbies, Entertainment, Holocaust & Anti-Semitism, Law, Communities & Synagogues, and many more.

http://www.maven.co.il/

Welcome to Virtual Jerusalem: The Jewish World From the Heart of Israel

OK, here is a joke: How do you flavor your virtual latkes? Answer: With CyberSpice! Besides acting as a gateway to the Web, Virtual Jerusalem's home page is a destination for Internet users seeking Israeli and Jewish headline news, daily features, study classes, an Israel vacation guide, an extensive online Jerusalem photo gallery, and advertisements. Virtual Jerusalem also provides a chat feature where kids can discuss issues with other kids from around the world. And the virtual tour itself is at *<http://virtual.co.il/communities/jerusalem/pathways/>*.

http://virtual.co.il/

ITALY

See also: VATICAN CITY

Learn to Speak Italian

Ragu, maker of Italian sauces and foods, presents Mama to teach you a little useful Italian. Some are actually phrases your parents might use, such as *Hai già fatto il tuo compito per casa?* (Have you done your homework yet?) It's funny and entertaining, plus there are Real Audio files so you can hear the phrases. For more beginner's Italian, try Tyler Jones' site at *<http://www.hardlink.com/~chambers/Italian/>*.

http://www.eat.com/learn-italian/

Lonely Planet -- Destination: Italy

In Italy, an archaeological treasure, historical building, or church is never far from sight. Learn about the history and culture of Italy, including a look at its regions and what makes them special. You can also click on further information about the major cities, including Rome and Florence, among others. And don't forget to have a look at the links!

http://www.lonelyplanet.com/dest/eur/ita.htm

Our Trip to the Pasta Factory

The second graders took a field trip to a pasta factory in Formia, Italy, and they made a Web site about it. Special flour is used to make the dough. The dough is forced through various molds to make the different pasta shapes. Then the pasta is dried, and finally boxed. The whole process takes about 12 hours! Find out more here. Then visit the main page of their school, the Naples Elementary School, which is a school for the kids of U.S. military and civilian Department of Defense personnel: *<http://www.naples.navy.mil/nes/nes.html>*

http://www.naples.navy.mil/nes/pasta.html

Welcome to Italy - Embassy of Italy - Washington, D.C.

If you need the sheet music to the national anthem of Italy, you can download a copy here. Then you can listen to the MIDI audio file and sing along. After all that exertion, you're probably hungry, and this site has plenty of wholesome Italian recipes to help you fill up those nooks and crannies in your tummy! In addition, you will find info on the government, history, and tourist regions. Check Pisa in the Tuscany section; it shows an aerial photo of the Leaning Tower that gives you an interesting new perspective.

http://www.italyemb.nw.dc.us/italy/

IVORY COAST

See CÔTE D'IVOIRE

JAMAICA
The Land of Jamaica

According to this site, Jamaica's name is derived from an Aarawak word *Xaymaca*, meaning "land of wood and water." After 300 years as a British colony, Jamaica became independent in 1962, although it remains part of the British commonwealth. Learn more about its history here.

http://www.webcom.com/~travel/jam1.html

The Unofficial Web Site on Jamaica

Sell mi tree poun a swimps (Sell me three pounds of shrimps). Can you speak patois? It's called either an island dialect of English or Real English, depending on who you are talking to! You can learn some phrases in Jamaican patois here, as well as get a look at island culture, music, and history. A caution to parents: Preview this site to see if it is appropriate for your family; some parts are mildly racy.

http://www.jamaicans.com/jam.htm

The World Factbook page on Jamaica

Need some hard facts for that report due on Monday? Maybe you just want to know what type of government Jamaica has (parliamentary democracy) or what the major exports are (bauxite, sugar, bananas). If so, you should definitely check out the listings for Jamaica here. This site contains information on everything from geography to defense forces.

http://www.odci.gov/cia/publications/nsolo/
factbook/jm.htm

JAPAN
ASIJ Elementary School Home Page

How would you feel about attending a Japanese tea ceremony for the first time? Would you know what to do? If someone gave you a chance to try playing a large stringed instrument—a *koto*—what would it be like? The kids at The American School in Japan have done all that and more! They've written about their experiences, and you'll learn all sorts of things from their Web page. For example, the tea used in a tea ceremony is bitter, so make sure you get a piece of candy in your mouth first! Be sure to read about Japanese holidays, too, especially the New Year's celebrations.

http://www.asij.ac.jp/elementary/Welcome.html

> **Surf,
> and you shall become
> empowered (or wet).**

Japan Information

This is the best general-interest site we could find. You can hear "Kimigayo," Japan's national anthem, plus try some links to Japanese sites on travel, culture, history, and more. You might try the Japanese art of origami, or bonsai, the art of growing small trees in miniature potted landscapes. This site even has a map of the subway system! You'll find it at <http://www.eccosys.com/CHIKA/index.html>. A similar-sounding site is also excellent. It's called the Japan Information Network at <http://www.jinjapan.org/> and is part of the Ministry of Foreign Affairs site.

http://SunSITE.sut.ac.jp/asia/japan/

The Japanese Tutor

This extensive guide to Japanese culture and language will let you hear everyday Japanese words and phrases. You'll also learn the polite way to count on your fingers and how to use chopsticks!

http://www.missouri.edu/~c563382/

Kid's Window

This is a great site for American and Japanese children. Here, kids can visit a virtual library with stories and a picture dictionary, a restaurant filled with delicious Japanese dishes (and how to pronounce them), a school with language and crafts areas, and a gallery of art created by kids aged 3 to 18. This site was a semifinalist in the 1996 National Information Infrastructure (NII) Awards.

http://jw.nttam.com/KIDS/kids_home.html

KIDS WEB JAPAN

This site provides a look into the life and culture of Japanese children. Many Japanese kids eat miso soup, pickled vegetables, and rice for breakfast. A school lunch might consist of fish, meat, sea vegetables, and fruit. But what do they like to eat in a fast-food restaurant? Hamburgers, fried chicken, and other delights! You can find out the answers to many questions about Japanese daily life at this entertaining and informative site. Finally, you will have an answer to the question, "Did real ninjas ever exist?" at <http://www.jinjapan.org/kidsweb/japan/i/q3.html>.

http://www.jinjapan.org/kidsweb/

Living in Tokyo is....

This excellent winner from last year's Cyberfair was created by over 40 kids from a school in Japan. They will tell you from experience that living in Tokyo is fun, delicious, interesting, challenging, and inspiring! You'll discover the fascinating material they present on Japanese customs, theater and music, sumo wrestling, foods, and more.

http://cyberfair.gsn.org/smis/contents.html

JERSEY

JerseyWeb - Home Page

Jersey Web has information on just about anything you need to know about this Channel Island. With links to other helpful sites, tourism info, and more, this is a great site if you are planning a trip or you just want some information about the island, which is only 14 miles from France. Heard of Jersey cows? (Or is that "herd" of Jersey cows?) They come from there.

http://www.jersey.co.uk/

States of Jersey Home Page

This page is the official site of Jersey's government. As the largest of the Channel Islands, it is a British Crown dependency. Heritage, sports, government, business, and tourism are covered at this site.

http://www.jersey.gov.uk/

JORDAN

ArabNet -- Jordan, Contents

Jordan's entry in ArabNet is one of the most fact-filled sites you can find concerning the country. It has an overview section that covers all the stuff you could find at the World Factbook site, plus it has a section devoted to history, geography, business, culture, government, transportation, a tour guide, and links, too. One of the crafts available in Jordan is blown glass. Although it used to be made from sand— Jordan's deserts supplied a lot of that—now these beautiful fragile artworks are made of recycled bottles. Hungry? Jordan's national dish is called mansaf, which is a whole stewed lamb cooked in a yogurt sauce and served on a bed of rice.

http://www.arab.net/jordan/jordan_contents.html

National Information System

King Hussein binTalal, the King of Jordan, ascended the throne when he was only 17 years old! He immediately instituted some reforms, notably freedom of speech and freedom of the press. So it's no wonder that his government has a very beautiful and informative Web site. You'll find information on the royal family, a history of Jordan, a map, and what attracts tourists to this land. Hint: Click on the map and the other pictures at the top of the page to get to the best parts of this site.

http://petra.nic.gov.jo/

KAZAKHSTAN

ICARP -Kazakhstan WWW VL

Part of the collaborative WWW Virtual Library project, the Interactive Central Asia Resource Project (ICARP) hosts a very informative site for those looking for information on Kazakhstan. With maps, flags, culture, links, and more, you can't go wrong. One we've selected for you contains a nice color map, a flag, and World Factbook information: <*http://www.bucknell.edu/ departments/russian/facts/kazakh.html*>.

http://www.rockbridge.net/personal/bichel/kazakh.htp

Waukesha-Kokshetau Sister City Page

Come see what a little cooperation can do. Two cities on opposite side of the globe have worked together to make a cultural link over thousands of miles. They give students from each city a chance to visit another culture and people. When Kokshetau needed a hand, Waukesha, Wisconsin, was there. After the breakdown of the Soviet Union, Waukesha began a relief effort, ultimately saving the lives of many Kokshetau kids.

http://www.execpc.com/~fdr5/sistercity.html

For happy hedgehogs see PETS AND PET CARE.

KENYA
Kenya

The author of this page has cobbled together lots of useful resources and links on Kenyan history and culture. The symbols on the Kenyan flag include a shield and two spears. You can hear the national anthem here and follow along with it in English or Swahili.

http://www.rcbowen.com/kenya/

KenyaWeb - Kenya's Definitive Internet Resource

KenyaWeb is the one-stop site for Kenya information and resources. You can find general information such as history, culture, and geography, as well as governmental information, commercial information, tourist information, and education information. There are over 40 ethnic groups in Kenya, and you can find information on many of them here. Also famous for its national parks, Kenya's wildlife is world-famous. Did you know that in Swahili, *safari* means "a journey"?

http://www.kenyaweb.com/

KIRIBATI
CHRISTMAS ISLAND, KIRIBATI

Because of its proximity to the equator, Kiritimati Atoll (also called Christmas Island) does not have seasons as most of us know them. With the mean daytime temperature hovering at 80 degrees Fahrenheit, temperatures in January are virtually identical to those in July. For those of us living anywhere up north where winter starts in October and sometimes lasts for six or seven months, this kind of climate is hard to imagine! When British explorer James Cook landed here on Christmas Eve in 1777, the island was uninhabited. Since then, it has been annexed by Britain, used as an airfield by the U.S. during World War II, and now is part of the nation of Kiribati. This tropical atoll is one of the largest islands formed by coral in the Pacific Ocean. Check this site to find out about many of the other unique features of this Pacific paradise.

http://www.earth.tohoku.ac.jp/kiribati/xmasi.html

KIRIBATI HOME PAGE

A country of many small coral atolls, Kiribati was a former colony of Great Britain. Its flag shows a yellow frigate bird flying in front of a sunrise over the blue sea. There are complex rules of behavior you need to know in case you ever visit: for example, never touch anyone on the head or walk across their outstretched legs! Read more about how to keep from offending the residents of this Pacific island nation.

http://www.earth.tohoku.ac.jp/kiribati/kiribati.html

KOREA, NORTH
The World Factbook page on Korea, North

Also known as the Democratic People's Republic of Korea, North Korea is currently suffering through a food shortage. They have appealed for help, but world powers are trying to tie food donations to peace talks between North Korea and South Korea. North Korea doesn't want that. Meanwhile, people are eating tree bark and roots to keep from starving. This stands in stark contrast to the "heroic-style" press releases you will read at <http://www.kcna.co.jp/>. We don't understand it, either, but then again, we don't know all the facts.

http://www.odci.gov/cia/publications/nsolo/
    factbook/kn.htm

KOREA, SOUTH
Information about South Korea

Pack your big suitcase and let's go! You'll visit museums, you'll meet the government officials, you'll hear the national anthem. Everything you could ever want to know about and see in South Korea is here at this site. Bon voyage, and give our regards to the President and his family. We all know about the White House in Washington, D.C., but do we know about the South Korean President's Blue House? It's called Chong Wa Dae, and you can visit it at <http://www.bluehouse.go.kr/eng/welcome.html>. While you're there, send the President a postcard in the special area for kids.

http://earth.library.pitt.edu/~ealib/skorea.htm

Korea Tour Home Page

This official site, from the Korea National Tourism Organization, is beautifully crafted. Sure, it has all the tourist information you'd want. But there is also some very unusual stuff. For example, in the Tourist Attractions area, you'll find sound files from several unique instruments. Listen to the Kayagum, a 12-stringed zither that dates back to the sixth century. For a larger Asian map and more facts, such as languages spoken in South Korea, climate, foods, and more, try <http://falcon.postech.ac.kr/ ~ipawb/misc/glance.html>.

http://www.knto.or.kr/

South Korea

If you're looking for environmental and energy resource information on South Korea, look no further. Check out this site to find the source of their natural resources and what they're doing to protect the environment. No pictures, but there is a good map—in case you want to include one in your report.

http://www.eia.doe.gov/emeu/cabs/skorea.html

NET FILES

Sand castles, algae-coated slime, and lava balls are some of the features you've come all this way to see. **Where are you, anyway?**

Answer: You've reached a vacation spot known as Ape Cave, a geologic feature near Mount St. Helens in Washington. It's an ancient lava tube with a hiking trail inside, where you can meet millipedes, banter with bats, and commune with the cave slime. Don't touch the slime, though, because it will die! The slime is really made of algae and bacteria, and it performs a special function in the cave. Read about Ape Cave at http://volcano.und.nodak.edu/vwdocs/msh/ov/ovb/ovbac.html

KUWAIT

The State of Kuwait - Ministry of Information Office, Washington, DC, USA

Do you have a question about Kuwait? Here's an official source of information. Although known for its oil production, Kuwait also has a long maritime tradition. In fact, the national emblem of Kuwait is a "falcon with outspread wings embracing a dhow (Boom) sailing on blue and white waves." There is also a special folk tradition called the "sea shanty." Special songs and dances accompany various types of work on the pearl diving ships. Find out more here!

http://www.kuwait.info.nw.dc.us/

KYRGYZSTAN

ICARP - Kyrgyzstan WWW VL

The WWW Virtual Library page on Kyrgyzstan includes loads of links to material on this nation in central Asia, carved out of the former Soviet Union. Another useful site on Kyrgyzstan is the Business and Tourist directory at <http://ourworld.compuserve.com/ homepages/dite/>. The history of the people is very interesting—the record goes back as far as 2 B.C.! The Kyrghyz people began as an alliance of nomadic tribes; in fact, one interpretation of the word *Kyrghyz* is "forty tribes."

http://www.rockbridge.net/personal/bichel/kyrgyz.htp

LAOS

Discovering Laos

Laos, or Lao People's Democratic Republic, used to be called Lane Xang, "The Land of a Million Elephants." My Travel in Laos at <http://www2.gol.com/users/ akihito/html/laos.html> is interesting for beautiful pictures of people, places, and events. It is unusual to see the things people have fashioned out of old U.S. bombs: horse troughs, park benches, and flower planters. The Lonely Planet Destination: Laos pages are another good source of information, at <http:// www.lonelyplanet.com/dest/sea/laos.htm>, and you need some background on the Hmong peoples' situation from the WWW Hmong Homepage at <http://www.stolaf.edu/people/cdr/hmong/>.

http://www.laoembassy.com/discover/

LATVIA

Embassy of Latvia - Washington, D.C.

Latvia is one of the Baltic nations (the others are Lithuania and Estonia) located on the Baltic Sea. It achieved independence in 1991 due to the breakup of the Soviet Union. The Ministry of Foreign Affairs has an excellent history of Latvia and notes on its culture and people at <http://www.mfa.bkc.lv/mfa/pub/public.htm>. Latvians have a long history of cultural and artistic tradition—and they love to sing! According to this page, "More than 1.4 million folk songs, or 'dainas,' almost always four-line couplets reflecting the ethics, morals and lifestyles of ancient Latvians, have been identified, thanks largely to the pioneering work of Krisjanis Barons (1835 -1923)." There is also an interesting history of the Latvian National Emblem at <http://home.earthlink.net/~ibezdechi/gerb.htm>. Lions, griffins, sun, and stars—what do they all mean?

http://www.seas.gwu.edu/guest/latvia/

Latvian Language

This resource teaches just a little Latvian, with audio files and crossword puzzles! You can also see and hear the letters of the alphabet and learn some of the history of the language.

http://www.codefusion.com/latvianasp/latonline.asp

LEBANON

Embassy of Lebanon

The Embassy of Lebanon in Washington, D.C., has a very nicely designed page that gives a lot of background information on the country. Lebanon has a narrow coastline on the Mediterranean Sea, backed by mountain ranges. They have an average of 300 sunny days a year, so bring your hat and sunglasses. Need a few photos for a project or report? You will surely find them at the Al Mashriq - Photographs page: <http://www.hiof.no/almashriq/base/photography.html>.

http://www.embofleb.org/

LESOTHO

Lesotho Page

This site contains a group of links to help you find information on that country. Travel advisories, statistics, and travel information are here, to name a few. One of the links is broken, but the new World Factbook page is at <http://www.odci.gov/cia/publications/nsolo/factbook/lt.htm>.

http://www.sas.upenn.edu/African_Studies/Country_Specific/Lesotho.html

Mphahlele Moruthane's Home Page

Letsotho is one of only two independent states in the world that are completely surrounded by another country. Lesotho is located inside the country of South Africa (the other independent state is Vatican City, surrounded by Italy). *O a utlwa?* In other words, are you listening? You should be! This page has a lot to say. You'll find a description and picture of the national flag of Lesotho, links (including one to learn some of the language), maps, and more.

http://www.msoe.edu/~morutham/lesotho/

NET FILES

How do you play "Chicken Skins"?

Answer: Chicken Skins refers to a version of competition golf where players play for points on each hole. In the popular "skins game," players get a point for each hole they win. If any two players tie, the point is added to the next hole (now worth two). In Chicken Skins, the points do not carry over to the next hole. Do you just love playing golf? Don't be chicken, try http://www.golfweb.com/glbb/glbbfun.htm to learn the rules of any golf game you can imagine!

LIBERIA

Liberia Page

On this page, you will find answers to questions about Liberian statistics, travel advisories, language, art, and technology. If you are doing research on Liberia, don't miss the page at <http://www.infinet.com/~ijoma/>. Ijoma Robert Flemister has been called to the special station of *fokpah*—someone who will put personal interests aside and try to heal the country and its people. His site is very interesting. Here is an example:

"We, Elders of the Land of Liberia, assembled at Zouzon by the Grace of the Almighty and under the commanding authority of the Ancestors, present these sentiments. Let them that have ears hear, know and act. We, Elders of the Land of Liberia, hear the roar of Liberia's silence. We fear the rumble of the storm of poverty and see the fury of ignorance. We hear the cry of our people... 'How long,...how long?' Our children have failed us and we have failed our children. We are on bended knee for the blood that has flowed across our land during these shameless dark days. Yet, we lift our eyes unto the hills from whence cometh our help. The incredible atrocities of war that we inflict on ourselves shall end; the blatant denial of hope shall pass; the rape and waste of our natural resources shall cease; the overwhelmimg fear of brother for brother shall fade away; peace, unity and common sense shall prevail; we shall sing and dance once again - soon, very soon...."

http://www.sas.upenn.edu:80/African_Studies/
Country_Specific/Liberia.html

> **Ask not what the Net can do for you, ask what you can do for the Net.**

LIBYA

Libya

This site is one of the most complete set of pages and links for the country of Libya we could discover. You'll find information about Libya, its people, maps and pictures, and information about its government and history here, as well as its human rights abuses. Libya has a long history of name changes. In 1951, it was Al-Mamlaka Al-Libiya Al-Motahidda (The United Kingdom of Libya). On September 1, 1969, the day of the Libyan revolution, it was Al-Jamhooriya Al-Arabiya Al-Libiyah (The Libyan Arab Republic). On March 8, 1977, it was Al-Jamahiriya Al-Arabiya Al-Libiyah Ash-Shabiya Al-Ishtrakia (The Socialist People's Libyan Arab Jamahiriya). The flag of the country has changed each time. Presently, it is a plain, dark green rectangle with no symbols or any other ornament on it.

http://ourworld.compuserve.com/homepages/
dr_ibrahim_ighneiwa/

Libya Home Page

This site is perfect for anyone needing information for a report on Libya. The outstanding maps are detailed and informative, and the links are useful. You can read about the Sahara Desert, "the great sand sea," and the oases scattered through it, which provide water and refuge. There is also a slide show you can watch and many other beautiful photos of this ancient land.

http://quic.queensu.ca/~hassan/libya/libya.html

LIECHTENSTEIN

Liechtenstein

Tiny Liechtenstein has an area of only 61 square miles, and it has a population of 300,000 people. This guide, from the Liechtenstein National Tourist Office, takes you on a virtual vacation to this beautiful country. Admire the pictures and learn the history of Liechtenstein. The actual date on which the Principality of Liechtenstein was founded was January 23, 1719, although there were settlements there since 800 B.C.

http://www.newsnet.li/tourist/

Liechtenstein News

This official newspaper site is more than just current events. It is also a history and information site. For example, you can find out about the history of the princely family (H.S.H. Prince Hans-Adam II and Royal Family) in one area, then you can shoot over to Art Market and check out some of the latest Liechtenstein art. Or if you are into stamp collecting, try that section. The first Liechtenstein postage stamps went on sale in early 1912. They are beautiful and cover many subjects. Sales of stamps account for about 3 percent of the country's revenues; you can order them online.

http://www.news.li/

LITHUANIA

Lithuanian Academic and Research Network Litnet

We know what you want. You want a great site that has Lithuanian information. Guess what? Here it is. You can find tourist tips, country statistics, geography, Lithuanian Internet information, and much more. The section on Traditions lists the following holiday, which sounds strangely familiar: "Zemaitija, the Lithuanian Lowlands in the western part of the country, is famous for its Uzgavenes masquerades when groups of both children and grown-ups, disguised as animals, birds, and fantastic beasts can be seen roaming the streets of villages and towns. Zemaitija is also famous for its woodcarvers specializing in masks for the Uzgavenes carnivals." Hmmm. We wonder how to say "Trick or Treat!" in Lithuanian.

http://www.ktl.mii.lt/

Lithuanian Folk Culture Centre

The highlight of this site is the great recipes for tasty Lithuanian food. After you stop drooling, you can check out a couple of online Lithuanian books or see what's coming up on the events schedule. If that doesn't satisfy you, click on the link to other cultural sites, where you can look at detailed color drawings of the national costume through history: <http://neris.mii.lt/heritage/costume/costume.html>.

http://neris.mii.lt/heritage/lfcc/lfcc.html

LKL - Lithuanian Basketball League

One of the fastest-growing crazes in Lithuania is basketball. Team Lithuania took a bronze at the Olympics, and now, more and more Lithuanians are getting excited about the sport. There are even two Lithuanians on NBA teams! You can learn about the Lithuanian Basketball League right here.

http://www.lkl.lt/

LUXEMBOURG

Home Page for Luxembourg

Here is the official home page for the Grand Duchy of Luxembourg. It is a constitutional monarchy, located between Belgium, France, and Germany. It is only 51 miles long and 36 miles wide. Its major export is steel, although it is known as a world financial center, too.

http://www.restena.lu/luxembourg/lux_welcome.html

MACAU

Welcome to Macau Tourism HomePage

This is an official site, created and maintained by the government. Macau is currently a Chinese territory under Portuguese administration, but it will return to China's sovereignty on the December 20, 1999. After that, it will be governed as a Special Administrative Region of Macau (SARM). It is an island off the southeast Chinese coast, connected to the mainland by two bridges. This Web page features a look at some of the sights, such as the oldest temple in Macau, the Temple of the Goddess A-Ma. "According to the legend, A-Ma, a poor girl looking for passage to Canton, was refused by the wealthy boat owners, but a lowly fisherman took her on board. A storm blew up and wrecked all but the boat carrying the girl. On arrival in Macau she vanished, to reappear as a Goddess on the spot where the fishermen built her temple."

http://turismo.macau.gov.mo/

Lots of monkey-business in MAMMALS.

The World Factbook page on Macau

Need some more facts about Macau? How about a lot of facts? This is the Macau page of the World Factbook. You will find sections on geography, population, government, transportation, and more. There is a simple map as well.

http://www.odci.gov/cia/publications/nsolo/
    factbook/mc.htm

MACEDONIA
Macedonia

The Republic of Macedonia is located on the Balkan Peninsula, an area situated at the crossroads of the three continents of Europe, Asia, and Africa. It borders on Greece, the Republic of Serbia, Bulgaria, and Albania. Archaeologists have found remnants of ancient cities in Macedonia, and so Macedonia is really a country of old and new. It has many cultural art treasures, religious icons, and natural beauty, including high mountains and thermal hot springs. It's amazing how much you can learn about the history and culture of a country by looking at its stamps: <http://WWW.ERC.MsState.Edu/~vkire/faq/ information/philately.html>. You'll see stamps honoring birds, local architecture, poets, inventions, and more!

http://www.soros.org.mk/mk/en/

MADAGASCAR
Madagasikara - The Rainbow Islands

Madagascar is an unusual country surrounded by the Indian Ocean. This Web site provides a wonderful look at this fascinating island. History, climate, and culture are described here, along with unusual subjects like fauna (it's a sanctuary for lemur species), music (listen to sound samples), and tourism (they say there are only two seasons in Madagascar: the rainy season and the season when it rains). If you want to learn about Madagascar, you've come to the right place.

http://www.dstc.edu.au/AU/staff/andry/Mada.html

The World Factbook page on Madagascar

Madagascar is an island nation off southern Africa. Here you will find the factual information to get you started on a report or an exciting journey. This site is mostly text (and a simple map), but it is packed with data and basic information to start you on your way. Let's go to the World Factbook!

http://www.odci.gov/cia/publications/nsolo/
    factbook/ma.htm

MALAWI
MALAWI

What would you like to know about the Republic of Malawi? Where is it? How is the weather? What is the capital? You can find the answers to those questions at this site and probably at many other sites, too. But do you have other questions? What about e-mail—is it available in Malawi? What is the latest news about Malawi? What does Malawi look like? There are answers to those and a lot more questions here as well. There are some great pictures, too! Find a little more information at <http://www.sas.upenn.edu/ African_Studies/Country_Specific/Malawi.html>.

http://spicerack.sr.unh.edu/~llk/

MALAYSIA
EDUCATION

Here's your opportunity to visit real schools in Malaysia. Many high schools in Malaysia have home pages, and most have text in English. By starting on this page of links for Malaysian universities, schools, and libraries, you can find high school and lower schools under the Schools section. Many of the school home pages include picture tours of the school and interesting histories. If you like to browse, and you would like to visit some schools in Malaysia, start right here! Maybe you can get your school to "link up" to a school in Malaysia.

http://www.jaring.my/msia/msia-link/educ.html

Surf today, smart tomorrow.

MALAYSIA HOMEPAGE

About 80 percent of the land of Malaysia is covered with tropical rain forests. This beautiful country is in Southeast Asia. To find out its history, go to this Web page! This home page is so full of wonderful information about Malaysia and its people that you could do a whole report just on Malaysia's national flower, the hibiscus. But there is a great deal more, complete with maps and pictures. You'll find the latest news, links to government and tourism sites, and a background section that is very educational, too.

http://www.jaring.my/

RTM.Net

If you've ever wondered what's on the radio or television in a foreign country, then you should visit this site. Here you can listen to six different radio stations in Malaysia. You will hear the actual, live broadcasts over the Internet, and you may hear Bahasa Malaysia, English, Mandarin, or Tamil. Check out the television schedule in Malaysia. How many TV programs do you recognize? You will also find information on the history of television and radio in Malaysia. Explore the many sounds of Malaysian radio broadcasts, from music to educational fare. Tune in!

http://www.asiaconnect.com.my/rtm-net/

Welcome To The Star Online Malaysia

Do you want to know what's happening in Malaysia? Extra, extra, you can read all about it! A weekly edition of The Star Online can be delivered right to your computer. Not all of this weekly online newspaper is light reading, but there is quality coverage of current Malaysian news in areas such as politics, sports, technology, education, business and weather. If you really want to know what's happening in Malaysia, you have to check it out.

http://www.jaring.my/~star/

MALDIVES

Maldives - The Last Paradise

The Maldives is a nation of over 1,000 small coral islands in the Indian Ocean. A quarter of a million tourists visit the Maldives each year. Visitors stay at resorts that are each built on their own island. At this commercial Web site, a tour of the Maldives, full of beautiful pictures and useful information, begins in the capital city of Malé (pronounced "maa lay"). Why not see the sights of the Maldives and learn about this unusual country, too?

http://www.asiaville.com/corporate/maldives/

Maldives Republic General

Only about 200 of the over 1,000 small islands of the Maldives are inhabited. This country is located off the southern tip of India. It is a favorite of tourists, but natives rarely mingle with the visitors. Many islands are covered with beautiful tropical vegetation and palm trees. Others are only sand and coral. Set sail for this site to find facts about the Maldives and a simple location map, as well as tourist information. You should also see the official Ministry of Tourism page at <http://www.visitmaldives.com/>.

http://www.wtgonline.com/country/mv/gen.html

MALI

An Introduction to Mali

True to its name, this site is a good introduction to this African nation. Most famous for the city of Timbuktu and the long Niger River, Mali is the largest country in western Africa. Get introduced to the legendary cities of Timbuktu and Djenne, the great river Niger, and the Sahara Desert. Now climb down off that camel and look around! There is a little more information at <http://www.sas.upenn.edu/African_Studies/Country_Specific/Mali.html>.

http://www.interknowledge.com/mali/

OPTICAL ILLUSIONS: now you see them, now you don't!

Real surfers get their feet wet in OUTDOOR RECREATION.

MALTA

Grazio's Malta Virtwali

This exceptionally thorough Web site includes lots of valuable information about Malta. Unfortunately, it is all on the same page, so the page takes forever to load. It is worth it, though, so hang in there! You may already know that Malta is an island in the Mediterranean Sea. Perhaps you know that Malta's currency is the Maltese lira. Maybe you even know that Malta has a president and a prime minister, but did you know that the voting system in Malta is very unusual? Check out <http://www.magnet.mt/election96/system.htm>. And did you know that ancient remains of small elephants and a giant swan were found on Malta? You can read about that at <http://www.aber.ac.uk/~jpg/malta/quatern.html>. That's not all—but why not visit this site and see for yourself!

http://www.fred.net/malta/

NET FILES

Keiko, the Free Willy whale, loves to watch videotapes in his new 2-million-gallon aquarium.

What are his favorite tapes?

Answer: According to Nolan Harvey, of the Oregon Coast Aquarium, "Keiko likes fast action movies and cartoons. He couldn't care less about videos with whales or dolphins. His favorite is professional wrestling. When we put the World Wrestling Federation tape in there, he'll watch it for the whole two hours." Find out more about Keiko at http://www.discovery.com/area/keiko/whale1.4.3.html then scroll all the way to the bottom of the page and click on Keiko Cam.

Malta National Tourist Office

Among the most popular recreational activities on Malta are scuba diving and golf. But other sports, such as windsurfing, boating, soccer, and tennis are popular, too. It's easy to see why the Maltese people are usually considered friendly and relaxed. And it's also easy to see why so many people visit Malta. Visiting Malta is even fun on the World Wide Web. See for yourself! You may also want to visit the official Web site of the Maltese government at <http://www.magnet.mt/>.

http://www.swift-tourism.com/malta/

MARTINIQUE

The Ever Radiant Welcome Of Martinique

Martinique is a popular vacation destination in the Caribbean Sea. In fact, many Web sites about Martinique are produced by commercial travel agencies. This colorful site includes a picture- and music-filled guided tour in which flowers, rain forests, and sandy white beaches are featured. You can sit back and tour while listening to Caribbean music! There are also brief overviews of history, geography, climate, and population. Travelers may be interested to learn about shopping and food on the island. Some commercial promotions are found at this site, but they are nicely mixed with some Web-based Caribbean fun. This site is available in English and French, since the island is an overseas department of France. You might also like Discover Martinique, at <http://www.magnet.mt/>.

http://www.martinique.org/

MAURITANIA

Mauritania

This site is comprised mainly of factual information commonly found in the *World Factbook,* except that this site includes a larger, more detailed map, in color. Mauritania is a hot and dry country in northwestern Africa that has suffered through many droughts. Start your journey to Mauritania here, gathering facts, and then cross the Sahara and search the Web for more! You might end up at the embassy in Washington, D.C., at <http://embassy.org/mauritania/>.

http://www.africaonline.com/AfricaOnline/countries/mauritania.html

MAURITIUS

Mauritius

Mauritius is a small island country in the Indian Ocean, located several hundred miles east of Madagascar. The island was formed by volcanoes, but they are no longer active. The now-extinct dodo bird originated here. Mauritius is a popular travel destination and features the attraction of the séga dance and music, which was connected with the early slave trade. You might also like the official Ministry of Tourism site at <http://www.mauritius.net/>.

http://www.zip.com.au/~lemurweb/Mauritius/
   mauritius.html

MAYOTTE

Mayotte

This site is based on information from the *World Factbook* entry, but with buttons for easy access to subjects and links to other atlas information. Mayotte is a small tropical island off of southern Africa, in the Mozambique Channel. It is a territory of France, and the almost 100,000 Mahoran people (the name for people from Mayotte) are Muslim. Mayotte flies the flag of France, exports something called *ylang-ylang* (a sweetly scented flower used in making perfume), and has no television stations! But there is much more to know about this island, and this fact-based site is a good place to get started.

http://www.intergo.com/Library/ref/atlas/
   africa/mf.htm

MEXICO

Art of Native Mexican Children

Kids everywhere like to paint and draw. True to form, kids in Mexico like to do artwork, and it's fantastic. See samples of drawings from Mayo, Tzeltal, and Mayan children at this Web page. The colors will grab you, and the world they paint is filled with animals, musicians, and festivals. Brighten your day and take a look now!

http://www.DocuWeb.ca/Mexico/1-engl/kids.html

The Azteca Web Page

Did you know many kids in the United States are of Mexican descent? They are proudly called *Chicanos y Chicanas.* Understanding what it means to be Chicano is about many things: music, history, culture, and language. To learn about this fascinating culture, this page is a good pace to start.

http://www.azteca.net/aztec/

Cinco de Mayo

Do you like a really good party? Well, every May 5, many Latino Americans and citizens of Mexico celebrate a grand event, and have a party in the process. In 1862, on Cinco de Mayo (that's Spanish for the fifth of May), a handful of Mexican troops defeated a much larger and better-armed force of soldiers from France. This victory showed that a small group, strengthened by unity, can overcome overwhelming odds. Ever since, Cinco de Mayo is celebrated with music, tasty food, parades, and a party. Read about the history behind this celebration, and learn a little more at <http://soundprint.brandywine.american.edu/~soundprt/more_info/nogales_history.html>.

http://latino.sscnet.ucla.edu/cinco.html

The Day of the Dead

On November 2, Mexicans celebrate the annual Day of the Dead. It's not a sad occasion. They make special foods and prepare a feast to honor their ancestors. They have picnics on their relatives' graves so the dead can join in the festivities, too. One of the special foods is called "Bread of the Dead" (*pan de muerto*). The baker hides a plastic skeleton in each rounded loaf, and it's good luck to bite into the piece with the skeleton! People also give each other candy skeletons, skulls, and other treats with a death design. The holiday has complex social, religious, and cultural meanings. Learn more about this celebration here.

http://www.public.iastate.edu/~rjsalvad/scmfaq/
   muertos.html

Expect a miracle in RELIGION!

Lotería: Mexican Bingo Games

Latinos like to play a fun game called *Lotería*. It's like Bingo, but it has colorful pictures with Spanish names instead of numbers and letters. Would you like to play the game? Go to the Lotería page on the World Wide Web. It's fun!

http://www.mercado.com/juventud/loteria/loteria.htm

MayaQuest

Who were the Mayans, and what happened to their civilization? This site tells you all about the history and cultures of this lost nation. The ancient Maya had an apparently healthy culture from around A.D. 250. They were masters of mathematics, building huge pyramids in the jungles of what is now Mexico and Central America. They had complex astronomical calendars and engineering for improving agriculture. During the ninth century, their civilization collapsed. No one knows exactly where they went or what happened to them. From this site, you can follow an expedition team called MayaQuest, searching the jungle for archaeological answers in 1995, 1996, and 1997.

http://www.mecc.com/mayaquest.html

Mexico: an Endless Journey

This is the official home page of the Ministry of Tourism. It describes the various states and regions of Mexico, which vary from temperate to torrid as the geography moves from the seaside to the jungle. Mexico has a long prehistory. Its original settlers may have come from Asia, over the Alaskan land bridge. According to this site, Olmec, Toltec, Maya, and Aztec cultures all left their marks on the land. "The architectural remnants of these civilizations can be found in virtually every corner of the country; more than 11,000 archaeological sites are registered." You can also read all about Mexican food and festivals here. And remember, the Mole Festival is *not* about small rodents. It celebrates mole (pronounced "MOH-lay"), which is "a rich, thick sauce made from various chiles, ground peanuts, spices, sesame seed, and chocolate." You will also want to read the Lonely Planet - Destination Mexico page at *<http://www.lonelyplanet.com/dest/cam/mexico.htm>*.

http://mexico-travel.com/

MOLDOVA

Virtual MOLDOVA - The Home Page

Moldova is a country in Eastern Europe, northeast of Romania. For a long time, Moldova was a part of the Soviet Union (U.S.S.R.), but it became independent in 1991. Moldova and Romania have many similarities; in fact, it would be very hard to tell if a person were speaking Moldovan or Romanian. The languages are almost the same! Find out more about this young independent nation by visiting this page. Another spot is the official Moldovan embassy page in Washington, D.C., at *<http://www.moldova.org/>*.

http://www.info.polymtl.ca/zuse/tavi/www/
Moldova.html

MONACO

The 700 Years of Grimaldi

Monaco's Grimaldi dynasty has ruled this small principality for the past seven hundred years! Your grandparents may remember how exciting it was in 1956, when the dashing Prince Rainier III married the American film star Grace Kelly. You can read about the stirring history of the Grimaldis, including biographies of Rainier and Prince Albert, his son. Surprisingly, Monaco did not join the United Nations until 1993.

http://www.monaco.mc/monaco/700ans/

Monaco

The Principality of Monaco is a tiny country on the southern border of France. Monaco's beautiful coastline is on the Mediterranean Sea. How small is Monaco? The land area is less than two square kilometers! If it's facts about Monaco's geography, people, government, and climate you're after, then you've come to the right little Web page. You should also look at the Monaco Government Tourist Office of New York at *<http://www.monaco.mc/usa/index.html>* for more.

http://www.intergo.com/Library/ref/atlas/
europe/mn.htm

The Monaco Guide

Monaco is one of the most fascinating places in the world. It has a long and captivating history of kings, lords, and princes. Today's Monaco is a favorite for tourists around the world. The climate is neither too hot nor too cold. Swim with the fishes, or travel a short distance to ski. Visit the glamorous city of Monte Carlo, with its exciting Casino Square flashing at night. There is a tremendous cultural side to Monaco, too, with much theater, music, and art. This page is very thorough, containing information on everything from history to entertainment. The sights are beautiful. See for yourself!

http://www.monaco.mc/monaco/

MONGOLIA

Mongolia Resource Page

Mongolia is one of the most unusual countries in the world. It is a beautiful country where lush forests meet stark deserts. Nomads still travel the lands as they did hundreds of years ago. But one major change in recent years is that Mongolia has now become a democracy, and it's recently gotten on the Net. Visit this informative Web page from the Soros Foundation and learn about Mongolia, including information on traditional tentlike homes, called *ger* (called yurts by non-Mongolians).

http://www.soros.org/mongolia.html

Virtual Mongol

Not everyone can travel to Mongolia. But you can virtually visit Mongolia on your screen! This WWW site contains dozens of quality pictures of beautiful and historic Mongolia. The picture index identifies the subject of each image. The shots are divided into categories: nature, people, religion, and history. There are links to other sites about this fascinating country, too. Don't miss the throat-singing pages, and see if you can learn to make those haunting multitoned sounds: <*http://avalon.phys.hokudai.ac.jp/throat-singing/throat-home.html*>.

http://www.kiku.com/electric_samurai/
  virtual_mongol/virtual_mongol.html

MONTSERRAT

Official Montserrat Tourist Board Web Site

Name a beautiful, tiny island in the Caribbean Sea. Well, there are several, but how about Montserrat? This small British dependency is a favorite for vacationers because of its warm, breezy climate and recreational opportunities, not to mention the live volcano on the island. A live volcano? This is some vacation place! Actually, the visible glow of the mountaintop is a popular sight, and tourists are kept a safe distance from the mountain. The island's tourist board maintains this page, which contains a great deal of useful information and images. Just stay on the safe side of the island! For volcano updates, check the official government volcano page at <*http://www.geo.mtu.edu/volcanoes/west.indies/soufriere/govt/*>.

http://www.mrat.com/

MOROCCO

Kingdom of Morocco

Click on the Foundation section to get to the facts on this country. You can also read a short biography of His Majesty, King Hassan II, and see photos of him and the rest of the royal family. There is a gallery of plant and animal life, too, and you can admire some of the minerals found in Morocco: agate, malachite, and desert rose, which does indeed look like a frozen flower. If you want to see beautiful floral patterns and other designs, try the link to the Carpets of Rabat.

http://www.mincom.gov.ma/

Morocco Guided Tour

When you take the guided tour of Morocco, you hear the music, see the sights, and even get a taste of Moroccan cooking. Well, maybe not an actual taste, but several recipes are here. You'll find a description of dining customs in Morocco, too. So even if your computer can't give you an actual taste of Moroccan food, with a little imagination, reading this page can be just like being there. Hey, do you smell *meshwee*?

http://www.dsg.ki.se/morocco/

MOZAMBIQUE

Mozambique

Mozambique is an African country fortunate enough to be rich in natural resources. Unfortunately, it struggled with a civil war for years. The war finally ended in 1992, and today the country is still rebuilding from its effects. The coastline of Mozambique is long, and fishing is important to the economy. Prawns and shrimp are major exports. Get the facts on Mozambique here.

http://www.sas.upenn.edu/African_Studies/
Country_Specific/Mozambique.html

MYANMAR (BURMA)

Lonely Planet -- Destination: Myanmar (Burma)

Although Myanmar (Burma) is trying to promote tourism, many people are refusing to travel there, because reports of an oppressive government, slave labor, and other disturbing stories have surfaced. You should be aware of the issues. This page collects not only general information on the country but also links to sites where you can learn more about the Free Burma movement. A caution to parents: The Myanmar (Burma) story is violent.

http://www.lonelyplanet.com/dest/sea/myan.htm

Myanmar Home Page

Myanmar is the new name of the country formerly known as Burma. It has a long history, with archaeological evidence of settlement as early as 5,000 years ago! This home page will give you a good introduction to its symbols and culture. For example, you can learn about the wet and wild holiday called the Thingyan Water Festival. Celebrated in April and lasting three days, it symbolizes the change (*Thingyan*) from the old year to the new. Since water is a symbol of cleanliness and rebirth, everybody is splashed with large amounts of water—even tourists, so bring your rain gear!

http://www.myanmar.com/

NAMIBIA

REPUBLIC OF NAMIBIA

Namibia is a large country in southwest Africa. Despite the country's size, its population is quite small! The reason is because Namibia is one of the driest countries on Earth. Almost half of Namibia is desert, and droughts are common. Incredibly, some areas are rich in wildlife. Namibia has been an independent country only since 1990. Learn about the struggles, and triumphs, of this interesting African country by visiting this official Web site.

http://www.republicofnamibia.com/

NAURU

The World Factbook page on Nauru

Coconut trees sway gently in the tropical breeze. You stretch out on the sandy beach and watch the sunset. You're uneasy. But why? Why wouldn't you be content on the pleasant South Pacific island of Nauru? There is no unemployment, and Nauruans have high incomes. Maybe it's the sinking feeling of knowing that the island's sustaining industry must end soon. The phosphate mining must end by 2000. Or it could be that you sense the danger of near-complete dependence on other nations for food and water, other than what rainwater can be collected in rooftop storage tanks (most fresh water is imported from Australia). Check out this site for clues to what makes life so uncertain for an island republic that is only a tenth the size of Washington, D.C.

http://www.odci.gov/cia/publications/nsolo/
factbook/nr.htm

**Explore underwater
archaeology in
SHIPS AND
SHIPWRECKS.**

NEPAL
A Visit to Nepal

"Please do not disturb the monkeys. This temple belongs to them." Oddities like this one, along with profound beauty are what Scott Yost found during a six-week visit to Nepal. Learn about this enchanting country and what it took to get there and back, through the eyes of a man who had admittedly "never done anything like this before." Now, he has made a way for us to discover Nepal through his detailed personal journal entries, which are linked to trek maps, a searchable index, and rich photography. Make your own cybervisit to Nepal through Yost's beautifully executed site. You might also like the Nepal Home Page at <http://www.info-nepal.com/> for basic information and lots more.

http://www.vic.com/nepal/

NETHERLANDS
The Flying Dutchman's Page

The name Netherlands is derived from the Dutch word *neder*, meaning "low," referring to the fact that much of this country is below sea level. A system of dikes and canals has allowed the Netherlands to reclaim land and use it for farming and other purposes. According to this page, "Approximately a third of the entire country lies below sea level at high tide. Another 25% is so low-lying that it would be subject to [flooding] if it were not for the surrounding dunes and dikes and the regular pumping of excess water. The lowest point is 6.7 m (22 ft.) below mean sea level, immediately to the northeast of Rotterdam." This page has lots of general interest info on the Netherlands and its people and culture.

http://www.proqc.com.tw/~jeroen/main.html

Become one with the Net.

Gouda

Yes, it's like the cheese. But Gouda is also the name of a medieval Dutch city. A stop at this site on the virtual Netherlands tour is rich with different things to do and see. Learn about the unique role that water has played in the life of Holland and the city of Gouda in particular. Read the illustrated stories of some of the more bizarre goings-on over the years. Take a look at the products of the region: cheese (of course), clay pipes, candles, and more. The beautiful, original photography will give you a feel for the Dutch way of life as you stroll Gouda's virtual streets.

http://www.xs4all.nl/~eleede/

The Holland Site

Windmills? Wooden shoes? Tulips? Strange women's headgear? Yes, you've got all those in Holland (also known as the Netherlands), but did you know about Van Gogh's connection to the "low country?" Did you know about the castles (over 300 of them) or extensive cycling opportunities? See it all, with lots of great color photos, as you easily navigate this attractive and informative site from the official Board of Tourism. From how to get there to how to get around once you're there, this is the place to go to glimpse the historic past and the future of this beautiful land. And with the 20 questions and answers for the "Holland uninitiated," you might just get by without the locals seeing "tourist" written all over your face.

http://www.nbt.nl/holland/

Teylers Museum

Teylers Museum is the oldest museum in Holland. It has the old, traditional stuff you'd expect from a great gallery. Boring, right? Wrong! In addition to its excellent permanent exhibits, it also has rotating exhibits that feature the coolest new stuff. This site has lots of graphics, whose clever design is to carry you from one great find to the next. If you can't make it to the Netherlands this year, do the next best thing and take a leisurely tour of the anything-but-boring Teylers Museum.

http://www.nedpunt.nl/teylersmuseum/engels/hal.html

NETHERLANDS ANTILLES

Caribbe.an - Netherlands Antilles

The Antilles island group is a Dutch protectorate. It is made up of two island groups; the largest islands are Curaçao and Bonaire. Papiamentu, the native tongue of many of these islands, is a mix of Spanish, Dutch, Portuguese, French, English, Caribbean Indian, and some African. At this page, you can listen to a sample of this unique language if your Web browser has audio capabilities. There's lots more to see, too, about history, industry, people, government, country facts, fun, and sun. The photos of local windsurfing are stunning and worth the download wait! So whether you talk your parents into a family vacation on these islands, make a virtual visit to the Netherlands Antilles to learn and enjoy. We also recommend the Bonaire Official Travel Guide at <http://www.interknowledge.com/bonaire/index.html> for a fascinating and detailed history of the area. The World Factbook page you'll want is at <http://www.odci.gov/cia/publications/nsolo/factbook/nt.htm>.

http://caribbe.an/islands/an/

NEW CALEDONIA

The World Factbook page on New Caledonia

It's a good news/bad news thing for New Caledonia. This group of islands east of Australia in the South Pacific boasts more than 20 percent of the world's nickel resources. That's good. It's too bad that in recent years the world demand for nickel has been slowing down. Crank up your Web browser and head to the site with all the facts on this French territory, which contrasts high mountains and dense forests with sparking lagoons and coral reefs. You might also like the info and photos at <http://www.new-caledonia.com/>.

http://www.odci.gov/cia/publications/nsolo/factbook/nc.htm

Have a whale of a time in MAMMALS.

NEW ZEALAND

Lonely Planet -- Destination: New Zealand

So this Polynesian guy named Kupe finds it in A.D. 950, names it Aotearoa ("Land of the Long White Cloud"), then poof, a thousand years later we've got New Zealand! Where else can you take in the Golden Shears Sheep-Shearing Contest, watch the earth bubble, hiss, and spew, learn about a fascinating native people, and snow ski from June through August (that's their winter, you know)? This cybersampler gets you in the mood to visit (virtually or otherwise) with great slide shows, interactive maps, and other cool links (including the Mountain Biking in New Zealand page). The only thing missing on this techno tour is the country's friendly people. Just browse it!

http://www.lonelyplanet.com.au/dest/aust/nz.htm

NET FILES

Why is the capital of the United States located in Washington, D.C.?

Answer: There weren't a lot of choices back in the late 1700s. Some people thought New York would be a good place; others favored Philadelphia. Finally they decided on a site on the Potomac River, about halfway between the original northern and southern states. The area was wilderness. It was marshy and full of mosquitoes. The area was drained, and construction began. According to the White House for Kids home page, the French city planner, Pierre L'Enfant, "decided to place the Capitol Building on one hill and the 'President's House' on another hill." In between were parks and grand boulevards. You can read more White House history at
http://www.whitehouse.gov/WH/kids/html/his_2.html

Lyall Bay School

If going to Lyall Bay School is as much fun as their Web site, these kids are having a blast! The animation, color, and fun of this New Zealand primary school's pages add to their excellent content. But be warned: with so much graphic multimedia, things here can slow down from time to time. Great reports on cool school happenings, visits to their classrooms, and an interactive story to which you contribute make it worth the wait, though. Take a New Zealand quiz, or link up to other kid-safe sites. But before you leave, be nice and drop the students (and maybe even the teachers) an e-mail like they ask you to!

http://ourworld.compuserve.com/homepages/
    LyallBaySchool/begin.htm

Merivale Scout Troop - New Zealand's First Cyber Scout Troop !!!

Scouting means campfires, merit badges, and good deeds, right? Right, but there's more. Whoever heard of a "cyber scout troop"? The Merivale Scouts in Christchurch, New Zealand have. They claim to be the first one in the land of the Kiwi. And based on their obvious self-confidence, it's easy to believe. If you're into scouting or even if you're just curious, hook up to this site and catch their excitement. Leave your impressions to be read by all (as others worldwide have). Experience their excellent adventures in the "join our troop" page. It is, as they say, "high velocity, heart pumping, eye popping, mind blowing." You can also learn a lot about Christchurch here, too!

http://www.netlink.co.nz/~rcthard/mainpage.html

I wonder what the
QUEENS, KINGS,
ROYALTY are
doing tonight?

Mount Ruapehu

It was clear the day Mount Ruapehu blew. We know, because this site's stunning photograph from the NOAA-14 satellite shows it. On that day in June of 1996, the photo from space showed the beautiful green North Island of New Zealand under the long, red ash cloud that spewed from this active volcano. Make a stop here for facts on the violent history of the mountain. Read about living near a volcano and what must be done when it erupts, and link to other great volcano sites. Whether you're interested in the five levels of a volcanic alert or the stunning pictures of Ruapehu's stormy past, these are must-see New Zealand pages.

http://www.mocd.govt.nz/nz_volcs/ruapehu/
    ruapehu.html

National Library of New Zealand Home Page

What will the library of the future look like? Sign on to the National Library of New Zealand's site to see. Check out how online versions of journals and books will become available in the "Library without Walls." But it's not all about the future. This online library has beautiful and interesting summaries of current and past local exhibits. And there are links to other New Zealand library resources, too. Here is a center of learning that reaches out to all of New Zealand's people and does it with cutting-edge flair. Of particular interest is the collection of Maori materials.

http://www.natlib.govt.nz/

New Zealand Government Online

At this site you can learn all about New Zealand's parliament, the cabinet, and governmental agencies. See a picture of the flag and learn about its symbols. You can even hear the national anthem and get the words in both English and Maori. The Treaty of Waitangi, considered New Zealand's founding document, was signed in 1840 by representatives of the British Crown and Maori chiefs; you can read English and Maori versions of it here.

http://www.govt.nz/

NICARAGUA

Lonely Planet -- Destination: Nicaragua

Ten thousand years ago, humans and animals ran toward the lake of Lago de Managua to escape nature's onslaught (we know because their footprints are buried under layers of volcanic ash). Another nearby lake, Lago de Nicaragua, is the largest lake in Central America. In it lives the world's only freshwater shark species. From its warthogs and boas to jaguars and howler monkeys, from its rain forest jungles to its plains, Nicaragua is a land waiting to be explored. Why did the Sandinistas come to power? Why did the Contra rebels fight them? What was Irangate? Come and learn of the history and culture of this beautiful tropical country. The World Factbook information is at <http://www.odci.gov/cia/publications/nsolo/factbook/nu.htm>.

http://www.lonelyplanet.com.au/dest/cam/nic.htm

NIGER

The World Factbook page on Niger

The market for Niger's largest export, uranium, was booming during the 1970s and 1980s. Now, for many reasons, there is less demand, and the country has seen uranium revenues drop almost 50 percent. How will they replace this income? You might find some ideas at the Focus on Niger page at <http://www.txdirect.net/users/jmayer/fon.html> where there are also some wonderful photos from former Peace Corps volunteers and others.

http://www.odci.gov/cia/publications/nsolo/factbook/ng.htm

NIGERIA

G. I. Jones -- S.E. Nigerian Art and Culture

In 1926, he traveled to Nigeria from England, where he served as an administrative officer until 1946. Armed with a Roloflex camera, G. I. Jones began taking photographs of the art and culture that he had come to profoundly respect. Now you can see 1930s southeastern Nigeria through the lens of a master. This site showcases the art and people of that time and place with simple brilliance. And after you've browsed a sample of his work, the world of African art is just a mouseclick away, with great links to places like the National Museum of African Art at the Smithsonian Institution. But don't leave before reading about the man himself (he was also called "Sherlock Jones"). If you are looking for just the facts, try the Nigeria pages at <http://www.webperfect.com/afrinet/nigeria/profile.html> or <http://www.odci.gov/cia/publications/nsolo/factbook/ni.htm>.

http://www.siu.edu/~anthro/mccall/jones/

Worldwide, what can you buy for the equivalent of about $4 of U.S. money?

Answer: In Singapore, you can buy five cans of Coca Cola or one Big Mac, or for something different, a bowl of laksa (a curry noodle dish), one glass of soybean milk, and a bowl of ice kachang (a multicolored, multi-ingredient ice dessert). In Nigeria, that much money could pay your monthly rent, or it could buy 50 pounds or more of rice, 50 pounds of flour, or 10 pounds of meat. Send in your own answers at http://www.wimmera.net.au/CurrComp/CurrComp.html

You can always count on the info in MATH AND ARITHMETIC.

NIUE

The World Factbook page on Niue

What do passion fruit products, pawpaw, footballs, and stamps have in common? They are all exports of Niue. This is a tiny, self-governing territory in free association with New Zealand. Niue, one of the world's largest coral islands, is situated in the South Pacific Ocean, east of Tonga. Visit the Niue page to find out one of the most interesting "important sources of revenue" that you're likely to see anywhere!

http://www.odci.gov/cia/publications/nsolo/
   factbook/ne.htm

NORFOLK ISLAND

Norfolk Island - The Web Site

Before the first white man stepped ashore on Norfolk Island from the good ship *Resolution*, the island had long been a stopover for sea-roving Polynesians. Today, migratory birds make this lush, green island in the South Pacific Ocean their temporary resting place. Here, among the famed Norfolk Pine trees that can reach 150 feet in height, no "fatal creature" dwells. Pretty peaceful, right? Yes, but it wasn't always like this. At one time, according to this site, it was home to "the most cruel British penal colony, ever." Set sail for the stunning images of Norfolk Island. Australia says Norfolk Island is an external territory of Australia. So does the World Factbook at *<http://www.odci.gov/cia/publications/nsolo/factbook/nf.htm>*. However, this page says there is no constitutional basis for that claim and that Norfolk Island is a British Crown colony.

http://www.ozemail.com.au/~jbp/pds/

NORTH KOREA

See KOREA, NORTH

NORTHERN IRELAND

See UNITED KINGDOM—NORTHERN IRELAND

The Sun never sets on the Internet.

NORWAY

Introducing Norway: Homepage

Brown goat's cheese is found in virtually every Norwegian home. It's "a rather sweet cheese made of goat's milk and cow's milk." Yum! This is just one of the things you'll learn at this very cool site designed just for kids. Norway does a lot of things just for kids. In fact, the government has a special official, called an ombudsman, whose job it is to take care of issues kids think are important. Kids can just call up the ombudsman if they have any problems! We wonder if they can get help with homework, too! Learn about Norway's history, culture, and much more at this page that combines great content with great fun. By the way, the paper clip is a Norwegian invention. Really, it is, come and see!

http://odin.dep.no/ud/publ/96/norway/

The Ministry of Foreign Affairs' article service

Do you want to know about Norse trolls and other folklore? How about snacking on some nice lutefisk? Or maybe you'd prefer learning about famous Norwegians, such as Roald Amundsen, who was the first person to reach the South Pole. This site has lots of information about Norwegian royalty, culture, and tourism.

http://odin.dep.no/ud/nornytt/

The Northern Lights Planetarium

Aurora borealis: it's otherwise known as the northern lights. People get to see it a lot in Norway. Norway's first public planetarium is now on the Web, and it explains this natural wonder and more! Learn about planetariums in general and this one in particular. See the northern lights in still photos or video. Peer backward at some of the early myths and explanations of this awesome light show. Read about Lars Vegard, the Norwegian scientist who first mapped the colors of the aurora, and his two distinguished compatriots who followed. See how these men broadened our understanding of the lights. Don't miss this show!

http://www.uit.no/npt/homepage-npt.en.html

The Viking Network Web

From A.D. 800 to A.D. 1050, they raided, they traded, and they sailed their longships and merchant ships. Sure we're talking about Vikings here, but do you really know them? This truly awesome site, with just the right balance of text and graphics, lets you breeze as easily through Viking history, culture, religion, and commerce as they sliced through the Atlantic. Use the site's maps and search features to sing Viking shipbuilder raps, visit the places that they visited, take Viking quizzes, and do Viking math (seriously, check it out). And while you're there, participate in a collaborative Viking project. Write a story, draw a picture, get involved! A Viking would.

http://odin.nls.no/viking/vnethome.htm

Who is Who in Norway - KING HARALD

His Majesty King Harald and Queen Sonja have the beginnings of a home page here. You can learn biographical facts about the King of Norway, including his sailing victories and involvement with the Olympics.

http://www.norway-info.com/history/people/
  kingharald.html

A WWW Railway Page for Norway

Norway has trains. Norwegians are serious about trains. And serious strategic planning about railroads is happening there. Immerse yourself in the towns and country of Norway with a visit to this train lover's paradise site. Read about railroad history in Norway, and see their trains of days gone by and of the not-too-distant future. If you're planning a trip, Norway's rail network information and timetables are here, too. All aboard!

http://www.ifi.uio.no/~terjek/rail/

It never rains in cyberspace.

OMAN
THE NOT-SO-LOST CITY OF UBAR

Frankincense was worth its weight in gold and was one of the treasures laid at the feet of the baby named Jesus. Ubar, the ancient Arab center of frankincense trade, is referred to in *The Thousand and One Nights* (The Arabian Nights) and the Koran. So was this city only mythical or was it real? Thanks to space-age technology, we find that it was very real indeed. In 1982, a remote spacecraft "peered" under the dry sand of modern-day Oman and found it! Come and hear this amazing tale and share the excitement of discovery. This beautiful site is rich with stunning information and photos, and it links you to other awesome sites on this great find, as well as a link to Oman's home page at *<http://paul.spu.edu/~kaltaei/oman.html>*.

http://www-dial.JPL.NASA.GOV/kidsat/exploration/
  Explorations_TEAM/Russell_Moffitt/ubarpage/

PAKISTAN
Lonely Planet -- Destination: Pakistan

The Islamic Republic of Pakistan is a land of contrast: the landscape is dotted with Buddhist monuments, Hindu temples, and Islamic palaces. Make this page on Pakistan your destination for history, geography, current events, links, and more.

http://www.lonelyplanet.com.au/dest/ind/pak.htm

PANAMA
PANAMA

The Republic of Panama is located in Central America. Running through it is the Panama Canal, which connects the Caribbean Sea to the Pacific Ocean. Over 14,000 trips through the canal are made each year by commercial vessels, cruise ships, and private pleasure yachts. Most people think the Panama Canal runs east-west, but it really goes northwest-southeast. According to this official site, "During their 50-mile (80 km) ocean-to-ocean voyage, ships pass through three sets of locks that raise vessels 85 feet to the man-made Lake Gatun and Gaillard Cut, and lower them again to sea level. Gatun Lake is the world's largest man-made body of water." A good map and other info are at the World Factbook page at *<http://www.odci.gov/cia/ publications/nsolo/factbook/pm.htm>*.

http://www.panamainfo.com/

The Panama Puzzle

Spin back in time to 1900 and take a trip with Major Walter Reed, U.S. Army Medical Corps. Your destination is Panama, where the now-famous Panama Canal is being dug. But there's a problem. Hundreds of men are dying of a disease they call "yellow jack." The major describes what was known of the disease and the popular theories at its outbreak, and he leads you down a series of paths that might explain it. Your answers will lead you closer to the cause that he and his colleagues discovered nearly a century ago. This site is rich in history and science and is a fun challenge to your reasoning skills. So put on your lab coat and get ready to sweat!

http://zeus.bioc.uvic.ca/Tutorials/Panama/
  Panama.html

PAPUA NEW GUINEA

The northwest patrol

It's 1926. An expeditionary force set out through the mountains to do what had not been done by the governments of Papua or the Mandated Territory of New Guinea. The force was to cross New Guinea at its widest point, not knowing what kind of reception they would get from the local tribe. How did they fare? Thankfully, only one life was lost to disease and not one shot was fired in anger. Fast-forward 70 years to a group of Australians and Papua New Guineans who sought to retrace the steps of the earlier Northwest Patrol, only this time with helicopter resupply and remote satellite data updates to this Web site. Read and see the bold story of both parties. For more contemporary information on the government, people, and culture of PNG (as it is shortened), try the Papua New Guinea page at <http://203.22.79.34/png/default.htm>.

http://rses.anu.edu.au/NWP/

If you feel funny, think what we went through when we wrote the JOKES AND RIDDLES section!

PARAGUAY

Lonely Planet -- Destination: Paraguay

These pages define *tranquilo* as a "state of mind that lulls you into a cheery, relaxed peace." Maybe *tranquilo* is found in the Chaco. The Chaco is one of South America's great wilderness areas and makes up 60 percent of Paraguay's landscape. In it live Indian peoples who trace their ancestry back to the 1500s. Animal life abounds: jaguar, puma, ocelot, and other wildlife. It hasn't always been cheery in Paraguay, though. Years of dictatorship and isolation are only recently giving way to brighter days. Today's Paraguay hears the strains of the oddly European native music and sees its people dance. Come, join in.

http://www.lonelyplanet.com.au/dest/sam/par.htm

PERU

NOVA Online/Ice Mummies of the Inca

Sometime in the 1500s, she was taken to the top of Sara Sara in the Cordillera Mountains of Peru and offered as a human sacrifice. The frozen and mummified remains of this child, now known as "Sarita," were recently uncovered there. Now, through NOVA Online, you can share in the discovery. Read the story of the expedition that reclaimed her from the ice, and see beautiful photographs of the Peruvian landscape, the local children, and the expedition and its discoveries. Listen to a native melody, a bilingual "Happy Birthday," and the sounds of the picks and shovels of the dig. This finely crafted site is a joy to experience. Don't miss it!

http://www.pbs.org/wgbh/pages/nova/peru/

PERU EXPLORER

In Peru are 84 of the world's known ecological zones and 28 different climates. The result is that kernels of corn grow as big as Buicks there (okay, a bit of an exaggeration). This site doesn't just give you the facts about Peru (loads of great "report stuff" like language, religion, currency, culture, climate, and history), it refuses to let you browse on by until you've had fun doing it. Walk the Inca Trail or visit the Sacred Valley, but by all means, have some of that corn! Maybe that's what the scarlet macaws at the top of the page are pecking. Okay, it's touristy, but it's, well, good.

http://www.peru-explorer.com/

Tales From the Peruvian Amazon

Have you ever dreamed about exploring the Amazon jungle? Ron Belliveau, Project Amazonas staff biologist, did more than dream—he packed his bags and did it! Ease your canoe into the water and join him as he tells his tale in words and pictures. Climb onto the river bank and into the dense rain forest that envelopes you. You almost hear the songs and screeches of exotic Amazon birds. You almost feel the shock of running your metal collection net into an electric eel (as did one unlucky adventurer). Whether you're looking at a photo of butterflies quietly sipping in a pool or the grin of a saber-toothed charicin (enough to make a piranha envious), you'll hardly believe your eyes.

http://www.contentpark.com/amazonas/tales/

PHILIPPINES
Collection of Legends

What a wonderfully simple site! From the knee of her Filipino mother to the pages of cyberspace come this Filipino woman's memories of the legends of her youth and culture. Whether you read of how the poison left a native plant or why the spiny pineapple looks like it does, these beautifully written stories will give you a look into the culture of the Philippines. From the legends, link to the games, mythology, superstitions, and even slang of the Philippines to broaden your view of this people and their land. At this site, there are no bells and no whistles, just lots of smiles and the warmth of visiting a site created with passion and with love.

http://www.pitt.edu/~filipina/legends.html

Filipino Kids on the Web

A good way to learn about another country is to hang out with someone who lives there. Talk to them. Hear them describe what it's like there. Well, that's just what this site offers for the non-Filipino surfer, since it highlights Filipino kids! Whether you stop at Anton or Lauren's page, Carmela or Liza's, you'll get to know their land by reading, listening, looking, and interacting. In addition to the home pages of some featured kids are Filipino folktales ("The Tortoise and the Monkey" and others) and kid-friendly Web links. So you want to learn about the Philippines from the real people? Come on over.

http://www.tridel.com.ph/user/ching/kids.html

Land of the Morning

Come to a virtual exhibit of the art and artifacts of Filipino culture from A.D. 500 to A.D. 1900. The stone carvings, ceramics, metalwork, wood carvings, textiles, and jewelry appear before you through the rich photography and text descriptions of each piece. Click on a map of the Philippines to read about the history and culture of the islands. Then view the objects in their context by hyperlinking to them as you read. This is a beautiful site; no Web study of the Philippines would be complete without a visit here. The gallery is always open!

http://www.laurasian.org/LOM_home.html

Lonely Planet -- Destination: The Philippines

The Philippines consists of over 7,100 islands, some of them with active volcanoes. Mount Pinatubo erupted in 1991 and left a moonlike landscape that tourists now visit by jeep. The Philippines are also notable for being the only Christian country in Asia. Ferdinand Magellan arrived in 1521 and erected the first cross, claiming the land for Spain. At the time, the natives did not think much of this idea. You'll find lots of general info at this site. You might also like the Philippines! Philippines! Philippines! Page at <http://www.filipino.com/>.

http://www.lonelyplanet.com/dest/sea/phil.htm

A Philippine Leaf

More than a thousand years ago, documents were written on leaves. In India and Southeast Asia, such communication was often made on palm leaves. Now, as we near a new millennium, a one-time aerospace computer systems engineer digs deeply into the ancient writing of the Philippines. He shares his results on the "leaf" of today's communication: the Web page. This site is rich in the history of the Philippines and Filipino writing systems, languages, and scripts that predates the Spaniards. Take a journey back to the ancient Philippines, "the way she was before the West found her."

http://WWW.BIBINGKA.COM/dahon/

Philippine Prehistory

Who were the Austronesians? How did they get where they were going? What three domestic animals were always with them (hint: Lassie, Porky, and Henny Penny)? The answers all tie in with today's Filipino people. In this "glimpse of the prehistory and pre-contact culture of the Philippines," we learn of their weapons, including the feared swivel gun. We discover their incredible ocean navigation and fishing skills and the religious beliefs of these very early people of the Philippines. And for those mystery lovers among you, see and read about the "tiger bells" and muse over their meaning.

http://www.he.net/~skyeagle/prehist.htm

Underwater Photos - Philippines

Who would have ever thought that a moray eel's eyes look like those on a cartoon fish? Normally, the first thing anyone would notice is the menacing jaws, but in Chuck Gardner's photographs the sea creature keeps its mouth shut long enough for us to notice its eyes. These brilliant pictures of what lies under the waves of the Philippines (and a few topside shots of the beaches, the palms, the dusty streets, and the landscape) are a feast for the eyes. And if you grow tired of stunning beauty, go to Chuck's home page and read about his role in the early development of the Internet and the World Wide Web in the Philippines. Don't miss this site!

http://members.nova.org/~cgardner/uw/

PITCAIRN ISLAND
Pitcairn Island Home Page

Isolation: see Pitcairn Island. This is a place where it takes months for mail and news to arrive. You could always call one of the 50 islanders on the phone. Not "their" phone, *the* phone. There is only one phone on the island. How could a place that is this far out of the mainstream possibly interest anyone? This site answers that question with a wealth of current local happenings, a list of who's who on the island, history (including the settlement by HMS *Bounty* mutineers), and more. View the local crafts and place your order. Look at the scenes and faces of the island. Read the musical scores, poems, and stories about Pitcairn. Just don't sail by! This is a great spot on the Web.

http://wavefront.wavefront.com/~pjlareau/pitc1.html

POLAND
Explore Poland

This is a jumpstation to many, many sites on Polish history, culture, and more. You might want to try the link to the State Ethnographical Museum in Warsaw, established in 1888. It features folk culture in Poland, Europe, and other continents. The museum owns 50,000 works from Central Europe and Poland and 20,000 from other countries. The works include folk costumes, sculpture and painting, handicrafts, and ritual objects. Small pictures of some of these items are shown on the home page. One exhibition of paintings is also featured.

http://www.explore-poland.pl/

New Polish Coins & Banknotes

It is said that money equivalent to one trillion dollars changes hands worldwide each day. Some of that money is Polish. On January 1, 1995, new banknotes and coins were made in Poland. You can see what the front and back of the notes look like here. This site is in Polish, but it is mostly graphics. You'll figure it out.

http://info.fuw.edu.pl/Zbigniew.Pasek/
    Money/money.html

Poland Country Guide

A tribe known as Polians, or "dwellers of the field," claimed Poland as their own in the early ninth century. Eleven centuries later, they put this site on the Web. You can learn about Polish history, people, and culture. If you explore the site, you'll find interesting details. For instance, defensive castles became an integral part of the Polish landscape in the fourteenth century in the reign of Casimir the Great, who "found Poland built of wood and left her built of stone." The education section includes links to the major universities in Poland.

http://ciesin.ci.uw.edu.pl/poland/poland-home.html

**Attention everyone.
The Internet is closing.
Please go play outside.**

Polish Homepages

Marek Kaminski, a Pole, is the only human to have reached both the North and the South Poles of our planet in the same year—on foot, and without support! You'll find his story and a link to his home page at this site (Kaminski appears in PolScapes: Impressions, Reminiscences). Stories of other Poles in Poland and abroad are also featured. You'll also learn about Polish ecology and Polish national parks. "About Poland" includes the national anthem, the Polish flag, and an interactive map of Poland. Check the Polish recipes and Christmas customs. And where else could you find the "Place of Poland" in the world rankings but in "Polish Statistics?" Poland is third in the world in potato production; 9.1 percent of all Earth's potatoes are grown there. The site also includes many links to other Polish sites.

http://www.infocom.net/~romanm/poland.html

The Warsaw Voice

The Warsaw Voice is Poland's only general-interest, English-language weekly newspaper. Get the Polish and Central European take on news, business, travel, and entertainment. The Buzz section gives a real sense of day-to-day life in Poland. Editorials are also a good source of what's happening there. One issue had a bike path map for Warsaw and notes on where you could stop to buy good ice cream!

http://www.contact.waw.pl/Pl-iso/voice/

PORTUGAL
The Algarve Home Page

This is a warm welcome from a mild climate. This part of Portugal receives many tourists, and this page explains everything a visitor might want to know about the area. There's information on weather, news, exchange rates, current Internet access, and links to various things Portuguese.

http://www.nexus-pt.com/algarve.htm

Don't be irrational, check on the numbers in MATH AND ARITHMETIC.

A collection of home pages about Portugal

Why did Portugal send so many explorers out to the New World? Maybe it's because Portugal is the westernmost point in Europe. It ranks as one of the world's longest-established countries. Portugal's boundaries have remained unchanged since the thirteenth century. Start your virtual journey at this huge collection of sites. Assembled are many of the available English language sources and some in Portuguese. You'll even find a "how to use the Net" guide here—in Portuguese!

http://www.well.com/user/ideamen/portugal.html

The Electronic News

The News is Portugal's national newspaper in English. At this site, catch the latest local and national news stories, sports shorts, and the classifieds. There is a link to Publico, the daily newspaper in Portuguese; even if you don't speak (or read) the language, you can get a sense of what's in the headlines. You'll also find sections on living in Portugal and doing business there. One classified ad offered a house in a windmill for sale.

http://www.nexus-pt.com/news/index.hts

Home Page de Portugal / Portugal Home Page

A fine map, with access to major cities, opens this page. Take a side trip to the Expo 98 site. This, the last exposition of the twentieth century, will take place in Lisbon, with the theme "The Oceans, a Heritage for the Future." (May 22 to September 30, 1998). "General information" leads you to lyrics to the national anthem (in Portuguese) and a detailed description and picture of the Portuguese flag. "Useful information" includes a chatty magazine (with articles on car culture and literacy in Portugal) called Irreal. If you're a passionate soccer fan, you'll find plenty of information on Portuguese soccer divisions and specific games. The satellite image might make a nice graphic for the first page of your report (try a screen shot).

http://s700.uminho.pt/homepage-pt.html

IPM HOME PAGE

If you like going to museums, this page will delight you. Tour the National Tile Museum or the National Museum of Ancient Art (with works from the twelfth through the nineteenth centuries). Sample contemporary art at the Chiado Museum, and take a peek at the sumptuous coaches in the unique National Coach Museum. Bring something to do—the graphics take a while to load, but they are worth the wait.

http://www.EUnet.pt/IPM/

QATAR

Ministry of Foreign Affairs, Qatar - Entrance

This, the official site of the Ministry of Foreign Affairs of Qatar, has absolutely splendid graphics. If you like the game of Myst, you'll appreciate this site. "Hot News" is offered in both English and Arabic. You'll find the emir's latest speeches and recent photos. Although the site is under construction, you'll get a feel for how Qatar sees itself. For more, try the ArabNet site at
<http://www.arab.net/qatar/qatar_contents.html>.

http://www.mofa.gov.qa/

REUNION ISLAND

Reunion Island

Reunion Island is a volcanic island off the coast of Africa. As Reunion Island is a department of France, you can polish up your *français* here (although most of the page is also in English). You'll see beautiful color photos of people, animals, plant life, and beaches. You'll get good background information on history, climate, and economic and social aspects of life there as well. A rainbow of people inhabit this island, which was first populated by 12 mutineers in 1646. You'll find good links to other pages here: official tourist information, the World Factbook, and individuals' home pages (in French, but with beautiful pictures).

http://www2.int-evry.fr/~narassig/run/eng/

ROMANIA

Discover Romania

In "News" be sure to look at Eu Romania, a Web site created and maintained by a Romanian high school. It has articles by students on youth in Romania, sports, begging in Bucharest, earthquake possibilities, and the parent-teen communication gap. Also on the main site you'll find a clickable map, general information, history, people, politics, economy, and sports. In "Celebrities," famous Romanians past and present, including Dracula and Ceausescu, are presented, with good descriptions of their lives. You may have to expand your browser window to see these choices.

http://students.missouri.edu/~romsa/romania.html

Embassy of Romania, Washington D.C.

Is the Black Sea in Romania really black? No, the Turks gave it the name Karadeniz ("black") because they feared the sea's storms. The embassy's FAQ section answers this and other questions you might have about Romania. You'll also find good links to other Romanian sites in "Romania on the Net" and "Other Official Romanian Sites on the Internet." And there are up-to-date links to newspapers and magazines, in Romanian and English.

http://embassy.org/romania/

ROMANIA

This Romanian source surveys everything from generalities, geography, and history to tourism and culture. A country in transition, Romania is still reeling from the fall of the Communist government in 1989. For decades, the Romania Communist party was the only party. After its demise, however, more than 200 parties sprang up. Cultural and political restructuring have been more difficult than anticipated. Transylvania is in Romania, and five centuries ago it was home to a man so infamous he is remembered to this day. This man was Vlad Tepes, also known as Vlad Dracula. "Tourism" contains a brief history of the man in history and in legend, as well as a portrait and pictures of two of his castles.

http://indis.ici.ro/romania/romania.html

Virtual ROMANIA

This up-to-date site has a little more depth than official sites. Explore news from Romania, facts about Romania, statistics, and culture (including fragments of Romanian folk music you can listen to). Also, in "Culture," enjoy Romanian/English quotations, such as *Întrebarea trece marea, Cine întreabă nu greseste* ("He that nothing questions, nothing learns"). A section called "Etc." includes information on Romanian adoption, recipes (Romanians apparently love sour foods), Romanian soccer, Jewish roots in Romania, computers in Romania, and much, much more.

http://www.info.polymtl.ca/zuse/tavi/www/
   rom_eng.html

RUSSIA
Friends of Tuva

We knew someone would eventually look up Tuva in this book, so we put this annotation in just for you! Tuva is an autonomous republic of Russia. You can find pictures of its flag and national symbols here. Richard Feynman made Tuva famous. Feynman was a physicist, bongo drum player, and engineer. He helped develop the atomic bomb in 1945, and he also helped solve the mystery behind the Challenger space shuttle disaster. Feynman was fascinated with Tuva, the land of triangular postage stamps and throat-singing. Many of Feynman's fans started an organization to advance the world's knowledge of Tuva, and Friends of Tuva was born.

http://www.feynman.com/tuva/

The Official Guide to Russia

This is the official site of the Russian National Tourist Office, and it gives good Web value. A clickable timeline presents basic Russian history, from ancient Russia through the Soviet era. You'll see pictures of cities and natural wonders. Read an enlightening essay on Russian art and architecture. The history and culture of Moscow and St. Petersburg are also presented. You can learn about the Trans-Siberian Railway and find out a little bit about the magnificent 13-foot Siberian tiger.

http://www.interknowledge.com/russia/

Research Exchange with PIN

A *dino*-mite exhibition is currently being shown at the University of California Museum of Paleontology site. It's a virtual visit to the Paleontological Institute in Moscow, the world's largest paleontological institute. The exhibit displays photographs of dinosaurs from Siberia and Mongolia, plus early mammals. The architectural features of the Moscow museum are also noted, including door hinges shaped like elk and three-story mosaics.

http://www.ucmp.berkeley.edu/pin/pin.html

Russia Alive!

Subtitled "Freedom, Information, Communication & Commerce in Russia," this site is part of the Alive! Global Network. This site is good for current news, weather, and culture of Russia. Newspapers such as the *St. Petersburg Times* and others publish up-to-the-minute reports. There are links to Russian magazines and an interview with Ovod, a 121-year-old former spy. If you need to know about a specific city, it's probably got a Web page on this site. Russia Alive! also includes a page just for children, where you'll find postings from kids in Kamchatka and Novgorod. For an interesting look at current Russian home pages, try the Incomparable All-Russian Hedgehog Award links.

http://www.alincom.com/russ/russmap.htm

Russian History

Russian history is like none other. The mix of cultures, invasions, religions, and politics creates a fascinating and complex entity. You can spend hours at this site. Learn about the very first settlements in Russia. Herodotus noted that Russian wheat sustained the builders of the Parthenon in the fifth century B.C. The Vikings, the Byzantine Empire, and Genghis Khan all played their parts in early Russian history. Find out why the Russians use the Cyrillic alphabet. And just how terrible was Ivan the Terrible? There is also information on the rise and fall of the Soviet Union and other recent happenings.

http://www.bucknell.edu/departments/russian/
   history.html

Russian Life

Russian Life is "The Monthly Magazine of Russian History, Culture, Business and Travel." Originally *USSR*, then *Soviet Life*, the newly named *Russian Life* was reborn in 1993. It is now a 32-page monthly magazine, a little bit like *Life* magazine in the U.S. *Russian Life* archives its front-page stories. You can find out about Catherine the Great, schools in Siberia, democracy in Russia, and marriage in Russia. Read about the birth of the samovar, and why the samovar is so important to Russians. There are also departments such as Survival Russian (which mixes Cyrillic text with English), Russian Cuisine, and Travel Journal. Also, you can read letters to the editor and follow links to other Russian pages. A caution to parents: Not all links have been viewed.

http://www.friends-partners.org/rispubs/RL-TOP.HTM

Russian Museums English Version

Tour major museums in Russia, from history (natural and otherwise) to literature to music to space flight. As you sift through this site, you'll find the menu for Nicholas and Alexandra's coronation dinner, hear "Flight of the Valkyrie," and see Russian portraits, architecture, and cultural artifacts. Most of the sites have English versions, but even the ones that don't are worth gazing at. Heavy on the graphics, this site may test your patience, but it's worth the wait.

http://www.museum.ru/DefEngl.htm

RWANDA
Rwanda Page

This page, assembled by the African studies department of the University of Pennsylvania, brings together many sources about Rwanda. You'll find Rwanda's constitution, the World Factbook article, maps, and background information about the civil war and genocide of 1994. There is also a link to the Ethnologue, a catalog of the world's languages, which describes the languages of Rwanda. A caution to parents: Violent events are described.

http://www.sas.upenn.edu/African_Studies/
  Country_Specific/Rwanda.html

SAINT HELENA
Saint Helena, South Atlantic Ocean

It's a good thing you can visit Saint Helena on the Web. It's very difficult to get there in person. Tiny Saint Helena is remote (1,200 miles from Africa, 1,800 miles from Brazil), and it's almost inaccessible. The only way you can get there is by mail boat, which sails six or seven times a year. The island's volcanic terrain has prevented any airports and runways from being built. But Saint Helena has a fascinating history and unique plant and animal life. Napoleon Bonaparte spent the last six years of his life there, in exile. At this page, you can see a picture of the wirebird, learn about island life today, and even find out how to get to the island. Take the spectacular photo tour, too, especially if you don't think you'll get there very soon. The island is a British dependent territory, and the people there are called "Saints." Larger islands dependent on Saint Helena are Ascension and Tristan da Cunha, even though they are miles and miles away!

http://geowww.gcn.uoknor.edu/WWW/Ascension/
  sh.htm

SAINT KITTS AND NEVIS
Accenting St. Kitts and Nevis - Official Travel Guide

These two islands look like a baseball and bat. Considering the colonial British history of the newly independent Caribbean nation, however, the residents would probably liken it more to a cricket ball and bat. This twin island nation became independent on September 19, 1983. At this site, you'll find more than just tourist information. There's a long article on Horatio Nelson, the famous British admiral, who married Francis Nisbet on Nevis in 1787. The Nelson Museum on Nevis has the largest collection of Nelson memorabilia in the Western Hemisphere. History and culture of Saint Kitts and Nevis are available. Nature is held in high regard there—by law, no building can be higher than the palm trees around it.

http://www.interknowledge.com/stkitts-nevis/

What TIME is it, anyway?

SAINT LUCIA
Official Guide to Saint Lucia

Part of the Lesser Antilles, Saint Lucia has the Atlantic Ocean lapping at its eastern shores, while its western beaches touch the Caribbean Sea. The terrain includes rain forests and volcanoes. There's much to celebrate in Saint Lucia—they have Independence Day in February, Emancipation Day in August, and National Day in December. This island is truly multicultural: a visitor can drive on the British (left) side of the road to a French town for an Indian meal. And, although French was outlawed by the British in the nineteenth century, Creole patois is commonly spoken. According to this page, Saint Lucia is the site of the world's only drive-in volcanic crater (Diamond Head on Oahu may make a similar claim).

http://www.interknowledge.com/st-lucia/

SAINT VINCENT AND THE GRENADINES
St. Vincent & the Grenadines

You'll find out about location and climate, as well as other background information here. Sites and Side Trips offers interesting anecdotes about the history and culture of the islands. For instance, St. George's Anglican Cathedral, which was built in the early 1800s, has a red-robed angel in a stained glass window. "The stained glass was originally commissioned by Queen Victoria to honour her first grandson, who later became King Edward VIII. Although it was destined to hang in St. Paul's Cathedral in London, the venerable queen took exception to the scarlet angel, believing the Bible specified that all angels wore white. As a result, the window found its way to Kingstown as a gift to the bishop and the diocese in St. Vincent."

http://www.cpscaribnet.com/stvgeni.html

Try actual reality.

SAINT-PIERRE AND MIQUELON
Welcome to Saint-Pierre et Miquelon

Saint-Pierre and Miquelon are the last remaining North American possession of France, located just off Newfoundland. This site has a detailed history of the islands, including a list of those who died in World War II. There are links to Basque and Breton sites, language and politics, and locally produced Web pages. Much of this material is in French, but about 20 percent has been translated into English. Portions of the site are also available in Portuguese, Euskara, Galego, and Spanish. Have you heard of all of those languages before? If not, learn more here!

http://www.cancom.net/~encyspm/English.html

SAN MARINO
Welcome to the Republic of San Marino

The opening page is written in a combination of Italian and English text. If you go about two-thirds of the way down the page, you'll find a clickable list of languages, including English. This leads you to basic information about "the ancient Republic of the world" (since A.D. 301). San Marino is a small but old nation. It is found within Italy, but it is a separate democratic republic that has been electing officials since 1243. The boundaries of San Marino have remained unchanged since 1463. In 1797, Napoleon Bonaparte offered to help the country expand its boundaries and increase revenue; the consuls politely declined. San Marino has a centuries-long tradition of asylum and hospitality. During the Second World War, it took in over 100,000 refugees, which is remarkable—especially when compared to their present population of only 24,000.

http://inthenet.sm/

What did grandma do when she was a kid? There is a list of questions to ask in GENEALOGY AND FAMILY HISTORY.

SAO TOME AND PRINCIPE

The Emerald Empire

These islands are off West Africa, straddling the equator. This site includes a flag, a map, and general information on population, geography, and economy of the area. Stay tuned: clickable buttons for Culture, Tourism, Real Estate, and News may be enabled in the future. Their major export is cocoa! You'll find a little more information at <http://www.sas.upenn.edu/African_Studies/Country_Specific/Sao_Tome.html>.

http://emerald-empire.com /geography/
   saotome/page00.htm

SAUDI ARABIA

ArabNet -- Saudi, Contents

Here you'll find fascinating tidbits among the population, government, and history facts. For instance, Saudi Arabia is home to the Arabian oryx, thought by some to be the inspiration for the legendary unicorn. This fabulous beast is perfectly suited to its desert habitat and can go for years, if necessary, without drinking. The oryx gets water from the plants it eats and from licking dew from desert plants. The site also explains the Islamic calendar, which is based on a lunar year instead of the solar one used in the West. Islamic months rotate, rather than coming in the same seasons each year. You'll learn a little bit about the *gahwa* ritual (coffee making). Also, the once-a-year hajj pilgrimage to Makkah (Mecca) is described in some detail. It differs from the pilgrimage to Mecca at any other time of year. There are even short articles on natural toothbrushes and Bedouin tents.

http://www.arab.net/saudi/saudi_contents.html

Royal Embassy of Saudi Arabia

This page is maintained by the Royal Embassy of Saudi Arabia in Washington, D.C. You'll find lots of information on the history, culture, economy, and government of the country. Religion is an important part of Saudi Arabian life. Be sure to take a look at the section on the history and practice of Islam. There is also a search engine that looks for terms appearing anywhere in the site. And look to the Multimedia Presentation for lots of pictures in categories such as health, Islam, sports and recreation, and energy.

http://imedl.saudi.net/

Saudi Arabia

Look in the Traveller's section to find the Arabic Language Center, which has eight common phrases in Arabic, with audio files to help you learn to say them (numbers and currency, too!). The History section (like the rest of the site) is illustrated with photos. It provides a capsule view of Saudi Arabia from 3000 B.C. to the present. Agricultural statistics are available; for example, there are six million sheep, and 3.5 million goats. And Saudi Arabia recently became an exporter of wheat. Cloak-and-dagger fans, look to the Saudi Arabian Intelligence Community link. You'll find Intelligence Watch Report Daily Updates that mention Saudi Arabia.

http://www.arablink.com/saudi-arabia/
   saudi-arabia.html

Saudi Arabia

This entry in the Encyclopedia of the Orient has brief articles on the political situation, the economy, health and education, religions and people, and history of Saudi Arabia. Look here for a more Western view of the country. Challenges facing Saudi Arabia are mentioned.

http://i-cias.com/e.o/saudi.htm

Welcome to Saudi Arabia

This site is less official than some, with links to recipes, Arabian horses, newsgroup postings, Operation Desert Storm, and Saudi Arabian resources. Note that it has not been updated in a while. While not all links work at all times, you will find information collected here that is hard to find elsewhere.

http://www.uoregon.edu/~kbatarfi/saudi.html

SCOTLAND

See UNITED KINGDOM—SCOTLAND

> **It's hard to remember, but mnemonic memory tricks are in WORDS.**

SENEGAL

The Official Home Page of the Republic of Sénégal

Senegal is the westernmost African country and a cultural crossroads. An overview of Senegal's current life and culture is provided on this home page. You can dip into information on art, recipes, and popular sporting events. "National Parks" gives you an idea of the kinds of animals native to the country (including hippos and warthogs). The World Factbook entry is included, so you can get the facts on population statistics and terrain.

http://www.earth2000.com/senegal/contents.shtml

SERBIA AND MONTENEGRO

Yugoslavia

Look at different sites for different views of Serbia and Montenegro. Although Serbia and Montenegro have asserted the formation of a joint independent state, it is unrecognized as yet by the United States. This site has information on culture, news, and economy of the area, plus a library of links. "Culture" is worth a look for the museums and descriptions of the people. You'll find lots of recipes here, too. And "Food" is a good place to look for Christmas customs. For another view of the region, try MonteNet at <http://www.netrover.com/~dragice/MonteNet.html> and especially "Why Yugoslavia again?"

http://www.yugoslavia.com/

SEYCHELLES

The Seychelles: An Unique Island Paradise

A group of islands in the Indian Ocean, northwest of Madagascar, Seychelles is a beautiful tropical nation. Seychelles is home to giant tortoises and unique fruit bats, as well as 72,300 people. Tourism is an important part of Seychelles' economy. It has been developed in an environmentally sound manner—only 4,000 tourists are allowed on the islands at a time. As the country didn't have an airport until 1971, it has developed its own unique culture.

http://www.bs.ac.cowan.edu.au/IOTO/
IOTO_SEYCHELLES/Seychelles1.htm

SIERRA LEONE

Sierra Leone Web

Current news of Sierra Leone will be found here. There are also news archives going back at least a year. You'll find language tidbits, too: proverbs and lorry (truck) slogans. Here's a sample in Krio: *Nius noh geht fut, boht i de waka* ("News has no feet, but it travels"). There are links to Sierra Leone pages maintained by Peace Corps volunteers and others with an interest in the country. Government information is also included. For a good map, climate information, and a picture of the Sierra Leone flag, try the Nations of the Commonwealth: Sierra Leone site at <http://www.tbc.gov.bc.ca/cwgames/ country/SierraL/sierral.html>.

http://www.winternet.com/~andersen/salone.htm

When a new state joins the United States, it gets its own star on the U.S. flag. When is the star officially sewn on?

Answer: The new star is added to the flag on the fourth of July following the admission of the new state. An Act of April 4, 1818, provided for this. Try http://www.icss.com/usflag/flag.evolution.html for more fascinating facts about the U.S. flag.

No lines at a virtual museum!

SINGAPORE

Makan Time in Singapore!

This is Singapore's unofficial food site. Foods from China, Thailand, Vietnam, and Malaysia all contribute to the delicious cuisine of Singapore. You can read about Asian restaurants in Singapore and all over the world. Also, there's a sizable collection of authentic recipes, with ingredients such as *pandan* leaves and *galangal*. Don't worry, another page of the site describes Asian ingredients, with pictures included. If you're traveling and want to find a good Asian restaurant, this site will clue you in to the best and the worst. Don't miss the "hawker food," which is what you'd find in the equivalent of a mall food court, at <http://www.sintercom.org/makan/foodcntr.html#list of popular hawker food>.

http://www.sintercom.org/makan/recipes.html

National Heritage Board: Homepage

"Preserving the heritage of the people of Singapore." This home page offers one-stop access to four of Singapore's museums. The National Archives of Singapore features building plans, old photographs, and audio clips (in Chinese). For instance, there's an interesting photograph collection of rickshaw drivers at the turn of the century. The Asian Civilisations Museum focuses on ancestral cultures of Singaporeans. Look for pictures and descriptions of art objects from all over Asia. The Singapore History Museum includes dioramas and famous monuments. When you've explored a little bit, take the Monuments Trail Quiz. And look for contemporary art at the Singapore Art Museum, with exhibitions and highlights.

http://www.museum.org.sg/nhb.html

SCHOOLS ONLINE

This Singapore-based resource is dedicated to schools, educators, and students. Some of the links will be of interest to students and teachers for their social or educational value. There are chat rooms and graffiti pages. Look for It Whiz, a new e-zine for kids. It has word puzzles, coloring pages, and key pals. Other links are Singapore-specific. Singapore information will be found on the Singapore Page in the Classroom Electric. You'll find links to Singapore's history, geography, art and culture.

http://www.sol.com.sg/

The Singapore Bookshop

Devoted book lovers are responsible for this site on the Net. It's the only bookstore on the Internet where you can buy books exclusively about Singapore or by Singaporean authors. Because so much information is given about each book, this site is like a heavily annotated bibliography. You can browse their "shelves," reading excerpts and getting background on the authors.

http://www.bookshop.canadasia.com.sg/

Singapore InfoMap

This site introduces and indexes Singapore resources on the Internet. Start with the FAQ, which serves as a descriptive index to the site. You may find everything you need in "One-Minute Singapore." It has links to basic information on climate, people, education, and government. If you have more time, delve into the many links related to sports and recreation, history, culture, business, and tourism. There are links to current newspaper articles as well.

http://www.sg/

SLOVAKIA

Slovakia Home Page - Central Europe Online

Take a look at "All That's New from the Old World" for Slovakian information, in as much detail as you chose. The very first page has basic information, like population and climate. There are also many links to sites on Slovakian daily life and culture, government, history, and many more. In the Main Section, the link to Travel & Culture has a Sights and Sounds of Central Europe site that may present information on the current holiday (Easter in the spring, Christmas in December). The archive also lists previous articles about the region.

http://www.centraleurope.com/ceo/slovakia/
  slkhome.html

DISNEY: a man, a plan, a land!

SLOVENIA

Connection to Slovenia Page

We hope you like accordion music—if you visit this site, you get a nice polka to listen to while you explore! You'll find lots of links here on the geography, economy, culture, history, government, language, and more. If you've got the time, this fine site has the info—tons of it. Other interesting places you might want to visit include the home page of the President of the Republic of Slovenia at *<http://www.sigov.si/upr/ang/>* and the General Information page at *<http://www.ijs.si/slo/country/visiting/general.html>* where you'll find the flag and the coat of arms. The Central Europe Online page for Slovenia at *<http://www.centraleurope.com/ceo/slovenia/slnhome.html>* is also recommended, although it is a lot quieter!

http://www.ualberta.ca/~mkozak/slovenia.htm

SOLOMON ISLANDS

Solomon Islands Home Page

The answer is 998! The question is exactly how many islands, atolls, and reefs make up the Solomon Islands? Furnished with a tropical climate, forests, mountain ranges, unspoiled beaches, butterflies as big as birds, underwater volcanoes, tons of history, and a location just a stone's throw from Australia, the Solomon Islands are truly the "happy isles." This site is a trove of information on the people, climate, geography, history, commerce, and government. Just one visit to this site will explain why the Solomon Islands are also referred to as the "pearl of the Pacific." The World Factbook page on this island group is at *<http://www.odci.gov/cia/publications/nsolo/factbook/bp.htm>*.

http://www.spacelab.net/~solomons/

SOMALIA

ArabNet -- Somalia, Contents

Did you ever wonder what frankincense is and where it comes from? It's a gum resin from the *Boswellia* tree, and it is an ingredient of incense and perfumes. Along with uranium, copper, gypsum, iron, marble, manganese, tin, and oil, it is one of the natural resources found in Somalia. Somalia is located in the easternmost part of the African continent. It has a hot and arid climate, rugged plateaus, and sandy coastal plains. Wildlife is plentiful in this African nation, but because of the harsh climate, plant life is limited. Much of the historical information here deals with Somalia's turbulent past, although its present is just as stormy.

http://www.arab.net/somalia/somalia_contents.html

SOUTH AFRICA

Nkosi Sikelel' iAfrika - South Africa's National Anthem

In many ways, the story of South Africa's national anthem mirrors the development of the country. The "Nkosi Sikelel' iAfrika" was composed in 1897 by Enoch Sontonga, from the Mpinga clan of the Xhosa nation. He taught at a Methodist Mission School. He wrote the tune and the first verse (in Xhosa), and the song of peace and healing always moved its audiences. In 1927, a further seven verses were published, added by a South African poet. It became an anthem of the oppressed, spreading beyond the borders of South Africa to Tanzania and Zambia. The problem was that white South Africa already had an official national anthem. When sweeping governmental reforms changed the policies that divided the races, South Africa also changed its national anthem. In 1994, parts of both anthems were combined. You can find the words to all three anthems here. Sontonga's burial site has been declared a national monument. Don't miss the story of the difficulty of locating his grave so that he could be honored.

http://www.anc.org.za/misc/nkosi.html

You won't believe how the GARDENS AND GARDENING section grew!

How is Kwanzaa celebrated? Find out in HOLIDAYS!

Pretoria Education Network

Judging by the list of schools in South Africa with Web sites—see <http://www.school.za/tes/websites.htm>—they have a good start. But this South African network won't rest until every school in their area is hooked up. And they aren't stopping there. Read the story of the e-mailing Sisters of Mercy at <http://www.mg.co.za/mg/pc/96june/18june-nuns.htm> and their mission.

http://www.moonbeam.co.za/pretnet/Welcome.html

Welcome to South Africa

For too many years, the mere thought of South Africa brought visions of a nation in which the black majority lived under a bigoted and constricting system known as apartheid. But that was then, and this is now. Apartheid has been abolished, Nelson Mandela has been released from prison and elected president, and South Africa is emerging into a world in which all of its people are citizens and all are represented. This official site, from the South African embassy in Washington, D.C., is a wonderful source for historical, cultural, and social information.

http://www.southafrica.net/

SOUTH GEORGIA AND THE SOUTH SANDWICH ISLANDS

The World Factbook page on South Georgia And The South Sandwich Islands

Name a large city in South Georgia. Atlanta, you say? Yes, that's right, but the world has more than one South Georgia. The one we're talking about is officially called South Georgia and the South Sandwich Islands. These islands are overseas British territories. But they are also claimed by the South American nation of Argentina. Fairly close to Antarctica, some of these islands have permanent ice and snow cover, and one has a herd of reindeer (the reindeer are not native; the species was brought there). There's a military fort and a bird sanctuary and not a lot else; see <http://www.nbs.ac.uk/public/info/birdis.html>. You might want to check out other island groups around Antarctica, which you can read about at <http://www.spri.cam.ac.uk/bob/periant.htm>.

http://www.odci.gov/cia/publications/nsolo/
  factbook/sx.htm

SOUTH KOREA

See KOREA, SOUTH

SPAIN

Discover Spain with the Tourist Office of Spain

Of course this site is tourist-oriented, but don't let that keep you from giving it a visit. It has all the usual country facts, such as geography, history, and government. But it also has really neat sections on people, social customs, transportation, communications, and things to do in the country. Be sure to check out the World Heritage in Spain section and the descriptions of the 15 World Heritage Site locations. For those really tough questions, there are even addresses for local tourist offices worldwide.

http://www.spaintour.com/

General Overview

Don't let the name of this site throw you off. This is more than just a general overview. Actually, this site has so much, it's hard to know where to begin. You'll find the usual: history, geography, customs, the people, a map. But you'll also find sports, cuisine, handicrafts, and a great section on the museums of Madrid. Did you know that one of the world's greatest art museums is located there? The Prado houses paintings from the eleventh through the nineteenth centuries and sculpture from ancient Sumeria and Egypt through the nineteenth century.

http://www.ozemail.com.au/~spain/overview.htm

Si, Spain

This official site is from the Directorate General for Cultural Affairs at the Spanish Foreign Ministry. It not only covers the history and culture of Spain but also gives practical information for tourists, including online Spanish lessons. If you are looking for specific info and can't seem to find it, then try the internal search engines here. There's even one just for fiestas! This site is also available in French and German.

http://www.DocuWeb.ca/SiSpain/

SRI LANKA
Embassy of Sri Lanka

This official site offers a wealth of beautiful pictures and history of this island republic. A great map is even included. By the way, did you know that Sri Lanka used to be called Ceylon? Its main exports are tea, rubber, coconuts, garments, gems, desiccated coconut, and cinnamon, among others. One of the fascinating things to see in Sri Lanka is the Sacred Bo Tree, which is in the city of Anuradhapura. According to this site, it is the world's oldest tree: "a branch of the very Bo Tree beneath which the Buddha himself found Enlightenment. It was brought to Sri Lanka in the 3rd century B.C."

http://wheat.symgrp.com/symgrp/srilanka/

Lonely Planet -- Destination: Sri Lanka

Where would you go to wash your elephant? The bathtub? No, it would leave footprints in the soap, and besides, your parents would never understand. The automatic car wash is probably out of the question, too—think of all the elephant wax you'd need. The only solution is to take your elephant to Sri Lanka, where they have elephant baths. You can see a picture of one at <http://www.lonelyplanet.com/dest/ ind/graphics/sri05.htm> and find out lots of other interesting facts about the country of Sri Lanka, including information about the ethnic unrest there.

http://www.lonelyplanet.com/dest/ind/sri.htm

SUDAN
Sudan

Sudan is the largest country on the continent of Africa. It also has some of the largest problems: civil war, border disputes, a declining economy, overpopulation, drought, and military coups, just to name a few. Each year, thousands of Sudanese citizens flee to the neighboring countries to escape the harsh conditions in their own country. Needless to say, the Sudan is not a popular tourist stop. This site does have a map and it does supply statistics, but that's about all. For balance, the Republic of Sudan page at <http://www.columbia.edu/~tm146/sudan.html> offers audio files of Sudanese music as well as lovely photographs, among other things.

http://www.arabworld.com/factbook/sd.htm

SURINAME
Lonely Planet -- Destination: Suriname

This Web page doesn't give a lot of encouragement to people wanting to visit Suriname. One of the problems with visiting very small countries is that they may not be able to accommodate the needs of tourists. Suriname has few roads, a hot, humid climate, and few accommodations. And then there's the high crime, both in the city and on the road. Unfortunately, a Tourist Board Web site is not yet up to balance this view. The World Factbook page on this South American country is at <http://www.odci.gov/cia/publications/nsolo/ factbook/ns.htm>.

http://www.lonelyplanet.com/dest/sam/sur.htm

Tropical Rainforests In Suriname

Save the rain forests! They are up for sale and are being destroyed at an alarming rate. This excellent site gives a close-up look at the rain forest, its plants, animals, people, and sounds. Don't miss it!

http://www.euronet.nl/users/mbleeker/suri_eng.html

SVALBARD
NN: Geography, history, religion, people - Svalbard

Svalbard is part of the kingdom of Norway. It is called the "land of cold coasts," and they're not kidding. One thing that keeps it so cold is the fact that the land never completely thaws out in the summer. Only the top few feet warm up, which means you won't find any deep-rooted vegetation. Still, some 164 species of plants are found on the island. Since the opening of an airport in 1979, tourism has increased. A vacation at Svalbard includes experiencing beautiful coastlines and desert—Arctic desert, that is. Don't pack a swimsuit, unless, of course, it's fur-lined! Another hazard is polar bears, and you can find out more about that and Svalbard at <http://www.svalbard.com/>.

http://odin.dep.no/ud/nornytt/uda-297.html

NTIN: Svalbard

The term "polar expedition" takes on a whole new meaning at this site, because your travel guide at <http://home.sn.no/~okleven/Svalbard.html> is a polar bear! Just follow the bear for some of the most exquisite photos you've ever seen, from hiking on snow-covered mountains in the summer to incredible shots of the aurora borealis (northern lights) in the winter. While Svalbard is a territory of Norway, you will see the strong cultural influences of both Scandinavia and Russia. The World Factbook page on Svalbard is at <http://www.odci.gov/cia/publications/nsolo/factbook/sv.htm>.

http://www.sn.no/rl/no/ntin/svalbard/

SWAZILAND
Swaziland

Swaziland, the "emerald of Africa." High mountains, grassy hills, tribal villages, luxury hotels, a temperate climate, and lions and rhino, and...well, you get the idea. There is plenty of wildlife. Much of it is protected in one of Swaziland's several huge wildlife preserves. This small, landlocked South African kingdom also has the last remaining ruling monarchy on the continent. Drop into this site and take a look, or try the World Factbook page at <http://www.odci.gov/cia/publications/nsolo/factbook/wz.htm>.

http://public-www.pi.se/~orbit/africa/swazi.html

SWEDEN
The Saami - people of the sun and wind

The Saami are northern Scandinavia's indigenous people. Their traditional homeland crosses five national borders, and about 20,000 Saami currently live in the Swedish part. Although originally hunters and gatherers, they are now better known for their large herds of reindeer. There are eight distinct seasons in reindeer herding; find out about them here. The Saami now have their own parliament under Swedish law, and its task is to provide the Saami with a way to determine their own future.

http://www.sametinget.se/english/

Sweden Information

If you happen to be doing a report on Sweden, this is the most comprehensive site you will find. Whatever facet of Swedish life you're interested in, you'll find it here. Everything from their history (starting with the Vikings), government, society, and industry to their food and recreation. For example, have you heard of Everyman's Right? According to this site,"The Right of Public Access (Allemansrätten) is unique and the most important base for recreation in Sweden, providing the possibility for each and everyone to visit somebody else's land, to take a bath in and to travel by boat on somebody else's waters, and to pick the wild flowers, mushrooms, berries." You can't destroy property, and if you want to pitch your tent for more than a day, you have to have permission of the landowner. You might also enjoy reading about the Swedish educational system and comparing it to the one you know.

http://www.smorgasbord.se/sweden/

Welcome to the Royal Court of Sweden

This is the official Web site of the Swedish monarchy. Carl XVI Gustaf, who ascended the throne in 1973, is the 74th King of Sweden. The monarchy goes back over a thousand years. You will learn about the King, Queen Silvia, and the rest of the royal family here. Check the information on the palace and why it has a different architectural style on each of its four sides.

http://www.royalcourt.se/eng/

Welcome to Virtual Sweden

Sweden is about the size and shape of California, and you'll find a good map here. You'll also find other information about their geography, their people (including King Carl XVI Gustaf), and their country in general. There's even a recipe section so you can try their food, although some of the ingredients might be a little hard to find: stinging nettles and reindeer heart! But you might try the recipe for delicious waffles, traditionally eaten on March 25, Annunciation Day. According to this site, "They are also very popular in Swedish mountain resorts, where they generally are served together with whipped cream and cloudberry jam." Now if we can just find some cloudberry jam, we will be all set!

http://www.sr.se/rs/virtual/

SWITZERLAND
Geneva Guide

Did you know that Geneva is the birthplace of the World Wide Web? Tim Berners-Lee started it, way back in 1989. That's just one of the fascinating things you'll learn about Geneva at this site. Check out the maps, the culture, the museums, and the art of Geneva. You can read about it in either French or English.

http://www.isoft.ch/GenevaGuide/home2e.html

Information About Switzerland

That's just exactly what this site provides: basic information about Switzerland, and more. You find the usual area, population, and government statistics and a map. An interesting section farther down lists famous people from Switzerland, such as William Tell (remembered for the famous apple incident), St. Nicholas (Santa Claus), and psychoanalyst Carl Jung, just to name a few. A good portion of this site is in German and English.

http://www.ethz.ch/swiss/Switzerland_Info.html

(NMBE) Saint Bernard Dog

It is winter, in the year 1800. At the summit of Switzerland's Great St. Bernard Pass, 8,100 feet above sea level, Napoleon Bonaparte's soldiers struggle against the "White Death" of snow and ice fog. They flounder in the deep snow, trying to find the way back to the right path. Just as they despair of ever finding it again, they hear a friendly bark! A huge fluffy dog bounds up to them. It's "Barry," one of the distinctive dogs owned by the nearby monastery. Since the eleventh century, the monks have offered travelers shelter from the fierce mountain storms, and their big working dogs have been adept at finding lost people and saving lives. The dog leads the soldiers back to the warm monastery buildings, called a hospice. As this site says, "The existence of such dogs has been documented in paintings and drawings dating back to 1695 and in written official documents of the Hospice since 1707." Read more about the early history of the Saint Bernard dog, and see wonderful pictures of this remarkable breed.

http://www-nmbe.unibe.ch/abtwt/saint_bernard.html

SYRIA
CITY.NET Syria

If you're looking for information on just about every subject having to do with Syria, then here it is. Syria boasts the oldest capital, Damascus. The first written alphabet came from Syria, and bronze was invented there. It was the scene of many battles during the Crusades. Three continents meet in Syria: Asia, Africa, and Europe. It was also a trade crossroads between the Caspian Sea, the Indian Ocean, the Black Sea, and the Nile River. The Silk Road, a trade route to China, also went through Syria. The ArabNet page on Syria is at <http://www.arab.net/syria/syria_contents.html>.

http://city.net/countries/syria/

TAIWAN
Taiwan General Information

You'll find lots of facts here! There's a good map to show you the location of Taiwan in relation to China, Japan, and the Philippines. Then there's general info about population, the monetary unit, and a brief history. Try some of the links. One of them goes to Traditional Chinese Culture in Taiwan at <http://www.gio.gov.tw/info/culture/culture.html> where you can learn about traditional calligraphy, folk arts, Chinese opera, jade, and the fine art of "chop carving." Not pork chops, but a special personalized signature stamp used to make a document official. A fascinating and beautiful site created by the Republic of China Tourist Board is at <http://www.tbroc.gov.tw/e_index2.html> with many cultural, historical, and spiritual sites.

http://www.softidea.com/twhakkausa/taiwan_info.html

Your family has a history—write it down! Hints in GENEALOGY AND FAMILY HISTORY.

TAJIKISTAN

Tajikistan

Formerly part of the Soviet Union, Tajikistan is bordered by China to the east, Uzbekistan to the west, Kyrgyzstan to the north, and Afghanistan and Pakistan to the south. It is a country of political unrest, and life there is uncertain. The Tajikistan Page at <*http://www.angelfire.com/sd/tajikistanupdate/*> collects updated information, personal pages, and travel information from all over the Web. Do yetis (Abominable Snowmen) really live in the inaccessible mountain wilderness there? Some people think so!

http://www.odci.gov/cia/publications/nsolo/
  factbook/ti.htm

TANZANIA

Tanzania

This country is properly called the United Republic of Tanzania. And though this site is only a single page, it is chock-full of great info on Tanzania's history, geography, natural resources, climate, population, education, culture, economy, and much more. There's even a small section on foreign policy. What more can you ask for? An animated giraffe? Oh, all right. You'll find one at the Tanzania Tourist Board site at <*http://www.tanzania-web.com/home.htm*> along with other tourist info!

http://parrett.net/~sti/tanz_doc.html

THAILAND

Lonely Planet -- Destination: Thailand

You'll find tons of all the usual info you'll ever need for reports, papers, or whatever. This is the site for Thailand. There's even a recommended reading section with books, articles, and travel guides. Just watch out for the land mines on the Cambodian border—read the warning here. For a more restful experience, run over to Amorn Chomchoey's Virtual Thai Music Cafe Home Page at <*http://www.inet.co.th/cyberclub/somsri/midipage.htm*> where you'll hear the Thai national anthem as well as a classical Thai piece called "Bat Eat Banana." On the other hand, we couldn't stop listening to another one on the page called "Sailom." Try it and see what you think!

http://www.lonelyplanet.com.au/dest/sea/thai.htm

Thai Heritage Page

The Emerald Buddha. The Golden Royal Barges. The Phanom Rung Sanctuary, designed in such a way that at least twice a year, the early morning rays of the sun shine through all 15 corridors, making the stone walls glow. Pictures, gorgeous pictures, even more gorgeous pictures, and a clickable map—that's what you'll find here. This well-written site gives you a fascinating history of Thailand, including its prehistory, plus biographies of the royal family.

http://www.cs.ait.ac.th/~wutt/wutt.html

Thailand: His Majesty King Bhumibol Adulyadej's Golden Jubilee Home Page

His Majesty King Bhumibol Adulyadej of Thailand was born in Cambridge, Massachusetts. He became King in 1946, and in 1996 he celebrated his Golden Jubilee—50 years as monarch. According to the information presented here, he is very popular among his subjects. He is involved in making technology and other scientific advances available to his people. Read about his agricultural and other reforms, and get a glimpse of the beautiful Jubilee celebration and its royal regalia.

http://kanchanapisek.or.th/index.en.html

TIBET

See CHINA

TOGO

Togo's OFFICIAL Web Page

This small African nation is about the size of West Virginia, with a population of about 4.5 million people. Its southernmost border is comprised of less than 30 miles of coastline on the North Atlantic. There's a map and lots of statistics about Togo that would be useful for writing a report for a geography class. The World Factbook page on Togo is at <*http://www.odci.gov/cia/publications/nsolo/factbook/to.htm*>.

http://www.afrika.com/togo/

TOKELAU

Tokelau

Tokelau is a territory of New Zealand. It's an island group that's approximately six square miles in total area. It has no airports, no railroads, and no port. It also has no official Web page or even a "Friends of Tokelau" page. Maybe it will next year!

http://www.odci.gov/cia/publications/nsolo/
factbook/tl.htm

TONGA

Welcome to the Kingdom of Tonga

If we ask you to meet us just west of where the international date line crosses the Tropic of Cancer, where would we be? In the Kingdom of Tonga! Made up of three island groups, Tonga has about 171 islands, the newest of which is Metis Shoal, created by volcanic activity in June 1995. With its coral reefs, rain forests and volcanic islands, Tonga was the first South Pacific nation to establish national parks and reserves to protect its unique ecology. While you're visiting this site, you can hear a welcome message from Tonga's Crown Prince Tupouto'a and even see a film of one of their native dances. You might also like Tonga Online at *<http://www.netstorage.com/ kami/index.html>* for more information on the culture of Tonga. You can also send an e-mail postcard "from Tonga" at this site.

http://www.vacations.tvb.gov.to/

TRINIDAD AND TOBAGO

FESTIVALS OF TRINIDAD AND TOBAGO

You're enjoying a holiday at a lush Caribbean resort, strolling through throngs of brightly dressed families playing music and singing and dancing. Suddenly you're doused with sprays of multicolored paint! Welcome to the Phagwa Festival, celebrated annually by the many Hindu residents of the islands of Trinidad and Tobago. This site explains Phagwa and the Carnival, two of the more unique festivals in this corner of the world. It is also part of the larger Yo! Trinidad pages featuring news and information about these islands.

http://www.yotrinidad.com/festival.htm

Welcome to Trinidad and Tobago!

The locals call it "T&T," and everyone knows this dual island nation as the birthplace of calypso and steelpan music. The islands are among the largest producers of oil and natural gas in the Caribbean. But with the festive and bustling cities of Trinidad and the quiet, unspoiled beaches of Tobago, they are a haven for tourists the world over. Look to this site for scads of reference material on T&T, including maps, history, government, art and cultural information, and much more.

http://www.tidco.co.tt/

TUNISIA

Rick's Tunisia Travel Photos

As you glance at these beautiful color photographs of Tunisian towns such as Tunis and Carthage, you may think that some of the views look familiar. The area known as Matmata, where people live underground to escape the heat of the Sahara Desert, was filmed in *Star Wars* as Luke Skywalker's home. Want more? The ArabNet page for Tunisia is at *<http://www.arab.net/ tunisia/tunisia_contents.html>*.

http://www.ricks.com/pages/travel/africa/tunisia/
tunisia.html

Wondrous Labyrinths: Tunisia Page 1

Thousands of years ago, Carthage was home to the Phoenicians, and it rivaled the Roman Empire. It was from there that Hannibal led an army—mounted on elephants—across the Alps to invade Rome itself. Years later, the Romans retaliated and destroyed Carthage, leveling it to the ground. The city that rose atop the ruins became the capital of Tunisia, and it is a living remnant of those ancient times. This Web site allows you to explore the wonders and history of Tunisia. It features magnificent color photographs of the people and landmarks by Ozan Yuksek.

http://www.turknet.com/atlas/february/tunisia/

TURKEY

History of Turkey

Mustafa Kemal, better known as Ataturk, founded modern Turkey by bringing down the 800-year-old Ottoman Empire in 1923. Here you can find a solid capsule history of his founding of the Republic of Turkey and the far-reaching modernization of his country. The page also includes a summary and review of a book concerning the Ottoman sultans from the year 1071 until 1923.

http://final.dystopia.fi/~emre/history.html

Information about Turkey

Here's where you need to go to get up to date on what's going on in Turkey. Yusuf Pisan has linked up to dozens of online Turkish newspapers, historical accounts, archeological digs, jazz festivals, sports events, recipes, city maps, name books, business reports, sailing information, and lots of other goodies.

http://www.CS.nwu.edu/~yusuf/turkey

Remember the legend of King Midas?

He asked the gods to turn everything he touched into gold. This became a problem when he wanted to eat, and his food turned to gold, too! Midas begged the gods to take their "gift" back, and they told him to bathe in the river Pactolus. Its sands have been golden ever since. Midas was the king of Phrygia, part of modern-day Turkey. Read more in Information about Turkey.

A Travel at Warp Speeds in Turkey

Hop aboard the Turkish time machine! Travel at warp speeds through ten thousand years and a multitude of civilizations. Mehmet Kurtkaya designed this clever cyberguide to Anatolia, now known as Turkey, as it developed from the Neolithic ages on through the twentieth century. It is truly amazing what is known about the people who lived in this area a hundred centuries ago. The time travel is complemented by a section entitled, "The Jewels of Anatolian History," featuring a dozen mind-boggling features and events of the region. According to legend, King Midas magically turned everything he touched to gold. While the legend is just a story, Midas was a real king of Gordion, located in central Turkey. And Gordion, too, is a place with its own legend: the Gordion Knot. Many wise and powerful people tried to untie the knot for years, believing that the one who could successfully untie it would be given magical powers. Alexander the Great conquered Gordion with his armies and came up with his own solution. He cut the knot open with his sword!

http://www.twarp.com/turkwarp.htm

Turknet

Nestled comfortably between Europe and Asia, Turkey is the home of ancient cities built along historical silk and spice trade routes. Once you've seen Turkey, you simply can't confuse it with anywhere else. This site explores the look of Turkish architecture and styles of its people. Click on the World of Wonders tag and see natural, historical, and cultural landscapes. Turkey is described here as the "crossroads of history," where East meets West. The Ottoman army blazed a trail across Europe in the sixteenth century, operating out of Turkey. They made it as far as the gates of Vienna in Austria, where they were driven back. The retreating armies left behind sacks of Turkish coffee, introducing the beverage to Europe. Even today, Vienna's coffee cafes are world-famous.

http://www.turknet.com/

You are your own network.

TURKMENISTAN
Turkmenistan Resource Page

This former Soviet Republic, now an independent nation, is wedged between Iran, Afghanistan, Uzbekistan, Kazakhstan, and the Caspian Sea. You can't get there by train, so most visitors go by airplane. Turkmenis have been famous for their wool carpets for over two thousand years, and the ones they make today are pretty much the same as the earliest ones. With so much wool, there are a lot of lamb recipes as well. This Web site (part of the Central Eurasia Resources Pages) organizes lots of useful information concerning Turkmenistan. Here you'll find the latest news, arts, culture, business, government, human rights information, and just about anything else you might want to know about this nation.

http://www.soros.org/turkstan.html

TURKS AND CAICOS ISLANDS
Caribbean Outpost - Turks and Caicos Islands

By putting together the information on this page, it is possible to paint a distinct picture of the Turks and Caicos Islands. Made up of 30 mostly uninhabited islands, it's about twice the size of Washington, D.C., yet it has a population of a little over 13,000. Most of these people make a living from fishing or tourism, and they have to endure frequent hurricanes. You'll find a lot more hard facts here as well, including the fact that this is a dependent territory of the United Kingdom.

http://www.cariboutpost.com/ff/tc.html

Turks & Caicos Islands

Recent evidence points to the Grand Turk Island as being the first place Columbus landed in the New World. Not too long afterward, the people who greeted Columbus vanished, and the islands were uninhabited for two hundred years. Pirates made the Turks and Caicos Islands their hideout for a long time. This site will provide you with a good overview of these Caribbean islands and why they are so popular with tourists and divers.

http://expedia.msn.com/wg/Places/TurksCaicosIslands/HSFS.htm

TUVALU
The World Factbook page on Tuvalu

Tuvalu, a stamp-sized nation of just 8,000 people living on nine tiny atolls, coincidentally lists postage stamps as its main source of international trade. A few more details for the Tuvalu fan is on the Tuvalu page at <http://www.tcol.co.uk/tuvalu/tuv.htm>.

http://www.odci.gov/cia/publications/nsolo/factbook/tv.htm

UGANDA
Uganda

Surprisingly, even though this page was developed by a travel agency trying to get people to vacation in Uganda, it is still quite frank about the brutal history of the country and its two terrible dictators. For good hard, historical facts about Uganda, this may be the site to see. For the Uganda Tourist Board's official site, see <http://www.tomco.net/~jssemwog/utb/utb.htm>.

http://www.kilimanjaro.com/uganda/uganda.htm

Uganda - Online

Winston Churchill called Uganda the "pearl of Africa." It is well represented at this site being constructed by Ugandans attempting to tell the rest of the world about their nation. Including information about Ugandan history, government, education, geography, business, health, and human rights and other important facts, it promises to offer rich insights into this developing nation. You might also get some information from the nicely designed and similar Uganda: The Pearl of Africa page at <http://www.uganda.co.ug/>.

http://imul.com/uganda/

> ## We like the INVERTEBRATES best. —The Nields

UKRAINE

Kiyiv-Pechesrsk Lavra

Continually evolving, Kiyiv-Pechesrsk Lavra explores the cultural side of the Ukraine. Most notable here is the truly in-depth exploration of the 900-year-old Lavra monastery and its network of caves and catacombs in Kiev, Ukraine's capital city. In fact, the Ukrainian word *pechery*, which means "caves," is where the monastery gets its name. Also to be found here is a look at a recently unearthed collection of carved stone artwork done by Cossack warriors of the eighteenth and nineteenth centuries. Plus, you'll discover an exhibition of breathtaking woodcuts by Ukrainian artist Jackues Hnizdovsky, a history of the last five years of Ukrainian independence, and much more.

http://www.lavra.kiev.ua/

Kyiv FreeNet

Ukrainians and people interested in the Ukraine from all over the world post questions and answers about the nation here on the FreeNet's discussion board. The topics are discussed mostly in English, making it a great place to ask questions you may have about the Ukraine. You can also find downloadable maps of the area and a FAQ file, among other features. There are many Ukraine-related links, too!

http://www.freenet.kiev.ua/

Ukraine Online

This site includes up-to-the-minute weather information about the area, a folk calendar offering listings of unique Ukrainian holidays, important resource information, and a terrific photo gallery.

http://www.gu.kiev.ua/

Did the groundhog see his shadow? Find out if it will be an early spring in HOLIDAYS.

Verkhovna rada of Ukraine

The Verkhovna rada is the Ukrainian parliament, which is the legislature of the nation. This is the body that makes the laws in the Ukraine, and the people in it have created this mostly English language site to explain how their nation works. While it has been over five years since the Ukraine became independent from the former Soviet Union, it took until June 1996 for the nation to adopt a constitution. The Ukraine, once dominated by a fierce dictatorship, has created what may be one of the most open societies on earth. Here you can read this fascinating government document in its entirety, including the portions that deal with the environmental disaster of the Chernobyl nuclear disaster of 1986. The people of this nation are committed to make public everything they can about this incident. You'll also find a colorful photo gallery and list of other Ukrainian-related Web sites.

http://www.rada.kiev.ua/welcome.html

UNITED ARAB EMIRATES

UAE - 25 Years - Home Page/Index

The etiquette and manners of other nations can sometimes be confusing. In the United Arab Emirates, for example, showing the sole of one's shoe can be an insult. Apparently, big business deals have been canceled because people have casually crossed their legs while sitting in chairs. It is proper to eat with your right hand only, and if your parents want to refuse a second, third, or fourth cup of coffee or tea, they need to cover the cup with their hands and shake it from side to side. Above all, be careful telling people that you admire something, for they may feel obligated to give it to you and expect something of equal value in return. In addition to these rules of manners, the site features detailed examinations of the environment, animals, heritage, culture, education, and industry of this oil-rich desert nation, as well as a sharply photographed collage of sights.

http://www.uaeu.ac.ae/25/

Get to know some famous AFRICAN AMERICANS.

United Arab Emirates: "infoemirates.com" Bookmarks

All the facts are in order here for a good look at the United Arab Emirates, a very young and extremely wealthy country. Here is a good starting point for research into this nation, offering links to government, history, travel, books, geography, business, and tourism.

http://infoemirates.com/bookmarks.html

UNITED KINGDOM

The British Monarchy

This is the official Web site of the British monarchy. Here you will learn about the monarchy as it exists today as well as how it was in the past. You'll visit the palaces, the crown jewels, even find out why Elizabeth II keeps corgis as pets! There is a section on a typical day in the life of Her Royal Highness, and you can find out about the many ceremonial duties she must perform. This site is very new, very popular, and very, very slow. If you're interested in exactly what was said, sung, and done back on June 2, 1953, when Elizabeth became an anointed sovereign, you can follow the complex procedure at <http://www.ely.anglican.org/~sjk/liturgy/cor1953.html>.

http://www.royal.gov.uk/

BritSpeak

In America, a man would have no trouble complimenting a woman on the pants she wears, but in Britain, "pants" refers to one's underwear! Other strange bits of Britspeak: "public school" means private school, "homely" means pleasant, "presently" means soon, and "pavement" is a sidewalk. A speed bump on the road is called a "sleeping policeman." "Bob's your uncle" is what Brits say instead of "That's all there is to it," and a really brainless person is as "thick as two short planks." You'll find British to American and American to British dictionaries here as well as links to other similar pages. A caution to parents: Some common American words translate into rude British language and vice versa.

http://pages.prodigy.com/NY/NYC/britspk/main.html

Dr. Dave's U. K. Pages

The United Kingdom includes England, Wales, Scotland, Northern Ireland, and the Isle of Man. Dr. Dave's pages give you a look at the assorted cultures that make up the kingdom. You will find detailed looks at the cities, towns, and villages and a wonderful collection of photographic images organized by subject matter, such as thatched cottages, pub signs, and British cartoons and caricatures.

http://www.neosoft.com/~dlgates/uk/ukgeneral.html

UNITED KINGDOM—ENGLAND

Guy Fawkes Day

On November 5 every year, people in England shoot off fireworks, light bonfires, and make a lot of noise. Why? They are celebrating a foiled plot to blow up the Parliament Buildings way back in 1605. It seems one Guy Fawkes and his group wanted to kill the King and all the members of Parliament. Thirty-six barrels of gunpowder were discovered just in time, and the traitors were executed. "Burning the Guy" is another tradition, where an *effigy*, or pretend figure, representing Guy Fawkes is thrown onto the bonfire. Children ask for "pennies for the Old Guy"—and they buy firecrackers with the money! It is the English version of trick or treating, and you can read about this holiday here. For an explanation with a little more detail, written by an English schoolgirl, try <http://www.kidlink.org/KIDPROJ/MCC/11.5.1.html>.

http://ezinfo.ucs.indiana.edu/~shyde/guyhome.html

Tower of London Virtual Tour

The Traitor's Gate. The Bloody Tower. The Ceremony of the Keys. The Crown Jewels. What an incredible history this building has. The Tower of London has been a treasury, a prison, and a government building for a thousand years. It is said that if the ravens that inhabit the Tower green ever leave, the Commonwealth of Great Britain will fall. You can take a tour of the Tower and its grounds right here. But don't scare the ravens!

http://www.voicenet.com/~dravyk/toltour/

Westminster Abbey - Place of Worship, and House of Kings

This London landmark has been the site of every British coronation since 1066. Many kings and queens are entombed at the Abbey, notably Elizabeth I. You'll also find Chaucer's grave in the Poets' Corner, along with those of other famous English authors, including Lewis Carroll. The Abbey has been the scene of numerous royal ceremonies, including royal weddings and other occasions. Admire the inspiring Gothic architecture as you wander around with the other tourists at this site.

http://www.westminster-abbey.org/

UNITED KINGDOM—NORTHERN IRELAND

Official Guide to Northern Ireland

This Tourist Board site offers a look at the historical and cultural context of Northern Ireland. But the site looks at the sweetness and light, and not the dark side of "the troubles," as the civil unrest there is called. For another view, try Project Children, which gives Northern Ireland's kids a summer away from the violence, staying with host families abroad. Maybe your family could host another kid or two for the summer—check into it here.

http://www.interknowledge.com/northern-ireland/

Small Schools Initiative Home Page

This neat little site contains links in the Small School Matters area to primary schools in Northern Ireland. At these schools' sites, you can see drawings, read poems, and learn what kids there are doing in school. One class wrote poems and made drawings to tell how they hate flies!

http://www.infm.ulst.ac.uk/~neelb/smallsi/ ssihome.html

UNITED KINGDOM—SCOTLAND

The Internet Guide to Scotland: the Highlands and Islands

It's really *Eigg*-citing news! The Isle of Eigg will soon be owned by a coalition of its residents and a nonprofit organization willing to help preserve the unique natural and cultural heritage of this small Hebridean Island, located ten miles offshore, south of the Isle of Skye. "It's 7,400 acres of heather moorland, wooded glens, fertile fields and spectacular beaches are dominated by the massive basalt ridge of An Sgurr." Doesn't it make you want to visit there? The island doesn't have a Net connection, but if you send them e-mail, they will print it out and hang it up in the local post office for everyone to read. Tell them you read about them in this book! This site has lots of info on all regions of Scotland, including all those small isles.

http://ourworld.compuserve.com/homepages/ RJWinters/scotland.htm

Scottish Tourist Board

This site is a rich treasure trove of kilts, Loch Ness monsters, castles, historic battlefields, and, yes, bagpipes. According to this site, the Scottish didn't invent bagpipes, although they have elevated the playing of them to a real art form. Bagpipes consist of a sheepskin bag and five wooden projections. One is the mouthpiece, three are drone pipes, and one is called the chanter, which is the one your fingers actually play. Bagpipes only have one volume: loud! You can't vary the volume level at all (this makes it difficult to find a time and a place to practice). Lucky Scotland has all those lonely heaths and moors. To read more about bagpipes and how you can get one, visit this excellent site.

http://www.holiday.scotland.net/

What's playing at the MOVIES?

People are the true treasures of the Net.

UNITED KINGDOM—WALES
Castles of Wales

At this site, you'll find pictures and descriptions of over 150 castles, most of them in Wales. The others are in England, on the often-disputed marcher lands between the English and Welsh borders. You can learn a lot of historical facts, including some hints about castle construction (should you ever get enough Legos to do such a thing). If you don't know a portcullis from a trebuchet, not to worry—there is a very cool dictionary of castle terms here. Don't forget the moat!

http://www.castlewales.com/home.html

NET FILES

What do the Uptown Movie Theater (Chicago, Illinois), the East Broad Top Railroad (Huntingdon County, Pennsylvania), and Central High School (Little Rock, Arkansas) have in common?

Answer: *They are on the 1996 America's most endangered historic sites list, published by the National Trust. You should visit these sites soon, because they may not be around for long. You can learn more about these sites and ten more at* http://www.nthp.org/daughter/02.html

Something fishy going on? Try AQUARIUMS.

Wales/Cymru - Land of Inspiration

Ireland has Saint Patrick, and Wales has March 1— Saint David's Day, which is celebrated by Welsh people all over the world. You wouldn't wear a shamrock, though, because the national emblems of Wales are the leek and the daffodil (in Welsh, the word for leek and the word for daffodil are almost the same: *cenhinen* means "leek," and *cenhinen pedr* means "daffodil"). As the legend goes at this site, "St. David advised the Britons, on the eve of a battle with the Saxons, to wear leeks in their caps so as to easily distinguish friend from foe. This helped to secure a great victory. It is also thought that the same thing occurred when Welsh archers fought with Henry V at the battle of Agincourt. Hence, the wearing of leeks on St. David's Day. It is still a surviving tradition that soldiers in the Welsh regiments eat a raw leek on St. David's Day." This excellent site explains many Welsh cultural themes and highlights lots of interesting regions and places to visit. Be sure to stop in at Llanfairpwllgwyngyllgogerychwyrndrobwllllanty-siliogogogoch, which has the longest name of any village in Wales. The name means "Saint Mary's (church) by the white aspen over the whirlpool and Saint Tysilio's (church) by the red cave." You can hear it pronounced at <http://www.tourism.wales.gov.uk/fculture/placename.html> so you can learn how to say it and amaze your friends!

http://www.tourism.wales.gov.uk/

UNITED STATES
See UNITED STATES—STATES *in the main section of this book.*

URUGUAY
Uruguay - Country of Encounter

Uruguay, once known as Banda Oriental, is one of the oldest democracies in South America. Its two political parties go back to the 1830s. On these award-winning pages, you will find a well-written history of the nation, a monthly calendar of events, tourism information, maps, weather reports, geological data, and lots more. This is the official Ministry of Tourism site. The pages are available in English, French, Spanish, and Portuguese. The front page has a great color photograph of Uruguay, and it changes to something different every time you hit the Reload button on your browser.

http://www.turismo.gub.uy/index-e.html

UZBEKISTAN

Cyber Uzbekistan

Uzbekistan, a former Soviet Republic, is a study in contrasts. The nation, standing at the crossroads of Asia, is mostly wide expanses of sandy nothingness. The capital city of Tashkent, however, despite being over 2,000 years old, is almost entirely modern. Most of the old city was destroyed in an earthquake in 1966, and the new city was built up over the ruins. There are factories, theaters, even a subway system. This Web site explores all of Uzbekistan, including photographs of Tamalane's Tomb, the Market Place of Bukhara, and the infamous Tower of Death. Get news reports and a short list of English-Uzbek phrases here as well.

http://www.cu-online.com/~k_a/uzbekistan

"Uzbekistan - Pearl of the East" by Kodir Norov

Kodirjon Norov is an Uzbek foreign exchange student who put this page together during his senior year in high school in Florida. It includes numerous colorful photographs, connections to other Uzbekistan pages, and an international pen pal link.

http://www.godby.leon.k12.fl.us/USERS/knorov/
 uzbek.html

VANUATU

Vanuatu - A Canadian's Perspective

Ever think what life would be like on a tropical island? There is a big difference between having a vacation and actually living there. The author of this site spent five years living and working in Vanuatu, where 170-mile-per-hour cyclones are a fact of life and lolling under a coconut tree can be deadly if a coconut happens to fall off. The author describes and contrasts life in Vanuatu's city and country areas and includes a number of photographs and links.

http://www.silk.net/personal/scombs/vanuatu.html

RAILROADS AND TRAINS
are on track.

VANUATU: AN INTRODUCTION

For people who have seen the movie and musical *South Pacific,* this very tiny island nation is more well-known as "Bali Hai." Actually, *South Pacific* wasn't really filmed there but in Hawaii instead (they just pretended to be there). The Robin Williams movie *Club Paradise,* which did not take place in Vanuatu, actually was filmed there. Formerly known as the New Hebrides, the islands were jointly run by the French and the English, but since 1980, it has been an independent country. This site is full of breathtaking photographs and written impressions of the place people think of when they envision tropical islands. There is much to explore, see, and even hear on these pages. The author recommends you take your time, just as you would if you were strolling around Vanuatu itself.

http://www.clark.net/pub/kiaman/vanuatu.html

VATICAN CITY

Città del Vaticano

The art treasures of the Vatican are truly astounding. This site includes hundreds of masterpieces in exquisite detail, including Michelangelo's remarkable Sistine Chapel ceiling. It is not to be missed for anyone who appreciates beautiful art and architecture.

http://www.christusrex.org/www1/citta/0-Citta.html

The Holy See

While Vatican City is just a tiny group of buildings entirely within the city of Rome, Italy, it is also considered an independent nation. As the global spiritual center of the entire Roman Catholic Church, its importance on the international scale is equal to that of many other countries. This is the official Web site of the Vatican, and it is the place to go for news from the Church, pronouncements and messages from the Pope, looks at some of the Church's vast collections of magnificent art, and the latest information on the upcoming celebration of the year 2000. You can find photographs, biographies, and other fascinating information on the last four Popes.

http://www.vatican.va

Welcome to Vatican Radio

Staff from 50 countries prepare 400 hours of broadcast material every week in 37 different languages. Radio Vatican broadcasts on short wave, medium wave, FM, satellite, and the Internet. You can download Real Audio files or ftp features in several languages. As they say: "Listen, for heaven's sake!"

http://www.wrn.org/vatican-radio/

VENEZUELA

La Cocina Venezolana

Venezuelans must love terrific food, judging by the variety of wonderful recipes in this site, translated as "The Venezuelan Cuisine." Many of the recipes are written in Spanish, but a large number of them are available here in English as well. Some are also translated into Japanese. You can discover how to make such delicious main dishes, such as Tequeños (fried cheese pastries) or Cachapas (corn pancakes), or sweet desserts, such as Churros or Flan. There are links to other Latin American recipe pages as well.

http://polaris.cs.uiuc.edu/~koufaty/yacb/

Lonely Planet -- Destination: Venezuela

Venezuela is home to a strange variety of animals, such as the jaguar, ocelot, tapir, armadillo, anteater, and the longest snake in the world, the anaconda. Angel Falls, the world's highest waterfall (16 times the height of Niagara Falls) is here, and the Amazonian jungles are full of beauty and mystery. Designed for travelers looking for exciting places to visit, the Lonely Planet Venezuelan page is chock-full of fascinating information about the country.

http://www.lonelyplanet.com/dest/sam/ven.htm

People in History Project

Part of a larger project created by students at Southside High School in Elmira, New York, this page gives a short explanation of Simon Bolivar's remarkable life. Bolivar, known as "The Liberator," is Venezuela's national hero, often considered the George Washington of Latin America. You will find a good picture of him on this site.

http://csc.sctboces.org/elmira/southside/islc/pih/
  bolivar.html

Venezuela for Kids

It is indeed appropriate that the Venezuelan embassy has created this page explaining their nation to kids, since the Venezuelan government spends about 20 percent of their budget on education, perhaps more than any other country in the world. Here you can find information on Venezuelan folk dances, such as the lively Joropo, or the traditional children's game, "The Dancing Devils of Yare," or exotic recipes such as Cachapas de Budare, Arepas, or Sancocho Soup. Venezuelan sports are included, and it may come as no surprise to learn that baseball is the most popular game to anyone familiar with the long list of Venezuelans playing pro ball in the U.S. There is a wealth of fascinating pages to explore. It is a site not to be missed!

http://venezuela.mit.edu/embassy/kids/

VIETNAM

Lonely Planet - Destination Vietnam

Since Vietnam was opened up to American travelers a couple of years ago, it has become a popular tourist destination. Vietnam's French and Asian traditions blend to make it the home of unique contrasts. Ho Chi Minh City (once known as Saigon) is full of hustling, bustling street vendors and exotic shops and peaceful, scenic pagodas and cathedrals. The Lonely Planet travel pages offer a surprisingly thorough and balanced guide to Vietnam's environment, culture, history, and well-known and off-the-beaten-track attractions. The fast-loading, mostly text page also offers links to beautiful photographs.

http://www.lonelyplanet.com/dest/sea/vietnam.htm

Vietconnection.com Home

Your parents probably have very strong emotional feelings concerning Vietnam. However, it has been over 20 years since the long war with that nation ended, and the people at Viet Connection have determined to use this Web site to take down cultural barriers between the Vietnamese people and the rest of the world. Here you can get news reports, shop for Vietnamese books, hear broadcasts from Radio Vietnam, and even get online language lessons! The news reports on the Web site have not been updated as frequently as promised, but we hope that this unique voice continues.

http://vietconnection.com/

WALES

See UNITED KINGDOM—WALES

WALLIS AND FUTUNA ISLANDS

The World Factbook page on Wallis and Futuna

This small South Pacific island group is an overseas territory of France. At this page, you'll find out that one of the big problems there is that the forests are being cut down for fuel. With no trees, the rocky ground is subject to erosion. The good soil washes into the sea, which affects how many crops they can grow. The islanders have to import a lot of food from other countries. How do they pay for it? They get money from selling off fishing rights to Japan and other countries. They also sell handicrafts.

http://www.odci.gov/cia/publications/nsolo/
factbook/wf.htm

WESTERN SAHARA

WESTERN SAHARA LINKS

Western Sahara is a nation that has been struggling for decades to keep its existence. Bordering Morocco has claimed the country as its own, and many of the Western Saharan people live in huge refugee camps. This desert country is the home of tent-dwelling nomads and has very little in the way of industry, cities, or farming. The site features a number of photographs that spell out the harsh conditions here better than words, and it offers links to an assortment of other Web pages offering background information. One that gives a view of life in the refugee camps is at *<http://heiwww.unige.ch/arso/index.htm>* in the Land and People section.

http://www.eaglenet.co.uk/sapn/

Never give your name or address to a stranger.

WESTERN SAMOA
BEACH HUTS

We usually don't put strictly commercial ads in this book—but the attitude here is engaging, and we thought you'd like it, too! Visiting this page may tempt you to hop on a plane and make your way to Western Samoa. On the Samoan island of Savali, you can rent a grass hut by the windswept, unspoiled beach, including meals, lagoons, lava tube caves, exotic flowers, and great surfing for $20 a night. Forget about business (no phones), and save your money (no shopping). Ahhh. Now if you want a more official site, try the Government Tourist Board site at *<http://www.interwebinc.com/samoa/>*.

http://www.pi.se/~orbit/samoa/29bch.html

NET FILES

What does a Van de Graaff generator generate, anyway?
(Hint: The story is shocking!)

Answer: The Van de Graaff generator makes static electricity from a revolving belt inside one of its towers. Read about its history and construction and all about lightning and electricity. You can see the huge original generator built by Dr. Robert J. Van de Graaff in the Theater of Electricity at the Museum of Science (Cambridge, Massachusetts) and on this World Wide Web site, http://www.mos.org/sln/toe/construction.html

Try actual reality.

WEST SAMOA

It may be hard to believe, but the tropical resort islands of Western Samoa are the home of World Rugby Cup Champions the Manu Samoa. The famous writer Robert Louis Stevenson ended his days here, and the island's natural beauty is much as it was for the last 5,000 years. This site, designed to promote environmentally friendly tourism, is a great place to take a virtual visit.

http://www.pi.se/~orbit/samoa/intro.html

YEMEN

ArabNet -- Yemen, Contents

Yemen, a small, mostly desert country on the Arabian peninsula, has pretty much avoided contact with the outside world for over a thousand years. This site is a good place to get an overview of Yemen's 3,000-year history. Around 2,700 years ago, a great dam was built there, making the area a rich agricultural center for growing spices that were shipped around the world. In the year A.D. 570, the dam burst, and Yemen quickly became arid desert. In the 1970s, Yemen split into two countries, one of which was the first Marxist Arabian state ever. More recently, the two states joined together to become a republic and began to open up to trade with the rest of the world.

http://www.arab.net/yemen/yemen_contents.html

Auracea Yemen

While most of the world considers Yemen to be a desert nation, it actually has a huge, mostly unexplored coastline teeming with underwater life. For the last 15 years, Daniel Jouvance and the International Marine Science Committee have been studying the wealth of the underwater world. Some of the things they discovered may lead to new antibiotics or other medicines. The Auracea Expedition explored ocean life off the coasts of Tunisia, Yemen, and Mozambique. See some of their incredible photographs here!

http://djouvance.com/history/h03c.html

NET FILES

It's the eighteenth century. Do you know where your augers, gimlets, and bitstocks are? What kind of work do you do, anyway?

Answer: You're a carpenter or woodworker of some kind. In Colonial times, these were very important tools for drilling holes of various sizes. Holes were needed to build everything from ships to harpsichords! Augers made the biggest holes, while gimlets drilled tiny pilot holes. Bitstocks were made of iron and had interchangeable bits, which could bore holes of several sizes. Find out more about Colonial tools at http://www.history.org/history/life/tools/tlaug.htm

ZAIRE

B&RD NEWS: Mountain Gorillas - Zaire

Zaire's Virunga National Park has protected animals in the wild since 1925. Its variety of ecosystems is home to over 200 mammals and 700 bird species. The mountain gorillas of Zaire are magnificent creatures and may be the most important tourist attraction there. Some of the gorilla groups are accustomed to humans, and others live deep within the mountains and avoid contact. In any event, the known number of gorillas (available in a chart on this page) is quite small, and they are threatened by poachers and illegal destruction of the forest by refugees from neighboring Rwanda. This page is a good starting place for information on these animals.

http://www.kilimanjaro.com/gorilla/brd/zaire.htm

Not everything on the Net is true.

NET FILES

Which large, plated dinosaur is known for having a brain the size of a walnut?

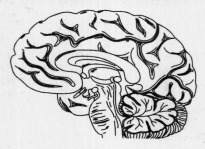

Answer: *The stegosaurus. This plant eater was really a strange combination of parts. Were those bony plates for protection or to help its body stay cool? And how about those spikes on the tail—what did they do? Check all the dinos out at* http://tyrell.magtech.ab.ca/tour/stego.html

Zaire

Zaire was once known as the Belgian Congo, until it gained its independence in 1960. While the country has a vast array of natural resources, such as gold, silver, oil, diamonds, copper, manganese, coal, and uranium, it is among the poorest nations on earth. Look to this site for strong, detailed facts and figures on the county's government, people, environment, and other useful information. An official home page of Zaire is at <http://www.xcom.it/zaire/> but if you go to <http://www.sas.upenn.edu/African_Studies/Country_Specific/Zaire.html> you will find other links, including one to paintings by Mbuti Women at <http://www.uampfa.berkeley.edu/exhibits/mbuti/>. You can watch a slide show and listen to Mbuti chants and music at the same time.

http://www.africaonline.com/AfricaOnline/ countries/zaire.html

ZAMBIA
Zambia Page

Prolific wildlife, spectacular sunsets, and unforgettable Victoria Falls (354 feet high)—all these are images of Zambia you may already know. For what you don't know, check this page or perhaps the World Factbook page on Zambia at <http://www.odci.gov/cia/publications/nsolo/factbook/za.htm>.

http://www.sas.upenn.edu/African_Studies/ Country_Specific/Zambia.html

ZIMBABWE
Welcome to Virtual Zimbabwe

Among the sites in Zimbabwe are Victoria Falls, one of the largest and most unspoiled major waterfalls in the world. The falls and the Zambezi River form a border with Zambia to the north, and Zambia claims the falls, too. Another popular tourist site is the Chipangali Wildlife Orphanage, where exotic animals once raised as pets are set loose in a protective environment. The Zimbabwe International Book Fair is held there every year, and it is the premiere event for publishers on the African continent. Zimbabwean industry and technology is highlighted at this site, as well as traditional crafts. If you have a Java-capable browser, you can have the *n'ganga* (a tribal healer and diviner) throw the Hakata Bones for you and tell you your fortune, at <http://www.mediazw.com/hakata/index.html>. You might also check the World Factbook page on this country at <http://www.odci.gov/cia/publications/nsolo/factbook/zi.htm>.

http://www.mediazw.com/

Mark Sensen, designer of the "Flags of the World" flag. We like to think of it as "The Flag of Cyberspace," but Mark doesn't make that claim.

"White on the hoist side stands for peace, blue on the fly side for progress. The six colours of the stars are the main colours used in flags around the world. The stars help to make one bigger symbol. The way the stars are all connected to each other represents the Internet."

The "Flags of the World" Flag

Designer: Mark Sensen,
          Weert, The Netherlands

You can find Mark's work at
Flags of the World: http://flags.cesi.it/flags/

And his own sites:
Flags of the 19th and 20th centuries:
  http://home.pi.net/~marksens

Vexillolinks: http://www.geocities.com/
  CapitolHill/8987/

Thank you for giving us permission to use your flag as our stamp for the postcards in this book. It's a beautiful flag. How did you get interested in flags? Were you interested in them when you were a child, or did it come later?
I think I was about ten when I became interested in flags, and two years later I bought my first flag book.

How did you happen to design this particular flag?
In December, 1995, "Flags of the World" webmaster Giuseppe Bottasini asked the members of the "Flag Mailing List" to design a flag for "FOTW." 12 proposals were sent in, and everyone on the mailing list voted. My design was chosen to become the flag for "FOTW."

What do the colors and symbols mean?
White on the hoist side stands for peace, blue on the fly side for progress. The six colours of the stars are the main colours used in flags around the world (from the top star, clockwise: green, white, yellow, red, blue, and black in the middle). The stars help to make one bigger symbol. The way the stars are all connected to each other represents the Internet.

You must hear from people all over the world! Can you think of an unusual request, question, or comment someone has sent to you?
Whenever I find a new flag, I post it to the "FOTW" site so others around the world can see it. Flags symbolize political ideas, and sometimes people disagree with those ideas, and I get mail about it. But I receive grateful mail all the time. For example, once I got mail from South Africa just saying "Mooie vlae" (beautiful flags).

If designing flags isn't your main job, what do you do?
At the moment, I work at a computer help desk. I have a chance to become a computer programmer at the same company.

Do you have a family? A dog? A lizard?
No, but I have a computer, an Internet account, and some flag books ;-)

What are your hopes and fears for the future of the Internet?
I hope the Internet will help people all over the world to communicate, so they will understand each other better. My fear is that they will communicate less with the people directly around them. (But I don't think both will come true.)

When you're not using the Net, what do you like to do?
I like to listen to music and I also like to play soccer. I enjoy reading about flags, history, and foreign countries.

If you could invite three people throughout history to your house for dinner, who would they be?
Because I'm a very bad cook I won't invite anybody :-)

Perhaps Mark might go to a restaurant! His guest might be the man whose quote appears in Mark's e-mail signature:
"Knowledge is of two kinds.
We know a subject ourselves, or we know where we can find information upon it."
—Samuel Johnson, 1775

The Flags of the World flag image is used with the kind permission of Mark Sensen. The image and design is copyrighted © 1996-1997 by Mark Sensen.

INTRODUCTION

THE SECRET GARDEN: WHAT PARENTS ASK ME ABOUT KIDS AND THE INTERNET

In each century since the beginning of the world wonderful things have been discovered. In the last century more amazing things were found out than in any century before. In this new century hundreds of things still more astounding will be brought to light. At first people refuse to believe that a strange new thing can be done, then they begin to hope it can be done, then they see it can be done—when it is done and all the world wonders why it was not done centuries ago. One of the new things people began to find out in the last century was that thoughts—just mere thoughts—are as powerful as electric batteries—as good for one as sunlight is, or as bad for one as poison. To let a sad thought or a bad one get into your mind is as dangerous as letting a scarlet fever germ get into your body. If you let it stay there after it has got in you may never get over it as long as you live....

Where you tend a rose, my lad, A thistle cannot grow.
—Frances Hodgson Burnett, *The Secret Garden* (1909)

When the children in Burnett's turn-of-the-century book stumbled into the Secret Garden[1], they found a wasteland of weeds and overgrown paths. With care, they restored it to a place of almost magical healing and peace, which eventually brought their family closer together.

I like to think of the Internet as the Secret Garden of today. Kids and parents stand at the gate, wondering what is inside the high walls. Everyone talks about the Internet, but much of the press coverage is about the weeds inside, not the dormant seeds and the promise of the buried bulbs. If you look for thistles, surely you will find them. This book chooses to concentrate on tending the roses instead.

The following is a collection, divided into three sections, of questions parents have asked me about the Internet and my answer to each one. Internet addresses for footnoted topics are included at the end of this introduction.

On the difficulty of finding the way into the Secret Garden

Q: Is using the Net too difficult and expensive?

A: Yes and no. Yes: Your time is a commodity. Like anything else, you have to expect to spend some time on the Net in order to learn how to use it and see if,

and how, it fits into your family's life. Some types of Net connections are still hard to set up, and some of the more esoteric applications are difficult to use, especially the ones that use multimedia. The good news is that for the most common uses, it is now easier to use the Net than it is to program your VCR. Expenses include the cost of the computer and phone line and the monthly Internet service or WebTV[2] subscription.

No: The Internet is not just for nerds anymore. Client software from America Online[3] or AT&T WorldNet[SM4], or even a traditional Internet service provider such as Mindspring[5], makes Internet life much simpler than it used to be. Search engines[6] and directories[7] are becoming faster and easier to use. There are even directories aimed at kids, such as Yahooligans[8]. People all over the world find my book to be a big help, too.

You can now decide on what news and information you want to come to you directly. One version of this customized broadcast can be seen at Pointcast.com[9], but this is only one example. Look for this server-push technology to really take off this year. If you don't want it "pushed" at you, you can "pull" customized news yourself. This variation is available at *my.yahoo.com*[10].

As for the question of expense, most U.S. Internet service providers will charge you about $20 per month as a flat rate. This includes e-mail, Web access, and sometimes your own Web page. Look for Internet service to become even more inexpensive. You can find a list of local and national Internet service providers (ISPs) at The List[11].

On creepy bugs and critters in the Secret Garden

Q: Isn't the Internet filled with pornography and pedophiles?

A: I wouldn't say "filled," that is, to the exclusion of everything else. Some of the "critters" we've seen in the course of the research for this book include: pornography, racism, hate speech, gambling, drugs, alcohol, weapons, Satanism, propaganda, and other political and cultural influences you may not want your family exposed to. These things are available on the Net, just as they are in real life.

It's important to remember that the Internet is not the enemy. The Net is only the transport method; in that regard, it's like the telephone system. What you may want to filter out are the places you can call, some of which may be too freewheeling for your family. The good news is that there are many tools to help you choose what you want to see.

Q: How do I find out about parental controls and filtering software?

A: Some of the commercial Internet services use parental controls of one type or another. Check with your Internet service provider (ISP). If your ISP does not provide this service, you can install software on your home computer that accomplishes the same thing. A good clearinghouse for information on parental controls is at PEDINFO[12]. Other resources are listed in the "Parenting and Families: Internet" section of this book.

Parental control software generally works with either blacklists or white lists. A blacklist is a collection of sites that are disallowed. If users try to go to a site that is not allowed, the filter notices and prevents it from appearing on the computer screen; this is also called "blocking" a site. A white list works the other way: it includes only "blessed" or rated sites, and users can go *only* to sites included on that list, not anywhere else.

There are problems with both of these lists. Who is rating the sites as "bad" or "good"? What is their agenda? Can you get a list of all the blocked sites, or all the blessed sites? Most companies keep these lists secret. Are they secret for competitive, or other, reasons?

In the last few months, several alleged lists did surface. You can read about this at Peacefire[13], which is a clearinghouse site for information on the flaws and perils of using filtering software. One oft-quoted example happened a few years back, when an online service blocked any communication with the word "breast" in it. This blocked not only potentially pornographic messages but also those involving breast cancer support groups and those exchanging recipes for chicken. This blocking was removed.

The danger remains that in the effort to keep the view of the Net as uncontroversial as possible, blocking will be done with too broad a brush, or worse, with a hidden, undisclosed agenda. Some filtering software blocks The National Organization for Women site. Some block animal rights sites. It is not hard to imagine a revisionist secretly blocking sites about Hiroshima or the Holocaust.

Do you wonder if a particular site, possibly even your own home page, is blocked? You may be able to find

out by using a service provided by the Netly News called Censorware Search Engine[14]. It allegedly gives you a peek into five filtering programs: CyberSitter, NetNanny, SurfWatch, The Internet Filter, and CyberPatrol. Enter a domain name, and see if it is blocked. The search will only return a few hits at a time, to keep you from downloading the entire blocked list.

Many parents and public facilities will elect to use filtering software. You should be aware of how the filtering is done: who chooses what is on the blacklist or the white list? How flexible it is for parents to modify the settings? Can parents make it more restrictive in general, or less restrictive, or can they choose to allow or restrict on a site-by-site basis? You should also find out how easy or difficult the software is to deinstall if you want to try something else!

I also believe filtering software companies must disclose their blacklists so that parents can be informed which sites are blocked. Currently, you have to try to go to a site and find it blocked before you can unblock it. I would like to be able to scan a printed list of blocked sites, so I could preallow a site for my family.

Q: What is PICS[15] and what is RSACi[16], and do I really need to know anything about them?

A: You should be aware of both. PICS stands for Platform for Internet Content Selection. It was developed by the World Wide Web Consortium (W3C) and is still in active development by member organizations. The W3C is located at the MIT Laboratory for Computer Science (LCS) in Cambridge, Massachusetts, and at the Institut National de Recherche en Informatique et en Automatique (INRIA) in Rocquencourt, France.

PICS is not software; it is a specification. It proposes a standard method of placing "metadata" tags within the source code of Web pages. These tags are readable by browsers, such as Microsoft's Internet Explorer, and some filtering software. You can get a complete list of PICS-compliant browsers and software at the PICS Web site mentioned in the footnote.

RSAC is the Recreational Software Advisory Council. It began life as a voluntary industry rating organization for disclosing levels of violence in video games. You can read about its history at the Web site noted, but what concerns us now is the fairly new RSACi or RSAC Internet ratings. They implement the PICS specifications, but they are by no means the only organization with a PICS-compliant ratings system.

However, the parental controls for Microsoft's Internet Explorer software use the RSACi ratings system by default. (Parents can choose to install and use other ratings systems.)

At publication date, less than 25,000 Web sites have rated themselves using the RSACi system. Yes, that's right: the RSACi ratings are not done by organizations but by webmasters themselves. Do you want to rate your own home page? Do you know a little basic HTML (hypertext markup language)? Just go to the RSACi site and answer a few simple questions about the level of nudity, violence, and other adult subjects at your site. Based on your answers, you will be given a metadata HTML tag to insert in the header of your pages. You're also supposed to insert the "We Rated with RSACi!" GIF on each of your pages and have it link back to the RSAC page. As you can tell, it involves some effort and extra steps for webmasters. Will it become the standard PICS implementation, or will one of the many others surface as the industry leader? Time and market share will tell.

Q: Is there any way to tell if a page has been rated?

A: Yes, if it is an implementation of the PICS standard. Did you know that (depending on the browser you're using) you may be able to view the source code behind any Web page? For example, in Netscape, use the VIEW pull-down menu and choose VIEW DOCUMENT SOURCE. Depending on how you have Netscape configured, the source code (with all those HTML tags) will either show up in a new browser window or will be saved to disk as a simple text file that can be opened with a word processor.

The metadata tags will be at the top of the file. You may find that a particular site has no rating. Or, it may be a collector of ratings: one from SafeSurf, a Safe for Kids rating, and a RSACi rating. You may even find others.

My RSACi Ratings Tag for http://www.well.com/user/polly/ is:

```
<META http-equiv="PICS-Label"
content='(PICS-1.0
"http://www.rsac.org/ratingsv01.html" l gen
true comment "RSACi North
America Server" by "polly@well.com" for
"http://www.well.com/user/polly" on
"1997.03.10T13:03-0500" exp
"1997.07.01T08:15-0500"
r (n 0 s 0 v 0 l 0))'>
```

Looks confusing, doesn't it? This translates into:

Nudity	0
Sex	0
Violence	0
Language	0

You might be able to set your browser or filtering software to allow only RSACi-rated levels of 0 if you wanted no adult content at all. There is an explanation of the ratings system at the RSACi site footnote.

Q: Filters, PICS—I still can't decide. Net-mom, what should I do?

A: Spend time on the Net with your kids. See what's out there. Better yet, teach kids how to deal with information and evaluate it for themselves, whether it's finding the "gotchas" in advertising or knowing when a resource of any kind is "too adult" for them.

Here at Net-mom's Pollywood Farm, we don't use filtering software. But we support the right of parents to evaluate it and see if it meets their needs.

Q: What can be done about e-mail? Won't my child get a lot of junk mail, some of it advertising adult services?

A: It's true that anyone with an electronic mailbox will get junk e-mail, and it is also true that some of it will be of the "make money fast!" variety and some will be advertising adult fare. This critter is called SPAM, but since that term is a registered trademark owned by the Hormel company, you will also see it referred to as UCE (unwanted commercial e-mail).

For those using America Online and other services, there are parental controls that let you control the addresses from which your child (or you!) can receive mail. There are also ways members can choose to not receive mail if it comes from anyone on AOL's Spammer's list. If you get mail that slips around these controls, you can also choose to ignore future mail from that person. Check with AOL to find out how to set your preferences to use these mail controls.

The problem is that many spammers/UCE-mailers use false e-mail addresses! You need to find out the real name of the Internet host machine that sent the mail and complain to abuse@hostname and postmaster@hostname (replace "hostname" with the actual host name of the offending site). These are standard, generic addresses—most legitimate host systems have them just for this purpose. How do you find out the real host name? Instructions are in the information below under the SPAM (UCE)[17] footnote.

What if you get no response to your complaints of abuse to the postmaster at the offending machine host name? Go to the next level: the Internet service provider who gave the transport for all that unwanted mail from the spammer. Send the unwanted mail and a complaint to the ISP. In many cases, they are not aware that the abuse is going on, and they often shut off service to spammers.

How can you trace the company that provides Internet service to the suspect host name? You can find out more about this at the SPAM (UCE) footnote.

Q: What about computer viruses?

A: A *virus* is a little program that piggybacks onto another program. This virus may slide unnoticed into your system, only to resurface later to do something cute or malevolent to your system or your files. You should have some type of virus protection on your computer. See some of the entries listed in the "Computers—Software Archives" section of this book for sources of virus protection software. Much of it is free.

Your computer can only get a virus from a program you run or execute. You can't get a virus from e-mail or from a text file. It's true.

Q: Hey, but what about the Good Times Virus[18]? It comes in e-mail!

A: It's a hoax! There is a link below from an even more authoritative source than Net-mom. Check Internet Hoaxes[19] to help sort out the truth from the hype. The U.S. Department of Energy's Computer Incident Advisory Capability says it spends more time debunking bogus virus reports than it does reporting real ones.

For other virus and security information on the Net, try the equally authoritative resource page at the Computer Emergency Response Team (CERT)[20] site.

Q: OK, but what about those "magic cookies" I keep hearing about?

A: Sounds like something from *Alice's Adventures in Wonderland*, doesn't it? A *cookie*[21] is a little file of settings a host computer tries to send you. You can set your browser to ask you before you accept a cookie. You *can* turn down a cookie! Net-mom refuses cookies all day (well, except chocolate chip!).

Cookies can be good: they let you set your preferences. For example, at an airline reservation site, cookies remember that you like aisle seats and Asian vegetarian meals. Cookies can be annoying, but harmless. For example, cookies can track which advertising has been shown to you—which things interested you, and which did not.

Cookies can also be bad if they report on your personal Web activities to others, and this fact isn't disclosed to you. For example, this information can include which ads you have clicked on, which pages you have seen, and what information you have requested.

You can control your cookies—and lose them if you have to! Browser software such as Netscape allows you to set a few security features, and one of them involves cookies. Look in the OPTIONS pull-down menu and select NETWORK PREFERENCES. From there, select PROTOCOLS and choose the option that tells Netscape to ask you for permission to accept a cookie each time one is presented. You will be shocked at how many cookies are offered to you at each Web page!

```
⚠   The server pathfinder.com
     wishes to set a cookie
     that will be sent only back to itself
     The name and value of the cookie are:
     OpenMarketSI=/@@nMNDyAcAN6SvkDLc

     Do you wish to allow the cookie to be set?

                    [  No  ]   [  Yes  ]
```

On weeds and broken pavements in The Secret Garden

Q: Isn't the Net mostly people's opinions, old information, and misinformation?

A: Misinformation is out there, just as misinformation is in any other kind of media. How do you recognize authoritative information in the things you read in newspapers and magazines? How do you recognize authenticity on radio and television?

You need the same skills to evaluate the information you discover on the Net. Just as you read *The New York Times*[22] instead of the *National Enquirer*[23] you may want to stick to authoritative hosts, such as NASA[24] or the Library of Congress[25] or CNN[26].

That's what we did when we picked the sites in this book!

Q: I hear the Net is slowing down and breaking all the time. Is it?

A: "Death of the Net predicted; film at 11" is a common theme on the Net these days. If you're dealing with pages that never seem to load, hosts that can't be reached, time outs, "not found" messages, and so many other annoyances, it may seem that the prediction is true.

What causes the "World Wide Wait"? First, you have the two end points: your desktop computer, which is trying to get the Web page, and the host computer, which is trying to send you the Web page. Then you have everything else in between.

Maybe your own computer is too pokey. Your processor can be slow to translate Web pages and display them to your screen—especially graphics. Many browsers allow you to turn graphics off (Auto Load Images under the Options menu in Netscape 3). You might find this mode useful when you're trying to quickly move through a familiar location and don't want to wait for all the graphics to load. With graphics turned off, you can still manually load images (Load Images under the View menu in Netscape). Perhaps the host computer system at the other end is busy with other users; if there is a general slowness of response, you may get a "Connection Refused" message. Or perhaps there has been a power failure and the host is truly unreachable—this happens more often than you might think!

Between these two end points, a lot can happen to your "send me this Web page" request. The first stop is the domain name system (DNS) server, which is probably operated by your ISP. (Your company or school may choose to run its own DNS instead, or in addition to the server operated by the ISP.)

Say you want to go to http://www.yahoo.com. You type that into your browser. Domain names are easy for humans to use, but computers understand only numerical Internet addresses. So, your yahoo.com request has to go through a DNS to be translated into its correct numerical address, in this case 204.71.177.71, before the actual request can go through.

What happens if the DNS server your ISP runs is down? Usually that is not a problem, because they operate more than one, and your Internet software should be set up to try several DNS servers. But if

both are down, or unreachable, your browser returns a message that "the server does not have a DNS entry." Obviously, you know Yahoo has a DNS entry! In most cases, you should just try again in a few minutes; the routes will probably come back to life in the interim. If this happens a lot, you should complain to your service provider. But if all is well and your Web page request to see www.yahoo.com is translated, then you're now on your way.

Simply put, the physical network connection itself can "break," or become so congested that you don't get the Web page you want, at three possible places:

- The line between you and your Internet service provider

- The line between the site you're trying to reach and its service provider

- Anywhere along the route between the two service providers—this route may be very indirect (once I traced the route of a message going from New York to California: it went via the United Kingdom).

If congestion appears anywhere along these connection paths, slowness and other problems can occur. The physical lines are connected by special computers called *routers*. These routers can "blink" or "flap" on and off. They can suffer power outages. That is not supposed to matter, since there are many ways to get from one place to another in cyberspace, but it can cause delays in your experience of using the Net.

In all the confusion, "dropped packets" can and do occur. I'll explain packets and why we don't want to see one dropped. Information is shuttled along the Internet not as a whole but broken up into "packets." Here's an example. Think of sending a physical photo print of your beagle to a friend. You put the photo in an envelope, address it, put a stamp on it, and go down to the post office. The mail moves by trucks, planes, and postal carriers, and in a few days your buddy can open the envelope, take out the photo, and admire it.

When you send a digitized photo over the Net, things are a little different. Internet protocols take the picture apart and divide it into neat jigsaw puzzle pieces. Each piece is deposited in its own packet—with reassembly instructions—and is sent on its merry way. At the other end, the packets are opened and reassembled, and your buddy gets to see your cute little dog.

Sometimes things go wrong. Some of the packets can get delayed along the way, which will make your friend wait longer to see the picture put back together. Worse, if the Internet connections between you and your friend have "blinked" during this transaction, packets can be dropped into la-la land, never to return. So packet #1 and packet #3 will sit around, waiting to join up with packet #2, which is never going to arrive. Eventually your browser says something to you like "Connection timed out."

What can you do? The best strategy is to just wait a few seconds, or minutes, or days, and try it again. For fun, try looking at the Internet Weather Report[27], which looks not at real-time weather fronts but Internet traffic jams.

You might also be able to use some of the new network monitoring tools for civilians, such as Net.Medic[28] or those from Keynote[29]. See the footnotes for more information.

"But is it getting better or not?" I hear you say. That depends on too many factors to go into here. But you can read an interview with Bob Metcalfe[30], leading doomsayer, for more information. You can take your pick of opposing views, which are legion. In fact, Bob recently "ate his words," using a copy of one of his interviews on the death of the Net, a blender, and a spoon.

Q: Can't you just wake me when this Internet thing is over?

A: Uh, no. Millions of users, hundreds of thousands of computers serving Web pages, a WWW address on

every TV commercial and print ad...it's everywhere. It's impossible to sleep through it anymore.

Still, Net-mom believes that people have the right to turn their backs on technology if they wish.

That said, welcome to the Secret Garden of delights and wonderful things we've found for you on the Net. You belong here; welcome home.

Here are the relevant links:

[1]*The Secret Garden* by Frances Hodgson Burnett: <http://www.teachersoft.com/Library/lit/burnet/garden/contents.htm>

[2]WebTV subscription: <http://www.webtv.net/>

[3]America Online: <http://www.aol.com/>

[4]AT&T WorldNet: <http://www.att.com/worldnet/>

[5]Mindspring: <http://www.mindspring.com/>

[6]Search engines: one example is AltaVista <http://www.altavista.digital.com/>

[7]Directories: one example is Yahoo! <http://www.yahoo.com/>

[8]Yahooligans: <http://www.yahooligans.com>

[9]Pointcast: <http://www.pointcast.com/>

[10]My.Yahoo.com: <http://my.yahoo.com/>

[11]The List: <http://thelist.iworld.com/>

[12]PEDINFO: <http://w3.lhl.uab.edu/pedinfo/Control.html>

[13]Peacefire: <http://www.peacefire.org>

[14]Censorware Search Engine: <http://cgi.pathfinder.com/netly/spoofcentral/censored/>

[15]PICS: <http://www.w3.org/pub/WWW/PICS/>

[16]RSACi: <http://www.rsac.org/>

[17]SPAM (UCE): An easy guide on what to do about unwanted e-mail <http://www.oitc.com/Disney/WhatToDo.html>. For even more info:

Tracing an E-mail message: <http://digital.net/~gandalf/spamfaq.html>

Blacklist of Internet Advertisers: <http://math-www.uni-paderborn.de/~axel/BL/>

People are the true treasures of the Net.

The Net Abuse FAQ:
<http://www.cybernothing.org/faqs/net-abuse-faq.html>
Among other things it details how the term Spam
came about; it's from a Monty Python sketch.

Spam Hater Program:
<http://www.compulink.co.uk/~net-services/spam/>

The Uselessness of Spam:
<http://www.go2net.com/internet/useless/useless/
spam.html> Pretty much all the tastiest Spam links on
the Net.

Spam Cam: <http://www.fright.com/cgi-bin/spamcam/>
The page that seeks to answer the question: IS SPAM
ORGANIC? Current experiment: Tofu and meat hot
dogs, Mini Spam, a Twinkie, and Cheese Whiz
on crackers.

[18]Good Times Virus Hoax:
<http://www.nsm.smcm.edu/News/GTHoax.html>

[19]Internet Hoaxes: PKZ300, Irina, Good Times,
Deeyenda, Ghost <http://ciac.llnl.gov/ciac/bulletins/
h-05.shtml>

[20]CERT: <http://www.cert.org/cert.faqintro.html>

[21]Cookies:
<http://www.incontext.ca/spidweb/may15_96/news/
cookie8.htm>

[22]*The New York Times*: <http://www.nyt.com/>

[23]*The National Enquirer*:
<http://www.nationalenquirer.com/>

[24]NASA: <http://www.nasa.gov/>

[25]The Library of Congress: <http://www.loc.gov/>

[26]CNN: <http://www.cnn.com/>

[27]Internet Weather Report:
<http://www.internetweather.com/>

[28]Net.Medic: <http://www.vitalsigns.com/>

[29]Keynote: <http://www.keynote.com/>

[30]Bob Metcalfe, leading doomsayer:
<http://www.packet.com/packet/hotseat/96/35/index4a.html

ADOPTION

Adoption.com

Baby Miguel was born in Paraguay. Van Hoa was born
in Vietnam. Jeevan was born in India. Natasha was
born in Russia. What these children all have in common
is that they are among the hundreds of children waiting
for a loving family to adopt them. At this site, you can
browse the international photolistings of children by
country, age, or gender. You'll also find answers to
frequently asked questions about international
adoption, general articles about adoption issues and
concerns, and a comprehensive listing of agencies
to contact for more information.

http://www.adoption.com/index.shtml

Faces Of Adoption Home Page

If your family is thinking about adopting but you still
have lots of unanswered questions, then be sure to
check out this site. First browse the photolistings of
American children waiting for adoption. Then check
the AdoptionQuest section for useful information on
how to begin the adoption process, what kinds of
questions to ask the agency, and articles on key issues,
such as single parent and older parent adoptions, tax
credits, and the latest court rulings. There are book
reviews and lists of books for both adults and
children, lists of state agency contacts, and links
to the National Adoption Center (NAC) and Children
Awaiting Parents (CAP) for additional information.
This site was the children's category winner of the
1996 National Information Infrastructure Awards.

http://www.inetcom.net/adopt/

**Sharpen your
digital crayons
for COLOR AND
COLORING
BOOKS!**

BABIES

THE BABIES PLANET

At this site, you'll find a thoughtful collection of briefly annotated links in subject areas such as Morning Sickness, Crack Babies, S.I.D.S, and more general topics, such as making your own baby food, the diaper dilemma, and more. It's definitely worth a look, even if this is not your first child or if you're a grandparent on baby-sitting duty!

http://www.thelastplanet.com/babyhp.htm

The Baby Booklet

Hey, you've got a new baby, who is so adorable when sleeping, but what do you do when he/she wakes up and cries, and wets, and needs a bath, and is hungry, and gets diaper rash, or some other kind of rash, and so on? If you are feeling a little overwhelmed and need answers to even the most basic baby care questions, then this is a good place to look. Written by Dr. Lewis Wasserman, a pediatrician from Florida, this booklet provides a guided tour to babies, with useful information about baby skin care, normal growth patterns (including weight tables), colic, and other common concerns of new parents (or "old" parents who may have forgotten!). Also useful is the health care schedule, which includes a complete list of vaccinations and the ages at which they should be given.

http://members.aol.com/AllianceMD/booklet.html

The HALLWAY At Tommy's CyberNursery Preemie Web Site

If you are a parent or grandparent of a premature baby (a *preemie*) or if you have friends going through this experience, you won't want to miss this site. You'll find emotional support as well as valuable information and insight about what families go through when their baby is born too early. The information here is written by a father whose son was born at 25 weeks (more than three months early) about his family's experiences in the neonatal unit at the hospital. The Babies On The Web section provides links to other parents' personal stories about their special baby. Whether you want information on the special feeding needs of preemies or a knitting pattern for a preemie hat, it's all here.

http://www.flash.net/~cyberkid

La Leche League International-Breast feeding Information

Breast milk is the best milk for most babies. Moms can breast-feed an adopted baby, too, and that info is here! This site will give you all the facts and encouragement you need to start it, continue it, or help other moms with it. The La Leche League is a nonprofit, nonsectarian group that gives education and support. Their Web page explains how they got their name: "La Leche is Spanish for 'the milk,' and is pronounced 'la LAY-chay.' The idea came from a statue in St. Augustine, Florida (USA) honoring 'Nuestra Senora de la Leche y Buen Parto,' which translated, means 'Our Lady of Happy Delivery and Plentiful Milk.' When La Leche League was founded in the mid 1950s, polite people didn't use words like 'breastfeeding' in public. The Spanish term became an informal code-word for our meetings and our function. La Leche League meetings could be listed in newspapers without offending anyone."

http://www.zipmall.com/llli/

Natal Care: Development of the Baby

Your kid has heard the big news: Mom, an aunt, or someone else is pregnant! What the heck is happening? The answer is available at FamilyWeb's page, which teaches the stages in pregnancy and what it feels like for a woman to be pregnant. Lots of technical terms are here, but you can share the pictures of the baby's growth with your child.

http://www.familyweb.com/pregnancy/natal/
    natpt103.html

Pampers Total Baby Care

Wow! Are you experiencing information overload, with nurses and doctors and well-meaning relatives and friends all giving you information and advice about caring for your new baby? It's hard to sort it all out, and you don't want to call your pediatrician with every little question. But *what* is this rash? And how do you take care of your newborn's belly button? You'll find Well Baby and Skin Care clinics, staffed by pediatricians, here. And everyone's favorite pediatrician, Dr. T. Berry Brazelton, is available here to answer your child development questions online.

http://www.pampers.com/

Search Dogwood's Baby Name Database

Your new family addition is on its way or maybe is already here; now all you need is a name! Over 3,000 of them are here, and you can search for names by gender, first letter, or meaning of the name. For example, searching for a boy's name meaning "wise" turned up Elvis, meaning "elf-wise friend" (perhaps Elvis isn't dead, he's just gone to live with those cookie-making elves?). For even more baby names, try the Baby Planet's compilation of links at <http://www.thelastplanet.com/bbnames.htm>.

http://www.parentsplace.com/shopping/dogwood/ search.html

BABY-SITTING

Babysitting Safety Tips

Your child's got a job baby-sitting. It's a very big and important job, and there is so much to remember! Help him or her learn to be a safe baby-sitter by taking a look at this page from the Phoenix Arizona Police Department, which has loads of commonsense tips to make baby-sitting easier and more fun. For example, before accepting the job, baby-sitters should get specific instructions about bedtimes, allowed snacks for themselves and the kids, and other information about what is expected. This will make both the baby-sitter and the parents feel more confident.

http://www.ci.phoenix.az.us/POLICE/babysit.html

> ## Ask not what the Net can do for you, ask what you can do for the Net.

CONSUMER

Consumer World

Teach your kids that they have consumer power and that manufacturers listen to consumers regardless of their age. While you're here, you can also find out how to avoid online scams, determine if products have been recalled, and link to the Better Business Bureau. You'll also find out how to contact many companies and other sources of consumer information.

http://www.consumerworld.org/

DEATH AND GRIEF

C_12: Life Changes And Family Options, Loss (Death, Grief)

The topic of death and dying is a very difficult one to talk about for parents and for kids. Here is a great list of books that may help you through the grieving process and understand each other's feelings better. Two good titles on the adult list are: *The Grieving Child: A Parents Guide* and *Talking About Death* and *Dialogue Between Parent and Child*. The list of books for kids includes two stories about coping with the death of a pet.

http://family.starwave.com/resource/pra/C_12_2.html

Children And Grief

Grief is a painful experience for both kids and grown-ups, and sometimes parents will try to protect their children from this pain by not allowing them to participate in the funeral of a loved one. Read about one little girl's struggle with the loss of a close family friend. The author of this article delivers some very useful advice on helping kids through a "healthy" grief process. Kids need the support of friends and family, too, and attending funeral services is often an important part of saying good-bye.

http://www.funeral.net/info/chilgrf.html

Children And Grief

Coping with the death of a family member is a really hard thing to do. It's OK to be sad, though, or even angry. The most important thing is to share your thoughts and feelings with other family members. This article lists some of the common emotions that grieving kids (and their parents) might experience. Also mentioned are some warning signs to watch for so that you can better help your child cope with and understand the loss. This site is available in English, French, and Spanish.

http://www.psych.med.umich.edu/web/aacap/
    factsFam/grief.htm

Pet Loss and Rainbow Bridge

If your very special pet has died, be sure to read this wonderful short story about Rainbow Bridge, a place just this side of heaven. The author knows that even though your pet may be gone from your life, it is never absent from your heart. Thinking about the animal you loved waiting for you at Rainbow Bridge may make your loss a little easier. You can also leave a remembrance of your pet here, for everyone to see. There are also links to other pet loss pages, including a Virtual Pet Cemetery.

http://www.primenet.com/~meggie/bridge.htm

Pets Grief Support

Loss of a beloved pet is a difficult time for both kids and parents. Many people like to remember their pets with the Monday Candle Ceremony, which is described at this site, both in English and Italian. There is also a list of online grief support groups that meet every week on many of the online services. Another place to find information, including a list of books for kids and families, is at the Pet Loss- A Reference to References page, at <http://www.superdog.com/petloss.htm>.

http://ourworld.compuserve.com/homepages/
    EdWilliams/

DIVORCE

CRC Catalog

Check out this link from the Children's Rights Council for a good list of books for children, parents, stepparents, and grandparents. Find out how your kids can subscribe to *Kids Express*, a newsletter especially for kids aged 7 to 12 about divorce and separation. The newsletter includes a kid-to-kid advice column, puzzles, and lots of answers to frequently asked questions.

http://www.vix.com/crc/catalog.htm

Family Law Advisor

This site presents lots of legal and other factual information about divorce. The On-line Newsletter covers all aspects of divorce, including child custody issues, visitation, and child support. There is an interactive bulletin board, where parents can post questions and read about the concerns of other families in similar situations. Separation and divorce are situations that affect all family members, so be sure to also check sites such as ParentsPlace at <http://www.parentsplace.com/> and Facts For Families at <http://www.aacap.org/web/aacap/factsFam/>, which periodically carry articles about children and divorce.

http://www.divorcenet.com/law/fla.html

EDUCATION

Classroom Connect

Classroom Connect is one of our favorite magazines. Their Web site doesn't disappoint, either. Check it out for info on upcoming conferences, a jumpstation to great Web links, newsgroups, ftp sites, a Web toolkit, and more. This is a commercial publisher, but they know their market, so stop in and browse!

http://www.wentworth.com/

DTS-L (Dead Teachers Society)

Education is the key to so many things, including our children's and nation's future. The Dead Teacher Society and its spin-off electronic discussion list, DTS-L, is a forum to discuss education. The conversations here are freewheeling and wide-ranging, but if you care about education, you will want to take part. Share your thoughts and learn from others.

List Address: dts-l@iubvm.ucs.indiana.edu
Subscription Address: listserv@iubvm.ucs.indiana.edu

EDUCATIONAL RESOURCES FOR PARENTS

Wow, talk about one-stop shopping! There are more than 160 links to sites of interest to parents, grandparents, and other caregivers. Articles range all the way from preparing yourself for parenthood to preparing your child for college, and every possible stage in between. Included are links to organizations, such as the National PTA and scouting, online magazines, and book reviews.

http://www.execpc.com/~dboals/parents.html

EdWeb Home Page

Are you sick and tired of those endless clickable lists that seem to lead nowhere? How do you find out what it all means to your students and your school? Let's talk about the history and impact of technology and the potential all this computer stuff has for good and bad. The Center for Networked Information Discovery and Retrieval knows what you want. This site is more than just a list of resources! Here you can also get the latest articles on technology and school reform. Find out how the World Wide Web relates to you and your classroom. Combine computers and kids in new, more exciting ways. This page will help you use the technology that's out there right now. Better hotlist this one—you'll want to come back.

http://k12.cnidr.org:90/

Crack open CODES AND CIPHERS.

ERIC - Celebrating 30 Years

Custom-build your own curriculum! The Educational Resources Information Center (ERIC) is a vast collection of data, ideas, research, lesson plans, literature, and more. This site will be of interest to parents who want to supplement their child's education at home or learn about parenting techniques. Teachers will find classroom ideas that go above and beyond textbook-type learning as well as professional information. They can also use the renowned AskERIC service. If you're an education professional (librarian, teacher, administrator, homeschooler, and so on) you can e-mail questions to AskERIC's Net-savvy information specialists; within 48 hours, you'll have suggestions and solutions drawn from customized ERIC database searches, ERIC digests, and Internet resources. If you've always wanted to talk to the reference librarian of the Internet, you can start with these folks. If you want to browse on your own, check AskERIC's Virtual Library, which contains over 700 lesson plans plus material drawn from the archives of *Newton's Apple, CNN Newsroom,* and the Discovery Channel.

http://www.aspensys.com/eric/

National PTA

One hundred years ago, the National PTA was founded by Alice McLellan Birney and Phoebe Apperson Hearst as the National Congress of Mothers. Birney said, "Let us have no more croaking as to what cannot be done; let us see what can be done." Today, this large organization is doing many things. Here, you can get more information about educational initiatives, health and welfare programs, and legislative issues.

http://www.pta.org/

PBS Teacher Connex

There are so many TV programs! How do you select the best ones for your kids? Here are descriptions of the shows on public television, grouped by month or subject area. Teacher guides, info on taping rights, and links to related sites—they're all here in one place.

http://www.pbs.org/tconnex/

U.S. Department of Education

The Department of Education has an easy-to-use site with some useful and welcome features. This site is worth a look if you're concerned with any of the following topics: improving education on a local or national level, learning from other schools in other communities, application procedures for education grants, and student financial aid. The Picks O' the Month section highlights important resources you won't see everywhere else.

http://www.ed.gov/

Urban Education Web

UEweb is connected with the ERIC (Educational Resources Information Center) clearinghouses. They offer vast numbers of articles, manuals, and other publications about urban education. Just one example is their "Strong Families, Strong Schools" handbook. One of UEweb's best features is its searchable ERIC databases. These hold lesson plans, publications, and educational research. Of course, if you'd rather gopher right to the ERIC files, you can also go to *<gopher://ericir.syr.edu/>*.

http://eric-web.tc.columbia.edu/

WebEd Curriculum Links

This page is the work of a librarian loose on the Web since 1993. The links are roughly categorized but are not annotated. Still, a browse through here will unearth some pretty arcane stuff. Be warned, though, that some of the sites are for older kids, so be sure to explore this site with your kids, and preview if you can.

**http://badger.state.wi.us/agencies/dpi/www/
   WebEd.html**

Yahoo! - Education

Here's a searchable page chock-full of education resources. Everything from special education to online teaching to alternative education is accessible from Yahoo. As an aside, did you know that two graduate students started Yahoo as a hobby and developed it into the indispensable information service we know today?

http://www.yahoo.com/Education/

DIFFERENTLY-ABLED KIDS

Gifted and Talented (TAG) Resources Home Page

Being gifted is being blessed—it means having special talents beyond the average. While being gifted is good, it can also lead to complications. Sometimes school can be boring and unchallenging for gifted kids. Finding other kids who share the same interests can be difficult. The Internet offers a way for gifted children to explore the world in a challenging environment and to find other kids with similar gifts. This is a good place to find information useful for gifted children!

http://www.eskimo.com/~user/kids.html

Internet Resources for Special Educators

OK, in your classroom you've got two gifted students, five with ADD, one with cerebral palsy, four learning-disabled kids, and three with behavior disorders. How do you mainstream them all? This collection will point you to the support you need.

http://www.interactive.net/~wader/sped.htm

HOMESCHOOLING

Christian Homeschool Forum WebPage

If you were to decide to homeschool, how would you get started? This information desk has tips to help you take the plunge. You'll also find answers to questions you might have, lists of books and magazines, links to support groups, and lots of tips. You'll find plenty of encouragement here!

http://www.gocin.com/homeschool/

> **Little Bo Peep
> lost her sheep,
> but she found them
> again in FARMING AND
> AGRICULTURE.**

HOME-ED and HOME-ED-POLITICS

Lots of kids don't walk very far to go to school. For them, it's right in their own homes! Home schooling is growing by leaps and bounds. With approximately one million students in home-school programs (up from a few thousand in the 1960s), there are increasingly more and more home-school parents and caregivers to share ideas with. HOME-ED is one Internet mailing list that gives parents a chance to do this. HOME-ED-POLITICS focuses on legislative and other governmental issues of concern for home-school providers.

List Address: home-ed@world.std.com
Subscription Address: Majordomo@world.std.com

List Address: home-ed-politics@Mainstream.net
Subscription Address: listproc@Mainstream.net

Homeschool World Home Page

Some kids don't go to school. Every state in the U.S. and many foreign countries permit homeschooling in some form. If you're thinking of making the switch to more independent learning at home, or if you already teach your kids at home, you'll find lots of ideas at this site.

http://www.home-school.com/

Jon's Homeschool Resource Page

If you could choose only one page on homeschooling, this would be it. Will your children fit into the "real world" if they don't go to school? Will they do as well academically in homeschool? Will they be able to get into college? Research shows that the answer to all of these questions is a loud Yes! This site also has a collection of home pages and photos from families; check out what they're doing and learning.

http://www.midnightbeach.com/hs/

> # You know something the Net doesn't. Make your own home page!

The Teel Family Web Site

Brrrr! Snow is falling all around, and you're harnessing the dogs to the sled. Get ready for a trip to Alaska to visit the Teel family. There is no such thing as a typical homeschooling family, but you'll find out what interests the Teels on their homeschool Web page. See what curriculum they are working on this week, and explore some of their favorite links. Watch out for the polar bears, though!

http://www.teelfamily.com/

The Unschooling Homeschooler

As Mark Twain said, "I have never let my schooling interfere with my education." The Bedford family doesn't study "subjects"; they follow their passions and interests as they "unschool." Now, you too can study and learn about what interests *you*! Lots of good links are here with resources for homeschoolers and others.

http://www2.islandnet.com/~bedford/home_lrn.html

Famous people who have been home-schooled include Alexander Graham Bell, Agatha Christie, Sandra Day O'Connor, Albert Einstein, Wolfgang Mozart, astronaut Sally Ride, Mark Twain, and George Washington.
Read more at
The Unschooling Homeschooler.

VLC.Homepage

The Village Learning Center (VLC) is a place where the future begins. If your kids are in grades seven through nine, they can take these lessons on the Web. They even get their own cyber-teacher! While they learn here, they begin to tie together different subject areas. Instead of spending one hour on math and then the next hour on social studies, they can make a model of a mosque and do both subjects at the same time. Note: There is a cost for subscriptions to the Village Learning Center, but you can look around for free.

http://www.snowcrest.net/villcen/vlchp.html

FAMILY FUN

See also FAMILY HOME PAGES

Family Explorer: Home Page

Have you ever wondered how to make butter at home? Maybe you'd like to experiment with some kitchen chemistry or try some nature crafts. This is a magazine you can have sent to your house, and a good number of their projects are up on the Web. It's an incredible assortment: invisible ink, an oatmeal box "camera," and a make-your-own "Surf in a Bottle" (the '90s version of the Lava Lamp). This is a fun site for families to explore together.

http://www.parentsplace.com/readroom/explorer/

Family Internet Home Page

OK, where do you go to find out how to make porcupine salad, decide whether or not to feed your Akita soybean dog food, read recent movie reviews, figure out how your family can save for a child's college education, and check today's headlines from the *Jerusalem Post*? This site has all this and lots more. If you and your family are new to the Internet, this is a great starting place. You can just click the buttons for categories such as Arts & Leisure, Medical Corner, Cooking With Blondee, Kids Corner, Daily News, and Education, to name a few. So, everyone pull up a chair and start surfing!

http://www.familyinternet.com/

KidsCom Home Page

You have to register here, but it's free. One fun thing is that you get to pick which language you want: English, French, Spanish, or German. Kids, if you are learning a foreign language in school, try picking that one and see how much you can understand! KidsCom is especially for kids aged 8 to 14. You can look here for a pen pal, post pictures and stories about your pets, or ask the Tobie Wan Kenobi expert anything you want to know about the Internet and where to find things you are interested in. Try guessing the country capitals in the Geography Game, and then read more about each country by clicking on the map. Parents, you can get support from your peers on how to cope with bringing up kids, and, if you're feeling technologically challenged yourself, there's a spot for you to ask the computer expert, too.

http://www.kidscom.com/

Steve and Ruth Bennett's Family Surfboard

Here's another great place for your family to start surfing the Net! As Steve and Ruth state, this site is for both the Web novice and the seasoned surfer. They definitely have something for everyone here. And what would any site be without its "best picks" list? Bennett's Picks include annotations to help you decide if you want to check them out or pass them by. Besides lots of links to museums, kids' publishing projects, and family vacations, you can also download some fun demo software in Kidding Around The Keyboard. The Public Service Announcements are neat things the Bennetts have found in literature and then converted to electronic format to include on their page.

http://www.familysurf.com/

Bring your shovel and meet me in the TREASURE AND TREASURE-HUNTING section.

HAY! Gallop over to HORSES AND EQUESTRIAN SPORTS.

Things with Kids

This site is for parents in a traditional family setting, as well as single moms or dads who are the primary parent. It was developed by a New Zealand dad who is separated and has four kids. It's not a fancy site, but you'll find a lot of things you can do here. For example, try some of the games, which require almost no equipment. Or prepare some of the recipes, which range from the simple (Popcorn) to the bizarre (Green Cake). You'll find puzzles, crafts, and lots of rainy-day ideas here. This is a thoughtful and useful site; be sure to say hi, and tell Stuart you found his site in this book.

http://www.massey.ac.nz/~KBirks/kids/kids.htm

Welcome to GusTown

Meet Gus, Rant, Rave, and the rest of the Cyberbuds in this colorful town full of animations, articles, games, recipes, crafts, and links for kids and parents! This book has a close-up look at the folks behind this page in a "Postcard from the Net" at the end of section C—check it out.

http://www.gustown.com/

HEALTH

Achoo On-Line Healthcare Services

With over 8,200 resources on health, you're sure to find some information on your topic. Whether it's baby care, parenting, alternative medical care, or even a directory to medical products, give this site a try. Don't miss the Site of the Week and the past archives for it. This will give you a good overview of some of the best resources on health the Net offers. This is a site for adults, not kids.

http://www.achoo.com/

The American Dental Association

This is the home page for the professional society of dentists, probably best known for bestowing the "American Dental Association Seal of Acceptance" on various dental gels, flosses, pastes, mouthwashes, and other products for both consumer and professional use. Surprisingly, the first report on toothpastes was published in 1866! You can get a list of all the approved products here, as well as lots of pamphlets on tooth sealants, kids' teeth, and more.

http://www.ada.org/

Ask the Dietitian(tm)

Staying healthy means practicing good nutrition, but it's hard to know what's good and bad for you and your kids. Some people say that some fat is good; others say it's all bad. Some say sugar is unhealthy; others say it's OK for you. What to do? You can ask a dietitian! Here, you'll find information on many frequently asked questions about nutrition from an expert who knows what foods are good for you.

http://www.dietitian.com/

Facts For Families

The American Academy of Child and Adolescent Psychiatry has an answer for almost any kind of family challenge you can imagine, from dealing with divorce to welcoming an adopted child. Parents will want to use this page with their children. It is available in English, French, and Spanish.

http://www.aacap.org/web/aacap/factsFam/

Family Health Home Page

Staying healthy means learning all kinds of facts. One way to learn some facts about staying healthy is to listen to doctors giving good information on how to be healthy. Here you'll find sound files, lasting approximately two minutes, on health topics from acne to weight loss. Give these a listen—it'll be good for your health!

http://www.tcom.ohiou.edu/family-health.html

Head Lice

Lice! Head lice (some people call them "cooties") are small insects that attach themselves to human hair. They itch and they make you feel terrible. The thing to know is that many people get head lice, and getting them doesn't mean you're an unclean person. To learn more about head lice and how to stop them if you get them, take a peek at this page on the University of Illinois Health Resource Center's Web site.

http://www.uiuc.edu/departments/mckinley/
    health-info/dis-cond/commdis/headlice.html

KidsHealth - Children's Health & Parenting Information

Quite simply, this is currently the best children's health resource on the Net. It is divided into sections for kids and parents, with a section for health professionals as well. The kids' section has Shockwave games and animations, tips on nutrition, fun recipes, and a sensitive section on feelings, including a Kid's Guide to Divorce. The resources for adults detail childhood diseases, explain medical tests, and answer questions like "How can I tell if my child has attention deficit disorder?" and "What do I tell my child about surgery?" plus many more. This site is well designed and built with love, and it doesn't go overboard with multimedia like so many others. It is sponsored by The Nemours Foundation and is staffed by professionals from The duPont Hospital for Children and The Nemours Children's Clinic, among others.

http://kidshealth.org/

Lynn Gazis-Sax's Children's Health Home Page

How do you pick a doctor for the kids? What are some of the ailments that affect kids? Where do really sick children get help? A good place to look to get answers to these questions is here. While there's nothing like chicken soup to help your kids stay healthy, this is a pretty good place to look for kids' health information.

http://www.best.com/~gazissax/chealth.html

Med Help International

If you or your child has been diagnosed with a particular medical condition and you'd like to talk to other families dealing with the same thing, you might try registering here in the Patient Network Support area. Let's face it—we all get sick once in a while. Sometimes it can just be annoying, and other times it can be scary. At the Med Help Library Search area, you can learn about all kinds of sicknesses. Sometimes just knowing what's happening can help you feel better. The texts are written in a nontechnical style, and relevant links out to the rest of the Internet are included for each entry. This site wants you to become a member ($120), but many of the areas are freely open to guests.

http://www.medhelp.org/

PEDINFO Home Page

This is an archive of information for pediatricians and others interested in children's health. Its keeper is a doctor at the Lister Hill Library of the Health Sciences at the University of Alabama at Birmingham. You'll find current information (and links!) on disorders, diseases, and syndromes. Visit many pediatrics departments in teaching hospitals all over the world, and examine some interesting information you won't find elsewhere. For example, in the International Pediatrics area, you'll find a letter to pediatricians everywhere from a mother and pediatrician who adopted a child in China. The letter describes conditions in Chinese orphanages and reasons why pediatricians might prescribe antibiotics and other medications to be taken to China by the adoptive parent, with appropriate instructions on if and when to administer them, because delay in treatment could be counterproductive. There is also a very useful collection of info on parental control of Internet access.

http://www.uab.edu/pedinfo/

From another galaxy? Learn about Earth in the ASTRONOMY SOLAR SYSTEM AND PLANETS area!

DRUGS

Growing Up Drug Free: A Parent's Guide to Prevention

Kids using drugs—it's bad news. Everybody knows that, but sometimes it's hard to know all the facts about drugs. Learn about why kids take drugs, what the effects of the drugs are, and how to help your kids learn how to "just say no."

http://seamless.com/alexanderlaw/txt/brochure/
   drgfree.shtml

KIDS WITH DISABILITIES

Assistive Technology On-Line

This site is so loaded with information about all kinds of assistive technologies (AT) that you won't want to miss it. Look for links to specific disability Internet resources, products and companies, U.S. government policy, and federally funded programs relating to AT. There's even information on regional and local programs, including local branches of national organizations, volunteer groups, and more. The Lists of Lists is very comprehensive and is a great place to start research on any particular type of disability.

http://www.asel.udel.edu/at-online/assistive.html

Autism Network International

Autism Network International (ANI) is an organization run "by and for autistic people." They promote peer support, information sharing, self-help, and help with educating the public about autism. There is also a wonderful collection of links to resources on other syndromes, such as ADD, Fragile X, hyperlexia, and Tourette's, among many others.

http://www.students.uiuc.edu/~bordner/ani.html

Autism Resources

This resource is a collection of autism-related sites on the Net. It includes an autism FAQ, autism mailing lists, advice to parents, treatment methods, facilitated communication, research information, and organizations.

http://web.syr.edu/~jmwobus/autism/

Children and Adults with Attention Deficit Disorder

ADD, ADHD—it's all just a bunch of letters. All you do know is that your child really has trouble paying attention in school. You're not alone! In the U.S., 3.5 million kids have been diagnosed with attention deficit disorder (ADD). At this site you can click on the map of the United States and see if a CH.A.D.D. (Children and Adults with ADD) chapter is near you (CH.A.D.D. is a nonprofit, parent-based organization providing family support, advocacy, and education). You'll find articles and information here on upcoming events and current laws relating to students with ADD.

http://www.chadd.org/

Cystic Fibrosis

It used to be that kids with cystic fibrosis, a lung disease, rarely lived long enough to become adults. That has changed. Many people with cystic fibrosis (CF) can look forward to a long life. If you have CF or if you know someone who does, you have to take a look at this page. You'll find some easy-to-understand information about CF and also the latest news about this disease.

http://www.ai.mit.edu/people/mernst/cf/

Down Syndrome WWW Page

The information here has been compiled by members of the Down listserv. It includes information about support organizations, conferences, educational issues, medical resources, and parenting (and brothering or sistering) your special child (or sibling).

http://www.nas.com/downsyn/

Visit the BRIDGES of Internet County in ARCHITECTURE!

Family Village

Although the main purpose of this site is to support families and friends of mentally disabled or other special needs kids, the site is a wealth of information for all parents. Check the Coffee Shop to find online groups, listservs, and other resources for parents, grandparents, and siblings. The Library has information on specific diagnoses. The Hospital has links to a current medical breakthroughs page, while the Mall has listings for special adaptive technologies, toys, clothing, and other items. Special Olympics links are also here, along with camps and other outdoor opportunities for special kids and special families. There is a lot to learn at this excellent site!

http://www.familyvillage.wisc.edu/

How Can I Help? (CP Booklet)

What's it like to raise a child with a disability? If you have not shared that unique experience, it may be hard for you to understand and imagine how it feels. "It's just a different place," says Emily Kingsley in her article, "Welcome To Holland." For friends or relatives of a child with cerebral palsy, this site offers valuable advice on how to provide empathy and support for the family, as well as information on what they may be experiencing and other ways you can help.

http://www.iinet.com.au/~scarffam/cpa.html

Med Help International

If you or your child has been diagnosed with a particular medical condition and you'd like to talk to other families dealing with the same thing, you might try registering here in the Patient Network Support area. Let's face it—we all get sick once in a while. Sometimes it can just be annoying, and other times it can be scary. At the Med Help Library Search area, you can learn about all kinds of sicknesses. Sometimes just knowing what's happening can help you feel better. The texts are written in a nontechnical style, and relevant links out to the rest of the Internet are included for each entry. This site wants you to become a member ($120), but many of the areas are freely open to guests.

http://www.medhelp.org/

Our Kids

Yum! You mean we can drink something that tastes great and is good for us, too? Peanut Butter Smoothie is just one of the high-calorie recipes listed here under nutritional tips. For a little support and a lot of information, browse the Our Kids archives and then join the hundreds of others on this e-mail discussion list who are sharing stories about their children's accomplishments and challenges with other families facing similar situations. If you are a parent, relative, or friend of a child with any kind of developmental delay, this site also provides a great reading list of books for kids and grown-ups. For the differently-abled child, there's a good list of adaptive technologies and how to contact the manufacturers. Be sure to try some of the links to special education institutions, medical research organizations, and others for more valuable information.

http://wonder.mit.edu/ok/

Our-Kids

Parents and caregivers of children with developmental delay can benefit from sharing with other parents and other caregivers. This is an Internet mailing list for just that opportunity. It's called "Our Kids" to avoid any labeling and just to provide a place where adults can interact about the special kids they love.

List Address: OUR-KIDS@SJUVM.stjohns.edu
Subscription Address: LISTSERV@SJUVM.stjohns.edu

INTERNET

Parental Control Product Review

There are a variety of software products you can place on your computer to filter your kids' use of the Internet and guide what they see. Get answers to questions about how these products compare. We support these types of products because we believe that this type of guidance should come from the home and not be imposed by the government.

http://www.neosoft.com/parental-control/

Parents Page

Do you need to know how to get a family Internet account? Are you looking for educational software reviews? This computer-oriented parenting site offers links to Internet filtering sites and software, "Computer Currents" articles for parents, and a hodgepodge of other interesting links.

http://www.currents.net/community/family/
  parent.html

PEDINFO Parental Control of Internet Access

There's been a lot of talk in the news about the Internet having stuff on it that is inappropriate for kids. The overwhelming majority of information is OK, but those news stories can make you nervous. Some people are even talking about keeping kids off the Net entirely, which would be terrible! We think that access to information is a good thing. But we also recognize that parents may want to use filtering software, and this page is a good place for you to look and see what's available.

http://www.uab.edu/pedinfo/Control.html

Web66 Home Page

If your kid's school or the school you teach in has its own Web server, it should be linked here. It's the largest collection of all the schools with Web sites in the world! If the school doesn't have a Web site yet, a cookbook here will give the recipe to create one: where to get the software, how to write the HTML, and more. Can't tell a LAN from a WAN? You just found out they want the fifth grade to run ethernet around the building? No fear, stop here. You'll find technical info anyone can understand, plus acceptable use policies as well as other technology planning musts. You want links on top of all that? No surprise, they got 'em.

http://web66.coled.umn.edu/

> ## Attention everyone.
> ## The Internet is closing.
> ## Please go play outside.

MOVING

Allied Van Lines, Inc. Home Page

This is a don't-miss site! You'll find lots of informative facts here, and the main reason we like this site is the thoughtful treatment it gives to taking care of kids' special needs before, during, and after a move. A psychologist offers answers to commonly asked questions about families on the move, including emotional support, school-related issues, and family teamwork. Also, a Carton Capers area gives step-by-step instructions on how to use empty Allied packing cartons to build a navy, an express train, and other exciting stuff (we're not really sure kids need directions on what to do with the huge empty boxes, but if they run out of ideas, try here!).

http://www.alliedvan.net/

The Atlas Van Lines Interchange

This page doesn't have lots of information on supporting the kids during the move, but it does have interesting articles you have to read. For example, how are you going to move that aquarium? Those plants? And your computer equipment? This site will tell you that, and more. Check the Sites area for links to places chock-full of stuff, like the Employee Relocation Council.

http://www.atlasvanlines.com/

C_12: Life Changes And Family Options, Moving

Your kids are probably worried that a Gila monster is going to meet you at the airport when you get to your new town, like in the book of the same name! To ease some of those fears, read Marjorie Sharmat's book and some of the others from this list of children's books dealing with moving. Find out how to order "Smooth Moves For Families And Kids," a resource packet filled with brochures, checklists, articles, and more to help your family adjust to relocating.

http://family.starwave.com/resource/pra/C_12_1.html

Children And Family Moves

Is your family getting ready for a move? Whether you're moving to a new neighborhood or a new state, it still means your kids have to leave their old friends behind and adjust to a new school. Here are some helpful suggestions for making the move easier on all of you and helping your kids through the transition. This site is also available in Spanish.

http://www.psych.med.umich.edu/web/aacap/
factsFam/fmlymove.htm

PARENTING

Arm Yourself with Facts and Solutions

This page points out some alarming statistics. Homicide is the second leading cause of death for all youths aged 15 to 24. It is the leading cause of death for young African American males in this age group. What can parents do to help stop the violence? One of the most powerful concepts found at this site is the following: "Help your child to adopt healthy responses to conflict. Avoid situations in which 'losing face' becomes an issue by recognizing the kind of behavior which leads to a fight. Assess the conflict for what you want, not for what the other person wants." Some good suggestions are found here, plus pointers to organizations and other resources across the Net.

http://www.dnai.com/~children/violence/
arm_yourself.html

Canadian Parents Online

Here is a good place for parents to help each other in a comfortable, community atmosphere in which to connect and communicate about diverse issues, such as stepparenting, foster parenting, or handling special-needs children. Be sure to check out the Library for monthly feature articles or ask one of the resident experts questions about nutrition, family finances, or child rearing.

http://www.canadianparents.com/

CHILD SAFETY FORUM

It's rough out there! So many things can be dangerous. From bathtubs to exercise walkers, just about anything can be harmful. To get the scoop on how to be safe (and to learn what can be unsafe), check here. You'll see monthly features on safety for kids, updates from parents around the world on child accidents, and great links to kids' safety all over the Internet.

http://www.xmission.com/~gastown/safe/safe2.htm

Consumer Information Center Main Page

Are you on a limited budget? Learn how to stretch it a bit further with publications from the Consumer Information Center. Many of them are right on this page in text or HTML format. Or you can order the publications online and have them sent to you. You can also find pamphlets on how to help your kids learn to read, book lists of great reading for kids, info on colleges, mortgages, online scams, birdhouses, landscaping, and more.

http://www.pueblo.gsa.gov/

D.O.S.A. PARENTING HOME PAGE

Psychologist Allan Hawkins, M.A., introduces this site with a humorous look at parenting kids and teens excerpted from Dr. Frank's article in *Psychology Today* magazine. Be sure to read both the "21 Tricks For Taming Children" and "21 Tricks For Taming Adolescents." You don't have to look too far, though, to see the truth and wisdom in many of these "tricks." Besides the treasure pick of the month, there are lots of links to other parenting sites and discussion groups and several psychology links, including *Practical Psychology* magazine, which routinely carries articles on family life issues.

http://www.mbnet.mb.ca/~ahawkins/

**Write your name
in hieroglyphics
in LANGUAGES AND
ALPHABETS.**

DAYCARE-L

Running a day care operation, whether from the home or in a center, is a challenging endeavor encompassing business skills, child psychology, parent psychology, and fun. To get in contact with other day care operators, subscribe to DAYCARE-L and learn with other professionals.

List Address: daycare-l@io.org
Subscription Address: majordomo@io.org

Facts For Families

The American Academy of Child and Adolescent Psychiatry provides 46 information fact sheets here. They provide concise and up-to-date material designed to educate parents and families about a wide variety of psychiatric disorders affecting children and adolescents. Issues covered include bedwetting, stepfamilies, learning disabilities, grief, adoption, AIDS, and much more. This material is revised and updated regularly and is offered in three languages: English, Spanish, and French.

http://www.aacap.org/web/aacap/factsFam/

Family Planet

Your fourth grader wants to subscribe to *Odyssey* magazine, but you've never heard of it and wonder what it's about. Is the bargain software you saw at the store really something your kids will enjoy? What kind of toys are appropriate and safe for three-year-olds? You've got a business meeting in Chicago on Friday and you decide to take the whole family for the weekend, but what are they going to do while you're at the meeting? This site has it all! The regular features include advice columns on a wide range of family-related topics. To skip to the columns, go to <http://family.starwave.com/experts/index.html>. The movie reviews include a "fidget factor" to help you decide if your seven-year-old and ten-year-old will really sit through the same movie: <http://family.starwave.com/reviews/conners/archive/connarch.html>. The Oppenheim Toy Portfolio <http://family.starwave.com/reviews/oppenheim/9611/index.html> has authoritative reviews of children's books, toys, and media. There are daily and monthly local activity calendars of family events for many U.S. cities. Families won't want to miss this site!

http://family.starwave.com/

Family.com

Is your family planning a vacation to another part of the country? Be sure to check the great events calendars at this site. Divided into four regions, the calendars include information about museums, county fairs, and other fun activities for families to do in different cities across the United States, including Alaska. And if you're not planning a trip, maybe reading about some of these events will spur your interest! Family World is really an interactive magazine with color graphics, sound, and hypertext links to lots of resources families need. More than 40 regional monthly parenting publications contribute feature articles on topics as diverse as connecting dads with play groups and recipes for summer parties. You'll also find talk about educational issues and book and software reviews. Make sure you bookmark this site so you can check it each month for new features.

http://www.family.com/

FATHER-L

Father-L is an e-mail conference dedicated to discussing the importance of fathers in children's lives. The American family is now rarely like the old TV show *Father Knows Best*. Roles are changing, families are being reconfigured, and the role of a father is not always clear. This site gives dads a chance to discuss how best to help raise kids as the paternal role changes.

List Address: father-l@tc.umn.edu
Subscription Address: listserv@tc.umn.edu

Bring an umbrella, we're going to read about WEATHER AND METEOROLOGY resources!

FatherNet

OK, dads, here is a parenting site especially for you that confirms the important role you play in your kids' lives. Check out the electronic bulletin board to read what other dads are thinking about, or read bimonthly issues of *Modern Dad Newsletter* for feature articles on topics as diverse as youth sports, potty training, summer hiking (including trail mix recipes), taking baby pictures, and planning for college expenses. Then you'll find even more information when you link to other Web resources on fatherhood, including two great quarterly newsletters: *Father Times* and *At-Home Dad*. In response to Vice President Al Gore's call to action, a father-to-father national effort to unite men and provide them with information, support, and encouragement in their roles as fathers has been initiated in many states. Read how you can get a Community Starter Kit and join this movement.

http://www.cyfc.umn.edu/Fathernet/

Fathers' Resource Center: Home Page

Whether you are a new dad, a single dad, or a seasoned dad, this site has something for you. The quarterly online newsletter, *Father Times*, offers insightful articles and advice designed to "support, educate, and advocate" fathers. The list of links to other father-focused resources, personal stories, and online magazines is great.

http://www.visi.com/~frc/

Foster Parent Home Page

Whoever said "I never promised you a rose garden" must have been referring to foster care. So says one dedicated foster parent, who shares her personal story here. This is a wonderful site for foster parents to find lots of information and support on all issues relating to foster care and the child welfare system. There are feature articles on topics such as foster care and the news media, medical, addiction, and educational concerns, plus transracial/cross-cultural issues. Intended as an interactive forum specifically for foster parents, this site has enlightening information for all parents.

http://worldaccess.com/FPHP/

Get Your ANGRIES Out!

Are you always yelling at your kids? Is there a bully bothering them at school? Are you mad and cranky a lot? This site gives you some useful ways to get your anger out in constructive ways, with hints for adults, couples, and kids. Here is a sample for kids: "Check your tummy, jaws and your fists. See if the mads are coming. Breathe! Blow your mad out. Get your control. Feel good about getting your control. Stop and think; make a good choice. People are not to be hurt with your hands, feet or voice. Remember to use your firm words, not your fists." There are many more good ideas here, and don't forget to check the links about peace here while you're dealing with your angries!

http://members.aol.com/AngriesOut/

Guide to Toys and Play

Play is essential to your child's development. But how do you know which toys are safe, which ones are best for which ages, and how to select the best toy for your child when faced with a mega-mall toy store? It's all so confusing; fortunately, this site provides articles and links to make it all seem like child's play.

http://www.kidsource.com/kidsource/content/
  toys_ply.html

Jeff Sam's Child Safety & Parenting Page

Here's everything from rollerblade safety to how to treat a sunburn, plus tips on how to keep your baby amused in the store while you shop for groceries. You'll find tons of stuff at this site!

http://www.enforcers.com/childsafety/

KidSource OnLine Welcome Page

Wasn't that toy recalled? Find out here! Families, be sure to check out this outstanding parenting site. The reviews of kid-tested software are written from a family perspective, with both negative and positive comments. The Education section includes articles and book lists and, best of all, links and more links! The Health section has everything from vaccination schedules to growth charts, and the ComputingEDGE is a way to match needy schools with computer equipment.

http://www.kidsource.com/

MelnikNotes, 10/95

Parents, if sibling rivalry is a daily concern in your household, and you feel like a United Nations peacekeeper much of the time, then read this overview of Faber and Mazlish's book, *Siblings Without Rivalry*. Tips are provided on how to foster cooperation, rather than competition, between your children. There are also recommendations on how you can develop a better sense of compassion and acceptance of each child's right to have envious and negative feelings about a brother or sister.

http://family.starwave.com/reviews/melnik/archive/
me100195.html

The Missing Kids Database

Some families are looking for their missing children. Check their photos. Have you seen any of these kids? Maybe you can help! This site lets you search by state, physical description, and other characteristics. If you have a Web page of your own, check the How You Can Help area. It will tell you how to put a link at your page that will show photos of recently missing kids to your Web site visitors, like the pictures on milk cartons.

http://www.missingkids.org/

National Parent Information Network

Do you find yourself stressed out and yelling at the kids all the time? You are not the only one out there struggling with issues such as how much TV your child should be watching or how to get your kids to clean up their rooms or develop better study habits. The National Parent Information Network (NPIN) is sponsored by the ERIC Clearinghouses on Urban Education and on Early Childhood Education. There are lots of choices: a parenting discussion list and a Q&A service through AskERIC are only two. You can search the ERIC database on all topics relating to child development, child rearing, and parenting children from birth to adolescence. *Parent News* monthly newsletter offers feature articles on a wide range of topics and periodically lists information about organizations of special interest to parents and how to subscribe to other publications, such as *Pp* (parents and preschoolers) *Newsletter* and *Single Mother Newsletter*.

http://ericps.ed.uiuc.edu/npin/npinhome.html

The National Parenting Center

The content changes daily here, with articles for parents of babies through teens. There's also a focus on soon-to-be parents, too! You'll find articles on how to prepare for a parent-teacher conference, how to deal with bedwetting, how to help your child change schools, and much, much more. There are also live chat opportunities as well as discussion groups. This site is programmed by ParentsPlace, which has a separate listing in this book.

http://www.tnpc.com/

NATURAL DISASTER PROGRAM FOR FAMILIES

Tornado! Flood! Hurricane! Forest Fire! Earthquake! Natural disasters are those times when Mother Nature seems to go a little crazy. You, and everyone in your family, can learn how to be prepared for natural disasters by looking at the Natural Disaster Preparedness pages from the North Carolina Cooperative Extension Service. Take the time and learn how to set up a Family Disaster Kit (remember to pack games for kids!), how to cook without electricity, how to save your saltwater-soaked plants, and much more helpful information.

http://www.ces.ncsu.edu/depts/fcs/disaster/

ParenthoodWeb -- The WWW Community for Parents and Families

Here new parents and parents of young children can "Ask the Pros," browse the library for child care and parenting articles, find out about children's product recalls, and participate in the open discussion board. Don't miss the links to software and movie reviews.

http://www.parenthoodweb.com/

Explore the past in ANCIENT CIVILIZATIONS AND ARCHAEOLOGY.

The Parenting Community: PARENTS PLACE.COM

Parents, whether you are on your first child, your tenth, or somewhere in between, join the hundreds of other parents who come to ParentsPlace to chat, get support, and share information on the adventures and challenges of child rearing. Whether you are looking for directions to make invisible ink or the latest in toy safety labeling requirements, you'll find it here. Feature articles in the reading rooms include information on parenting twins, stepparenting, at-home dads, and single parents; but that's just the beginning. You can "Ask the Pediatrician" questions about children's health or look at sample articles from the *Family Explorer Newsletter* for some fun science and nature activities to do with your kids. And the S.O.S. (Search Our Site) feature is great! This Web site is sure to be one of your favorites.

http://www.parentsplace.com/

ParentNews

Daily parent tips offer good advice for all of us! The five professionally hosted forums include current topics, such as stepparenting and divorce. This site includes some unique links.

http://www.parent.net/

Parents Helping Parents (PHP)

PHP—The Family Resource Center provides links to many other sites of interest to parents and their children. If you haven't found what you are looking for at any of the other sites mentioned in this section, be sure to try this one. There are links to disability, health, and child care information, legal, parents' rights, and support services, the Electronic School House and other educational sites for families, and lots, lots more.

http://www.php.com/

Parents' Resource Almanac: Table of Contents

Beth DeFrancis has compiled this lifesaver for moms, dads, and other caregivers as a guide through the labyrinth of information on parenting and caring for children. Here you can find lists of the best books, magazines, products, and services as recommended by various child development experts. The information is arranged in broad topics, including Parenting Approaches and Techniques, Child Safety, Education, Work and Childcare, and so much more. The more you dig, the more you'll find, like these: what to do about separation anxiety; how to raise "purchasing savvy" kids; fun activities to do on rainy days, like building forts; free resources and catalogs for homeschoolers; travel agencies specializing in travel planning for kids and their grandparents; and more and more.

http://family.starwave.com/resource/pra/
   Table_of_Contents.html

PBS Teacher Connex

There are so many TV programs! How do you select the best ones for your kids? Here are descriptions of the shows on public television, grouped by month or subject area. Teacher guides, info on taping rights, and links to related sites—they're all here in one place.

http://www.pbs.org/tconnex/

POSITIVE PARENTING (ON-LINE!)

All of us who are parents know that dealing with kids can be a real battle of the wills. This site provides support and advice on how to handle the most difficult situations with your kids and includes a great set of parenting links.

http://www.positiveparenting.com/

Staring off into space? Discover ASTRONOMY!

The wonderful world of worms may be admired in the section called INVERTEBRATES.

SmartParenting (tm) On-Line

If you feel you need some fun and useful ways to reduce the stresses and strains of parenting in today's hectic world, then try some of Dr. Favaro's techniques. At this site, the child psychologist provides an electronic edition of *The Parent's Answer Book: 101 Solutions To Everyday Parenting Problems.* You can also download free copies of the SmartParenting Electronic News and the SmartParenting Catalog. If you are a single parent, Dr. Favaro also gives advice on managing custody and visitation issues.

http://www.garlic.com/parents/

Usenet Newsgroups

Usenet is a huge electronic e-mail messaging system. Created about 15 years ago, it now covers almost every imaginable topic. The topics discussed range from the boring to the bizarre. Obtaining access to Usenet depends on your Internet service provider, and not all Usenet discussions (called newsgroups) are available through all providers. You can read newsgroups through many World Wide Web browsers, or you can use a separate application. Ask your provider for suggestions.

To search for information contained in newsgroups, or to find newsgroups of potential interest to you, we recommend DejaNews. You can find it at *<http://www.dejanews.com>*.

Here are some potentially worthwhile Usenet newsgroups for parents and caregivers:

- *misc.kids* If you have a question about kids, this is a good place to post a message. This is a very active newsgroup, and many good ideas are exchanged.

- *misc.kids.computers* This is a more focused newsgroup, with participants sharing ideas and tips on kids and their computers. This is also good place to learn about software, CD-ROMs, and multimedia titles for children.

- *misc.kids.consumers* If you want to learn about products for kids, this is a good newsgroup to read.

- *misc.kids.health* If you have questions about your child's health, first contact your doctor. After that, you might find this newsgroup helpful.

http://www.dejanews.com/

Welcome to Parent Soup!

Remember the story of Stone Soup? Some soldiers boasted that they could make a nourishing soup out of stones. Then they said, does anyone have an onion? A carrot? A potato? Some salt? And soon, everyone in the village brought something to add to the simmering pot. In the end, everyone marveled that such a good soup could be made out of simple stones! This site is sort of like that. It's made up of a community of parents just like you, each bringing some new element to the pot. The content here is based on what other users can add to the mix of real-time chat and discussion groups. Want to ask for help with your shy preschooler? Want someone to talk to while your partner watches football? Want some health, crafts, or entertainment suggestions? Try the Parent Soup community!

http://www.parentsoup.com/

Welcome to the Ultimate Band List

This is a good place to preview lyrics for CDs your kids want to buy. For other uses, please explore this with your children. Prepare to spend the day sifting through this vast list. It's an "interactive guide" to band Web pages and digitized music and lyrics servers. There are also listings by genre, such as pop/rock/alternative, metal/hard rock/industrial, country/western, jazz/blues/R&B, even classical and new age. You can browse alphabetically or by type of music or resource, which includes newsgroups, mailing lists, FAQ files, lyrics, guitar tablature, digitized songs, and many, many WWW pages.

http://www.ubl.com/

What did grandma do when she was a kid? There is a list of questions to ask in GENEALOGY AND FAMILY HISTORY.

Westcoast Families Reading Room

At this site, you'll read tips on how to know if your kids are exercising too hard, how to be a good beach visitor, and how to pack a picnic. Pick up some brown-bagging lunch ideas or some reading or video recommendations for the little ones.

http://www.westcoastfamilies.com/reading.htm

TRAVEL

Family.com: Travel

Whether you're traveling by car or by plane, don't miss the great information here on how to keep your kids entertained. There are activities and games, travel snacks (what would any family trip be without food?), packing tips, and lots more in the Advice section.

http://www.family.com/Categories/Travel.html

HEALTHY FLYING With Diana Fairechild

Flying takes less time than going by car, but it can be less comfortable. The airplane air is drier. The pressure changes quickly as the plane takes off and lands. Flying to places in different time zones can leave passengers with *jet lag*, that tired feeling that surfaces when you are in one place but your body thinks it is still someplace else! The solutions to most of these problems are inexpensive and can be brought with you on the plane. Read Diana's secrets for comfortable flying and share them with your family. She should know: she's a retired flight attendant.

http://www.flyana.com/

The Penny Whistle Traveling With Kids Book

This site has tons of great ideas for you and your kids. For example, how about helping your kids make their own "passports" to keep track of their travels? Or maybe you'd like to try some of the take-along snacks and recipes, or the backseat travel games to pass the time. Are you there yet?

http://family.starwave.com/funstuff/pwhistle/
pwtravel/pwttoc.html

You've made it into the Forbidden City, home of Chinese emperors of long ago. Now, can you find your way out? How many rooms are there?

Answer: Beijing is the capital city of China. At its center is the Forbidden City, which was the home and audience hall of the Ming and Qing emperors. The Forbidden City contains over 9,000 rooms and covers over 720,000 square meters of land. It was originally built in the early 1400s. Read more about Beijing's 3,000-year-old history at http://www.ihep.ac.cn/tour/bj.html

ART is more
than crayons and
finger paint!

See what's shakin' in
EARTH SCIENCE
GEOLOGY-EARTHQUAKES.

Index

Main subject headings are shown in bold

Main subject headings are shown in bold

*Main subject headings are shown in **bold***

*Main subject headings are shown in **bold***

*Main subject headings are shown in **bold***

*Main subject headings are shown in **bold***

*Main subject headings are shown in **bold***

*Main subject headings are shown in **bold***

*Main subject headings are shown in **bold***

*Main subject headings are shown in **bold***

*Main subject headings are shown in **bold***

*Main subject headings are shown in **bold***

*Main subject headings are shown in **bold***

*Main subject headings are shown in **bold***

*Main subject headings are shown in **bold***

*Main subject headings are shown in **bold***

*Main subject headings are shown in **bold***

*Main subject headings are shown in **bold***

*Main subject headings are shown in **bold***

Main subject headings are shown in **bold**

Main subject headings are shown in bold

*Main subject headings are shown in **bold***

Main subject headings are shown in **bold**

Main subject headings are shown in bold

*Main subject headings are shown in **bold***

*Main subject headings are shown in **bold***

*Main subject headings are shown in **bold***

*Main subject headings are shown in **bold***

*Main subject headings are shown in **bold***

*Main subject headings are shown in **bold***

*Main subject headings are shown in **bold***

*Main subject headings are shown in **bold***

*Main subject headings are shown in **bold***

*Main subject headings are shown in **bold***

*Main subject headings are shown in **bold***